THE POLITICAL HISTORY OF ENGLAND.

Seventy-five years have passed since Lingard completed his HISTORY OF ENGLAND, which ends with the Revolution of 1688. During that period historical study has made a great advance. Year after year the mass of materials for a new History of England has increased; new lights have been thrown on events and characters, and old errors have been corrected. Many notable works have been written on various periods of our history; some of them at such length as to appeal almost exclusively to professed historical students. It is believed that the time has come when the advance which has been made in the knowledge of English history as a whole should be laid before the public in a single work of fairly adequate size. Such a book should be founded on independent thought and research, but should at the same time be written with a full knowledge of the works of the best modern historians and with a desire to take advantage of their teaching wherever it appears sound.

The vast number of authorities, printed and in manuscript, on which a History of England should be based, if it is to represent the existing state of knowledge, renders co-operation almost necessary and certainly advisable. The History, of which this volume is an instalment, is an attempt to set forth in a readable form the results at present attained by research. It will consist of twelve volumes by twelve different writers, each *of them chosen as being specially capable of dealing with the period which he undertakes, and the editors, while leaving to each author as free a hand as possible, hope to insure a general similarity in method of treatment, so that the twelve volumes may in their contents, as well as in their outward appearance, form one History.*

As its title imports, this History will primarily deal with politics, with the History of England and, after the date of the union with Scotland, Great Britain, as a state or body politic; but as the life of a nation is complex, and its condition at any given time cannot be understood without taking into account the various forces acting upon it, notices of religious matters and of intellectual, social, and economic progress will also find place in these volumes. The footnotes will, so far as is possible, be confined to references to authorities, and references will not be appended to statements which appear to be matters of common knowledge and do not call for support. Each volume will have an Appendix giving some account of the chief authorities, original and secondary, which the author has used. This account will be compiled with a view of helping students rather than of making long lists of books without any notes as to their contents or value. That the History will have faults both of its own and such as will always in some measure attend co-operative work, must be expected, but no pains have been spared to make it, so far as may be, not wholly unworthy of the greatness of its subject.

Each volume, while forming part of a complete History, will also in itself be a separate and complete book, will be sold separately, and will have its own index, and two or more maps.

Vol. I. to 1066. By Thomas Hodgkin, D.C.L., Litt.D., Fellow of University College, London; Fellow of the British Academy.

Vol. II. 1066 to 1216. By George Burton Adams, M.A., Professor of History in Yale University, New Haven, Connecticut.

Vol. III. 1216 to 1377. By T. F. Tout, M.A., Professor of Medieval and Modern History in the Victoria University of Manchester; formerly Fellow of Pembroke College, Oxford.

Vol. IV. 1377 to 1485. By C. Oman, M.A., Fellow of All Souls' College, and Deputy Professor of Modern History in the University of Oxford.

Vol. V. 1485 to 1547. By H. A. L. Fisher, M.A., Fellow and Tutor of New College, Oxford.

Vol. VI. 1547 to 1603. By A. F. Pollard, M.A., Professor of Constitutional History in University College, London.

Vol. VII. 1603 to 1660. By F. C. Montague, M.A., Professor of History in University College, London ; formerly Fellow of Oriel College, Oxford.

Vol. VIII. 1660 to 1702. By Richard Lodge, M.A., Professor of History in the University of Edinburgh; formerly Fellow of Brasenose College, Oxford.

Vol. IX. 1702 to 1760. By I. S. Leadam, M.A., formerly Fellow of Brasenose College, Oxford.

Vol. X. 1760 to 1801. By the Rev. William Hunt, M.A., D.Litt., Trinity College, Oxford.

Vol. XI. 1801 to 1837. By the Hon. George C. Brodrick, D.C.L., late Warden of Merton College, Oxford, and J. K. Fotheringham, M.A., Magdalen College, Oxford, Lecturer in Classics at King's College, London.

Vol. XII. 1837 to 1901. By Sidney J. Low, M.A., Balliol College, Oxford, formerly Lecturer on History at King's College, London.

The Political History of England

IN TWELVE VOLUMES

EDITED BY WILLIAM HUNT, D.LITT., AND
REGINALD L. POOLE, M.A.

III.

THE HISTORY OF ENGLAND
FROM THE ACCESSION OF HENRY III. TO THE
DEATH OF EDWARD III.

1216-1377

THE
HISTORY OF ENGLAND

FROM THE ACCESSION OF HENRY III.
TO THE DEATH OF EDWARD III.

(1216-1377)

BY

T. F. TOUT, M.A.

PROFESSOR OF MEDIÆVAL AND MODERN HISTORY IN THE
UNIVERSITY OF MANCHESTER

LONGMANS, GREEN, AND CO.
39 PATERNOSTER ROW, LONDON
NEW YORK AND BOMBAY
1905

CONTENTS.

CHAPTER I.

THE REGENCY OF WILLIAM MARSHAL.

CHAPTER II.

THE RULE OF HUBERT DE BURGH.

CHAPTER III.

THE ALIEN INVASION.

CHAPTER IV.

POLITICAL RETROGRESSION AND NATIONAL PROGRESS.

CHAPTER V.

THE BARONS' WAR.

CHAPTER VI.

THE RULE OF MONTFORT AND THE ROYALIST RESTORATION.

CHAPTER VII.

THE EARLY FOREIGN POLICY AND LEGISLATION OF EDWARD I.

CHAPTER VIII.

THE CONQUEST OF NORTH WALES.

CHAPTER IX.

THE SICILIAN AND THE SCOTTISH ARBITRATIONS.

CHAPTER X.

THE FRENCH AND SCOTTISH WARS AND THE CONFIRMATION OF THE CHARTERS.

CHAPTER XI.

THE SCOTTISH FAILURE.

CHAPTER XII.

Gaveston, the Ordainers, and Bannockburn.

CHAPTER XIII.

Lancaster, Pembroke, and the Despensers.

CHAPTER XIV.

THE FALL OF EDWARD II. AND THE RULE OF ISABELLA AND MORTIMER.

CHAPTER XV.

THE PRELIMINARIES OF THE HUNDRED YEARS' WAR.

CHAPTER XVI.

THE EARLY CAMPAIGNS OF THE HUNDRED YEARS' WAR.

CHAPTER XVII.

FROM THE BLACK DEATH TO THE TREATY OF CALAIS.

CHAPTER XVIII.

The Hundred Years' War from the Treaty of Calais to the Truce of Bruges.

CHAPTER XIX.

ENGLAND DURING THE LATTER YEARS OF EDWARD III.

APPENDIX.

ON AUTHORITIES.

(1216-1377.)

MAPS.

(AT THE END OF THE VOLUME.)

1. Map of Wales and the March at the end of the XIIIth century.
2. Map of Southern Scotland and Northern England in the XIIIth and XIVth centuries.
3. Map of France in the XIIIth and XIVth centuries.

CHAPTER I.

THE REGENCY OF WILLIAM MARSHAL.

WHEN John died, on October 19, 1216, the issue of the war between him and the barons was still doubtful. The arrival of Louis of France, eldest son of King Philip Augustus, had enabled the barons to win back much of the ground lost after John's early triumphs had forced them to call in the foreigner. Beyond the Humber the sturdy north-country barons, who had wrested the Great Charter from John, remained true to their principles, and had also the support of Alexander II., King of Scots. The magnates of the eastern counties were as staunch as the northerners, and the rich and populous southern shires were for the most part in agreement with them. In the west, the barons had the aid of Llewelyn ap Iorwerth, the great Prince of North Wales. While ten earls fought for Louis, the royal cause was only upheld by six. The towns were mainly with the rebels, notably London and the Cinque Ports, and cities so distant as Winchester and Lincoln, Worcester and Carlisle. Yet the baronial cause excited little general sympathy. The mass of the population stood aloof, and was impartially maltreated by the rival armies.

John's son Henry had at his back the chief military resources of the country; the two strongest of the earls, William Marshal, Earl of Pembroke, and Randolph of Blundeville, Earl of Chester; the fierce lords of the Welsh March, the Mortimers, the Cantilupes, the Cliffords, the Braoses, and the Lacys; and the barons of the West Midlands, headed by Henry of Neufbourg, Earl of Warwick, and William of Ferrars, Earl of Derby. This powerful phalanx gave to the royalists a stronger hold in the west than their opponents had in any one part of the much wider territory within their sphere of influence. There was no baronial counterpart to the successful raiding of the north and east, which John had carried through in the last months of his life. A baronial centre, like Worcester, could not hold its own long in the west. Moreover, John had not entirely forfeited his hereditary advantages. The administrative families, whose chief representative was the justiciar Hubert de Burgh, held to their tradition of unswerving loyalty, and joined with the followers of the old king, of whom William Marshal was the chief survivor. All over England the royal castles were in safe hands, and so long as they remained unsubdued, no part of Louis' dominions was secure. The crown had used to the full its rights over minors and vacant fiefs. The subjection of the south-west was assured by the marriage of the mercenary leader, Falkes de Bréauté, to the mother of the infant Earl of Devon, and by the grant of Cornwall to the bastard of the last of the Dunstanville earls. Though Isabella, Countess of Gloucester, John's repudiated wife, was as zealous as her new husband, the Earl of Essex, against John's son, Falkes kept a tight hand over Glamorgan, on which the military power of the house of Gloucester largely depended. Randolph of Chester was custodian of the earldoms of Leicester and Richmond, of which the nominal earls, Simon de Montfort and Peter Mauclerc, were far away, the one ruling Toulouse, and the other Brittany. The band of foreign adventurers, the mainstay of John's power, was still unbroken. Ruffians though these hirelings were, they had experience, skill, and courage, and were the only professional soldiers in the country.

The vital fact of the situation was that the immense moral and spiritual forces of the Church remained on the side of the king. Innocent III. had died some months before John, but his successor, Honorius III., continued to uphold his policy. The papal legate, the Cardinal Gualo, was the soul of the royalist cause. Louis and his adherents had been excommunicated, and not a single English bishop dared to join openly the foes of Holy Church. The most that the clerical partisans of the barons could do was to disregard the interdict and continue their ministrations to the excommunicated host. The strongest English prelate, Stephen Langton, Archbishop of Canterbury, was at Rome in disgrace. Walter Grey, Archbishop of York, and Hugh of Wells, Bishop of Lincoln, were also abroad, while the Bishop of London, William of Sainte-Mère-Eglise, was incapacitated by illness. Several important sees, including Durham and Ely, were vacant. The ablest resident bishop, Peter des Roches of Winchester, was an accomplice in John's misgovernment.

The chief obstacle in the way of the royalists had been the character of John, and the little Henry of Winchester could have had no share in the crimes of his father. But the dead king had lately shown such rare energy that there was a danger lest the accession of a boy of nine might not weaken the cause of monarchy. The barons were largely out of hand. The war was assuming the character of the civil war of Stephen's days, and John's mercenaries were aspiring to play the part of feudal potentates. It was significant that so many of John's principal supporters were possessors of extensive franchises, like the lords of the Welsh March, who might well desire to extend these feudal immunities to their English estates. The triumph of the crown through such help might easily have resolved the united England of Henry II. into a series of lordships under a nominal king.

The situation was saved by the wisdom and moderation of the papal legate, and the loyalty of William Marshal, who forgot his interests as Earl of Pembroke in his devotion to the house of Anjou. From the moment of John's death at Newark, the cardinal and the marshal took the lead. They met at Worcester, where the tyrant was buried, and at once made preparations for the coronation of Henry of Winchester. The ceremony took place at St. Peter's Abbey, Gloucester, on October 28, from which day the new reign was reckoned as beginning. The marshal, who had forty-three years before dubbed the "young king" Henry a knight, then for a second time admitted a young king Henry to the order of chivalry. When the king had recited the coronation oath and performed homage to the pope, Gualo anointed him and placed on his head the plain gold circlet that perforce did duty for a crown.[1]

---

[1] There is some conflict of evidence on this point, and Dr. Stubbs, following Wendover, iv., 2, makes Peter of Winchester crown Henry. But the official account in *Fœdera*, i., 145, is confirmed by *Ann. Tewkesbury*, p. 62; *Histoire de G. le Maréchal*, lines 15329-32; *Hist. des ducs de Normandie, et des rois d'Angleterre*, p. 181, and *Ann. Winchester*, p. 83. Wykes, p. 60, and *Ann. Dunstable*, p. 48, which confirm Wendover, are suspect by reason of other errors.

I *

CHAP.   Next day Henry's leading supporters performed homage, and
I.   before November 1 the marshal was made justiciar.

On November 11 a great council met at Bristol. Only four earls appeared, and one of these, William of Fors, Earl of Albemarle, was a recent convert. But the presence of eleven bishops showed that the Church had espoused the cause of the little king, and a throng of western and marcher magnates made a sufficient representation of the lay baronage. The chief business was to provide for the government during the minority. Gualo withstood the temptation to adopt the method by which Innocent III. had ruled Sicily in the name of Frederick II. The king's mother was too unpopular and incompetent to anticipate the part played by Blanche of Castile during the minority of St. Louis. After the precedents set by the Latin kingdom of Jerusalem, the barons took the matter into their own hands. Their work of selection was not an easy one. Randolph of Chester was by far the most powerful of the royalist lords, but his turbulence and purely personal policy, not less than his excessive possessions and inordinate palatine jurisdictions, made him unsuitable for the regency. Yet had he raised any sort of claim, it would have been hardly possible to resist his pretensions.[1] Luckily, Randolph stood aside, and his withdrawal gave the aged earl marshal the position for which his nomination as justiciar at Gloucester had already marked him out. The title of regent was as yet unknown, either in England or France, but the style, "ruler of king and kingdom," which the barons gave to the marshal, meant something more than the ordinary position of a justiciar. William's friends had some difficulty in persuading him to accept the office. He was over seventy years of age, and felt it would be too great a burden. Induced at last by the legate to undertake the charge, from that moment he shrank from none of its responsibilities. The personal care of the king was comprised within the marshal's duties, but he delegated that branch of his work to Peter des Roches.[2] These two, with Gualo, controlled the whole policy of the new reign.

---

[1] The fears and hopes of the marshal's friends are well depicted in *Histoire de Guillaume le Maréchal*, lines 15500-15708.

[2] The panegyrist of the marshal emphasises strongly the fact that Peter's charge was a delegation, *ibid.*, lines 17993-18018.

Next to them came Hubert de Burgh, John's justiciar, whom the marshal very soon restored to that office. But Hubert at once went back to the defence of Dover, and for some time took little part in general politics.

On November 12, the legate and the regent issued at Bristol a confirmation of the Great Charter. Some of the most important articles accepted by John in 1215 were omitted, including the "constitutional clauses" requiring the consent of the council of barons for extraordinary taxation. Other provisions, which tied the hands of the government, were postponed for further consideration in more settled times. But with all its mutilations the Bristol charter of 1216 marked a more important moment than even the charter of Runny-mede. The condemnation of Innocent III. would in all probability have prevented the temporary concession of John from becoming permanent. Love of country and love of liberty were doubtless growing forces, but they were still in their infancy, while the papal authority was something ultimate against which few Christians dared appeal. Thus the adoption by the free will of the papal legate, and the deliberate choice of the marshal of the policy of the Great Charter, converted, as has well been said, "a treaty won at the point of the sword into a manifesto of peace and sound government ".[1] This wise change of policy cut away the ground from under the feet of the English supporters of Louis. The friends of the young Henry could appeal to his innocence, to his sacred unction, and to his recognition by Holy Church. They offered a programme of limited monarchy, of the redress of grievances, of vested rights preserved, and of adhesion to the good old traditions that all Englishmen respected. From that moment the Charter became a new starting-point in our history.

In strange contrast to this programme of reform, the aliens, who had opposed the charter of Runnymede, were among the lords by whose counsel and consent the charter of Bristol was issued. In its weakness the new government sought to stimulate the zeal both of the foreign mercenaries and of the loyal barons by grants and privileges which seriously entrenched upon the royal authority. Falkes de Bréauté was confirmed in the custody of a compact group of six midland shires,

[1] Stubbs, *Const. Hist.*, ii., 21.

besides the earldom of Devon, and the "county of the Isle of Wight,"[1] which he guarded in the interests of his wife and stepson. Savary de Mauléon, who in despair of his old master's success had crossed over to Poitou before John's death, was made warden of the castle of Bristol. Randolph of Chester was consoled for the loss of the regency by the renewal of John's recent grant of the Honour of Lancaster which was by this time definitely recognised as a shire.[2]

The war assumed the character of a crusade. The royalist troops wore white crosses on their garments, and were assured by the clergy of certain salvation. The cruel and purposeless ravaging of the enemy's country, which had occupied John's last months of life, became rare, though partisans, such as Falkes de Bréauté, still outvied the French in plundering monasteries and churches. The real struggle became a war of castles. Louis endeavoured to complete his conquest of the south-east by the capture of the royal strongholds, which still limited his power to the open country. At first the French prince had some successes. In November he increased his hold on the Home counties by capturing the Tower of London, by forcing Hertford to surrender, and by pressing the siege of Berkhampsted. As Christmas approached the royalists proposed a truce. Louis agreed on the condition that Berkhampsted should be surrendered, and early in 1217 both parties held councils, the royalists at Oxford and the barons at Cambridge. There was vague talk of peace, but the war was renewed, and Louis captured Hedingham and Orford in Essex, and besieged the castles of Colchester and Norwich. Then another truce until April 26 was concluded, on the condition that the royalists should surrender these two strongholds.

Both sides had need to pause. Louis, at the limit of his resources, was anxious to obtain men and money from France. He was not getting on well with his new subjects. The eastern counties grumbled at his taxes. Dissensions arose between the English and French elements in his host. The English lords resented the grants and appointments he gave to his countrymen. The French nobles professed to despise the English as traitors. When Hertford was taken, Robert

[1] *Histoire des ducs de Normandie*, etc., p. 181.
[2] Tait, *Medieval Manchester and the Beginnings of Lancashire*, p. 180.

FitzWalter demanded that its custody should be restored to
him. Louis roughly told him that Englishmen, who had betrayed their natural lord, were not to be entrusted with such
charges. It was to little purpose that he promised Robert
that every man should have his rights when the war was over.
The prospects of ending the war grew more remote every day.
The royalists took advantage of the discouragement of their
opponents. The regent was lavish in promises. There should
be no inquiry into bygones, and all who submitted to the young
king should be guaranteed all their existing rights. The result
was that a steady stream of converts began to flow from the
camp of Louis to the camp of the marshal. For the first time
signs of a national movement against Louis began to be manifest. It became clear that his rule meant foreign conquest.

Louis wished to return to France, but despite the truce
he could only win his way to the coast by fighting. The
Cinque Ports were changing their allegiance. A popular
revolt had broken out in the Weald, where a warlike squire,
William of Cassingham,[1] soon became a terror to the French
under his nickname of Wilkin of the Weald. As Louis
traversed the disaffected districts, Wilkin fell upon him near
Lewes, and took prisoners two nephews of the Count of
Nevers. On his further march to Winchelsea, the men of
the Weald broke down the bridges behind him, while on his
approach the men of Winchelsea destroyed their mills, and
took to their ships as avowed partisans of King Henry. The
French prince entered the empty town, and had great difficulty
in keeping his army alive. "Wheat found they there," says
a chronicler, "in great plenty, but they knew not how to grind
it. Long time were they in such a plight that they had to
crush by hand the corn of which they made their bread. They
could catch no fish. Great store of nuts found they in the town ;
these were their finest food."[2] Louis was in fact besieged by
the insurgents, and was only released by a force of knights
riding down from London to help him. These troops dared
not travel by the direct road through the Weald, and made
their way to Romney through Canterbury. Rye was strongly

---

[1] Mr. G. J. Turner has identified Cassingham with the modern Kensham,
between Rolvenden and Sandhurst, in Kent.

[2] *Histoire des ducs de Normandie*, etc., p. 183.

CHAP.
I.
held against them and the ships of the Cinque Ports dominated the sea, so that Louis was still cut off from his friends at Romney. A relieving fleet was despatched from Boulogne, but stress of weather kept it for a fortnight at Dover, while Louis was starving at Winchelsea. At last the French ships appeared off Winchelsea. Thereupon the English withdrew, and Louis finding the way open to France returned home.

A crowd of waverers changed sides. At their head were William Longsword, Earl of Salisbury, the bastard great-uncle of the little king, and William, the young marshal, the eldest son of the Earl of Pembroke. The regent wandered from town to town in Sussex, receiving the submission of the peasantry, and venturing to approach as near London as Dorking. The victorious Wilkin was made Warden of the Seven Hundreds of the Weald. The greatest of the magnates of Sussex and Surrey, William, Earl Warenne, followed the example of his tenantry, and made his peace with the king. The royalists fell upon the few castles held by the barons. While one corps captured Odiham, Farnham, Chichester, and other southern strongholds, Falkes de Bréauté overran the Isle of Ely, and Randolph of Chester besieged the Leicester-shire fortress of Mount Sorrel. Enguerrand de Coucy, whom Louis had left in command, remained helpless in London. His boldest act was to send a force to Lincoln, which occupied the town, but failed to take the castle. This stronghold, under its hereditary warden, the valiant old lady, Nichola de Cam-ville,[1] had already twice withstood a siege.

Louis found no great encouragement in France, for Philip Augustus, too prudent to offend the Church, gave but grudging support to his excommunicated son. When, on the eve of the expiration of the truce, Louis returned to England, his reinforcements comprised only 120 knights. Among them, however, were the Count of Brittany, Peter Mauclerc, anxious to press in person his rights to the earldom of Richmond, the Counts of Perche and Guînes, and many lords of Picardy, Artois and Ponthieu. Conscious that everything depended on the speedy capture of the royal castles, Louis introduced for the first time into England the *trébuchet*, a recently invented

---

[1] On Nichola de Camville or de la Hay see M. Petit-Dutaillis in *Mélanges Julien Havet*, pp. 369-80.

machine that cast great missiles by means of heavy counter-   CHAP.
poises. " Great was the talk about this, for at that time few   I.
of them had been seen in France." [1] On April 22, Louis
reached Dover, where the castle was still feebly beset by the
French. On his nearing the shore, Wilkin of the Weald and
Oliver, a bastard of King John's, burnt the huts of the French
engaged in watching the castle. Afraid to land in their
presence, Louis disembarked at Sandwich. Next day he went
by land to Dover, but discouraged by tidings of his losses, he
gladly concluded a short truce with Hubert de Burgh. He
abandoned the siege of Dover, and hurried off towards Winchester, where the two castles were being severely pressed by
the royalists. But his progress was impeded by his siege train,
and Farnham castle blocked his way.

Saer de Quincy, Earl of Winchester, joined Louis outside
the walls of Farnham. Saer's motive was to persuade Louis
to hasten to the relief of his castle of Mount Sorrel. The
French prince was not in a position to resist pressure from
a powerful supporter. He divided his army, and while the
Earl of Winchester, along with the Count of Perche and
Robert FitzWalter, made their way to Leicestershire, he completed his journey to Winchester, threw a fresh force into the
castles, and, leaving the Count of Nevers in charge, hurried to
London. There he learnt that Hubert de Burgh at Dover had
broken the truce, and he at once set off to renew the siege of the
stronghold which had so continually baulked his plans. But
little good came of his efforts, and the much-talked-of *trébuchet*
proving powerless to effect a breach, Louis had to resign
himself to a weary blockade. While he was besieging Dover,
Saer de Quincy had relieved Mount Sorrel, whence he marched
to the help of Gilbert of Ghent, the only English baron whom
Louis ventured to raise to comital rank as Earl of Lincoln.
Gilbert was still striving to capture Lincoln Castle, but Nichola
de Camville had resisted him from February to May. With
the help of the army from Mount Sorrel, the castle and its
châtelaine were soon reduced to great straits.

The marshal saw that the time was come to take the
offensive, and resolved to raise the siege. Having no field

[1] *Histoire des ducs de Normandie*, etc., p. 188; cf. *English Hist. Review*,
xviii. (1903), 263-64.

CHAP.
I.

army, he stripped his castles of their garrisons, and gave rendezvous to his barons at Newark. There the royalists rested three days, and received the blessing of Gualo and the bishops. They then set out towards Lincoln, commanded by the regent in person, the Earl of Chester, and the Bishop of Winchester, whom the legate appointed as his representative. The strong water defences of the rebel city on the south made it unadvisable for them to take the direct route towards it. Their army descended the Trent to Torksey, where it rested the night of May 19. Early next day, the eve of Trinity Sunday, it marched in four "battles" to relieve Lincoln Castle.

There were more than 600 knights besieging the castle and holding the town, and the relieving army only numbered 400 knights and 300 cross-bowmen. But the barons dared not risk a combat that might have involved them in the fate of Stephen in 1141. They retreated within the city and allowed the marshal to open up communications with the castle. The marshal's plan of battle was arranged by Peter des Roches, who was more at home in the field than in the church. The cross-bowmen under Falkes de Bréauté were thrown into the castle, and joined with the garrison in making a sally from its east gate into the streets of the town. While the barons were thus distracted, the marshal burst through the badly defended north gate. The barons taken in front and flank fought desperately, but with no success. Falkes' cross-bowmen shot down their horses, and the dismounted knights soon failed to hold their own in the open ground about the cathedral. The Count of Perche was slain by a sword-thrust through the eyehole of his helmet. The royalists chased the barons down the steep lanes which connect the upper with the lower town. When they reached level ground the baronial troops rallied, and once more strove to reascend the hill. But the town was assailed on every side, and its land defences yielded with little difficulty. The Earl of Chester poured his vassals through one of the eastern gates, and took the barons in flank. Once more they broke, and this time they rallied not again, but fled through the Wigford suburb seeking any means of escape. Some obstruction in the Bar-gate, the southern exit from the city, retarded their flight, and many of the leaders were captured. The remnant fled to London, thinking that "every bush was full of marshals," and suffering severely from the hostility of the peasantry. Only three persons were slain in the battle, but there was a cruel massacre of the defenceless citizens after its close. So vast was the booty won by the victors that in scorn they called the fight the Fair of Lincoln.[1]

Louis' prospects were still not desperate. The victorious army scattered, each man to his own house, so that the marshal was in no position to press matters to extremities. But there was a great rush to make terms with the victor, and Louis thought it prudent to abandon the hopeless siege of Dover, and take refuge with his partisans, the Londoners. Meanwhile the marshal hovered round London, hoping eventually to shut up the enemy in the capital. On June 12, the Archbishop of Tyre and three Cistercian abbots, who had come to England to preach the Crusade, persuaded both parties to accept provisional articles of peace. Louis stipulated for a complete amnesty to all his partisans; but the legate declined to grant pardon to the rebellious clerks who had refused to obey the interdict, conspicuous among whom was the firebrand Simon Langton, brother of the archbishop. Finding no compromise possible, Louis broke off the negotiations rather than abandon his friends. Gualo urged a siege of London, but the marshal saw that his resources were not adequate for such a step. Again many of his followers went home, and the court abode first at Oxford and afterwards at Gloucester. It seemed as if the war might go on for ever.

Blanche of Castile, Louis' wife, redoubled her efforts on his behalf. In response to her entreaties a hundred knights and several hundred men-at-arms took ship for England. Among the knights was the famous William des Barres, one of the heroes of Bouvines, and Theobald, Count of Blois. Eustace the Monk, a renegade clerk turned pirate, and a hero of later romance, took command of the fleet. On the eve of St. Bartholomew, August 23, Eustace sailed from Calais towards the mouth of the Thames. Kent had become royalist; the marshal and Hubert de Burgh held Sandwich, so that the long voyage up the Thames was the only way of taking succour to Louis. Next day the old earl remained on shore, but sent out Hubert

---

[1] For a discussion of the battle, see *English Hist. Review*, xviii. (1903), 240-65.

CHAP.
I.

with the fleet. The English let the French pass by, and then, manœuvring for the weather gage, tacked and assailed them from behind.[1] The fight raged round the great ship of Eustace, on which the chief French knights were embarked. Laden with stores, horses, and a ponderous *trébuchet*, it was too low in the water to manœuvre or escape. Hubert easily laid his own vessel alongside it. The English, who were better used to fighting at sea than the French, threw powdered lime into the faces of the enemy, swept the decks with their crossbow bolts and then boarded the ship, which was taken after a fierce fight. The crowd of cargo boats could offer little resistance as they beat up against the wind in their retreat to Calais; the ships containing the soldiers were more fortunate in escaping. Eustace was beheaded, and his head paraded on a pole through the streets of Canterbury.

The battle of St. Bartholomew's Day, like that of Lincoln a triumph of skill over numbers, proved decisive for the fortunes of Louis. The English won absolute control of the narrow seas, and cut off from Louis all hope of fighting his way back to France. As soon as he heard of the defeat of Eustace, he reopened negotiations with the marshal. On the 29th there was a meeting between Louis and the Earl at the gates of London. The regent had to check the ardour of his own partisans, and it was only after anxious days of deliberation that the party of moderation prevailed. On September 5 a formal conference was held on an island of the Thames near Kingston. On the 11th a definitive treaty was signed at the archbishop's house at Lambeth.

The Treaty of Lambeth repeated with little alteration the terms rejected by Louis three months before. The French prince surrendered his castles, released his partisans from their oaths to him, and exhorted all his allies, including the King of Scots and the Prince of Gwynedd, to lay down their arms. In return Henry promised that no layman should lose his inheritance by reason of his adherence to Louis, and that the baronial prisoners should be released without further payment

---

[1] This successful attempt of the English fleet to manœuvre for the weather gage, that is to secure a position to the windward of their opponents, is the first recorded instance of what became the favourite tactics of British admirals. For the legend of Eustace see *Witasse le Moine*, ed. Förster (1891).

of ransom.   London, despite its pertinacity in rebellion, was
to retain its ancient franchises.   The marshal bound himself
personally to pay Louis 10,000 marks, nominally as expenses,
really as a bribe to accept these terms.   A few days later Louis
and his French barons appeared before the legate, barefoot
and in the white garb of penitents, and were reconciled to the
Church.   They were then escorted to Dover, whence they
took ship for France.   Only on the rebellious clergy did
Gualo's wrath fall.   The canons of St. Paul's were turned
out in a body ; ringleaders like Simon Langton were driven
into exile, and agents of the legate traversed the country
punishing clerks who had disregarded the interdict.   But
Honorius was more merciful than Gualo, and within a year
even Simon received his pardon.   The laymen of both camps
forgot their differences, when Randolph of Chester and William
of Ferrars fought in the crusade of Damietta, side by side with
Saer of Winchester and Robert FitzWalter.   The reconciliation
of parties was further shown in the marriage of Hubert de Burgh
to John's divorced wife, Isabella of Gloucester, a widow by the
death of the Earl of Essex, and still the foremost English heiress.
On November 6 the pacification was completed by the reissue
of the Great Charter in what was substantially its final form.
The forest clauses of the earlier issues were published in a
much enlarged shape as a separate Forest Charter, which laid
down the great principle that no man was to lose life or
limb for hindering the king's hunting.

It is tempting to regard the defeat of Louis as a triumph
of English patriotism.   But it is an anachronism to read the
ideals of later ages into the doings of the men of the early
thirteenth century.   So far as there was national feeling in
England, it was arrayed against Henry.   To the last the
most fervently English of the barons were steadfast on the
French prince's side, and the triumph of the little king had
largely been procured by John's foreigners.   To contemporary
eyes the rebels were factious assertors of class privileges and
feudal immunities.   Their revolt against their natural lord
brought them into conflict with the sentiment of feudal duty
which was still so strong in faithful minds.   And against
them was a stronger force than feudal loyalty.   From this
religious standpoint the Canon of Barnwell best sums up the

situation : "It was a miracle that the heir of France, who had won so large a part of the kingdom, was constrained to abandon the realm without hope of recovering it.   It was because the hand of God was not with him.   He came to England in spite of the prohibition of the Holy Roman Church, and he re-mained there regardless of its anathema."

The young king never forgot that he owed his throne to the pope and his legate.   "When we were bereft of our father in tender years," he declared long afterwards, "when our subjects were turned against us, it was our mother, the Holy Roman Church, that brought back our realm under our power, anointed us king, crowned us, and placed us on the throne."[1]   The papacy, which had secured a new hold over England by its alliance with John, made its position permanent by its zeal for the rights of his son.   By identifying the monarchy with the charters, it skilfully retraced the false step which it had taken.   Under the ægis of the Roman see the national spirit grew, and the next generation was to see the temper fostered by Gualo in its turn grow impatient of the papal supremacy.   It was Gualo, then, who secured the confirmation of the charters.   Even Louis unconsciously worked in that direction, for, had he not gained so strong a hold on the country, there would have been no reason to adopt a policy of conciliation.   We must not read the history of this generation in the light of modern times, or even with the eyes of Matthew Paris.

The marshal had before him a task essentially similar to that which Henry II. had undertaken after the anarchy of Stephen's reign.   It was with the utmost difficulty that the sum promised to Louis could be extracted from the war-stricken and famished tillers of the soil.   The exchequer was so empty that the Christmas court of the young king was celebrated at the expense of Falkes de Bréauté.   Those who had fought for the king clamoured for grants and rewards, and it was necessary to humour them.   For example, Randolph of Blundeville, with the earldom of Lincoln added to his Cheshire palatinate and his Lancashire Honour, had acquired a position nearly as strong as that of the Randolph of the reign of Stephen.   "Adulterine castles" had grown up in such numbers that the new issue of the Charter insisted upon their destruc-

[1] Grosseteste, *Epistolæ*, p. 339.

tion. Even the lawful castles were held by unauthorised custodians, who refused to yield them up to the king's officers. Though Alexander, King of Scots, purchased his reconciliation with Rome by abandoning Carlisle and performing homage to Henry, the Welsh remained recalcitrant. One chieftain, Morgan of Caerleon, waged war against the marshal in Gwent, and was dislodged with difficulty. During the war Llewelyn ap Iorwerth conquered Cardigan and Carmarthen from the marchers, and it was only after receiving assurances that he might retain these districts so long as the king's minority lasted that he condescended to do homage at Worcester in March, 1218.

In the following May Stephen Langton came back from exile and threw the weight of his judgment on the regent's side. Gradually the worst difficulties were surmounted. The administrative machinery once more became effective. A new seal was cast for the king, whose documents had hitherto been stamped with the seal of the regent. Order was so far restored that Gualo returned to Italy. He was a man of high character and noble aims, caring little for personal advancement, and curbing his hot zeal against "schismatics" in his desire to restore peace to England. His memory is still commemorated in his great church of St. Andrew, at Vercelli, erected, it may be, with the proceeds of his English benefices, and still preserving the manuscript of legends of its patron saint, which its founder had sent thither from his exile.

At Candlemas, 1219, the aged regent was smitten with a mortal illness. His followers bore him up the Thames from London to his manor of Caversham, where his last hours were disturbed by the intrigues of Peter of Winchester for his succession, and the importunity of selfish clerks, clamouring for grants to their churches. He died on May 14, clad in the habit of the Knights of the Temple, in whose new church in London his body was buried, and where his effigy may still be seen. The landless younger son of a poor baron, he had supported himself in his youth by the spoils of the knights he had vanquished in the tournaments, where his successes gained him fame as the model of chivalry. The favour of Henry, the "young king," gave him political importance, and his marriage with Strongbow's daughter made him a mighty man in England, Ireland, Wales, and Normandy. Strenuous and upright, simple and dignified, the young soldier of fortune bore easily the weight of office and honour which accrued to him before the death of his first patron. Limited as was his outlook, he gave himself entirely to his master-principle of loyalty to the feudal lord whom he had sworn to obey. This simple conception enabled him to subordinate his interests as a marcher potentate to his duty to the English monarchy. It guided him in his difficult work of serving with unbending constancy a tyrant like John. It shone most clearly when in his old age he saved John's son from the consequences of his father's misdeeds. A happy accident has led to the discovery in our own days of the long poem, drawn up in commemoration of his career[1] at the instigation of his son. This important work has enabled us to enter into the marshal's character and spirit in much the same way as Joinville's *History of St. Louis* has made us familiar with the motives and attributes of the great French king. They are the two men of the thirteenth century whom we know most intimately. It is well that the two characters thus portrayed at length represent to us so much of what is best in the chivalry, loyalty, statecraft, and piety of the Middle Ages.

[1] *Histoire de Guillaume le Maréchal*, published by P. Meyer for the Soc. de l'histoire de France. Petit-Dutaillis, *Étude sur Louis VIII.* (1894), and G. J. Turner, *Minority of Henry III.*, part i., in *Transactions of the Royal Hist. Soc.*, new ser., viii. (1904), 245-95, are the best modern commentaries on the history of the marshal's regency.

CHAPTER II.

THE RULE OF HUBERT DE BURGH.

WILLIAM MARSHAL had recognised that the regency must end with him. "There is no land," he declared, "where the people are so divided as they are in England. Were I to hand over the king to one noble, the others would be jealous. For this reason I have determined to entrust him to God and the pope. No one can blame me for this, for, if the land is not defended by the pope, I know no one who can protect it." The fortunate absence of Randolph of Chester on crusade made it easy to carry out this plan. Accordingly the king of twelve years was supposed to be capable of acting for himself. But the ultimate authority resided with the new legate Pandulf, who, without any formal designation, was the real successor of the marshal. This arrangement naturally left great power to Peter des Roches, who continued to have the custody of the king's person, and to Hubert the justiciar, who henceforth acted as Pandulf's deputy. Next to them came the Archbishop of Canterbury. Langton's share in the struggle for the charters was so conspicuous, that we do not always remember that it was as a scholar and a theologian that he acquired his chief reputation among his contemporaries. On his return from exile he found such engrossing occupation in the business of his see, that he took little part in politics for several years. His self-effacement strengthened the position of the legate.

Pandulf was no stranger to England. As subdeacon of the Roman Church he received John's submission in 1213, and stood by his side during nearly all his later troubles. He had been rewarded by his election to the bishopric of Norwich, but was recalled to Rome before his consecration, and only came back to England in the higher capacity of legate on December 3, 1218, after the recall of Gualo. He had been the cause of Langton's suspension, and there was probably no love lost between him and the archbishop. It was in order to avoid troublesome questions of jurisdiction that Pandulf, at the pope's suggestion, continued to postpone his consecration as bishop, since that act would have subordinated him to the Archbishop of Canterbury. But neither he nor Langton was disposed to push matters to extremities. Just as Peter des Roches balanced Hubert de Burgh, so the archbishop acted as a makeweight to the legate. When power was thus nicely equipoised, there was a natural tendency to avoid conflicting issues. In these circumstances the truce between parties, which had marked the regency, continued for the first years after Earl William's death. In all doubtful points the will of the legate seems to have prevailed. Pandulf's correspondence shows him interfering in every matter of state. He associated himself with the justiciar in the appointment of royal officials; he invoked the papal authority to put down "adulterine castles," and to prevent any baron having more than one royal stronghold in his custody; he prolonged the truce with France, and strove to pacify the Prince of North Wales; he procured the resumption of the royal domain, and rebuked Bishop Peter and the justiciar for remissness in dealing with Jewish usurers; he filled up bishoprics at his own discretion. Nor did he neglect his own interests; his kinsfolk found preferment in his English diocese, and he appropriated certain livings for the payment of his debts, "so far as could be done without offence". But in higher matters he pursued a wise policy. In recognising that the great interest of the Church was peace, he truly expressed the policy of the mild Honorius. For more than two years he kept Englishmen from flying at each other's throats. If they paid for peace by the continuance of foreign rule, it was better to be governed by Pandulf than pillaged by Falkes.

The principal events of these years were due to papal initiative.[1] Honorius looked askance on the maimed rites of

[1] H. R. Luard, *On the Relations between England and Rome during the Earlier Portion of the Reign of Henry III.* (1877), illustrates papal influence at this period.

the Gloucester coronation, and ordered a new hallowing to take place at the accustomed place and with the accustomed ceremonies. This supplementary rite was celebrated at Westminster on Whitsunday, May 17, 1220. Though Pandulf was present, he discreetly permitted the Archbishop of Canterbury to crown Henry with the diadem of St. Edward. " This coronation," says the Canon of Barnwell, "was celebrated with such good order and such splendour that the oldest magnates who were present declared that they had seen none of the king's predecessors crowned with so much goodwill and tranquillity." Nor was this the only great ecclesiastical function of the year. On July 7 Langton celebrated at Canterbury the translation of the relics of St. Thomas to a magnificent shrine at the back of the high altar. Again the legate gave precedence to the archbishop, and the presence of the young king, of the Archbishop of Reims, and the Primate of Hungary, gave distinction to the solemnity. It was a grand time for English saints. When Damietta was taken from the Mohammedans, the crusaders dedicated two of its churches to St. Thomas of Canterbury and St. Edmund the King. A new saint was added to the calendar, who, if not an Englishman, had done good work for the country of his adoption. In 1220 Honorius III. canonised Hugh of Avalon, the Carthusian Bishop of Lincoln, on the report of a commission presided over by Langton himself.

No real unity of principle underlay the external tranquillity. As time went on Peter des Roches bitterly resented the growing preponderance of Hubert de Burgh. Not all the self-restraint of the legate could commend him to Langton, whose obstinate insistence upon his metropolitical authority forced Pandulf to procure bulls from Rome specifically releasing him from the jurisdiction of the primate. In these circumstances it was natural for Bishop Peter and the legate to join together against the justiciar and the archbishop. Finding that the legate was too strong for him, Langton betook himself to Rome, and remained there nearly a year. Before he went home he persuaded Honorius to promise not to confer the same benefice twice by papal provision, and to send no further legate to England during his lifetime. Pandulf was at once recalled, and left England in July, 1221, a month before his

rival's return.   He was compensated for the slight put up n
him by receiving his long-deferred consecration to Norwich at
the hands of the pope.   There is small reason for believing that
he was exceptionally greedy or unpopular.   But his withdrawal
removed an influence which had done its work for good, and
was becoming a national danger.   Langton henceforth could
act as the real head of the English Church.   In 1222, he
held an important provincial council at Oseney abbey, near
Oxford, where he issued constitutions, famous as the first provincial canons still recognised as binding in our ecclesiastical
courts.   He began once more to concern himself with affairs
of state, and Hubert found him a sure ally.   Bishop Peter,
disgusted with his declining influence, welcomed his appointment as archbishop of the crusading Church at Damietta.   He
took the cross, and left England with Falkes de Bréauté as
his companion.   Learning that the crescent had driven the
cross out of his new see, he contented himself with making the
pilgrimage to Compostella, and soon found his way back to
England, where he sought for opportunities to regain power.

Relieved of the opposition of Bishop Peter, Hubert insisted on depriving barons of doubtful loyalty of the custody
of royal castles, and found his chief opponent in William
Earl of Albemarle.   In dignity and possessions, Albemarle
was not ill-qualified to be a feudal leader.   The son of
William de Fors, of Oléron, a Poitevin adventurer of the type
of Falkes de Bréauté, he represented, through his mother,
the line of the counts of Aumâle, who had since the Conquest
ruled over Holderness from their castle at Skipsea.   The
family acquired the status of English earls under Stephen, retaining their foreign title, expressed in English in the form of
Albemarle, being the first house of comital rank abroad to hold
an earldom with a French name unassociated with any English
shire.   During the civil war Albemarle's tergiversations, which
rivalled those of the Geoffrey de Mandeville of Stephen's time,
had been rewarded by large grants from the victorious party.
Since 1219 he suffered slight upon slight, and in 1220 was
stripped of the custody of Rockingham Castle.   Late in that
year Hubert resolved to enforce an order, promulgated in
1217, which directed Albemarle to restore to his former subtenant Bytham Castle, in South Kesteven, of which he was

overlord, and of which he had resumed possession on account of the treason of his vassal. The earl hurried away in indignation from the king's Christmas court, and in January, 1221, threw himself into Bytham, eager to hold it by force against the king. For a brief space he ruled over the country-side after the fashion of a baron of Stephen's time. He plundered the neighbouring towns and churches, and filled the dungeons of Castle Bytham with captives. On the pretext of attending a council at Westminster he marched southwards, but his real motive was disclosed when he suddenly attacked the castle of Fotheringhay. His men crossed the moat on the ice, and, burning down the great gate, easily overpowered the scanty garrison. "As if he were the only ruler of the kingdom," says the Canon of Barnwell, "he sent letters signed with his seal to the mayors of the cities of England, granting his peace to all merchants engaged in plying their trades, and allowing them free licence of going and coming through his castles." Nothing in the annals of the time puts more clearly this revival of the old feudal custom that each baron should lord it as king over his own estates.

Albemarle's power did not last long. He incurred the wrath of the Church, and both in Kesteven and in Northamptonshire set himself against the interests of Randolph of Chester. Before January was over Pandulf excommunicated him, and a great council granted a special scutage, "the scutage of Bytham," to equip an army to crush the rebel. Early in February a considerable force marched northwards against him. The Earl of Chester took part in the campaign, and both the legate and the king accompanied the army. Before the combined efforts of Church and State, Albemarle dared not hold his ground, and fled to Fountains, where he took sanctuary. His followers abandoned Fotheringhay, but stood a siege at Bytham. After six days this castle was captured on February 8. Even then secret sympathisers with Albemarle were able to exercise influence on his behalf, and Pandulf himself was willing to show mercy. The earl came out of sanctuary, and was pardoned on condition of taking the crusader's vow. No effort was made to insist on his going on crusade, and within a few months he was again in favour. "Thus," says Roger of Wendover, "the king set the worst of

CHAP.
II.

examples, and encouraged future rebellions." Randolph of Chester came out with the spoils of victory. He secured as the price of his ostentatious fidelity the custody of the Honour of Huntingdon, during the nonage of the earl, his nephew, John the Scot.

A tumult in the capital soon taught Hubert that he had other foes to fight against besides the feudal party. At a wrestling match, held on July 25, 1222, between the city and the suburbs, the citizens won an easy victory. The tenants of the Abbot of Westminster challenged the conquerors to a fresh contest on August 1 at Westminster. But the abbot's men were more anxious for revenge than good sport, and seeing that the Londoners were likely to win, they violently broke up the match. Suspecting no evil, the citizens had come without arms, and were very severely handled by their rivals. Driven back behind their walls, the Londoners clamoured for vengeance. Serlo the mercer, their mayor, a prudent and peace-loving man, urged them to seek compensation of the abbot. But the citizens preferred the advice of Constantine FitzAthulf, who insisted upon an immediate attack on the men of Westminster. Next day the abbey precincts were invaded, and much mischief was done. The alarm was the greater because Constantine was a man of high position, who had recently been a sheriff of London, and had once been a strenuous supporter of Louis of France. It was rumoured that his followers had raised the cry, "Montjoie! Saint Denis!" The quarrels of neighbouring cities were as dangerous to sound rule as the feuds of rival barons, and Hubert took instant measures to put down the sedition. With the aid of Falkes de Bréauté's mercenaries, order was restored, and Constantine was led before the justiciar. Early next day Falkes assembled his forces, and crossed the river to Southwark. He took with him Constantine and two of his supporters, and hanged all three, without form of trial, before the city knew anything about it. Then Falkes and his soldiers rushed through the streets, capturing, mutilating, and frightening away the citizens. Constantine's houses and property were seized by the king. The weak Serlo was deposed from the mayoralty, and the city taken into the king's hands. It was the last time that Hubert and Falkes worked together, and something of the violence of

the *condottiere* captain sullied the justiciar's reputation. As
the murderer of Constantine, Hubert was henceforth pursued
with the undying hatred of the Londoners.

During the next two years parties became clearly defined.
Hubert more and more controlled the royal policy, and strove
to strengthen both his master and himself by marriage alliances.
Powerful husbands were sought for the king's three sisters.
On June 19, 1221, Joan, Henry's second sister, was married to
the young Alexander of Scotland, at York. At the same
time Hubert, a widower by Isabella of Gloucester's death,
wedded Alexander's elder sister, Margaret, a match which compensated the justiciar for his loss of Isabella's lands. Four
years later, Isabella, the King of Scot's younger sister, was
united with Roger Bigod, the young Earl of Norfolk, a grandson of the great William Marshal, whose eldest son and successor, William Marshal the younger, was in 1224 married to
the king's third sister, Eleanor. The policy of intermarriage
between the royal family and the baronage was defended by
the example of Philip Augustus in France, and on the ground
of the danger to the royal interests if so strong a magnate as
the earl marshal were enticed away from his allegiance by an
alliance with a house unfriendly to Henry.[1]

The futility of marriage alliances in modifying policy was
already made clear by the attitude of Llewelyn ap Iorwerth,
the husband of Henry's bastard sister Joan. This resourceful
prince had already raised himself to a high position by a statecraft which lacked neither strength nor duplicity. Though
fully conscious of his position as the champion of a proud
nation, and posing as the peer of the King of Scots, Llewelyn
saw that it was his interest to continue the friendship with the
baronial opposition which had profited him so greatly in the
days of the French invasion. The pacification arranged in
1218 sat lightly upon him, and he plunged into a war with
William Marshal the younger that desolated South Wales for
several years. In 1219 Llewelyn devastated Pembrokeshire so
cruelly that the marshal's losses were currently, though ab-
surdly, reported to have exceeded the amount of the ransom of
King Richard. There was much more fighting, but Llewelyn's
progress was impeded by difficulties with his own son Griffith,

[1] *Royal Letters*, i., 244-46.

CHAP.
II.

and with the princes of South Wales, who bore impatiently the growing hold of the lord of Gwynedd upon the affections of southern Welshmen. There was war also in the middle march, where in 1220 a royal army was assembled against Llewelyn; but Pandulf negotiated a truce, and the only permanent result of this effort was the fortification of the castle and town at Montgomery, which had become royal demesne on the extinction of the ancient house of Bollers a few years earlier. But peace never lasted long west of the Severn, and in 1222 William Marshal drove Llewelyn out of Cardigan and Carmarthen. Again there were threats of war. Llewelyn was excommunicated, and his lands put under interdict. The marshal complained bitterly of the poor support which Henry gave him against the Welsh, but Hubert restored cordiality between him and the king. In these circumstances the policy of marrying Eleanor to the indignant marcher was a wise one. Llewelyn however could still look to the active friendship of Randolph of Chester. While the storm of war raged in South Wales, the march between Cheshire and Gwynedd enjoyed unwonted peace, and in 1223 a truce was patched up through Randolph's mediation.

Earl Randolph needed the Welsh alliance the more because he definitely threw in his lot with the enemies of Hubert de Burgh. In April, 1223, a bull of Honorius III. declared Henry competent to govern in his own name, a change which resulted in a further strengthening of Hubert's power. Towards the end of the year Randolph joined with William of Albemarle, the Bishop of Winchester and Falkes de Bréauté, in an attempt to overthrow the justiciar. The discontented barons took arms and laid their grievances before the king. They wished, they said, no ill to king or kingdom, but simply desired to remove the justiciar from his counsels. Hot words passed between the indignant Hubert and Peter des Roches, and the conference broke up in confusion. The barons still remained mutinous, and, while the king held his Christmas court at Northampton, they celebrated the feast at Leicester. At last Langton persuaded both parties to come to an agreement on the basis of king's friends and barons alike surrendering their castles and wardships. This was a substantial victory for the party of order, and during the next few months much was done to transfer the castles to loyal hands. Randolph himself surrendered Shrewsbury and Bridgnorth.

Comparative peace having been restored, and the judicial bench purged of feudal partisans, private persons ventured to complain of outrageous acts of "novel disseisin," or unlawful appropriation of men's lands. In the spring of 1224 the king's justices went throughout the country, hearing and deciding pleas of this sort. Sixteen acts of novel disseisin were proved against Falkes de Bréauté. Despite all the efforts of Langton and Hubert, that able adventurer, though stripped of some of his castles, fully maintained the position which he first acquired in the service of John. He was not the man to put up tamely with the piecemeal destruction of his power by legal process, and, backed up secretly by the feudal leaders, resolved to take the law into his own hands. One of the most active of the judges in hearing complaints against him was Henry of Braybrook. Falkes bade his brother, William de Bréauté, fall upon the justice, who had been hearing suits at Dunstable, and take him prisoner. William faithfully fulfilled his brother's orders, and on June 17 the unlucky judge was safely shut up in a dungeon of Bedford Castle, of which William had the custody, as his brother's agent. So daring an outrage on the royal authority was worse than the action of William of Albemarle four years before. Hubert and the archbishop immediately took strong measures to enforce the sanctity of the law. While Langton excommunicated Falkes and his abettors, Hubert hastily turned against the traitor the forces which were assembling at Northampton with the object of reconquering Poitou. Braybrook was captured on Monday. On Thursday the royal troops besieged Bedford.

The siege lasted from June 20 to August 14. The "noble castle of Bedford" was new, large, and fortified with an inner and outer baily, and two strong towers. Falkes trusted that it would hold out for a year, and had amply provided it with provisions and munitions of war. In effect, though William de Bréauté and his followers showed a gallant spirit, it resisted the justiciar for barely two months. When called upon to surrender the garrison answered that they would only yield at their lord's orders, and that the more as they were not bound to the king by homage or fealty. Nothing was left

but a fight to the death.   The royalists made strenuous efforts.
A new scutage, the "scutage of Bedford," was imposed on the
realm.   Meanwhile Falkes fled to his accomplice, the Earl of
Chester, and afterwards took refuge with Llewelyn.   But the
adventurer found such cold comfort from the great men who
had lured him to his ruin that he perforce made his way back
to England, along with a motley band of followers, English
and French, Scottish and Welsh.[1]   A hue and cry was raised
after him, and, like William of Albemarle, he was forced to
throw himself into sanctuary, while Randolph of Chester
openly joined the besiegers of Bedford.   In his refuge in
a church at Coventry, Falkes was persuaded to surrender to
the bishop of the diocese, who handed him over to Langton.

During Falkes's wanderings his brother had been struggling
valiantly against overwhelming odds.   *Petrariae* and man-
gonels threw huge stones into the castle, and effected breaches
in keep and curtain.   Miners undermined the walls, while over-
against the stronghold two lofty structures of wood were raised,
from which the crossbowmen, who manned them, were able
to command the whole of the interior.   At last the castle was
captured in four successive assaults.   In the first the barbican
was taken ; in the next the outer baily was stormed ; in the
third the interior baily was won; and in the last the keep was
split asunder.   The garrison then allowed the women and captives, including the wife of Falkes and the unlucky Braybrook,
to make their way to the enemies' lines.   Next day the defenders themselves surrendered.   The only mercy shown to
these gallant men was that they were allowed to make their
peace with the Church before their execution.   Of the eighty
prisoners, three Templars alone were spared.

Falkes threw himself upon the king's mercy, appealing to
his former services to Henry and his father.   He surrendered
to the King the large sums of money which he had deposited
with his bankers, the Templars of London, and ordered his
castellans in Plympton and the other west-country castles of
his wife to open their gates to the royal officers.   In return
for these concessions he was released from excommunication.
His life was spared, but his property was confiscated, and he

[1] The names of his *familia* taken with him are in *Patent Rolls of Henry
III.*, 1216-1227, pp. 461-62.

was ordered to abjure the realm.   Even his wife deserted him, CHAP.
protesting that she had been forced to marry him against her II.
will.   On October 26 he received letters of safe conduct to
go beyond sea.   As he left England, he protested that he had
been instigated by the English magnates in all that he had
done.   On landing at Fécamp he was detained by his old
enemy Louis, then, by his father's death, King of France.   But
Louis VIII. was the last man to bear old grudges against the
Norman adventurer, especially as Falkes's rising had enabled
him to capture the chief towns of Poitou.

Even in his exile Falkes was still able to do mischief.   He
obtained his release from Louis' prison about Easter, 1225,
on the pretence of going on crusade.   He then made his
way to Rome where he strove to excite the sympathy of
Honorius III., by presenting an artful memorial, which throws
a flood of light upon his character, motives, and hopes.   Honorius earnestly pleaded for his restitution, but Hubert and
Langton stood firm against him.   They urged that the pope
had been misinformed, and declined to recall the exile.
Honorius sent his chaplain Otto to England, but the nuncio
found it impossible to modify the policy of the advisers of
the king.   Falkes went back from Italy to Troyes, where he
waited for a year in the hope that his sentence would be
reversed.   At last Otto gave up his cause in despair, and devoted himself to the more profitable work of exacting money
from the English clergy.   Falkes died in 1226.   With him
disappears from our history the lawless spirit which had
troubled the land since the war between John and his barons.
The foreign adventurers, of whom he was the chief, either went
back in disgust to their native lands, or, like Peter de Mauley,
became loyal subjects and the progenitors of a harmless stock
of English barons.   The ten years of storm and stress were
over.   The administration was once more in English hands,
and Hubert enjoyed a few years of well-earned power.

New difficulties at once arose.   The defeat of the feudalists
and their Welsh allies involved heavy special taxation, and
the king's honour required that an effort should be made both
to wrest Poitou from Louis VIII., and to strengthen the English hold over Gascony.   Besides national obligations, clergy
and laity alike were still called upon to contribute towards the

cost of crusading enterprises, and in 1226 the papal nuncio, Otto, demanded that a large proportion of the revenues of the English clergy should be contributed to the papal coffers. To the Englishman of that age all extraordinary taxation was a grievance quite irrespective of its necessity. The double incidence of the royal and papal demands was met by protests which showed some tendency towards the splitting up of the victorious side into parties. It was still easy for all to unite against Otto, and the papal agent was forced to go home empty handed, for councils both of clergy and barons agreed to reject his demands. Whatever other nations might offer to the pope, argued the magnates, the realms of England and Ireland at least had a right to be freed from such impositions by reason of the tribute which John had agreed to pay to Innocent III. The demand of the king's ministers for a fifteenth to prosecute the war with France was reluctantly conceded, but only on the condition of a fresh confirmation of the charters in a form intended to bring home to the king his personal obligation to observe them. Hubert de Burgh, however, was no enthusiast for the charters. His standpoint was that of the officials of the age of Henry II. To him the re-establishment of order meant the restoration of the prerogative. There he parted company with the archbishop, who was an eager upholder of the charters, for which he was so largely responsible. The struggle against the foreigner was to be succeeded by a struggle for the charters.

In January, 1227, a council met at Oxford. The king, then nearly twenty years old, declared that he would govern the country himself, and renounced the tutelage of the Bishop of Winchester. Henry gave himself over completely to the justiciar, whom he rewarded for his faithful service by making him Earl of Kent. In deep disgust Bishop Peter left the court to carry out his long-deferred crusading vows. For four years he was absent in Palestine, where his military talents had ample scope as one of the leaders of Frederick II.'s army, while his diplomatic skill sought, with less result, to preserve some sort of relations between the excommunicated emperor and the new pope, Gregory IX., who in this same year succeeded Honorius. In April Gregory renewed the bull of 1223 in which his predecessor recognised Henry's competence to govern.

Thus ended the first minority since the Conquest. The successful restoration of law and order when the king was a child, showed that a strong king was not absolutely necessary for good government. From the exercise of royal authority by ministers without the personal intervention of the monarch arose the ideas of limited monarchy, the responsibility of the official, and the constitutional rights of the baronial council to appoint ministers and control the administration. We also discern, almost for the first time, the action of an inner ministerial Council which was ultimately to develop into the *consilium ordinarium* of a later age.

No sudden changes attended the royal majority. Those who had persuaded Henry to dismiss Bishop Peter had no policy beyond getting rid of a hated rival. The new Earl of Kent continued to hold office as justiciar for five years, and his ascendency is even more marked in the years 1227 to 1232 than it had been between 1224 and 1227. Hubert still found the task of ruling England by no means easy. With the mitigation of home troubles foreign affairs assumed greater importance, and England's difficulties with France, the efforts to establish cordial relations with the empire, the ever-increasing aggressions of Llewelyn of Wales, and the chronic troubles of Ireland, involved the country in large expenses with little compensating advantage. Not less uneasy were the results of the growing encroachments of the papacy and the increasing inability of the English clergy to face them. Papal taxation, added to the burden of national taxation, induced discontent that found a ready scapegoat in the justiciar. The old and the new baronial opposition combined to denounce Hubert as the true cause of all evils. The increasing personal influence of the young king complicated the situation. In his efforts to deal with all these problems Hubert became involved in the storm of obloquy which finally brought about his fall.

At the accession of Henry III., the truce for five years concluded between his father and Philip Augustus on September 18, 1214, had still three years to run. The expedition of Louis to England might well seem to have broken it, but the prudent disavowal by Philip II. of his son's sacrilegious enterprise made it a point of policy for the French King to regard it as still in force, and neither John nor the earl marshal had a mind to face the enmity of the father as well as the invasion of the son. Accordingly the truce ran out its full time, and in 1220 Honorius III., ever zealous for peace between Christian sovereigns, procured its prolongation for four years. Before this had expired, the accession of Louis VIII. in 1223 raised the old enemy of King Henry to the throne of France. Louis still coveted the English throne, and desired to complete the conquest of Henry's French dominions in France. His accession soon involved England in a new struggle, luckily delayed until the worst of the disorders at home had been overcome.

Peace was impossible because Louis, like Philip, regarded the forfeiture of John as absolute, and as involving the right to deny to Henry III. a legitimate title to any of his lands beyond sea. Henry, on the other hand, was still styled Duke of Normandy, Count of Anjou, Count of Poitou, and Duke of Aquitaine. Claiming all that his father had held, he refused homage to Philip or Louis for such French lands as he actually possessed. For the first time since the Conquest, an English king ruled over extensive French territories without any feudal subjection to the King of France. However, Henry's French lands, though still considerable, were but a shadow of those once ruled by his father. Philip had conquered all Normandy, save the Channel Islands, and also the whole of Anjou and Touraine. For a time he also gained possession of Poitou, but before his death nearly the whole of that region had slipped from his grasp. Poitiers, alone of its great towns, remained in French hands. For the rest, both the barons and cities of Poitou acknowledged the over-lordship of their English count. Too much importance must not be ascribed to this revival of the English power. Henry claimed very little domain in Poitou, which practically was divided between the feudal nobles and the great communes. So long as they maintained a virtual freedom, they were indifferent as to their overlord. If they easily transferred their allegiance from Philip to Henry, it was because the weakness of absentee counts was less to be dreaded than the strength of a monarch near at hand. Meanwhile the barons carried on their feuds one against the other, and all alike joined in oppressing the townsmen.

During Henry's minority the crown was not strong enough

to deal with the unruly Poitevins. Seneschals quickly succeeded each other; the barons expected the office to be filled
by one of their own order, and the towns, jealous of hostile
neighbours, demanded the appointment of an Englishman. At
last, in 1221, Savary de Mauléon, one of King John's mercenaries, a poet, and a crusader against infidels and Albigenses,
was made seneschal. His English estates ensured some measure of fidelity, and his energy and experience were guarantees
of his competence, though, as a younger member of the great
house of Thouars, he belonged by birth to the inner circle of
the Poitevin nobility, whose treachery, levity, and self-seeking
were proverbial. The powerful Viscounts of Thouars were constantly kept in check by their traditional enemies the Counts
of La Marche, whose representative, Hugh of Lusignan, was
by far the strongest of the local barons. His cousin, and sometime betrothed, Isabella, Countess of Angoulême, the widow
of King John, had left England to resume the administration
of her dominions. Early in 1220 she married Hugh, justifying
herself to her son on the ground that it would be dangerous
to his interests if the Count of La Marche should contract an
alliance with the French party. But this was mere excuse.
The union of La Marche and Angoulême largely increased
Count Hugh's power, and he showed perfect impartiality in
pursuing his own interests by holding a balance between his
stepson and the King of France. Against him neither Savary
nor the Poitevin communes could contend with success. The
anarchy of Poitou was an irresistible temptation to Louis VIII.
" Know you," he wrote to the men of Limoges, " that John, king
of England, was deprived by the unanimous judgment of his
peers of all the lands which he held of our father Philip. We
have now received in inheritance all our father's rights, and
require you to perform the service that you owe us." While
the English government weakly negotiated for the prolongation of the truce, and for the pope's intervention, Louis concluded treaties with the Poitevin barons, and made ready an
army to conquer his inheritance. Foremost among his local
partisans appeared Henry's stepfather.

The French army met at Tours on June 24, 1224, and
marched through Thouars to La Rochelle, the strongest of
the Poitevin towns, and the most devoted to England. On

the way Louis forced Savary de Mauléon to yield up Niort, and to promise to defend no other place than La Rochelle, before which city he sat down on July 15. At first Savary resisted vigorously. The siege of Bedford, however, prevented the despatch of effective help from England, and Savary was perhaps already secretly won over by Louis. Be this as it may, the town surrendered on August 3, and with it went all Aquitaine north of the Dordogne. Savary took service with the conqueror, and was made warden of La Rochelle and of the adjacent coasts, while Lusignan received the reward of his treachery in a grant of the Isle of Oléron. When Louis returned to the north, the Count of La Marche undertook the conquest of Gascony. He soon made himself master of St. Emilion, and of the whole of Périgord. The surrender of La Réole opened up the passage of the Garonne, and the capture of Bazas gave the French a foothold to the south of that river. Only the people of Bordeaux showed any spirit in resisting Hugh. But their resistance proved sufficient, and he withdrew baffled before their walls.

The easiness of Louis' conquests showed their instability. "I am sure," wrote one of Henry's officers, "that you can easily recover all that you have lost, if you send speedy succour to these regions." After the capture of Bedford, Hubert undertook the recovery of Poitou and the defence of Gascony. Henry's younger brother Richard, a youth of sixteen, was appointed Earl of Cornwall and Count of Poitou, dubbed knight by his brother, and put in nominal command of the expedition despatched to Gascony in March, 1225. His experienced uncle, William Longsword, Earl of Salisbury, and Philip of Aubigny, were sent with him as his chief counsellors. Received with open arms by Bordeaux, he boasted on May 2 that he had conquered all Gascony, save La Réole, and had received the allegiance of every Gascon noble, except Elie Rudel, the lord of Bergerac. The siege of La Réole, the only serious military operation of the campaign, occupied Richard all the summer and autumn, and it was not until November 13 that the burgesses opened their gates. As soon as the French had retired, the lord of Bergerac, "after the fashion of the Poitevins," renounced Louis and professed himself the liegeman of Earl Richard. Then the worst trouble was that Savary de

Mauléon's ships commanded the Bay of Biscay, and rendered communication between Bordeaux and England very difficult.[1] Once more the men of the Cinque Ports came to the king's aid, and there was severe fighting at sea, involving much plunder of merchant vessels and dislocation of trade.

The English sought to supplement their military successes by diplomacy. Richard of Cornwall made an alliance with the counts of Auvergne, and the home administration negotiated with all possible enemies of the French King. A proposal to affiance Henry's sister, Isabella, to Henry, King of the Romans, the infant son of Frederick II., led to no results, for the Archbishop of Cologne, the chief upholder of the scheme in Germany, was murdered, and the young king found a bride in Austria. Yet the project counteracted the negotiations set on foot by Louis to secure Frederick II. for his own side, and induced the Emperor to take up a position of neutrality. An impostor appeared in Flanders who gave out that he was the old Count Baldwin, sometime Latin Emperor of the East, who had died in prison in Bulgaria twenty years before. Baldwin's daughter, Joan, appealed to Louis for support against the false Baldwin, whereupon Henry recognised his claims and sought his alliance. Nothing but the capture and execution of the impostor prevented Henry from effecting a powerful diversion in Flanders. Peter Mauclerc, Count of Brittany, was won over by an offer of restitution to his earldom of Richmond, and by a promise that Henry would marry his daughter Iolande. Intrigues were entered into with the discontented Norman nobles, and the pope was importuned to save Henry from French assaults at the same moment that the king made a treaty of alliance with his first cousin, the heretical Raymond VII. of Toulouse. Honorius gave his ward little save sympathy and good advice. His special wish was to induce Louis to lead a French expedition into Languedoc against the Albigensian heretics. As soon as Louis resolved on this, the pope sought to prevent Henry from entering into unholy alliance with Raymond. It was the crusade of 1226, not the good-will of the Pope or the fine-drawn English negotiations, which gave Gascony a short respite. Louis VIII. died on November 8 in the course of his expedition, and the Capetian

[1] *Patent Rolls of Henry III.*, 1225-1232, ii., 25.

monarchy became less dangerous during the troubles of a minority, in which his widow, Blanche, strove as regent to uphold the throne of their little son, Louis IX.

The first months of Louis IX.'s reign showed how unstable was any edifice built upon the support of the treacherous lords of Poitou. Within six weeks of Louis VIII.'s death, Hugh of Lusignan, the viscount of Thouars, Savary de Mauléon, and many other Poitevin barons, concluded treaties with Richard of Cornwall, by which in return for lavish concessions they went back to the English obedience. In the spring of 1227, however, the appearance of a French army south of the Loire caused these same lords to make fresh treaties with Blanche. Peter of Brittany also became friendly with the French regent, and gave up his daughter's English marriage. With allies so shifty, further dealings seemed hopeless. Before Easter, Richard patched up a truce and went home in disgust. The Capetians lost Poitou, but Henry failed to take advantage of his rival's weakness, and the real masters of the situation were the local barons. Fifteen more years were to elapse before the definitive French conquest of Poitou.

During the next three years the good understanding between the Bretons, the Poitevins, and the regent Blanche came to an end, and the progress of the feudal reaction against the rule of the young King of France once more excited hopes of improving Henry's position in south-western France. Henry III. was eager to win back his inheritance, though Hubert de Burgh had little faith in Poitevin promises, and, conscious of his king's weakness, managed to prolong the truce, until July 22, 1229. Three months before that, Blanche succeeded in forcing the unfortunate Raymond VII. to accept the humiliating treaty of Meaux, which assured the succession to his dominions to her second son Alfonse, who was to marry his daughter and heiress, Joan. The barons of the north and west were not yet defeated, and once more appealed to Henry to come to their aid. Accordingly, the English king summoned his vassals to Portsmouth on October 15 for a French campaign. When Henry went down to Portsmouth he found that there were not enough ships to convey his troops over sea. Thereupon he passionately denounced the justiciar as an "old traitor," and accused him of being bribed by the French queen.

Nothing but the intervention of Randolph of Chester, Hubert's
persistent enemy, put an end to the undignified scene.

Count Peter of Brittany, who arrived at Portsmouth on the 9th, did homage to Henry as King of France, and received the earldom of Richmond and the title of Duke of Brittany which he had long coveted, but which the French government refused to recognise. He persuaded Henry to postpone the expedition until the following spring. When that time came Henry appointed Ralph Neville, the chancellor, and Stephen Segrave, a rising judge, as wardens of England, and on May 1, 1230, set sail from Portsmouth. It was the first time since 1213 that an English king had crossed the seas at the head of an army, and every effort was made to equip a sufficient force. Hubert the justiciar, Randolph of Chester, William the marshal, and most of the great barons personally shared in the expedition, and the ports of the Channel, the North Sea, and the Bay of Biscay were ransacked to provide adequate shipping. Many Norman vessels served as transports, apparently of their owners' free will.

On May 3 Henry landed at St. Malo, and thence proceeded to Dinan, the meeting-place assigned for his army, the greater part of which landed at Port Blanc, a little north of Tréguier. Peter Mauclerc joined him, and a plan of operations was discussed. The moment was favourable, for a great number of the French magnates were engaged in war against Theobald, the poet-count of Champagne, and the French army, which was assembled at Angers, represented but a fraction of the military strength of the land. Fulk Paynel, a Norman baron who wished to revive the independence of the duchy, urged Henry to invade Normandy. Hubert successfully withstood this rash proposal, and also Fulk's fatal suggestion that Henry should divide his army and send two hundred knights for the invasion of Normandy. Before long the English marched through Brittany to Nantes, where they wasted six weeks. At last, on the advice of Hubert, they journeyed south into Poitou. The innate Poitevin instability had again brought round the Lusignans, the house of Thouars, and their kind to the French side, and Henry found that his own mother did her best to obstruct his progress. He was too strong to make open resistance safe, and his long progress from Nantes

3 *

to Bordeaux was only once checked by the need to fight his way. This opposition came from the little town and castle of Mirambeau, situated in Upper Saintonge, rather more than half-way between Saintes and Blaye.[1] From July 21 to 30 Mirambeau stoutly held out, but Henry's army was reinforced by the chivalry of Gascony, and by a siege-train borrowed from Bordeaux and the loyal lords of the Garonne. Against such appliances of warfare Mirambeau could not long resist. On its capitulation Henry pushed on to Bordeaux.

Useless as the march through Poitou had been, it was then repeated in the reverse way. With scarcely a week's rest, Henry left the Gascon capital on August 10, and on September 15 ended his inglorious campaign at Nantes. Although he was unable to assert himself against the faithless Poitevins, the barons of the province were equally impotent to make head against him. On reaching Brittany, Hubert once more stopped further military efforts. After a few days' rest at Nantes, Henry made his way by slow stages through the heart of Brittany. It was said that his army had no better occupation than teaching the local nobles to drink deep after the English fashion. The King had wasted all his treasure, and the poorer knights were compelled to sell or pawn their horses and arms to support themselves. The farce ended when the King sailed from St. Pol de Léon, and late in October landed at Portsmouth. He left a portion of his followers in Brittany, under the Earls of Chester and Pembroke. Randolph himself, as a former husband of Constance of Brittany, had claims to certain dower lands which appertained to Count Peter's mother-in-law. He was put in possession of St. James de Beuvron, and thence he raided Normandy and Anjou. By this time the coalition against the count of Champagne had broken down, and Blanche was again triumphant. It was useless to continue a struggle so expensive and disastrous, and on July 4, 1231, a truce for three years was concluded between France, Brittany, and England. Peter des Roches, then returning through France from his crusade, took an active part in negotiating the treaty. Just as the king was disposed to make the justiciar the scapegoat of his failure,

---

[1] E. Berger, *Bibl. Ecole des Chartes*, 1893, pp. 35-36, shows that Mirambeau, not Mirebeau, was besieged by Henry; see also his *Blanche de Castille* (1895).

Hubert's old enemy appeared once more upon the scene. The responsibility for blundering must be divided among the English magnates, and not ascribed solely to their monarch. If Hubert saved Henry from reckless adventures, he certainly deserves a large share of the blame for the Poitevin fiasco.

The grave situation at home showed the folly of this untimely revival of an active foreign policy. The same years that saw the collapse of Henry's hopes in Normandy and Poitou, witnessed troubles both in Ireland and in Wales. In both these regions the house of the Marshals was a menace to the neighbouring chieftains, and Hugh de Lacy, Earl of Ulster, and Llewelyn ap Iorwerth, made common cause against it and vigorously attacked their rivals both in Leinster and in South Wales. Nor was this the only disturbance. The summons of the Norman chieftains of Ireland to Poitou gave the king of Connaught a chance of attacking the justiciar of Ireland, Geoffrey Marsh, who ultimately drove the Irish back with severe loss. Llewelyn was again as active and hostile as ever. Irritated by the growing strength of the new royal castle of Montgomery, he laid siege to it in 1228. Hubert de Burgh, then castellan of Montgomery, could only save his castle by summoning the levies of the kingdom. At their head Hubert went in person to hold the field against Llewelyn, taking the king with him. The Welsh withdrew as usual before a regular army, and Hubert and the king, late in September, marched a few miles westwards of Montgomery to the vale of Kerry, where they erected a castle. But Llewelyn soon made the English position in Kerry untenable. Many of the English lords were secretly in league with him, and the army suffered severely from lack of food. In the fighting that ensued the Welsh got the better of the English, taking prisoner William de Braose, the heir of Builth, and one of the greatest of the marcher lords. At last king and justiciar were glad to agree to demolish the new castle on receiving from Llewelyn the expenses involved in the task. The dismantled ruin was called " Hubert's folly ". " And then," boasts the Welsh chronicler, "the king returned to England with shame."

In 1230 Llewelyn inflicted another slight upon his overlord. William de Braose long remained the Welsh prince's captive, and only purchased his liberty by agreeing to wed his daughter to Llewelyn's son, and surrendering Builth as her marriage portion. The captive had employed his leisure in winning the love of Llewelyn's wife, Joan, Henry's half-sister. At Easter, Llewelyn took a drastic revenge on the adulterer. He seized William in his own castle at Builth, and on May 2 hanged him on a tree in open day in the presence of 800 witnesses. Finding that neither the king nor the marchers moved a finger to avenge the outrage done to sister and comrade, Llewelyn took the aggressive in regions which had hitherto been comparatively exempt from his assaults. In 1231 he laid his heavy hand on all South Wales, burning down churches full of women, as the English believed, and signalling out for special attack the marshal's lands in Gwent and Pembroke. Once more the king penetrated with his barons into Mid Wales, while the pope and archbishop excommunicated Llewelyn and put his lands under interdict. Yet neither temporal nor spiritual arms were of avail against the Welshman. Henry's only exploit in this, his second Welsh campaign, was to rebuild Maud's Castle in stone. He withdrew, and in December agreed to conclude a three years' truce, and procure Llewelyn's absolution. Hubert once more bore the blame of his master's failure.

On July 9, 1228, Stephen Langton died. Despite their differences as to the execution of the charters, his removal lost the justiciar a much-needed friend. Affairs were made worse by the unteachable folly of the monks of Christ Church. Regardless of the severe warning which they had received in the storms that preceded the establishment of Langton's authority, the chapter forthwith proceeded to the election of their brother monk, Walter of Eynsham. The archbishop-elect was an ignorant old monk of weak health and doubtful antecedents, and Gregory IX. wisely refused to confirm the election. On the recommendation of the king and the bishops, Gregory himself appointed as archbishop Richard, chancellor of Lincoln, an eloquent and learned secular priest of handsome person, whose nickname of "le Grand" was due to his tall stature. The first Archbishop of Canterbury since the Conquest directly nominated by the pope—for even in Langton's case there was a form of election—Richard le Grand at once began to quarrel with the justiciar, demanding that he

should surrender the custody of Tunbridge castle on the ground CHAP.
of some ancient claim of the see of Canterbury. Failing to ^{II.} obtain redress in England, Richard betook himself to Rome in the spring of 1231. There he regaled the pope's ears with the offences of Hubert, and of the worldly bishops who were his tools. In August, Richard's death in Italy left the Church of Canterbury for three years without a pastor.

While Gregory IX. did more to help Henry against Louis than Honorius III., the inflexible character and lofty hier-archical ideals of this nephew of Innocent III. made his hand heavier on the English Church than that of his predecessor. Above all, Gregory's expenses in pursuing his quarrel with Frederick II. made the wealth of the English Church a sore temptation to him. With his imposition of a tax of one-tenth on all clerical property to defray the expenses of the crusade against the emperor, papal taxation in England takes a newer and severer phase. The rigour with which Master Stephen, the pope's collector, extorted the tax was bitterly resented. Not less loud was the complaint against the increasing numbers of foreign ecclesiastics forced into English benefices by papal authority, and without regard for the rights of the lawful patrons and electors. A league of aggrieved tax-payers and patrons was formed against the Roman agents. At Eastertide, 1232, bands of men, headed by a knight named Robert Twenge, who took the nickname of William Wither, despoiled the Romans of their gains, and distributed the proceeds to the poor. These doings were the more formidable from their excellent organisation, and the strong sympathy everywhere extended to them. Hubert, who hated foreign interference, did nothing to stop Twenge and his followers. His inaction further precipitated his ruin. Arch-bishop Richard had already poisoned the pope's mind against him, and his suspected connivance with the anti-Roman move-ment completed his disfavour. Bitter letters of complaint arrived in England denouncing the outrages inflicted on the friends of the apostolic see. It is hard to dissociate the pope's feeling in this matter from his rejection of the nomination of the king's chancellor, Ralph Neville, Bishop of Chichester, to the see of Canterbury, as an illiterate politician.

The dislike of the taxes made necessary by the Welsh

and French wars, such as the " scutage of Poitou " and the " scutage of Kerry," swelled the outcry against the justiciar. So far back as 1227 advantage had been taken of Henry's majority to exact large sums of money for the confirmation of all charters sealed during his nonage.   The barons made it a grievance that his brother Richard was ill-provided for, and a rising in 1227 extorted a further provision for him from what was regarded as the niggardliness of the justiciar.   Nor did Hubert, with all his rugged honesty, neglect his own interests.   He secured for himself lucrative wardships, such as the custody for the second time of the great Gloucester earldom, and of several castles, including the not very profitable charge of Montgomery, and the important governorship of Dover.   On the very eve of his downfall he was made justice of Ireland. His brother was bishop of Ely, and other kinsmen were promoted to high posts.   He was satisfied that he spent all that he got in the King's service, in promoting the interests of the kingdom, but his enemies regarded him as unduly tenacious of wealth and office.   All classes alike grew disgusted with the justiciar.   The restoration of the malign influence of Peter of Winchester completed his ruin.   The king greedily listened to the complaints of his old guardian against the minister who overshadowed the royal power.   At last, on July 29, 1232, Henry plucked up courage to dismiss him.

With Hubert's fall ends the second period of Henry's reign. William Marshal expelled the armed foreigner.   Hubert restored the administration to English hands.   Matthew Paris puts into the mouth of a poor smith who refused to fasten fetters on the fallen minister words which, though probably never spoken, describe with sufficient accuracy Hubert's place in history : " Is he not that most faithful Hubert who so often saved England from the devastation of the foreigners and restored England to England ? "   Hubert was, as has been well said, perhaps the first minister since the Conquest who made patriotism a principle of policy, though it is easy in the light of later developments to read into his doings more than he really intended.   But whatever his motives, the results of his action were clear.   He drove away the mercenaries, humbled the feudal lords, and set limits to the pope's interference.   He renewed respect for law and obedience to the law courts.

Even in the worst days of anarchy the administrative system did not break down, and the records of royal orders and judicial judgments remain almost as full in the midst of the civil war as in the more peaceful days of Hubert's rule. But it was easy enough to issue proclamations and writs. The difficulty was to get them obeyed, and the work of Hubert was to ensure that the orders of king and ministers should really be respected by his subjects. He made many mistakes. He must share the blame of the failure of the Kerry campaign, and he was largely responsible for the sorry collapse of the invasion of Poitou. He neither understood nor sympathised with Stephen Langton's zeal for the charters. A straightforward, limited, honourable man, he strove to carry out his rather old-fashioned conception of duty in the teeth of a thousand obstacles. He never had a free hand, and he never enjoyed the hearty support of any one section of his countrymen. Hated by the barons whom he kept away from power, he alienated the Londoners by his high-handed violence, and the tax-payers by his heavy exactions. The pope disliked him, the aliens plotted against him, and the king, for whom he sacrificed so much, gave him but grudging support. But the reaction which followed his retirement made many, who had rejoiced in his humiliation, bitterly regret it.

Three notable enemies of Hubert went off the stage of history within a few months of his fall. The death of Richard le Grand has already been recorded. William Marshal, the brother-in-law of the king, the gallant and successful soldier, the worthy successor of his great father, came home from Brittany early in 1231. His last act was to marry his sister, Isabella, to Richard of Cornwall. Within ten days of the wedding his body was laid beside his father in the Temple Church at London. In October, 1232, died Randolph of Blundeville, the last representative of the male stock of the old line of the Earls of Chester, and long the foremost champion of the feudal aristocracy against Hubert. The contest between them had been fought with such chivalry that the last public act of the old earl was to protect the fallen justiciar from the violence of his foes. For more than fifty years Randolph had ruled like a king over his palatine earldom; had, like his master, his struggles with his own vassals, and had perforce to grant to his own barons and boroughs liberties which he strove to wrest from his overlord for himself and his fellow nobles. He was not a great statesman, and hardly even a successful warrior. Yet his popular personal qualities, his energy, his long duration of power, and his enormous possessions, give him a place in history. His memory, living on long in the minds of the people, inspired a series of ballads which vied in popularity with the cycle of Robin Hood,[1] though, unfortunately, they have not come down to us. His estates were divided among his four sisters. His nephew, John the Scot, Earl of Huntingdon, received a re-grant of the Chester earldom ; his Lancashire lands had already gone to his brother-in-law, William of Ferrars, Earl of Derby ; other portions of his territories went to his sister, the Countess of Arundel, and the Lincoln earldom, passing through another sister, Hawise of Quincy, to her son-in-law, John of Lacy, constable of Chester, raised the chief vassal of the palatinate to comital rank. None of these heirs of a divided inheritance were true successors to Randolph. With him died the last of the great Norman houses, tenacious beyond its fellows, and surpassing in its two centuries of unbroken male descent the usual duration of the medieval baronial family. Its collapse made easier the alien invasion which threatened to undo Hubert's work.

[1] " Ich can rymes of Robyn Hode, and of Randolf erl of Chestre," *Vision of Piers Plowman*, i., 167 ; ii., 94.

CHAPTER III.

THE ALIEN INVASION.

WITH the dismissal of Hubert on July 29, 1232, Peter des Roches resumed his authority over Henry III. Mindful of past failures, the bishop's aim was to rule through dependants, so that he could pull the wires without making himself too prominent. His chief agents in pursuing this policy were Peter of Rivaux, Stephen Segrave, and Robert Passelewe. Of these, Peter of Rivaux was a Poitevin clerk, officially described as the bishop's nephew, but generally supposed to have been his son. Stephen Segrave, the son of a small Leicestershire landholder, was a lawyer who had held many judicial and administrative posts, including the regency during the king's absence abroad in 1230. He abandoned his original clerical profession, received knighthood, married nobly, and was the founder of a baronial house in the midlands. His only political principle was obedience to the powers that were in the ascendant. Passelewe, a clerk who had acted as the agent of Randolph of Chester and Falkes of Bréauté at the Roman court, was, like Segrave, a mere tool.

The Bishop of Winchester began to show his hand. Between June 26 and July 11, nineteen of the thirty-five sheriffdoms were bestowed on Peter of Rivaux for life. As Segrave was sheriff of five shires, and the bishop himself had acquired the shrievalty of Hampshire, this involved the transference of the administration of over two-thirds of the counties to the bishop's dependants. On the downfall of Hubert, Segrave became justiciar. He was not the equal of his predecessors either in personal weight or in social position, and did not aspire to act as chief minister. The appointment of a mere lawyer to the great Norman office of state marks the first stage in the decline, which before long degraded the justiciarship into a simple position of headship over the judges, the chief justiceship of the next generation. Hubert's offices and lands were divided among his supplanters. Peter of Rivaux became keeper of wards and escheats, castellan of many castles on the Welsh march, and the recipient of even more offices and wardships in Ireland than in England. The custody of the Gloucester earldom went to the Bishop of Winchester. The last steps of the ministerial revolution were completed at the king's Christmas court at Worcester. There Rivaux, who had yielded up before Michaelmas most of his shrievalties, was made treasurer, with Passelewe as his deputy. Of the old ministers only the chancellor, Ralph Neville, Bishop of Chichester, was suffered to remain in office. Finally the king's new advisers imported a large company of Poitevin and Breton mercenaries, hoping with their help to maintain their newly won position. The worst days of John seemed renewed.

The Poitevin gang called upon Hubert to render complete accounts for the whole period of his justiciarship. When he pleaded that King John had given him a charter of quittance, he was told that its force had ended with the death of the grantor. He was further required to answer for the wrongs which Twenge's bands had inflicted on the servants of the pope. He was accused of poisoning William Earl of Salisbury, William Marshal, Falkes de Bréauté, and Archbishop Richard. He had prevented the king from contracting a marriage with a daughter of the Duke of Austria; he had dissuaded the king from attempting to recover Normandy; he had first seduced and then married the daughter of the King of Scots; he had stolen from the treasury a talisman which made its possessor invincible in war and had traitorously given it to Llewelyn of Wales; he had induced Llewelyn to slay William de Braose; he had won the royal favour by magic and witchcraft, and finally he had murdered Constantine FitzAthulf.

Many of these accusations were so monstrous that they carried with them their own refutation. It was too often the custom in the middle ages to overwhelm an enemy with incredible charges for it to be fair to accuse the enemies of Hubert of any excessive malignity. The substantial innocence of Hubert is clear, for the only charges brought against him were either errors of judgment and policy, or incredible crimes. Nevertheless he was in such imminent danger that he took sanctuary with the canons of Merton in Surrey. Thereupon the king called upon the Londoners to march to Merton and bring their ancient foe, dead or alive, to the city. Randolph of Chester interposed between his fallen enemy and the royal vengeance. He persuaded Henry to countermand the march to Merton and to suffer the fallen justiciar to leave his refuge with some sort of safe conduct. But the king was irritated to hear that Hubert had journeyed into Essex. Again he was pursued, and once more he was forced to take sanctuary, this time in a chapel near Brentwood. From this he was dragged by some of the king's household and brought to London, where he was imprisoned in the Tower. The Bishop of London complained to the king of this violation of the rights of the Church, and Hubert was allowed to return to his chapel. However, the levies of Essex surrounded the precincts, and he was soon forced by hunger to surrender. He offered to submit himself to the king's will, and was for a second time confined in the Tower. On November 10, he was brought before a not unfriendly tribunal, in which the malice of the new justiciar was tempered by the baronial instincts of the Earls of Cornwall, Warenne, Pembroke, and Lincoln. He made no effort to defend himself, and submitted absolutely to the judgment of the king. It was finally agreed that he should be allowed to retain the lands which he had inherited from his father, and that all his chattels and the lands that he had acquired himself should be forfeited to the crown. Further, he was to be kept in prison in the castle of Devizes under the charge of the four earls who had tried him.

Peter des Roches was soon in difficulties. The earls who had saved Hubert began to oppose the whole administration. Their leader was Richard, Earl of Pembroke, the second son of the great regent, and since his brother's death head of the house of Marshal. Richard was bitterly prejudiced against the king and his courtiers by an attempt to refuse him his brother's earldom. A gallant warrior, handsome and eloquent, pious, upright, and well educated, Richard, the best of the marshal's sons, stood for the rest of his short life at the head of the opposition. He incited his friends to refuse to attend a council summoned to meet at Oxford, on June 24, 1233. The king would have sought to compel their presence, had not a Dominican friar, Robert Bacon, when preaching before the court, warned him that there would be no peace in England until Bishop Peter and his son were removed from his counsels. The friar's boldness convinced him that disaffection was widespread, and he promised the magnates at a later council at London that he would, with their advice, correct whatever he found there was need to reform. Meanwhile the Poitevins brought into England fresh swarms of hirelings from their own land, and Peter des Roches urged Henry to crush rebellion in the bud. As a warning to greater offenders, Gilbert Basset was deprived of a manor which he had held since the reign of King John, and an attempt was made to lay violent hands upon his brother-in-law, Richard Siward. The two barons resisted, whereupon all their estates were transferred to Peter of Rivaux. Yet Richard Marshal still continued to hope for peace, and, after the failure of earlier councils, set off to attend another assembly fixed for August 1, at Westminster. On his way he learnt from his sister Isabella, the wife of Richard of Cornwall. that Peter des Roches was laying a trap for him. In high indignation he took horse for his Welsh estates, and prepared for rebellion.

The king summoned the military tenants to appear with horses and arms at Gloucester on the 14th. There Richard Marshal was declared a traitor and an invasion of his estates was ordered. But the king had not sufficient resources to carry out his threats, and October saw the barons once more wrangling with Henry at Westminster, and claiming that the marshal should be tried by his peers. Peter of Winchester declared that there were no peers in England as there were in France, and that in consequence the king had power to condemn any disloyal subject through his justices. This daringly unconstitutional doctrine provoked a renewed outcry. The bishops joined the secular magnates, and threatened their colleague with excommunication. A formidable civil war broke out. Siward and Basset harried the lands of the Poitevins, while the marshal made a close alliance with Llewelyn of Wales. The king still had formidable forces on his side. Richard of Cornwall was persuaded by Bishop Peter to take up arms for his brother, and the two new earls, John the Scot of Chester, and John de Lacy of Lincoln, joined the royal forces. Hubert de Burgh took advantage of the increasing confusion to escape from Devizes castle to a church in the town. Dragged back with violence to his prison, he was again, as at Brentwood, restored to sanctuary through the exertions of the bishop of the diocese. There he remained, closely watched by his foes, until October 30, when Siward and Basset drove away the guard, and took him off with them to the marshal's castle of Chepstow.

The tide of war flowed to the southern march of Wales. Llewelyn and Richard Marshal devastated Glamorgan, which, as a part of the Gloucester inheritance, was under the custody of the Bishop of Winchester. They took nearly all its castles, including that of Cardiff. Thence they subdued Usk, Abergavenny, and other neighbouring strongholds, while an independent army, including the marshal's Pembrokeshire vassals and the men of the princes of South Wales, wasted months in a vain attack on Carmarthen. The king's vassals were again summoned to Gloucester, whence Henry led them early in November towards Chepstow, the centre of the marshal's estates in Gwent. Earl Richard devastated his lands so effectively that the king could not support his army on them, and was compelled to move up the Wye valley towards the castles of Monmouth, Skenfrith, Whitecastle, and Grosmont, the strong quadrilateral of Upper Gwent which still remained in the hands of the king's friends. Marching to the most remote of these, Grosmont, on the upper Monnow, Henry spent several days in the castle, while his army lay around under canvas. On the night of November 11, the sleeping soldiers were suddenly set upon by the barons and their Welsh allies; they fled unarmed to the castle, or scattered in confusion. The assailants seized their horses, harness, arms and provisions, but refrained from slaying or capturing them. The royal forces never rallied. Many gladly went home, giving as their excuse that they were unable to fight since they had lost their equipment. Henry and his ministers withdrew to Gloucester. More convinced than ever of the treachery of Englishmen, the king entrusted the defence of the border castles to mercenaries from Poitou.

The fighting centred round Monmouth, which Richard approached on the 25th with a small company. A sudden sortie almost overwhelmed the little band. The marshal held his own heroically against twelve, until at last Baldwin of Guînes, the warden of the castle, took him prisoner. Thereupon Baldwin fell to the ground, his armour pierced by a lucky bolt from a crossbow. His followers, smitten with panic, abandoned the marshal, and bore their leader home. By that time, however, the bulk of the marshal's forces had come upon the scene. A general engagement followed, in which the Anglo-Welsh army drove the enemy back into Monmouth and took possession of the castle. This set the marshal free to march northwards and join Llewelyn in a vigorous attack upon Shrewsbury. In January, 1234, they burnt that town and retired to their own lands loaded with booty. Meanwhile Siward devastated the estates of the Poitevins and of Richard of Cornwall. Afraid to be cut off from his retreat to England the king abandoned Gloucester, where he had kept his melancholy Christmas court, and found a surer refuge in Bishop Peter's cathedral city. Thereupon Gloucestershire suffered the fate of Shropshire. " It was a wretched sight for travellers in that region to see on the highways innumerable dead bodies lying naked and unburied, to be devoured by birds of prey, and so polluting the air that they infected healthy men with mortal sickness." [1]

The king swore that he would never make peace with the marshal, unless he threw himself on the royal mercy as a confessed traitor with a rope round his neck. Having, however, exhausted all his military resources, he cunningly strove to entice Richard from Wales to Ireland. The two Peters wrote to Maurice Fitzgerald, then justiciar of Ireland, and to the chief foes of the marshal, urging them to fall upon his Irish estates and capture the traitor, dead or alive. Many of the most powerful nobles of Ireland lent themselves to the conspiracy. The Lacys of Meath, his old enemies, joined with Fitzgerald, Geoffrey Marsh, and Richard de Burgh, the greatest of the Norman lords of Connaught, and the nephew of Hubert, in carrying out the plot. The confederates fell suddenly upon the marshal's estates and devastated them with fire and sword. On hearing of this attack Richard immediately left Wales, and, accompanied by only fifteen knights, took ship for Ireland. On his arrival Geoffrey Marsh, the meanest of the conspirators,

[1] Wendover, iv., 291.

received him with every profession of cordiality, and urged him to attack his enemies without delay. Geoffrey was an old man; he had long held the great post of justiciar of Ireland; and he was himself the liegeman of the marshal. Richard therefore implicitly trusted him, and forthwith took the field.

The first warlike operations of Earl Richard were successful. After a short siege he obtained possession of Limerick, and his enemies were fain to demand a truce. Richard proposed a conference to be held on April 1, 1234, on the Curragh of Kildare. The conference proved abortive, for Geoffrey Marsh cunningly persuaded the marshal to refuse any offer of terms which the magnates would accept, and Richard found that he had been duped into taking up a position that he was not strong enough to maintain. Marsh withdrew from his side, on the ground that he could not fight against Lacy, whose sister he had married. The marshal foresaw the worst. "I know," he declared, "that this day I am delivered over to death, but it is better to die honourably for the cause of justice than to flee from the field and become a reproach to knighthood."

The forsworn Irish knights slunk away to neighbouring places of sanctuary or went over to the enemy. When the final struggle came, later on the same April 1, Richard had few followers save the faithful fifteen knights who had crossed over with him from Wales. The little band, outnumbered by more than nine to one, struggled desperately to the end. At last the marshal, unhorsed and severely wounded, fell into the hands of his enemies. They bore him, more dead than alive, to his own castle of Kilkenny, which had just been seized by the justiciar. After a few days Richard's tough constitution began to get the better of his wounds. Then his enemies, showing him the royal warranty for their acts, induced him to admit them into his castles. An ignorant or treacherous surgeon, called in by the justiciar, cauterised his wounds so severely that his sufferings became intense. He died of fever on the 16th, and was buried, as he himself had willed, in the Franciscan church at Kilkenny. No one rejoiced at the death of the hero save the traitors who had lured him to his doom and the Poitevins who had suborned them. Their victim, the weak king, mourned for his friend as David had lamented Saul and

Jonathan.[1] The treachery of his enemies brought them little profit. While Richard Marshal lay on his deathbed, a new Archbishop of Canterbury drove the Poitevins from office.

In the heyday of the Poitevins' power the Church sounded a feeble but clear note of alarm. The pope expostulated with Henry for his treatment of Hubert de Burgh, and Agnellus of Pisa, the first English provincial of the newly arrived Franciscan order, strove to reconcile Richard Marshal with his sovereign in the course of the South-Welsh campaign. More drastic action was necessary if vague remonstrance was to be translated into fruitful action. The three years' vacancy of the see of Canterbury, after the death of Richard le Grand, paralysed the action of the Church. After the pope's rejection of the first choice of the convent of Christ Church, the chancellor, Ralph Neville, the monks elected their own prior, and him also Gregory refused as too old and incompetent. Their third election fell upon John Blunt, a theologian high in the favour of Peter des Roches, who sent him to Rome, well provided with ready money, to secure his confirmation. Simon Langton, again restored to England, and archdeacon of Canterbury, persuaded the pope to veto Blunt's appointment on the ground of his having held two benefices without a dispensation. His rejection was the first check received by the Poitevin faction. It was promptly followed by a more crushing blow. Weary of the long delay, Gregory persuaded the Christ Church monks then present at Rome to elect Edmund Rich, treasurer of Salisbury. Edmund, a scholar who had taught theology and arts with great distinction at Paris and Oxford, was still more famous for his mystical devotion, for his asceticism and holiness of life. He was however an old man, inexperienced in affairs, and, with all his gracious gifts, somewhat wanting in the tenacity and vigour which leadership involved. Yet in sending so eminent a saint to Canterbury, Rome conferred on England a service second only to that which she had rendered when she secured the archbishopric for Stephen Langton.

Before his consecration as archbishop on April 2, 1234, Edmund had already joined with his suffragans on February 2 in upholding the good fame of the marshal and in warning the king

---

[1] *Dunstable Ann.*, p. 137.

of the disastrous results of preferring the counsels of the Poitevins   CHAP.
to those of his natural-born subjects. A week after his con-   III.
secration Edmund succeeded in carrying out a radical change
in the administration. On April 9 he declared that unless
Henry drove away the Poitevins, he would forthwith pronounce
him excommunicate. Yielding at once, Henry sent the Bishop
of Winchester back to his diocese, and deprived Peter of Rivaux
of all his offices. The followers of the two Peters shared their
fate, and Henry, despatching Edmund to Wales to make peace
with Llewelyn and the marshal, hurried to Gloucester in order
to meet the archbishop on his return. His good resolutions
were further strengthened by the news of Earl Richard's death.
On arriving at Gloucester he held a council in which the ruin
of the Poitevins was completed. A truce, negotiated by the
archbishop with Llewelyn, was ratified. The partisans of the
marshal were pardoned, even Richard Siward being forgiven
his long career of plunder. Gilbert Marshal, the next brother
of the childless Earl Richard, was invested with his earldom
and office, and Henry himself dubbed him a knight. Hubert
de Burgh was included in the comprehensive pardon. Indignant
that his name and seal should have been used to cover his ex-
ministers' treachery to Earl Richard, Henry overwhelmed them
with reproaches, and strove by his violence against them to
purge himself from complicity in their acts. The Poitevins
lurked in sanctuary, fearing for the worst. Segrave forgot his
knighthood, resumed the tonsure, and took refuge in a church
in Leicester. The king's worst indignation was reserved for
Peter of Rivaux. Peter protested that his orders entitled him
to immunity from arrest, but it was found that he wore a mail
shirt under his clerical garments, and, without a word of reproach
from the archbishop, he was immured in a lay prison on the
pretext that no true clerk wore armour. Of the old ministers
Ralph Neville alone remained in office.

With Bishop Peter's fall disappeared the last of the influences that had prevailed during the minority. The king, who
felt his dignity impaired by the Poitevin domination, resolved
that henceforward he would submit to no master. He soon
framed a plan of government that thoroughly satisfied his
jealous and exacting nature. Henceforth no magnates, either
of Church or State, should stand between him and his subjects.

4 *

He would be his own chief minister, holding in his own hands all the strings of policy, and acting through subordinates whose sole duty was to carry out their master's orders. Under such a system the justiciarship practically ceased to exist. The treasurership was held for short periods by royal clerks of no personal distinction. Even the chancellorship became overshadowed. Henry quarrelled with Ralph Neville in 1238, and withdrew from him the custody of the great seal, though he allowed him to retain the name and emoluments of chancellor. On Neville's death the office fell into abeyance for nearly twenty years, during which time the great seal was entrusted to seven successive keepers. Like his grandfather, Henry wished to rule in person with the help of faithful but unobtrusive subordinates. This system, which was essentially that of the French monarchy, presupposed for success the constant personal supervision of an industrious and strong-willed king. Henry III. was never a strenuous worker, and his character failed in the robustness and self-reliance necessary for personal rule. The magnates, who regarded themselves as the king's natural-born counsellors, were bitterly incensed, and hated the royal clerks as fiercely as they had disliked the ministers of his minority. Opposed by the barons, distrusted by the people, liable to be thrown over by their master at each fresh change of his caprice, the royal subordinates showed more eagerness in prosecuting their own private fortunes than in consulting the interests of the State. Thus the nominal government of Henry proved extremely ineffective. Huge taxes were raised, but little good came from them. The magnates held sullenly aloof ; the people grumbled ; the Church lamented the evil days. Yet for five and twenty years the wretched system went on, not so much by reason of its own strength as because there was no one vigorous enough to overthow it.

The author of all this mischief was a man of some noble and many attractive qualities. Save when an occasional outburst of temper showed him a true son of John, Henry was the kindest, mildest, most amiable of men. He was the first king since William the Conqueror in whose private life the austerest critics could find nothing blameworthy. His piety stands high, even when estimated by the standards of the thirteenth century. He was well educated and had a touch of the artist's temperament, loving fair churches, beautiful sculpture, delicate gold-smith's work, and richly illuminated books. He had a horror of violence, and never wept more bitter tears than when he learned how treacherously his name had been used to lure Richard Marshal to his doom. But he was extraordinarily deficient in stability of purpose. For the moment it was easy to influence him either for good or evil, but even the ablest of his counsellors found it impossible to retain any hold over him for long. One day he lavished all his affection on Hubert de Burgh ; the next he played into the hands of his enemies. In the same way he got rid of Peter des Roches, the preceptor of his infancy, the guide of his early manhood. Jealous, self-asser-tive, restless, and timid, he failed in just those qualities that his subjects expected to find in a king. Born and brought up in England, and never leaving it save for short and infrequent visits to the continent, he was proud of his English ancestors and devoted to English saints, more especially to royal saints such as Edward the Confessor and Edmund of East Anglia. Yet he showed less sympathy with English ways than many of his foreign-born predecessors. Educated under alien in-fluences, delighting in the art, the refinement, the devotion, and the absolutist principles of foreigners, he seldom trusted a man of English birth. Too weak to act for himself, too suspicious to trust his natural counsellors, he found the friend-ship and advice for which he yearned in foreign favourites and kinsmen. Thus it was that the hopes excited by the fall of the Poitevins were disappointed. The alien invasion, checked for a few years, was renewed in a more dangerous shape.

During the ten years after the collapse of Peter des Roches, swarms of foreigners came to England, and spoiled the land with the king's entire good-will. Henry's marriage brought many Provençals and Savoyards to England. The renewed troubles between pope and emperor led to a renewal of Roman interference in a more exacting form. The continued inter-course with foreign states resulted in fresh opportunities of alien influence. A new attempt on Poitou brought as its only result the importation of the king's Poitevin kinsmen. The continued close relationship between the English and the French baronage involved the frequent claim of English estates and titles by men of alien birth. Even such beneficial movements as the establishment of the mendicant orders in England, and the cosmopolitan outlook of the increasingly important academic class contributed to the spread of outlandish ideas. As wave after wave of foreigners swept over England, Englishmen involved them in a common condemnation. And all saw in the weakness of the king the very source of their power.

The first great influx of foreigners followed directly from Henry's marriage. For several years active negotiations had been going on to secure him a suitable bride. There had also at various times been talk of his selecting a wife from Brittany, Austria, Bohemia, or Scotland, and in the spring of 1235 a serious negotiation for his marriage with Joan, daughter and heiress of the Count of Ponthieu, only broke down through the opposition of the French court. Henry then sought the hand of Eleanor, a girl twelve years old, and the second of the four daughters of Raymond Berengar IV., Count of Provence, and his wife Beatrice, sister of Amadeus III., Count of Savoy. The marriage contract was signed in October. Before that time Eleanor had left Provence under the escort of her mother's brother, William, bishop-elect of Valence. On her way she spent a long period with her elder sister Margaret, who had been married to Louis IX. of France in 1234. On January 14, 1236, she was married to Henry at Canterbury by Archbishop Edmund, and crowned at Westminster on the following Sunday.

The new queen's kinsfolk quickly acquired an almost unbounded ascendency over her weak husband. With the exception of the reigning Count Amadeus of Savoy, her eight maternal uncles were somewhat scantily provided for. The prudence of the French government prevented them from obtaining any advantage for themselves at the court of their niece the Queen of France, and they gladly welcomed the opportunity of establishing themselves at the expense of their English nephew. Self-seeking and not over-scrupulous, able, energetic, and with the vigour and resource of high-born soldiers of fortune, several of them play honourable parts in the history of their own land, and are by no means deserving of the complete condemnation meted out to them by the English annalists.[1] The

---

[1] For Eleanor's countrymen see Mugnier, *Les Savoyards en Angleterre au XIIIe siècle, et Pierre d'Aigueblanche, évêque d'Héreford* (1890).

bishop-elect of Valence was an able and accomplished warrior. CHAP. He stayed on in England after accomplishing his mission, and III. with him remained his clerk, the younger son of a house of Alpine barons, Peter of Aigueblanche, whose cunning and dexterity were as attractive to Henry as the more martial qualities of his master. Weary of standing alone, the king eagerly welcomed a trustworthy adviser who was outside the entanglements of English parties, and made Bishop William his chief counsellor. It was believed that he was associated with eleven others in a secret inner circle of royal advisers, whose advice Henry pledged himself by oath to follow. Honours and estates soon began to fall thickly on William and his friends. He made himself the mouthpiece of Henry's foreign policy. When he temporarily left England, he led a force sent by the king to help Frederick II. in his war against the cities of northern Italy. His influence with Henry did much to secure for his brother, Thomas of Savoy, the hand of the elderly countess Joan of Flanders. With Thomas as the successor of Ferdinand of Portugal, the rich Flemish county, bound to England by so many political and economic ties, seemed in safe hands, and preserved from French influence. In 1238 Thomas visited England, and received a warm welcome and rich presents from the king.

Despite the establishment of the Savoyards, the Poitevin influence began to revive. Peter des Roches, who had occupied himself after his fall by fighting for Gregory IX. against the revolted Romans, returned to England in broken health in 1236, and was reconciled to the king. Peter of Rivaux was restored to favour, and made keeper of the royal wardrobe. Segrave and Passelewe again became justices and ministers. England was now the hunting-ground of any well-born Frenchmen anxious for a wider career than they could obtain at home.[1] Among the foreigners attracted to England to prosecute legal claims or to seek the royal bounty came Simon of Montfort, the second son of the famous conqueror of the Albigenses. Amice, the mother of the elder Simon, was the sister and heiress of Robert of Beaumont, the last of his line to hold the earldom of

[1] This is well illustrated by Philip de Beaumanoir's well-known romance, *Jean de Dammartin et Blonde d'Oxford* (ed. by Suchier, Soc. des anciens Textes français, and by Le Roux de Lincy, Camden Soc.).

Leicester. After Amice's death her son used the title and claimed the estates of that earldom. But these pretensions were but nominal, and since 1215 Randolph of Chester had administered the Leicester lands as if his complete property. However, Amaury of Montfort, the Count of Toulouse's eldest son, ceded to his portionless younger brother his claims to the Beaumont inheritance, and in 1230 Simon went to England to push his fortunes. Young, brilliant, ambitious and attractive, he not only easily won the favour of the king, but commended himself so well to Earl Randolph that in 1231 the aged earl was induced to relax his grasp on the Leicester estates. In 1239 the last formalities of investiture were accomplished. Amaury renounced his claims, and after that Simon became Earl of Leicester and steward of England. A year before that he had secured the great marriage that he had long been seeking. In January, 1238, he was wedded to the king's own sister, Eleanor, the childless widow of the younger William Marshal. Simon was for the moment high in the affection of his brother-in-law. To the English he was simply another of the foreign favourites who turned the king's heart against his born subjects.

In 1238 Peter des Roches died. With all his faults the Poitevin was an excellent administrator at Winchester,[1] and left his estates in such a prosperous condition that Henry coveted the succession for the bishop-elect of Valence, though William already had the prospect of the prince-bishopric of Liége. But the monks of St. Swithun's refused to obey the royal order, and Henry sought to obtain his object from the pope. Gregory gave William both Liége and Winchester, but in 1239 death ended his restless plans. William's death left more room for his kinsfolk and followers. His clerk, Peter of Aigueblanche, returned to the land of promise, and in 1240 secured his consecration as Bishop of Hereford. William's brother, Peter of Savoy, lord of Romont and Faucigny, was invited to England in the same year. In 1241 he was invested with the earldom of Richmond, which a final breach with Peter of Brittany had left in the king's hands. Peter, the ablest member of his house, thus became its chief representative in England.[2]

---

[1] See H. Hall, *Pipe Roll of the Bishop of Winchester*, 1207-8.
[2] For Peter see Wurstemberger, *Peter II., Graf von Savoyen* (1856).

With the Provençals and Savoyards came a fresh swarm
of Romans.   In 1237 the first papal legates *a latere* since the
recall of Pandulf landed in England. The deputy of Gregory IX.
was the cardinal-deacon Otto, who in 1226 had already discharged the humbler office of nuncio in England.   It was
believed that the legate was sent at the special request of
Henry III., and despite the remonstrances of the Archbishop
of Canterbury.   Those most unfriendly to the legate were won
over by his irreproachable conduct.   He rejected nearly all gifts.
He was unwearied in preaching peace; travelled to the north
to settle outstanding differences between Henry and the King
of Scots, and thence hurried to the west to prolong the truce
with Llewelyn.   His zeal for the reformation of abuses made
the canons of the national council, held under his presidency
at St. Paul's on November 18, 1237, an epoch in the history of
our ecclesiastical jurisprudence.

Despite his efforts the legate remained unpopular.   The
pluralists and nepotists, who feared his severity, joined with
the foes of all taxation and the enemies of all foreigners in
denouncing the legate.   To avoid the danger of poison, he
thought it prudent to make his own brother his master cook.
During the council of London it was necessary to escort him
from his lodgings and back again with a military force.   In
the council itself the claim of high-born clerks to receive
benefices in plurality found a spokesman in so respectable a
prelate as Walter of Cantilupe, the son of a marcher baron,
whom Otto had just enthroned in his cathedral at Worcester,
and the legate, " fearing for his skin," was suspected of mitigating the severity of his principles to win over the less greedy
of the friends of vested interests.   His Roman followers knew
and cared little about English susceptibilities, and feeling was
so strong against them that any mischance might excite an
explosion.   Such an accident occurred on St. George's day,
April 23, 1238, when the legate was staying with the Austin
Canons of Oseney, near Oxford, while the king was six miles
off at Abingdon.   Some of the masters of the university went
to Oseney to pay their respects to the cardinal, and were rudely
repulsed by the Italian porter.   Irritated at this discourtesy,
they returned with a host of clerks, who forced their way
into the abbey.   Amongst them was a poor Irish chaplain,

who made his way to the kitchen to beg for food. The chief cook, the legate's brother, threw a pot of scalding broth into the Irishman's face. A clerk from the march of Wales shot the cook dead with an arrow. A fierce struggle followed, in the midst of which Otto, hastily donning the garb of his hosts, took refuge in the tower of their church, where he was besieged by the infuriated clerks, until the king sent soldiers from Abingdon to release him. Otto thereupon laid Oxford under an interdict, suspended all lectures, and put thirty masters into prison. English opinion, voiced by the diocesan, Grosseteste, held that the cardinal's servants had provoked the riot, and found little to blame in the violence of the clerks.

In 1239 Gregory IX. began his final conflict with Frederick II., and demanded the support of all Europe. As before, from 1227 to 1230, the pressure of the papal necessity was at once felt in England. The legate had to raise supplies at all costs. Crusaders were allowed to renounce their vows for ready money. Every visitation or conference became an excuse for procurations and fees. Presents were no longer rejected, but rather greedily solicited. On the pretence that it was necessary to reform the Scottish Church, "which does not recognise the Roman Church as its sole mother and metropolitan," Otto excited the indignation of Alexander II. by attempts to extend his jurisdiction to Scotland, hitherto unvisited by legates. In England his claims soon grew beyond all bearing. At last he demanded a fifth of all clerical goods to enable the pope to finance the anti-imperial crusade. Even this was more endurable than the order received from Rome that 300 clerks of Roman families should be "provided" to benefices in England in order that Gregory might obtain the support of their relatives against Frederick. Both as feudal suzerain and as spiritual despot, the pope lorded it over England as fully as his uncle Innocent III.

Weakness, piety, and self-interest combined to make Henry III. acquiesce in the legate's exactions. "I neither wish nor dare," said he, "to oppose the lord pope in anything." The union of king and legate was irresistible. The lay opposition was slow and feeble. Gilbert Marshal, though showing no lack of spirit, was not the man to play the part which his brother Richard had filled so effectively. Richard, Earl of Cornwall, who constituted himself the spokesman of the magnates, made a special grievance of the marriage of Simon of Montfort with his sister Eleanor.   England, he said, was like a vineyard with a broken hedge, so that all that went by could steal the grapes.   He took arms, and subscribed the first of the long series of plans of constitutional reform that the reign was to witness, according to which the king was to be guided by a chosen body of counsellors.   But at the crisis of the movement he held back, having accomplished nothing.

There was more vigour in the ecclesiastical opposition. Robert Grosseteste,[1] a Suffolk man of humble birth, had already won for himself a position of unique distinction at Oxford and Paris.   A teacher of rare force, a scholar of unexampled range, a thinker of daring originality, and a writer who had touched upon almost every known subject, he was at the height of his fame when, in 1235, his appointment as Bishop of Lincoln gave the fullest opportunities for the employment of his great gifts in the public service.   He was convinced that the preoccupation of the clergy in worldly employment and the constant aggressions of the civil upon the ecclesiastical courts lay at the root of the evils of the time.   His conviction brought him into conflict with the king rather than the legate, though for the moment his absorption in the cares of his diocese distracted his attention from general questions.   The bishops generally had become so hostile that Otto shrank from meeting them in another council, and strove to get money by negotiating individually with the leading churchmen.   The old foe of papal usurpations, Robert Twenge, renewed his agitation on behalf of the rights of patrons, and the clergy of Berkshire drew up a remonstrance against Otto's extortions.

Archbishop Edmund saw the need of opposing both legate and king ; but he was hampered by his ecclesiastical and political principles, and still more, perhaps, by the magnitude of the rude task thrown upon him.   He had set before himself the ideal of St. Thomas, not only in the asceticism of his private life, but in his zeal for his see and the Church.   But few men were more unlike the strong-willed and bellicose martyr of Canterbury than the gentle and yielding saint of Abingdon.   A plentiful crop

[1] For Grosseteste, see F. S. Stevenson, *Robert Grosseteste, Bishop of Lincoln* (1899).

of quarrels, however, soon showed that Edmund had, in one respect, copied only too faithfully the example of his predecessor. He was engaged in a controversy of some acerbity with the Archbishop of York, and he was involved in a long wrangle with the monks of his cathedral, which took him to Rome soon after the legate's arrival. He got little satisfaction there, and found a whole sea of troubles to overwhelm him on his return. At last came the demand of the fifth from Otto. Edmund joined in the opposition of his brethren to this exaction, but his attitude was complicated by his other difficulties. Leaning in his weakness on the pope, he found that Gregory was a taskmaster rather than a director. At last he paid his fifth, but, broken in health and spirits, he was of no mind to withstand the demands of the Roman clerks for benefices. If he could not be another St. Thomas defending the liberties of the Church, he could at least withdraw like his prototype from the strife, and find a refuge in a foreign house of religion. Seeking out St. Thomas's old haunt at Pontigny, he threw himself with ardour into the austere Cistercian life. On the advice of his physicians, he soon sought a healthier abode with the canons of Soisy, in Brie, at whose house he died on November 16, 1240. His body was buried at Pontigny in the still abiding minster which had witnessed the devotions of Becket and Langton, and miracles were soon wrought at his tomb. Within eight years of his death he was declared a saint; and Henry, who had thwarted him in life, and even opposed his canonisation, was among the first of the pilgrims who worshipped at his shrine. It needed a tougher spirit and a stronger character than Edmund's to grapple with the thorny problems of his age.

The retirement of the archbishop enabled Otto to carry through his business, and withdraw from England on January 7, 1241. On August 21 Gregory IX. died, with his arch-enemy at the gates of Rome and all his plans for the time frustrated. High-minded, able and devout, he wagered the whole fortunes of the papacy on the result of his secular struggle with the emperor. In Italy as in England, the spiritual hegemony of the Roman see and the spiritual influence of the western Church were compromised by his exaltation of ecclesiastical politics over religion.

The monks of Christ Church won court favour by electing as archbishop, Boniface of Savoy, Bishop-elect of Belley, one

of the queen's uncles. There was no real resistance to the appointment, though a prolonged vacancy in the papacy made it
impossible for him to receive formal confirmation until 1243,
and it was not until 1244 that he condescended to visit his new
province. Meanwhile his kinsmen were carrying everything
before them. Richard of Cornwall lost his first wife, Isabella,
daughter of William Marshal, in 1240, an event which broke
almost the last link that bound him to the baronial opposition.
He withdrew himself from the troubles of English politics by
going on crusade, and with him went his former enemy, Simon
of Leicester. Richard was back in England early in 1242, and
on November 23, 1243, his marriage with Sanchia of Provence,
the younger sister of the queens of France and England, completed his conversion to the court party.

Henry III.'s cosmopolitan instincts led him to take as
much part in foreign politics as his resources allowed. In 1235
he married his sister Isabella to Frederick II., and henceforth
manifested a strong interest in the affairs of his imperial brother-
in-law. His relations with France were still uneasy, and he
hoped to find in Frederick's support a counterpoise to the
steady pressure of French hostility. All England watched
with interest the progress of the emperor's arms. Peter of
Savoy led an English contingent to fight for Frederick against
the Milanese, and Matthew Paris, the greatest of the English
chroniclers, narrates the campaign of Corte Nuova with a detail
exceeding that which he allows to the military enterprises of
his own king. Frederick constantly corresponded with both
the king and Richard of Cornwall, and it was nothing but
solicitude for the safety of the heir to the throne that led the
English magnates to reject the emperor's request that Richard
should receive a high command under him. Even Frederick's
breach with the pope in 1239 did not destroy his friendship
with Henry. The situation became extremely complicated,
since Innocent IV. derived large financial support for his
crusade from the unwilling English clergy, while Henry still
professed to be Frederick's friend. The king allowed Otto to
proclaim Frederick's excommunication in England, and then
urged the legate to quit the country because the emperor
strongly protested against the presence of an avowed enemy
at his brother-in-law's court. Neither pope nor emperor could

rely upon the support of so half-hearted a prince. Renewed trouble with France explains in some measure the anxiety of Henry to remain in good relations with the emperor despite Frederick's quarrel with the pope.

The position of the French monarchy was far stronger than it had been when Henry first intervened in continental politics. Blanche of Castile had broken the back of the feudal coalition, and even Peter Mauclerc had made his peace with the monarchy at the price of his English earldom. Louis IX. attained his majority in 1235, and his first care was to strengthen his power in his newly won dominions. If Poitou were still in the hands of the Count of La Marche and the Viscount of Thouars, the royal seneschals of Beaucaire and Carcassonne after 1229 ruled over a large part of the old dominions of Raymond of Toulouse. In 1237 the treaty of Meaux was further carried out by the marriage of Raymond's daughter and heiress, Joan, to Alfonse, the brother of the French king. In 1241 Alfonse came of age, and Louis at once invested him with Poitou and Auvergne. The lords of Poitou saw that the same process which had destroyed the feudal liberties of Normandy now endangered their disorderly independence. Hugh of Lusignan and his wife had been present at Alfonse's investiture, and the widow of King John had gone away highly indignant at the slights put upon her dignity.[1] She bitterly reproached her husband with the ignominy involved in his submission. Easily moved to new treasons, Hugh became the soul of a league of Poitevin barons formed at Parthenay, which received the adhesion of Henry's seneschal of Gascony, Rostand de Sollers, and even of Alfonse's father-in-law, the depressed Raymond of Toulouse. At Christmas Hugh openly showed his hand. He renounced his homage to Alfonse, declared his adhesion to his step-son, Richard of Cornwall, the titular count of Poitou, and ostentatiously withdrew from the court with his wife. The rest of the winter was taken up with preparations for the forthcoming struggle.

Untaught by experience, Henry III. listened to the appeals of his mother and her husband. Richard of Cornwall, who came back from his crusade in January, 1242, was persuaded that he had another chance of realising his vain title of Count

---

[1] See the graphic letter of a citizen of La Rochelle to Blanche, published by M. Delisle in *Bibliothèque de l'Ecole des Chartes*, série ii., iv., 513-55 (1856).

of Poitou.   But the king had neither men nor money and the
parliament of February 2 refused to grant him sums adequate
for his need, so that, despairing of dealing with his barons in
a body, Henry followed the legate's example of winning men
over individually.   He made a strong protest against the King
of France's breach of the existing truce, and his step-father
assured him that Poitou and Gascony would provide him with
sufficient soldiers if he brought over enough money to pay them.
Thereupon, leaving the Archbishop of York as regent, Henry
took ship on May 9 at Portsmouth and landed on May 13 at
Royan at the mouth of the Gironde.   He was accompanied by
Richard of Cornwall, seven earls, and 300 knights.

Meanwhile Louis IX. marshalled a vast host at Chinon,
which from April to July overran the patrimony of the house
of Lusignan, and forced many of the confederate barons to
submit.   Peter of Savoy and John Mansel, Henry's favourite
clerk, then made seneschal of Gascony, assembled the Aquitanian levies, while Peter of Aigueblanche, the Savoyard Bishop
of Hereford, went to Provence to negotiate the union between
Earl Richard and Sanchia, and, if possible, to add Raymond
Berengar to the coalition against the husband of his eldest
daughter.   Henry hoped to win tactical advantages by provoking Louis to break the truce, and mendaciously protested
his surprise at being forced into an unexpected conflict with his
brother-in-law.   Towards the end of July, Louis, who had
conquered all Poitou, advanced to the Charente, and occupied
Taillebourg.   If the Charente were once crossed, Saintonge
would assuredly follow the destinies of Poitou ; and the Anglo-
Gascon army advanced from Saintes to dispute the passage of
the river.   On July 21 the two armies were in presence of each
other, separated only by the Charente.   Besides the stone bridge
at Taillebourg, the French had erected a temporary wooden
structure higher up the stream, and had collected a large
number of boats to facilitate their passage.   Seeing with dis-
may the oriflamme waving over the sea of tents which, "like
a great and populous city," covered the right bank, the soldiers
of Henry retreated precipitately to Saintes.   There was imminent danger of their retreat being cut off, but Richard of
Cornwall went to the French camp, and obtained an armistice
of a few hours, which gave his brother time to reach the town.

Next day Louis advanced at his ease to the capital of Saintonge. The Anglo-Gascons went out to meet him, and, despite their inferior numbers, fought bravely amidst the vineyards and hollow lanes to the west of the city. But the English king was the first to flee, and victory soon attended the arms of the French. Immediately after the battle, the lords of Poitou abandoned Richard for Alfonse. Henry fled from Saintes to Pons, from Pons to Barbezieux, and thence sought a more secure refuge at Blaye, leaving his tent, the ornaments of his chapel, and the beer provided for his English soldiers as booty for the enemy. The outbreak of an epidemic in the French army alone prevented a siege of Bordeaux, by necessitating the return of St. Louis to the healthier north. Henry lingered at Bordeaux until September, when he returned to England.[1] Meanwhile the French dictated peace to the remaining allies of Henry. On the death of Raymond of Toulouse, in 1249, Alfonse quietly succeeded to his dominions. The next twenty years saw the gradual extension of the French administrative system to Poitou, Auvergne, and the Toulousain. English Gascony was reduced to little more than the districts round Bordeaux and Bayonne. Even a show of hostility was no longer useful, and on April 7, 1243, a five years' truce between Henry and Louis was signed at Bordeaux. The marriage of Beatrice of Provence, the youngest of the daughters of Raymond Berengar, to Charles of Anjou, Louis' younger brother, removed Provence from the sphere of English influence. On his father-in-law's death in 1245, Charles of Anjou succeeded to his dominions to the prejudice of his two English brothers-in-law, and became the founder of a Capetian line of counts of Provence, which brought the great fief of the empire under the same northern French influences which Alfonse of Poitiers was diffusing over the lost inheritances of Eleanor of Aquitaine and the house of Saint-Gilles.

A minor result of Louis' triumph was the well-deserved ruin of Hugh of Lusignan and Isabella of Angoulême. The proud spirit of Isabella did not long tolerate her humiliation. She

---

[1] The only good modern account of this expedition is that by M. Charles Bémont, *La campagne de Poitou, 1242-3*, in *Annales du Midi*, v., 289-314 (1893). For the Lusignans see Boissonade, *Quomodo comites Engolismenses erga reges Angliæ et Franciæ se gesserint*, 1152-1328 (1893).

retired to Fontevraud and died there in 1246. Hugh X. followed
her to the tomb in 1248. Their eldest son, Hugh XI., succeeded him, but the rest of their numerous family turned for
support to the inexhaustible charity of the King of England.
Thus in 1247 a Poitevin invasion of the king's half-brothers and
sisters recalled to his much-tried subjects the Savoyard invasion
of ten years earlier. In that single year three of the king's
brothers and one of his sisters accepted his invitation to make
a home in England. Of these, Guy, lord of Cognac, became
proprietor of many estates. William, called from the Cistercian
abbey in which he was born William of Valence, secured, with
the hand of Joan of Munchensi, a claim to the great inheritance that was soon to be scattered by the extinction of the
male line of the house of Marshal. Aymer of Valence, a very
unclerical churchman, obtained in 1250 his election as bishop
of Winchester, though his youth and the hostility of his chapter
delayed his consecration for ten years. Alice their sister found
a husband of high rank in the young John of Warenne, Earl of
Warenne or Surrey, while a daughter of Hugh XI. married
Robert of Ferrars, Earl of Ferrars or Derby. Others of their
kindred flocked to the land of promise. Any Poitevin was
welcome, even if not a member of the house of Lusignan.
Thus the noble adventurer John du Plessis, came over to
England, married the heiress of the Neufbourg Earls of
Warwick, and in 1247 was created Earl of Warwick. The
alien invasion took a newer and more grievous shape.

The expenses of the war were still to be paid ; and in 1244
Henry assembled a council, declaring that, as he had gone to
Gascony on the advice of his barons, they were bound to
make him a liberal grant towards freeing him from the debts
which he had incurred beyond sea. Prelates, earls, and barons
each deliberated apart, and a joint committee, composed of four
members of each order, drew up an uncompromising reply. The
king had not observed the charters ; previous grants had been
misapplied, and the abeyance of the great offices of state made
justice difficult and good administration impossible. The committee insisted that a justiciar, a chancellor, and a treasurer
should forthwith be appointed. This was the last thing that
the jealous king desired. Helpless against a united council, he
strove to break up the solidarity between its lay and clerical

elements by laying a papal order before the prelates to furnish him an adequate subsidy. The leader of the bishops was now Grosseteste, who from this time until his death in 1253 was the pillar of the opposition. " We must not," he declared, " be divided from the common counsel, for it is written that if we be divided we shall all die forthwith." At last a committee of twelve magnates was appointed to draw up a plan of reform. The unanimity of all orders was shown by the co-operation on this body of prelates such as Boniface of Savoy with patriots of the stamp of Grosseteste and Walter of Cantilupe, while among the secular lords, Richard of Cornwall and Simon of Leicester worked together with baronial leaders like Norfolk and Richard of Montfichet, a survivor of the twenty-five executors of Magna Carta. The obstinacy of the king may well have driven the estates into drawing up the remarkable paper constitution pre-served for us by Matthew Paris.[1] By it the execution of the charters and the supervision of the administration were to be entrusted to four councillors, chosen from among the magnates, and irremovable except with their consent. It is unlikely that the scheme was ever carried out ; but its conception shows an advance in the claims of the opposition, and anticipates the policy of restraining an incompetent ruler by a committee re-sponsible to the estates, which, for the next two centuries, was the popular specific for royal maladministration. For the mo-ment neither side gained a decided victory. Though the barons persisted in their refusal of an extraordinary grant, they agreed to pay an aid to marry the king's eldest daughter to the son of Frederick II.

Further demands arose from the quarrel between Innocent IV. and the emperor. A new papal envoy, Master Martin, came to England to extort from the clergy money to enable Innocent to carry on his war against Frederick. The lords told Martin that if he did not quit the realm forthwith he would be torn in pieces. In terror he prayed for a safe conduct. " May the devil give you a safe conduct to hell," was the only reply that the angry Henry vouchsafed. Even his complais-ance was exhausted by Master Martin.

On July 26, 1245, a few weeks before Martin's expulsion,

[1] *Chron. Maj.*, iv., 366-68.

Innocent IV. opened a general council at Lyons, in which CHAP. Frederick was deposed from the imperial dignity. Grosseteste, III. the chief English prelate to attend the gathering, was drawn in conflicting directions by his zeal for pope against emperor and by his dislike of curialist exactions. This attitude of the bishop is reflected in the remonstrance, in the name of the English people, laid before Innocent, declaring the faithfulness of England to the Holy See and the wrongs with which her fidelity had been requited. The increasing demands for money, the intrusion of aliens into English cures, and Martin's exactions were set forth at length. Innocent refused to entertain the petition, forced all the bishops at Lyons to join in the deprivation of the emperor, and required every English bishop to seal with his own seal the document by which John had pledged the nation to a yearly tribute. No one could venture to stand up against the successor of St. Peter, and so, despite futile remonstrance, Innocent still had it all his own way. In 1250 Grosseteste again met Innocent face to face at Lyons, and urged him to "put to flight the evils and purge the abominations" which the Roman see had done so much to foster. But this outspoken declaration was equally without result. Bold as were Grosseteste's words, he fully accepted the curialist theory which regarded the pope as the universal bishop, the divinely appointed source of all ecclesiastical jurisdiction. He could therefore do no more than protest. If the pope chose to disregard him, there was nothing to be done but wait patiently for better times. The plague of foreign ecclesiastics was still to torment the English Church for many a year.

The king's difficulties were increased by fresh troubles in Scotland and Wales. The friendship between Henry and his brother-in-law, Alexander II., was weakened by the death of the Queen of Scots and by Alexander's marriage to a French lady in 1239. At last, in 1244, relations were so threatening that the English levies were mustered for a campaign at Newcastle. However, on the mediation of Richard of Cornwall, Alexander bound himself not to make alliances with England's enemies, and the trouble passed away. In Wales the difficulties were more complicated. Llewelyn ap Iorwerth died in 1240, full of years and honour. In the last years of his reign broken health and the revolts of his eldest son Griffith made the

5 *

old chieftain anxious for peace with England, as the best way
of securing the succession to all his dominions of David, his
son by Joan of Anjou. Henry III., anxious that David as his
nephew should inherit the principality, granted a temporary
cessation of hostilities. After Llewelyn's death David was
accepted as Prince of Snowdon, and made his way to Gloucester, where he performed homage, and was dubbed knight
by his uncle. Next year, however, hostilities broke out, and
Henry, disgusted with his nephew, made a treaty with the
wife of Griffith, Griffith himself being David's prisoner. In
1241 Henry led an expedition from Chester into North Wales,
and forced David to submit. He surrendered Griffith to his
uncle's safe keeping and promised to yield his principality to
Henry if he died without a son. Three years later Griffith
broke his neck in an attempt to escape from the Tower. The
death of his rival emboldened David to take up a stronger line
against his uncle. A fresh Welsh expedition was necessary
for the summer of 1245, in which the English advanced to the
Conway, but were speedily forced to retire. David held his
own until his death, without issue, in March, 1246, threw open
the question of the Welsh succession.

CHAPTER IV.

POLITICAL RETROGRESSION AND NATIONAL PROGRESS.

THE ten years from 1248 to 1258 saw the continuance of the misgovernment, discontent, and futile opposition which have already been sufficiently illustrated. The history of those years must be sought not so much in the relations of the king and his English subjects as in Gascony, in Wales, in the crusading revival, and in the culmination of the struggle of papacy and empire. In each of these fields the course of events reacted sharply upon the domestic affairs of England, until at last the failures of Henry's foreign policy gave unity and determination to the party of opposition whose first organised success, in 1258, ushered in the Barons' War.

The relations between England and France remained anomalous. Formal peace was impossible, since France would yield nothing, and the English king still claimed Normandy and Aquitaine. Yet neither Henry nor Louis had any wish for war. They had married sisters : they were personally friendly, and were both lovers of peace. In such circumstances it was not hard to arrange truces from time to time, so that from 1243 to the end of the reign there were no open hostilities. In 1248 the friendly feeling of the two courts was particularly strong. Louis was on the eve of departure for the crusade and many English nobles had taken the cross. Henry, who was himself contemplating a crusade, was of no mind to avail himself of his kinsman's absence to disturb his realm.

The French could afford to pass over Henry's neglect to do homage, for Gascony seemed likely to emancipate itself from the yoke of its English dukes without any prompting from Paris. After the failure of 1243, a limited amount of territory between the Dordogne and the Pyrenees alone acknowledged Henry.

This narrower Gascony was a thoroughly feudalised land : the
absentee dukes had little authority, domain, or revenue : and
the chief lordships were held by magnates, whose relations to
their overlord were almost formal, and by municipalities almost
as free as the cities of Flanders or the empire.   The disastrous
campaign of Taillebourg lessened the prestige of the duke, and
Henry quitted Gascony without so much as attempting to
settle its affairs.   In the following years weak seneschals, with
insufficient powers and quickly succeeding each other, were unable to grapple with ever-increasing troubles.   The feudal lords
dominated the countryside, pillaged traders, waged internal war
and defied the authority of the duke.   In the autonomous towns
factions had arisen as fierce as those of the cities of Italy.
Bordeaux was torn asunder by the feuds of the Rosteins and
Colons.   Bayonne was the scene of a struggle between a few
privileged families, which sought to monopolise municipal office,
and a popular opposition based upon the seafaring class.   The
neighbouring princes cast greedy eyes on a land so rich, divided,
and helpless.   Theobald IV., the poet, Count of Champagne
and King of Navarre, coveted the valley of the Adour.   Gaston,
Viscount of Béarn, the cousin of Queen Eleanor, plundered and
destroyed the town of Dax.   Ferdinand the Saint of Castile
and James I. of Aragon severally claimed all Gascony.   Behind
all these loomed the agents of the King of France.   Either
Gascony must fall away altogether, or stronger measures must
be taken to preserve it.

In this extremity Henry made Simon of Montfort seneschal
or governor of Gascony, with exceptionally full powers and an
assured duration of office for seven years.   Simon had taken the
crusader's vow, but was persuaded by the king to abandon his intention of following Louis to Egypt.   He at once threw himself
into his rude task with an energy that showed him to be a true
son of the Albigensian crusader.   In the first three months he
traversed the duchy from end to end ; rallied the royal partisans ;
defeated rebels ; kept external foes in check, and administered
the law without concern for the privileges of the great.   In
1249 he crushed the Rostein faction at Bordeaux.   The same
fate was meted out to their partisans in the country districts.
Order was restored, but the seneschal utterly disregarded impartiality or justice.   He sought to rule Gascony by terrorism

and by backing up one faction against the other. It was the same with minor cities, like Bazas and Bayonne, and with the tyrants of the countryside. The Viscount of Fronsac saw his castle razed and his estates seized. Gaston of Béarn, tricked by the seneschal out of the succession of Bigorre, was captured, sent to England, and only allowed to return to his home, humiliated and powerless to work further evil. The lesser barons had to acknowledge Simon their master. On the death of Raymond of Toulouse in 1249, his son-in-law and successor, Alfonse of Poitiers, had all he could do to secure his inheritance, and was too closely bound by the pacific policy of his brother to give Simon much trouble. The truce with France was easily renewed by reason of St. Louis' absence on a crusade. The differences between Gascony and Theobald of Navarre were mitigated in 1248 at a personal interview between Leicester and the poet-king.

Gascony for the moment was so quiet that the rebellious hordes called the *Pastoureaux*, who had desolated the royal domain, withdrew from Bordeaux in terror of Simon's threats. But the expense of maintaining order pressed heavily on the seneschal's resources, and his master showed little disposition to assist him. Moreover Gascony could not long keep quiet. There were threats of fresh insurrections, and the whole land was burning with indignation against its governor. Complaints from the Gascon estates soon flowed with great abundance into Westminster. For the moment Henry paid little attention to them. His son Edward was ten years of age, and he was thinking of providing him with an appanage, sufficient to support a separate household and so placed as to train the young prince in the duties of statecraft. Before November, 1249, he granted to Edward all Gascony, along with the profits of the government of Ireland, which were set aside to put Gascony in a good state of defence. Simon's strong hand was now more than ever necessary to keep the boy's unruly subjects under control. The King therefore continued Simon as seneschal of Gascony, though henceforth the earl acted as Edward's minister. " Complete happily," Henry wrote to the seneschal, " all our affairs in Gascony and you shall receive from us and our heirs a recompense worthy of your services." For the moment Leicester's triumph seemed complete, but the Gascons, who had hoped that Edward's estab-

lishment meant the removal of their masterful governor, were
bitterly disappointed at the continuance of his rule. Profiting
by Simon's momentary absence in England, they once more
rose in revolt. Henry wavered for the moment. " Bravely,"
declared he to his brother-in-law, " hast thou fought for me,
and I will not deny thee help. But complaints pour in against
thee. They say that thou hast thrown into prison, and condemned to death, folk who have been summoned to thy court
under pledge of thy good faith." In the end Simon was sent
back to Gascony, and by May, 1251, the rebels were subdued.

Next year Gaston of Béarn stirred up another revolt, and,
while Simon was in England, deputies from the Aquitanian
cities crossed the sea and laid new complaints before Henry.
A stormy scene ensued between the king and his brother-in-law.
Threatened with the loss of his office, Simon insisted that he
had been appointed for seven years, and that he could not be
removed without his own consent. Henry answered that he
would keep no compacts with traitors. "That word is a lie,"
cried Simon; "were you not my king it would be an ill hour
for you when you dared to utter it." The sympathy of the
magnates saved Leicester from the king's wrath, and before
long he returned to Gascony, still seneschal, but with authority
impaired by the want of his sovereign's confidence. Though
the king henceforth sided with the rebels, Simon remained
strong enough to make headway against the lord of Béarn.
Before long, however, Leicester unwillingly agreed to vacate
his office on receiving from Henry a sum of money. In
September, 1252, he laid down the seneschalship and retired
into France. While shabbily treated by the king, he had certainly shown an utter absence of tact or scruple. But the
tumults of Gascony raged with more violence than ever now
that his strong hand was withdrawn. Those who had professed to rise against the seneschal remained in arms against
the king. Once more the neighbouring princes cast greedy
eyes on the defenceless duchy. In particular, Alfonso the
Wise, King of Castile, who succeeded his father Ferdinand
in 1252, renewed his father's claims to Gascony.

The only way to save the duchy was for Henry to go there
in person. Long delays ensued before the royal visit took
place, and it was not until August, 1253, that Bordeaux saw

her hereditary duke sail up the Gironde to her quays. The
Gascon capital remained faithful, but within a few miles of
her walls the rebels were everywhere triumphant. It required
a long siege to reduce Benauge to submission, and months
elapsed before the towns and castles of the lower Garonne
and Dordogne opened their gates. Even then La Réole,
whither all the worst enemies of Montfort had fled, held out
obstinately. Despairing of military success, Henry fell back
upon diplomacy. The strength of the Gascon revolt did not
lie in the power of the rebels themselves but in the support of
the neighbouring princes and the French crown. By renewing
the truce with the representatives of Louis, Henry protected
himself from the danger of French intervention, and at the
same time he cut off a more direct source of support to the
rebels by negotiating treaties with such magnates as the lord
of Albret, the Counts of Comminges and Armagnac, and the
Viscount of Béarn. His master-stroke was the conclusion, in
April, 1254, of a peace with Alfonso of Castile, whereby the
Spanish king abandoned his Gascon allies and renounced his
claims on the duchy. In return it was agreed that the lord
Edward should marry Alfonso's half-sister, Eleanor, heiress
of the county of Ponthieu through her mother, Joan, whom
Henry had once sought for his queen. As Edward's appanage included Aquitaine, Alfonso, in renouncing his personal
claims, might seem to be but transferring them to his sister.

In May, 1254, Queen Eleanor joined Henry at Bordeaux.
With her went her two sons, Edward and Edmund, her uncle,
Archbishop Boniface, and a great crowd of magnates. In
August Edward went with his mother to Alfonso's court at
Burgos, where he was welcomed with all honour and dubbed
to knighthood by the King of Castile, and in October he and
Eleanor were married at the Cistercian monastery of Las
Huelgas. His appanage included all Ireland, the earldom of
Chester, the king's lands in Wales, the Channel Islands, the
whole of Gascony, and whatsoever rights his father still had
over the lands taken from him and King John by the Kings
of France. Thus he became the ruler of all the outlying dependencies of the English crown, and the representative of all
the claims on the Aquitanian inheritance of Eleanor and the
Norman inheritance of William the Conqueror. The caustic

St. Alban's chronicler declared that Henry left to himself such scanty possessions that he became a "mutilated kinglet".[1] But Henry was too jealous of power utterly to renounce so large a share of his dominions. His grants to his son were for purposes of revenue and support, and the government of these regions was still strictly under the royal control.[2] Yet from this moment writs ran in Edward's name, and under his father's direction the young prince was free to buy his experience as he would. Soon after his son's return with his bride, Henry III. quitted Gascony, making his way home through France, where he visited his mother's tomb at Fontevraud and made atonement at Pontigny before the shrine of Archbishop Edmund. Of more importance was his visit to King Louis, recently returned from his Egyptian captivity. The cordial relations established by personal intercourse between the two kings prepared the way for peace two years later.

Edward remained in Gascony about a year after his father. He checked with a stern hand the disorders of his duchy, strove to make peace between the Rosteins and Colons, and failing to do so, took in 1261 the decisive step of putting an end to the tumultuous municipal independence of the Gascon capital by depriving the jurats of the right of choosing their mayor. Thenceforth Bordeaux was ruled by a mayor nominated by the duke or his lieutenant. Edward's rule in Gascony has its importance as the first experiment in government by the boy of fifteen who was later to become so great a king. Returning to London in November, 1255, he still forwarded the interests of his Gascon subjects, and an attempt to protect the Bordeaux wine-merchants from the exactions of the royal officers aroused the jealousy of Henry, who declared that the days of Henry II. had come again, when the king's sons rose in revolt against their father. Despite this characteristic wail, Edward gained his point. Yet his efforts to secure the well-being of Gascony had not produced much result. The hold of the English duke on Aquitaine was as precarious under Edward as it had been in the days of Henry's direct rule.

The affairs of Wales and Cheshire involved Edward in responsibilities even more pressing than those of Gascony.

[1] Matthew Paris, *Chron. Maj.*, v., 450.
[2] See Bémont, *Rôles Gascons*, i., supplément, pp. cxvi.-cxviii.

On the death of John the Scot without heirs in 1237, the CHAP.
palatinate of Randolph of Blundeville became a royal escheat. IV.
Its grant to Edward made him the natural head of the marcher
barons. The Cheshire earldom became the more important
since the Welsh power had been driven beyond the Conway.
Since the death of David ap Llewelyn in 1246, divisions in
the reigning house of Gwynedd had continued to weaken the
Welsh. Llewelyn and Owen the Red, the two elder sons of
the Griffith ap Llewelyn who had perished in attempting to
escape from the Tower, took upon themselves the government
of Gwynedd, dividing the land, by the advice of the "good
men," into two equal halves. The English seneschal at Carmarthen took advantage of their weakness to seize the outlying dependencies of Gwynedd south of the Dovey. War
ensued, for the brothers resisted this aggression. But in April,
1247, they were forced to do homage at Woodstock for
Gwynedd and Snowdon. Henry retained not only Cardigan
and Carmarthen, but the debatable lands between the eastern
boundary of Cheshire and the river Clwyd, the four cantreds
of the middle country or Perveddwlad, so long the scene of
the fiercest warfare between the Celt and the Saxon. Thus
the work of Llewelyn ap Iorwerth was completely undone, and
his grandsons were confined to Snowdon and Anglesey, the
ancient cradles of their house.

It suited English policy that even the barren lands of
Snowdon should be divided. As time went on, other sons
of Griffith ap Llewelyn began to clamour for a share of
their grandfather's inheritance. Owen, the weaker of the two
princes, made common cause with them, and David, another
brother, succeeded in obtaining his portion of the common
stock. Llewelyn showed himself so much the most resourceful and energetic of the brethren that, when open war broke
out between them in 1254, he easily obtained the victory.
Owen was taken prisoner, and David was deprived of his
lands. Llewelyn, thus sole ruler of Gwynedd, at once aspired
to follow in the footsteps of his grandfather. He overran
Merioneth, and frightened the native chieftains beyond the
Dovey into the English camp. His ambitions were, however,
rudely checked by the grant of Cheshire and the English lands
in Wales to Edward.

Besides the border palatinate, Edward's Welsh lands included the four cantreds of Perveddwlad, and the districts of
Cardigan and Carmarthen. Young as he was, he had competent advisers, and, while he was still in Aquitaine, designs
were formed of setting up the English shire system in his
Welsh lands, so as to supersede the traditional Celtic methods
of government by feudal and monarchical centralisation. Efforts
were made to subject the four cantreds to the shire courts at
Chester; and Geoffrey of Langley, Edward's agent in the south,
set up shire-moots at Cardigan and Carmarthen, from which
originated the first beginnings of those counties. The bitterest
indignation animated Edward's Welsh tenants, whether on
the Clwyd or on the Teivi and Towy. They rose in revolt
against the alien innovators, and called upon Llewelyn to
champion their grievances. Llewelyn saw the chance of extending his tribal power into a national principality over all
Wales by posing as the upholder of the Welsh people. He
overran the four cantreds in a week, finding no resistance save
before the two castles of Deganwy and Diserth. He conquered
Cardigan with equal ease, and prudently granted out his acquisition to the local chieftain Meredith ap Owen. Nor were
Edward's lands alone exposed to his assaults. In central Wales
Roger Mortimer was stripped of his marches on the upper
Wye, and Griffith ap Gwenwynwyn, the lord of upper Powys,
driven from the regions of the upper Severn. In the spring
of 1257 the lord of Gwynedd appeared in regions untraversed
by the men of Snowdon since the days of his grandfather. He
devastated the lands of the marchers on the Bristol Channel
and slew Edward's deputy in battle. "In those days," says
Matthew Paris, "the Welsh saw that their lives were at stake,
so that those of the north joined together in indissoluble
alliance with those of the south. Such a union had never
before been, since north and south had always been opposed."
The lord of Snowdon assumed the title of Prince of Wales.

Edward was forced to defend his inheritance. Henry III.
paid little heed to his misfortunes, and answered his appeal for
help by saying: "What have I to do with the matter? I have
given you the land; you must defend it with your own resources.
I have plenty of other business to do." Nevertheless, Henry
accompanied his son on a Welsh campaign in August, 1257.

The English army got no further than Deganwy, and therefore
did not really invade Llewelyn's dominions at all.   After waiting idly on the banks of the Conway for some weeks, it retired
home, leaving the open country to be ruled by Llewelyn as he
would, and having done nothing but revictual the castles of the
four cantreds.   Next year a truce was made, which left Llewelyn
in possession of the disputed districts.   Troubles at home were
calling off both father and son from the Welsh war, and thus
Llewelyn secured his virtual triumph.   Though fear of the
progress of the lord of Gwynedd filled every marcher with
alarm, yet the dread of the power of Edward was even more
nearly present before them.   The marcher lords deliberately
stood aside, and the result was inevitable disaster.   Edward
found that the territories handed over to him by his father
had to be conquered before they could be administered, and
Henry III.'s methods of government made it a hopeless business
to find either the men or the money for the task.

England still resounded with complaints of misgovernment,
and demands for the execution of the charters.   Before going
to Bordeaux in 1253, Henry obtained from the reluctant
parliament a considerable subsidy, and pledged himself as "a
man, a Christian, a knight, and a crowned and anointed king,"
to uphold the charters.   During his absence a parliament,
summoned by the regents, Queen Eleanor and Richard of Cornwall, for January, 1254, showed such unwillingness to grant a
supply that a fresh assembly was convened in April, to which
knights of the shire, for the first time since the reign of John,
and representatives of the diocesan clergy, for the first occasion
on record, were summoned, as well as the baronial and clerical
grandees.   Nothing came of the meeting save fresh complaints.
The Earl of Leicester became the spokesman of the opposition.
Hurrying back from France he warned the parliament not to
fall into the "mouse-traps" laid for them by the king.   In default
of English money, enough to meet the king's necessities was
extorted from the Jews, recently handed over to the custody of
Richard of Cornwall.   After his return from France at the end
of 1254, Henry's renewed requests for money gave coherence
to the opposition.   Between 1254 and 1258 the king's exactions, and an effective organisation for withstanding them, developed on parallel lines.   To the old sources of discontent were

added grievances proceeding from enterprises of so costly a nature that they at last brought about a crisis.

The foremost grievance against the king was still his co-operation with the papacy in spoiling the Church of England. Though the death of the excommunicated Frederick II. in 1250 was a great gain for Innocent IV., the contest of the papacy against the Hohenstaufen raged as fiercely as ever. Both in Germany and in Italy Innocent had to carry on his struggle against Conrad, Frederick's son. After Conrad's death, in 1254, there was still Frederick's strenuous bastard, Manfred, to be reckoned with in Naples and Sicily. Innocent IV. died in 1254, but his successor, Alexander IV., continued his policy. A papalist King of Naples was wanted to withstand Manfred, and also a papalist successor to the pope's phantom King of the Romans, William of Holland, who died in 1256.

Candidates to both crowns were sought for in England. Since 1250 Innocent IV. had been sounding Richard, Earl of Cornwall, as to his willingness to accept Sicily. The honourable scruple against hostility to his kinsman, which Richard shared with the king, prevented him from setting up his claims against Conrad. But the deaths both of Conrad and of Frederick II.'s son by Isabella of England weakened the ties between the English royal house and the Hohenstaufen, and Henry was tempted by Innocent's offer of the Sicilian throne for his younger son, Edmund, a boy of nine, along with a proposal to release him from his vow of crusade to Syria, if he would prosecute on his son's behalf a crusading campaign against the enemies of the Church in Naples. Innocent died before the negotiations were completed, but Alexander IV. renewed the offer, and in April, 1255, Peter of Aigueblanche, Bishop of Hereford, accepted the proferred kingdom in Edmund's name. Sicily was to be held by a tribute of money and service, as a fief of the holy see, and was never to be united with the empire. Henry was to do homage to the pope on his son's behalf, to go to Italy in person or send thither a competent force, and to reimburse the pope for the large sums expended by him in the prosecution of the war. In return the English and Scottish proceeds of the crusading tenth, imposed on the clergy at Lyons, were to be paid to Henry. On October 18, 1255, a cardinal invested Edmund with a ring that symbolised his appointment.

Henry stood before the altar and swore by St. Edward that he CHAP.
would himself go to Apulia, as soon as he could safely pass IV.
through France.

The treaty remained a dead letter. Henry found it quite
impossible to raise either the men or the money promised, and
abandoned any idea of visiting Sicily in person. Meanwhile
Naples and Sicily were united in support of Manfred, and discomfited the feeble forces of the papal legates who acted against
him in Edmund's name. At last the Archbishop of Messina
came from the pope with an urgent request for payment of
the promised sums. It was in vain that Henry led forth his
son, clothed in Apulian dress, before the Lenten parliament of
1257, and begged the magnates to enable him to redeem his
bond. When they heard the king's speech "the ears of all men
tingled". Nothing could be got save from the clergy, so that
Henry was quite unable to meet his obligations. He besought
Alexander to give him time, to make terms with Manfred, to
release Edmund from his debts on condition of ceding a large
part of Apulia to the Church,—to do anything in short save
insist upon the original contract. The pope deferred the payment, but the respite did Henry no good. Edmund's Sicilian
monarchy vanished into nothing, when, early in 1258, Manfred
was crowned king at Palermo. Before the end of the year,
Alexander cancelled the grant of Sicily to Edmund. Yet his
demands for the discharge of Henry's obligations had contributed not a little towards focussing the gathering discontent.[1]

While Henry was seeking the Sicilian crown for his son,
his brother Richard was elected to the German throne. Since
William of Holland's death in January, 1256, the German magnates, divided between the Hohenstaufen and the papalist
parties, had hesitated for nearly a year as to the choice of his
successor. As neither party was able to secure the election
of its own partisan, a compromise was mooted. At last the
name of Richard of Cornwall was brought definitely forward.
He was of high rank and unblemished reputation; a friend of
the pope yet a kinsman of the Hohenstaufen; he was moderate
and conciliatory; he had enough money to bribe the electors

[1] For Edmund's Sicilian claims, see W. E. Rhodes' article on *Edmund,
Earl of Lancaster*, in the *English Historical Review*, x. (1895), 20-27.

handsomely, and he was never likely to be so deeply rooted in
Germany as to stand in the way of the princes of the empire.
The Archbishop of Cologne became his paid partisan, and the
Count Palatine of the Rhine accepted his candidature on conditions. The French party set up as his rival Alfonso X. of
Castile, who, despite his newly formed English alliance, was
quite willing to stand against Richard. At last, in January,
1257, the votes of three electors, Cologne, Mainz, and the Palatine, were cast for Richard, who also obtained the support of
Ottocar, King of Bohemia. However, in April, Trier, Saxony,
and Brandenburg voted for Alfonso. The double election of two
foreigners perpetuated the Great Interregnum for some sixteen
years. Alfonso's title was only an empty show, but Richard took
his appointment seriously. He made his way to Germany, and
was crowned King of the Romans on May 17, 1257, at Aachen.
He remained in the country nearly eighteen months, and succeeded in establishing his authority in the Rhineland, though
beyond that region he never so much as showed his face.[1] The
elevation of his brother to the highest dignity in Christendom
was some consolation to Henry for the Sicilian failure.

The nation was disgusted to see maladministration grow
worse and worse; the nobles were indignant at the ever-increasing sway of the foreigners; and several years of bad harvests,
high prices, rain, flood, and murrain sharpened the chronic
misery of the poor. The withdrawal of Earl Richard to his
new kingdom deprived the king and nation of an honourable if
timid counsellor, though a more capable leader was at last provided in the disgraced governor of Gascony. Simon still deeply
resented the king's ingratitude for his services, and had become
enough of an Englishman to sympathise with the national feel-
ings. Since his dismissal in 1253 he had held somewhat aloof
from politics. He knew so well that his interests centred in
England that he declined the offer of the French regency on
the death of Blanche of Castile. He prosecuted his rights over
Bigorre with characteristic pertinacity, and lawsuits about his
wife's jointure from her first husband exacerbated his relations
with Henry. It cannot, however, be said that the two were as

---

[1] See for Richard's career, Koch's *Richard von Cornwallis*. 1209-1257, and
the article on *Richard, King of the Romans*, in the *Dictionary of National
Biography*.

yet fiercely hostile.   Simon went to Henry's help in Gascony   CHAP.
in 1254, served on various missions and was nominated on others   IV.
from which he withdrew.   His chosen occupations during these
years of self-effacement were religious rather than political; his
dearest comrades were clerks rather than barons.

Among Montfort's closer intimates, Bishop Grosseteste was
removed by death in 1253.   But others of like stamp still
remained, such as Adam Marsh, the Franciscan mystic, whose
election to the see of Ely was quashed by the malevolence
of the court; Eudes Rigaud, the famous Archbishop of Rouen,
and Walter of Cantilupe, Bishop of Worcester, who formed a
connecting link between the aristocracy and the Church.   Despite the ineffectiveness of the clerical opposition to the papacy,
the spirit of independence expressed in Grosseteste's protests
had not yet deserted the churchmen.   Clerks had felt the pinch
of the papal exactions, had been bled to the uttermost to support the Sicilian candidature, and had seen aliens and non-
residents usurping their revenues and their functions.   More
timid and less cohesive than the barons, they had quicker brains,
more ideas, deeper grievances, and better means of reaching
the masses.   If resentment of the Sicilian candidature was the
spark that fired the train, the clerical opposition showed the
barons the method of successful resistance.   The rejection of
Henry's demands for money in the assemblies of 1257 started
the movement that spread to the baronage in the parliaments
of 1258.   In the two memorable gatherings of that year the
discontent, which had smouldered for a generation, at last burst
into flame.   In the next chapter we shall see in what fashion
the fire kindled.

The futility of the political history of the weary middle
period of the reign suggests, to those who make the history
of the state the criterion of every aspect of the national fortunes,
a corresponding barrenness and lack of interest in other aspects
of national life.   Yet a remedy for Henry's misrule was only
found because the age of political retrogression was in all other
fields of action an epoch of unexampled progress.   The years
during which the strong centralised government of the Angevin
kings was breaking down under Henry's weak rule were years
which, to the historian of civilisation, are among the most fruitful in our annals.   In vivid contrast to the tale of misrule, the

historian can turn to the revival of religious and intellectual life, the growing delight in ideas and knowledge, the consummation of the best period of art, and the spread of a nobler civilisation which make the middle portion of the thirteenth century the flowering time of English medieval life. It is part of this strange contrast that Henry, the obstacle to all political progress, was himself a chief supporter of the religious and intellectual movements which were so deeply influencing the age.

Much has been said of the alien invasion, and of the strong national opposition it excited. But insularity is not a good thing in itself, and the natural English attitude to the foreigners tended to confound good and bad alike in a general condemnation. Even the Savoyards were by no means as evil as the English thought them, and Henry in welcoming his kinsmen was not merely moved by selfish and unworthy motives; he believed that he was showing his openness to ideas and his welcome to all good things from whencesoever they came. There were, in fact, two tendencies, antagonistic yet closely related, which were operative, not only in England but all over western Europe, during this period. Nations, becoming conscious and proud of their unity, dwelt, often unreasonably, on the points wherein they differed from other peoples, and strongly resented alien interference. At the same time the closer relations between states, the result of improved government, better communications, increased commercial and social intercourse, the strengthening of common ideals, and the development of cosmopolitan types of the knight, the scholar, and the priest, were deepening the union of western Christendom on common lines. Neither the political nor the military nor the ecclesiastical ideals of the early middle ages were based upon nationality, but rather on that ecumenical community of tradition which still made the rule of Rome, whether in Church or State, a living reality. In the thirteenth century the papal tradition was still at its height. The jurisdiction of the papal *curia* implied a universal Christian commonwealth. World-wide religious orders united alien lands together by ties more spiritual than obedience to the papal lawyers. The academic ideal was another and a fresh link that connected the nations together. To the ancient reasons for union—symbolised by the living Latin speech of all clerks, of all scholars,

of all engaged in serious affairs—were added the newer bonds of
connexion involved in the common knightly and social ideals,
in the general spread of a common art and a common vernacular language and literature.

As Latin expressed the one series of ties, so did French
represent the other. The France of St. Louis meant two things.
It meant, of course, the French state and the French nationality, but it meant a great deal more than that. The influence
of the French tongue and French ideals was wider than the
political influence of the French monarchy. French was the
common language of knighthood, of policy, of the literature that
entertained lords and ladies, of the lighter and less technical
sides of the cosmopolitan culture which had its more serious
embodiments in Latin. To the Englishman of the thirteenth
century the French state was the enemy; but the English
baron denounced France in the French tongue, and leant a
ready ear to those aspects of life which, cosmopolitan in reality,
found their fullest exposition in France and among French-
speaking peoples. In the age which saw hostility to Frenchmen become a passion, a Frenchman like Montfort could
become the champion of English patriotism, English scholars
could readily quit their native land to study at Paris, the
French vernacular literature was the common property of the
two peoples, and French words began to force their way into
the stubborn vocabulary of the English language, which for
two centuries had almost entirely rejected these alien elements.
In dwelling, however briefly, on the new features which were
transforming English civilisation during this memorable period,
we shall constantly see how England gained by her ever-increasing intercourse with the continent, by necessarily sharing
in the new movements which had extended from the continent
to the island, no longer, as in the eleventh century, to be
described as a world apart. Neither the coming of the friars,
nor the development of university life and academic schools
of philosophy, theology, and natural science, nor the triumph
of gothic art, nor the spread of vernacular literature, not even
the scholarly study of English law nor the course of English
political development—not one of these movements could have
been what it was without the close interconnexion of the
various parts of the European commonwealth, which was

6 *

becoming more homogeneous at the same time that its units were acquiring for themselves special characteristics of their own.

In the early days of Henry III.'s reign, a modest alien invasion anticipated the more noisy coming of the Poitevin or the Provençal. The most remarkable development of the "religious" life that the later middle age was to witness had just been worked out in Italy. St. Francis of Assisi had taught the cult of absolute poverty, and his example held up to his followers the ideal of the thorough and literal imitation of Christ's life. Thus arose the early beginnings of the Minorite or Franciscan rule. St. Dominic yielded to the fascination of the Umbrian enthusiast, and inculcated on his Order of Preachers a complete renunciation of worldly goods which made a society, originally little more than a new type of canons regular, a mendicant order like the Franciscans, bound to interpret the monastic vow of poverty with such literalness as to include corporate as well as individual renunciation of possessions, so that the order might not own lands or goods, and no member of it could live otherwise than by labour or by alms. In the second chapter of the Dominican order, at Whitsuntide, 1221, an organisation into provinces was carried out; and among the eight provinces, each with its prior, then instituted, was the province of England, where no preaching friar had hitherto set foot, and over it Gilbert of Freynet was appointed prior. Then Dominic withdrew to Bologna, where he died on August 6. Within a few days of the saint's death, Friar Gilbert with thirteen companions made his way to England. In the company of Peter des Roches the Dominican pioneers went to Canterbury, where Archbishop Langton was then residing. At the archbishop's request Gilbert preached in a Canterbury church, and Langton was so much delighted by his teaching that henceforth he had a special affection for the new order. From Canterbury the friars journeyed to London and Oxford. Mindful of the work of their leaders at Paris and Bologna, they built their first English chapel, house, and schools in the university town. Soon these proved too small for them, and they had to seek ampler quarters outside the walls. From these beginnings the Dominicans spread over England.

The Franciscans quickly followed the Dominicans. On September 10, 1224, there landed at Dover a little band of four

clerks and five laymen, sent by St. Francis himself to extend
the new teaching into England. At their head was the
Italian, Agnellus of Pisa, a deacon, formerly warden of the
Parisian convent, who was appointed provincial minister in
England. His three clerical companions were all Englishmen,
though the five laymen were Italians or Frenchmen. Like the
Dominican pioneers, the Franciscan missionaries first went to
Canterbury, where the favour of Simon Langton, the archdeacon, did for them what the goodwill of his brother Stephen
had done for their precursors. Leaving some of their number
at Canterbury, four of the Franciscans went on to London, and
thence a little later two of them set out for Oxford. Alike
at London and at Oxford, they found a cordial welcome from
the Dominicans, eating in their refectories, and sleeping in their
dormitories, until they were able to erect modest quarters in
both places. The brethren of the new order excited unbounded
enthusiasm. Necessity and choice combined to compel them
to interpret their vow of poverty as St. Francis would have
wished. They laboured with their own hands at the con-
struction of their humble churches. The friars at Oxford
knew the pangs of debt and hunger, rejected pillows as a vain
luxury, and limited the use of boots and shoes to the sick and
infirm. The faithful saw the brethren singing songs as they
picked their way over the frozen mud or hard snow, blood
marking the track of their naked feet, without their being
conscious of it. The joyous radiance of Francis himself illuminated the lives of his followers. " The friars," writes their
chronicler, " were so full of fun among themselves that a deaf
mute could hardly refrain from laughter at seeing them." With
the same glad spirit they laboured for the salvation of souls,
the cure of sickness, and the relief of distress. The emotional
feeling of the age quickly responded to their zeal. Within a
few years other houses had arisen at Gloucester, at Nottingham,
at Stamford, at Worcester, at Northampton, at Cambridge, at
Lincoln, at Shrewsbury. In a generation there was hardly
a town of importance in England that had not its Franciscan
convent, and over against it a rival Dominican house.

The esteem felt for the followers of Francis and Dominic
led to an extraordinary extension of the mendicant type. New
orders of friars arose, preserving the essential attribute of abso-

lute poverty, though differing from each other and from the
two prototypes in various particulars. Some of these lesser
orders found their way to England. In the same year as
Agnellus, there came to England the Trinitarian friars, called
also the Maturins, from the situation of their first house in Paris,
an order whose special function was the redemption of captives.
In 1240 returning crusaders brought back with them the first
Carmelite friars, for whom safer quarters had to be found than
in their original abodes in Syria. This society spread widely,
and in 1287, to the disgust of the older monks, it laid aside
the party-coloured habit, forced upon it in derision by the
infidels, and adopted the white robe, which gave them their
popular name of White Friars. Hard upon these, in 1244,
came also the Crutched Friars, so called from the red cross set
upon their backs or breasts ; but these were never deeply rooted
in England. The multiplication of orders of friars became an
abuse, so that, at the Council of Lyons of 1245, Innocent IV.
abolished all save four. Besides Dominicans and Franciscans
the pope only continued the Carmelites, and an order first seen
in England a few years later, the Austin friars or the hermits
of the order of St. Augustine. These made up the traditional
four orders of friars of later history. Yet even the decree of
a council could not stay the growth of new mendicant types.
In 1257 the Friars of the Penance of Jesus Christ, popularly
styled Friars of the Sack, from their coarse sackcloth garb,
settled down in London, exempted by papal dispensation from
the fate of suppression ; and even later than this King Richard's
son, Edmund of Cornwall, established a community of Bon-
hommes at Ashridge in Buckinghamshire.

The friars were not recluses, like the older orders, but
active preachers and teachers of the people. The parish
clergy seldom held a strong position in medieval life. The
estimation in which the monastic ideal was held limited their
influence. They were, as a rule, not much raised above the
people among whom they laboured. If the parish priest were
a man of rank or education, he was too often a non-resident
and a pluralist, bestowing little personal attention on his pa-
rishioners. Nor were the numerous parishes served by monks
in much better plight. The monastery took the tithes and
somehow provided for the services ; but the efforts of Grosseteste

to secure the establishment of permanent stipendiary vicarages CHAP.
in his diocese exemplify the reluctance of the religious to give IV.
their appropriations the benefit of permanent pastors, paid on
an adequate scale. It was an exceptional thing for the parish
clergymen to do more than discharge perfunctorily the routine
duties of their office, and preaching was almost unknown among
them. The friars threw themselves into pastoral work with
such devotion as to compel the reluctant admiration of their
natural rivals, the monks. "At first," says Matthew Paris,[1]
"the Preachers and the Minorites lived a life of poverty and
extreme sanctity. They busied themselves in preaching, hearing confessions, the recital of divine service, in teaching and
study. They embraced voluntary poverty for God's sake,
abandoning all their worldly goods and not even reserving for
themselves their food for to-morrow." A special field of labour
was in the crowded suburbs of the larger towns, where so often
they chose to erect their first convents. The care of the sick
and of lepers was their peculiar function. Their sympathy and
charity carried everything before them, and they remained the
chief teachers of the poor down to the Reformation. They in-
gratiated themselves with the rich as much as with the poor,
Henry III. and Edward selected mendicants as their confessors. The strongest and holiest of the bishops, Grosseteste,
became their most active friend. Simon of Montfort sought
the advice and friendship of a friar like Adam Marsh. The
mere fact that Stephen Langton and Peter des Roches were
their first patrons in England shows how they appealed alike
to the best and worst clerical types of the time.

Men and women of all ranks, while still living in the world
and fulfilling their ordinary occupations, associated themselves
to the mendicant brotherhoods. Besides these *tertiaries*, as
they were called, still wider circles sought the friars' direction
in all spiritual matters and showed eagerness to be buried within
their sanctuaries. Nor did the friars limit themselves to pastoral
care. They won a unique place in the intellectual history of the
time. They made themselves the spokesmen of all the movements of the age. They were eager to make peace, and Agnellus himself mediated between Henry III. and the earl marshal.

[1] *Chron. Maj.*, v., 194.

They were the strenuous preachers of the crusades, whether against the infidel or against Frederick II. The Franciscans taught a new and more methodical devotion to the Virgin Mother. The friars upheld the highest papal claims, were constantly selected as papal agents and tax-gatherers, and yet even this did not deprive them of their influence over Englishmen. Their zeal for truth often made them defenders of unpopular causes, and it was much to their honour that they did not hesitate to incur the displeasure of the Londoners by their anxiety to save innocent Jews accused of the murder of Christian children. The parish clergy hated and envied them as successful rivals, and bitterly resented the privilege which they received from Alexander IV. of hearing confessions throughout the world. Not less strong was the hostility of the monastic orders which is often expressed in Matthew Paris's free-spoken abuse of them. They were accused of terrorising dying men out of their possessions, of laxity in the confessional, of absolving their friends too easily, of overweening ambition and restless meddlesomeness. They were violent against heretics and enemies of the Church. They answered hate with hate. They despised the seculars as drones and the monks as lazy and corrupt. The dissensions between the various orders of friars, and particularly between the sober and intellectual Dominicans and the radical and mystic Franciscans, were soon as bitter as those between monks and friars, or monks and seculars. But when all allowances have been made, the good that they wrought far outbalanced the evil, and in England at least, the mendicant orders exhibited a nobler conception of religion, and of men's duty to their fellowmen than had as yet been set before the people. If the main result of their influence was to strengthen that cosmopolitan conception of Christendom of which the papacy was the head and the friars the agents, their zeal for righteousness often led them beyond their own rigid platform, and Englishmen honoured the wandering friar as the champion of the nation's cause.

Like the religious orders, the universities were part of the world system and only indirectly represented the struggling national life. The ferment of the twelfth century revival crystallised groups of masters or doctors into guilds called universities, with a strong class tradition, rigid codes of rules, and intense corporate spirit. The schools at Oxford, whose continuous history can be traced from the days of Henry II., had acquired a considerable reputation by the time that his grandson had ascended the throne. Oxford university, with an autonomous constitution of its own since 1214, was presided over by a chancellor who, though in a sense the representative of the distant diocesan at Lincoln, was even in the earliest times the head of the scholars, and no mere delegate of the bishop. Five years earlier the Oxford schools were sufficiently vigorous to provoke a secession, from which the first faint beginnings of a university at Cambridge arose. A generation later there were other secessions to Salisbury and Northampton, but neither of these schools succeeded in maintaining themselves. Cambridge itself had a somewhat languid existence throughout the whole of the thirteenth century, and was scarcely recognised as a *studium generale* until the bull of John XXII. in 1318 made its future position secure. In early days the university owed nothing to endowments, buildings, social prestige, or tradition. The two essentials was the living voice of the graduate teacher and the concourse of students desirous to be taught. Hence migrations were common and stability only gradually established. When, late in Henry III.'s reign, the chancellor, Walter of Merton, desired to set up a permanent institution for the encouragement of poor students, he hesitated whether to establish it at Oxford, or Cambridge, or in his own Surrey village. Oxford, though patriots coupled it with Paris and Bologna, only gradually rose into repute. But before the end of Henry III.'s reign it had won an assured place among the great universities of western Europe, though lagging far behind that of the supreme schools of Paris.

The growing fame of the university of Oxford was a matter of national importance. Down to the early years of the thirteenth century a young English clerk who was anxious to study found his only career abroad, and was too often cut off altogether from his mother country. Among the last of this type were the Paris mathematician, John of Holywood or Halifax, Robert Curzon, cardinal, legate, theologian, and crusader, and Alexander of Hales. Stephen Langton, who did important work in revising the text of the Vulgate, might well have been one of those lost to England but for the

wisdom of Innocent III. who restored him, in the fulness of his
reputation and powers, to the service of the English Church.
Not many years younger than Langton was his successor Edmund of Abingdon, but the difference was enough to make the
younger primate a student of the Oxford schools in early life.
Though he left Oxford for Paris, Edmund returned to an active
career in England, when experience convinced him of the vanity
of scholastic success.   Bishop Grosseteste, another early Oxford
teacher of eminence, probably studied at Paris, for so late as
1240 he held up to the Oxford masters of theology the example
of their Paris brethren for their imitation.   The double allegiance of Edmund and Grosseteste was typical.   A long catalogue of eminent names adorned the annals of Oxford in the
thirteenth century, but the most distinguished of her earlier sons
were drawn away from her by the superior attractions of Paris.
England furnished at least her share of the great names of
thirteenth century scholasticism, but of very few of these
could it be said that their main obligation was to the English
university.   It was at Paris that the academic organisation
developed which Oxford adopted.   At Paris the great intellectual conflicts of the century were fought.   There the ferment
seethed round that introduction of Aristotle's teaching from
Moorish sources which led to the outspoken pantheism of an
Amaury of Bène.   There also was the reconciliation effected
between the new teacher and the old faith which made Aristotle
the pillar of the new scholasticism that was to justify by reason
the ways of God to man.   In Paris also was fought the contest
between the aggressive mendicant friars and the secular doctors
whom they wished to supplant in the divinity schools.

There is little evidence of even a pale reflection of these
struggles in contemporary Oxford.   English scholars bore their
full share in the fight.   It was the Englishman Curzon who
condemned the heresies of Amaury of Bène.   Another Englishman, Alexander of Hales, issued in his *Summa Theologiæ*
the first effective reconciliation of Aristotelian metaphysic with
Christian doctrine which his Paris pupils, Thomas Aquinas, the
Italian, and Albert the Great, the German, were to work out
in detail in the next generation.   Hales was the first secular
doctor in Europe who in 1222, in the full pride of his powers,
abandoned his position in the university to embrace the volun-

tary poverty of the Franciscans and resume his teaching, not
in the regular schools but in a Minorite convent.   And at the
same time another English doctor at Paris, John of St. Giles,
notable as a physician as well as a theologian, dramatically
marked his conversion to the Dominican order by assuming its
habit in the midst of a sermon on the virtues of poverty.   All
these famous Englishmen worked and taught at Paris, and it
was only a generation later that their successors could establish on the Thames the traditions so long upheld on the
banks of the Seine.

The establishment of the Dominicans and Franciscans at
Oxford gave an immense impetus to the activity of the university.   The Franciscans appointed as the first *lector* of their
Oxford convent the famous secular teacher Grosseteste, who
ever after held the Minorites in the closest estimation.   Grosseteste was the greatest scholar of his day, knowing Greek and
Hebrew as well as the accustomed studies of the period.   A
clear and independent thinker, he was not, like so many of his
contemporaries, overborne by the weight of authority, but appealed to observation and experience in terms which make him
the precursor of Roger Bacon.   Grosseteste's successor as *lector*
was himself a Minorite, Adam Marsh, whose reputation was so
great that Grosseteste was afraid to leave him when sick in
a French town, lest the Paris masters should persuade him to
teach in their schools.   Adam's loyalty to his native university
withstood any such temptation, and from that time Oxford
began to hold up its head against Paris.   Even before this,
Grosseteste persuaded John of St. Giles to transfer his teaching
from Paris to Oxford, where he remained for the rest of his life.

The intense intellectual activity of the thirteenth century
flowed in more than one channel, and Englishmen took their
full share both in building up and in destroying.   Two Englishmen of the next generation mark in different ways the reaction
against the moderate Aristotelianism and orthodox rationalism
which their countryman Hales first brought into vogue.   These
were the Franciscan friars, Roger Bacon and Duns Scotus.
Bacon, though he studied at Paris as well as at Oxford, is
much more closely identified with England than with the Continent.   His sceptical, practical intellect led him to heap scorn
on Hales and his followers and to plunge into audacities of

speculation which cost him long seclusions in his convent and
enforced abstinence from writing and study.   In his war against
the Aristotelians, the intrepid friar upheld recourse to experiment and observation as superior to deference to authority, in
language which stands in strange contrast to the traditions of
the thirteenth century.   Grosseteste, who also had preferred the
teachings of experience to the appeal to the sages of the past,
was the only academic leader that escaped Bacon's scathing
censure.   When his order kept him silent, Roger was bidden to
resume his pen by Pope Clement IV.   A generation still later,
Duns Scotus, probably a Lowland Scot, who taught at Paris
and died at Cologne in 1308, emphasised, sharply enough, but
in less drastic fashion, the reaction against the teaching of Hales
and Aquinas, by accepting a dualism between reason and
authority that broke away from the Thomist tradition of the
thirteenth century and prepared the way for the scholastic
decadence of the fourteenth.   After France, England took a
leading part in all these movements; and even in France
English scholars had a large share in making that land the
special home of the *Studium*, as Italy was of the *Sacerdotium*
and Germany of the *Imperium*.

   This intellectual ferment had its results on practical life.
Though the university was cosmopolitan, the individual members of it were not the less good citizens.   A patriot like
Grosseteste strove to his uttermost to keep Englishmen for
Oxford or to win them back from Paris.   Oxford clerks fought
the battle of England against the legate Otto, and we shall see
them siding with Montfort.   The eminently practical temper
of the academic class could not neglect the world of action for
the abstract pursuit of science.   Eager as men were to know,
to prove, and to inquire, the age had little of the mystical
temperament about it.   The studies which made for worldly
success, such as civil and canon law, attracted the thousands
for whom philosophy or theology had little attraction.   Never
before was there a career so fully opened to talent.   The
academic teacher's fame took him from the lecture-room to the
court, from the university to the episcopal throne, and so it was
that the university influenced action almost as profoundly as
it influenced thought, and affected all classes of society alike.
The struggles of poor students like Edmund of Abingdon or

Grosseteste must not make us think that the universities of this CHAP.
period were exclusively frequented by humble scholars. The   IV.
academic career of a rich baron's son like Thomas of Cantilupe,
living in his own hired house at Paris with a train of chaplains
and tutors, receiving the visits of the French king, and feeding
poor scholars with the remnants from his table, is as characteristic as the more common picture of the student begging his way
from one seat of learning to another, and suffering the severest
privations rather than desert his studies. Yet the function of
the *studium* as promoting a healthy circulation between the
various orders of medieval society, must not be ignored.

Partly to help on the poor, partly to encourage men to
devote themselves to the pursuit of knowledge, endowments
began to arise which soon enhanced the splendour of universities
though they lessened their mobility and their freedom. The
mendicant convents at Paris and Oxford prepared the way for
secular foundations, at first small and insignificant, like that
which, in the days of Henry III., John Balliol established at
Oxford for the maintenance of poor scholars, but soon increasing in magnitude and distinction. The great college set up by
St. Louis' confessor at Paris for the endowment of scholars, desirous of studying the unlucrative but vital subject of theology,
was soon imitated by the chancellor of Henry III. Side by
side with Robert of Sorbon's college of 1257, arose Walter of
Merton's foundation of 1263, and twenty years later Bishop
Balsham's college of Peterhouse extended the "rule of Merton"
to Cambridge.

The academic movement was not all clear gain. The
humanism of the twelfth century was crushed beneath the
weight of the specialised science and encyclopædic learning
of the thirteenth. We should seek in vain among most theo-
logians or the philosophers of our period for any spark of
literary art; and the tendency dominant in them affected for
evil all works written in Latin. Even the historians show a
falling away from the example of William of Malmesbury or
of Roger of Hoveden. The one English chronicler of the
thirteenth century who is a considerable man of letters, Matthew Paris, belongs to the early half of it, before the academic
tradition was fully established, and even with him prolixity
impairs the art without injuring the colour of his work. The

age of Edward I., the great time of triumphant scholasticism, is recorded in chronicles so dreary that it is hard to make the dry bones live. Walter of Hemingburgh, the most attractive historian of the time, belongs to the next generation : and his excellencies are only great in comparison with his fellows. Something of this decadence may be attributed to the falling away of the elder monastic types, whose higher life withered up from want of able recruits, for the secular and mendicant careers offered opportunities so stimulating that few men of purpose, or earnest spiritual character, cared to enter a Benedictine or a Cistercian house of religion. Something more may be assigned to the growing claims of the vulgar tongue on literary aspirants. But the chief cause of the literary defects of thirteenth century writers must be set down to the doctrine that the study of "arts"—of grammar, rhetoric and the rest— was only worthy of schoolboys and novices, and was only a preliminary to the specialised faculties which left little room for artistic presentation. Science in short nearly killed literature.

It was the same with the vulgar tongues as with Latin. French remained the common language of the higher classes of English society, and the history of French literature belongs to the history of the western world rather than to that of England. The share taken in it by English-born writers is less important than in the great age of romance when the contact of Celt and Norman on British soil added the Arthurian legend to the world's stock of poetic material. The practical motive, which destroyed the art of so many Latin writers, impaired the literary value of much written in the vernacular. We have technical works in French and even in English, such as Walter of Henley's treatise on *Husbandry*, composed in French for the guidance of stewards of manors, and translated, it is said by Grosseteste, into English for the benefit of a wider public. Grosseteste is also said to have drawn up in French a handbook of rules for the management of a great estate, and he certainly wrote French poetry. The legal literature, written in Latin or French, and illustrated by such names as Bracton, Britton, and " Fleta," shows that there was growing up a school of earnest students of English law who, though anxious, like Bracton, to bring their conclusions under the rules of Roman jurisprudence, began to treat their science with an independence which secured for English custom the opportunity of independent development. Of more literary interest than such technicalities were the rhyming chronicles, handed on from the previous age, of which one of the best, the recently discovered history of the great William Marshal, has already been noticed. The spontaneity of this poem proves that its language was still the natural speech of the writer, and impels its French editor to claim for it a French origin. As the century grew older there was no difficulty in deciding whether French works were written by Englishmen or Frenchmen. The Yorkshire French of Peter Langtoft's *Chronicle*, and the jargon of the *Year Books*, attest how the political separation of the two lands, and the preponderance in northern France of the dialect of Paris, placed the insular French speech in strong contrast to the language of polite society beyond the Channel. Yet barbarous as Anglo-French became, it retained the freshness of a living tongue, and gained some ground at the expense of Latin, notably in the law courts and in official documents.

English was slowly making its way upwards. There was a public ready to read vernacular books, and not at home with French. For their sake a great literature of translations and adaptations was made, beginning with Layamon's English version of Wace's *Brut*, which by the end of the century made the cycle of French romance accessible to the English reader. Many works of edification and devotion were written in English; and Robert of Gloucester's rhyming history appealed to a larger public than the Yorkshire French of Langtoft. It is significant of the trend of events that the early fourteenth century saw Langtoft himself done into English by Robert Mannyng, of Bourne. While as yet no continuous works of high merit were written in English, there was no lack of experiments, of novelties, and of adaptations. Much evidence of depth of feeling, power of expression, and careful art lies hidden away in half-forgotten anonymous lyrics, satires, and romances. The language in which these works were written was steadily becoming more like our modern English. The dialectical differences become less acute; the inflections begin to drop away; the vocabulary gradually absorbs a larger romance element, and the prosody drops from the forms of the West Saxon period into measures and modes that reflect a living connexion with

the contemporary poetry of France. Thus, even in the literature of a not too literary age, we find abundant tokens of that
strenuous national life which was manifesting itself in so many
different ways.

Art rather than literature reflected the deeper currents
of the thirteenth century. Architecture, the great art of the
middle age, was in its perfection. The inchoate gothic which
the Cistercians brought from Burgundy to the Yorkshire dales,
and William of Sens transplanted from his birthplace to Canterbury, was superseded by the more developed art of St.
Hugh's choir at Lincoln. In the next generation the new
style, imported from northern France, struck out ways of its
own, less soaring, less rigidly logical, yet of unequalled grace
and picturesqueness, such as we see in Salisbury cathedral,
which altogether dates from the reign of Henry III. Here
also, as in literature, foreign models stood side by side with
native products. Henry III.'s favourite foundation at Westminster reproduced on English soil the towering loftiness, the
vaulted roofs, the short choir, and the ring of apsidal chapels,
of the great French minsters. This was even more emphatically
the case with the decorations, the goldsmith's and metal work,
the sculpture, painting, and glass, which the best artists of
France set up in honour of the English king's favourite saint.
In these crafts English work would not as yet bear a comparison with foreign, and even the glories of the statuary of the
façade of Wells cannot approach the sculptured porches of
Amiens or Paris. As the century advanced some of the
fashions of the French builders, notably as regards window
tracery, were taken up in the early "Decorated" of the reign
of Edward I.; and here the claims of English to essential
equality with French building can perhaps be better substantiated than in the infancy of the art. But all these comparisons
are misleading. The impulse to gothic art came to England
from France, like the impulse to many other things. Its working out was conducted on English local lines, ever becoming
more divergent from those of the prototype, though not seldom
stimulated by the constant intercourse of the two lands.

The new gothic art enriched the medieval town with a
splendour of buildings hitherto unknown, which symbolised
the growth of material prosperity as well as of a keener artistic

appreciation. In the greater towns the four orders of friars erected their large and plain churches, designed as halls for preaching to great congregations. The development of domestic architecture is even more significant than the growth of ecclesiastical and military buildings. Stone houses were no longer the rare luxuries of Jews or nobles. Never were the towns more prosperous and more energetic. They were now winning for themselves both economic and administrative independence. Magnates, such as Randolph of Chester, followed the king's example by granting charters to the smaller towns. Even the lesser boroughs became not merely the abodes of agriculturists but the homes of organised trading communities. It was the time when the merchant class first began to manifest itself in politics, and the power of capital to make itself felt. Capital was almost monopolised by Jews, Lombards, or Tuscans, and the fierce English hatred of the foreigner found a fresh expression in the persecution of the Hebrew money-lenders and in the increasing dislike felt for the alien bankers and merchants who throve at Englishmen's expense. The fact that so much of English trade with the continent was still in the hands of Germans, Frenchmen, and Italians made this feeling the more intense. But there were limits even to the ill-will towards aliens. The foreigner could make himself at home in England, and the rapid naturalisation of a Montfort in the higher walks of life is paralleled by the absorption into the civic community of many a Gascon or German merchant, like that Arnold FitzThedmar,[1] a Bremen trader's son, who became alderman of London and probably chronicler of its history. Yet even the greatest English towns did not become strong enough to cut themselves off from the general life of the people. They were rather a new element in that rich and purposeful nation that had so long been enduring the rule of Henry of Winchester. The national energy spurned the feebleness of the court, and the time was at hand when the nation, through its natural leaders, was to overthrow the wretched system of misgovernment under which it had suffered. Political retrogression was no longer to bar national progress.

---

[1] See for Arnold the *Chronica majorum et vicecomitum Londoniarum* in *Liber de antiquis legibus*, and Riley's introduction to his translation of *Chronicles of the Mayors and Sheriffs of London* (1863).

CHAPTER V.

THE BARONS' WAR.

DURING the early months of 1258, the aliens ruled the king and realm, added estate to estate, and defied all attempts to dislodge them. Papal agents traversed the country, extorting money from prelates and churches. The Welsh, in secret relations with the lords of the march, threatened the borders, and made a confederacy with the Scots. The French were hostile, and the barons disunited, without leaders, and helpless. A wretched harvest made corn scarce and dear. A wild winter, followed by a long late frost, cut off the lambs and destroyed the farmers' hopes for the summer. A murrain of cattle followed, and the poor were dying of hunger and pestilence. Henry III. was in almost as bad a plight as his people. He had utterly failed to subdue Llewelyn. A papal agent threatened him with excommunication and the resumption of the grant of Sicily. He could not control his foreign kinsfolk, and the rivalry of Savoyards and Poitevins added a new element of turmoil to the distracted relations of the magnates. His son had been forced to pawn his best estates to William of Valence, and the royal exchequer was absolutely empty. Money must be had at all risks, and the only way to get it was to assemble the magnates.

On April 2 the chief men of Church and State gathered together at London. For more than a month the stormy debates went on. The king's demands were contemptuously waved aside. His exceptional misdeeds, it was declared, were to be met by exceptional measures. Hot words were spoken, and William of Valence called Leicester a traitor. "No, no, William," the earl replied, "I am not a traitor, nor the son of a traitor; your father and mine were men of a different stamp."

An opposition party formed itself under the Earls of Gloucester,
Leicester, Hereford, and Norfolk. Even the Savoyards partially fell away from the court, and a convocation of clergy at Merton, presided over by Archbishop Boniface, drew up canons in the spirit of Grosseteste. In parliament all that Henry could get was a promise to adjourn the question of supply until a commission had drafted a programme of reform. On May 2 Henry and his son Edward announced their acceptance of this proposal; parliament was forthwith prorogued, and the barons set to work to mature their scheme.

On June 11 the magnates once more assembled, this time at Oxford. A summons to fight the Welsh gave them an excuse to appear attended with their followers in arms. The royalist partisans nicknamed the gathering the Mad Parliament, but its proceedings were singularly business-like. A petition of twenty-nine articles was presented, in which the abuses of the administration were laid bare in detail. A commission of twenty-four was appointed who were to redress the grievances of the nation, and to draw up a new scheme of government. According to the compact Henry himself selected half this body. It was significant of the falling away of the mass of the ruling families from the monarchy, that six of Henry's twelve commissioners were churchmen, four were aliens, three were his brothers, one his brother-in-law, one his nephew, one his wife's uncle. The only earls that accepted his nomination were the Poitevin adventurer, John du Plessis, Earl of Warwick, and John of Warenne, who was pledged to a royalist policy by his marriage to Henry's half-sister, Alice of Lusignan. The only bishops were the queen's uncle, Boniface of Canterbury, and Fulk Basset of London, the richest and noblest born of English prelates, who, though well meaning, was too weak in character for continued opposition. Yet these two were the most independent names on Henry's list. The rest included the three Lusignan brothers, Guy, William, and Aymer, still eight years after his election only elect of Winchester; Henry of Almaine, the young son of the King of the Romans; the pluralist official John Mansel; the chancellor, Henry Wingham; the Dominican friar John of Darlington, distinguished as a biblical critic, the king's confessor and the pope's agent; and the Abbot of Westminster, an old man pledged by long years of dependence to do

the will of the second founder of his house.   In strong contrast
to these creatures of court favour were the twelve nominees of
the barons.   The only ecclesiastic was Walter of Cantilupe,
Bishop of Worcester, and the only alien was Earl Simon of
Leicester.   With him were three other earls, Richard of Clare,
Earl of Gloucester, Roger Bigod, earl marshal and Earl of
Norfolk, and Humphrey Bohun, Earl of Hereford.   Those of
baronial rank were Roger Mortimer, the strongest of the
marchers, Hugh Bigod, the brother of the earl marshal, John
FitzGeoffrey, Richard Grey, William Bardolf, Peter Montfort,
and Hugh Despenser.

The twenty-four drew up a plan of reform which left little
to be desired in thoroughness.   The Provisions of Oxford, as
the new constitution was styled, were speedily laid before the
barons and adopted.   By it a standing council of fifteen was
established, with whose advice and consent Henry was henceforth to exercise all his authority.   Even this council was not
to be without supervision.   Thrice in the year another committee of twelve was to treat with the fifteen on the common
affairs of the realm.   This rather narrow body was created, we
are told, to save the expense involved in too frequent meetings
of the magnates.   A third aristocratic junto of twenty-four was
appointed to make grants of money to the crown.   All aliens
were to be expelled from office and from the custody of royal
castles.   New ministers, castellans, and escheators were appointed under stringent conditions and under the safeguard
of new oaths.   The original twenty-four were not yet discharged from office.   They had still to draw up schemes for
the reform of the household of king and queen, and for the
amendment of the exchange of London.   Moreover, "Be it
remembered," ran one of the articles, "that the estate of Holy
Church be amended by the twenty-four elected to reform the
realm, when they shall find time and place".

For the first time in our history the king was forced to stand
aside from the discharge of his undoubted functions, and suffer
them to be exercised by a committee of magnates.   The conception of limited monarchy, which had been foreshadowed in
the early struggles of Henry's long reign, was triumphantly
vindicated, and, after weary years of waiting, the baronial victors
demanded more than had ever been suggested by the most free

interpretation of the Great Charter. The body that controlled CHAP. the crown was, it is true, a narrow one. But whatever was lost V. by its limitation, was more than gained by the absolute freedom of the whole movement from any suspicion of the separatist tendencies of the earlier feudalism. The barons tacitly accepted the principle that England was a unity, and that it must be ruled as a single whole. The triumph of the national movement of the thirteenth century was assured when the most feudal class of the community thus frankly abandoned the ancient baronial contention that each baron should rule in isolation over his own estates, a tradition which, when carried out for a brief period under Stephen, had set up " as many kings or rather tyrants as lords of castles ". The feudal period was over : the national idea was triumphant. This victory becomes specially significant when we remember how large a share the barons of the Welsh march, the only purely feudal region in the country, took in the movement against the King.

The unity of the national government being recognised, it was another sign of the times that its control should be transferred from the monarch to a committee of barons. At this point the rigid conceptions of the triumphant oligarchy stood in the way of a wide national policy. Since the reign of John the custom had arisen of consulting the representatives of the shire-courts on matters of politics and finance. In 1258 there is not the least trace of a suggestion that parliament could ever include a more popular element than the barons and prelates. On the contrary, the Provisions diminished the need even for those periodical assemblies of the magnates which had been in existence since the earliest dawn of our history. For all practical purposes small baronial committees were to perform the work of magnates and people as well as of the crown. Yet it must be recognised that the barons showed self-control, as well as practical wisdom, in handing over functions discharged by the baronage as a whole to the various committees of their selection. The danger of general control by the magnates was that a large assembly, more skilled in opposition than in constructive work, was almost sure to become infected by faction. By strictly limiting and defining who the new rulers of England were to be, the barons approached a combination of aristocratic control with the stability and continuity resulting from limited numbers

and defined functions. It is likely, however, that in bestowing
such extensive powers on their nominees, they were influenced
by the well-grounded belief that the new constitution could only
be established by main force, and that, even when abandoned
by the king, the aliens would make a good fight before they
gave up all that they had so long held in England. The
success of the new scheme largely depended upon the immediate execution of the ordinance for the expulsion of the
foreigners.

The first step taken to carry out the Provisions was the
appointment of the new ministers. The barons insisted on the
revival of the office of justiciar, and a strenuous and capable
chief minister was found in Hugh Bigod. It was advisable
to go cautiously, and some of the king's ministers were
allowed to continue in office. An appeal to force was necessary before the new constitution could be set up in detail. The
Savoyards bought their safety by accepting it ; but the Poitevins,
seeing that flight or resistance were the only alternatives before
them, were spirited enough to prefer the bolder course. They
were specially dangerous because Edward and his cousin, Henry
of Almaine, the son of the King of the Romans, were much
under their influence. In the Dominican convent at Oxford
the baronial leaders formed a sworn confederacy not to desist
from their purpose until the foreigners had been expelled.
There were more hot words between Leicester and William,
the most capable of the Lusignans. The Poitevins soon found
that they could not maintain themselves in the face of the
general hatred. On June 22 they fled from Oxford in the
company of their ally, Earl Warenne. They rode straight for
the coast, but failing to reach it, occupied Winchester, where
they sought to maintain themselves in Aymer's castle of Wolvesey. The magnates of the parliament then turned against
them the arms they professed to have prepared against the
Welsh. Headed by the new justiciar, Hugh Bigod, they besieged Wolvesey. Warenne abandoned the aliens, and they
gladly accepted the terms offered to them by their foes.
They were allowed to retain their lands and some of their
ready money, on condition of withdrawing from the realm and
surrendering their castles. By the middle of July they had
crossed over to France. With them disappeared the whole of

the organised opposition to the new government. Edward,
deprived of their support, swore to observe the Provisions.

Immediately on the flight of the Lusignans the council of
Fifteen was chosen after a fashion which seemed to give the
king's friends an equal voice with the champions of the aristocracy. Four electors appointed it, and of these two were the
nominees of the baronial section, and two of the royalist section
of the original twenty-four. The result of their work showed
that there was only one party left after the Wolvesey fiasco.
While only three of the king's twelve had places on the permanent council, no less that nine of the fifteen were chosen
from the baronial twelve. It was useless for Archbishop Boniface, John Mansel, and the Earl of Warwick to stand up against
the Bishop of Worcester, the Earls of Leicester, Norfolk,
Hereford, and Gloucester, against John FitzGeoffrey, Peter
Montfort, Richard Grey, and Roger Mortimer. Moreover, of
the three, John Mansel alone could still be regarded as a royalist
partisan. There were three of the fifteen chosen from outside
the twenty-four. Of these, Peter of Savoy, Earl of Richmond,
might, like his brother Boniface, be regarded as an alien, though
hatred of the Poitevins had by this time made Englishmen
of the Savoyards. The other two, the marcher-lord James
of Audley and William of Fors, Earl of Albemarle, were of
baronial sympathies. It was the same with the other councils.

Inquiry was made as to abuses. Gradually the royal
officials were replaced by men of popular leanings. The
sheriffs were changed and were strictly controlled, and four
knights from each shire assembled in October to present to
the king the grievances of the people against the out-going
sheriffs. The custody of the castles was put into trusty and,
for the most part, into English hands. Finally the king was
forced to issue a proclamation, in which he commanded all true
men " steadfastly to hold and to defend the statutes that be
made or are to be made by our counsellors ". This document was issued in English as well as in French and Latin.
A copy of the English version was sent to every sheriff, with
instructions to read it several times a year in the county court,
so that a knowledge of its contents might be attained by every
man. It is perhaps the first important proclamation issued in
English since the coming of the Normans. Early in 1259

CHAP.
V.

Richard, King of the Romans, set out to revisit England. He was met at Saint Omer by a deputation of magnates, who told him that he could only be allowed to land after taking an oath to observe the Provisions. Richard blustered, but soon gave in his submission. His adhesion to the reforms marks the last step in the revolution.

The new constitution worked without interruption until the end of 1259. Throughout that period domestic affairs were uneventful, and the efforts of the ministry were chiefly concerned in securing peace abroad. In 1258 Wales had been in revolt, Scotland unfriendly, and France threatening. A truce, ill observed, was made with Llewelyn, who found it worth while to be cautious, seeing that his natural enemies, but sometime associates, the marchers, had a preponderant share in the government. The Scots were easier to satisfy, for there was at the time no real hostility between either kings or peoples. The chief event of this period is the conclusion of the first peace with France since the wars of John and Philip Augustus. The protracted negotiations which preceded it took the king and his chief councillors abroad, and that made it easier to carry on the new domestic system without friction.

Since the friendly personal intercourse held between Henry and Louis IX. in 1254, the relations between England and France had become less cordial. The revival of the English power in Gascony, the Anglo-Castilian alliance, and the election of Richard of Cornwall to the German kingship irritated the French, to whom the persistent English claim to Normandy and Anjou, and the repudiation of the Aquitanian homage, were perpetual sources of annoyance. The French championship of Alfonso against Richard achieved the double end of checking English pretensions, and cooling the friendship between England and Castile. St. Louis, however, was always ready to treat for peace, while the revolution of 1258 made all parties in England anxious to put a speedy end to the unsettled relations between the two realms. Negotiations were begun as early as 1257, and made some progress ; but the decisive step was taken immediately after the prorogation of the reforming parliament in the spring of 1258. During May a strangely constituted embassy treated for peace at Paris, where Montfort and Hugh Bigod worked side by side with two of the Lusignans and Peter of

Savoy. They concluded a provisional treaty in time for the negotiators to take their part in the Mad Parliament. The unsettled state of affairs in England, however, delayed the ratification of the treaty. Arrangements had been made for its publication at Cambrai, but the fifteen dared not allow Henry to escape from their tutelage, and Louis refused to treat save with the king himself. There were difficulties as to the relation of the pope and the King of the Romans to the treaty, while Earl Simon's wife Eleanor and her children refused to waive their very remote claims to a share in the Norman and Angevin inheritances, which her brother was prepared to renounce. As ever, Montfort held to his personal rights with the utmost tenacity, and the self-seeking obstinacy of the chief negotiator of the treaty caused both bad blood and delay. At last he was bought off by the promise of a money payment, and the preliminary ratifications were exchanged in the summer of 1259. On November 14 Henry left England for Paris for the formal conclusion of the treaty. There were great festivities on the occasion of the meeting of the two kings, but once more Montfort and his wife blocked the way. Not until the very morning of the day fixed for the final ceremony were they satisfied by Henry's promise to deposit on their behalf a large sum in the hands of the French. Immediately afterwards Henry did homage to Louis for Gascony.

The chief condition of the treaty of Paris was Henry's definitive renunciation of all his claims on Normandy, Anjou, Maine, Touraine, and Poitou, and his agreement to hold Gascony as a fief of the French crown. In return for this, Louis not only recognised him as Duke of Aquitaine, but added to his actual possessions there by ceding to him all that he held, whether in fief or in demesne, in the three dioceses of Limoges, Cahors, and Périgueux. Besides these immediate cessions, the French king promised to hand over to Henry certain districts then held by his brother, Alfonse of Poitiers, and his brother's wife Joan of Toulouse, in the event of their dominions escheating to the crown by their death without heirs. These regions included Agen and the Agenais, Saintonge to the south of the Charente, and in addition the whole of Quercy, if it could be proved by inquest that it had been given by Richard I. to his sister Joan, grandmother of Joan of Poitiers, as her marriage portion. Moreover the French king promised to pay to Henry the sums necessary to maintain for two years five hundred knights to be employed "for the service of God, or the Church, or the kingdom of England ".[1]

The treaty was unpopular both in France and England. The French strongly objected to the surrender of territory, and were but little convinced of the advantage gained by making the English king once more the vassal of France. English opinion was hostile to the abandonment of large pretensions in return for so small an equivalent. On the French side it is true that Louis sacrificed something to his sense of justice and love of peace. But the territory he ceded was less in reality than in appearance. The French king's demesnes in Quercy, Périgord, and Limousin were not large, and the transference of the homage of the chief vassals meant only a nominal change of overlordship, and was further limited by a provision that certain "privileged fiefs" were still to be retained under the direct suzerainty of the French crown. As to the eventual cessions, Alfonse and his wife were still alive and likely to live many years. Even the cession of Gascony was hampered by a stipulation that the towns should take an " oath of security," by which they pledged themselves to aid France against England in the event of the English king breaking the provisions of the treaty. Perhaps the most solid advantage Henry gained by the treaty was financial, for he spent the sums granted to enable him to redeem his crusading vow in preparing for war against his own subjects. It was, however, an immense advantage for England to be able during the critical years which followed to be free from French hostility. If, therefore, the French complaints against the treaty were exaggerated, the English dissatisfaction was unreasonable. The real difficulty for the future lay in the fact that the possession of Gascony by the king of a hostile nation was incompatible with the proper development of the French monarchy. For fifty years, however, a chronic state of war had not given Gascony to the French ; and Louis IX. was, perhaps, politic as well as scrupulous in abandoning the way of force and beginning a new

---

[1] For the treaty and its execution see M. Gavrilovitch, *Étude sur le traité de Paris de 1259* (1899).

method of gradual absorption, that in the end gained the Gascon CHAP.
fief for France more effectively than any conquest. The treaty V.
of Paris was not a final settlement. It left a score of questions
still open, and the problems of its gradual execution involved
the two courts in constant disputes down to the beginning of
the Hundred Years' War. For seventy years the whole history
of the relations between the two nations is but a commentary
on the treaty of Paris.

During his visit to Paris Henry arranged a marriage between
his daughter Beatrice and John of Brittany, the son of the reigning duke. In no hurry to get back to the tutelage of the
fifteen, he prolonged his stay on the continent till the end of
April, 1260. Yet, abroad as at home, he could not be said to
act as a free man. It was not the king so much as Simon
of Montfort who was the real author of the French treaty.
Indeed, it is from the conclusion of the Peace of Paris that
Simon's preponderance becomes evident. He was at all stages
the chief negotiator of the peace and, save when his personal
interests stood in the way, he controlled every step of the
proceedings. If in 1258 he was but one of several leaders of
the baronial party in England, he came back from France in
1260 assured of supremacy. During his absence abroad, events
had taken place in England which called for his presence.

After their triumph in 1258, the baronial leaders relaxed
their efforts. Contented with their position as arbiters of the
national destinies, they made little effort to carry out the
reforms contemplated at Oxford. The ranks of the victors
were broken up by private dissensions. Before leaving for
France, Earl Simon violently quarrelled with Richard, Earl of
Gloucester. It was currently believed that Gloucester had
grown slack, and Simon rose in popular estimation as a
thorough-going reformer who had no mind to substitute the
rule of a baronial oligarchy for the tyranny of the king. His
position was strengthened by his personal qualities which made
him the hero of the younger generation; and his influence began
to modify the policy of Edward the king's son, who, since the
flight of his Poitevin kinsmen, was gradually arriving at broader
views of national policy. Even before his father's journey to
France, Edward took up a line of his own. In the October
parliament of 1259, he listened to a petition presented to the

CHAP.
V.

council by the younger nobles[1] who complained that, though the king had performed all his promises, the barons had not fulfilled any of theirs. Edward thereupon stirred up the oligarchy to issue an instalment of the promised reforms in the document known as the Provisions of Westminster. During Henry's absence in France the situation became strained. The oligarchic party, headed by Gloucester, was breaking away from Montfort; and Edward was forming a liberal royalist party which was not far removed from Montfort's principles. Profiting by these discords, the Lusignans prepared to invade England. The papacy was about to declare against the reformers. When the monks of Winchester elected an Englishman as their bishop in the hope of getting rid of the queen's uncle, Alexander IV. summoned Aymer to his court and consecrated him bishop with his own hands.

Early in 1260, Montfort went back to England and made common cause with Edward. Despite the king's order that no parliament should be held during his absence abroad, Montfort insisted that the Easter parliament should meet as usual at London. The discussions were hot. Montfort demanded the expulsion of Peter of Savoy from the council, and Edward and Gloucester almost came to blows. The Londoners closed their gates on both parties, but the mediation of the King of the Romans prevented a collision. Henry hurried home, convinced that Edward was conspiring against him. The king threw himself into the city of London, and with Gloucester's help collected an army. Meanwhile Montfort and Edward, with their armed followers, were lodged at Clerkenwell, ready for war. Again the situation became extremely critical, and again King Richard proved the best peacemaker. Henry held out against his son for a fortnight, but such estrangement was hard for him to endure. "Do not let my son appear before me," he cried, "for if I see him, I shall not be able to refrain from kissing him." A reconciliation was speedily effected, and nothing remained of the short-lived alliance of Edward with Montfort save that his feud with Gloucester continued until the earl's death.

---

[1] "Communitas bacheleriae Angliae," *Burton Ann.*, p. 471. See on this, *Engl. Hist. Review*, xvii. (1902), 89-94.

The dissensions among the barons encouraged Henry to shake off the tutelage of the fifteen. As soon as he was reconciled with his son, he charged Leicester with treason.[1] " But, thanks be to God, the earl answered to all these points with such force that the king could do nothing against him." Unable to break down his enemy by direct attack, Henry followed one of the worst precedents of his father's reign by beseeching Alexander IV. to relieve him of his oath to observe the Provisions. On April 13, 1261, a bull was issued annulling the whole of the legislation of 1258 and 1259, and freeing the king from his sworn promise.

William of Valence was already back in England, and re- stored to his old dignities. His return was the easier because his brother, Aymer, the most hated of the Poitevins, had died soon after his consecration to Winchester. On June 14, 1261, the papal bull was read before the assembled parliament at Winchester. There Henry removed the baronial ministers and replaced them by his own friends. Chief among the sufferers was Hugh Despenser, who had succeeded Hugh Bigod as justiciar; and Bigod himself was expelled from the custody of Dover Castle. In the summer Henry issued a proclamation, declaring that the right of choosing his council and garrisoning his castles was among the inalienable attributes of the crown. England was little inclined to rebel, for the return of prosperity and good harvests made men more contented.

The repudiation of the Provisions restored unity to the baronage. The defections had been serious, and it was said that only five of the twenty-four still adhered to the opposition. But the crisis forced Leicester and Gloucester to forget their recent feuds, and co-operate once more against the king. They saw that their salvation from Henry's growing strength lay in appealing to a wider public than that which they had hitherto addressed. Still posing as the heads of the government estab- lished by the Provisions, they summoned three knights from each shire to attend an assembly at St. Alban's. This appeal to the landed gentry alarmed the king so much that he issued counter-writs to the sheriffs ordering them to send the knights, not to the baronial camp at St. Alban's, but to his own court

---

[1] Bémont, *Simon de Montfort*, Appendix xxxvii., pp. 343-53.

at Windsor.   Neither party was as yet prepared for battle. The death of Alexander IV. soon after the publication of his bull tied the hands of the king.   At the same time the renewed dissensions of Leicester and Gloucester paralysed the baronage.   Before long Simon withdrew to the continent, leaving everything in Gloucester's hands.   At last, on December 7, a treaty of pacification was patched up, and the king announced that he was ready to pardon those who accepted its conditions. But there was no permanence in the settlement, and the king, the chief gainer by it, was soon pressing the new pope, Urban IV., to confirm the bull of Alexander.   On February 25, 1262, Urban renewed Henry's absolution from his oath in a bull which was at once promulgated in England.   Montfort then came back from abroad and rallied the baronial party.   In January, 1263, Henry once more confirmed the Provisions, and peace seemed restored.   The death of Richard of Gloucester during 1262 increased Montfort's power.   His son, the young Earl Gilbert, was Simon's devoted disciple, but he was still a minor and the custody of his lands was handed over to the Earl of Hereford.   Montfort's personal charm succeeded in like fashion in winning over Henry of Almaine.

The events of 1263 are as bewildering and as indecisive as those of the two previous years.   Amidst the confusion of details and the violent clashing of personal and territorial interests, a few main principles can be discerned.   First of all the royalist party was becoming decidedly stronger, and fresh secessions of the barons constantly strengthened its ranks. Conspicuous among these were the lords of the march of Wales, who in 1258 had been almost as one man on the side of the opposition, but who by the end of 1263 had with almost equal unanimity rallied to the crown.[1]   The causes of this change of front are to be found partly in public and partly in personal reasons.   In 1258 Henry III., like Charles I. in 1640, had alienated every class of his subjects, and was therefore entirely at the mercy of his enemies.   By 1263 his concessions had procured for him a following, so that he now stood in the same position as Charles after his concessions to the Long

---

[1] On this, and the whole marcher and Welsh aspect of the period, 1258-1267, see my essay on *Wales and the March during the Barons' Wars* in *Owens College Historical Essays*, pp. 76-136 (1902).

Parliament made it possible for him to begin the Civil War CHAP. in 1642. A new royalist party was growing up with a wider V. policy and greater efficiency than the old coterie of courtiers and aliens. Of this new party Edward was the soul. He had dissociated himself from Earl Simon, but he carried into his father's camp something of Simon's breadth of vision and force of will. He set to work to win over individually the remnant that adhered to Leicester. What persuasion and policy could not effect was accomplished by bribes and promises. Edward won over the Earl of Hereford, whose importance was doubled by his custody of the Gloucester lands, the ex-justiciar Roger Bigod, and above all Roger Mortimer.

The change of policy of the marchers was partly at least brought about by their constant difficulties with the Prince of Wales. During the period immediately succeeding the Provisions of Oxford, Llewelyn ceased to devastate the marches. A series of truces was arranged which, if seldom well kept, at least avoided war on a grand scale. Within Wales Llewelyn fully availed himself of the respite from English war. Triumphant over the minor chiefs, he could reckon upon the support of every Welsh tenant of a marcher lord, and at last grew strong enough to disregard the truces and wage open war against the marchers. It was in vain that Edward, the greatest of the marcher lords, persuaded David, the Welsh prince's brother, to rise in revolt against him. Llewelyn devastated the four cantreds to the gates of Chester, and at last, after long sieges, forced the war-worn defenders of Deganwy and Diserth to surrender the two strong castles through which alone Edward had retained some hold over his Welsh lands. It was the same in the middle march, where Llewelyn turned his arms against the Mortimers, and robbed them of their castles. Even in the south the lord of Gwynedd carried everything before him. "If the Welsh are not stopped," wrote a southern marcher, "they will destroy all the lands of the king as far as the Severn and the Wye, and they ask for nothing less than the whole of Gwent." Up to this point the war had been a war of Welsh against English, but Montfort sought compensation for his losses in England by establishing relations with the Welsh. The alliance between Montfort and their enemy had a large share in bringing about the secession of the marchers.   Their alliance with Edward neutralised the action of Montfort, and once more enabled Henry to repudiate the Provisions.

In the summer of 1263, Edward and Montfort both raised armies.   Leicester made himself master of Hereford, Gloucester, and Bristol, and when Edward threw himself into Windsor Castle, he occupied Isleworth, hoping to cut his enemy off from London, where the king and queen had taken refuge in the Tower.   But the hostility of the Londoners made the Tower an uneasy refuge for them.   On one occasion, when the queen attempted to make her way up the Thames in the hope of joining her son at Windsor, the citizens assailed her barge so fiercely from London Bridge that she was forced to return to the Tower.   The foul insults which the rabble poured upon his mother deeply incensed Edward and he became a bitter foe of the city for the rest of his life.   For the moment the hostility of London was decisive against Henry.   Once more the king was forced to confirm the Provisions, agree to a fresh banishment of the aliens, and restore Hugh Despenser to the justiciarship.   This was the last baronial triumph.   In a few weeks Edward again took up arms, and was joined by many of Montfort's associates, including his cousin, Henry of Almaine. Even the Earl of Gloucester was wavering.   The barons feared the appeal to arms, and entered into negotiations.   Neither side was strong enough to obtain mastery over the other, and a recourse to arbitration seemed the best way out of an impossible situation.   Accordingly, on December, 1263, the two parties agreed to submit the question of the validity of the Provisions to the judgment of Louis IX.

The king and his son at once crossed the channel to Amiens, where the French king was to hear both sides.   A fall from his horse prevented Leicester attending the arbitration, and the barons were represented by Peter Montfort, lord of Beaudesert castle in Warwickshire, and representative of an ancient Anglo-Norman house that was not akin to the family of Earl Simon. Louis did not waste time, and on January 23, 1264, issued his decision in a document called the "Mise of Amiens," which pronounced the Provisions invalid, largely on the ground of the papal sentence.   Henry was declared free to select his own wardens of castles and ministers, and Louis expressly annulled "the statute that the realm of England should henceforth be governed by native-born Englishmen". "We ordain," he added, "that the king shall have full power and free jurisdiction over his realm as in the days before the Provisions." The only consolation to the barons was that Louis declared that he did not intend to derogate from the ancient liberties of the realm, as established by charter or custom, and that he urged a general amnesty on both parties. In all essential points Louis decided in favour of Henry. Though the justest of kings, he was after all a king, and the limitation of the royal authority by a baronial committee seemed to him to be against the fundamental idea of monarchy. The pious son of the Church was biassed by the authority of two successive popes, and he was not unmoved by the indignation of his wife, the sister of Queen Eleanor. A few weeks later Urban IV. confirmed the award.

The Mise of Amiens was too one-sided to be accepted. The decision to refer matters to St. Louis had been made hastily, and many enemies of the king had taken no part in it. They, at least, were free to repudiate the judgment and they included the Londoners, the Cinque Ports, and nearly the whole of the lesser folk of England. The Londoners set the example of rebellion. They elected a constable and a marshal, and joining forces with Hugh Despenser, the baronial justiciar, who still held the Tower, marched out to Isleworth, where they burnt the manor of the King of the Romans. "And this," wrote the London Chronicler, "was the beginning of trouble and the origin of the deadly war by which so many thousand men perished." The Londoners did not act alone. Leicester refused to be bound by the award, though definitely pledged to obey it. It was, he maintained, as much perjury to abandon the Provisions as to be false to the promise to accept the Mise of Amiens. After a last attempt at negotiation at a parliament at Oxford, he withdrew with his followers and prepared for resistance. "Though all men quit me," he cried, "I will remain with my four sons and fight for the good cause which I have sworn to defend—the honour of Holy Church and the good of the realm." This was no mere boast. The more his associates fell away, the more the Montfort family took the lead. While Leicester organised resistance in the south, he sent his elder sons, Simon and Henry, to head the revolt in the midlands and the west.

There was already war in the march of Wales when Henry Montfort crossed the Severn and strove to make common cause with Llewelyn. But the Welsh prince held aloof from him, and Edward himself soon made his way to the march. At first all went well for young Montfort. Edward, unable to capture Gloucester and its bridge, was forced to beg for a truce. Before long he found himself strong enough to repudiate the armistice and take possession of Gloucester. Master of the chief passage over the lower Severn, Edward abandoned the western campaign and went with his marchers to join his father at Oxford, where he at once stirred up the king to activity. The masters of the university, who were strong partisans of Montfort, were chased away from the town. Then the royal army marched against Northampton, the headquarters of the younger Simon, who was resting there, and, on April 4, the king and his son burst upon the place. Their first assault was unsuccessful, but next day the walls were scaled, the town captured, and many leading barons, including young Simon, taken prisoner. The victors thereupon marched northwards, devastated Montfort's Leicestershire estates, and thence proceeded to Nottingham, which opened its gates in a panic.

Leicester himself had not been idle. While his sons were courting disaster in the west and midlands, he threw himself into London, where he was rapturously welcomed. The Londoners, however, became very unruly, committed all sorts of excesses against the wealthy royalists, and cruelly plundered and murdered the Jews. Montfort himself did not disdain to share in the spoils of the Jewry, though he soon turned to nobler work. He was anxious to open up communications with his allies in the Cinque Ports. But Earl Warenne, in Rochester castle, blocked the passage of the Dover road over the Medway. Accordingly Montfort marched with a large following of Londoners to Rochester, captured the town, and assaulted the castle with such energy that it was on the verge of surrendering. The news of Warenne's peril reached Henry in the midlands. In five days the royalists made their way from Nottingham to Rochester, a distance of over 160 miles. On their approach Montfort withdrew into London.

Flushed with their successes at Northampton and Rochester, the royalists marched through Kent and Sussex, plundering

and devastating the lands of their enemies. Though masters CHAP.
of the open country, they had to encounter the resistance of V.
the Clare castles, and the solid opposition of the Cinque Ports.
Their presence on the south coast was specially necessary, for
Queen Eleanor, who had gone abroad, was waiting, with an
army of foreign mercenaries, on the Flemish coast, for an
opportunity of sailing to her husband's succour. The royal
army was hampered by want of provisions, and was only
master of the ground on which it was camped. As a first
fruit of the alliance with Llewelyn, Welsh soldiers lurked
behind every hedge and hill, cut off stragglers, intercepted
convoys, and necessitated perpetual watchfulness. At last the
weary and hungry troops found secure quarters in Lewes, the
centre of the estates of Earl Warenne.

Montfort then marched southwards from the capital. Besides the baronial retinues, a swarm of Londoners, eager for the
fray, though unaccustomed to military restraints, accompanied
him. On May 13 he encamped at Fletching, a village hidden
among the dense oak woods of the Weald, some nine miles
north of Lewes. A last effort of diplomacy was attempted
by Bishop Cantilupe of Worcester who, despite papal censures,
still accompanied the baronial forces. But the royalists would
not listen to the mediation of so pronounced a partisan.
Nothing therefore was left but the appeal to the sword.

The royal army was the more numerous, and included
the greater names. Of the heroes of the struggle of 1258
the majority was in the king's camp, including most of the
lords of the Welsh march, and the hardly less fierce barons of
the north, whose grandfathers had wrested the Great Charter
from John. The returned Poitevins with their followers
mustered strongly, and the confidence of the royalists was so
great that they neglected all military preparations. The poverty
of Montfort's host in historic families attested the complete
disintegration of the party since 1263. Its strength lay in
the young enthusiasts, who were still dominated by the strong
personality and generous ideals of Leicester, such as the Earl
of Gloucester, or Humphrey Bohun of Brecon, whose father,
the Earl of Hereford, was fighting upon the king's side.
Early on the morning of May 14 Montfort arrayed his troops
and marched southward in the direction of Lewes. Dawn had

8 *

hardly broken when the troops were massed on the summit of
the South Downs, overlooking Lewes from the north-west.

Lewes is situated on the right bank of a great curve of
the river Ouse, which almost encircles the town. To the south
are the low-lying marshes through which the river meanders
towards the sea, while to the north, east, and west are the bare
slopes of the South Downs, through which the river forces its
way past the gap in which the town is situated. To the north
of the town lies the strong castle of the Warennes, wherein
Edward had taken up his quarters, while in the southern suburb
the Cluniac priory of St. Pancras, the chief foundation of the
Warennes, afforded lodgings for King Henry and the King
of the Romans. When Simon reached the summit of the
downs, his movements were visible from the walls. But the
royal army was still sleeping and its sentinels kept such bad
watch that the earl was able to array his troops at his leisure.

From the summit of the hills two great spurs, separated by
a waterless valley, slope down towards the north and west
sides of the town. The more northerly led straight to the
castle, and the more southerly to the priory. Montfort's plan
was to throw his main strength on the attack on the priory,
while deluding the enemy into the belief that his chief object
was to attack the castle. He was not yet fully recovered from
his fall from his horse, and it was known that he generally
travelled in a closed car or horse-litter. This vehicle he posted
in a conspicuous place on the northerly spur, and planted over
it his standard. In front of it were massed the London militia,
mainly infantry and the least effective element in his host.
Meanwhile the knights and men-at-arms were mustered on the
southerly spur under the personal direction of Montfort, who
held himself in the rear with the reserve, while the foremost
files were commanded by the young Earl of Gloucester, whom
Simon solemnly dubbed to knighthood before the assembled
squadrons. Then the two divisions of the army advanced towards Lewes, hoping to find their enemies still in their beds.

At the last moment the alarm was given, and before the
barons approached the town, the royalists, pouring out of castle,
town, and priory, hastily took up their position face to face to
the enemy. All turned out as Montfort had foreseen. Edward,
emerging from the castle with his cousin Henry of Almaine,

his Poitevin uncles, and the warriors of the march, observed CHAP.
the standard of Montfort on the hill, and supposing that the   V.
earl was with his banner, dashed impetuously against the left
wing of Leicester's troops.   He soon found himself engaged
with the Londoners, who broke and fled in confusion before his
impetuous charge.   Eager to revenge on the flying citizens the
insults they had directed against his parents, he pursued the
beaten militia for many a mile, inflicting terrible damage upon
them.   On his way he captured Simon's standard and horse-
litter, and slew its occupants, though they were three royalist
members of the city aristocracy detained there for sure keeping.
When the king's son drew rein he was many miles from Lewes,
whither he returned, triumphant but exhausted.

The removal of Edward and the marchers from the field
enabled Montfort to profit by his sacrifice of the Londoners.
The followers of the two kings on the left of the royalist lines
could not withstand the weight of the squadrons of Leicester
and Gloucester.   The King of the Romans was driven to take
refuge in a mill, where he soon made an ignominious surrender.
Henry himself lost his horse under him and was forced to yield
himself prisoner to Gilbert of Gloucester.   The mass of the
army was forced back on to the town and priory, which were
occupied by the victors.   Scarcely was their victory assured
when Edward and the marchers came back from the pursuit of
the Londoners.   Thereupon the battle was renewed in the
streets of the town.   It was, however, too late for the weary
followers of the king's son to reverse the fortunes of the day.
Some threw themselves into the castle, where the king's
standard still floated ; Edward himself took sanctuary in the
church of the Franciscans ; many strove to escape eastwards
over the Ouse bridge or by swimming over the river.   The
majority of the latter perished by drowning or by the sword :
but two compact bands of mail-clad horsemen managed to cut
their way through to safety.   One of these, a force of some two
hundred, headed by Earl Warenne himself, and his brothers-
in-law, Guy of Lusignan and William of Valence, secured their
retreat to the spacious castle of Pevensey, of which Warenne
was constable, and from which the possibility of continuing
their flight by sea remained open.   Of greater military consequence was the successful escape of the lords of the Welsh

march, whose followers were next day the only section of the royalist army which was still a fighting force. This was the only immediate limitation to the fulness of Montfort's victory. After seven weary years, the judgment of battle secured the triumph of the "good cause," which had so long been delayed by the weakness of his confederates and the treachery of his enemies. Not the barons of 1258, but Simon and his personal following were the real conquerors at Lewes.

CHAPTER VI.

THE RULE OF MONTFORT AND THE ROYALIST RESTORATION.

ON the day after the battle, Henry III. accepted the terms
imposed upon him by Montfort in a treaty called the "Mise of Lewes," by which he promised to uphold the Great Charter, the Charter of the Forests, and the Provisions of Oxford. A body of arbitrators was constituted, in which the Bishop of London was the only Englishman, but which included Montfort's friend, Archbishop Eudes Rigaud of Rouen; the new papal legate, Guy Foulquois, cardinal-bishop of Sabina; and Peter the chamberlain, Louis IX.'s most trusted counsellor, with the Duke of Burgundy or Charles of Anjou, to act as umpire. These arbitrators were, however, to be sworn to choose none save English councillors, and Henry took oath to follow the advice of his native-born council in all matters of state. An amnesty was secured to Leicester and Gloucester; and Edward and Henry of Almaine surrendered as hostages for the good behaviour of the marchers, who still remained under arms. By the establishment of baronial partisans as governors of the castles, ministers, sheriffs, and conservators of the peace, the administration passed at once into the hands of the victorious party. Three weeks later writs were issued for a parliament which included four knights from every shire. In this assembly the final conditions of peace were drawn up, and arrangements made for keeping Henry under control for the rest of his life, and Edward after him, for a term of years to be determined in due course. Leicester and Gloucester were associated with Stephen Berkstead, the Bishop of Chichester, to form a body of three electors. By these three a Council of Nine was appointed, three of whom were to be in constant attendance at court; and without their advice the king was to do nothing.

CHAP.   Hugh Despenser was continued as justiciar, while the chancery
VI.   went to the Bishop of Worcester's nephew, Thomas of Cantilupe, a Paris doctor of canon law, and chancellor of the University of Oxford.

Once more a baronial committee put the royal authority
into commission, and ruled England through ministers of its
own choice. While agreeing in this essential feature, the
settlement of 1264 did not merely reproduce the constitution
of 1258. It was simpler than its forerunner, since there was
no longer any need of the cumbrous temporary machinery for
the revision of the whole system of government, nor for the
numerous committees and commissions to which previously so
many functions had been assigned. The main tasks before the
new rulers were not constitution-making but administration
and defence. Moreover, the later constitution shows some
recognition of the place due to the knights of the shire and
their constituents. It is less closely oligarchical than the
previous scheme. This may partly be due to the continued
divisions of the greater barons, but it is probably also in large
measure owing to the preponderance of Simon of Montfort.
The young Earl of Gloucester and the simple and saintly
Bishop of Chichester were but puppets in his hands. He was
the real elector who nominated the council, and thus controlled
the government. Every act of the new administration reflects
the boldness and largeness of his spirit.

The pacification after Lewes was more apparent than real,
and there were many restless spirits that scorned to accept the
settlement which Henry had so meekly adopted. The marchers
were in arms in the west, and were specially formidable because
they detained in their custody the numerous prisoners captured
at the sack of Northampton. The fugitives from Lewes were
holding their own behind the walls of Pevensey, though Earl
Warenne and other leaders had made their escape to France,
where they joined the army which Queen Eleanor had collected
on the north coast for the purpose of invading England and
restoring her husband to power. The papacy and the whole
official forces of the Church were in bitter hostility to the new
system. The collapse of Henry's rule had ruined the papal plans
in Sicily, where Manfred easily maintained his ground against so
strong a successor of the unlucky Edmund as Charles of Anjou.

The papal legate, Guy Foulquois, was waiting at Boulogne for admission into England, and, far from being conciliated by his appointment as an arbitrator, was dexterously striving to make the arbitration ineffective, by summoning the bishops adhering to Montfort to appear before him, and sending them back with orders to excommunicate Earl Simon and all his supporters. The only gleam of hope was to be found in the unwillingness of the King of France to interfere actively in the domestic disputes of England. The death of Urban IV. for the moment brought relief, but, after a long vacancy, the new pope proved to be none other than the legate Guy, who in February, 1265, mounted the papal throne as Clement IV. It was to no purpose that Walter of Cantilupe assembled the patriotic bishops and appealed to a general council, or that radical friars like the author of the *Song of Lewes* formulated the popular policy in spirited verse. The greatest forces of the time were steadily opposed to the revolutionary government, and rare strength and boldness were necessary to make head against them.

Before the end of 1264 the vigour of Earl Simon triumphed over some of his immediate difficulties. In August he summoned the military forces of the realm to meet the threatened invasion. Adverse storms, however, dispersed Queen Eleanor's fleet, and her mercenaries, weary of the long delays that had exhausted her resources, went home in disgust. This left Simon free to betake himself to the west, and on December 15 he forced the marcher lords to accept a pacification called the Provisions of Worcester, by which they agreed to withdraw for a year and a day to Ireland, leaving their families and estates in the hands of the ruling faction.

On the day after the signature of the treaty, Henry, who accompanied Simon to the west, issued from Worcester the writs for a parliament that sat in London from January to March in 1265. From the circumstances of the case this famous assembly could only be a meeting of the supporters of the existing government. So scanty was its following among the magnates that writs of summons were only issued to five earls and eighteen barons, though the strong muster of bishops, abbots, and priors showed that the papal anathema had done little to shake the fidelity of the clergy to Montfort's cause. The special feature of the gathering, however, was the summoning of two knights from every shire, side by side with the barons of the faithful Cinque Ports and two representatives from every city and borough, convened by writs sent, not to the sheriff, after later custom, but to the cities and boroughs directly. It was the presence of this strong popular element which long caused this parliament to be regarded as the first really representative assembly in our history, and gained for Earl Simon the fame of being the creator of the House of Commons. Modern research has shown that neither of these views can be substantiated. It was no novelty for the crown to strengthen the baronial parliaments by the representatives of the shire-moots, and there were earlier precedents for the holding meetings of the spokesmen of the cities and boroughs. What was new was the combination of these two types of representatives in a single assembly, which was convoked, not merely for a particular administrative purpose, but for a great political object. The real novelty and originality of Earl Simon's action lay in his giving a fresh proof of his disposition to fall back upon the support of the ordinary citizen against the hostility or indifference of the magnates, to whom the men of 1258 wished to limit all political deliberation. This is in itself a sufficient indication of policy to give Leicester an almost unique position among the statesmen to whom the development of our representative institutions are due. But just as his parliament was not in any sense our first representative assembly, so it did not include in any complete sense a House of Commons at all. We must still wait for a generation before the rival and disciple of Montfort, Edward, the king's son, established the popular element in our parliament on a permanent basis. Yet in the links which connect the early baronial councils with the assemblies of the three estates of the fourteenth century, not one is more important than Montfort's parliament of January, 1265.

The chief business of parliament was to complete the settlement of the country. Simon won a new triumph in making terms with the king's son. Edward had witnessed the failure of his mother's attempts at invasion, the futility of the legatine anathema, and the collapse of the marchers at Worcester. He saw it was useless to hold out any longer, and unwillingly bought his freedom at the high price that Simon exacted. He transferred to his uncle the earldom of Chester, including all the

lands in Wales that might still be regarded as appertaining to
it. This measure put Simon in that strong position as regards
Wales and the west which Edward had enjoyed since the days
of his marriage. It involved a breach in the alliance between
Edward and the marchers, and the subjection of the most
dangerous district of the kingdom to Simon's personal authority.
It was safe to set free the king's son, when his territorial position and his political alliances were thus weakened.

At the moment of his apparent triumph, Montfort's authority began to decline. It was something to have the commons
on his side : but the magnates were still the greatest power in
England, and in pressing his own policy to the uttermost, Simon
had fatally alienated the few great lords who still adhered to
him. There was a fierce quarrel in parliament between Leicester
and the shifty Robert Ferrars, Earl of Derby. For the moment
Leicester prevailed, and Derby was stripped of his lands and
was thrown into prison. But his fate was a warning to others,
and the settlement between Montfort and Edward aroused the
suspicions of the Earl of Gloucester. Gilbert of Clare was now
old enough to think for himself, and his close personal devotion
to Montfort could not blind him to the antagonism of interests
between himself and his friend. He was gallant, strenuous,
and high-minded, but quarrelsome, proud, and unruly, and his
strong character was balanced by very ordinary ability. His
outlook was limited, and his ideals were those of his class ;
such a man could neither understand nor sympathise with the
broader vision and wider designs of Leicester. Moreover,
with all Simon's greatness, there was in him a fierce masterful-
ness and an inordinate ambition which made co-operation with
him excessively difficult for all such as were not disposed to
stand to him in the relation of disciple to master. And behind
the earl were his self-seeking and turbulent sons, set upon
building up a family interest that stood directly in the way of
the magnates' claim to control the state. Thus personal rivalries
and political antagonisms combined to lead Earl Gilbert on in
the same course that his father, Earl Richard, had traversed.
The closest ally of Leicester became his bitterest rival. The
victorious party split up in 1265, as it had split up in 1263.
And the dissolution of the dominant faction once more gave
Edward a better chance of regaining the upper hand than

was to be hoped for from foreign mercenaries and from papal support.

Gloucester was the natural leader of the lords of the Welsh march. He was not only the hereditary lord of Glamorgan, but had received the custody of William of Valence's forfeited palatinate of Pembroke. He had shown self-control in separating himself so long from the marcher policy; and his growing suspicion of the Montforts threw him back into his natural alliance with them. Even after the treaty of Worcester, the marchers remained under arms. They had obtained from the weakness of the government repeated prolongations of the period fixed for their withdrawal into Ireland. It was soon rumoured that they were sure of a refuge in Gloucester's Welsh estates, and Leicester, never afraid of making enemies, bitterly reproached Earl Gilbert with receiving the fugitives into his lands. Shortly after the breaking up of parliament, Gloucester fled to the march, and a little later William of Valence and Earl Warenne landed in Pembrokeshire with a small force of men-at-arms and crossbowmen. There was no longer any hope of carrying out the Provisions of Worcester, and once more Montfort was forced to proceed to the west to put down rebellion.

By the end of April Montfort was at Gloucester, accompanied by the king and Edward, who, despite his submission, remained virtually a prisoner. Earl Gilbert was master of all South Wales, and closely watched his rival's movements from the neighbouring Forest of Dean. It was with difficulty that Earl Simon and his royal captives advanced from Gloucester to Hereford, but Earl Gilbert preferred to negotiate rather than to push matters to extremities. He went in person to Hereford and renewed his homage to the king. Arbitrators were appointed to settle the disputes between the two earls, and a proclamation was issued declaring that the rumour of dissension between them was "vain, lying, and fraudulently invented". For the next few days harmony seemed restored.

Gloucester's submission lured Leicester into relaxing his precautions. His enemies took advantage of his remissness to hatch an audacious plot which soon enabled them to renew the struggle under more favourable conditions. Since his nominal release, Edward had been allowed the diversions of riding and hunting, and on May 28 he was suffered to go out for a ride

under negligent or corrupt guard.　Once well away from Hereford, the king's son fled from his lax custodians and joined
Roger Mortimer, who was waiting for him in a neighbouring
wood.　On the next day he was safe behind the walls of Mortimer's castle of Wigmore, and, the day after, met Earl Gilbert
at Ludlow, where he promised to uphold the charters and
expel the foreigners.　Valence and Warenne hurried from
Pembrokeshire and made common cause with Edward and
Gilbert.　Edward then took the lead in the councils of the
marchers, who, from that moment, obtained a unity of purpose
and policy that they had hitherto lacked.　He and his allies
could claim to be the true champions of the Charters and
the Provisions of Oxford against the grasping foreigner who
strove to rule over king and barons alike.

Montfort's small force was cut off from its base by the
rapidity of the marchers' movements.　It was in vain that all
the supporters of the existing government were summoned to
the assistance of the hard-pressed army at Hereford.　Before
the end of June, Edward completed the conquest of the Severn
valley by the capture of the town and castle of Gloucester.
A broad river and a strong army stood between Montfort and
succour from England.　Leicester then turned to Llewelyn of
Wales, who took up his quarters at Pipton, near Hay.　There,
on June 22, a treaty was signed between the Welsh prince and
the English king by which Henry was forced to make huge
concessions to Llewelyn in order to secure his alliance.　Llewelyn was recognised as prince of all Wales.　The overlordship over all the barons of Wales was granted to him, and the
numerous conquests, which he had made at the expense of the
marchers, were ceded to him in full possession.

Thus Llewelyn, like his grandfather in the days of the
Great Charter, profited by the dissensions of the English to
obtain the recognition of his claims which had invariably been
refused when England was united.　The Welsh prince gained a
unique opportunity of making his weight felt in general English
politics, but with all his ability he hardly rose to the occasion.
Montfort had pressing need of his help.　A few days after the
treaty of Pipton, Gloucester Castle opened its gates to Edward,
and the marchers advanced westwards to seek out Earl Simon
at Hereford.　Leicester fled in alarm before their overwhelm-

ing forces. He was driven from the Wye to the Usk, and, beaten in a sharp fight on Newport bridge, found refuge only by retreating up the Usk valley, whence he escaped northwards into the hilly region where Llewelyn ruled over the lands once dominated by the Mortimers. Before long Montfort's English followers grew weary of the hard conditions of mountain warfare. With their heavy armour and barbed horses it was difficult for them to emulate the tactics of the Welsh, and they revolted against the simple diet of milk and meat that contented their Celtic allies. They could not get on without bread, and, as bread was not to be found among the hills, they forced their leader to return to the richer regions of the east. Llewelyn did little to help them in their need, and did not accompany them in their march back to the Severn valley, though a large but disorderly force of Welsh infantry still remained with Simon as the fruit of the alliance with their prince.

By the end of July, Simon was once more in the Severn valley, seeking for a passage over the river. On August 2 he found a ford over the stream some miles south of Worcester. There he crossed with all his forces and encamped for the night at Kempsey, one of Bishop Cantilupe's manors on the left bank. His skill as a general had extricated him from a position of the utmost peril. All might yet be regained if he could join forces with an army of relief which his son Simon had slowly levied in the south and midlands. But his quarrel with Gloucester and his alliance with the Welsh had done much to undermine Montfort's popularity, and the younger Simon had no appreciation of the necessity for decisive action. Summoned from the long siege of Pevensey by his father's danger, he wasted time in plundering the lands of the royalists, and only left London on July 8, whence he led his men by slow stages to Kenilworth. On July 31 young Simon's troops took up their quarters for the night in the open country round Kenilworth castle. They had no notion that the enemy was at hand and troubled neither to defend themselves nor to keep watch. Edward, warned by spies of their approach, abandoned his close guard of the Severn fords, and in the early morning of August 1 fell suddenly upon the sleeping host and scattered it with little difficulty. The younger Simon and a few of his followers took refuge in the castle. As a fighting force the army of relief ceased to exist.

Leicester, knowing nothing of his son's disaster, made his way, on August 3, from Kempsey to Evesham, where he rested for the night. Next morning, after mass and breakfast, the army was about to continue its march, when scouts descried troops advancing upon the town. At first it was hoped that they were the followers of young Simon, but their near approach revealed them to be the army of the marchers. With extraordinary rapidity Edward led his troops back to Worcester as soon as he had won the fight at Kenilworth. Learning there that Simon had crossed the river in his absence, he at once turned back to meet him, seeking to elude his vigilance by a long night march by circuitous routes. The result was that for the second time he caught his enemy in a trap.

Evesham, like Lewes, stands on a peninsula. It is situated on the right bank of a wide curve of the Avon, and approachable only by crossing over the river, or by way of the sort of isthmus between the two bends of the Avon a little to the north of the town. Edward occupied this isthmus with his best troops, and thus cut off all prospect of escape by land. The other means of exit from the town was over the bridge which connects it with its south-eastern suburb of Bengeworth, on the left bank of the river. Edward, however, took the precaution to detach Gloucester with a strong force to hold Bengeworth, and thus prevent Simon's escape over the bridge. The weary and war-worn host of Montfort, then, was outgeneralled in such fashion that effective resistance to a superior force, flushed by recent victory, was impossible. Simon himself saw that his last hour was come; yet he could not but admire the skilful plan which had so easily discomfited him. " By the arm of St. James," he declared, " they come on cunningly. Yet they have not taught themselves that order of battle; they have learnt it from me. God have mercy upon our souls, for our bodies are theirs."

Edward and Gloucester both advanced simultaneously to the attack. A storm broke at the moment of the encounter, and the battle was fought in a darkness that obscured the brightness of an August day. Leicester's Welsh infantry broke at once before the charge of the mail-clad horsemen, and took refuge behind hedges and walls, where they were hunted out and butchered after the main fight was over. But the men-at-arms struggled valiantly against Edward's superior forces, though they were soon borne down by sheer numbers. Simon fought like a hero and met a soldier's death. With him were slain his son Henry, his faithful comrade Peter Montfort, the baronial justiciar Hugh Despenser, and many other men of mark. A large number of prisoners fell into the victor's hands, and King Henry, who unwillingly followed Simon in all his wanderings, was wounded in the shoulder by his son's followers, and only escaped a worse fate by revealing his identity with the cry: "Slay me not! I am Henry of Winchester, your King." The marchers gratified their rage by massacring helpless fugitives, and by mutilating the bodies of the slain. Earl Simon's head was sent as a present to the wife of Roger Mortimer; and it was with difficulty that the mangled corpse found its last rest in the church of Evesham Abbey. His memory long lived in the hearts of his adopted countrymen, and especially among monks and friars, who despite the ban of the Church, hailed him as another St. Thomas, for he too had lain down his life for the cause of justice and religion. Miracles were worked at his tomb; liturgies composed in his honour, and an informal popular canonisation, which no papal censures could prevent, kept his memory green. His faults were forgotten in the pathos of his end. His work survived the field of Evesham and the reaction which succeeded it. His victorious nephew learnt well the lesson of his career, and the true successor of the martyred earl was the future Edward I.

No thoughts of policy disturbed the fierce passion of revenge which possessed the victorious marchers. On August 7 Henry issued a proclamation announcing that he had resumed the personal exercise of the royal power. The baronial ministers and sheriffs were replaced by royalist partisans. The acts of the revolutionary government were denounced as invalid. The faithful city of London was cruelly humiliated for its zeal for Earl Simon. The exiles, headed by Queen Eleanor and Archbishop Boniface, returned from their long sojourn beyond sea. With them came to England a new legate, the Cardinal Ottobon, specially sent from the papal court to punish the bishops and clergy that had persisted in their adherence to the popular cause. Four prelates were excommunicated and suspended from their functions, including Berkstead of Chichester and Cantilupe of Worcester. But the aged Bishop of Worcester was delivered from persecution by death; "snatched away," as a kindly foe says, "lest he should see evil days". His nephew, Thomas of Cantilupe, the baronial chancellor, fled to Paris, where he forsook politics for the study of theology. The widowed Countess of Leicester was not saved by her near kindred to the king from lifelong banishment. At last a general sentence of forfeiture was pronounced against all who had fought against Edward, either at Kenilworth or Evesham. There was a greedy scramble for the spoils of victory. The greatest of these, Montfort's forfeited earldom of Leicester, went to Edmund, the king's younger son. Edward took back the earldom of Chester and all his old possessions. Roger Mortimer was rewarded by grants of land and franchises which raised the house of Wigmore to a position only surpassed by that of the strongest of the earldoms.

At first the Montfort party showed an inclination to accept the defeat at Evesham as decisive. Even young Simon of Montfort, who still held out at Kenilworth, considered it prudent to restore his prisoner, the King of the Romans, to liberty. But the victors' resolve to deprive all their beaten foes of their estates, drove the vanquished into fresh risings. The first centre of the revolt of the disinherited was at Kenilworth, but before long the younger Simon abandoned the castle to join a numerous band which had found a more secure retreat in the isle of Axholme, amidst the marshes of the lower Trent. There they held their own until the winter, when they were persuaded by Edward to accept terms. A little later, Simon again revolted and joined the mariners of the Cinque Ports, whose towns still held out against the king, save Dover, which Edward had captured after a siege. Under Simon's leadership the Cinque Ports played the part of pirates on all merchants going to and from England. At last in March, 1266, Edward forced Winchelsea to open its gates to him. He next turned his arms against a valiant freebooter, Adam Gordon, who lurked with his band of outlaws in the dense beech woods of the Chilterns. With the capture of Adam Gordon, after a hand-to-hand tussle with Edward in

CHAP.
VI.

which the king's son narrowly escaped with his life, the resistance in the south was at an end.

As one centre of rebellion was pacified other disturbances arose. In the spring of 1266, Robert Ferrars, Earl of Derby, newly released from the prison into which Earl Simon had thrown him, raised a revolt in his own county. On May 15, 1266, Derby was defeated by Henry of Almaine at Chesterfield. His earldom was transferred to Edmund, the king's son, already Montfort's successor as Earl of Leicester, and in 1267 also Earl of Lancaster, a new earldom, deriving its name from the youngest of the shires.[1] Reduced to the Staffordshire estate of Chartley, the house of Ferrars fell back into the minor baronage. Kenilworth was still unconquered. Its walls were impregnable except to famine, and before his flight to Axholme young Simon had procured provisions adequate for a long resistance. The garrison harried the neighbourhood with such energy that the whole levies of the realm were assembled to subdue it. After a fruitless assault, the royalists settled down to a blockade which lasted from midsummer to Christmas. The legate, Ottobon, appearing in the besiegers' camp to excommunicate the defenders, they in derision dressed up their surgeon in the red robes of a cardinal, in which disguise he answered Ottobon's curses by a travesty of the censures of the Church.

The blockade soon tried the patience of the barons. It was hard to keep any medieval army long together, and the lords, anxious to go back to their homes, complained of the harsh policy that compelled their long attendance. The royalist host split up into two parties, led respectively by Roger Mortimer and Earl Gilbert of Gloucester. The cruel lord of Wigmore was the type of the extreme reaction. Intent only on vengeance, booty, and ambition, Mortimer clamoured for violent measures, and was eager to reject all compromises. Gloucester, on the other hand, posed as the mediator, and urged the need of pacifying the disinherited by mitigating the sentence of forfeiture which had driven them into prolonged resistance. In the first flush of victory, Edward had been altogether on Mortimer's side, but gradually statecraft and humanity turned

[1] For Edmund's estates and whole career, see W. E. Rhodes' *Edmund, Earl of Lancaster*, in *Engl. Hist. Review*, x. (1895), 19-40 and 209-37.

him from the reckless policy of the marcher. Edward's adhesion to counsels of moderation changed the situation. While Mortimer pressed the siege of Kenilworth, Edward and Gloucester met a parliament at Northampton which agreed to uphold the policy of 1258 and mitigate the hard lot of the disinherited. A document drawn up in the camp at Kenilworth received the approval of parliament and was published on October 31. The *Dictum de Kenilworth*, as it was called, was largely taken up with assertions of the authority of the crown, and denunciations of the memory of Earl Simon. More essential points were the re-enactment of the Charters and the redress of some of the grievances against which the Provisions of 1258 were directed. The vital article, however, laid down that the stern sentence of forfeiture against adherents of the fallen cause was to be remitted, and allowed rebels to redeem their estates by paying a fine, which in most cases was to be assessed at five years' value of their lands. Hard as were these terms, they were milder than those which had previously been offered to the insurgents. Yet the defenders of Kenilworth could not bring themselves to accept them until December, when disease and famine caused them to surrender. Despite their long-deferred submission, the garrison was admitted to the terms of the *Dictum*.

Even then resistance was not yet over. A forlorn hope of the disinherited, headed by John d'Eyville, established themselves about Michaelmas in the isle of Ely, where they made themselves the terror of all East Anglia, plundering towns so far apart as Norwich and Cambridge, maltreating the Jews, and holding the rich citizens to ransom. Early in 1267 the north-country baron, John of Vescy, rose in Northumberland, and violently resumed possession of his forfeited castle of Alnwick. While Henry tarried at Cambridge, Edward went north and soon won over Vescy by the clemency which made the lord of Alnwick henceforth one of his most devoted servants.

More formidable than the revolt of Eyville or Vescy was the ambiguous attitude of Earl Gilbert of Gloucester. Roger Mortimer was once more intriguing against him, and striving to upset the Kenilworth compromise. After a violent scene between the two enemies in the parliament at Bury, Gloucester withdrew to the march of Wales, where he waged war against Mortimer. In April, 1267, he made his way with a great following to London, professing that he wished to hold a conference with the legate. It was a critical moment. Edward was still in the north; Henry was wasting his time at Cambridge; the Londoners welcomed Earl Gilbert as a champion of the good old cause; the legate took refuge in the Tower, and the earl did not hesitate to lay siege to the stronghold. Before long Gloucester was joined by Eyville and many of the Ely fugitives. It seemed as if Gloucester was in as strong position as Montfort had ever won, and that after two years of warfare the verdict of Evesham was about to be reversed.

Edward marched south and joined forces with his father, who had moved from Cambridge to Stratford, near London. Everything seemed to suggest that the eastern suburbs of London would witness a fight as stubborn as Lewes or Evesham. But Gloucester was not the man to press things to extremities, and Edward though firm was conciliatory. He delivered Ottobon from the hands of the rebels,[1] and then arranged a peace upon terms which secured Gloucester's chief object of procuring better conditions for the disinherited. Not only Earl Gilbert but Eyville and his associates were admitted to the royal favour. A few desperadoes still held out until July in the isle of Ely, and Edward devoted himself to tracking them to their lairs. He built causeways of wattles over the fens, which protected the disinherited in their last refuge. When he had clearly shown his superiority, he offered the garrison of Ely the terms of the *Dictum de Kenilworth*. With their acceptance of these conditions the English struggle ended, in July, 1267, nearly two years after the battle of Evesham.

Llewelyn still remained under arms. He had profited by the two years of strife to deal deadly blows against the marchers. He conquered the Mid-Welsh lands which had been granted to Mortimer, and devastated Edward's Cheshire earldom. When Gloucester grew discontented with the course of events, the old friend of Montfort became the close ally of the man who had ruined Montfort's cause. A Welsh chronicler treats Gloucester's march to London as a movement which naturally followed the alliance of Gloucester and Llewelyn. On Gloucester's submission, Llewelyn was left to his own resources. Edward had it in his power to avenge past injuries

[1] *Engl. Hist. Review*, xvii. (1902), 522.

by turning all his forces against his old enemy. But the country was weary of war, and Edward preferred to end the struggle. The legate Ottobon urged both Edward and the Welsh prince to make peace, and in September, 1267, Henry and his son went down to Shrewsbury, accompanied by Ottobon, who received from the king full powers to treat with Llewelyn, and a promise that Henry would accept any terms that he thought fit to conclude. Llewelyn thereupon sent ambassadors to Shrewsbury, and the negotiations went on so smoothly that on September 25 a definite treaty of peace was signed. On Michaelmas day Henry met Llewelyn at Montgomery, received his homage, and witnessed the formal ratification of the treaty.

By the treaty of Shrewsbury Llewelyn was recognised as Prince of Wales, and as overlord of all the Welsh magnates, save the representative of the old line of the princes of South Wales. The four cantreds, Edward's old patrimony, were ceded to him ; and though he promised to surrender many of his conquests, he was allowed to remain in possession of great tracts of land in Mid and South Wales, in the heart of the marcher region.[1] Substantially the Welsh prince was recognised as holding the position which he claimed from Montfort in the days of the treaty of Pipton. Alone of Montfort's friends, Llewelyn came out of an unsuccessful struggle upon terms such as are seldom obtained even by victory in the field. The triumph of the Welsh prince is the more remarkable because Edward and his ally, Mortimer, were the chief sufferers by the treaty. But Edward had learnt wisdom during his apprenticeship. He recognised that the exhaustion of the country demanded peace at any price, and he dreaded the possibility of the alliance of Llewelyn and Earl Gilbert. But whatever Edward's motives may have been in concluding the treaty, it left Llewelyn in so strong a position that he was encouraged to those fresh aggressions which in the next reign proved the ruin of his power. The Welsh wars of Edward I. are the best elucidation of the importance of the treaty of Shrewsbury. The Welsh principality, which Edward as king was to destroy, was as much the creation of the Barons' War

---

[1] For the growth of Llewelyn's power see the maps of Wales in 1247 and 1267 in *Owens College Historical Essays,* pp. 76 and 135.

as the outcome of the fierce Celtic enthusiasm which found its bravest champion in the son of Griffith.

It was time to redeem the promises by which the moderate party had been won over to the royalist cause. The statute of Marlborough of 1267 re-enacted in a more formal fashion the chief of the Provisions of Westminster of 1259, and thus prevented the undoing of all the progress attained during the years of struggle. Ottobon in 1268 held a famous council at London, in which important canons were enacted with a view to the reformation of the Church. A little later the Londoners received back their forfeited charters and the disinherited were restored to their estates. After these last measures of reparation, England sank into a profound repose that lasted for the rest of the reign of Henry III. A happy beginning of the years of peace was the dedication of the new abbey of Westminster, and the translation of the body of St. Edward to the new shrine, whose completion had long been the dearest object of the old king's life.

At this time Louis IX. was meditating his second crusade, and in every country in Europe the friars were preaching the duty of fighting the infidel. Nowhere save in France did the Holy War win more powerful recruits than in England. In 1268 Edward himself took the cross,[1] and with him his brother Edmund of Lancaster, his cousin Henry of Almaine, and many leading lords of both factions. Financial difficulties delayed the departure of the crusaders, and it was not until 1270 that Edward and Henry were able to start. On reaching Provence, they learnt that Louis had turned his arms against Tunis, whither they followed him with all speed. On Edward's arrival off Tunis, he found that Louis was dead and that Philip III., the new French king, had concluded a truce with the misbelievers. Profoundly mortified by this treason to Christendom, Edward set forth with his little squadron to Acre, the chief town of Palestine that still remained in Christian hands. Henry of Almaine preferred to return home at once, but on his way through Italy was murdered at Viterbo by the sons of Earl Simon of Montfort, a deed of blood which

---

[1] For Edward's crusade see Riant's article in *Archives de l'Orient Latin*, i., 617-32 (1881).

revived the bitterest memories of the Barons' War. Edward remained in Palestine until August, 1272, and threw all his wonted fire and courage into the hopeless task of upholding the fast-decaying Latin kingdom. At last alarming news of his father's health brought him back to Europe.

On November 16, 1272, Henry III., then in his sixty-sixth year, died at Westminster. His remains were laid at rest in the neighbouring abbey church, hard by the shrine of St. Edward. With him died the last of his generation. St. Louis' death in August, 1270, has already been recorded. The death of Clement IV. in 1268 was followed by a three years' vacancy in the papacy. This was scarcely over when Richard, King of the Romans, prostrated by the tragedy of Viterbo, preceded his brother to the tomb. Still earlier, Boniface of Canterbury had ended his tenure of the chair of St. Augustine. The new reign begins with fresh actors and fresh motives of action.

CHAPTER VII.

THE EARLY FOREIGN POLICY AND LEGISLATION OF EDWARD I.

THE Dominican chronicler, Nicholas Trivet, thus describes the personality of Edward I. : " He was of elegant build and lofty stature, exceeding the height of the ordinary man by a head and shoulders. His abundant hair was yellow in childhood, black in manhood, and snowy white in age. His brow was broad, and his features regular, save that his left eyelid drooped somewhat, like that of his father, and hid part of the pupil. He spoke with a stammer, which did not, however, detract from the persuasiveness of his eloquence. His sinewy, muscular arms were those of the consummate swordsman, and his long legs gave him a firm hold in the saddle when riding the most spirited of steeds. His chief delight was in war and tournaments, but he derived great pleasure from hawking and hunting, and had a special joy in chasing down stags on a fleet horse and slaying them with a sword instead of a hunting spear. His disposition was magnanimous, but he was intolerant of injuries, and reckless of dangers when seeking revenge, though easily won over by a humble submission." [1] The defects of his youth are well brought out by the radical friar who wrote the *Song of Lewes*. Even to the partisan of Earl Simon, Edward was "a valiant lion, quick to attack the strongest, and fearing the onslaught of none. But if a lion in pride and fierceness, he was a panther in inconstancy and mutability, changing his word and promise, cloaking himself by pleasant speech. When he is in a strait he promises whatever you wish, but as soon as he has escaped he forgets his promise. The treachery or falsehood, whereby he is advanced, he calls prudence ; the way whereby he arrives whither he will, crooked

---

[1] *Annals*, pp. 181-82.

though it be, he regards as straight; whatever he likes he says
is lawful, and he thinks he is released from the law, as though
he were greater than a king." [1]

Hot and impulsive in disposition, easily persuaded that his
own cause was right, and with a full share in the pride of caste,
Edward committed many deeds of violence in his youth, and
never got over his deeply rooted habit of keeping the letter
of his promise while violating its spirit.   Yet he learnt to curb
his impetuous temper, and few medieval kings had a higher idea
of justice or a more strict regard to his plighted word.   "Keep
troth" was inscribed upon his tomb, and his reign signally
falsified the prediction of evil which the Lewes song-writer
ventured to utter.   A true sympathy bound him closely to his
nobles and people.   His unstained family life, his piety and
religious zeal, his devotion to friends and kinsfolk, his keen
interest in the best movements of his time, showed him a true
son of Henry III.   But his strength of will and seriousness of
purpose stand in strong contrast to his father's weakness and
levity.   A hard-working, clear-headed, practical, and sober temperament made him the most capable king of all his line.   He
may have been wanting in originality or deep insight, yet it is
impossible to dispute the verdict that has declared him to be
the greatest of all the Plantagenets.

The broad lines of Edward's policy during the thirty-five
years of his kingship had already been laid down for him
during his rude schooling.   The ineffectiveness of his father's
government inspired him with a love of strong rule, and this
enabled him to grapple with the chronic maladministration
which made even a well-ordered medieval kingdom a hot-bed
of disorder.   The age of Earl Simon had been fertile in new
ideals and principles of government.   Edward held to the best
of the traditions of his youth, and his task was not one of creation so much as of selection.   His age was an age of definition.
The series of great laws, which he made during the earlier half
of his reign, represented a long effort to appropriate what was best
in the age that had gone before, and to combine it in orderly
sequence.   The same ideals mark the constitutional policy of
his later years.   The materials for the future constitution of

---

[1] *Song of Lewes*, pp. 14-15, ed. Kingsford.

CHAP.
VII.

England were already at his hand. It was a task well within Edward's capacity to strengthen the authority of the crown by associating the loyal nobles and clergy in the work of ruling the state, and to build up a body politic in which every class of the nation should have its part. Yet he never willingly surrendered the most insignificant of his prerogatives, and if he took the people into partnership with him, he did so with the firm belief that he would be a more powerful king if his subjects loved and trusted him. Though closely associated with his nobles by many ties of kinship and affection, he was the uncompromising foe of feudal separatism, and hotly resented even the constitutional control which the barons regarded as their right. In the same way the unlimited franchises of the lords of the Welsh march, the almost regal authority which the treaty of Shrewsbury gave to the Prince of Wales, the rejection of his claims as feudal overlord of Scotland, were abhorrent to his autocratic disposition. True son of the Church though he was, he was the bitter foe of ecclesiastical claims which, constantly encroaching beyond their own sphere, denied kings the fulness of their authority.

Edward's policy was thoroughly comprehensive. He is not only the "English Justinian" and the creator of our later constitution; he has rightly been praised for his clear conception of the ideal of a united Britain which brought him into collision with Welsh and Scots. His foreign policy lay as near to his heart as the conquest of Wales or Scotland, or the subjection of priests and nobles. He was eager to make Gascony obey him, anxious to keep in check the French king, and to establish a sort of European balance of power, of which England, as in Wolsey's later dreams, was to be the tongue of the balance. Yet, despite his severe schooling in self-control, he undertook more than he could accomplish, and his failure was the more signal because he found the utmost difficulty in discovering trustworthy subordinates. Moreover, the limited resources of a medieval state, and the even more limited control which a medieval ruler had over these resources, were fatal obstacles in the way of too ambitious a policy. Edward had inherited his father's load of debt, and could only accomplish great things by further pledging his credit to foreign financiers, against whom his subjects raised unending complaints. Yet, if his methods

of attaining his objects were sometimes mean and often violent, CHAP.
there was a rare nobility about his general purpose. VII.

Every precaution was taken to secure Edward's succession
and the establishment of the provisional administration which
was to rule until his return. Before leaving England in 1270,
Edward had appointed as his agents Walter Giffard, Archbishop of York, Roger Mortimer, and Robert Burnell, his
favourite clerk. The vacancy of the see of Canterbury after
Boniface's death placed Giffard in a position of peculiar eminence. Appointed first lord of the council, he virtually became
regent; and he associated with himself in the administration of
the realm his two colleagues in the management of the new
king's private affairs. Early in 1273 a parliament of magnates
and representatives of shires and boroughs took oaths of allegiance to the king and continued the authority of the three
regents. By the double title of Edward's personal delegation
and the recognition of the estates, Giffard, Mortimer, and
Burnell ruled the country for the two years which were to
elapse before the sovereign's return. Their government was
just, economical, and peaceful. Even Gilbert of Gloucester
remained quiet, and, save for the refusal of the Prince of Wales
to perform his feudal obligations, the calm of the last years
of the old reign continued. It is evidence of constitutional
progress that the administration was carried on with so little
friction in the absence of the monarch. Roger Mortimer, the
most formidable of the feudal baronage, was himself one of the
agents of this salutary change. The marcher chieftain put
down with promptitude an attempted revolt of north-country
knights which threatened public tranquillity.

Edward first heard of his father's death in Sicily, but the
tidings of the maintenance of peace rendered it unnecessary
for him to hasten his return, and he made his way slowly
through Italy. In Sicily he was entertained by his uncle,
Charles of Anjou. Thence he went to Orvieto, where the new
pope, Gregory X., who, as archdeacon of Liège, had been the
comrade of his crusade, was then residing. From king and
pope alike Edward earnestly sought vengeance for the murder
of Henry of Almaine. Proceeding northwards, he was received
with great pomp by the cities of Lombardy, and made personal
acquaintance with Savoy and its count, Philip, his aged great-

uncle.　Crossing the Mont Cenis, he was welcomed by bands of
English magnates who had gone forth to meet him.　He was
soon at the head of a little army, and in the true spirit of a hero
of romance halted to receive the challenge of the boastful Count
of Chalon.　The tournament between the best knights of England
and Burgundy was fought out with such desperation that it became a serious battle.　At last Edward unhorsed the count in
a personal encounter, which added greatly to his fame.　This
" Little Battle of Chalon " was the last victory of his irresponsible
youth.

　　The serious business of kingcraft began when Edward met
his cousin, Philip III., at Paris.　The news from England was
still so good that Edward resolved to remain in France with
the twofold object of settling his relations with the French
monarchy and of receiving the homage and regulating the
affairs of Aquitaine.　Despite the treaty of Paris of 1259, there
were so many subjects of dispute between the English and
French kings that, beneath the warm protestations of affection
between the kinsmen, there was, as a French chronicler said,
but a cat-and-dog love between them.[1]　The treaty had not
been properly executed, and the English had long complained
that the French had not yielded up to England their king's
rights over the three bishoprics of Limoges, Cahors, and Périgueux, which St. Louis had ceded.　New complications arose
after the death of Alfonse of Poitiers in the course of the
Tunisian crusade.　By the treaty of Paris the English king
should then have entered into possession of Saintonge south of
the Charente, the Agenais, and lower Quercy.　But the ministers
of Philip III. laid hands upon the whole of Alfonse's inheritance and refused to surrender these districts to the English.
The welcome which Edward received from his cousin at Paris
could not blind him to the incompatibility of their interests, nor
to the impossibility of obtaining at the moment the cession
of the promised lands.　He did not choose to tarry at Paris
while the diplomatists unravelled the tangled web of statecraft.
Nor would he tender an unconditional homage to the prince
who withheld from him his inheritance.　Already a stickler for
legal rights, even when used to his own detriment, Edward was

---

[1] " Hic amor dici potest amor cati et canis," *Chron. Limov.*, in *Recueil
des Hist. de la France*, xxi., 784.

unable to deny his subjection to the overlord of Aquitaine. He therefore performed homage, but he phrased his submission in terms which left him free to urge his claims at a more convenient season. "Lord king," he said to Philip, "I do you homage for all the lands which I ought to hold of you." The vagueness of this language suggested that, if Edward could not get Saintonge, he might revive his claim to Normandy. The king appointed a commission to continue the negotiations with the French court, and then betook himself to Aquitaine.[1]

It was nearly ten years since the presence of the monarch had restrained the turbulence of the Gascon duchy. Edward had before him the task of watching over its internal administration, and checking the subtle policy whereby the agents of the French crown were gradually undermining his authority. Two wars, the war of Béarn and the war of Limoges, desolated Gascony from the Pyrenees to the Vienne. It was Edward's first task to bring these troubles to an end. Age and experience had not diminished the ardour which had so long made Gaston of Béarn the focus of every trouble in the Pyrenean lands. He defied a sentence of the ducal court of Saint Sever, and was already at war with the seneschal, Luke of Tany, when Edward's appearance brought matters to a crisis. During the autumn and winter of 1273-74, Edward hunted out Gaston from his mountain strongholds, and at last the Béarnais, despairing of open resistance, appealed to the French king. Philip accepted the appeal, and ordered Edward to desist from molesting Gaston during its hearing. The English king, anxious not to quarrel openly with the French court, granted a truce. The suit of Gaston long occupied the parliament of Paris, but the good-will of the French lawyers could not palliate the wanton violence of the Viscount of Béarn. The French, like the English, were sticklers for formal right, and were unwilling to push matters to extremities. Edward had the reward of his forbearance, for Philip advised Gaston to go to England and make his submission. Gratified by his restoration to Béarn in 1279, Gaston remained faithful for the next few years.

Edward was less successful in dealing with Limoges. There

---

[1] C. V. Langlois' *Le Règne de Philippe le Hardi* (1887), and Gavrilovitch's *Le Traité de Paris*, give the best modern accounts of Edward's early dealings with the French crown.

CHAP.
VII.

had been for many years a struggle between the commune of the castle, or *bourg*, of Limoges and Margaret the viscountess. It was to no purpose that the townsfolk had invoked the treaty of Paris, whereby, as they maintained, the French king transferred to the King of England his ancient jurisdiction over them. They were answered by a decree of the parliament of Paris that the homage of the commune of Limoges belonged not to the crown but to the viscountess, and that therefore the treaty involved no change in their allegiance. Edward threw himself with ardour on to the side of the burgesses. Guy of Lusignan, still the agent of his brother abroad, though prudently excluded from England, was sent to Limoges, where he incited the commune to resist the viscountess. In May, 1274, Edward himself took up his quarters in Limoges, and for a month ruled there as sovereign. But the French court reiterated the decree which made the commune the vassal of the viscountess. To persevere in upholding the rebels meant an open breach with the French court in circumstances more unfavourable than in the case of Gaston of Béarn. Once more Edward refused to allow his ambition to prevail over his sense of legal obligation. With rare self-restraint he renounced the fealty of Limoges, and abandoned his would-be subjects to the wrath of the viscountess. This was an act of loyalty to feudal duty worthy of St. Louis. If Edward, on later occasions, pressed his own legal claims against his vassals, he set in his own case a pattern of strict obedience to his overlord.

While Edward was still abroad, his friend Gregory X. held from May to July, 1274, the second general council at Lyons, wherein there was much talk of a new crusade, and an effort was made, which came very near temporary success, towards healing the schism of the Eastern and Western Churches. At Gregory's request Edward put off his coronation, lest the celebration might call away English prelates from Lyons. When the council was over, he at last turned towards his kingdom. At Paris he was met by the mayor of London, Henry le Waleis, and other leading citizens, who set before him the grievous results of the long disputes with Flanders, which had broken off the commercial relations between the two countries, and had inflicted serious losses on English trade. Edward strove to bring the Flemings to their senses by prohibiting the export of wool from England to the weaving towns of Flanders. The looms of Ghent and Bruges were stopped by reason of the withholding of the raw material, and the distress of his subjects made Count Guy of Flanders anxious to end so costly a quarrel. On July 28 Edward met Guy at Montreuil and signed a treaty which re-established the old friendship between lands which stood in constant economic need of each other. There was no longer any occasion for further delay, and on August 2 Edward and his queen crossed over to Dover. Received with open arms by his subjects, he was crowned at Westminster on August 19 by the new Archbishop of Canterbury, Robert Kilwardby, philosopher, theologian, and Dominican friar, whom Gregory X. had placed over the church of Canterbury, despite the vigorous efforts which Edward made to secure the primacy for Robert Burnell. He had been absent from England for four years.

Edward's sojourn in France was fruitful of results which he was unable to reap for the moment. Conscious of the inveterate hostility of the French king, he strove to establish relations with foreign powers to counterbalance the preponderance of his rival. When the death of Richard of Cornwall reopened the question of the imperial succession, Charles of Anjou had been anxious to obtain the prize for his nephew, Philip III., on the specious pretext that the headship of Christendom would enable the King of France to "collect chivalry from all the world" and institute the crusade which both Gregory X. and Edward so ardently desired. But the most zealous enthusiast for the holy war could hardly be deceived by the false zeal with which the Angevin cloaked his overweening ambition. It was a veritable triumph for Edward, when Gregory X., though attracted for a moment by the prospect of a strong emperor capable of landing a crusade, accepted the choice of the German magnates who, in terror of France, elected as King of the Romans the strenuous but not overmighty Swabian count, Rudolf of Hapsburg. As Alfonso of Castile's pretensions were purely nominal, this election ended the Great Interregnum by restoring the empire on a narrower but more practical basis. Though Gregory strove to reconcile the French to Rudolf's accession, common suspicion of France bound Edward and the new King of the Romans in a common friendship.

CHAP.
VII.   Family disputes soon destroyed the unity of policy of the
Capetian house.   Philip III., well meaning but weak, was drifting
into complete dependence on Charles of Anjou, whom Edward
distrusted, alike as the protector of the murderers of Henry of
Almaine and as the supplanter of his mother in the Provençal
heritage.   Margaret of Provence, the widow of St. Louis, had a
common grievance with Edward and his mother against Charles
of Anjou.   She hated him the more inasmuch as he was depriving
her of all influence over her son, King Philip.   It was easy in
such circumstances for the two widowed queens of France and
England to form grandiose schemes for ousting Charles from
Provence.   Rudolf lent himself to their plans by investing
Margaret with the county.   Edward's filial piety and political
interests made him a willing partner in these designs.   In 1278
he betrothed his daughter Joan of Acre to Hartmann, the son
of the King of the Romans.   The plan of Edward and Rudolf
was to revive in some fashion the kingdom of Arles[1] in favour
of the young couple.   Though Rudolf was unfaithful to this
policy, and abandoned the proposed English marriage in favour
of a match between his daughter and the son of the King of
Sicily, the two queens persisted in their plans, and new combinations against Charles and Philip for some years threatened
the peace of Europe.

It is unlikely that Edward hoped for serious results from
schemes so incoherent and backed with such slender resources.
Besides his alliance with the emperor, he strove to injure the
French king by establishing close relations with his brother-in-
law, Alfonso of Castile, who since 1276 was at war with the
French.   Earlier than this, he made himself the champion of
Blanche of Artois, the widow of Henry III. of Navarre and
Champagne.   He wished that Joan, their only child, should
bring her father's lands to one of his own sons, and, though
disappointed in this ambition, he managed to marry his younger
brother, Edmund of Lancaster, to Blanche.   Though the French
took possession of Navarre, whereby they alike threatened
Gascony and Castile, they suffered Blanche to rule in Champagne in her daughter's name, and Edmund was associated
with her in the government of that county.   The tenure of a

---

[1] Fournier's *Le Royaume d'Arles et de Vienne* (1891) gives the best modern
account of Edward's relations to the Middle Kingdom.

great French fief by the brother of the English king was a fresh
security against the aggressions of the kings of France and Sicily.
It probably facilitated the conclusion of the long negotiations
as to the interpretation of the treaty of Paris, and the partition
of the inheritance of Alfonse of Poitiers. Edward's position
against France was further strengthened in 1279 by the death
of his wife's mother, Joan of Castile, the widow of Ferdinand
the Saint and the stepmother of Alfonso the Wise, whereupon
he took possession of Ponthieu in Eleanor's name. Scarcely
had he established himself at Abbeville, the capital of the
Picard county, than the negotiations at Paris were so far ripened
that Philip III. went to Amiens, where Edward joined him.
On May 23 both kings agreed to accept the treaty of Amiens
by which the more important of the outstanding difficulties
between the two nations were amicably regulated. By it Philip
recognised Eleanor as Countess of Ponthieu, and handed over
a portion of the inheritance of Alfonse of Poitiers to Edward.
Agen and the Agenais were ceded at once, and a commission
was appointed to investigate Edward's claims over lower Quercy.
In return for this Edward yielded up his illusory rights over
the three bishoprics of Limoges, Périgueux, and Cahors. It
was a real triumph for English diplomacy.

No lasting peace could arise from acts which emphasised
the essential incompatibility of French and English interests
by enlarging the territory of the English kings in France.
The undercurrent of hostility still continued ; and the proposal
of Pope Nicholas III. that Edward should act as mediator
between Philip III. and Alfonso of Castile led to difficulties
that deeply incensed Edward, and embroiled him once more
both with France and Spain. Under Angevin influence, both
Philip and Alfonso rejected Edward's mediation in favour of
that of the Prince of Salerno, Charles of Anjou's eldest son.
Disgust at this unfriendliness made Edward again support the
plans of Margaret of Provence against the Angevins. In 1281
Margaret's intrigues formed a combination of feudal magnates
called the League of Mâcon, with the object of prosecuting
her claims over Provence by force of arms. Edward and his
mother, Eleanor, his Savoyard kinsfolk, and Edmund of Lancaster all entered into the league. But it was hopeless for a
disorderly crowd of lesser chieftains, with the nominal support

of a distant prince like Edward, to conquer Provence in the teeth of the hostility of the strongest and the ablest princes of the age. The League of Mâcon came to nothing, like so many other ambitious combinations of a time in which men's capacity to form plans transcended their capacity to execute them. Margaret herself soon despaired of the way of arms and was bought off by a money compensation. The league mainly served to keep alive the troubles that still separated England and France. In 1284 Philip gained a new success in winning the hand of Joan of Champagne, Count Edmund's step-daughter, for his son, the future Philip the Fair. When Joan attained her majority, Edmund lost the custody of Champagne, which went to the King of France as the natural protector of his son and his son's bride. With his brother's withdrawal from Provins to Lancaster, Edward lost one of his means of influencing the course of French politics.

A compensation for these failures was found in 1282 when the Sicilian vespers rang the knell of the Angevin power in Sicily. When the revolted islanders chose Peter, King of Aragon, as their sovereign, Charles, seeking to divert him from Sicily by attacking him at home, inspired his partisan, Pope Martin IV., to preach a crusade against Aragon. It was in vain that Edward strove to mediate between the two kings. The only response made to his efforts was a fantastic proposal that they should fight out their differences in a tournament at Bordeaux with him as umpire, but Edward refused to have anything to do with the pseudo-chivalrous venture. At last, in 1285, Philip III. lent himself to his uncle's purpose so far as to lead a papalist crusade over the Pyrenees. The movement was a failure. Philip lost his army and his life in Aragon, and his son and successor, Philip IV., at once withdrew from the undertaking. In the year of the crusade of Aragon, Charles of Anjou, Peter of Aragon, and Martin IV. died. With them the struggles, which had begun with the attack on Frederick II., reached their culminating point. Their successors continued the quarrel with diminished forces and less frantic zeal, and so gave Edward his best chance to pose as the arbiter of Europe. Though Edward's continental policy lay so near his heart that it can hardly be passed over, it was fuller of vain schemes than of great results. Yet it was not altogether fruitless, since twelve

years of resolute and moderate action raised England, which CHAP.
under Henry III. was of no account in European affairs, to VII.
a position only second to that of France, and that under conditions more nearly approaching the modern conception of a
political balance and a European state system than feudalism,
imperialism, and papalism had hitherto rendered possible.

In domestic policy, seven years of monotonous administration had in a way prepared for vigorous reforms. Edward's
return to England in 1274 was quickly followed by the dismissal of Walter of Merton, the chancellor of the years of
quiescence. He was succeeded by Robert Burnell, who, though
foiled in his quest of Canterbury, obtained an adequate standing
by his preferment to the bishopric of Bath and Wells. For
the eighteen years of life which still remained to him, Bisho
Burnell held the chancery and possessed the chief place i
Edward's counsels. The whole of this period was mark d
by a constant legislative activity which ceased so soon a er
Burnell's death that it is tempting to assign at least as larg a
part of the law-making of the reign to the minister as to the
sovereign. A consummate lawyer and diplomatist, Burnell
served Edward faithfully. Nor was his fidelity impaired either
by the laxity which debarred him from higher ecclesiastical
preferment or by his ambitious endeavours to raise the house of
Shropshire squires from which he sprang into a great territorial
family. Edward gave him his absolute confidence and was
blind even to his defects.

The first general parliament of the reign to which the king
summoned the commons was held at Westminster in the spring
of 1275. Its work was the statute of Westminster the First, a
comprehensive measure of many articles which covered almost
the whole field of legislation, and is especially noteworthy
for the care which its compilers took to uphold sound administration and put down abuses. Not less important was the
provision of an adequate revenue for the debt-burdened king.
The same parliament made Edward a permanent grant of a
custom on wool, wool-fells, and leather, which remained henceforth a chief source of the regular income of the crown. The
later imposition of further duties soon caused men to describe
the customs of 1275 as the " Great and Ancient Custom ". It
was significant of the economic condition of England that

10 *

the great custom was a tax on exports, not imports, and that, with the exception of leather, it was a tax on raw materials. Granted the more willingly since the main incidence of it was upon the foreign merchants, who bought up English wool for the looms of Flanders and Brabant, the custom proved a source of revenue which could easily be manipulated, increased, and assigned in advance to the Italian financiers, willing to lend money to a necessitous king. A new step in our financial history was attained when this tax on trade steps into the place so long held by the taxes on land, from which the Normans and Angevins had derived their enormous revenue.

The statute of Westminster the First had a long series of fellows. Next year came the statute of Rageman, which supplemented an earlier inquest into abuses by instituting a special inquiry in cases of trespass. In 1277 the first Welsh war interrupted the current of legislation. The break was compensated for in 1278 by the passing of the important statute of Gloucester, the consummation of a policy which Edward had adopted as soon as he set foot on English soil. The troubles of Edward's youth had made clear to him the obstacles thrown in the path of orderly government by the great territorial franchises. He had been forced to modify his policy to gratify the lord of Glamorgan, and win over the house of Mortimer by the erection of a new franchise that was a palatinate in all but name. But such great "regalities" were, after all, exceptional. Much more irritating to an orderly mind were the innumerable petty immunities which made half the hundreds in England the appendages of baronial estates, and such common privileges as "return of writs," which prevented the sheriff's officers from executing his mandates on numerous manors where the lords claimed that the execution of writs must be entrusted to their bailiffs.[1] These widespread powers in private hands were the more annoying to the king since they were commonly exercised with no better warrant than long custom, and without direct grant from him.

Bracton had already laid down the doctrine that no prescription can avail against the rights of the crown, and it was a commonplace with the lawyers of the age that nothing less than a clear grant by royal charter could justify such delegation

---

[1] See on "return of writs" and a host of similar immunities, Pollock and Maitland's *History of English Law*, i., 558-82.

of the sovereign's powers into private hands. Within a few CHAP. VII.
months of his landing, Edward sent out commissioners to inquire
into the baronial immunities. The returns of these inquests,
which were carried out hundred by hundred, are embodied in
the precious documents called the Hundred Rolls. The study
of these reports inspired the procedure of the statute of Gloucester, by which royal officers were empowered to traverse the
land demanding by what warrant the lords of franchises exercised their powers. The demand of the crown for documentary
proof of royal delegation would have destroyed more than half
the existing liberties. But aristocratic opinion deserted Edward
when he strove to carry out so violent a revolution. The irritation of the whole baronage is well expressed in the story of how
Earl Warenne, unsheathing a rusty sword, declared to the commissioners: "Here is my warrant. My ancestors won their
lands with the sword. With my sword I will defend them
against all usurpers." Nor was this mere boasting. The return
of the king's officers tells us that Warenne would not say of
whom, or by what services, he held his Yorkshire stronghold of
Conisborough, and that his bailiffs refused them entrance into
his liberties and would not suffer his tenants to answer or appear
before them.[1] Edward found it prudent not to press his claims.
He disturbed few men in their franchises, and was content to
have collected the mass of evidence embodied in the *placita de
quo warranto*, and thus to have stopped the possibility of any
further growth of the franchises. A few years later he accepted
the compromise that continuous possession since the coronation
of Richard I. was a sufficient answer to a writ of *quo warranto*.
In this lies the whole essence of Edward's policy in relation to
feudalism, a policy very similar to that of St. Louis. Every
man is to have his own, and the king is not to inquire too
curiously what a man's own was. But no extension of any
private right was to be tolerated. Thus feudalism as a principle
of political jurisdiction gradually withered away, because it was
no longer suffered to take fresh root. The later land legislation
of Edward's reign pushed the idea still further.

In 1278 it had been the turn of the barons to suffer. Next
came the turn of the Church. Though Edward was a true son

---

[1] *Kirkby's Quest for Yorkshire*, pp. 3, 227, 231, Surtees Soc.

of the Church, he saw as clearly as William the Conqueror and Henry II. the essential incompatibility between the royal supremacy and the pretensions of the extreme ecclesiastics. The limits of Church and State, the growth of clerical wealth and immunities, and the relations of the world-power of the pope to the local authority of the king, were problems which no strong king could afford to neglect, and perhaps were incapable of solution on medieval lines. Edward saw that the most practical way of dealing with clerical claims was for him to stand in good personal relations to the chief dispensers of ecclesiastical jurisdiction. With a pope like Gregory X. it was easy for Edward to be on friendly terms; but it was more difficult to feel any cordiality for the dogmatic canonists or the furious Guelfic partisans who too often occupied the chair of St. Peter. Yet Edward was shrewd enough to see that it was worth while making sacrifices to keep on his side the power which, alike under Innocent III. and Clement IV., had given valuable assistance to his grandfather and father in their struggle against domestic enemies. Moreover the enormous growth of the system of papal provisions had given the papacy the preponderating authority in the selection of the bishops of the English Church. It was only by yielding to the popes, whenever it was possible, that Edward could secure the nomination of his own candidates to the chief ecclesiastical posts in his own realm.

In the earlier years of his reign Edward was luckier in his relations to the popes than to his own archbishops. But he found that his power at Rome broke down just where he wanted to exercise it most. He was disgusted to find how little influence he had in the selection of the Archbishops of Canterbury. Gregory X. sent to Canterbury the Dominican Robert Kilwardby, the first mendicant to hold high place in the English Church. Kilwardby was translated in 1278 to the cardinal bishopric of Porto, a post of greater dignity but less emolument and power than the English archbishopric. A cardinal bishop was bound to reside at Rome, and the real motive for this doubtful promotion was the desire to remove Kilwardby from England and to send a more active man in his place. Edward's indiscreet devotion to Bishop Burnell led him again to press his friend's claims, but, though he persuaded the monks of Christ Church to elect him, Nicholas III. quashed the appointment, and selected the Franciscan friar, John Peckham, as archbishop. Peckham, a famous theologian and physicist, had been a distinguished professor at Paris, Oxford, and Rome. He was high-minded, honourable and zealous, a saint as well as a scholar, an enthusiast for Church reform and a vigorous upholder of the extremest hierarchical pretensions. Fussy, energetic, tactless, he was the true type of the academic ecclesiastic, and alike in his personal qualities and his wonderful grasp of detail, he may be compared to Archbishop Laud. Though received by Edward with a rare magnanimity, Friar John allowed no personal considerations of gratitude to interpose between him and his duty. Reaching England in June, 1279, he presided, within six weeks of his landing, at a provincial council at Reading. In this gathering canons were passed against pluralities which frightened every benefice hunter among the clerks of the royal household. Orders were also issued for the periodical denunciation of ecclesiastical penalties against all violators of the Great Charter in a fashion that suggested that the king was an habitual offender against the fundamental laws of his realm.

Edward wrathfully laid the usurpations of the new primate before parliament, and forced Peckham to withdraw all the canons dealing with secular matters, and particularly those which concerned the Great Charter. The king set up the counter-claims of the State against the pretensions of the Church, and the estates passed the statute of Mortmain of 1279 as the layman's answer to the canons of Reading. Like most of Edward's laws the statute of Mortmain was based on earlier precedents. The wealth of the Church had long inspired statesmen with alarm, and a true follower of St. Francis like Peckham was specially convinced of the need of reducing the clergy to apostolic poverty. By the new law all grants of land to ecclesiastical corporations were expressly prohibited, under the penalty of the land being forfeited to its supreme lord. The statute was not a mere political weapon of the moment. It had a wider importance as a step in the development of Edward's anti-feudal policy, and may be regarded as a counterpart of the inquest into franchises, and as a means of protecting the State as well as of disciplining the Church. A corporation never died, and never paid reliefs or wardships. Its property never escheated for want of heirs, and, as scutages were passing out of fashion, ecclesiastics were less valuable to the king in times of war than lay lords.   The recent exigencies of the Welsh war had emphasised the need of strengthening the military defences of the crown, and the new statute secured this by preventing the further devolution of lands into the dead hand of the Church.   But all medieval laws were rather enunciations of an ideal than measures which practical statesmen aimed at carrying out in detail.   The statute of Mortmain hardly stayed the creation of fresh monasteries and colleges, or the further endowment of old ones.   All that was necessary for the pious founder was to obtain a royal dispensation from the operation of the statute.   There was little need to fear that the new law would stand in the way of the power of the ecclesiastical estate.

A more distinct challenge to the Church was provoked by a further aggression of Peckham in 1281.   In that year the primate summoned a council at Lambeth, wherein he sought to withdraw from the cognisance of the civil courts all suits concerning patronage and the disposition of the personal effects of ecclesiastics.   To extend the jurisdiction of the *forum ecclesiasticum* was the surest way of exciting the hostility of the common lawyers and the king.   Once more Edward annulled the proceedings of a council, and once more the submission of Peckham saved the land from a conflict which might have assumed the proportions of Becket's struggle against Henry II.   Four years later Edward pressed his advantage still further by the royal ordinance of 1285, called *Circumspecte agatis*, which, though accepting the supremacy of the Church courts within their own sphere, narrowly defined the limits of their power in matters involving a temporal element.   Again Peckham was fain to acquiesce.   His policy had not only irritated the king, but alienated his fellow bishops.   He visited his province with pertinacity and minuteness, and he was the less able to stand up against the king as he was engaged in violent quarrels with all his own suffragans.   The leader of the bishops in resisting his claims was Thomas of Cantilupe.   Restored to England by the liberal policy of Edward, Montfort's chancellor after Lewes had been raised to the see of Hereford, where his sanctity and devotion won him the universal love of his flock.   Involved in costly lawsuits with the litigious primate, Thomas was forced to leave his diocese to plead his cause before the papal *curia.* He died in Italy in 1282, and his relics, carried back by his followers to his own cathedral, won the reputation of working miracles. A demand arose for his canonisation, and Edward before his death had secured the appointment of the papal commission, which, a few years later, added St. Thomas of Hereford to the list of saints.[1] Thus the chancellor of Montfort obtained the honour of sanctity through the action of the victor of Evesham.

The second Welsh war interrupted both the conflict between Edward and the archbishop, and the course of domestic legislation. Yet even in the midst of his campaigns Edward issued the statute of Acton Burnell of 1283, which provided a better way of recovering merchants' debts, and the statute of Rhuddlan of 1284 for the regulation of the king's exchequer. The king's full activity as a lawgiver was renewed after the settlement of his conquest by the statute of Wales of 1284, and the legislation of his early years culminated in the two great acts of 1285, the statute of Westminster the Second, and the statute of Winchester. That year, which also witnessed the passing of the *Circumspecte agatis,* stands out as the most fruitful in law-making in the whole of Edward's reign.

The second statute of Westminster, passed in the spring parliament, partook of the comprehensive character of the first statute of that name. There were clauses by which, as the Canon of Oseney puts it, "Edward revived the ancient laws which had slumbered through the disturbance of the realm : some corrupted by abuse he restored to their proper form : some less evident and apparent he declared : some new ones, useful and honourable, he added". Among the more conspicuous innovations of the second statute of Westminster was the famous clause *De donis conditionalibus,* which forms a landmark in the law of real property. It facilitated the creation of entailed estates by providing that the rights of an heir of an estate, granted upon conditions, were not to be barred on account of the alienation of such an estate by its previous tenant. Thus arose those estates for life, which in later ages became a special feature of the English land system, and which, by re-

---

[1] The *processus canonisationis* of Cantilupe, printed in the Bollandist *Acta Sanctorum,* Oct. 1, 539-705, illustrates many aspects of this period.

stricting the control of the actual possessor of a property over his land, did much to perpetuate the worst features of medieval land-holding.   It is a modern error to regard the legitimation of estates in tail as a triumph of reactionary feudalism over the will of Edward.   Apart from the fact that there is not a tittle of contemporary evidence to justify such a view, it is manifest that the interest of the king was in this case exactly the same as that of each individual lord of a manor.   The greater prospect of reversion to the donor, and the other features of the system of entails, which commended them to the petty baron, were still more attractive to the king, the greatest proprietor as well as the ultimate landlord of all the realm.   Other articles of the Westminster statute were only less important than the clause *De donis*, notable among them being the institution of justices of *nisi prius*, appointed to travel through the shires three times a year to hear civil causes.   This was part of the simplification and concentration of judicial machinery, whereby Edward made tolerable the circuit system which under Henry III. had been a prolific source of grievances.

While in the statute of Westminster Edward prepared for the future, the companion statute of Winchester, the work of the autumn parliament, revived the jurisdiction of the local courts ; reformed the ancient system of watch and ward, and brought the ancient system of popular courts into harmony with the jurisdiction emanating from the crown, which had gone so far towards superseding it.   This measure marks the culmination of Edward's activity as a lawgiver.   During the five next years there were no more important statutes.

CHAPTER VIII.

THE CONQUEST OF NORTH WALES.

THE treaty of Shrewsbury of 1267 had not brought enduring peace to Wales and the march. The pacification was in essentials a simple recognition of accomplished facts, but, so far as it involved promises of restitution and future good behaviour, its provisions were barely carried out, even in the scanty measure in which any medieval treaty was executed. Moreover, the treaty by no means covered the whole ground of variance between the English and the Welsh. Like the treaty of Paris of 1259, it was as much the starting-point of new difficulties as the solution of old ones. Many troublesome questions of detail had been postponed for later settlement, and no serious effort was made to grapple with them. Even during the life of the old king, there had been war in the south between the Earl of Gloucester and Llewelyn. However, the Welsh prince paid, with fair regularity, the instalments of the indemnity to which he had been bound, and there was no disposition on the part of the English authorities to question the basis of the settlement. Even the marchers maintained an unwonted tranquillity. They had lost so much during the recent war that they had no great desire to take up arms again. Llewelyn himself was the chief obstacle to peace. The brilliant success of his arms and diplomacy seems somewhat to have turned his brain. Visions of a wider authority constantly floated before him. His bards prophesied the expulsion of the Saxon, and he had done such great deeds in the first twenty years of his reign, that a man of more practical temperament might have been forgiven for indulging in dreams of future success. Three obstacles stood in the way of the development of his power. These were his vassalage to the English crown, the hostility of the marcher barons, and the impatience with which the minor Welsh chieftains submitted to his authority.   For five years he impatiently endured these restraints.   He then took advantage of the absence of the new king to rid himself of them.

Five days after the accession of Edward I., the lieutenants of the king received the last payment of the indemnity which Llewelyn condescended to make.   Their demand that the Welsh prince should take an oath of fealty to his new sovereign was answered by evasive delays.   Arrears of the indemnity accumulated, and the state of the march became more disturbed.   The regents showed moderation, though one of them, Roger Mortimer, had himself been the greatest sufferer from the treaty of Shrewsbury.   In the south, Humphrey Bohun, grandson of the old Earl of Hereford and earl himself in 1275 by his grandfather's death, was engaged in private war with Llewelyn.   In direct defiance of the terms of 1267, Humphrey strove to maintain himself in the march of Brecon, which had been definitely ceded to Llewelyn.   It was to the credit of the regents that they refused to countenance this glaring violation of the treaty.   Meanwhile Llewelyn busied himself with erecting a new stronghold on the upper Severn, which was a menace alike to the royal castle of Montgomery and to his own vassal, Griffith ap Gwenwynwyn, the tributary lord of Powys.   Yet the regents were content to remonstrate, and to urge on all parties the need of strict adherence to the terms of the treaty.   The Earl of Warwick was appointed in the spring of 1274 as head of a commission, empowered to do justice on all transgressions of the peace, and Llewelyn was ordered to meet him at Montgomery Ford.   But Llewelyn was busy at home, where his brother David had joined hands with Griffith ap Gwenwynwyn in a plot against him.   Llewelyn easily crushed the conspiracy; David, after a feeble attempt to maintain himself in his own patrimony, took flight to England, and Griffith of Powys, driven from his dominions, was also obliged to seek the protection of Edward.   Henceforth Llewelyn ruled directly over Powys as well as Gwynedd.   His success encouraged him to persevere in defying his overlord.

Rash as he was, Llewelyn recognised that he was not strong enough to stand up single-handed against England.   Former experience, however, suggested that it was an easy matter to make a party with the barons against the crown. But times had changed since the Great Charter and the Barons' War; and a policy, which could obtain concessions from John or Henry III., was powerless against a king who commanded the allegiance of all his subjects. Yet there was enough friction between the new king and his feudatories to make the attempt seem feasible, and Llewelyn revived the Montfort tradition, by claiming the hand of Eleanor, Earl Simon's daughter, which had been promised to him since 1265. The alarm created by this shows that Edward perceived the danger that it might involve. But his policy of conciliation had now restored to their estates the last of the " disinherited," and, since the murder of Henry of Almaine, the name of Montfort was no longer one to conjure with. The exiled sons of Earl Simon welcomed Llewelyn's advances, and, in 1275, Eleanor was despatched from France to Wales under the escort of her clerical brother Amaury. On their way, Eleanor and Amaury were captured by English sailors. Edward detained the lady at the queen's court, and gave some scandal to the stricter clergy by shutting up Amaury in Corfe castle. He had foiled the Welsh prince's game, but he had given him a new grievance.

During these transactions negotiations had been proceeding between the English court and Llewelyn. In November, 1274, Edward went to Shrewsbury in the hope of receiving the prince, but he was delayed by illness, and Llewelyn made this an excuse for non-appearance. Next year the king journeyed to Chester with the same object, but his mission was equally fruitless. Summons after summons was despatched to the recalcitrant vassal. Llewelyn heeded them no more than requests to pay up the arrears which he owed the English crown. After two years of hesitation Edward lost all patience. Irritated to the quick by Llewelyn's offer to perform homage in a border town on conditions altogether impossible of acceptance, the king summoned a council of magnates for November 12, 1276, and laid the whole case before them. It was agreed that the king should go against Llewelyn as a rebel and disturber of the peace; and the feudal levies were summoned to meet at Worcester on June 24, 1277. As a preliminary to the great effort, Warwick was sent to Chester, Roger Mortimer to Montgomery, and Payne of

Chaworth to Carmarthen.   All the available marcher forces and every trooper of the royal household were despatched to enable them to operate during the winter and spring.   Their movements were brilliantly successful.   On the reappearance of its ancient lord, the middle march threw off the yoke of Llewelyn and went back to its obedience to Mortimer.   Griffith ap Gwenwynwyn was restored to upper Powys ; the sons of Griffith of Bromfield cast off their allegiance to Llewelyn and were received back as direct vassals of the king.   A Tony was once more ruling in Elvael, a Gifford in Llandovery, and a Bohun in Brecon.   Rhys ap Meredith yielded up Dynevor, and was content to be recognised as lord of the humbler stronghold of Drysllwyn.   Chaworth's bands conquered all Cardiganshire.   Thus the wider " principality " of Llewelyn was shattered at the first assault, and when the decisive moment came, Llewelyn was thrown back upon his hereditary clansmen of Gwynedd.   Of all the acquisitions of the treaty of Shrewsbury, the four cantreds alone still held for their prince.[1]

When the baronial levies mustered at Worcester, the work was already half accomplished.   Of the thousand lances that there assembled, small forces were detached to help Mortimer in mid Wales and to reinforce the marcher army in west Wales, which was now commanded by Edmund of Lancaster, the king's brother.   The mass of the troops followed Edward to Chester, whence the main attack was to be made.   Edward's plan of operations was simplicity itself.   He knew that the Welsh desired no pitched battle, and he was indisposed to lose his soldiers in unnecessary conflict.   Swarms of workmen cleared a wide road through the dense forests of the four cantreds.   The route chosen was as near as possible to the coast, where a strong fleet, mainly from the Cinque Ports, kept up communications with the land forces.   The advance was cautious and slow, with long halts at Flint and at Rhuddlan, where hastily erected forts secured the king's base and safeguarded a possible retreat.   By the end of August the king was at Deganwy, and the four cantreds were conquered.   During all this time fresh forces were hurried up.   Some 15,000 in-

[1] On the whole subject of this chapter Mr. J. E. Morris's *Welsh Wars of Edward I.* throws a flood of new light, especially on the military history, the organisation of the Edwardian army, and the political condition of the march.

fantry, largely drawn from southern and central Wales, swelled
the king's host.

Llewelyn was closely shut up in the Snowdon country. His position was safe enough from a direct assault, and his only fear was want of provisions. He trusted, however, that supplies would come in from Anglesea, whose rich cornfields were yellowing for the harvest. But the fleet of the Cinque Ports cut off communications between Anglesea and the mainland, and ferried over a strong detachment of Edward's troops, which occupied the island. English harvest-men gathered for Edward the crops of Welsh corn, and left Llewelyn to face the beginnings of a mountain-winter without the means of feeding his followers. By September the real fight was over. Edward withdrew to Rhuddlan and dismissed the greater part of his followers. Enough were left to block the approaches to Snowdon, and Llewelyn, seeing no gain in further delay, made his submission on November 9.

The treaty of Aberconway, which Edward dictated, reduced Llewelyn to the position of a petty North Welsh chieftain, which he had held thirty years before. He gave up the homage of the greater Welsh magnates, and resigned all his former conquests. The four cantreds thus passed away from his power, and even Anglesea was only allowed to him for life and subject to a yearly tribute. He was compelled to do homage, and ordered to pay a crushing indemnity, twice as much as the expenses of the war. But Edward was in a generous mood. After Llewelyn's personal submission at Rhuddlan, the king remitted the indemnity and the rent for Anglesea. It was a boon to Llewelyn that the treacherous David received his reward not in Gwynedd itself but in Duffryn Clwyd and Rhuvoniog, two of the four cantreds of the Perveddwlad. Llewelyn's humiliation was completed by his enforced attendance at Edward's Christmas court at Westminster. Next year, however, he received a further sign of royal favour. He was allowed to marry Eleanor Montfort, and Edward himself was present at their wedding. But on the morning of the ceremony, Llewelyn was forced to make a promise not to entertain the king's fugitives and outlaws.

The treaty of Aberconway left Edward free to revive in the rest of Wales the policy which, when originally begun in 1254,[1] had, like a rising flood, floated Llewelyn into his wider principality. The lords marchers resumed their ancient limits. Princes like Griffith of Powys and Rhys of Drysllwyn sank into a position which is indistinguishable from that of their Anglo-Norman neighbours. David, in the vale of Clwyd had no better prospects. The heirs of lower Powys were put under the guardianship of Roger Mortimer's younger son, another Roger, who, on the death of his wards by drowning, received possession of their lands, and henceforth, as Roger Mortimer of Chirk, became a new marcher baron. Meanwhile Edward busied himself with schemes for establishing settled government in the conquered territories. To a man of his training and temperament, this meant the establishment of English law and administration. He could see no merits in the archaic Welsh customs which regarded all crimes as capable of atonement by a money payment, treated a wrecked ship as the lawful perquisite of the local proprietor, and hardly distinguished legitimate from illegitimate children in determining the descent of property. He convinced himself that the land laws of Wales were already those of Anglo-Norman feudalism. He subjected the cantreds of Rhos and Englefield to the Cheshire county court, and breathed a new life into the decayed shire organisation of Cardiganshire and Carmarthenshire. Flint and Rhuddlan dominated the two former, Aberystwyth and Carmarthen the latter. Round the king's castles grew up petty boroughs of English traders, who would, it was believed, teach the Welsh to love commerce and peaceful ways.

For five years all seemed to go well, though underneath the apparent calm a storm was gradually gathering. The Welsh of the ceded districts bitterly resented the imposition of a strange yoke and complained that the king had broken his promise to respect their laws. "Are the Welsh worse than Jews?" was their cry, "and yet the king allows the Jews to follow their own laws in England." But Edward coldly answered that, though it would be a breach of his coronation oath to maintain customs of Howel the Good, which were contrary to the Decalogue, he was willing to listen to specific complaints. It was, however, a very difficult matter to persuade

[1] See page 76.

Edward's bailiffs and agents to carry out his commands, and CHAP.
VIII. many acts of oppression were wrought for which there was no redress. Nobles like David and Rhys found their franchises threatened by the encroachments of the neighbouring shire-courts. Lesser Welshmen were liable to be robbed and insulted by the workmen who were building Edward's castles, or by the soldiers who were garrisoning them. At last even the Welsh who had helped Edward to put down Llewelyn saw that they had been preparing their own ruin, and turned to their former enemy for the redress refused them at Westminster. David himself made common cause with his brother, and the spirit of resistance spread among the half-hearted Cymry of the south. Edward's oppression did more than Llewelyn's triumphs to weld together the Welsh clans into a single people. A rising was planned in the strictest secrecy; and on the eve of Palm Sunday, March 21, 1282, David swooped down on Hawarden, a weak castle in private hands, and captured it. Llewelyn promptly crossed the Conway and turned his arms against the royal strongholds of Flint and Rhuddlan, which withstood him, though he devastated the countryside in every direction. Meanwhile David hurried south and found the local lords in Cardigan and the vale of Towy already in arms. With their help he captured the castles of the upper Towy, but lower down the river Rhys remained staunch to the king, whereupon David hurried over the hills to Cardiganshire and took Aberystwyth. North and south were in full revolt.

Edward, taken unawares, prepared to reassert his authority. Certain faithful barons were "affectionately requested" to serve the king for pay, and a fairly large army was gathered together, though the scattered character of the rebellion necessitated its acting in small bands. Meanwhile the military tenants and the Cinque Ports were summoned to join in an attack on Llewelyn on the lines of the campaign of 1277. Edward's task was more difficult than on the previous occasion. Though Rhuddlan, not Chester as in 1277, had become his starting-point against Gwynedd, he dared not advance so long as David threatened his left flank from Denbigh, and the rising in the south was far more formidable than that of five years before. A considerable part of the levies had to be despatched to the help of Earl Gilbert of Gloucester, who was charged with the reconquest of the vale of Towy. On June 17 as the earl's soldiers were returning, laden with plunder, to their headquarters at Dynevor, they were suddenly attacked by the Welsh at Llandilo, and were driven back on their base. Gloucester hastily retreated to Carmarthen. He was superseded by William of Valence, whose activity against the Welsh had been quickened by the loss of his son at Llandilo. Llewelyn then came south, and pressed the English so hard that for several weeks nothing of moment was accomplished.

The advance against Gwynedd was delayed until the late summer. Edward still tarried at Rhuddlan, with a host constantly varying in numbers, for his soldiers had long overpassed the period of feudal service. Every effort was made to bring fresh troops to the field, and Luke de Tany, seneschal of Gascony, came upon the scene with a small levy of the chivalry of Aquitaine. To Tany was assigned the task of conquering Anglesey, but it was not until September that he was able to occupy the island. In the same month a strenuous effort was made to dislodge the hostile Welsh in the vale of Clwyd; the Earl of Lincoln at last took Denbigh from David; Reginald Grey, justice of Chester, captured Ruthin, higher up the valley, and Earl Warenne seized Bromfield and Yale. Each noble fought for his own hand, and Edward was forced to reward their services by immediately granting to them their conquests, and thus created a new marcher interest which, later on, stood in the way of an effective settlement. But things were getting desperate, and it was well for Edward that the security of his left flank at last enabled him to advance to the Conway. Thereupon Llewelyn returned to Snowdon, where he was joined by the homeless David. Meanwhile Tany, then master of Anglesey, opened up communications with the coast of Arvon by a bridge of boats over the Menai Straits. Winter was already at hand when Llewelyn and his brother were at last shut up amidst the fastnesses of Snowdon.

Late in October Archbishop Peckham appeared on the scene. He had excommunicated Llewelyn at the beginning of the war, but was still anxious to negotiate a peace. Edward did his best to put him off, but Peckham's importunity extorted from him a short truce, during which the primate visited Snowdon, taking with him an offer of an ample estate in England if

the prince would surrender his patrimony. Llewelyn furnished
Peckham with long catalogues of grievances. He was quite
willing to gain time by discussing his wrongs.

Edward's army shared his irritation at Peckham's interference, and, while the archbishop was still in Snowdon, a breach
of the truce destroyed any hopes of peace. On November 6
Tany led his troops over the bridge of boats at low water and
marched inland. But his operations were ill-planned, and the
Welsh came down from the hills and easily put him to flight.
Meanwhile the tide had risen and the flood cut off access to the
bridge over the Menai. In their panic the soldiers rushed into
the water rather than face the enemy. Many leading men were
drowned, including Tany himself, the author of the treachery.
Flushed with this success Llewelyn rejected Peckham's terms.
In great disgust the archbishop went back to England, bitterly
denouncing the Welsh. But defeat only strengthened the iron
resolution of Edward. He issued fresh summonses for men and
money. Contrary to all precedent, he determined to continue
the campaign through the winter.

Llewelyn was probably ignorant of the perilous plight into
which the king had fallen. With the approach of bad weather
he became afraid that he would be starved out in Snowdon.
Any risk was better than being caught like a rat in a trap, and,
fearing lest a cordon should be drawn round the mountains, he
made his way southwards, leaving David in command. His
enemy, Roger Mortimer, was just dead, and Mortimer's eldest
son Edmund, a youth brought up for the clerical profession, was
not likely to hold the middle marches with the same strong
grasp as his father. Thither accordingly Llewelyn made his
way, hoping that on his approach the tribesmen of the upper Wye,
over whom he had ruled so long, would abandon their English
lord for their Cymric chieftain. A force gathered round him, and
he occupied a strong position on a hill overlooking the river
Yrvon, which flows into the right bank of the Wye, just above
Builth. The right bank of the Yrvon was held by the English
of Builth. But the only way over the stream was by Orewyn
bridge, which was held by a detachment of the Welsh. Their
position seemed so secure that, on December 11, Llewelyn left
his troops to confer with some of the local chieftains. The
English were, however, shown a ford over the river; a band

11 *

CHAP.
VIII.

Death of Llewelyn.

crossed in safety, and, taking the defenders of Orewyn bridge in the rear, opened up the passage over it to their comrades. The English ascended the hill, their mail-clad squadrons interlaced with archers, in order that the Welsh infantry might be assailed by missiles before they were exposed to the shock of a cavalry charge. In the absence of their leader, the Welsh were a helpless mass of sheep, and were easily put to flight. Meanwhile Llewelyn, hearing the din of battle, hurried back to direct his followers. On the way he was slain by Stephen of Frankton, a Shropshire veteran of the Barons' War, who fought under the banner of Roger l'Estrange. The discovery of important papers on the body first told the conquerors the rank of their victim.

Thus perished the able and strenuous chief, who had struggled so long to win for himself in Wales a position similar to that occupied by the King of Scots in the north. His death did not end, but it much simplified, the struggle. The south and midland districts were entirely subdued, and the interest of the war again shifted to the mountains of Snowdon, where David strove to maintain himself as Prince of Wales. His best chance lay in the exhaustion of his enemy, but Edward stuck grimly to his task. His coffers were exhausted, and his army for the most part went home. Yet Edward tarried at Rhuddlan for over six months, dividing his energy between watching the Welsh and replenishing his treasure and troops. His treasurer, John Kirkby, wandered from shire to shire soliciting voluntary contributions. Then in January, 1283, an anomalous parliament was summoned, consisting mainly of ecclesiastics, knights of the shire, and burgesses, and meeting in two divisions, at York and at Northampton, according as the members came from the northern or southern ecclesiastical provinces. The grant of a thirtieth so little satisfied the king that he laid violent hands on the crusading-tenth, which was deposited in the Temple. Meanwhile the chivalry of Gascony and Ponthieu were tempted by high wages to supply the void left by the retirement of the English.

Early in 1283 a gallant force from beyond sea, among which figured the Counts of Armagnac and Bigorre, reached Rhuddlan. After their arrival the king took the offensive, crossed the Conway and transferred his headquarters to the

Cistercian abbey of Aberconway. Fearful once more of being enclosed in the mountains, David sought a new hiding-place among the heights of Cader Idris. He shifted his quarters to the castle of Bere, hidden away in a remote valley sloping down from the mountain to the sea. The unwearied Edward once more issued summonses for a fresh campaign. David was at the extremity of his resources. Before the new arrivals enabled Edward to move, William of Valence marched up from the south, and in April forced Bere to surrender. David fled before the siege began ; but he was a fugitive without an army, and the campaign was reduced to a weary tracking out of the last little bands that still scorned to surrender. In June David was betrayed by men of his own tongue, and Edward summoned for Michaelmas at Shrewsbury a parliament whose chief business was the trial of David. On October 3 the last Cymric Prince of Wales suffered the ignominious doom of a traitor, a murderer, and a blasphemer. The magnates then adjourned to the chancellor's neighbouring seat of Acton Burnell, where the rejoicings incident to the king's visit to his friend's new mansion were combined with passing the statute of Merchants.

Edward's love of thoroughness made him linger in Wales to settle the government of the newly won lands. His first care was to hold Snowdon with the ring of fortresses which, in their ruin, still bear abiding witness to the solidity of the conqueror's work. Round each castle arose a new town, created as artificially as were the *bastides* of Aquitaine, within whose walls English traders and settlers were tempted by high privileges to take up their abodes, and whose strictly military character was emphasised by the general provision that the constable of the castle was to be *ex officio* the mayor of the municipality. Chief among these was Aberconway, whose strategic importance Edward understood so fully that he forced the Cistercian monks to take up new quarters at Maenan, higher up the valley, in order that there might be room for the castle and town which were henceforth to guard the entrance to Snowdon. Equally important was the future capital of Gwynedd, Carnarvon, where on April 25, 1284, a son was born to Edward and Eleanor, who seventeen years later was to become the first English Prince of Wales. Elsewhere fortresses of Welsh origin were rebuilt and enlarged to complete the stone circuit round the mountains.

Such were Criccieth, the key of Lleyn; Dolwyddelen, which dominated the upper Conway; and Harlech and Bere, the two strongholds that curbed the mountaineers of Merioneth. In the south the same policy was carried out. Alike in Gwynedd and in the vale of Towy, both in his castle building and in his town foundations, Edward was simply carrying on the traditions of earlier ages, and applying to his new lands those principles of government which, since the Norman Conquest, had become the tradition of the marcher lords. Even in his architectural schemes there was nothing novel in Edward's policy. Gilbert of Gloucester at Caerphilly, and Payne of Chaworth at Kidwelly, had already worked out the pattern of "concentric" defences that were to find their fullest expression in the new castles of the principality. In each of these strongholds an adequate garrison of highly trained and well-paid troops kept the Welsh in check.

The civil government of the Edwardian conquests was provided for by the statute of Wales, issued on Mid-Lent Sunday, 1284, at Rhuddlan, Edward's usual headquarters. It declared that the land of Wales, heretofore subject to the crown in feudal right, was entirely transferred to the king's dominion. To the whole of the annexed districts the English system of shire government was extended, though such local customs as appealed to Edward's sense of justice were suffered to be continued. Gwynedd and its appurtenances were divided into the three shires of Anglesey, Carnarvon, and Merioneth, and were collectively put under the justice of Snowdon, whose seat was to be at Carnarvon, where courts of chancery and exchequer for north Wales were set up. The shires of Cardigan and Carmarthen were re-organised so as to include the southern districts which had been subject to Llewelyn, or to the Welsh lords who had fallen with him. These were put under the justice of west Wales, whose chancery and exchequer were established at Carmarthen. It is significant that Edward prepared the way for making these districts into shires by persuading his brother Edmund, to whom they had been granted, to abandon his claims over them in return for ample compensation elsewhere. Without this step the new shires would only have been palatinates of the Glamorgan or Pembroke type, and the creation of such franchises was directly contrary to Edward's policy. It was different

in the vale of Clwyd, where it would have been natural for
Edward to have extended the shire system to the four cantreds.
Military exigences had, however, already erected most of these
lands into new marcher lordships, and Edward was perforce
content with the union of some fragments of Rhos to the shire
of Carnarvon, and with joining together Englefield and some
adjoining districts in the new county of Flint. This arrangement secured the strongholds of Flint and Rhuddlan for the
king. But the district was too small to make it worth while
to set up a separate organisation for it, and Flintshire was put
under the justice and courts of Chester, so that it became a
dependency of the neighbouring palatinate.[1]

The lordships of the march were not directly influenced
by this legislation. They continued to hold their position as
franchises until the reign of Henry VIII., and under Edward
III. were declared by statute to be no part of the principality
but directly subject to the English crown. Yet the removal
of the pressure of a native principality profoundly affected these
districts. The policy of definition made its mark even here.
The liberties of each marcher were defined and circumscribed,
and, while scrupulously respected, were incapable of further extension. The vague jurisdictions of the sheriffs of the border
shires were cleared up, and if this process involved some limitation of the royal authority in districts like Clun and Oswestry,
which virtually ceased to be parts of Shropshire, there was a
compensating advantage in the increased clearness with which
the border line was drawn and the royal authority consolidated.
Gradually the marcher lordships passed by lapse into the royal
hands, and even from the beginning there were regions, such as
Montgomery and Builth, which knew no lord but the king. All
this was, however, an indirect result of the Edwardian conquest.
Strictly speaking it was no conquest of all Wales but merely
of the principality, the ancient dominions of Llewelyn, to which
most of the crown lands in Wales were joined.

Ecclesiastical settlement followed the political reorganisa-
tion. Peckham was as zealous as Edward in compelling the
conquered to follow the law-abiding traditions of the king's
ancient inheritance. He laboured strenuously for the rebuild-

[1] For the shires of Wales see my paper on *The Welsh Shires* in *Y Cymmrodor*,
ix. (1888), 201-26.

ing of churches, the preservation and extension of ecclesiastical property, the education of the clergy, and the extirpation of clerical matrimony and simony. Despite his unsympathetic attitude, he did good work for the Welsh Church by his manful resistance to all attempts of Edward and his subordinates to encroach upon her liberties. He quaintly thought it would promote the civilisation of Wales if the people were forced to "learn civility" by living in towns and sending their children to school in England. His assiduous visitation of the Welsh dioceses in 1284 did something to kindle zeal, and win the Welsh clergy from the idleness wherein, he believed, lay the root of all their shortcomings.

In the autumn of 1284 Edward went on an extended progress in Wales. He passed through the four cantreds into Gwynedd, and thence worked his way southwards through Cardigan and Carmarthen, ending his tour by visits to the marcher lords of the south. He crossed over from Glamorgan, where he had been entertained by Gilbert of Clare, to Bristol, where he held his Christmas court. Wales was to see no more of its new ruler for seven years. During that time the principality gave Edward little trouble, though the marchers, as will be seen, were a constant anxiety to him. In 1287, while Edward was in Gascony, the regent, Edmund of Cornwall, was called upon to deal with a revolt of Rhys, son of Meredith, the loyalist lord of the vale of Towy, who resented the authority of the justice of Carmarthen over his patrimony. His grievances were those of a marcher rather than those of a Welshman. Yet his rising in 1287 was formidable enough to require the raising of a great army for its suppression. The Welsh chieftain could not long hold out against the odds brought against him, and the confiscation of his lands swelled the district directly depending on the sheriff of Carmarthen. The support of the countryside enabled Rhys to evade his pursuers for nearly three years. At last he was captured, and with the execution of the last of the lords of Dynevor, the triumph of Edward became complete.

CHAPTER IX.

THE SICILIAN AND THE SCOTTISH ARBITRATIONS.

EDWARD I. had now attained the height of his fame. He had conquered Llewelyn; he had reformed the administration; he had put himself as a lawmaker in the same rank as St. Louis or Frederick II.; and he had restored England to a leading position in the councils of Europe. Moreover, he had won a character for justice and fairness which did him even greater service, since the several deaths of prominent sovereigns during 1285 left him almost alone of his generation among princes of a lesser stature. Of the chief rulers of Europe in the early years of Edward's reign, Rudolf of Hapsburg alone survived; and the King of the Romans had little weight outside Germany. Edward had outlived his brother-in-law Alfonso of Castile, his cousin Philip the Bold, his uncle Charles of Anjou, and Peter of Aragon. But the conflicts, in which these kings had been engaged, were continued by their successors. Above all, the contest for Sicily still raged. The successors of Martin IV., though deprived of the active support of France, would not abandon the claims of the captive Charles of Salerno; and James of Aragon, Peter's second son, maintained himself in Sicily, despite papal censures and despite the virtual desertion of his cause by his elder brother, Alfonso III., the new king of Aragon. Each side was at a standstill, though each side struggled on. The personal hatreds, which made it impossible to reconcile the older generation, were dying out, and the chief obstacle in the way of a settlement was the stubbornness of the papacy. If any one could reconcile the quarrel, it was the King of England; and to him Charles' sons and the nobles of his dominions appealed to procure his release.

Edward was anxious to proffer his services as a peacemaker.

The dream of a Europe, united for the liberation of the holy places, had not been expelled from his mind by his schemes for the advancement of his kingdom. If he could inspire his neighbour kings with something of his spirit, the crusade might still be possible. Other matters also called Edward's attention to the continent. He had to do homage to the new French king; he had to press for the execution of the treaty of Amiens, and his presence was again necessary in Gascony. His realm was in such profound peace that he could safely leave it. Accordingly in May, 1286, he took ship for France. With him went his wife Eleanor of Castile, his chancellor Bishop Burnell, and a large number of his nobles. He entrusted the regency to his cousin, Edmund, Earl of Cornwall, the son and successor of Earl Richard; and England saw him no more until August, 1289. Edward first made his way to Amiens, where he met the new King of France, Philip the Fair. The two kings went together to Paris, where Edward spent two months. There he performed homage for Gascony, and made a new agreement as to the execution of the treaty of Amiens, by which he renounced his claims over Quercy for a money payment, and was put in possession of Saintonge, south of the Charente. The settlement was the easier as for the moment neither king had his supreme interest in Gascony. Edward's real business was to make peace between Anjou and Aragon, and Philip IV. showed every desire to help him. Before Edward left Paris, he had negotiated a truce between the Kings of France and Aragon. Soon afterwards he went to Bordeaux. He made Gascony his headquarters for three years, and strove with all his might to convert the truce into a peace.

Grave obstacles arose, chief among which was the determination of the papacy to make no terms with the King of Aragon so long as his brother still reigned over Sicily. Honorius IV., in approving Edward's preliminary action, and exhorting him to obtain the liberation of the Prince of Salerno, carefully guarded himself against recognising the schismatic Aragonese. Edward himself was no partisan of either side. He was heartily anxious for peace and desirous to free his kinsman from the rigours of his long imprisonment. His wish for a close alliance between England and Aragon was unacceptable to the partisanship both of Honorius IV. and his

successor Nicholas IV. Papal coldness, however, did not turn
Edward from his course.   In the summer of 1287 he met
Alfonso at Oloron in Béarn, where a treaty was drawn up by
which the Aragonese king agreed to release Charles of Salerno
on condition that he would either, within three years, procure
from the pope the recognition of James in Sicily, or return
to captivity and forfeit Provence.   Besides this, an alliance
between England and Aragon was to be cemented by the
marriage of one of Edward's daughters to Alfonso.   Delighted
with the success of his undertaking, Edward, on his return
to Bordeaux, again took the cross and prepared to embark
on the crusade.

Nicholas IV. interposed between Edward and his vows by
denouncing the treaty of Oloron.[1]   Though well-meaning, he
was not strong enough to shake himself free from partisan traditions, and though honestly anxious to bring about a crusade,
he could not see that he made the holy war impossible by
interposing obstacles in the way of the one prince who seriously
intended to take the cross.   While denouncing Edward's treaty,
Nicholas encouraged his crusading zeal by granting him a new
ecclesiastical tenth for six years, a tax made memorable by the
fact that it occasioned the stringent valuation of benefices, called
the taxation of Pope Nicholas, which was the standard clerical
rate-book until the reign of Henry VIII.   Despite the pope,
Edward still persevered in his mediation, and in October, 1288,
a new treaty for Charles' liberation was signed at Canfranc, in
Aragon, which only varied in details from the agreement of
1287.   Charles was released, but he straightway made his way
to Rome, where Nicholas absolved him from his oath and
crowned him King of Sicily.   Edward was bitterly disappointed.   He tarried in the south until July, 1289, usefully
employed in promoting the prosperity of his duchy, crushing
conspiracies, furthering the commerce of Bordeaux, and founding new *bastides*.   At last tidings of disorder at home called
him back to his kingdom before the purpose of his continental
sojourn had been accomplished.   But he still pressed on his
thankless task, and in 1291 peace was made at Tarascon, between Aragon and the Roman see, on the hard condition of

---

[1] For his policy, see O. Schiff, *Studien zur Geschichte P. Nikolaus IV.* (1897).

CHAP.
IX.

Alfonso abandoning his brother's cause. On Alfonso's death soon afterwards the war was renewed, for James then united the Sicilian and Aragonese thrones and would not yield up either. It was not until 1295 that Boniface VIII., a stronger pope than Nicholas, ended the struggle on terms which left the stubborn Aragonese masters of Sicily.

Things had not gone well in England during Edward's absence. Edmund of Cornwall had shown vigour in putting down the revolt of Rhys, but he was not strong enough to control either the greater barons or the officers of the crown. Grave troubles were already brewing in Scotland. A fierce quarrel between the Earls of Gloucester and Hereford broke out with regard to the boundaries of Glamorgan and Brecon, and the private war between the two marchers proved more formidable to the peace of the realm than the revolt of the Welsh prince. Even more disastrous to the country was the scandalous conduct of the judges and royal officials, who profited by the king's absence to pile up fortunes at the expense of his subjects. The highest judges of the land forged charters, condoned homicides, sold judgments, and practised extortion and violence. A great cry arose for the king's return. In the Candlemas parliament of 1289 Earl Gilbert of Gloucester met a request for a general aid by urging that nothing should be granted until Englishmen once more saw the king's face. Alarmed at this threat, Edward returned, and landed at Dover on August 12, 1289.

The whole situation was changed by the king's arrival. Edward met the innumerable complaints against his subordinates by dismissing nearly all the judges from office, and appointing a special commission to investigate the charges brought against royal officials of every rank. Thomas Weyland, chief justice of the common pleas, anticipated inquiry by taking sanctuary with the Franciscan friars of Bury St. Edmunds. A knight and a married man, he had taken subdeacon's orders in early life and sought to little purpose to be protected by his clergy. His refuge was watched by the local sheriffs; finally, he was starved into surrender, and suffered to abjure the realm.[1] He fled to France, whence he never returned. For some years the

[1] For the *abjuratio regni* see A. Réville in the *Revue Historique*, l. (1892), 1-42.

commission investigated the offences of the ministers of the crown. Though much that was irregular was proved against them, many charges broke down under inquiry, and, as time went on, the official class saw that their interest lay in condoning rather than in punishing scandals. Some of the worst offenders, such as the greedy and corrupt Adam of Stratton, were never restored to office ;[1] but Hengham, the chief justice of the King's Bench, was soon reinstated. There were not enough good lawyers in England to make it prudent for Edward to dispense with the services of such a man. A rigorous maintenance of a high standard of official morality meant getting rid of nearly all the king's ministers, and any successors would have been inferior in experience and not superior in honesty. Edward had to work with such material as he had, and on the whole he made the best of it. Scandalous as were the proceedings of his agents, their iniquities are but trifles as compared with the offences of the counsellors of Philip the Fair.

Fear of Edward drove nobles into obedience as well as ministers into honesty. Gloucester desisted unwillingly from his attacks on Brecon, and was constrained to divorce his wife and marry the king's daughter, Joan of Acre. In becoming the king's son-in-law, he was forced to surrender his estates to the crown, receiving them back entailed on the heirs of the marriage or, in their default, on the heirs of Joan. Thus the system of entails made possible by the statute *De donis* was used by Edward to strengthen his hold over the most powerful of his feudatories and increase the prospect of his estates escheating to the crown. Considered in this light, Gilbert's marriage with the king's daughter seems less a reward of loyalty than a punishment for lawlessness. In the same year as this marriage, Edward passed another law directed against the baronage. This was the statute of Westminster the Third, called from its opening words, *Quia emptores.* It enacted that, when part of an estate was alienated by its lord, the grantee should not be permitted to become the subtenant of the grantor, but should stand to the ultimate lord of the fief in the same feudal relation

---

[1] For Adam of Stratton see Hall, *Red Book of the Exchequer*, iii., cccxv.-cccxxxi. Extracts from the Assize rolls recording the proceedings of the special commission will soon be published by the Royal Historical Society.

CHAP.
IX.

as the grantor himself. This prohibition of further subinfeuda-tion stopped the creation of new manors and prevented the rivetting of new links in the feudal chain, which were the necessary condition of its strength. Though passed at the re-quest of the barons, it was a measure much more helpful to the king than to his vassals. It stood to the barons as the statute of Mortmain stood to the Church.

Edward was bent on showing that he was master, and his new son-in-law and the Earl of Hereford became the victims of his policy. He forced the reluctant Gloucester to admit that the pretensions of the lord of Glamorgan to be the overlord of the bishop of Llandaff and the guardian of the temporalities of the see during a vacancy were usurpations. Seeing that his marcher prerogatives were thus rapidly becoming undermined, Gloucester put the most cherished marcher right to the test by renewing the private war with the Earl of Hereford which had disturbed the realm during Edward's absence. The king issued peremptory orders for the immediate cessation of hos-tilities. These mandates Hereford obeyed, but Gloucester did not. Resolved that law not force was henceforth to settle disputes in the march, Edward summoned a novel court at Ystradvellte, in Brecon, wherein a jury from the neighbouring shires and liberties was to decide the case between the two earls in the presence of the chief marchers. Gloucester refused to appear, and the marchers declined to take part in the trial, pleading that it was against their liberties. The case was adjourned to give the recalcitrants every chance, and after a preliminary report by the judges, Edward resolved to hear the suit in person. In October, 1291, he presided at Abergavenny over the court before which the earls were arraigned. They were condemned to imprisonment and forfeiture. Content with humbling their pride and annihilating their privileges, Edward suffered them to redeem themselves from captivity by the pay-ment of heavy fines, and before long gave them back their lands. The king's victory was so complete that neither of the earls could forgive it. In 1295, Gloucester died, without op-portunity of revenge ; but Hereford lived on, brooding over his wrongs, and in later years signally avenged the trial at Abergavenny. Meanwhile the conqueror of the principality had shown unmistakably that the liberties of the march were

an anachronism, since the marchers had no longer the work of
defending English interests against the Welsh nation.[1]

Another measure that followed Edward's home-coming was the expulsion of the Jews. Despite constant odium and intermittent persecution, the Jewish financiers who had settled in England after the Norman conquest steadily improved their position down to the reign of Henry III. The personal dependants of the crown, they were well able to afford to share their gains from usury with their protectors. They lived in luxury, built stone houses, set up an organisation of their own, and even purchased lands. Henry III.'s financial embarrassments forced him to rely upon them, and the alliance of the Jews and the crown stimulated the religious bigotry of the popular party to ill-treat the Jews during the Barons' War. Stories of Jews murdering Christian children were eagerly believed; and the cult of St. Hugh of Lincoln and St. William of Norwich,[2] two pretended victims of Hebrew cruelty, testified to the hatred which Englishmen bore to the race.

Under Edward I. the condition of the Jews became more precarious. The king hated them alike on religious and economical grounds. He rigorously insisted that they should wear a distinctive dress, and at last altogether prohibited usury. Driven from their chief means of earning their living, the Jews had recourse to clipping and sweating the coin. Indiscriminate severities did little to abate these evils. Meanwhile active missionary efforts were made to win over the Jews to the Christian faith. They were compelled to listen to long sermons from mendicant friars, and their obstinacy in adhering to their own creed was denounced as a deliberate offence against the light. Peckham shut up their synagogues, and Eleanor of Provence, who had entered a convent, joined with the archbishop in urging her son to take severe measures against them. There was a similar movement in France, and Edward, during his long stay abroad, had expelled the Jews from Aquitaine. In 1290 he applied the same policy to England, and their exile was so popular an act that parliament made him a special

---

[1] Mr. J. E. Morris in chap. vi. of his *Welsh Wars of Edward I.* has admirably summarised this suit. See also G. T. Clark's *Land of Morgan.*

[2] See for this saint, Thomas of Monmouth, *Life and Miracles of St. William of Norwich*, ed. Jessopp and James (1896).

CHAP. grant as a thankoffering. But though Edward thus drove the
IX. Jews to seek new homes beyond sea, he allowed them to carry
their property with them, and punished the mariners who took
advantage of the helplessness of their passengers to rob and
murder them. Though individual Jews were found from time
to time in England during the later middle ages, their official
re-establishment was only allowed in the seventeenth century.[1]

Two generations at least before their expulsion, the Jews
had been outrivalled in their financial operations by societies of
Italian bankers, whose admirable organisation and developed
system of credit enabled them to undertake banking operations of a magnitude quite beyond the means of the Hebrews.
First brought into England as papal agents for remitting to
Rome the spoils of the Church, they found means of evading
the canonical prohibitions of usury, and became the loan-
mongers of prince and subject alike. To the crown the Italians
were more useful than the Jews had been. The value of the
Jews to the monarch had been in the special facilities enjoyed
by him in taxing them. The utility of the Italian societies was
in their power of advancing sums of money that enabled the
king to embark on enterprises hitherto beyond the limited
resources of the medieval state. The Italians financed all
Edward's enterprises from the crusade of 1270 to his Welsh
and Scottish campaigns. From them Edward and his son
borrowed at various times sums amounting to almost half a
million of the money of the time. In return the Italians, chief
among whom was the Florentine Society of the Frescobaldi,
obtained privileges which made them as deeply hated as ever
the Hebrews had been.[2]

Among the troubles which had called Edward back from
Gascony was the condition of Scotland, where a long period
of prosperity had ended with the death of Edward's brother-
in-law, Alexander III., in 1286. Alexander III. attended his

---

[1] For the Jews see J. Jacobs, *Jews in Angevin England;* Tovey, *Anglia
Judaica;* J. M. Rigg, *Select Pleas of the Jewish Exchequer;* and for their exile
B. L. Abrahams, *Expulsion of the Jews from England in 1290.*

[2] See on this subject E. A. Bond's article in *Archæologia*, vol. xxviii., pp.
207-326; W. E. Rhodes, *Italian Bankers in England under Edward I. and II.*
in *Owens Coll. Historical Essays,* pp. 137-68; and R. J. Whitwell, *Italian
Bankers and the English Crown* in *Transactions of Royal Hist. Soc.,* N.S.,
xvii. (1903), pp. 175-234.

brother-in-law's coronation in 1274, and the irritation excited by his limiting his homage to his English lordships of Tynedale and Penrith did not cause any great amount of friction. But the homage question was only postponed, and at Michaelmas, 1278, Alexander was constrained to perform unconditionally this unwelcome act. " I, Alexander King of Scotland," were his words, " become the liege man of the lord Edward, King of England, against all men." But by carefully refraining from specifying for what he became Edward's vassal, Alexander still suggested that it was for his English lordships. Edward with equal caution declared that he received the homage, "saving his right and claim to the homage of Scotland when he may wish to speak concerning it". Both parties were content with mutual protestations. Edward was so friendly to Alexander that he allowed him to appoint Robert Bruce, Earl of Carrick, his proxy in professing fealty, so as to minimise the king's feeling of humiliation. The King of Scots went home loaded with presents, and for the rest of his life his relations with Edward remained cordial.

The closing years of Alexander's reign were overshadowed by domestic misfortunes and the prospects of difficulties about the succession. His wife, Margaret of England, had died in 1275, and was followed to the tomb by their two sons, Alexander and David. A delicate girl, Margaret, then alone represented the direct line of the descendants of William the Lion. Margaret was married, when still young, to Eric, King of Norway, and died in 1283 in giving birth to her only child, a daughter named Margaret. No children were born of Alexander's second marriage; and in March, 1286, the king broke his neck, when riding by night along the cliffs of the coast of Fife. Before his death, however, he persuaded the magnates of Scotland to recognise his granddaughter as his successor. The Maid of Norway, as Margaret was called, was proclaimed queen, and the administration was put into the hands of six guardians, who from 1286 to 1289 carried on the government with fair success. As time went on, the baronage got out of hand and a feud between the rival south-western houses of Balliol and Bruce foreshadowed worse troubles.

William Fraser, Bishop of St. Andrews, the chief of the regents, visited Edward in Gascony and urged the necessity of

CHAP.
IX.

action. The best solution of all problems was that the young Queen of Scots should be married to Edward of Carnarvon, a boy a few months her junior. But both the Scots nobles and the King of Norway were jealous and suspicious, and any attempt to hurry forward such a proposal would have been fatal to its accomplishment. However, negotiations were entered into between England, Scotland, and Norway. In 1289 the guardians of Scotland agreed to nominate representatives to treat on the matter. Edward took up his quarters at Clarendon, while his agents, conspicuous among whom was Anthony Bek, Bishop of Durham, negotiated with the envoys of Norway and Scotland. On November 6 the three powers concluded the treaty of Salisbury, by which they agreed that Margaret should be sent to England or Scotland before All Saints' Day, 1290, "free and quit of all contract of marriage or espousals". Edward promised that if Margaret came into his custody he would, as soon as Scotland was tranquil, hand her over to the Scots as "free and quit" as when she came to him; and the "good folk of Scotland" engaged that, if they received their queen thus free, they would not marry her "save with the ordinance, will, and counsel of Edward and with the agreement of the King of Norway". In March, 1290, a parliament of Scots magnates met at Brigham, near Kelso, and ratified the treaty. Fresh negotiations were begun for the marriage of Edward of Carnarvon and the Queen of Scots, resulting in the treaty of Brigham of July 18, which Edward confirmed a month later at Northampton. By this Edward agreed that, in the event of the marriage taking place, the laws and customs of Scotland should be perpetually maintained. Should Margaret die without issue, Scotland was to go to its natural heir, and in any case was to remain "separate and divided from the realm of England".

The treaty of Brigham was as wise a scheme as could have been devised for bringing about the unity of Britain. In the care taken to meet the natural scruples of the smaller nation we are reminded of the treaty of Union of 1707. But a nearer parallel is to be found in the conditions under which the union between France and Brittany was gradually accomplished after the marriage of Anne of Brittany. In both cases alike, in France and in England, the stronger party was content with securing the personal union of the two crowns, and strove to

reconcile the weaker party by providing safeguards against CHAP.
violent or over-rapid amalgamation.   It was left for the future   IX.
to decide whether the habit of co-operation, continued for generations, might not ultimately involve a more organic union.
Unluckily for this island, the policy which ultimately made
the stubborn Celts of Brittany content with union with France,
never had a chance of being carried out here.   Edward made
every preparation for bringing over the Maid of Norway
to her kingdom and her husband, and neither the Scots nor
the Norwegians grudged his leading share in accomplishing
their common wishes.   But the child's health gave way before
the hardships of the journey.   Before All Saints' day had come
round, she died in one of the Orkneys, where the ship which
conveyed her had put in.

The death of the queen threatened Scotland with revolution.
The regents' commission became of doubtful legality, and a
swarm of claimants for the vacant throne arose, whose resources,
if not their rights, were sufficiently evenly balanced to make civil
strife inevitable.   Since southern Scotland had become a wholly
feudal, largely Norman, and partly English state, there had been
no grave difficulties with regard to the succession.   Now that
they arose, there was doubt as to the principles on which claims
to the throne should be settled.   There was no legitimate representative left of the stock of William the Lion.   The male
line of his brother David, Earl of Huntingdon, had died out
with John the Scot, the last independent Earl of Chester.   The
nearest claimants to the succession were therefore to be found
in the descendants of David's three daughters.   But there was
no certainty that any rights could be transmitted through the
female line.   Moreover there was a doubt whether, allowing
that a woman could transmit the right to rule, the succession
should proceed according to primogeniture or in accordance
with the nearness of the claimant to the source of his claim.
If the former view were held then John of Balliol, lord of
Barnard castle in Durham and of Galloway in Scotland, had
the best right as the grandson of Earl David's eldest daughter.
Yet less than a century before, the passing over of Arthur of
Brittany in favour of his uncle John, had recalled to men's mind
the ancient doctrine that a younger son is nearer to the parent
stock than a grandson sprung from his elder brother; and if the

CHAP.
IX.

view, then expressed in the *History of William the Marshal*,[1] was still to hold good, Robert Bruce, lord of Skelton in Yorkshire, and of Annandale in the northern kingdom, was the nearest in blood to David of Huntingdon as the son of his second daughter. Beyond this there was the further question of the divisibility of the kingdom. So fully was southern Scotland feudalised that it seemed arguable that the monarchy, or at least its demesne lands, might be divided among all the representatives of the coheiresses, after the fashion in which the Huntingdon estates had been allotted to all the representatives of Earl David. In that case John of Hastings, lord of Abergavenny, put in a claim as the grandson of Earl David's youngest daughter.

When so much was uncertain, every noble who boasted any connexion with the royal house safeguarded his interests, or advertised his pedigree, by enrolling himself among the claimants. Five or six of the competitors had no better ground of right than descent from bastards of the royal house, especially from the numerous illegitimate offspring of William the Lion. The others went back to more remote ancestors. A foreign prince, Florence, Count of Holland, demanded the succession as a descendant of a sister of Earl David, declaring that David had forfeited his rights by rebellion. John Comyn, lord of Badenoch, brought forward his descent from Donaldbane, brother of Malcolm Canmore. One claim reads like a fairy tale, with stories of an unknown king dying, leaving a son to be murdered by a wicked uncle, and a daughter to escape to obscurity in Ireland, where she married and transmitted her rights to her children. There was no authority in Scotland strong enough to decide these claims. Once more Robert Bruce raised the standard of disorder, and the appeal of Bishop Fraser to Edward to undertake the settlement of the question showed that the English king's mediation was the readiest way of restoring order.

In 1291 Edward summoned the magnates of both realms,

---

[1] *Hist. de Guillaume le Maréchal*, ii., 64, ll. 11899-902.
　　Oïl, sire, quer c'est raison
　　Quer plus près est sanz achaison
　　Le filz de la terre son père
　　Que le niés : dreiz est qu'il i père.

along with certain popular representatives, to meet at Norham, CHAP.
Bishop Bek's border castle on the Tweed. Trained civilians and IX.
canonists also attended, while abbeys and churches contributed
extracts from chronicles, carefully compiled by royal order, with
a view of illustrating the king's claims. On May 10 Edward met
the assembly in Norham parish church. Roger Brabazon, the
chief justice, declared in the French tongue that Edward was
prepared to do justice to the claimants as "superior and direct
lord of Scotland". Before, however, he could act, his master
required that his overlordship should be recognised by the
Scots. It is likely that this demand was not unexpected.
Even in the treaty of Brigham Edward had been careful not to
withdraw his claim of superiority, and his action with relation
to Alexander III.'s homage was well known. But the sensi-
tiveness which their late king had shown in the face of Edward's
earlier claims was shared by the Scots lords, and shrinking from
recognising facts which they ought to have faced before they
solicited his intervention, they begged for delay and drew up
remonstrances. Edward granted them a respite for three
weeks, though he swore by St. Edward that he would rather die
than diminish the rights due to the Confessor's crown. He had
already summoned the northern levies, and was prepared to
enforce his claim by force. His uncompromising attitude put
the Scots in an awkward position. But they had gone to
Norham to get his help, and they were not prepared to run the
risk of an English invasion as well as civil war. Most of the
claimants had as many interests in England as in Scotland, and
a breach with Edward would involve the forfeiture of their
southern lands as well as the loss of a possible kingdom in
the north. When the magnates reassembled, the competitors
set the example of acknowledging Edward as overlord. Fresh
demands followed their submission, and were at once conceded.
Edward was to have seisin of Scotland and its royal castles,
though he pledged himself to return both land and fortresses
to him who should be chosen king.

Edward then undertook the examination of the suit. He
delegated the hearing of the claims to a commission, of whom
the great majority, eighty, were Scotsmen, nominated in equal
numbers by Bruce and Balliol, the two senior competitors,
while the remaining twenty-four consisted of Englishmen, and

included many of Edward's wisest counsellors. In deference to Scottish feeling, Edward ordered the court to meet on Scottish territory, at Berwick, and appointed August 2 for the opening day. Meanwhile the full consequences of the Scottish submission were carried out. On Edward's taking seisin of Scotland, the regency came to an end. The nomination of the provisional government resting with Edward, he reappointed the former regents, and allowed the Scots barons to elect their chancellor. But with the regents Edward associated a northern baron, Brian Fitzalan of Bedale, and the Scottish bishop, who was appointed chancellor, had to act jointly with one of Edward's clerks. Edward then made a short progress, reaching as far as Stirling and St. Andrews. He was back at Berwick for the meeting of the commissioners on August 2.

The first session of the court was a brief one. The twelve competitors put in their claims, and Bruce and Balliol supported theirs by argument. However, on August 12, the trial was adjourned for nearly a year, until June 2, 1292. On its resumption in Edward's presence, the more difficult issues were carefully worked out. A new and fantastic claim, sent in by Eric of Norway, as the nearest of kin to his daughter, did not delay matters. The judges were instructed to settle in the first instance the relative claims of Bruce and Balliol, and also to decide by what law these should be determined. On October 14, they declared their first judgment. They rejected Bruce's plea that the decision should follow the "natural law by which kings rule," and accepted Balliol's contention that they should follow the laws of England and Scotland. They further laid down that the law of succession to the throne was that of other earldoms and dignities. They pronounced in favour of primogeniture as against proximity of blood.

These decisions practically settled the case, but a further adjournment was resolved upon, and upon the reassembling of the court on November 6 the only question still open, that of whether the kingdom could be divided, was taken up. John of Hastings came on the scene with the contention that the monarchy should be divided among the representatives of Earl David's daughters. Bruce had the effrontery to associate himself with Hastings' demand. A short adjournment was arranged to settle this issue, and on November 17 the final scene

took place in the hall of Berwick castle.   Besides the commissioners, the king was there in full parliament, and eleven
claimants, who still persevered, were present or represented by
proxy.   Nine of these were severally told that they would
obtain nothing by their petitions.   Bruce was informed that his
claim to the whole was incompatible with his present claim for
a third.   It was laid down that the kingdom of Scotland was
indivisible, and that the right of Balliol had been established.

The seal of the regency was broken : Edward handed over
the seisin of Scotland to John Balliol, who three days later
took the oath of fealty as King of Scots, promising that he
would perform all the service due to Edward from his kingdom.
Balliol hurried to his kingdom, and was crowned at Scone on
St. Andrew's day.   He then returned to England, and kept
Christmas with his overlord at Newcastle, where, on December
26, he did homage to Edward in the castle hall.   But within a
few days a difficulty arose.   John resented Edward's retaining
the jurisdiction over a law-suit in which a Berwick merchant,
a Scotsman, was a party.   He was reassured by Edward that
he only did so, because the case had arisen during the vacancy,
when Edward was admittedly ruling Scotland.   But Edward
significantly added a reservation of his right of hearing appeals,
even in England; and when the King of Scots went back to
his realm, early in January, he must have already foreseen that
there was trouble to come.

Edward never lost sight of his own interests, and it is clear
that he took full advantage of the needs of the Scots to establish a close supremacy over the northern kingdom.   Making
allowance for this sinister element, his general policy in dealing
with the great suit had been singularly prudent and correct.
He was anxious to ascertain the right heir ; he gave the Scots
a preponderating voice in the tribunal ; he rejected the temptation which Bruce and Hastings dangled before him of splitting
up the realm into three parts, and he restored the land and its
castles as soon as the suit was settled.   There is nothing to
show that up to this point his action had produced any resentment in Scotland, and little evidence that there was any strong
national feeling involved.   Scottish chroniclers, who wrote after
the war of independence, have given a colour to Edward's policy
which contemporary evidence does not justify.   From the stand-

point of his generation, his action was just and legal. He had, in fact, performed a signal service to Scotland in vindicating its unity; and by maintaining the rigid doctrines of Anglo-Norman jurisprudence, he rescued it from the vague philosophy which Bruce called natural law, and the recrudescence of Celtic custom that gave even bastards a hope of the succession. The real temptation came when, after his triumph, Edward sought to extract from the submission of the Scots consequences which had no warranty in custom, and made Scottish resistance inevitable.

The expulsion of the Jews, the reform of the administration, the statute *Quia emptores*, the treaty of Tarascon, the humiliation of Gloucester, and the successful issue of the Scottish arbitration, mark the culminating point in the reign of Edward I. The king had ruled twenty years with almost uniform success, and his only serious disappointment had been the failure of the crusade. The last hope of the Latin East faded when, in 1291, Acre, so long the bulwark of the crusaders against the Turks, opened its gates to the infidel. With the fall of Acre went the last chance of the holy war. Before long the peace of Europe, which Edward thought that he had established, was once more rudely disturbed. Difficulties soon arose with Scotland, with France, with the Church, and with the barons. These troubles bore the more severely on the king because this period saw also the removal of nearly all of those in whom he had placed special trust. The gracious Eleanor of Castile died in 1290, at Harby, in Nottinghamshire, near Lincoln,[1] and the devotion of the king to the partner of his youth found a striking expression in the sculptured crosses, which marked the successive resting-places of her corpse on its last journey from Harby to Westminster Abbey. A few months later Edward's mother, Eleanor of Castile, ended her long life in the convent of Amesbury, in Wiltshire. The ministers of Edward's early reign were also removed by death. Bishop Kirkby, the treasurer, died in 1290, and Burnell, the chancellor, in 1292, soon after he had performed his last public act in the declaration of the king's judgment as to the Scottish succession. Archbishop Peckham died in the same year. New domestic ties were formed,

---

[1] See for this W. H. Stevenson, *Death of Eleanor of Castile*, in *English Hist. Review*, iii. (1888), pp. 315-318.

and fresh ministers were found, but the ageing king became CHAP. IX.
more and more lonely, as he was compelled to rely upon a
younger and a less faithful generation. Of his old comrades
the chief remaining was Henry Lacy, Earl of Lincoln, while
the removal of Burnell brought forward to the first rank
prelates whose position had hitherto been somewhat obscured
by his predominance. Prominent among these were the
brothers Thomas Bek, Bishop of St. David's, and Anthony
Bek, Bishop of Durham, members of a conspicuous Lincolnshire
baronial family. Both of these for a time strikingly combined
devotion to the royal service with loyalty to those clerical
and aristocratic traditions which, strictly interpreted, were
almost incompatible with faithful service to a secular monarch.
Even more important henceforth was the king's treasurer,
Walter Langton, Bishop of Lichfield, the most trusted minister
of Edward's later life, a faithful but not too scrupulous prelate
of the ministerial type, who stood to the second half of the
reign in almost the same close relation as that in which Burnell
stood to the years which we have now traversed.

CHAPTER X.

THE FRENCH AND SCOTTISH WARS AND THE CONFIRMATION OF THE CHARTERS.

CHAP.
X.

TROUBLES arose between France and England soon after Edward had settled the Scottish succession. Neither Edward nor Philip the Fair sought a conflict. Edward was satisfied with his diplomatic successes, and Philip's designs upon Gascony were better pursued by chicane than by warfare. But questions arose of a different kind from the disputes as to feudal right, which had been hitherto the principal matters in debate between the two crowns.

There had long been keen commercial rivalry between the Cinque Ports and the traders of Normandy. The sailors of Bayonne and other Gascon harbours had associated themselves with the English against the Normans, and both sides loudly complained to their respective rulers of the piracies and homicides committed by their enemies. Edward and Philip did what they could to smooth over matters, but were alike unable to prevent their subjects flying at each other's throats. The story spread that a Norman ship was to be seen in the Channel with English sailors and dogs hanging suspended from her yard-arms: "And so," says Hemingburgh, "they sailed over the sea, making no difference between a dog and an Englishman". Indignation at this outrage drove the English to act together in large organised squadrons. The French adopted the same tactics, and a collision soon ensued. On May 15, 1293, an Anglo-Gascon merchant fleet encountered a Norman fleet off Saint Mahé in Brittany. A pitched battle, probably prearranged, at once ensued. It ended in a complete victory for the less numerous English squadron, which immediately returned to Portsmouth, laden with booty.

Even after this, Edward strove to keep the peace, and CHAP.
endeavoured to exact compensation from his subjects. They ^X.^
answered with a highly coloured narrative of the dispute which
threw the whole blame upon the Normans. Philip, changing
his policy, took up his subjects' cause, and summoned Edward
to answer in January, 1294, before the Parliament of Paris for
the piracy exercised by his mariners, the misdeeds of his Gascon
subjects, and the violent measures taken by his officers against
any who appealed to the court of Paris. Edward sent his
brother, Edmund, to reply for him. As Count of Champagne
and the step-father of Philip's wife, Joan, Edmund seemed a
peculiarly acceptable negotiator. After long debates, the personal intervention of the French queen, and Philip's step-mother,
Mary of Brabant, resulted in an agreement being arranged. The
overlord's grievances could not be denied, and it was urged that
the formal surrender of part of Gascony might be made by way
of recognising them. French garrisons were therefore to be
admitted into six Gascon strongholds; twenty Gascon hostages
were to be delivered over to Philip, while the seisin of the duchy
was also to be transferred to the French king, who pledged
himself not to change the officials nor to occupy the land in
force. The whole business was in fact to be as formal as the
delivery of the seisin of Scotland to Edward during the suit for
the succession. Meanwhile, Edward and Philip were to arrange
a meeting at Amiens to settle the conditions of a permanent
peace, by which Edward was to take Philip's sister, Margaret, as
his second wife, and the Gascon duchy was to be settled upon
the offspring of the union. That Edward or Edmund should
ever have contemplated such terms is a strong proof of their
zeal for peace. It soon became clear that Edmund had been
outrageously duped, and that the whole negotiation was a trick
to secure for Philip the permanent possession of Gascony. The
constable of France appeared on the Aquitanian frontier. The
English seneschal surrendered the six castles and the seisin of
the land. Gradually the French king began to take actual
possession of the government. Moreover, after three months,
the proceedings against Edward in the parliament of Paris were
resumed; Edward was declared contumacious on the ground
of his non-appearance, and sentence of forfeiture was passed.

Philip's treachery was thus manifest, and in great disgust

CHAP.   Edmund withdrew from France.   Edward was deeply indignant.
  X.   In a parliament, held in June, 1294, which was attended by
       the King of Scots, war was resolved upon.   The feudal tenants
       were summoned to assemble at Portsmouth on September 1 ;
       and Edward appealed for help to his Gascon subjects, beseech-
       ing their pardon for having negotiated the fatal treaty, and
       promising a speedy effort to restore them to his obedience.
       He sent them his nephew, John of Brittany, as his lieutenant
       and captain-general, under whom John of St. John was to act
       as seneschal of Gascony.   Ambassadors were despatched to all
       neighbouring courts to build up a coalition against the French.
       Strenuous efforts were made to get together men and money,
       and the clergy were forced to make a grant of a half of their
       spiritual income.   Edward overbore their opposition amidst a
       scene of excitement in which the Dean of St. Paul's fell dead
       at the king's feet.   The shires were mulcted of a tenth and the
       boroughs of a sixth.   And besides these constitutional exactions,
       the king laid violent hands on all the coined money deposited
       in the treasuries of the churches, and appropriated the wool of
       the merchants, which he only restored on the payment of a
       heavy pecuniary redemption.   Meanwhile, about Michaelmas
       the lieutenant and the seneschal sailed with a fairly strong force.
       Further levies were summoned to assemble at Portsmouth at
       later dates.   Besides the ordinary tenants of the crown, writs
       were sent to the chief magnates of Ireland and Scotland ; and
       Wales and its march were called upon to furnish all the men
       that could be mustered.   The Earls of Cornwall and Lincoln
       were appointed to the command, and Edward himself proposed
       to follow them to Gascony as soon as he could.

           At the moment of the departure of John of Brittany a
       sudden insurrection in Wales frustrated Edward's plans.   All
       Wales was ripe for revolt.   In the principality the Cymry re-
       sented English rule, and the sulky marchers stood aloof in
       sullen discontent, while their native tenants, seeing in the recent
       humiliation of Gloucester and Hereford the degradation of all
       their lords, lost respect for such powerless masters.   Both in
       the principality and in the marches, Edward's demand for
       compulsory service in Gascony was universally regarded as a
       new aggression.   The intensity of the resistance to his demand
       can be measured by the general nature of the insurrection, and

by the admirable way in which it was organised. As by a common signal all Wales rose at Michaelmas, 1294. One Madog, probably a bastard son of Llewelyn, son of Griffith, raised all Gwynedd, took possession of Carnarvon castle, and closely besieged the other royal strongholds. In west Wales a chieftain named Maelgwn was equally successful in Carmarthen and Cardigan. The marches were in arms equally with the principality. In the north, Lincoln's tenants in Rhos and Rhuvoniog besieged Denbigh, and threatened the king's fortresses in Flint. Maelgwn's sphere of operations included the earldom of Pembroke, while Brecon rose against Hereford, and Glamorgan against Gilbert of Gloucester. Morgan, the leader of the Glamorganshire rebels, loudly declared that he did not rebel against the king but against the Earl of Gloucester. With the beginning of winter the state of Wales was more critical than in the worst times of the winter of 1282.

Edward postponed his attack on Philip in order to throw all his energies into the reduction of Wales. The levies assembled at Portsmouth for the Gascon expedition were hurried beyond the Severn. The king held another parliament and exacted a fresh supply. Criminals were offered pardon and good wages, if they would serve, first in Wales and then in Gascony. Before Christmas about a thousand men-at-arms were mustered at various border centres under the royal standards, while every marcher lord was busily engaged in putting down his own rebels. Before so great a force the Welsh could do but little, and the spring saw the extinction of the rebellion. But there was hard fighting both in the south and in the north. Edward himself undertook the reconquest of Gwynedd. He was at Conway before the end of the year, and in his haste he threw himself into the town while the mass of his army remained on the right bank of the river. High tides and winter floods made the crossing of the stream impossible, and for a short time the king was actually besieged by the rebels. Conway was unprepared for resistance and almost destitute of supplies. The garrison thought it a terrible hardship that they had to live on salt meat and bread, and to drink water mixed with honey. They were encouraged by Edward refusing to taste better fare than his troopers, and declining to partake of the one small measure of wine reserved for his use. William Beauchamp,

CHAP.   Earl of Warwick, conveyed his troops across the estuary and
 X.   raised the siege. Yet the insurgents were still able to fight a
pitched battle. About January 22, 1295, Warwick found the
Welsh established in a strong position in a plain between two
woods. They had fixed the butts of their lances into the ground,
hoping thus to resist the shock of a cavalry charge. Improving
on the tactics of Orewyn bridge, the earl stationed between his
squadrons of knights, archers and crossbowmen, whose missiles
inflicted such loss on the Welsh lines that the cavalry soon
found it safe to charge. The Welsh were utterly broken, and
never in a single day did they suffer such enormous losses.
Even more important than its results in breaking the back of
Madog's insurrection, this battle of Maes Madog—or Madog's
field, as the Welsh called the place of their defeat—is of the
highest importance in the development of infantry tactics.
The order of the victorious force strikingly anticipates the
great battles in Scotland and France of a later generation. In
obscure fights, like Orewyn bridge and Maes Madog, the English learnt the famous battle array which was to overwhelm
the Scots in the later years of Edward's reign and prepare the
way for the triumphs of Crecy and Poitiers.

Madog still held out, and with the advent of spring, 1295,
Edward began to hunt him from his lairs. Gwynedd was cleared
of the enemy and Anglesey was reconquered. Carnarvon castle
arose from its ruins in the stately form that we still know, while
on the Anglesey side of the Menai the new stronghold of
Beaumaris arose, to ensure the subjection of the granary of
Gwynedd. In May Edward felt strong enough to undertake
a progress in South Wales. After receiving the submissions of
the rebels of Cardigan and Carmarthen, he won back for the
lords of Brecon and Glamorgan the lands which, without his
help, they had been unable to conquer. The Welsh chieftains
were leniently treated. While Madog was imprisoned in the
Tower, Morgan was at once set at liberty. By July Edward
was able to leave Wales. Yet his triumph had taxed all his
resources, and left him, overwhelmed with debt, to face the
irritation of subjects unaccustomed to such demands upon their
loyalty and patriotism. But nothing broke his dauntless spirit,
and once more he busied himself in obtaining revenge on the
false King of France.

It was inevitable that the Welsh war should have reduced to slender proportions the expedition of John of Brittany and John of St. John for the recovery of Gascony. After a tedious voyage the English expedition sailed up the Gironde late in October, 1294. Their forces, strong enough to capture Bourg and Blaye, were not sufficient to attack Bordeaux. Leaving the capital in the hands of its conquerors, the English sailed past Bordeaux to Rioms, where they disembarked. The small towns of the neighbourhood were taken and garrisoned, and the Gascon lords began to flock to the camp of their duke. Before long the army was large enough to be divided. John of Brittany remained at Rioms, while John of St. John marched overland to Bayonne. The French garrison was unable to overpower the enthusiasm of the Bayonnais for Edward, and the capture of the second town of Gascony was the greatest success attained by the invaders. With the spring of 1295, however, Charles of Valois, brother of the King of France, was sent to operate against John of Brittany. The English and Gascons found themselves unable to make head against him. There was ill-feeling between the two nations that made up the army, and also between the nobly-born knights and men-at-arms and the foot soldiers. The infantry mutinied, and John of Brittany fled by night down the river from Rioms, leaving many of his knights and all his horses and armour in the town. Next day Rioms opened its gates to Charles of Valois, who gained immense spoils and many distinguished prisoners. Save for the capture of Bayonne, the expedition had been a disastrous failure.

Edward failed even more signally in his efforts to defeat Philip by diplomacy. He had left no effort unspared to build up a great coalition against the French king. He "sent a great quantity of sterling money beyond the sea," and made alliances with all the princes and barons that he could find.[1] At first it seemed that he had succeeded. Adolf of Nassau, the poor and dull, but strenuous and hard-fighting King of the Romans, concluded a treaty with England, and did not think it beneath the dignity of the lord of the world to take the pay of the English monarch. Many vassals of the empire, especially in the Netherlands, the Rhineland, and Burgundy followed Adolf's

---

[1] See a contemporary notice printed by F. Funck-Brentano in *Revue Historique*, xxxix. (1889), pp. 329-30.

example. Edward strengthened his party further by marrying three of his daughters to the Duke of Brabant, the son of the Count of Holland, and the Count of Bar as the price of their adherence to the coalition. He made closer his ancient friendship with Guy of Dampierre, the old Count of Flanders, by betrothing Edward of Carnarvon to his daughter Philippine. At the same time he sought the friendship of the lords of the Pyrenees, such as the Count of Foix, and of the kings of the Spanish peninsula. But nothing came of the hopes thus excited, save fair promises and useless expenditure. Before long Philip of France was able to build up a French party in appearance as formidable—in reality as useless as Edward's attempted confederation. Edward's most important ally, Guy of Flanders, was forced to renounce his daughter's marriage to the heir of England and hand her over to Philip's custody. The time was not yet come for effective European coalitions; the real fighting had to be done by the parties directly interested in the quarrel.

The command of the sea continued to be a vital question. The Norman sailors were eager to avenge their former defeats, and Philip saw that the best way to preserve his hold over Gascony was to be master of the Channel and the Bay of Biscay. Edward prepared to meet attack by establishing an organisation of the English navy which marks an epoch in the history of our admiralty. He divided the vessels told off to guard the sea into three classes, and set over each a separate admiral. John of Botecourt was made admiral of the Yarmouth and eastern fleet ; William of Leyburn was set over the navy at Portsmouth ; and the western and Irish squadron was put under a valiant knight of Irish origin. Meanwhile the French planned an invasion of England, and promised James of Aragon that, when England was conquered, its king should be considered his personal prize. Galleys were hired at Marseilles and Genoa for service in the Channel, and Sir Thomas Turberville, a Glamorganshire knight captured at Rioms, turned traitor and was restored to England in the hope that he might obtain the custody of some seaport and betray it to the enemy. Turberville strove in vain to induce Morgan to head another revolt in Glamorgan, and urged upon Philip the need of an alliance with the Scots. At last the invasion was attempted, and the French admiral, Matthew of Montmorenci, sacked and burnt the town of Dover.

Luckily, however, Turberville's treason was discovered, and the Yarmouth fleet soon avenged the attack on Dover by burning Cherbourg. In the face of such resistance, Philip IV. abandoned his plan of invasion and tried to establish a sort of "continental blockade" of English ports in which a modern writer has seen an anticipation of the famous dream of Napoleon.[1] Though nothing came of these grandiose schemes, yet the efforts made to organise invasion had their permanent importance as resulting in the beginnings of the French royal navy. As late as 1297 a Genoese was appointed admiral of France in the Channel, and strongly urged the invasion of England and its devastation by fire and flame. But the immediate result of Philip's efforts to cut off England from the continent was that his Flemish allies found in his policy a new reason for abandoning his service. On January 7, 1297, a fresh treaty of alliance between Edward and Guy, Count of Flanders, was concluded.

More effective than Philip's efforts to combine the Continent against the English were his endeavours to stir up opposition to Edward in Britain. The Welsh rising of 1294 had taken place independently of him, but it was not Philip's fault that Morgan did not once more excite Glamorgan to rebellion. A better opening for intrigue was found in Scotland. Ever since the accession of John Balliol, there had been appeals from the Scottish courts to those of Edward. Certain suits begun under the regency, which had acted in Edward's name from 1290 to 1292, gave the overlord an opportunity of inserting the thin end of the wedge; and it looked as if, after a few years, appeals from Edinburgh to London would be as common as appeals from Bordeaux to Paris. But whatever were the ancient relations of England and Scotland, it is clear that the custom of appeals to the English king had never previously been established. It was no wonder then that what seemed to Edward an inevitable result of King John's submission, appeared to the Scots an unwarrantable restriction of their independence.

The weakness and simplicity of King John left matters to take their course for a time, but the king, who was not strong

---

[1] See for this Jourdain, *Mémoire sur les Commencements de la Marine française sous Philippe le Bel* (1880), and C. de la Roncière, *Le Blocus continental de l'Angleterre sous Philippe le Bel* in *Revue des Questions historiques,* lx. (1896), 401-41.

enough to stand up against Edward, was not the man to resist the pressure of his own subjects. On his return from the London parliament of June, 1294, the Scots barons virtually deposed him. A committee was set up by parliament consisting of four bishops, four earls, and four barons which, though established professedly on the model of the twelve peers of France, had a nearer prototype in the fifteen appointed under the Provisions of Oxford. To this body the whole power of the Scottish monarchy was transferred, so that John became a mere puppet, unable to act without the consent of his twelve masters. Under this new government the relations of England and Scotland soon became critical. The Scots denied all right of appeal to the English courts, and expelled from their country the nobles whose possessions in England gave them a greater interest in the southern than in the northern kingdom. Among the dispossessed barons was Robert Bruce, son of the claimant, by marriage already Earl of Carrick, and now by his father's recent death lord of Annandale. In defiance of Edward's prohibition the Scots received French ships, and subjected English traders at Berwick to many outrages. At last, on July 5, 1295, an alliance was signed between Scotland and France, by which Edward Balliol, the eldest son of King John, was betrothed to Joan, the eldest daughter of Charles of Valois, the brother of the French king. On this, Edward demanded the surrender of three border castles, and on the refusal of the Scots, cited John to appear at Berwick on March 1, 1296. Thus, by a process similar to that which had embroiled Edward with his French overlord, the King of Scots also was forced to face the alternative of certain war or humiliating surrender.

To Edward a breach with Scotland was unwelcome. In 1294 the Welsh had prevented him using all his power against France, and in 1295 the Scots troubles further postponed his prospects of revenge. But no suggestion of compromise or delay came from him. On his return to London early in August, 1295, he busied himself with preparing to resist the enemies that were gathering around him on every side. It was the moment of the raid on Dover, and the French question was still the more pressing. In a parliament of magnates at London, Edmund of Lancaster told the story of his Paris embassy with such effect that two cardinal-legates, whom the new pope, Boni-

face VIII., had sent in the hope of making peace, were put off CHAP.
politely, on the ground that Edward could make no treaty with- X.
out the consent of his ally, the King of the Romans. Edmund
was appointed commander of a new expedition to Gascony,
though his weak health delayed his departure. Meanwhile
Edward called upon every class of his subjects to co-operate
with him in his defence of the national honour. He was statesman enough to see that he could only cope with the situation,
if England as a whole rallied round him. His best answer to
the Scots and the French was the convention of the "model
parliament" of November, 1295.

The deep political purpose with which this parliament was
assembled is reflected even in the formal language of the writs.
"Inasmuch as a most righteous law of the emperors," wrote
Edward, " ordains that what touches all should be approved by
all, so it evidently appears that common dangers should be met
by remedies agreed upon in common. You know well how the
King of France has cheated me out of Gascony, and how he
still wickedly retains it. But now he has beset my realm with
a great fleet and a great multitude of warriors, and proposes, if
his power equal his unrighteous design, to blot out the English
tongue from the face of the earth." To avert this peril, Edward
summoned not only a full and representative gathering of magnates, but also two knights from every shire and two burgesses
from every borough. Moreover, the lower clergy were also
required to take part in the assembly, the archdeacons and
deans in person, the clergy of every cathedral church by one
proctor, the beneficed clerks of each diocese by two proctors.
Thus the assembly became so systematic a representation of the
three estates that after ages have regarded it as the type upon
which subsequent popular parliaments were to be modelled.
This gathering marks the end of the parliamentary experiments
of the earlier part of the reign. It met on November 27, and
each estate, deliberating separately, contributed its quota to the
national defence. The barons and knights offered an eleventh,
and the boroughs a seventh. It was a bitter disappointment
to Edward that the clergy could not be induced to make a
larger grant than a tenth. Enough, however, was obtained to
equip the two armies which, in the spring of 1296, were to
operate against the French and the Scots.

The Gascon expedition was the first to start.   Early in March, 1296, Edmund of Lancaster, accompanied by the Earl of Lincoln, landed at Bourg and Blaye.   John of St. John was still maintaining himself in that district as well as at Bayonne. On the appearance of the reinforcements the Gascon lords began to flock to the English camp, and a large force was at once able to take the field.   On March 28 an attempt was made to capture Bordeaux by a sudden assault.   On its failure Edmund, who did not possess the equipment necessary for a formal siege, sailed up the river to Saint-Macaire and occupied the town. But the castle held out gallantly, and after a three weeks' siege Edmund retired to his original position on the lower Gironde. Even there he found difficulty in holding his own, and before long shifted his quarters to Bayonne.   He had exhausted his resources, and found that his army could not be kept together without pay.   " Thereupon," writes Hemingburgh, " his face fell and he sickened about Whitsuntide.   So with want of money came want of breath too, and after a few days he went the way of all flesh."   Lincoln, his successor, managed still to stand his ground against Robert of Artois.   At last Artois made a successful night attack upon the English, captured St. John, and destroyed all his war-train and baggage.   The darkness of the night and the shelter of the neighbouring woods alone saved the English army from total destruction.   " After this," boasted William of Nangis, " no Englishman or Gascon dared to go out to battle against the Count of Artois and the French."   At Easter, 1297, a truce was concluded which left nearly all Gascony in French hands.

Soon after the departure of his brother for Gascony, Edward went to war against the Scots, regarding the non-appearance of King John on March 1 at Berwick as a declaration of hostility. The lord of Wark offered to betray his castle to the Scots, and Edward's successful effort to save it first brought him to the Tweed.   Meanwhile the men of Annandale under their new lord, the Earl of Buchan, engaged in a raid on Carlisle, but failed to capture the city, and speedily returned home.   On March 28, the day on which his brother attacked Bordeaux, Edward crossed the Tweed at Coldstream, and marched down its left bank towards Berwick.   On March 30 Berwick was captured.   The townsmen fought badly, and the heroes of the

resistance were thirty Flemish merchants, who held their factory, CHAP.
called the Red Hall, until the building was fired, and the de-   X.
fenders perished in the flames.   The garrison of the castle, commanded by Sir William Douglas, laid down their arms at once.

Edward spent a month in Berwick, strengthening the fortifications of the town, and preparing for an invasion of Scotland.
Early in April, King John renounced his homage and, immediately afterwards, the Scots lords who had attacked Carlisle
devastated Tynedale and Redesdale, penetrating as far as Hexham.   Edward's command of the sea made it impossible for
the raiders to cut off his communications with his base, and
they quickly returned to their own land, where they threw
themselves into Dunbar.   Though the lord of Dunbar, Patrick,
Earl of March, was serving with the English king, his countess,
who was at Dunbar, invited them into the fortress.   Dunbar
blocked the road into Scotland, and Edward sent forward
Earl Warenne with a portion of the army in the hope of re-
capturing the position.   Warenne laid siege to Dunbar, but on
the third day, April 27, the main Scots army came to its relief.
Leaving some of the young nobles to continue the siege, Warenne
drew up his army in battle array.   The Scots thought that the
English were preparing for flight, and rushed upon them with
loud cries and blowing of horns.   Discovering too late that
the enemy was ready for battle, they fell back in confusion
as far as Selkirk Forest.   Next day Edward came up from
Berwick and received the surrender of Dunbar.   Henceforth
his advance was but a military promenade.

Edward turned back from Dunbar to receive the submission
of the Steward of Scotland at Roxburgh, and to welcome a
large force of Welsh infantry, whose arrival enabled him to dismiss the English foot, fatigued with the slight effort of a month's
easy campaigning.   Thence he made his way to Edinburgh,
which yielded after an eight days' siege.   Stirling castle, the
next barrier to his progress, was abandoned by its garrison,
and there Edward was reinforced by some Irish contingents.
He then advanced to Perth, keeping St. John's feast on June
24 in St. John's own town.   On July 10 Balliol surrendered to
the Bishop of Durham at Brechin, acknowledging that he had
forfeited his throne by his rebellion.   Edward continued his
triumphal progress, preceded at every stage by Bishop Bek at

CHAP.
X.

the head of the warriors of the palatinate of St. Cuthbert. He made his way through Montrose up the east coast to Aberdeen, and thence up the Don and over the hills to Banff and Elgin, the farthest limit of his advance. He returned by a different route, bringing back with him from Scone the stone on which the Scots kings had been wont to sit at their coronation. This he presented as a trophy of victory to the monks of Westminster, where it was set up as a chair for the priest celebrating mass at the altar over against the shrine of St. Edward, though soon used as the coronation seat of English kings.

In less than five months Edward had conquered a kingdom. On August 22 he was back at Berwick, whither he had summoned a parliament of the nobles and prelates of both kingdoms, in order that the work of organising the future government of Scotland might be completed. Meanwhile a crowd of Scots of every class flocked to the victor's court and took oaths of fealty to him. Their names, along with those of the persons who made similar recognitions of his sovereignty during his Scottish progress, were recorded with notarial precision in one of those formal documents with which Edward delighted to mark the stages in the accomplishment of his task. This record, popularly styled the Ragman Roll, containing the names of about two thousand freeholders and men of substance in Scotland, is of extreme value to the Scottish genealogist and antiquary.[1] The last entries are dated August 28, the day on which Edward met his parliament at Berwick. The administration of Scotland was provided for. John, Earl Warenne, became the king's lieutenant, Hugh Cressingham, treasurer, and William Ormesby, justiciar. When the land was subdued Edward showed a strong desire to treat the people well. The only precaution taken by him against the renewal of disturbances was an order that the former King of Scots, John Comyn of Buchan, John Comyn of Badenoch, and other magnates of the patriotic party were to dwell in England, south of the Trent, until the conclusion of the war with France. As soon as his business was accomplished at Berwick, Edward turned his steps southwards. At last he seemed free to lead a great

---

[1] It is printed by the Bannatyne Club, and summarised in *Cal. Doc. Scot.*, ii., 193-214.

army against Philip the Fair; and, in order to prepare for the CHAP.
French expedition, he summoned another parliament to meet at X.
Bury St. Edmunds on the morrow of All Souls' day, November
3. At Bury the barons, knights, and burgesses made liberal
offerings for the war. But a new difficulty arose in the absolute
refusal of the clergy to vote any supplies. Once more the cup
of hope was dashed from Edward's lips, and he found himself
forced to enter into another weary conflict, this time with his
English liegemen.

So long as Peckham had lived, there had always been a
danger of a conflict between Church and State. Friar John had
ended his restless career in 1292, and Edward showed natural
anxiety to secure as his successor a prelate more amenable to
the secular authority and more national in his sentiments.
The papacy remained vacant after the death of Nicholas IV.
in 1292, so that there was no danger of Rome taking the appointment into its own hands, and the happy accident, which
had given the monks of Christchurch a statesmanlike prior in
Henry of Eastry, minimised the chances of a futile conflict between the king and the canonical electors. Eastry took care
that the archbishop-elect should be a person acceptable to the
sovereign. Robert Winchelsea, the new primate, was an Englishman and a secular clerk, who had taught with distinction
at Paris and Oxford, but had received no higher ecclesiastical
promotion than the archdeaconry of Essex and a canonry of
St. Paul's, and was mainly conspicuous for the sanctity of his
life, his ability as a preacher, and his zeal for making the
cathedral of London a centre of theological instruction. The
vacancy in the papacy forced upon the archbishop-elect a
wearisome delay of eighteen months in Italy; but at last in
September, 1294, he received consecration and the *pallium*
from the newly elected hermit-pope, Celestine V. Winchelsea
on his return strove to show that a secular archbishop could be
as austere in life, and as zealous for the rights of Holy Church,
as his mendicant predecessors. His desire to walk in the steps
of Peckham soon brought him into conflict with the king, and
in this conflict he showed an appreciation of the political situation, and a power of interpreting English opinion, which made
him the most formidable of Edward's domestic opponents. He
gained his first victory in the parliament of 1295 by preventing

CHAP. the clergy from making a larger grant than a tenth. But this
X.   triumph sank into insignificance as compared with the refusal of
all aid by the parliament of Bury.

A change in the papacy immensely strengthened Winchelsea's position against Edward. In December, 1294, Celestine,
overpowered with the burden of an office too heavy for his
strength, made his great renunciation and sought to resume
his hermit life. The Cardinal Benedict Gaetano was at once
elected his successor and took the style of Boniface VIII. The
son of a noble house of the neighbourhood of Anagni, a canonist,
a politician, and a zealot, the new pope had made personal
acquaintance with Edward and England from having attended
Cardinal Ottobon on his English legation, and was eager to
appease discord between Christian princes in order to forward
the crusade. He hated war the more because it was largely
waged with the money drawn from the clergy, and was indignant that the custom of taxing the Church, which was begun
under the guise of crusading tenths, had become so frequent
that both Philip and Edward applied it in order to raise
revenue from ecclesiastics for frankly secular warfare. Within
a few weeks of his accession he despatched two cardinals to
mediate peace between the Kings of France and England, and
was disgusted at the long delays with which both kings had
sought to frustrate his intervention. On February 29, 1296,
Boniface issued his famous bull *Clericis laicos*, in which he
declared it unlawful for any lay authority to exact supplies
from the clergy without the express authority of the apostolic
see. Princes imposing, and clerics submitting to such exactions
were declared *ipso facto* excommunicate.

Boniface's contention had been urged by his predecessors,
and it is improbable that he sought to do more than assert
the ancient law of the Church and save the clergy all over the
Latin world from exactions which were fast becoming intolerable. His object was quite general, though a pointed reference
to the extortions of Edward in 1294 showed that he had the
case of England before his mind. He had no wish to throw
down the gauntlet to the princes of Christendom, or to quarrel
with Edward and Philip, between whom he was still conducting
negotiations. It was his misfortune that he was constantly
forced to face fresh conditions which rendered it almost im-

possible to apply the ancient doctrines. Strong national kings, CHAP. like Edward and Philip, had already shown impatience with X. such traditions of the Church as limited their temporal authority. The pope's untimely re-statement of the theories of the twelfth century at once involved him in his first fierce difference with Philip the Fair, and put him into a position in which he could only win peace by explaining away the doctrine of *Clericis laicos*. While on the continent the conflict of Church and State took the form of a dispute between the French king and the papacy, in England it assumed the shape of a struggle between Edward and the Archbishop of Canterbury.

In November, 1296, at Bury, Winchelsea admitted the justice of the French war, but pleaded the pope's decretal as an absolute bar to any grant from the clerical estate. No decision was arrived at, and the problem was discussed again in the convocation of Canterbury in January, 1297. "We have two lords over us," declared the archbishop to his clergy, "the king and the pope; and, although we owe obedience to both of these, we owe greater obedience to our spiritual than to our temporal lord." All that they could do was to entreat the pope's permission to allow them to pay Cæsar that which Cæsar by himself had no right to demand. Edward burst into a fury on hearing of this new pretext for delay. He declared that the clergy must pay a fifth, under penalty of his withdrawing his protection from a body which strove to stand outside the commonwealth. The clergy remained firm, and separated without making any grant. Thereupon, on January 30, the chief justice, John of Metingham, sitting in Westminster Hall, pronounced the clergy to be outlaws. "Henceforth," he declared, "there shall be no justice meted out to a clerk in the court of the lord king, however atrocious be the injury from which he may have suffered. But sentence against a clerk shall be given at the instance of all who have a complaint against him." Winchelsea retaliated by publishing the sentence of excommunication against violators of the papal bull. Two days later the king ordered the sheriffs to take possession of the lay fees held by clerks in the province of Canterbury. A few ecclesiastics, who privately made an offering of a fifth, were alone exempted from this command.

Edward's conflict with the Church was followed within a month by a dispute of almost equal gravity with a section of

CHAP.
X.

the barons. He summoned a baronial parliament to assemble on February 24 at Salisbury, and went down in person to explain his plan of campaign. One force was to help his new ally, Guy of Flanders, while another was to act in Gascony. Edward himself was to accompany the army to Flanders. He requested some of the earls, including Norfolk and Hereford, to fight for him in Gascony. The deaths of Edmund of Lancaster, Gilbert of Gloucester, and William of Pembroke had robbed the baronage of its natural leaders. Earl Warenne was fully engaged in the north, and Lincoln was devoted to the king's side. The removal of other possible spokesmen made Norfolk and Hereford the champions of the party of opposition. For years the friends of aristocratic authority had been smarting under the growing influence of the crown. The time was ripe for a revival of the baronial opposition which a generation earlier had won the Provisions of Oxford. Moreover both the earls had personal slights to avenge. Hereford bitterly resented the punishment meted out to him for waging private war against Earl Gilbert in the march. Norfolk was angry because, during the last Welsh campaign, Edward had suspended him from the exercise of the marshalship. The form of Edward's request at Salisbury gave them a technical advantage which they were not slow to seize. Ignoring the broader issues which lay between them and the king, they took their stand on their traditional rights as constable and marshal to attend the king in person. "Freely," declared the earl marshal, "will I go with thee, O king, and march before thee in the first line of thy army, as my hereditary duty requires." Edward answered: "Thou shalt go without me along with the rest to Gascony". The marshal replied: "I am not bound to go save with thee, nor will I go". Edward flew into a passion: "By God, sir earl, thou shalt either go or hang". Norfolk replied with equal spirit: "By that same oath, sir king, I will neither go nor hang". The parliament broke up in disorder. Before long a force of 1,500 men-at-arms gathered together under the leadership of the constable and marshal.

During these stormy times Edward had been straining every nerve to equip an adequate army for foreign service. Once more he laid violent hands upon the wool and hides of the merchants, while a huge male-tolt, varying from forty shillings a sack for raw wool to sixty-six shillings and eightpence a sack for carded wool, was exacted for such wool as the king's officers suffered to remain in the owner's possession. Moreover, vast stores of wheat, barley, and oats, salt pork and salt beef were requisitioned all over the land. Men said that the king's tyranny could no longer be borne, and that the rights decreed to all Englishmen by the Great Charter were in imminent danger. The movement, which had begun as a defence of feudal right, became a popular revolt in favour of national liberty. The commons joined the barons and clergy in the general opposition to the headstrong king.

Edward saw that he must divide his enemies if he wished to effect his purpose. The clergy were the easiest to deal with. Boniface VIII. was already yielding in his struggle against Philip the Fair. In the bull *Romana mater* of February 2, 1297, he had authorised voluntary contributions of the French clergy in the case of pressing necessity, without previous recourse to the permission of the apostolic see. The same attitude had already been taken up by the royalist clergy in England, who redeemed their outlawry by offering to the king the fifth of their revenues. In March Edward made things easier for the recalcitrants by suspending the edict confiscating the lay fees of the Church. Even Winchelsea saw the wisdom of abandoning his too heroic attitude. In a convocation, held on March 24, he practically applied the doctrine of *Romana mater* to the English situation. "Let each man," he declared, "save his own soul and follow his own conscience. But my conscience does not allow me to offer money for the king's protection or on any other pretext." In the event nearly all the clergy bought off the king's wrath by the voluntary payment of a fifth. Winchelsea was obdurate. His estates remained for five months in the king's hands, and he was forced, like another St. Francis, to depend on the charity of the faithful. But even Winchelsea did not hold out indefinitely. On July 14 he was publicly reconciled with the king outside Westminster Hall, and a few days later his goods were restored. On July 31 Boniface entirely receded from the doctrine of *Clericis laicos* in the bull *Etsi de statu*. Before this could be known in England, Winchelsea told his clergy that the king had agreed to confirm the Great Charter, if they would but make a grant to carry on the

French war.   A little later Edward of his own authority exacted a third from all clerical revenues.   This persistence in his high-handed policy made any real reconciliation between Edward and Winchelsea impossible.   The king never forgave the arch-bishop, whose action demonstrated to all England the divided allegiance of his clergy between their two masters.   Winchelsea still retained his profound distrust of the king, who had set at naught the liberties of Church and realm.

The baronial opposition was broken up by devices not dissimilar to those which neutralised the antagonism of the clergy.   By strenuous efforts Edward obtained a fair sum of money for his expenses.   He let it be understood that, if he took his subjects' wool, the talleys given in exchange would be redeemed when better times had arrived, and he scrupulously paid for the corn and meat that his officers had requisitioned. Meanwhile he summoned all possible fighting men from Eng-land, Wales, and Ireland to meet at London on July 7.   The prospect of subjects of the crown being forced, whatsoever their feudal obligations might be, to wage war beyond sea, threatened to provoke a fresh crisis.   But after many long altercations, Edward announced that neither the feudal tenants nor the twenty-pound freeholders had any legal obligation to go with him to Flanders, and offered pay to all who were willing to hearken to his "affectionate request" for their services.   Under these conditions a considerable force of stipendiaries was levied without much difficulty.

Hereford and Norfolk abandoned active in favour of passive hostility.   They refused to serve as constable and marshal, and Edward appointed barons of less dignity and greater loyalty to act in their place.   While all England was busy with the equipment of troops and the provision of supplies, they sullenly held aloof.   At last, when all was ready, Edward issued an appeal to his subjects, protesting the purity of his motives, and emphasising the inexorable necessity under which he was forced to play the tyrant in the interests of the whole realm.   By the beginning of August such barons as were willing to go to Flanders began to assemble in arms at London.   The young Edward of Carnarvon was appointed regent during his father's absence, and among the councillors who were to act in his name was the Archbishop of Canterbury.   At last the king set off to embark at Winchelsea. While there, the earls presented to him a belated list of grievances. He refused to deal with their demand for the confirmation of the charters. " My full council," he declared to the envoys of the earls, " is not with me, and without it I cannot reply to your requests. Tell those who have sent you that, if they will come with me to Flanders, they will please me greatly. If they will not come, I trust they will do no harm to me, or at any rate to my kingdom." On August 24 he took ship for Flanders, and a few days later he and his troops safely landed at Sluys, whence they made their way to Ghent. Nearly a thousand men-at-arms and a great force of infantry, largely Welsh and Irish, swelled the expedition to considerable proportions. After all his troubles, Edward found that the loyalty of his subjects enabled him to carry out the ideal which he had formulated two years before. King and nation were to meet common dangers by action undertaken in common.

Everything else was ruthlessly sacrificed in order that the king might take an army to Flanders. The Gascon expedition was quietly dropped. But the gravest difficulty arose not from Gascony but Scotland. Edward's choice of agents to carry out his Scottish policy had been singularly unhappy. Warenne, the governor, was a dull and lethargic nobleman more than sixty-six years of age. He complained of the bad climate of Scotland, and passed most of his time on his Yorkshire estates. In his absence Cressingham, the treasurer, and Ormesby, the justiciar, became the real representatives of the English power. Cressingham was a pompous ecclesiastic, who appropriated to his own uses the money set aside for the fortification of Berwick, and was odious to the Scots for his rapacity and incompetence. Ormesby was a pedantic lawyer, rigid in carrying out the king's orders but stiff and unsympathetic in dealing with the Scots. Under such rulers Scotland was neither subdued nor conciliated. No real effort was made to track to their hiding-places in the hills the numerous outlaws, who had abandoned their estates rather than take an oath of fealty to Edward. When the English governors took action, they were cruel and indiscriminating ; and often too were lax and careless. Matters soon became serious. William Wallace of Elderslie slew an English official in Clydesdale, and threw in

CHAP.   his lot with the outlaws.   He was joined by Sir William Douglas,
X.   the former defender of Berwick.   By May, 1297, Scotland was
in full revolt.   In the north, Andrew of Moray headed a rising
in Strathspey.   In central Scotland the justiciar barely escaped
capture, while holding his court at Scone.   The south-west, the
home both of Wallace and Douglas, proved the most dangerous district.   There the barons, imitating Bohun and Bigod,
based their opposition to Edward on his claim upon their com-
pulsory service in the French wars.   Before long the son of the
lord of Annandale, Robert Bruce, now called Earl of Carrick,
Robert Wishart, Bishop of Glasgow, and other magnates were
in arms, and in close association with Douglas and Wallace.

Edward made light of this rebellion.   Resolved to go to
Flanders at all costs, he contented himself with calling upon
the levies of the shires north of the Trent to protect his
interests in Scotland.   Early in July, Henry Percy, Warenne's
grandson, rode through south-western Scotland, at the head of
the Cumberland musters, and on July 7, the local insurgent
leaders, with the exception of Wallace, made their submission
to him at Irvine.   Moreover, Edward released the two Comyns
from their veiled imprisonment, and sent them back to Scotland to help in suppressing the insurrection.   Henry Percy
boasted that the Scots south of the Forth had been reduced
to subjection.   But a few days later Wallace was found to be
strongly established in Ettrick forest and was threatening Roxburgh.   At last Edward stirred up Warenne to return to his
government.   The king took the precaution of leaving some of
his best warriors in England in case their services were needed
against the recalcitrant barons or the Scots.   Then, as has
been said, on August 24 he crossed over to Flanders.

The constable and marshal were still in arms, and Winchelsea, who, in spite of his reconciliation with Edward, was
in close communication with them, declined to take an active
part on the council of regency.   Two days before Edward
took ship, Hereford and Norfolk appeared in arms at the exchequer at Westminster, and forbade the officials to continue
the collection of supplies, until the Great Charter and the
Charter of the Forest had been confirmed.   They strove to
win the support of the Londoners, who had long had a grievance against Edward for depriving them of their right to elect

their own mayor, and for subjecting the city to the arbitrary
rule of a warden nominated by the crown.   They forbade their
followers to commit acts of violence, but they made it clear
that there could be no peace until the charters were confirmed.

In August, Warenne grappled with the Scottish rising, but
his own incompetence, and the half-heartedness of the Scottish
magnates, on whom he relied, made his task very difficult.
Wallace retreated beyond the Forth, and Warenne reached
Stirling on September 10 in pursuit of him.   He learnt that
Wallace was holding the wooded heights, immediately to the
north of Stirling bridge on the left bank of the Forth, not far
from the abbey of Cambuskenneth.   The Steward of Scotland,
who, after the collapse of the revolt in the south-west, served
under Warenne, offered his mediation.   But no good result
came from his action, and the English suspected treachery.
Wallace took up a bold attitude, scorning either compromise
or retreat.   He had only a small following of cavalry, but
his infantry was numerous and enthusiastic.   The English resolved to attack him on September 11.   The Forth at Stirling
was crossed by a long wooden bridge, so narrow that only two
horsemen could pass abreast.   It was madness to send an
army over the river by such a means in the face of a watchful
enemy.   But not only was the English plan of battle foolish
it was also carried out weakly.   Warenne overslept himself, and
his subordinates wasted the early morning in useless discussions
and altercations.   When at last he woke up, he rejected the
advice of a Scottish knight to send part of his cavalry over the
river by a ford which thirty horsemen could traverse abreast,
and ordered all his troops to cross by the bridge.

Wallace, seeing that the enemy had delivered themselves
into his hands, remained in the woods until a fair proportion of
the English men-at-arms had made their way over the stream.
He then suddenly swooped down upon the bridge, cutting off
the retreat of those who had traversed it, and blocking all
possibility of reinforcement.   After a short fight the English
to the north of the Forth were cut down almost to a man.
The English on the Stirling side, seeing the fate of their
comrades, fled in terror, and their Scots allies went over to
their countrymen.   Among the slain was the greedy Cressingham, whose skin the Scots tanned into leather.   Warenne did

CHAP.
X.

not draw rein until he reached Berwick, and in one day all Scotland was lost. The castles of Roxburgh and Berwick alone upheld the English flag. Wallace and Moray governed all Scotland as "generals of the army of King John". Within a few weeks of their victory, they raided the three northern counties of England.

Wallace had freed Scotland, but his wonderful success taught the contending factions in England the plain duty of union against the common enemy. A new parliament of the three estates was summoned for September 30. The opposition leaders came armed, and declared that there could be no supply of men or money until their demand for the confirmation of the charters was granted. No longer content with simple confirmation, they drew up, in the form of a statute, a petition requiring that no tallage or aid should henceforth be taken without the assent of the estates. This was the so-called *statutum de tallagio non concedendo* which seventeenth-century parliaments and judges erroneously accepted as a statute. The helpless regency substantially accepted their demands, and, on October 12, issued a confirmation of the charters, to which fresh clauses were added, providing, with less generality than in the baronial request, that no male-tolts, or such manner of aids as had recently been extorted, should be imposed in the future without the common consent of all the realm, but making no reference to tallage.[1] Liberal supplies were then voted by all the three estates, and Winchelsea, who all through these proceedings acted as the brain of the baronage, exerted himself to explain away the last of the clerical difficulties raised by the *Clericis laicos*.

On November 5 the king ratified, at Ghent, the action of his son's advisers. Thus the constitutional struggle was ended by the complete triumph of the baronial opposition. And the victory was the more signal, because it was gained not over a weak king, careless of his rights, but over the strongest of

---

[1] The Latin, *Articuli inserti in magna carta*, given by Hemingburgh, ii., 152, is quoted as a statute in the Petition of Right of 1628, under the title *De tallagio non concedendo*. The view of its relation to the French *Confirmatio cartarum* is that taken by M. Bémont, *Chartes des libertés anglaises*, especially pp. xliii., xliv. and 87. It is based on Bartholomew Cotton's nearly contemporary statement (*Hist. Angl.*, p. 337).

the Plantagenets, greedy to retain every scrap of authority. It is with good reason that the Confirmation of the Charters of 1297 is reckoned as one of the great turning points in the history of our constitution. Its provisions sum up the whole national advance which had been made since Gualo and William the marshal first identified the English monarchy with the principles wrested from John at Runnymede. In the years that immediately followed, it might well seem that the act of 1297, like the submission of John, was only a temporary expedient of a dexterous statecraft which consented with the lips but not with the heart. But in later times, when the details of the struggle were forgotten and the noise of the battle over, the event stood out in its full significance. Edward had been willing to take the people into partnership with him when he thought that they would be passive partners, anxious to do his pleasure. He was taught that the leaders of the people were henceforth to have their share with the crown in determining national policy. Common dangers were still to be met by measures deliberated in common, but the initiative was no longer exclusively reserved to the monarch. The sordid pedantry of the baronial leaders and the high-souled determination of the king compel our sympathy for Edward rather than his enemies. But all that made English history what it is, was involved in the issue, and the future of English freedom was assured when the obstinacy of the constable and marshal prevailed over the resolution of the great king.

CHAPTER XI.

THE SCOTTISH FAILURE.

THE expedition of Edward to Flanders lost its best chance of success through the events which retarded its despatch. While the English king was wrangling with his barons, the French king was active. On the news of the alliance of Count Guy with the English, Robert of Artois was summoned from Gascony to the north. While Philip besieged Lille, and finally took it, Robert of Artois gained a brilliant victory over the Flemings at Furnes on August 20. Meanwhile John of Avesnes, Count of Hainault, was closely co-operating with the French, and kept Edward's son-in-law and ally, John, Duke of Brabant, from sending effective help to the Flemings. Moreover, the Flemish townsmen, in their dislike of their count, were largely on the side of the French. Edward's little army could do nothing to redress a balance that already inclined so heavily on the other side. The Flemings were disappointed at the scanty numbers of the English men-at-arms, and stared with wonder and contempt at the bare-legged Welsh archers and lancemen, with their uncouth garb, strange habits of eating and fighting, and propensity to pillage and disorder, though they recognised their hardihood and the effectiveness of their missiles.[1] The same disorderly spirit that had marred the Rioms campaign still prevailed among the English engaged on foreign service. No sooner were the troops landed at Sluys on August 28, than the mariners of the Cinque Ports renewed their old feud with the men of Yarmouth, and many ships were destroyed and lives lost in this untimely conflict. Edward advanced to Bruges, where he was joined by

---

[1] See for Flemish criticisms of the Welsh, L. van Velthem, *Spiegel Historiaal*, pp. 215-16, ed. Le Long, partly translated by Funck Brentano in his edition of *Annales Gandenses*, p. 7, a work giving full details of these struggles.

the Count of Flanders, but the disloyalty of the townsmen and CHAP.
the approach of King Philip forced the king and the earl to XI.
take shelter behind the stronger walls of Ghent.   Immediately
on their retreat, Philip occupied Bruges and Damme, thus cutting
off the English from the direct road to the sea.   The Anglo-
Flemish army was afraid to attack the powerful force of the
French king.   But the French had learnt by experience a
wholesome fear of the English and Welsh archers, and did
not venture to approach Ghent too closely.   The ridiculous
result followed that the Kings of France and England avoided
every opportunity of fighting out their quarrel, and lay, wasting
time and money, idly watching each other's movements.

The only dignified way of putting an end to this impossible
situation lay in negotiation.   Edward's faithful servant, William
of Hotham, the Dominican friar whom the pope had appointed
Archbishop of Dublin, was in the English camp.   Hotham, who
had enjoyed Philip's personal friendship while teaching theology in the Paris schools, was an acceptable mediator between
the two kings.   A short truce was signed at Vyve-Saint-Bavon
on the Lys on October 7.   This allowed time for more elaborate negotiations to be carried on at Courtrai and Tournai, and
on January 31, 1298, a truce, in which the allies of both kings
were included, was signed at Tournai, to last until January 6,
1300.   It was agreed to refer all questions in dispute to the
arbitration of Boniface VIII., "not as pope but as a private
person, as Benedict Gaetano".   Both kings despatched their
envoys to Rome, where with marvellous celerity Boniface issued,
on June 30, 1298, a preliminary award.   It suggested the
possibility of a settlement on the basis of each belligerent retaining the possessions which he had held at the beginning of
the struggle, and entering into an alliance strengthened by a
double marriage.   Edward was to marry the French king's sister
Margaret, while Edward of Carnarvon was to be betrothed to
Philip's infant daughter Isabella.   The latter match involved
the repudiation of the betrothal of Edward of Carnarvon with
the daughter of the Count of Flanders.   But all through the
award there was no mention of the allies of either party.   Boniface was too eager for peace to be over-scrupulous as to the
honourable obligations of the two kings who sought his mediation.

14 *

The English regency, which grappled so courageously with the baronial opposition, showed an equal energy in protecting the northern counties from the Scots. About the time of the confirmation of the charters, Wallace crossed the border and spread desolation and ruin from Carlisle to Hexham. Warenne and Henry Percy, who had attended the October parliament at London, were soon back in the north. By December the largest army which was ever assembled during Edward I.'s reign [1] was collected together on the borders, and preparations were made for a winter campaign after the fashion which had proved so effective in Wales. But all that Warenne was able to accomplish was the relief of Roxburgh. The quality of the troops was not equal to their quantity, and all his misfortunes had not taught him wisdom. Early in Lent Edward stopped active campaigning by announcing that no great operations were to be attempted until his return. Thereupon Warenne sent the bulk of the troops home, and remained at Berwick, awaiting the king's arrival.

Edward landed at Sandwich on March 14, 1298, and at once set about preparing to avenge Stirling Bridge. He met his parliament on Whitsunday, May 25, at York. The Scots barons were summoned to this assembly, but as they neither attended nor sent proxies, their absence was deemed to be proof of contumacy. A month later a large army was concentrated at Roxburgh. The earls and barons with their retinues mustered to the number of 1,100 horse, while 1,300 men-at-arms served under the king's banners for pay. Though Gascony was still in Philip's hands, the good relations that prevailed between England and France allowed the presence in Edward's host of a magnificent troop of Gascon lords, headed by the lord of Albret and the Captal de Buch, and conspicuous for the splendour of their armour and the costliness and beauty of their chargers. On this occasion Edward set little store on infantry, and was content to accept the services of those who came of their own free will. Yet even under these conditions some 12,000 foot were assembled, more than 10,000 of whom came from Wales and its march.

The leaders of the opposition were present in Edward's

[1] Morris, *Welsh Wars of Edward I.*, pp. 284-86.

host. On the eve of the invasion, the impatient king was kept
back by the declaration of Hereford and Norfolk that they would
not cross the frontier, until definite assurances were given that
the king would carry out the confirmation of the charters which
he had informally ratified on foreign soil. Etiquette or pride
prevented Edward himself satisfying their demand, but the
Bishop of Durham and three loyal earls pledged themselves that
the king would fulfil all his promises on his return. Then the
two earls suffered the expedition to proceed ; and on July 6 the
army left Roxburgh, proceeding by moderate marches to Kirk-
liston on the Almond, where it encamped on the 15th. Here
there was a few days' delay, while Bishop Bek captured some of
the East Lothian castles which were threatening the English
rear. Already there was a difficulty in obtaining supplies from
the devastated country-side, and northerly winds prevented the
provision ships from sailing from Berwick to the Forth. The
worst hardships fell upon the Welsh infantry, who began to
mutiny and talked of joining the Scots. Matters grew worse on
the arrival of a wine ship, for such ample rations of wine were
distributed to the Welsh that very many of them became drunk.
So threatening was the state of affairs that Edward thought of
retreating to Edinburgh. On July 21, however, the news was
brought that Wallace and his followers were assembled in great
force at Falkirk, some seventeen miles to the west. The prospect of battle at once restored the courage and discipline of
the army, and Edward ordered an advance. That night the host
bivouacked on the moors east of Linlithgow, "with shields for
pillows and armour for beds ". During the night the king, who
was sleeping in the open field like the meanest trooper, received a kick from his horse which broke two of his ribs. Yet
the early morning of July 22, the feast of St. Mary Magdalen,
saw him riding at the head of his troops through the streets
of Linlithgow. At last the Scots lances were descried on the
slopes of a hill near Falkirk, and the English rested while the
bishop and king heard mass. Then the army, which had eaten
nothing since the preceding day, advanced to the battle.

Wallace had a large following of infantry, but a mere handful of mounted men-at-arms. He ordered the latter to occupy
the rear, and grouped his pikemen, the flower of his army, into
four great circles, or "schiltrons," which, with the front ranks

kneeling or sitting and the rear ranks standing, presented to the enemy four living castles, each with a bristling hedge of pikes, dense enough, it was hoped, to break the fierce shock of a cavalry charge. The spaces between the four schiltrons were occupied by the archers, the best of whom came from Ettrick Forest. The front was further protected by a morass, and perhaps also by a row of stout posts sunk into the ground and fastened together by ropes.

Edward ordered the Welsh archers to prepare the way with their missiles for the advance of the men-at-arms. But the Welsh refused to move, so that Edward was forced to proceed by a direct cavalry charge. For this purpose he divided his men-at-arms into four "battles". The first of these was commanded by the Earl of Lincoln, with whom were the constable and marshal, who at last had an opportunity of serving the king in battle in the offices which belonged to them by hereditary right. On approaching the morass this first line was thrown into some confusion, and paused in its advance. Behind it the second battle, under command of the Bishop of Durham, who, perhaps, knew the ground better, wheeled to the east and took the Scots on their left flank. But Bek's followers disobeyed his orders to wait until the rest of the army came up, and they suffered heavy losses in attacking the left schiltron. Before long, however, Lincoln found a way round the morass westwards to the enemy's right, while the two rearmost battles, headed by the king and Earl Warenne, also advanced to the front. The combat thus became general. The Scots cavalry fled without striking a blow, and some of the English thought that Wallace himself rode off the field with them. The archers between the schiltrons were easily trampled down, so that the only effective resistance came from the circles of pikemen. The yeomanry of Scotland steadily held their own against the fierce charges of the mail-clad knights, and it looked for a time as if the day was theirs. But the despised infantry at last made their way to the front and poured in showers of arrows that broke down the Scottish ranks. Friend and foe were at such close quarters that the English who had no bows threw stones against the Scottish circles. When the way was thus prepared, the horsemen easily penetrated through the gaps made in the circles, and before long the Scottish pikemen were a crowd of

panic-stricken fugitives. Edward's brilliant victory was won
with comparatively little loss.

It was years before the Scots again ventured to meet the English in the open field. Yet the king's victory was not followed by any real conquest even of southern Scotland. Edward advanced to Stirling, where he rested until he had recovered from his accident, while detachments of his troops penetrated as far as Perth and St. Andrews. Meanwhile the south-west rose in revolt, under Robert Bruce, Earl of Carrick, whose father had fought at Falkirk. Late in August, Edward made his way to Ayr and occupied it, while Bruce fled before him. Provisions were still scarce, and the army was weary of fighting. The Durham contingent deserted in a body,[1] and the earls were so lukewarm that Edward was fain to return by way of Carlisle, capturing Lochmaben, Bruce's Annandale stronghold, on the way. On September 8 the king reached Carlisle, where the constable and marshal declared that they had lost so many men and horses that they could no longer continue the campaign. Edward tried to stem the tide of desertion by promises of Scottish lands to those who would remain with his banners. But the distribution of these rewards proved only a fresh source of discontent. At last Edward was forced to dismiss the greater part of his forces. He lingered in the north until the end of the year, but there was no more real fighting ; with the beginning of 1299 he returned to the south, convinced that the disloyalty of his barons had neutralised his triumphs in the field. The few castles which still upheld the English cause in Scotland were soon closely besieged.

During the whole of 1299 Edward was prevented by other work from prosecuting the war against the Scots. Even the borderers were sick of fighting, and Bishop Bek, who had hitherto afforded him an unswerving support with all the forces of his palatinate, was forced to desist from warlike operations by the refusal of his tenants to serve any longer beyond the bounds of the lands of St. Cuthbert. While the men of Durham abandoned the war, there was little reason to wonder at the indifference of the south country as to the progress of the Scots. In the Lenten parliament at London, the Earls of Hereford and Nor-

[1] Lapsley, *County Palatine of Durham*, p. 128.

folk pressed Edward once more to fulfil his promise to carry
out the confirmation of the charters. The king would not yield
to their demand yet dared not refuse it. In his perplexity he
had recourse to evasions which further embittered his relations
with them. He promised that he would give an answer the
next day, but when the morrow came, he secretly withdrew from
the city. The angry barons followed him to his retreat and
reminded him of his broken promise. Edward coolly replied
that he left London because his health was suffering from the
corrupt air of the town, and bade the barons return, as his council
had his reply ready. The barons obeyed the king's orders, but
their indignation passed all bounds when they found that the
king's promised confirmation of the charters was vitiated by a
new clause saving all the rights of the crown, and that nothing
was said as to the promised perambulation of the forests. In
bitter wrath the parliament broke up, and the Londoners, who
shared the anger of the barons, threatened a revolt. After
Easter these stormy scenes were repeated in a new parliament,
and Edward was at last forced to yield a grudging assent to all
the demands of the opposition, and even to appoint a commission for the perambulation of the forests. By the time the
summer was at hand, the progress of the negotiations with
France occupied Edward so fully that he had abundant excuse
for not precipitating a new rupture with his barons, by insisting
upon a fresh campaign against the Scots.

A papal legate presided over a congress of English and French
ambassadors at Montreuil-sur-mer, which belonged to Edward
by right of the late queen, Eleanor as Countess of Ponthieu.
The outcome of these deliberations was the treaty of Montreuil,
concluded on June 19, 1299. It was not the final pacification
which had been hoped for. Edward indeed abandoned his
Flemish allies, but Philip would not relax his hold upon Gascony, and without that a definitive peace was impossible. The
treaty of Montreuil was simply a marriage treaty. Edward
was forthwith to marry Margaret, and his son was to be betrothed to Isabella of France. Neither the prolongation of
the truce nor the affairs of the Flemings were mentioned in it,
while all that Philip did for the Scots was to provide for the
liberation of the deposed King John from his English prison.
As soon as the ratifications were exchanged the king, who was

then sixty years of age, and his youthful bride were married on
September 9 at Canterbury by Archbishop Winchelsea.

Edward's willingness to marry the sister of the king who
still kept him out of Gascony can best be explained by his
overmastering desire to renew operations in Scotland.   Shortly
after his marriage, he again busied himself with preparations for
the long-delayed Scots campaign.   It was high time that he
took action.   The English garrisons were surrendering one by
one, and the Scottish magnates were deserting the English cause.
Their conversion to patriotic principles was made easier by the
decay of Wallace's power consequent on his defeat at Falkirk.
After stormy scenes with his aristocratic rivals, Wallace withdrew from Scotland and went to the continent, where he implored the help of the King of France.   Philip proved true to
his new brother-in-law, and put Wallace in prison, only releasing
him that he might go to Rome and enlist the sympathy of
Boniface VIII.   Meanwhile the Scots chose a new regency at
the head of which was the younger John Comyn of Badenoch.
Under these changed conditions the Scottish earls rapidly rallied
round the national cause.   Stirling, Edward's chief stronghold
in central Scotland, was so hardly pressed that the men-at-arms
were forced to eat their chargers.   Yet when the English
barons assembled about the beginning of winter, in obedience
to Edward's summons, they stubbornly declared that they
would not endure the hardships of a winter campaign until the
king had fulfilled his pledges as regards the charters.   Thus
left to their own resources, the sorely tried garrison of Stirling
surrendered to the Scots.

In March, 1300, Edward met his parliament at Westminster.
Despite the straits to which he was reduced, he was still unwilling to make a complete surrender.   He avoided a formal
re-issue of the charters by giving his sanction to a long series
of articles, drawn up apparently by the barons.   These articles
provided for the better publication of the charters, and the appointment in every shire of a commission to punish all offences
against them which were not already provided for by the common law ; together with numerous technical clauses "for the
relief of the grievances that the people have had by reason of
the wars that have been, and for the amendment of their estate,
and that they may be more ready in the king's service and more

willing to aid him when he has need of them". This document
was known as *Articuli super cartas*.[1] At the same time the
forest perambulation, which had long been ordered, was directed
to be proceeded with at once. For this reason a chronicler
calls this assembly "the parliament of the perambulation".[2]
The reconciliation between the king and his subjects was attested by a grant of a twentieth.

Edward's concessions once more enabled him to face the
Scots, and the summer saw a gallant army mustered at Carlisle,
though some of the earls, including Roger Bigod, still held aloof.
A two months' campaign was fought in south-western Scotland
in July and August. But the peasants drove their cattle to the
hills, and rainy weather impeded the king's movements. The
chief exploit of the campaign was the capture of Carlaverock
castle, though even in the glowing verse of the herald, who has
commemorated the taking of this stronghold,[3] the military insignificance of the achievement cannot be concealed. Edward
returned to the same district in October, but he effected so little
that he was glad to agree to a truce with the Scots, which Philip
the Fair urged him to accept. The armistice was to last until
Whitsuntide, and Edward immediately returned to England.
He had not yet satisfied his subjects, and was again forced to
meet his estates.

A full parliament assembled on January 20, 1301, at Lincoln. The special business was to receive the report of the
forest perambulation; and the first anticipation of the later
custom of continuing the same parliament from one session to
another can be discerned in the direction to the sheriffs that
they should return the same representatives of the shires and
boroughs as had attended the Lenten parliament of 1300, and
only hold fresh elections in the case of such members as had
died or become incapacitated. During the ten days that the
commons were in session stormy scenes occurred. Edward
would only promise to agree to the disafforestments recom-
mended by the perambulators, if the estates would assure him
that he could do so, without violating his coronation oath or
disinheriting his crown. The estates refused to undertake this

---

[1] It is published in Bémont's *Chartes*, pp. 99-108, with valuable comments;
cf. another draft analysed in *Hist. MSS. Comm.*, 6th Report, i., p. 344.

[2] Langtoft, ii., 320.   [3] *The Siege of Carlaverock*, ed. Nicolas (1828).

grave responsibility, and a long catalogue of their grievances CHAP. was presented to Edward by Henry of Keighley, knight of the XI. shire for Lancashire, and one of the first members of the third estate of whose individual action history has preserved any trace. The commons demanded a fresh confirmation of the charters; the punishment of the royal ministers who had infringed them, or the *Articuli super cartas* of the previous session, and the completion of the proposed disafforestments. In addition, the prelates declared that they could not assent to any tax being imposed upon the clergy contrary to the papal prohibition. Among the ministers specially signalled out for attack was the treasurer, Bishop Walter Langton, and in this Edward discerned the influence of Winchelsea, for he was Langton's personal enemy. The king's disgust at the primate's action was the more complete since Bishop Bek now arrayed himself on the side of the opposition. Edward showed his ill-will by consigning Henry of Keighley to prison. But the coalition was too formidable to be withstood. The king agreed to all the secular demands of the estates, accepted the hated disafforestments and directed the re-issue of a further confirmation of the charters, but refused his assent to the demand of the prelates. A grant of a fifteenth was then made, and Edward dismissed the popular representatives on January 30, retaining the prelates and nobles for further business. On February 14, the last confirmation of the charters concluded the long chapter of history, which had begun at Runnymede.

Edward strove to separate his baronial and his clerical enemies, and found an opportunity, which he was not slow to use, in the uncompromising papalism of Winchelsea. Boniface VIII. had no sooner settled the relations of England and France than he threw himself with ardour into an attempt to establish peace between England and Scotland. Scottish emissaries, including perhaps Wallace himself, gave Boniface their version of the ancient relations of the two crowns. On June 27, 1299, the pope issued the letter *Scimus, fili*, in which he claimed that Scotland specially belonged to the apostolic see, on the ground that it was converted through the relics of St. Andrew. He denied all feudal dependence of Scotland on Edward, and explained away the submissions of 1291 as arising from such momentary fear as might fall upon the most steadfast. If

Edward persisted in his claims, he was to submit them to the judgment of the Roman *curia* within the next six months. In 1300 Winchelsea, who fully accepted the new papal doctrine, sought out Edward in the midst of the Carlaverock campaign and presented him with Boniface's letter. Edward's hot temper fired up at the archbishop's ill-timed intervention, and subsequent military failures had not smoothed over the situation. His wrath reached its climax when Winchelsea once more stirred up opposition in the Lincoln parliament, and his refusal of a demand, which the primate had astutely added to the commons' requests, showed that he was prepared for war to the knife. Edward laid the papal letter before the earls and barons that still tarried with him at Lincoln. His appeal to their patriotism was not unsuccessful. A letter was drawn up, which was sealed, then and subsequently, by more than a hundred secular magnates, in which Boniface was roundly told that the King of England was in no wise bound to answer in the pope's court as to his rights over the realm of Scotland or as to any other temporal matter, and that the papal claim was unprecedented, and prejudicial to Edward's sovereignty. A longer historical statement was composed by the king's order in answer to Boniface. It is not certain that the two documents ever reached the pope, but they had great effect in influencing English opinion and in breaking down the alliance between the baronage and the ecclesiastical party.[1] Winchelsea's influence was fatally weakened, and the period of his overthrow was at hand.

The triumph over Winchelsea made Edward's position stronger than it had been during the first days of the Lincoln parliament. That assembly ended amidst the festivities which attended the creation of Edward of Carnarvon as Prince of Wales, Earl of Chester, and Count of Ponthieu. The new prince, already seventeen years of age, had made his first campaign in the previous year. But all the pains that Edward took in training his son in warfare and in politics bore little fruit, and Edward of Carnarvon's introduction to active life was only to add another trouble to the many that beset the king.

When the truce with Scotland expired, in the summer of 1301, Edward again led an army over the border, in which the

---

[1] See, on the barons' letter, the *Ancestor*, for July and October, 1903, and Jan., 1904.

Prince of Wales appeared, at the head of a large Welsh contingent.   Little of military importance happened.   Edward
remained in Scotland over the cold season, and kept his Christmas court at Linlithgow.   Men and horses perished amidst the
rigours of the northern winter, and, before the end of January,
1302, the king was glad to accept a truce, suggested by Philip
of France, to last until the end of November.   Immediately
afterwards he was called to the south by the negotiations for a
permanent peace with France, which still hung fire despite his
marriage to the French king's sister.   The earlier stages of the
negotiation were transacted at Rome, but it was soon clear to
Edward that no good would come to him from the intervention
of the *curia*.   The fundamental difficulty still lay in the refusal
of Philip to relax his grasp on Gascony.   Not even the exaltation, consequent on the success of the famous jubilee of
1300, blinded Boniface to the patent fact that he dared not
order the restitution of Gascony.   "We cannot give you an
award," declared the pope to the English envoys in 1300.   "If
we pronounced in your favour, the French would not abide by it,
and could not be compelled, for they would make light of any
penalty."   "What the French once lay hold of," he said again,
"they never let go, and to have to do with the French is to
have to do with the devil." [1]   A year later Boniface could do no
more than appeal to the crusading zeal of Edward not to allow
his claim on a patch of French soil to stand between him and his
vow.   With such commonplaces the papal mediation died away.

Two events in 1302 indirectly contributed towards the
establishment of a permanent peace.   These were the successful revolt of Flanders from French domination, and the renewed quarrel between Philip and Boniface.   On May 18, the
Flemings, in the "matins of Bruges," cruelly avenged themselves for the oppressions which they had endured from Philip's
officials, and on July 11 the revolted townsfolk won the battle
of Courtrai, in which their heavy armed infantry defeated the
feudal cavalry of France, a victory of the same kind as that
Wallace had vainly hoped to gain at Falkirk.   Even before
the Flemish rising, the reassertion of high sacerdotal doctrine
in the bull *Ausculta, fili* had renewed the strife between Boni-

CHAP.
XI.

---

[1] See the remarkable report of the Bishop of Winchester to Edward printed
in *Engl. Hist. Review*, xvii. (1902), pp. 518-27.

CHAP.
XI.

face and the French king.   A few months later the bull *Unam sanctam* laid down with emphasis the doctrine that those who denied that the temporal sword belongs to St. Peter were heretics, unmindful of the teachings of Christ.   Thus began the famous difference that went on with ever-increasing fury until the outrage at Anagni, on September 7, 1303, brought about the fall of Boniface and the overthrow of the Hildebrandine papacy.   Meanwhile Philip was devoting his best energies to constant, and not altogether vain, attempts to avenge the defeat of Courtrai, and re-establish his hold on Flanders.   With these two affairs on his hands, it was useless for him to persevere in his attempt to hold Gascony.

In the earlier stages of his quarrel with Philip, Boniface built great hopes on Edward's support, and strongly urged him to fight for holy Church against the impious French king.   But Edward had suffered too much from Boniface to fall into so obvious a trap.   His hold over his own clergy was so firm that Winchelsea himself had no chance of taking up the papal call to battle.   Thus it was that *Unam sanctam* produced no such clerical revolt in England as *Clericis laicos* had done.   It was Edward's policy to make use of Philip's necessities to win back Gascony, and cut off all hope of French support from the Scottish patriots.   Philip himself was the more disposed to agree with his brother-in-law's wishes, because about Christmas, 1302, Bordeaux threw off the French yoke and called in the English.   The best way to save French dignity was by timely concession.   Accordingly, on May 20, 1303, the definitive treaty of Paris was sealed, by which the two kings were pledged to "perpetual peace and friendship".   Gascony was restored, and Edward agreed that he, or his son, should perform liege homage for it.   With the discharge of this duty by the younger Edward at Amiens, in 1304, the last stage of the pacification was accomplished.   For the rest of the reign, England and France remained on cordial terms.   Neither Edward nor Philip had resources adequate to the accomplishment of great schemes of foreign conquest.   Though Edward got back Gascony, he owed it, not to his own power, but to the embarrassment of his rival.

While completing his pacification with Philip the Fair, Edward was busily engaged in establishing his power at home, at the expense of the clerical and baronial opposition, which had stood for so many years in the way of the conquest of Scotland. Since the parliament of Lincoln, Winchelsea was no longer dangerous. He failed even to get Boniface on his side in a scandalous attack which he instigated on Bishop Langton. His constant efforts to enlarge his jurisdiction raised up enemies all over his diocese and province, and the mob of his cathedral city broke open his palace, while he was in residence there. His inability to introduce into England even a pale reflection of the struggle of Philip and the pope showed how clearly he had lost influence since the days of *Clericis laicos*. A more recent convert to higher clerical pretensions also failed. Bishop Bek of Durham lost all his power, and was deprived of his temporalities by the king in 1302. Two years later the insignificant Archbishop of York also incurred the royal displeasure, and was punished in the same fashion. With Durham, Norhamshire, and Hexhamshire all in the royal hands, the road into Scotland was completely open.

The heavy hand of Edward fell upon earls as well as upon bishops. Even in the early days of his reign when none, save Gilbert of Gloucester, dared uplift the standard of opposition, Edward had not spared the greatest barons in his efforts to eliminate the idea of tenure from English political life. A subtle extension of his earlier policy began to emphasise the dependence of the landed dignitaries on his pleasure. The extinction of several important baronial houses made this the easier, and Edward took care to retain escheats in his own hands, or at least to entrust them only to persons of approved confidence. The old leaders of opposition were dead or powerless. Ralph of Monthermer, the simple north-country knight who had won the hand of Joan of Acre, ruled over the Gloucester-Glamorgan inheritance on behalf of his wife and Edward's little grandson, Gilbert of Clare. The Earl of Hereford died in 1299, and in 1302 his son and successor, another Humphrey Bohun, was bribed by a marriage with the king's daughter, Elizabeth, the widowed Countess of Holland, to surrender his lands to the crown and receive them back, like the Earl of Gloucester in 1290, entailed on the issue of himself and his consort. In the same year the childless earl marshal, Roger Bigod, conscious of his inability to continue any longer his struggle against royal assumptions and at variance with his

CHAP.
XI.

brother and heir, made a similar surrender of his estates, which was the more humiliating since the estate in tail, with which he was reinvested, was bound to terminate with his life.   In 1306, on the marshal's death, the Bigod inheritance lapsed to the crown.   Much earlier than that, in 1293, Edward had extorted on her deathbed from the great heiress, Isabella of Fors, Countess of Albemarle and Devon, the bequest of the Isle of Wight and the adjacent castle of Christchurch.   In 1300, on the death of the king's childless cousin, Earl Edmund, the wealthy earldom of Cornwall escheated to the crown.   To Edward's contemporaries the acquisition of the earldoms of Norfolk and Cornwall seemed worthy to be put alongside the conquests of Wales and Scotland.[1]

Even more important as adding to Edward's resources than these direct additions to the royal domains, was the increasing dependence of the remaining earls upon the crown.   His sons-in-law of Gloucester and Hereford were entirely under his sway. In 1304 the aged Earl Warenne had died, and in 1306 his grandson and successor was bound closely to the royal policy by his marriage with Joan of Bar, Edward's grand-daughter.   In the same way Edward's young nephew, Thomas of Lancaster, ruled over the three earldoms of Lancaster, Derby, and Leicester, and by his marriage to the daughter and heiress of Henry Lacy, was destined to add to his immense estates the additional earldoms of Lincoln and Salisbury.   Edward of Carnarvon was learning the art of government in Wales, Cheshire, and Ponthieu. The policy of concentrating the higher baronial dignities in the royal family was no novelty, but Edward carried it out more systematically and successfully than any of his predecessors. He reaped the immediate advantages of his dexterity in the extinction of baronial opposition and in the zeal of the baronial levies against the Scots during the concluding years of his reign. Yet the later history of the Middle Ages bears witness to the grievous dangers to the wielder of the royal power which lurked beneath a system so attractive in appearance.

The truce with the Scots ended in November, 1302, and Edward despatched a strong force to the north under John Segrave.   On February 24, 1303, Segrave, attacked unex-

---

[1] See John of London, *Commendatio lamentabilis* in *Chron. of Edw. I. and Edw. II.*, ii., 8-9.   See for the earldoms my *Earldoms under Edward I.* in *Transactions of the Royal Historical Society*, new ser., viii. (1894), 129-155.

pectedly by the enemy at Roslin, near Edinburgh, suffered a CHAP.
severe defeat. The conclusion of the treaty of Paris gave Ed-   XI.
ward the opportunity for avenging the disaster. He summoned
his levies to assemble at Roxburgh for Whitsuntide and, a
fortnight before that time, appeared in person in Tweeddale.
After seven weary years of waiting and failure, he was at
last in a position to wear down the obstinate Scots by the
same systematic and deliberate policy that had won for him
the principality of Wales. The invasion of Scotland was
henceforth to continue as long as the Scottish resistance.
Adequate resources were procured to enable the royal armies
to hold the field, and a politic negotiation with the foreign
merchants resulted in a *carta mercatoria* by which additional
customs were imposed upon English exports. These imposts,
known as the "new and small customs," as opposed to the "old
and great customs" established in 1275, were not sanctioned by
parliamentary grant : but for the moment they provoked no
opposition. Thus Edward was equipped both with men and
money for his undertaking. At last the true conquest of Scotland began.

No attempt was made in the Lothians to stop Edward's advance, but the Scots, under the regent, John Comyn of Badenoch,
made a vigorous effort to hold the line of the Forth against him.
Their plan seemed to promise well, for Stirling castle was still
in Scottish hands. Edward crossed the river by a ford, and all
organised efforts to oppose him at once ceased. Prudently leaving Stirling to itself for the present, he hurried to Perth. After
spending most of June and July at Perth, he led his army
northwards, nearly following the line of his advance in 1296,
through Perth, Brechin, and Aberdeen, to Banff and Elgin.
The most remote point reached was Kinloss, a few miles west
of Elgin, in which neighbourhood he spent much of September.
Then he slowly retraced his steps and took up his winter
quarters at Dunfermline. In all this long progress, the only
energetic resistance which Edward encountered was at Brechin.
Flushed with his triumph, he ordered Stirling to be besieged,
and from April, 1304, directed the operations himself. The
garrison held out with the utmost gallantry, but at last a breach
was effected in the walls, and on July 24 the defenders laid
down their arms. Long before the Scots people despaired of

withstanding the invader, the nobles grew cold in the defence of their country.   In February, 1304, the regent and many of the earls made their submission.   It was more than suspected that this result was brought about by the threat of Edward to divide their lands among his English followers.   But on Comyn and his friends showing a desire to yield, the king readily promised them their lives and estates.   Believing that his task was over, Edward returned to England in August after an absence of nearly fifteen months.   He crossed the Humber early in December, kept his Christmas court at Lincoln, and reached London late in February.   As a sign of the completion of the conquest, he ordered that the law courts, which since 1297 had been established at York, should resume their sessions in London.

A few heroes still upheld the independence of Scotland. Foremost among them was Sir William Wallace, who, since his mission to France in 1298, had disappeared from history. The submission of the barons to Edward gave him another chance.   He took a strenuous part in the struggle of 1303-4, and he was specially exempted from the easy pardons with which Edward purchased the submission of the greater nobles.   It was the daring and skill of Wallace that prolonged the Scots' struggle until the spring of 1305.   But he was then once more an outlaw and a fugitive, only formidable by his hold over the people, and by the possibility that the smallest spark of resistance might at any time be blown into a flame.   At last he was captured through the zeal, or treachery, of a Scot in Edward's service.   In August, Wallace was despatched to London to stand a public trial for treason, sedition, sacrilege, and murder.   He denied that he had ever become Edward's subject, but did not escape conviction.   With his execution, the last stage of Edward's triumph in Scotland was accomplished. Though the full measure of Wallace's fame belongs to a later age rather than his own, yet it was a sure instinct that made the Scottish people celebrate him as the popular hero of their struggle for independence.   His courage, persistency, and daring stands in marked contrast to the self-seeking opportunism of the great nobles, who afterwards appropriated the results of his endeavours.   Yet we can hardly blame Edward for making an example of him, when he fell into his power.   Even if Wallace had successfully evaded the oath of fealty to Edward, it is scarcely reasonable to expect that the king would consider this technical plea as availing against his doctrine that all Scots were necessarily his subjects since the submission of 1296. It was Wallace's glory that he fought his fight and paid the penalty of it.

A full parliament of the three estates sat with the king at Westminster from February 28 to March 21, 1305. The proceedings of this assembly are known with a fulness exceeding that of the record of any of the other parliaments of the reign.[1] Among the matters enumerated in the writs as specially demanding attention was the "establishment of our realm of Scotland". Three Scottish magnates, Robert Wishart, Bishop of Glasgow, Robert Bruce, Earl of Carrick, and John Mowbray were particularly called upon to give their advice as to how Scotland was to be represented in a later parliament, in which the plans for its future government were to be drawn up. They informed the king that two bishops, two abbots, two barons, and two representatives of the commons, one from the south of the Forth and the other from the north thereof, would be sufficient for this purpose. This further "parliament" assembled on September 15, three weeks after the execution of Wallace. It consisted simply of twenty councillors of Edward, and the ten Scottish delegates. From the joint deliberations of these thirty sprang the "ordinance made by the lord king for the establishment of the land of Scotland".

Following the general lines of the settlement of the principality of Wales, the ordinance combined Edward's direct lordship over Scotland with a legal and administrative system separate from that of England. John of Brittany, Earl of Richmond, the king's sister's son, was made Edward's lieutenant and warden of Scotland, and under him were a chancellor, a chamberlain, and a controller. Scotland was to be split up for judicial purposes into districts corresponding to its racial and political divisions. Four pairs of justices were appointed for each of these regions, two for Lothian, two for Galloway and the southwest, two for the lands "between Forth and the mountains," that is the Lowland districts of the north-east, and two for the lands "beyond the mountains," that is for the Highlands and islands. Sheriffs "natives either of England or Scotland" were

---

[1] See *Memoranda de parliamento* (1305), ed. F. W. Maitland (Rolls Series).

15 *

nominated for each of the shires, and it was significant that the great majority of them were Scots and that the hereditary sheriffdoms of the older system were still continued. The " custom of the Scots and the Welsh," that is the Celtic laws of the Highlanders and the Strathclyde Welsh, was "henceforth prohibited and disused ". John of Brittany was to " assemble the good people of Scotland in a convenient place " where " the laws of King David and the amendments by other kings " were to be rehearsed, and such of these laws as are " plainly against God and reason " were to be reformed, all doubtful matters being referred to the judgment of Edward. The king's lieutenant was bidden to " remove such persons as might disturb the peace " to the south of the Trent, but their deportation was to be in " courteous fashion " and after taking the advice of the " good people of Scotland ". Care for the preservation of the peace, and for administrative reform, is seen in the oath imposed upon officials and in the pains taken to secure the custody of the castles. The Scots parliament was to be retained, and recent precedents also suggested the probability of Scottish representation in the parliament of England. If Scotland were to be ruled by Edward at all, it would have been difficult to devise a wiser scheme for its administration. Yet the Scottish love of independence was not to be bartered away for better government. Within six months the new constitution was overthrown, and the chief part in its destruction was taken by the Scots by whose advice Edward had drawn it up.

Edward at last felt himself in a position to take his long deferred revenge on Winchelsea. The primate still kept aloof from the councils of the king, and his spirit was as irreconcilable as ever. He gained his last victory in the Lenten parliament of 1305, when he prevented the promulgation of a statute, passed on the petition of the laity, but agreed to by all the estates, which forbade taxes on ecclesiastical property involving the exportation of money out of the country.[1] At this moment the long vacancy of the papacy, which followed the pontificate of Benedict XI., Boniface VIII.'s short-lived successor, had not yet come to an end. Soon, however, Winchelsea's zeal on

---

[1] *Memoranda de parliamento*, preface, p. li.   The statement in the text is an inference suggested by Professor Maitland's account of the statute *De asportis religiosorum*.   For the last struggle of Edward and Winchelsea, see Stubbs's preface to *Chron. of Edw. I. and Edw. II.*, i., xcix.-cxiii.

behalf of papal taxation was to be ill requited. On June 5, 1305, CHAP.
Bertrand de Goth, a Gascon nobleman who since 1299 had XI.
been archbishop of Bordeaux, was elected to the papacy as
Clement V., through the management of Philip the Fair. A
dependant of the King of France and a subject of the King of
England, the new pope showed a complaisance towards kings
which stood in strong contrast to the ultramontane austerity of
his predecessors. He refused to visit Italy, received the papal
crown at Lyons, and spent the first years of his pontificate in
Poitou and Gascony. Ultimately establishing himself at Avignon, he began that seventy years of Babylonish captivity of
the apostolic see which greatly degraded the papacy. Though
Clement's main concern was to fulfil the exacting conditions
which, as it was believed, Philip had imposed upon him, he
was almost as subservient to Edward as to the King of
France. His deference to his natural lord enabled Edward
to renounce the most irksome of the obligations which he had
incurred to his subjects, to punish Winchelsea, and to restrain
Roman authority by laws which anticipate the legislation of
the age of Edward III.

At Clement V.'s coronation at Lyons, in November, England
was represented by Winchelsea's old enemy, Bishop Walter Langton, and by the Earl of Lincoln. The first result of their work was
the promulgation, on December 29, of the bull *Regalis devotionis*,
by which the pope annulled the additions made to the charters
in 1297 and succeeding years, and dispensed Edward from the
oath which he had taken to observe them, on the ground that it
was in conflict with his coronation vows. Next year Edward
took advantage of this bull to revoke the disafforestments made,
by the parliament of Lincoln in 1301. It may be a sign either
of the moderation, or of the well-grounded fears of the king, that
he made no further use of the papal absolution. But, like his
father and grandfather, he used the papal authority to set aside
his plighted word, and his conduct in this respect suggests that
it was well for England that the renewal of the Scottish troubles
reduced for the rest of the reign the temptation, which the
bull held out to him, to play fast and loose with the liberties
of his subjects. The standards of contemporary morality were
not, however, infringed by Edward's action, dishonourable and
undignified as it seems to us of later times.

Winchelsea's turn was at last come.   On February 12, 1306, Clement suspended him from his office, and summoned him to appear before the *curia*.   On March 25 the archbishop humbled himself before Edward and begged for his protection.   But the king overwhelmed him with reproaches and refused to show him any mercy.   Within two months, the primate took ship for France and made his way to the papal court, which was then established at Bordeaux.   He remained in exile, though in the English king's dominions, for the rest of Edward's life. A less harsh punishment was meted out to the Bishop of Durham, who then came back from the court of Clement with the magnificent title of Patriarch of Jerusalem.   For a second time Edward laid violent hands upon the rich temporalities of the see, and Bek, like Winchelsea, remained under a cloud for the remainder of the reign.

Clement expected to be paid for yielding so much to the king.   A papal agent, William de Testa, was sent to England, and to him Edward gave the administration of the temporalities of Canterbury.   William's energy in collecting first-fruits aroused a storm of opposition from the clergy.   The laity, disgusted to find that the king was negotiating for the transference of a crusading tenth to himself, associated themselves with their protest.   Clement thereupon despatched the Cardinal Peter of Spain to England, that he might attempt to arrange a general pacification, and complete the marriage of the Prince of Wales to Isabella of France, which had been agreed upon in 1303. Before the cardinal's arrival, Edward's last parliament met in January, 1307, at Carlisle.   The renewed disturbances in Scotland necessitated a meeting on the border, but the main transactions of the estates bore upon matters ecclesiastical.   The lords and commons joined in demanding from the king a remedy against the oppressions of the apostolic see.   A spirited and strongly worded protest was addressed to the pope.   Nor were the estates contented with mere remonstrances.   The statute of Carlisle renewed the abortive measure of 1305, *De asportis religiosorum*, by prohibiting tallages of religious houses being sent out of the realm.   Had the petition of the estates been drafted into a statute, the parliament of Carlisle would have anticipated the statute of *Præmunire* and many other anti-papal enactments. But Peter of Spain arrived, and Edward thought it injudicious to provoke a contest with the papacy. Even the petition actually approved was left in suspense to await further negotiations between the king and the cardinal. Before any decision was come to, Edward died, and this anti-Roman movement, like so many which had preceded it, resulted in little more than brave words. When, two generations later, a more resolute temper seized upon king and estates, they fell back upon the petitions and proceedings of the parliament of Carlisle for precedents for resisting the papal authority. With all its pitiful conclusion, Edward's ecclesiastical policy at least marks a step in advance upon the dependent attitude of Henry III.

In the period of peace after the conquest of Scotland, Edward busied himself with strengthening the administration of his own kingdom and with enforcing the laws against violence and outrage. Under the strongest of medieval kings, the state of society was very disorderly, and even a ruler like Edward had often to be contented with holding up in his legislation an ideal of conduct which he was powerless to enforce in detail. Complaints had long been made that the greater nobles encroached upon poor men's inheritances, that gangs of marauders ranged over the country, wreaking every sort of violence and outrage, and that the law courts would give no redress to the sufferers from such outrageous deeds, since judges and juries were alike terrorised by overmighty offenders and dared not administer equal justice. Accordingly in the Lenten parliament of 1305 was drawn up the ordinance of Trailbaston, by which the king was empowered to issue writs of inquiry, addressed to special justices in the various shires, and authorising them to take vigorous action against these *trailbastons*, or men with clubs, whose outrages had become so grievous. It was not so much a new law as an administrative act; but it formed a precedent for later times, and the energy of the justices of trailbaston effected a real, if temporary, improvement in the condition of the country. So important was the measure that a chronicler calls the year in which this was enacted the "year of trailbaston".[1]

Never did Edward's prospects seem brighter than in the early days of 1306. Scotland was obedient; the French alliance was firmly cemented; the pope was complacent; the Archbishop

---

[1] *Liber de antiquis legibus*, p. 250.

of Canterbury was in exile and the Bishop of Durham in disgrace; the commons were grateful for the better order secured
by the commissions of trailbaston, and the king had in the papal
absolution a weapon in reserve, which he could always use
against a renewal of baronial opposition, though, for the moment,
neither nobles nor commons seemed likely to give trouble.
Once more there was some talk of Edward leading a crusade,
and the French lawyer, Peter Dubois, at this time dedicated to
him the first draft of his remarkable treatise on the recovery of
the Holy Land.[1]   Nor did the project seem altogether impracticable.   Though Edward was sixty-seven years of age, he remained slim, vigorous and straight as a palm tree.   He could
mount his horse and ride to the hunt or the field with the
activity of youth.   His eyes were not dimmed with age and his
teeth were still firm in his jaws.[2]   The worst trouble which
immediately beset him, was the undutiful conduct of the young
Prince of Wales, who foolishly quarrelled with Bishop Langton,
and preferred to amuse himself with unworthy favourites rather
than submit himself to the severe training in arms and affairs
to which Edward had long striven to inure him.   When all
thus seemed favourable, a sudden storm burst in Scotland which
plunged the old king into renewed troubles.

In 1304 Robert Bruce, Earl of Carrick, became by his
father's death the head of his house.   Though he had long adhered to the regency which had governed Scotland in Balliol's
name, he had now made terms with Edward, and had taken
a conspicuous part in bringing about the pacification of Scotland
under its new constitution.   But the double policy, which had
involved him in the shifts and tergiversations of his earlier
career, still dominated the mind of the ambitious earl.   At the
moment of his submission to Edward, he entered into an intimate alliance with Bishop Lamberton of St. Andrews, the old
partisan of Wallace.   Lamberton was then, like Bruce, on Edward's side, and as John of Brittany had not yet personally taken
up his new charge, the blind confidence of Edward entrusted
him with the foremost place among the commissioners who acted
as wardens of Scotland during the king's lieutenant's absence.

[1] *De recuperatione terre sancte*, ed. C. V. Langlois (1891).
[2] John of London, *Commendatio lamentabilis*, pp. 5-6.

Bruce, still remembering his grandfather's claim on the throne, welcomed the definitive setting aside of Balliol. While Edward believed that Scotland was quieting down under its new constitution, Bruce was secretly conspiring with the Scottish magnates, with the view of making himself king. His chief difficulty was with the late regent, John Comyn the Red, lord of Badenoch. The Bruces and the Comyns had long been at variance, and the Red Comyn, who was the nephew of the deposed King John, regarded himself as the representative of the Balliol claim to the throne, and was not unmindful how his father had withdrawn his pretensions in 1291 rather than divide the Balliol interest. Meanwhile the antagonism of the two houses was the best safeguard for the continuance of Edward's rule.

Bruce was violent as well as able and ambitious. He invited Comyn to a conference for January 10, 1306, in the Franciscan friary at Dumfries. On that day the king's justices were holding the assizes in the castle, and Bruce and Comyn, with a few followers, met in the cloister of the convent. Hot words were exchanged, and Bruce drew his sword and wounded Comyn. The lord of Badenoch took refuge in the church, and some of Bruce's friends followed him and slew him on the steps of the high altar. This cruel murder involved a violent breach between Bruce and the king. The earl took to the hills, declared himself the champion of national independence, and renewed his claim to the crown. He was joined by a great multitude of the people and by a certain number of the magnates. Conspicuous among the latter was Bishop Wishart of Glasgow, who broke his sixth oath of fealty, using the timber given him by Edward for building the steeple of his cathedral in constructing military engines to besiege the castles which were still held for the English king. Before long Bishop Lamberton, the chief of the Edwardian government, also went over. The support of the two bishops enabled Bruce to be crowned on March 25 at Scone. All Scotland was soon in revolt, and only the garrisons and a few magnates remained faithful to Edward.

News of the death of Comyn and the revolt of Bruce reached Edward, while engaged in hunting in Dorset and Wiltshire. He at once called upon Church and State to unite against the sacrilegious murderer and traitor. Clement V. excommunicated the Earl of Carrick, and deprived Lamberton and Wishart of their bishoprics.   The warlike zeal of the English barons was stimulated by liberal grants of the forfeited estates of Bruce and his partisans.   Feeling the infirmities of age coming upon him, Edward saw that his best chance of success was to inspire his son with something of his spirit.   The Prince of Wales accordingly received a grant of Gascony, and on Whitsunday, May 22, was dubbed knight at Westminster along with over two hundred other aspirants to arms.   A magnificent feast in Westminster Hall succeeded the ceremony.   Two swans, adorned with golden chains, were brought in, and the old king set to all the revellers the example of vowing on the swans to revenge the murder of Comyn.   Edward swore that when he had expiated this wrong to Holy Church, he would never more bear arms against Christian man, but would immediately turn his steps towards the Holy Land to redeem the Holy Sepulchre. The Prince of Wales' vow was never to rest two nights in the same spot until he had reached Scotland to assist his father in his purpose.   Then all the young knights were despatched northwards to overthrow the Scottish pretender.

A liberal grant from the estates facilitated the military preparations. But since the beginning of the year, Edward's strength had rapidly broken.   He was no longer able to ride, and his movements were consequently very tedious.   His army gathered together with more than the usual slowness, and Aymer of Valence, Earl of Pembroke, the king's cousin, was sent forward as warden of Scotland to meet Bruce with such forces as were ready.   On June 26 Aymer fell upon Bruce at Methven, near Perth, and inflicted a severe defeat upon him.   The power of the pretender died away as rapidly as it had arisen.   The Bishops of St. Andrews and Glasgow were made prisoners, and Bruce's brothers, wife, and daughter fell into the enemy's hands. The brothers were promptly beheaded, though one of them was an ecclesiastic, and the ladies were confined in English nunneries.   Bruce himself fled to Kintyre, and thence to Rathlin island, off the coast of Antrim.

Edward went north in July, and, after a long stay in Northumberland, took up his quarters early in October with the Austin canons of Lanercost, near Carlisle.   There he remained for above five months.   In January, 1307, the parliament, whose anti-clerical policy has already been recounted, assembled at Carlisle, and remained in session until March. With the spring, Bruce crossed over from Ireland, and re-appeared in his own lands in the south-west. In May he revenged the rout of Methven by inflicting a bloody check on Aymer of Valence near Ayr, and within three days gained another victory over Edward's son-in-law, Earl Ralph of Gloucester. These blows only spurred on Edward to increased efforts. The levies were summoned to meet at Carlisle and, regardless of his infirmities, the old king resolved to lead his troops in person. On July 3 he once more mounted his horse and started for the border. But his constitution could not respond to the demands made on it by his unbroken spirit. After a journey of two miles he was forced to rest for the night. Next day he could only traverse a similar distance, and his exertions so fatigued him that he was compelled to remain at his lodgings all the following day. This repose enabled him to make his way, on July 6, to Burgh-on-Sands, less than seven miles from Carlisle, where he spent the night. On July 7, as he was being raised in his bed by his attendants to take his morning meal, he fell back in their arms and expired.

CHAPTER XII.

GAVESTON, THE ORDAINERS, AND BANNOCKBURN.

CHAP.
XII.

EDWARD OF CARNARVON was over twenty-three years of age when he became king. Tall, graceful, and handsome, with magnificent health and exceptional bodily strength, the young king was, so far as externals went, almost as fine a man as his father. Yet no one could have been more absolutely destitute of all those qualities which constitute Edward I.'s claims to greatness. An utter want of serious purpose blasted his whole career. It was in vain that his father subjected him to a careful training in statecraft and in military science. Though not lacking in intelligence, the young prince from the first to the last concerned himself with nothing but his own amusements. A confirmed gambler and a deep drinker, Edward showed a special bent for unkingly and frivolous diversions. Save in his devotion for the chase, his tastes had nothing in common with the high-born youths with whom he was educated. He showed himself a coward on the battlefield, and shirked even the mimic warfare of the tournament. He repaid the contempt and dislike of his own class by withdrawing himself from the society of the nobles, and associating himself with buffoons, singers, play-actors, coachmen, ditchers, watermen, sailors, and smiths. Of the befitting comrades of his youth, the only one of the higher aristocracy with whom he had any true intimacy was his nephew, Gilbert of Clare, while the only member of his household for whom he showed real affection was the Gascon knight, Peter of Gaveston.[1] Attributing his son's levity to Gaveston's corrupting influence, the old king had banished the foreign favourite early in 1307. But no change in his surroundings could stir up the prince's frivolous nature to fulfil the duties of his station. Edward's most kingly qualities were

[1] That is Gabaston, dep. Basses Pyrénées, cant. Morlaas.

236

love of fine clothes and of ceremonies. Passionately fond of rowing, driving, horse-breeding, and the rearing of dogs, his ordinary occupations were those of the athlete or the artisan. He was skilful with his hands, and an excellent mechanic, proficient at the anvil and the forge, and proud of his skill in digging ditches and thatching roofs. Interested in music, and devoted to play-acting, he was badly educated, taking the coronation oath in the French form provided for a king ignorant of Latin. Vain, irritable, and easily moved to outbursts of childish wrath, he was half-conscious of the weakness of his will, and was never without a favourite, whose affection compensated him for his subjects' contempt. The household of so careless a master was disorderly beyond the ordinary measure of the time. While Edward irritated the nobles by his neglect of their counsel, he vexed the commons by the exactions of his purveyors.

The task which lay before Edward might well have daunted a stronger man. The old king had failed in the great purpose of his life. Scotland was in full revolt and had found a man able to guide her destinies. The crown was deeply in debt; the exchequer was bare of supplies, and the revenues both of England and Gascony were farmed by greedy and unpopular companies of Italian bankers, such as the Frescobaldi of Florence, the king's chief creditors. The nobles, though restrained by the will of the old king, still cherished the ideals of the age of the Barons' War, and were convinced that the best way to rule England was to entrust the machinery of the central government, which Edward I. had elaborated with so much care, to the control of a narrow council of earls and prelates. Winchelsea, though broken in health, looked forward in his banishment to the renewal of the alliance of baronage and clergy, and to the reassertion of hierarchical ideals. The papal *curia*, already triumphant in the last days of the reign of the dead king, was anticipating a return to the times of Henry III., when every dignity of the English Church was at its mercy. The strenuous endeavour which had marked the last reign gave place to the extreme of negligence.

Edward at once broke with the policy of his father. After receiving, at Carlisle, the homage of the English magnates, he crossed the Solway to Dumfries, where such Scottish barons as had not joined Robert Bruce took oaths of fealty to him. He soon relinquished the personal conduct of the war, and travelled slowly to Westminster on the pretext of following his father's body to its last resting-place. He replaced his father's ministers by dependants of his own. Bishop Walter Langton, the chief minister of the last years of Edward I., was singled out for special vengeance. He was stripped of his offices, robbed of his treasure, and thrown into close confinement, without any regard to the immunities of a churchman from secular jurisdiction. Langton's place as treasurer was given to Walter Reynolds, an illiterate clerk, who had won the chief place in Edward's household through his skill in theatricals. Ralph Baldock, Bishop of London, was replaced in the chancery by John Langton, Bishop of Chichester. The barons of the exchequer, the justices of the high courts, and the other ministers of the old king were removed in favour of more complacent successors. Signal favour was shown to all who had fallen under Edward I.'s displeasure. Bishop Bek, of Durham, was restored to his palatinate, and the road to return opened to Winchelsea, though ill-health detained him on the Continent for some time longer. Conspicuous among the returned exiles was Peter of Gaveston, whom the king welcomed with the warmest affection. He at once invested his " brother Peter " with the rich earldom of Cornwall, which the old king, with the object of conferring it on one of his sons by his second marriage, had kept in his hands since Earl Edmund's death. A little later Edward married the favourite to his niece, Margaret of Clare, the eldest sister of Earl Gilbert of Gloucester. Of the tried comrades of Edward I. the only one who remained in authority was Henry Lacy, Earl of Lincoln. The abandonment of the Scottish campaign soon followed. It was no wonder that the Scots lords, who had performed homage to Edward at Dumfries, began to turn to Bruce. Already king of the Scottish commons, Robert was in a fair way to become accepted by the whole people.

The readiness with which the barons acquiesced in Edward's reversal of his father's policy shows that they had regarded the late king's action with little favour. Lincoln, the wisest and most influential of the earls, even found reasons for the grant of Cornwall to Gaveston, and kept in check his son-in-law, Earl Thomas of Lancaster, who was the most disposed to grumble

at the elevation of the Gascon favourite. Gilbert of Gloucester
was but newly come to his earldom. He was personally attached to the king, his old playmate and uncle, and was not
unfriendly to his Gascon brother-in-law. The recent concentration of the great estates in the hands of a few individuals
gave these three earls a position of overwhelming importance
both in the court and in the country, and with their good-will
Edward was safe. But the weakness of the king and the rash-
ness of the favourite soon caused murmurs to arise.

Early in 1308 Edward crossed over to France, leaving
Gaveston as regent, and was married on January 25, at Boulogne, to Philip the Fair's daughter Isabella, a child of
twelve, to whom he had been plighted since 1298. The
marriage was attended by the French king and a great gathering of the magnates of both countries. Opportunity was taken
of the meeting for Edward to perform homage for Aquitaine.
After the arrival of the royal couple in England, their coronation took place on February 25. Time had been when
the reign began with the king's crowning; but Edward had
taken up every royal function immediately on his father's
death, and set a precedent to later sovereigns by dating his own
accession from the day succeeding the decease of his predecessor. The coronation ceremony, minutely recorded, provided
precedents for later ages. It was some recognition of the work
of the last generation that the coronation oath was somewhat
more rigid and involved a more definite recognition of the
rights of the community than on earlier occasions. Winchelsea
was still abroad, and the hallowing was performed by Henry
Woodlock, Bishop of Winchester.

Discontent was already simmering. Not even Lincoln's
weighty influence could overcome the irritation of the earls at
the elevation of the Gascon knight into their circle. The very
virtues of the vigorous favourite turned to his discredit. At a
tournament given by him, at his own castle of Wallingford, to
celebrate his marriage with the king's niece, the new-made earl,
with a party of valiant knights, challenged a troop, which included the Earls of Hereford, Warenne, and Arundel, and
utterly discomfited his rivals.[1] The victory of the upstart over
magnates of such dignity was accounted for by treachery, and

---

[1] *Ann. Paulini*, p. 258, and Monk of Malmesbury, p. 156, are to be preferred to Trokelowe, p. 65.

the prohibition of a coronation tournament, probably a simple measure of police, was ascribed to the unwillingness of Peter to give his opponents a legitimate opportunity of vindicating their skill.   There had been much resentment at Gaveston's appointment as regent during the king's absence in France.   A further outburst of indignation followed when the Gascon, magnificently arrayed and bedecked with jewels, bore the crown of St. Edward in the coronation procession.   The queen's uncles, who had escorted her to her new home, left England disgusted that Edward's love for Gaveston led him to neglect his bride, and the want of reserve shown in the personal dealings of the king and his "idol" suggested the worst interpretation of their relations, though this is against the weight of evidence.   Rumours spread that the favourite had laid hands on the vast treasures which Bishop Walter Langton had deposited at the New Temple, and had extorted from the king even larger sums, which he had sent to his kinsfolk in Gascony by the agency of the Italian farmers of the revenue.

Gaveston was a typical Gascon, vain, loquacious, and ostentatious, proud of his own ready wit and possessed of a fatal talent for sharp and bitter sayings.   He seems to have been a brave and generous soldier.   There is little proof that he was specially vicious or incompetent, and, had he been allowed time to establish himself, he might well have been the parent of a noble house, as patriotic and as narrowly English as the Valence lords of Pembroke had become in the second generation.   But his sudden elevation rather turned his head, and the dull but dignified English earls were soon mortally offended by his airs of superiority, and by his intervention between them and the sovereign.   "If," wrote the annalist of St. Paul's, London, "one of the earls or magnates sought any special favour of the king, the king forthwith sent him to Peter, and whatever Peter said or ordered at once took place, and the king ratified it.   Hence the whole people grew indignant that there should be two kings in one kingdom, one the king in name, the other the king in reality."   Gaveston's vanity was touched by the sullen hostility of the earls.   He returned their suspicion by an openly expressed contempt.   He amused himself and the king by devising nicknames for them.   Thomas of Lancaster was the old pig or the play-actor, Aymer of Pembroke was Joseph the Jew, Gilbert

of Gloucester was the cuckoo, and Guy of Warwick was the
black dog of Arden. Such jests were bitterly resented. " If
he call me dog," said Warwick on hearing of the insult, " I
will take care to bite him." The barons formed an association,
bound by oath to drive Gaveston into exile and deprive him
of his earldom. All over the country there were secret meetings
and eager preparations for war. The outlook became still more
alarming when the Earl of Lincoln at last changed his policy.
Convinced of the unworthiness of Gaveston, he turned against
him, and the whole baronage followed his lead. Only Hugh
Despenser and a few lawyers adhered to the favourite. Gloucester did not like to take an active part against his brother-
in-law, but his stepfather, Monthermer, was conspicuous among
the enemies of the Gascon. Winchelsea, too, came to England
and threw his powerful influence on the side of the opposition.

In April, 1308, a parliament of nobles met and insisted upon
the exile of the favourite. The magnates took up a high line.
" Homage and the oath of allegiance," they declared, " are due
to the crown rather than to the person of the king. If the king
behave unreasonably, his lieges are bound to bring him back to
the ways of righteousness." On May 18 letters patent were
issued promising that Gaveston should be banished before June
25. Gaveston, bending before the storm, surrendered his earldom and prepared for departure, while Winchelsea and the
bishops declared him excommunicate if he tarried in England
beyond the appointed day. The king did his best to lighten
his friend's misfortune. Fresh grants of land and castles
compensated for the loss of Cornwall and gave him means for
armed resistance. The grant of Gascon counties, jurisdictions,
cities and castles to the value of 3,000 marks a year provided
him with a dignified refuge. The pope and cardinals were besought to relieve him from the sentence hung over his head
by the archbishop. It is significant of Edward's early intention
to violate his promise, that in his letters to the *curia* he still
describes Gaveston as Earl of Cornwall. Peter was soon appointed
the king's lieutenant in Ireland. This time he was called Earl
of Cornwall in a document meant for English use. As midsummer approached, Edward accompanied him to Bristol
and bade him a sorrowful farewell. Attended by a numerous
and splendid household, Gaveston crossed over to Ireland and

CHAP.
XII.

took up the government of that country, where his energy and liberality won him considerable popularity.

Edward was inconsolable at the loss of his friend. For the first time in his reign he threw himself into politics with interest, and intrigued with rare perseverance to bring about his recall. Meanwhile the business of the state fell into deplorable confusion. No supplies were raised; no laws were passed; no effort was made to stay the progress of Robert Bruce. The magnates refused to help the king, and in April, 1309, Edward was forced to meet a parliament of the three estates at Westminster. There he received a much-needed supply, but the barons and commons drew up a long schedule of grievances, in which they complained of the abuses of purveyance, the weakness of the government, the tyranny of the royal officials, and the delays in obtaining justice. The estates refused point blank the king's request for the recall of Gaveston and demanded an answer to their petitions in the next parliament.

Edward saw in submission to the estates the only way of bringing back his brother Peter from his gilded exile. He persuaded the pope to annul the ecclesiastical censures with which Winchelsea had sought to prevent Gaveston's return, and then recalled his friend on his own authority. Gaveston at once quitted Ireland and was met at Chester by Edward. Together they attended a parliament of magnates held in July at Stamford. There Edward announced that he accepted the petitions of the estates and issued a statute limiting purveyance. But the real work of this assembly was the ratification of the recall of the favourite, which was assured since Edward had won over some of the chief earls to agree to it. Gloucester was easily moved to champion his brother-in-law's cause. Lincoln reverted to his former friendship for the Gascon, and managed both to overbear the hostility of Lancaster and to induce Earl Warenne, "who had never shown a cheerful face to Peter since the Wallingford tournament," to become his friend. Warwick, alone of the earls, was irreconcilable. But Edward had gained his point. It was even agreed that the returned exile should regain his earldom of Cornwall.

The annalists moralise on the instability of the magnates; and the sudden revolution may perhaps be set down as much to their incapacity as to the dexterity of the king. But Peter's second period of power was even shorter than his first. He had learnt nothing from his misfortunes, save perhaps increased contempt for his enemies. He was more insolent, greedy, and bitter in speech than ever. Early in 1310 the barons were again preparing to renew their attacks. The second storm burst in a parliament of magnates held at London in March, 1310. The barons came to this parliament in military array, and Edward once more found himself at their mercy. The conditions of 1258 exactly repeated themselves. Once more an armed baronial parliament made itself the mouthpiece of the national discontent against a weak king, an incompetent administration, and foreign favourites. The magnates were no longer contented with simply demanding the banishment of Gaveston. They were ready with a constructive programme of reform, and they went back to the policy of the Mad Parliament. As the king could not be trusted, the royal power must once more be put into commission in the hands of a committee of magnates. So stiff were the barons in their adhesion to the precedents of 1258, that they made no pretence of taking the commons into partnership with them. To them the work of Edward I. had been done to no purpose. Baronial assemblies and full parliaments of the estates were still equally competent to transact all the business of the nation. It is vain to see in this ignoring of the commons any aristocratic jealousy of the more popular element in the constitution. There can be no doubt but that any full parliament would have co-operated with the barons as heartily in 1310 as it had done in 1309. It was simply that popular co-operation was regarded as unnecessary. As in 1258, the magnates claimed to speak for the whole nation.

The barons drew up a statement of the "great perils and dangers" to which England was exposed through the king's dependence on bad counsellors. The franchises of Holy Church were threatened; the king was reduced to live by extortion; Scotland was lost; and the crown was "grievously dismembered" in England and Ireland. "Wherefore, sire," the petition concludes, "your good folk pray you humbly that, for the salvation of yourself and them and of the crown, you will assent that these perils shall be avoided and redressed by ordinance of your baronage." Edward at once surrendered at discretion, perhaps in the vain hope of saving Gaveston. On March 16 he issued a

16 *

charter, which empowered the barons to elect certain persons to draw up ordinances to reform the realm and the royal household. The powers of the committee were to last until Michaelmas, 1311. A barren promise that the king's concession should not be counted a precedent made Edward's submission seem a little less abject. Four days later the ordainers were appointed, the method of their election being based upon the precedents of 1258.

Twenty-one lords ordainers represented in somewhat unequal proportions the three great ranks of the magnates. At the head of the seven bishops was Winchelsea, while both Bishop Baldock of London, the dismissed chancellor, and his successor, John Langton of Chichester, were included among the rest. All the eight earls attending the parliament became ordainers. Side by side with moderate men, such as Gloucester, Lincoln, and John of Brittany, Earl of Richmond, were the extreme men of the opposition, Lancaster, Pembroke, Warwick, Hereford, the king's brother-in-law, and Edmund Fitzalan, Earl of Arundel. Warenne and the insignificant Earl of Oxford do not seem to have been present in parliament, and are therefore omitted. With these exceptions, and of course that of the Earl of Cornwall, the whole of the earls were arrayed against the king. The six barons, who completed the list of nominees, were either colourless in their policy or dependent on the earls and their episcopal allies. The ordainers set to work at once. Two days after their appointment, they issued six preliminary ordinances by which they resolved that the place of their sitting should be London, that none of the ordainers should receive gifts from the crown, that no royal grants should be valid without the consent of the majority, that the customs should be paid directly into the exchequer, that the foreign merchants who had lately farmed them should be arrested, and that the Great Charter should be firmly kept. During the next eighteen months they remained hard at work.

Gaveston, conscious of his impending doom, betook himself to the north as early as February. As soon as he could escape, Edward hurried northwards to join him. An expedition against the Scots was then summoned for September. It was high time that something should be done. During the three years that Edward had reigned, Robert Bruce had made alarming progress.

One after the other the Scottish magnates had joined his cause, and a few despairing partisans and some scattered ill-garrisoned, ill-equipped strongholds alone upheld the English cause north of the Tweed. But even then Edward did not wage war in earnest. His real motive for affecting zeal for martial enterprise was his desire to escape from his taskmasters, and to keep Gaveston out of harm's way. The earls gave him no encouragement. On the pretext that their services were required in London at the meetings of the ordainers, the great majority of the higher baronage took no personal part in the expedition. Gloucester was the only ordainer who was present, and the only other earls in the host were Warenne and Gaveston himself. The chief strength of Edward's army was a swarm of ill-disciplined Welsh and English infantry, more intent on plunder than on victory. In September Edward advanced to Roxburgh and made his way as far as Linlithgow. No enemy was to be found, for Bruce was not strong enough to risk a pitched battle, even against Edward's army. He hid himself in the mountains and moors, and contented himself with cutting off foraging parties, destroying stragglers, and breaking down the enemy's communications. Within two months Edward discreetly retired to Berwick, and there passed many months at the border town. Technically he was in Scotland; practically he might as well have been in London for all the harm he was doing to Bruce. However, Gaveston showed more martial zeal than his master. He led an expedition which penetrated as far as Perth, and reduced the country between the Forth and the Grampians to Edward's obedience. Gloucester also pacified the forest of Ettrick. To these two all the little honour of the campaign belonged.

The Earl of Lincoln governed England as regent during the king's absence. In February, 1311, he died, and Gloucester abandoned the campaign to take up the regency. The death of the last of Edward I.'s lay ministers was followed in March by that of another survivor of the old generation, Bishop Bek of Durham. The old landmarks were quickly passing away, and the forces that still made for moderation were sensibly diminished. Gilbert of Gloucester, alone of the younger generation, still aspired to the position of a mediator. The most important result of Lincoln's death was the unmuzzling of his son-in-law, Thomas of Lancaster. In his own right the lord of the three earldoms of Lancaster, Leicester, and Derby, Thomas then received in addition his father-in-law's two earldoms of Lincoln and Salisbury. The enormous estates and innumerable jurisdictions attached to these five offices gave him a territorial position greater by far than that of any other English lord. " I do not believe," writes the monk of Malmesbury, "that any duke or count of the Roman empire could do as much with the revenues of his estates as the Earl of Lancaster." Nor were Earl Thomas' personal connexions less magnificent than his feudal dignities. As a grandson of Henry III., he was the first cousin of the king. Through his mother, Blanche of Artois, Queen of Navarre and Countess of Champagne, he was the grandson of the valiant Robert of Artois, who had fallen at Mansura, and the great-grandson of Louis VIII. of France. His half-sister, Joan of Champagne, was the wife of Philip the Fair, so that the French king was his brother-in-law as well as his cousin, and Isabella, Edward's consort, was his niece. Unluckily, the personality of the great earl was not equal to his pedigree or his estates. Proud, hard to work with, jealous, and irascible, he was essentially the leader of opposition, the grumbler, and the *frondeur*. When the time came for a constructive policy, Thomas broke down almost as signally as Edward himself. His ability was limited, his power of application small, and his passions violent and ungovernable. Greedy, selfish, domineering, and narrow, he had few scruples and no foresight, little patriotism, and no breadth of view. At this moment he had to play a part which was within his powers. The simple continuance of the traditions of policy, which he inherited with his pedigree and his estates, was all that was necessary. As the greatest of the English earls, the head of a younger branch of the royal house, and the inheritor of the estates and titles of Montfort and Ferrars, he was trebly bound to act as leader of the baronial opposition, the champion of the charters, the enemy of kings, courtiers, favourites, and foreigners. He was steadfast in his prejudices and hatreds, and the ordainers found in him a leader who could at least save them from the reproach of inconstancy and the lack of fixed purpose shown at the parliament of Stamford.

It was the first duty of Earl Thomas to perform homage and fealty for his new earldoms of Lincoln and Salisbury.

Attended by a hundred armed knights, he rode towards the   CHAP.
border.   Edward was at Berwick, and Thomas declined to   XII.
proffer his homage outside the kingdom.   On Edward refusing
to cross the Tweed, Thomas declared that he would take forcible possession of his lands.   Civil war was only avoided by
Edward giving way.   The king met Thomas on English soil at
Haggerston, four miles from Berwick.   There the earl performed homage, and exchanged the kiss of peace with his king,
but he would not even salute the upstart Earl of Cornwall,
who injudiciously accompanied Edward, and the king departed
deeply indignant at this want of courtesy.   Returning to Berwick, Edward lingered there until the completion of the work
of the ordainers made it necessary for him to face parliament.
Leaving Gaveston protected by the strong walls of Bamburgh,
the king quitted the border at the end of July, and met his
parliament a month later in London.   Though the ordainers
had been appointed by a baronial parliament, the three estates
were summoned to hear and ratify the results of their labours.
Thirty-five more ordinances, covering a very wide field, were
then laid before them.   Disorderly and disproportioned, like most
medieval legislation, they ranged from trivial personal questions
and the details of administration to the broadest schemes for
the future.   Many of them were simply efforts to get the recognised law enforced.   There were clauses forbidding alienation of
domain, the abuses of purveyance, the usurpations of the courts of
the royal household, the enlargement of the forests, and the employment of unlawful sources of revenue.   Under the last head,
the new custom, which Edward I. had persuaded the foreign
merchants to pay, was specifically abolished.   Provisions of such
a character show that the king had made no effort to observe
either the Great Charter or the laws of Edward I.   Even the
recent statute of Stamford, and the six ordinances of the previous year, had to be re-enacted.   Similar restatements of sound
principles were too common in the fourteenth century to
make the ordinances an epoch.   The vital clauses were those
providing for the control of the king and for penalties against
his favourites.

Under the first of these heads, the ordainers worked out to
the uttermost consequences their favourite distinction between
the crown and the king.   The crown was to be strengthened,

but the king was to be deprived of every shred of power. The great offices of state in England, Ireland, and Gascony were to be filled up with the counsel and consent of the barons, a provision which, if literally interpreted, meant that the barons intended to govern Gascony as well as England. The king was not to go to war, raise an army, or leave the kingdom without the permission of parliament. He was to "live of his own," however scanty a living that might be. Special judges were to hear complaints against royal ministers and bailiffs. Parliaments were to meet once or twice a year. It was a complete programme of limited monarchy. But there was no reference to the commons and clergy. We are still in the atmosphere of the Provisions of Oxford, and there is no Earl Simon to emphasise the fuller conception of national control.

To Edward and to the barons, the penal clauses were the very essence of the ordinances. The twentieth ordinance declared that Peter of Gaveston, "as a public enemy of the king and kingdom, be forthwith exiled, for all time and without hope of return," from all dominions subject to the English king. He was to leave England before All Saints' day, and the port of Dover was to be his place of embarkation. Other ordinances dealt with lesser offenders. Exile was once more to be the doom of the Frescobaldi, and the other alien merchants who had acted as Edward's financial agents; Gaveston's kinsfolk, followers and abettors incurred their master's fate. All Gascons were to be sent to their own country, their allegiance to the crown in no wise saving them from the hatred meted out to all aliens. Neither high nor low were spared: Henry de Beaumont, the grandson of an Eastern emperor, and his sister, the lady Vescy, were to leave the realm; John Charlton, the pushing Shropshire squire who was worming his way by court favour into the estates of the degenerate descendants of the house of Gwenwynwyn, was, with the other English partisans of the favourite, to be driven from the royal service.

Edward made a last desperate attempt to save Gaveston. He would agree to all the other ordinances, if he were still allowed to keep his brother Peter in England and in possession of the earldom of Cornwall. But the estates refused to yield the root of the whole matter. Threatened with the prospect of a new battle of Lewes, if he remained obdurate, Edward bowed

to his destiny.   The ordinances were published in every shire,
and new ministers, chosen with the approval of the estates, deprived the king of the government of the country.

Early in November, Gaveston sailed to Flanders, but within
a few weeks Edward insisted upon his return.   Rumours spread
that Gaveston was in England, hiding himself away in his former
castles of Wallingford and Tintagel, or in the king's castle of
Windsor.   The thin veil of mystery was soon withdrawn.   Early
in 1312, Peter openly accompanied the king to York, where,
on January 18, Edward issued a proclamation to the effect that
Gaveston had been unlawfully exiled, that he was back in England by the king's command, and prepared to answer to all
charges against him.   A few weeks later, Edward restored him
to his earldom and estates.   King and favourite still tarried
in the north, preparing for the inevitable struggle.   It was
believed that they intrigued with Robert Bruce for a refuge
in Scotland.   Bruce, according to the story, declined to have
anything to do with them.   "If the King of England will not
keep faith with his own subjects," he is reported to have said,
"how then will he keep faith with me?"

The ordainers looked upon Gaveston's return as a declaration of war.   Winchelsea pronounced him excommunicate, and
five of the eight earls who sat among the ordainers, bound
themselves by oaths to maintain the ordinances and pursue the
favourite to the death.   These were Thomas of Lancaster, Aymer
of Pembroke, Humphrey of Hereford, Edmund of Arundel, and
Guy of Warwick.   Gilbert of Gloucester declined to take part in
the confederacy, but promised to accept whatever the five earls
might determine.   Moreover, John, Earl Warenne, who had
hitherto kept aloof from the ordainers, at last threw in his lot
with them, won over, it was believed, by the eloquence of Archbishop Winchelsea.   The ordainers then divided England into
large districts, appointing one of the baronial leaders to the
charge of each.   Gloucester himself undertook the government
of the south-east, while Robert Clifford and Henry Percy agreed
to guard the march, to prevent Gaveston escaping to the Scots.
Pembroke and Warenne marched to the north to lay hands on
the favourite, and Lancaster himself followed them.

While the ordainers were acting, Edward and Gaveston
were aimlessly wandering about in the north.   They failed to

raise an army or to win the people to their side, and on the approach of Lancaster, they fled before him from York to Newcastle. The earl followed quickly. On the afternoon of Ascension day, May 4, Lancaster, Clifford, and Percy suddenly swooped down on Newcastle. The king and his friend escaped with the utmost difficulty to Tynemouth, leaving their luggage, jewels, horses, and other possessions to the victor. Next day they fled by sea to Scarborough. The queen, left behind at Tynemouth, fell into her uncle Lancaster's power.

The royal castle of Scarborough, whose Norman keep and spacious wards occupy a rocky peninsula surrounded, except on the town side, by the North Sea, had lately been transferred from the custody of Henry Percy, one of the confederate barons, to that of Gaveston. There was no fitter place wherein the favourite could stand at bay against his pursuers. Accordingly Edward left Gaveston, after a tender parting, and betook himself to York. Lancaster thereupon occupied a position midway between Scarborough and Knaresborough, while Pembroke, Warenne, and Henry Percy laid siege to Scarborough. Gaveston soon found that he was unable to resist them. His troops, scarcely adequate to man the extensive walls, were too many for the scanty store of provisions which the castle contained. After less than a fortnight's siege, he persuaded the two earls and Percy to allow him easy terms of surrender. The three baronial leaders pledged themselves on the Gospels to protect Gaveston from all manner of evil until August 1. During the interval parliament was to decide as to what was to be his future fate. If the terms agreed upon by parliament were unsatisfactory to him, he was to return to Scarborough, which was still to be garrisoned by his followers, with leave to purchase supplies.

Pembroke undertook the personal custody of the prisoner, and escorted him by slow stages from Scarborough to the south, where he was to be retained in honourable custody at his own castle of Wallingford. Three weeks after the surrender, the convoy reached Deddington, a small town in Oxfordshire, a few miles south of Banbury. There Gaveston was lodged in the house of the vicar of the parish, and told to take a few days' rest after the fatigues of the journey. Pembroke himself did not remain at Deddington, but went on to Bampton in the Bush, where his countess then was. Thereupon on June 10, at sunrise, the Earl of Warwick, the most rancorous of Peter's enemies, occupied Deddington with a strong force. Bursting into the bedchamber of his victim, Earl Guy exclaimed in a loud voice : " Arise, traitor, thou art taken ". Peter was at once led with every mark of indignity to Warwick castle. Thus the black dog of Arden showed that he could bite.

Warwick was not personally pledged to Gaveston's safety, though, as one of the confederates, he was clearly bound by their acts. His seizure of Peter was only warrantable by the fear that Pembroke, with his royalist leanings, was likely to play the extreme party false ; but in any case Warwick was as much obliged as Pembroke to observe the terms of the capitulation. Neither Warwick nor his allies took this view of the matter. They rejoiced at the good fortune which had remedied the disastrous capitulation of Scarborough, and resolved to put an end to the favourite without delay. Lancaster was then at Kenilworth ; Hereford, Arundel, and other magnates were also present, and all agreed in praising Warwick's energy. On Monday morning, June 19, the three earls rode the few miles from Kenilworth to Warwick, and Earl Guy handed over Peter to them. They then escorted their captive to a place called Blacklow hill, about two miles out of Warwick on the Kenilworth road, but situated in Lancaster's lands. The crowd following the cavalcade was moved to tears when Peter, kneeling to Lancaster, cried in vain for mercy from the " gentle earl ". On reaching Blacklow hill, the three earls withdrew, though remaining near enough to see what was going on. Then two Welshmen in Lancaster's service laid hands upon the victim. One drove his sword through his body, the other cut off his head. The corpse remained where it had fallen, but the head was brought to the earls as a sign that the deed was done. After this the earls rode back to Kenilworth. Guy of Warwick remained all the time in his castle. He had already taken his share in the cruel act of treachery. It was, however, important that Lancaster should take the responsibility for the deed. Four cobblers of Warwick piously bore the headless corpse within their town. But the grim earl sent it back, because it was not found on his fee. At last some Oxford Dominicans took charge of the body and deposited it temporarily in their convent, not daring to inter it in holy ground, as Gaveston had died excommunicate.

The ostentatious violence of the confederate earls broke up their party. Aymer of Pembroke, indignant at their breach of faith, regarded the whole transaction as a stain on his honour. He besought Gloucester's intervention, but was only told that he should be more cautious in his future negotiations. He harangued the clerks and burgesses of Oxford, but university and town agreed that the matter was no business of theirs. Then in disgust he betook himself to the king, whom he found still surrounded with the Beaumonts, Mauleys, and other friends of Gaveston, against whom the ordinances had decreed banishment. Warenne, whose honour was only less impeached than Pembroke's, also deserted the ordainers for the court. Edward bitterly deplored the death of his friend. He gladly welcomed the deserters, and prepared to wreak vengeance on the ordainers.

Edward plucked up courage to return to London, where in July he addressed the citizens, and persuaded them to maintain the peace of the city against the barons. He next visited Dover, and there he strengthened the fortifications of the castle, took oaths of fealty from the Cinque Ports, and negotiated with the King of France. Thence he returned to London, hoping that the precautions he had taken would secure his position in the parliament which he had summoned to meet at Westminster. But the four earls still held the field, and answered the summons to parliament by occupying Ware with a strong military force. A thousand men-at-arms were drawn by Lancaster from his five earldoms, while the Welsh from Brecon, who followed the Earl of Hereford, and the vigorous foresters of Arden, who mustered under the banner of Warwick, made a formidable show. Yet at the last moment neither side was eager to begin hostilities. The four earls' violence damaged their cause, and many who had no love of Gaveston, or desire to avenge him, inclined to the king's party. Gilbert of Gloucester busied himself with mediating between the two sides. At this juncture two papal envoys, sent to end the interminable outstanding disputes with France, arrived in England, along with Louis, Count of Evreux, the queen's uncle. Edward availed himself of the presence of French jurists in the count's train to

obtain legal opinion that the ordinances were invalid, as against
natural equity and civil law. These technicalities did little service to the king's cause, and better work was done when Louis
and the papal envoys joined with Gloucester in mediating
between the opposing forces. At length moderate counsels
prevailed. Edward could only resist the four earls through
the support of his new allies, and Pembroke and Warenne were
as little anxious to fight as Gloucester himself. They were
quite willing to make terms which seemed to the king treason
to his friend's memory.

The negotiations were still proceeding when, on November
13, 1312, the birth of a son to Edward and Isabella revived the
almost dormant feeling of loyalty to the sovereign. The king
ceased to brood over the loss of his brother Peter, and became
more willing to accept the inevitable. He gave some pleasure
to his subjects by refusing the suggestion of the queen's uncle
that the child should be called Louis, and christened him Edward
after his own father. At last, on December 22, terms of peace
were agreed upon. The earls and barons concerned in Gaveston's death were to appear before the king in Westminster
Hall, and humbly beg his pardon and good-will. In return
for this the king agreed to remit all rancour caused by the
death of the favourite. Lancaster and Warwick, who took no
personal part in the negotiations, sent in a long list of objections
to the details of the treaty. Nearly a year elapsed before the
earls personally acknowledged their fault. During that interval
there was no improvement in the position of affairs. Parliament granted no money ; and Edward only met his daily expenses by loans, contracted from every quarter, and by keeping
tight hands on the confiscated estates of the Templars. Both
the king and the leading earls made every excuse to escape
attending the ineffective parliaments of that miserable time.
Two short visits to France gave Edward a pretext for avoiding his subjects. There were some hasty musterings of armed
men on pretence of tournaments. But the king was still formidable enough to make it desirable for the barons to carry
out the treaty. Finally, in October, 1313, Lancaster, Hereford,
and Warwick made their public submission in Westminster
Hall. Pardons were at once issued to them and to over four
hundred minor offenders. Feasts of reconciliation were held,

and it seemed as if the old feuds were at last ended. Gaveston's corpse was removed from Oxford to Langley, in Hertfordshire, and buried in the church of a new convent of Dominicans set up by Edward to pray for the favourite's soul.

Just before the end of the disputes Archbishop Winchelsea died in May, 1313. He left behind him the reputation of a saint and a hero, and a movement was undertaken for his canonisation. With all his faults, he was the greatest churchman of his time, and the most steadfast and unselfish of ecclesiastical statesmen. Despite his palsy, he had shown wonderful activity since his return. The brain and soul of the ordainers, he equally made it his business to uphold extreme hierarchical privilege. Bitterly as he hated Walter Langton, he was indignant that a bishop should be imprisoned and despoiled by the lay power, and took up his cause with such energy that he effected his liberation, only to find that Langton made peace with the king and turned his back on the ordainers. The after-swell of the storms, excited by the petition of Lincoln and the statute of Carlisle, still continued troublous during Winchelsea's later years. The pope complained of the violated privileges of the Church and of the accumulated arrears of King John's tribute ; and Winchelsea was anxious to promote the papal cause. But the barons in Edward's early parliaments still used the bold language of the magnates of 1301, and the letter of 1309, drawn up by the parliament of Stamford, is no unworthy pendant of the Lincoln letter. As time went on, the disorders of the government and the weakness of the king surrendered everything to the pope. It was soon as it had been in the days of Henry III., when pope and king combined to despoil the English Church.

The suppression of the order of the Temple shows how absolutely England was forced to follow in the wake of the papacy and the King of France. There was no spontaneous movement against the society as in France ; there was not even the fierce malice and insatiable greed which could find their only satisfaction in the ruin of the brethren ; and there is not much evidence that the Templars were unpopular. The whole attack was the result of commands given from without. It was at the repeated request of Philip of France and Clement V. that Edward reluctantly ordered the apprehension of all the Templars within England, Scotland, and Ireland on January 8, 1308. Their property was taken into the king's hands, and their persons were confined in the royal prisons under the custody of the sheriffs. For their trial, Clement appointed a mixed commission including Winchelsea, Archbishop Greenfield of York, several English bishops, one French bishop, and certain papal inquisitors specially assigned for the purpose, the chief of whom were the Abbot of Lagny and Sicard de Lavaur, Canon of Narbonne, who came to England in 1309. At last the victims were collected at London and York, where the trials were to be conducted for the southern and northern provinces. There was much hesitation among the English bishops. The foes of the Templars lamented the prelates' lack of zeal and their scruples in collecting evidence, and suggested that the torture, which had so freely been used in France, would soon extract confessions. But the northern bishops declared that torture was unknown in England, and asked, if it were to be adopted, whether it was to be applied by clerks or laymen, and whether torturers should be imported from beyond sea. In the end, torture was used, but not to any great extent.

A great mass of depositions, mostly vague and worthless, or derived from the suspicious confessions of apostates and weaklings, was gathered together, and in 1311 laid before provincial councils, but neither province came to any fixed decision. "Inasmuch," says Hemingburgh, "as the Templars were not found altogether guilty or altogether innocent, they referred the dubious matter to the pope." They sent the evidence they had collected to swell the mass of testimony from all Christendom, which was laid before the council of Vienne. When the pope suppressed the order in April, 1312, and transferred its lands to the Knights of St. John, the papal decrees were quietly carried out in England. One or two Templars died in prison, but none were executed ; and the majority were dismissed with pensions or secluded in monasteries. Edward and his nobles took good care to make a large profit out of the transaction. The resources of the Temple alone kept the king from destitution during the period between the death of Gaveston and his reconciliation with the earls. Many barons laid violent hands on estates belonging to the order, and long held on to them despite papal expostulation. The Hospitallers found that the lands of their rivals came to them so slowly, and encumbered

CHAP.
XII.

with so many charges, that their new property became burdensome rather than helpful to their society.   Thus it was that they never made any use of the New Temple in London, and, before long, let it out to the common-lawyers.   In the fall of the Templars, the pope and the Church set the first great example of the suppression of a religious order to kings, who before long bettered the precedent given them.   The sordid story is mainly important to our history as an example of the completeness of the influence of the papal autocracy, and of the submissiveness of clergy and laity to its behests.   It was a lurid commentary on the practical working of the ecclesiastical system that the business of condemning an innocent order first brought into England the papal inquisitor and the use of torture.   Yet the whole process was but so pale a reflection of the horrors wrought in France that the conclusion arises that England owed more to the weakness of Edward II. than France to the strength of Philip IV.

Winchelsea's death removed a real check on Edward, especially as the king was on such good terms with the papacy that he had little difficulty in obtaining a successor amenable to his will.   Undeterred by Clement's bull reserving to himself the appointment, the monks of Christ Church at once proceeded to elect Thomas of Cobham, a theologian and a canonist of distinction, a man of high birth, great sanctity, and unblemished character, and in every way worthy of the primacy.   But his merits did not weigh for a moment with Clement against the wishes of the king.   He rejected Cobham and conferred the primacy on Edward's favourite, Walter Reynolds, who had already obtained the bishopric of Worcester through the king's influence.   A good deal of money, it was believed, found its way to the coffers of the *curia ;* and the indignation of the English Church found voice in the impassioned protests of the chroniclers.   "Lady Money rules everything in the pope's court," lamented the monk of Malmesbury.   "For eight years Pope Clement has ruled the Universal Church : but what good he has done escapes memory.   England, alone of all countries, feels the burden of papal domination.   Out of the fulness of his power, the pope presumes to do many things, and neither prince nor people dare contradict him.   He reserves all the fat benefices for himself, and excommunicates all who resist him : his legates come and spoil the land : those armed with his bulls come and

demand prebends. He has given all the deaneries to foreigners,
and cut down the number of resident canons. Why does the
pope exercise greater power over the clergy than the emperor
over the laity? Lord Jesus! either take away the pope from our
midst or lessen the power which he presumes to have over the
people." Such lamentations bore no fruit, and the simoniacal
nomination of Reynolds was but the first of a series of appointments which robbed the episcopate of dignity and moral worth.

While Church and State in England were thus distressed,
the cause of Robert Bruce was making steady progress in
Scotland. It is some measure of the difficulties against which
Bruce had to contend that, after six years, he was still by
no means master of all that land. But least of all among the
causes which retarded his advance can be placed the armed
forces of England. During six years Edward II.'s one personal
expedition had been a complete failure. A more formidable
obstacle in Bruce's way was the stubborn resistance offered to
him by the valour and skill of the small but highly trained
garrisons which the wisdom of Edward I. had established in
the fortresses of southern and central Scotland. Each castle
took a long time to subdue, and demanded engineering resources
and a persistency of effort, which were difficult to obtain from
a popular army. The garrisons co-operated with the Scottish
nobles who still adhered to Edward through jealousy of the
upstart Bruces and love of feudal independence, rather than by
reason of any sympathy with the English cause. Additional
obstacles to Robert's progress were the hostility of the Church,
to which he was still the excommunicated murderer of Comyn;
the captivity of so many Scottish prelates and barons in England; the efforts of the pope and the King of France to bring
about suspensions of hostilities, and the grievous famines which
desolated Scotland no less than southern Britain. But during
these years the King of Scots gradually overcame these difficulties. His hardest fighting in the field was with rival Scots
rather than with the English intruders. In 1308 he defeated
the Comyns of Buchan, and established himself on the ruins of
that house in the north-east. In the same year his brother,
Edward Bruce, conquered Galloway, where the Balliol tradition long prevented the domination of the rival family.

Secure from retaliation so long as domestic troubles lasted, the Scots devastated the northern counties of England, whose inhabitants were forced to purchase relief from further attacks by paying large sums of money to the invaders. Formal truces were more than once made, but they were ill observed, and each violation of an armistice involved some loss to Edward and some gain to Robert. Meanwhile the garrisons were carefully isolated, and one by one signalled out for attack. In 1312 Berwick itself was only saved from surprise by the opportune barking of a dog. In January, 1313, Perth was captured by assault. Next day Robert slew the leading native burgesses who had adhered to the English, while he permitted the English inhabitants to return freely to their own country. The whole town was destroyed, since walled towns, like castles, had given the English their chief hold upon the country.

Such was the state of Scotland when the reconciliation between Edward and the earls restored England to the appearance of unity. As if conscious that no time was to be lost in strengthening his position, Bruce redoubled his efforts to make himself master of the fortresses which still remained in the enemy's hands. Regardless of the rigour of the season, he set actively to work in the early weeks of 1314, and remarkable success attended his efforts. In February, the border stronghold of Roxburgh was taken by a night attack. "And all that fair castle, like the other castles which he had acquired, they pulled down to the ground, lest the English should afterwards by holding the castle bear rule over the land."[1] In March, Edinburgh castle was secured by some Scots who climbed up the precipitous northern face of the castle rock, overpowered the garrison, and opened the gates to their comrades outside. Flushed with this great success, Bruce began the siege of Stirling, the only important English garrison then held by the English in the heart of Scotland. He pressed the besieged so hard that they agreed to surrender to the enemy, if they were not relieved before Midsummer day, the feast of St. John the Baptist. While Robert was watching Stirling, his brother Edward devastated the country round Carlisle, lording it for three days at the bishop's castle of Rose, and levying heavy blackmail on the men of Cumberland.

---

[1] *Lanercost Chronicle*, p. 223.

If Stirling were lost, all Scotland would be at Bruce's mercy. Even Edward was stirred by the disgrace involved in the utter abandonment of his father's conquest; and from March onwards he began to make spasmodic efforts to collect men and ships to enable him to advance to the relief of the beleaguered garrison. At first it seemed sufficient to raise the feudal levies and a small infantry force from the northern shires, but as time went on the necessity of meeting the Scottish pikemen by corresponding levies of foot soldiers became evident, and over 20,000 infantry were summoned from the northern counties and Wales.[1] But the notice given was far too short, and June was well advanced before anything was ready.

Even the Scottish peril could not quicken the sluggish patriotism of the ordainers. Four earls, Lancaster, Warenne, Warwick, and Arundel, answered Edward's summons by reminding him that the ordinances prescribed that war should only be undertaken with the approval of parliament, and by declining to follow him to a campaign undertaken on his own responsibility. They would send quotas, but begged to be excused from personal attendance. Yet even without them, a gallant array slowly gathered together at Berwick, and one at least of the opposition earls, Humphrey of Hereford, was there, with Gilbert of Gloucester and Aymer of Pembroke and 2,000 men-at-arms. An enormous baggage train enabled the knights and barons to appear in the field in great magnificence, though it destroyed the mobility of the force. " The multitude of waggons," wrote the monk of Malmesbury, " if they had been extended in a single line would have occupied the space of twenty leagues." The splendour and number of the army inspired the king and his friends with the utmost confidence. Though the host started from Berwick less than a week before the appointed day, the king moved, says the Malmesbury monk, not as if he were about to lead an army to battle, but rather as if he were going on a pilgrimage to Compostella. " There was but short delay for sleep, and a shorter delay for taking food. Hence horses, horsemen, and infantry were worn out with fatigue and hunger." There was no order

---

[1] For the numbers at Bannockburn, see *Fœdera*, ii., 248, and Round, *Commune of London*, pp. 289-301.

or method in the proceedings of the host. The presence of the king meant that there was no effective general, and Hereford and Gloucester quarrelled for the second place.

It was not until Sunday, June 23, that Edward at last took up his quarters a few miles south of Stirling, with a worn-out and dispirited army. Yet, if Stirling were to be saved, immediate action was necessary. Gloucester and Hereford made a vigorous but unsuccessful effort to penetrate at once into the castle, and Bruce came down just in time to throw himself between them and the walls. Henry Bohun, who had forced his way forward at the head of a force of Welsh infantry, was slain, and his troops dispersed. Gloucester was unhorsed, and thereupon the English retreated to their camp. Fearing an attack under cover of darkness, they had little sleep that night, and many of the watchers consoled themselves with revelry and drunkenness. When St. John's day dawned, they were too weary to fight effectively. Bruce advanced from the woods and stationed his troops on the low ridge bounding the northern slope of the little brook, called the Bannockburn, which runs about two miles south of Stirling on its course towards the Forth. Of the three divisions, or battles, into which the Scots were divided, two stood on the same front, side by side, while King Robert commanded the rear battle, which was to serve as a reserve. He marshalled his forces much in the same way that Wallace had adopted at Falkirk. There was the same close array of infantry, protected by a wall of shields and a thick hedge of pikes. Each man wore light but adequate armour, and, besides the pike, bore an axe at his side for work at close quarters. Pits were dug before the Scots lines, and covered over with hurdles so light that they would not bear the weight of a mail-clad warrior and his horse. Save for a small cavalry force kept in reserve in the rear, the men-at-arms were ordered to dismount and take their place in the dense array, lest, like their comrades at Falkirk, they should ride off in alarm when they saw the preponderance of the enemy's horse. The Scots were less numerous than the English, but they were an army and not a mob; their commander was a man of rare military insight, and their tactics were those which, twelve years before, had defeated the chivalry of France at Courtrai.

The English had feared that the Scots would not fight a pitched battle, and were astonished to see them at daybreak prepared to receive an attack. Their contempt for their enemy made them eager to accept the challenge, but Gloucester, who, though only twenty-three, had more of the soldier's eye than most of the magnates, urged Edward to postpone the encounter for a day, that the army might recover from its fatigue, and the clergy advised delay out of respect to St. John the Baptist. Unmoved by prudence or piety, Edward denounced his nephew as a coward, and ordered an immediate advance.

The English, forgetting the lessons of the Welsh wars, sent on the archers in front of the cavalry. Bruce, seeing that their missiles were playing havoc on his dense ranks, directed his small cavalry force to charge the archers on their left flank. The unsupported bowmen at once fell back in confusion, leaving the cavalry to do its work. Meanwhile the English men-at-arms were advancing in three "battles," the first of which then came into action. Many of the English fell into the pits prepared for them, and the Scottish shields and pikes broke the attack of those who evaded these obstacles. Gloucester fought with rare gallantry, but was badly seconded by his followers. At last his horse was slain under him, and he was knocked down and killed. The troop which he led fled panic-stricken from the field. The Scots then advanced with such vigour that the English never recovered from the disorder into which their first disaster had thrown them. While these things were going on, the second and third English "battles" had been making feeble efforts to take their part in the fight. But the first line cut them off from direct access to the foe, and the archers of the second battle did more harm to their friends than to their enemies by shooting wildly, straight in front of them. There was no single directing force, nor after Gloucester's fall, even one conspicuous leader who would set an example of blind valour. Hundreds of English knights, who had not drawn their swords, were soon fleeing in terror before the enemy. Edward, who had taken up his station in the rear battle, rode off the field and never dismounted until he reached Dunbar, whence he fled by sea to Berwick.

Abandoned by their leaders, the English retreated as best they could. Many of their best knights lay dead on the field, and more were drowned in the Forth or Bannock, or swallowed up in the bogs, than were slain in the fight. The Scots, whose losses were slight, showed a prudent tendency to capture rather than slay the knights and barons, in order that they might hold them up to ransom, and though many desisted from the pursuit to plunder the baggage train, those who followed the English fugitives reaped an abundant harvest of captives. Hereford was chased into Bothwell castle, which was still held for the English. But next day the Scottish official who commanded there for Edward opened the gates to Bruce, and the earl became a prisoner. Pembroke escaped with difficulty on foot, along with a contingent of Welsh infantry. The mighty English army had ceased to exist; and with the surrender of Stirling, next day, Bruce's career attained its culminating point. His long years of trial were at last over, and the clever adventurer could henceforth enjoy in security the crown which he had so gallantly won.

The military results of Bannockburn were of extreme importance. The ablest of contemporary annalists aptly compared Bruce's victory to the battle of Courtrai. An even nearer analogy was the fight at Morgarten where, within two years, the pikemen of the Forest Cantons were to scatter the chivalry of the Hapsburgers as effectively as the Flemings won the day at Courtrai or the Scots at Bannockburn. The English had forgotten the military lessons of Edward I. as completely as they had forgotten his political lessons, and their reliance on the obsolete and unsupported cavalry charge was their undoing. Bruce, on the other hand, had improved upon the teaching of Wallace and Edward I. His use of his men-at-arms on foot anticipates the English tactics of the Hundred Years' War. The presence of these heavily armed troopers in his ranks gave him a strength in defence, and an impetuosity in attack, which made it a simple matter to break up the undisciplined squadrons opposed to him. Bannockburn rang the death-knell of the tactics which since Hastings had been regarded as the perfection of military art.

The political lessons of the victory were of not less importance. It is almost too much to say that Bannockburn won for Scotland its independence, for Scottish independence had already been vindicated. But the easy victory brought home to men's minds the full measure of the Scottish triumph. It was already clear that so long as Edward lived, England would never make the continued effort which, as Edward I.'s wars both in Wales and Scotland had shown, could alone systematically conquer a nation. Bruce's difficulties were not so much with the English as with the Scots. It was no small task to unite the English of the Lothians, the Welsh of the south-west, the Norsemen of the extreme north, and the Celts of the hills into a single Scottish nation. He had against him the separatist local feeling which Scottish history and ethnology made inevitable, and it took time for him to obtain that prestige, which should hedge a king, and raise him above the crowd of feudal earls and clan chieftains, who thought themselves as good as the sometime Earl of Carrick. Such dignity and distinction Bannockburn supplied, and such measure of national unity and strong monarchical authority as Scotland ever enjoyed, came from the triumph of him who became, even more than Wallace, the hero of the new nation. For the next few years the Scots took the aggressive. They induced the French kings to renew the alliance which Philip IV. had made with them in the early years of the contest. They obtained papal recognition for their king and the withdrawal of the ban of the Church on Comyn's murderer ; they plundered northern England from end to end, and broke down Anglo-Norman rule in Ireland ; they plotted for the resurrection of the Welsh principality ; and, worse than all, they made common cause with the baronial opposition. Hence it followed that the political results of the victory were as important to England as they were to Scotland itself. The troubled history of the next eight years reveals in detail the effects of Bannockburn on England. Edward's defeat threw him into the power of the ordainers. The ordainers, when called upon to govern, showed themselves as incapable as ever Edward or his favourites had been. The results were misrule, aristocratic faction, popular distress, and mob violence. Ineffective as are the first seven years of the reign of Edward of Carnarvon, the eight years which followed Bruce's victory plunged England deeper into the pit of degradation, from which neither the king nor the king's foes were strong, wise, or honest enough to release her.

CHAPTER XIII

CHAP.
XIII.
BANNOCKBURN was almost welcomed by the ordainers, for it afforded new opportunities of humiliating the defeated king. While Edward tarried at Berwick, Lancaster was in his castle of Pontefract with a force far larger than his cousin's. Loudly declaring that the true cause of the disaster was Edward's neglect to carry out the ordinances, he announced his intention of immediately enforcing their observance. At a parliament at York, in September, Edward delivered himself altogether into Thomas's hands, ordering the immediate execution of the ordinances, and replacing his ministers and sheriffs by nominees of the ordainers. The only boon that he obtained was that the earls postponed the removal from court of Hugh Despenser and Henry Beaumont, the two faithful friends who had guarded him in his flight from Bannockburn. Despenser, however, thought it prudent to avoid his enemies by going into hiding. Edward's submission did not help him against the Scots. The earls resolved that the question of an expedition was to be postponed until the next parliament, on the ground that it was imprudent to take action until Hereford and the other captives had been released. It was a sorry excuse, for King Robert and his brother were devastating the northern counties with fire and sword, and it gave new ground to the suspicion of an understanding between the Scottish king and the ordainers. But the victor of Bannockburn showed surprising moderation. He suffered the bodies of Gloucester and the slain barons to be buried among their ancestors, and released Gloucester's father-in-law, Monthermer, without ransom, declaring that the thing in the world which he most desired was to live in peace with the English. He welcomed an exchange of prisoners, by which

his wife, Elizabeth de Burgh, his sister, his daughter, and the
Bishop of Glasgow were restored to Scotland. The release
of Hereford soon added to the king's troubles.

In January, 1315, Edward's humiliation was completed at
a London parliament. Hugh Despenser and Walter Langton
were removed from the council. The "superfluous members"
of the royal household, denounced as "excessively burdensome
to the king and the land," were dismissed, and drastic ordinances
were drawn up for the regulation of the diminished following
still allowed to the king. Edward was put on an allowance
of £10 a day, and the administration of his revenues taken
out of his hands. The grant made was accompanied by the
condition that its spending should be entirely in the hands of
the barons, and the estates arranged after their own fashion
for the new Scottish campaign. When summer came, Lancaster insisted on taking the command himself, and thus gave a
new grievance to Pembroke, who had already been appointed
general. Lancaster was henceforth the indispensable man.
When parliament met at Lincoln, in January, 1316, the few
magnates who attended would transact no business until his
arrival. On his tardy appearance in the last days of the
session, it was resolved "that the lord king should do nothing
grave or arduous without the advice of the council, and that
the Earl of Lancaster should hold the chief place in the
council". It was only after some hesitation that the earl accepted this position. Once more the king was forced to confirm the ordinances. Liberal grants were made by the estates,
and every rural township was called upon to furnish and pay a
foot soldier to fight the Scots.

The commander of the army and the chief counsellor of
the king, Lancaster, was in a stronger position than any subject
since the days of Simon of Montfort. He could afford to
despise aristocratic jealousy and royal malignity. To the commons he was the good earl, who was standing up for the rights
of the people. He was the darling of the clergy, who looked
upon him as the pillar of orthodoxy, the disciple of Winchelsea,
and the upholder of the rights of Holy Church. The warlike
and energetic barons of the north were his sworn followers,
and, apart from his hold upon public opinion, he could always
fall back on the resources of his five earldoms. But events

were soon to show that the successful leader of opposition was absolutely incapable of carrying out a constructive policy. He had no ideals, no principles, no feeling of the importance of administrative efficiency, no sense of responsibility, no power of controlling his followers. He never understood that his business was no longer to oppose but to act. The clear-headed monk of Malmesbury paints the disastrous results of his inaction : " Whatsoever pleased the king, the earl's servants strove to overthrow; and whatever pleased the earl, was declared by the king's servants to be treasonable; and so, at the suggestion of the evil one, the households of earl and king put themselves in the way and would not allow their masters, by whom the land should have been defended, to be of one accord ". Even the implied understanding with the King of Scots was not abandoned by the man on whom the responsibility rested of defeating him. When Bruce devastated the north of England he still spared the lands of the king's " chief counsellor," as of old he had spared the lands of the opposition leader. When, in 1316, Lancaster mustered his forces at Newcastle against the Scots, Edward repaid him for his inaction in 1314 by declining to accompany him over the border. " Thereupon," wrote the border annalist,[1] "the earl at once went back; for neither trusted the other." Edward, who forgot and forgave nothing, secretly negotiated with the pope for absolution from his oath to the ordinances. He gradually built up a court party, and soon restored Hugh Despenser to his position in the household. As might be expected in such circumstances no effective resistance was made to the Scots.

It was a time of severe distress in England. In 1315 a rainy summer ruined the harvest. Great floods swept away the hay from the fields, and drowned the sheep and cattle. In 1316 famine raged, especially in the north. For a hundred years, we are told, such scarcity of corn had not been known. A bushel of wheat was sold at London for forty pence, and the Northumbrians were driven to feed on dogs, horses, and other unwonted food. Pestilence followed in the train of famine. It was in vain that parliament passed laws, limiting the repasts of the barons' households to two courses of meat, and fixing the price of the chief sorts of victuals. The only result was

---

[1] *Lanercost Chronicle,* p. 233.

that dealers refused to bring their produce to market.   Then
the legislation, passed in a panic, was repealed in a panic.   " It
is better," said a chronicler, "to buy things at a high rate than
not to be able to buy them at all."

Private wars raged from end to end of south Britain.   On the
upper Severn, Griffith of Welshpool, the younger son of Griffith
ap Gwenwynwyn, laid regular siege to Powys castle, the stronghold of John Charlton, his niece's husband and his rival for the
lordship of upper Powys.   As Charlton was a courtier, Griffith
attached himself to the ordainers.   After Bannockburn, the
captivity of Hereford, the lord of Brecon, and the death without
heirs of Gloucester, the lord of Glamorgan, removed the strongest
restraints on the men of south Wales.   The royal warden of
Glamorgan, Payne of Turberville, displaced Gloucester's old
officers.   One of the sufferers was Llewelyn Bren, "a great and
powerful Welshman in those parts," who had held high office
under Earl Gilbert.   In 1315 Llewelyn, after seeking justice in
vain at the king's court, rose in revolt against Turberville.   He
gathered the Welshmen on the hills, burst upon Caerphilly,
while the constable was holding a court outside the castle, took
the outer ward by surprise and burnt it to ashes.   There was
fear lest this revolt should be the starting-point of a general
Welsh rising.   Llewelyn's hill strongholds threatened Brecon
on the north and the vale of Glamorgan on the south ; and Hereford, then released from his Scottish captivity, was entrusted
with the suppression of the revolt.   Before long all the lords
of the march joined Hereford in stamping out the movement.
Among them were the two Roger Mortimers, the Montagues
and the Giffords, and Henry of Lancaster, Earl Thomas's
brother, and lord in his own right of Monmouth and Kidwelly.
Overwhelmed by such mighty opponents, Llewelyn surrendered
to Hereford, hoping thus to save his followers.

Lancaster himself suffered from the spirit of anarchy that
was abroad.   His own Lancashire vassals rose against his
authority, under Adam Banaster, a former member of his
household.   Adam belonged to an important Lancashire family,
which had long stood in close relations to Wales, and had committed a homicide for which he despaired of pardon.   He
now posed as the champion of the king against the earl, believing that anything that caused trouble to Thomas would

CHAP.
XIII.

give no small delight at court. Lancaster showed more energy in upholding his own rights than in maintaining the honour of England. He raised such an overwhelming force that Banaster, unable to hold the field against him, shut himself up in his house. His refuge was stormed and his head brought to Earl Thomas as a trophy of victory. While Banaster was raiding Lancashire and Llewelyn south Wales, the Scots were devastating the country as far south as Furness, and Edward Bruce, King Robert's brother, was conquering Ireland. There was little wonder that Edward Bruce hoped to cross over to Wales when he had done his work in Ireland, or that the Welsh, buoyed up, as in the last generation, by the prophesies of Merlin, believed that the time was come when they would expel the Saxons, and win back the empire of Britain.

Of much longer duration than the wars of Llewelyn Bren and Adam Banaster, were the formidable disturbances which raged for many years at Bristol. Fourteen Bristol magnates had long a preponderating influence in the government of the town. The commons bitterly resented their superiority and declared that every burgess should enjoy equal rights. A royal inquiry was ordered, but the judges, bribed, as was believed, by the fourteen, gave a decision which was unacceptable to the commons. Lord Badlesmere, warden of the castle, sided with the oligarchs, and thus the whole authority of the state was brought to bear against the popular party. But it was an easy matter to resist the government of Edward II. The commons took arms and a riot broke out in court. Twenty men were killed in the disturbances, and the judges fled for their lives. Eighty burgesses were proved by inquest at Gloucester to have been the ringleaders. As they refused to appear to answer the charges, they were outlawed. Indignation at Bristol then rose to such a height that the fourteen fled in their turn, and for more than two years Bristol succeeded in holding out against the royal mandate. At last, in 1316, the town was regularly besieged by the Earl of Pembroke. The castle was not within the burgesses' power, and its *petrariae*, breaking down the walls and houses of the borough, compelled the townsmen to surrender. A few of the chief rebels were punished, but a pardon was issued to the mass of the burgesses.

More dangerous than any of these troubles was the attack

made by Edward Bruce on the English power in Ireland. That power had been on the wane during the last two genera- tions. Edward I. had formed schemes for the better adminis- tration of the country, but little had come of them. The English government in Dublin gradually lost such control as it had possessed over the remoter parts of the island. The shire organisation, set up in an earlier generation, became little more than nominal. The constitutional movement of the thirteenth century extended to the island, and the Irish parliament, then growing up out of the old council, reflected in a blurred fashion the organisation of the English parliament of the three estates. But royal lieutenants and councils, shires and sheriffs, parliaments and justices had only the most superficial influence on Irish life. Real authority was divided between the Norman lords of the plain and the Celtic chieftains of the hills. Each feudal lord hated his fellows, and bitter as were the feuds of Fitzgeralds and Burghs, they were mild as compared with the rancorous hereditary fac- tions which divided the native septs from each other. These divisions alone made it possible for the king's officers to keep up some semblance of royal rule. If they were seldom obeyed, the divisions in the enemies' camps prevented any chance of their being overthrown. Thus the Irish went on living a rude, turbulent life of perpetual purposeless war and bloodshed. Ire- land was a wilder, larger, more remote Welsh march, and the resemblance was heightened by the fact that many of the Anglo-Norman principalities were in the hands of great Eng- lish or marcher families, and that the Irish foot-soldier played only a less important part than the Welsh archer and pikeman among the light-armed soldiers of the English crown.

The easiest way to keep up a show of English government was to form an alliance between the crown and some of the baronial houses. Richard de Burgh, Earl of Ulster, the most powerful of the feudal lords of Ireland, was the only one who at that period bore the title of earl. He had long been in- terested in general English affairs, and his kinswomen had intermarried into great British houses. One of his daughters married Robert Bruce when he was Earl of Carrick, and another was more recently wedded to Earl Gilbert of Gloucester. Des- pite the Bruce connexion, the Earl of Ulster was still trusted by the English party, and the king gave him the command

CHAP.
XIII.

of an Irish army which he had intended to send against Scotland in 1314. Richard was too busy fighting the Ulster clans of O'Donnell and O'Neil, and too jealous of the Fitzgeralds, his feudal rivals, to throw his heart into the hopeless task of gathering together the two nations and many clans of Ireland into a single host. The death of Earl Gilbert at Bannockburn broke his nearest tie with England, and the release of Elizabeth Bruce in exchange for Hereford gave his daughter the actual enjoyment of the throne of Scotland. His natural instincts as an Irishman and as a baron were to restrain the power of his overlord. When the news of Bruce's victory produced a great stir among the Irish clans, he stood aside and let events take their course.

Though the Gael of the Scottish Highlands played little part at Bannockburn, the Irish rejoiced at the Scots' success as that of their kinsmen. " The Kings of the Scots," said the Irish Celts, " derive their origin from our land. They speak our tongue and have our laws and customs." However little true this was in fact, it was a good excuse for some of the Irish clans to offer the throne of Ireland to the King of Scots. Robert rejected the proposal for himself, but was willing to give his able and adventurous brother Edward the chance of winning another crown for his house. Edward, " who thought that Scotland was too little for his brother and himself," cheerfully fell in with the scheme. On May 25, 1315, he landed near Carrickfergus and received a rapturous welcome from the O'Neils, the greatest of the septs of the north-east. Before long all Celtic Ulster flocked to his banners, and Edmund Butler, then justice of Ireland, strove with little success to make head against the Scottish invasion. The completeness of Bruce's union with the native Irish gave him his best chance of attaining his object. Up to this point the attitude of the Earl of Ulster had been most undecided. He at last threw in his lot with the justiciar. When parties began to shape themselves it was clear that "all the Irish of Ireland" were in league with Bruce. The danger was that "a great part of the great lords and lesser English folk" also joined the invader. Conspicuous among these were the Lacys of Meath.

Edward Bruce showed energy and vigour. He made his way southwards, and in September won a victory over the forces of

the Earl of Ulster and the justiciar at Dundalk, then in the
south of Ulster.   After this he pushed into Meath and Leinster
and was joined by the O'Tooles and the other clans of the
Wicklow mountains, while the adhesion of Phelim O'Connor,
King of Connaught, brought the whole of the Celtic west into
his alliance.   The barons, however, took the alarm.   During
the winter Butler contracted friendship with many of the Norman colonists.   From that time the struggle assumed the character of a war between Celtic Ireland and feudal Ireland, the
native clansmen and the Anglo-Norman settlers.   Thus, though
Bruce and his wild allies found it easy to make themselves
masters of the open country, all the castles and towns were
closed to them and could only be won by long-continued efforts.
Before long, Butler drove them to the hills.   Ere the winter
was over, Edward found it prudent to retire to Ulster.

During 1316 the struggle raged unceasingly.   Bruce was
crowned King of Ireland, the O'Neil, it was said, having ab-
dicated his rights in his favour.   But the summer saw the utter
defeat of the O'Connors by the justiciar at the bloody battle
of Athenry, where King Phelim and the noblest of his sept
perished.   A little later the King of Scots came to the help of
his brother.   With his aid, Edward was able to reduce Carrickfergus, which had hitherto defied his efforts.   Then the brothers
led their forces from one end of Ireland to the other.   Dublin
prepared for a siege by burning its suburbs and devastating
the country around.   But though the two Bruces penetrated
as far as Limerick, they did not capture a single castle or a
walled town.   They lost so many men during their winter campaign, that they were forced in the spring to retire to Ulster.
The hopeless disunion of both parties in Ireland seemed likely
to prolong the struggle indefinitely.   The men of Dublin and
the Earl of Ulster were at feud with each other, and the
citizens captured the earl and shut him up in Dublin castle.
However little the earl could be trusted, this was a step likely to
throw all Ulster into the arms of the Bruces.   But a stronger
justice of Ireland then superseded Edmund Butler.   Roger Mortimer of Wigmore, the mightiest baron of the Welsh march,
and a man of real ability, rare energy, extreme ruthlessness, and
savage cruelty, crossed over from Haverfordwest early in 1317
at the head of a large force of marcher knights and men-at-

arms, versed from their youth up in the traditions of Celtic warfare. Mortimer set himself to work to break up the ill-assorted coalition that supported Bruce. He released the Earl of Ulster from his Dublin prison ; he procured the banishment of the heads of the house of Lacy ; he won over some of the Irish septs to his side ; he stimulated the civil war which had devastated Connaught since the fall of the O'Connors. Edward Bruce was once more confined to Ulster, where he still struggled on bravely. In the autumn of 1318 he led a foray southwards, and met his fate in a skirmish near Dundalk on October 14, when his force was scattered in confusion by John of Bermingham, one of the neighbouring lords. The four quarters of the luckless King of Ireland were exposed in the four chief towns of the island as a trophy of victory, and Bermingham was re-warded by the new earldom of Louth.

Edward Bruce's enterprise ended with his death, and Ireland rapidly settled down into its normal condition of impotent turbulence. Though at first sight the invader utterly failed, yet he pricked the bubble of the English power in Ireland. His gallant attempt at winning the throne is the critical event in a long period of Irish history. From the days of Henry III. to the days of Edward Bruce, the lordship of the English kings in Ireland was to some extent a reality. From 1315 to the reign of Henry VIII. the English dominion was little more than a name as regards the greater part of Ireland.

No one attained success, in the years after Bannockburn,—neither Banaster, nor Llewelyn Bren, nor the Bristol commons, nor Edward Bruce and his Irish allies. Before long, the incompetence of Lancaster became as manifest as the incompetence of Edward II. Lancaster's failure led to the dissolution of the baronial opposition into fiercely opposing factions. Personal and territorial jealousies slowly undermined a unity which had always been more apparent than real. The Earl of Pembroke had never forgiven the treachery of Deddington. Though Warwick was dead, Pembroke still pursued Lancaster with unrelenting hatred. No partisan of prerogative, and an enemy of Edward's personal following, Earl Aymer separated himself from his old associates and strove to form a middle party between the faction of the king and the faction of Lancaster. Warenne, coarse, turbulent, and vicious, at once violent

and crafty, still acted with him. The lord of Conisborough had
long grudged the master of Pontefract and Sandal his great
position in Yorkshire. The natural rivalries of neighbouring
potentates were further emphasised by personal animosity of the
deadliest kind. Lancaster had long been at variance with his
wife, Alice Lacy. On May 9, 1317, the Countess of Lancaster
ran away from him, with the active help of Warenne and by
the secret contrivance of the king. Private war at once broke
out between the two earls. Lancaster was too strong for his
enemy. Before winter had begun, Conisborough and Warenne's
other Yorkshire castles fell into his hands. Lancaster's partisans
even laid hold of the king's castle of Knaresborough, while other
Lancastrian bands occupied Alton castle in Staffordshire. Intermittent hostilities continued until the summer of 1318. Twice
Edward himself went to the north, and on one occasion appeared
in force outside Pontefract. But the more moderate of the
baronage managed to prevent open hostilities between the king
and the earl. Lancaster was, as ever, fighting for his own
hand. His self-seeking narrowness gave Pembroke the chance
of winning for his middle party a preponderating authority.

Pembroke found more trustworthy allies than Warenne in
Bartholomew, Lord Badlesmere, the sometime instigator of
the Bristol troubles, and a bitter opponent of Lancaster, and
in Roger of Amory, the husband of one of the three co-heiresses
who now divided the Gloucester inheritance. Edward, who
had profited by the divisions of his enemies to revive the
court party, formed a coalition between his friends and the
followers of Pembroke. All lovers of order, of moderation,
and of the supremacy of the law necessarily made common
cause with them. Thus it followed that the same machinery,
which Lancaster a few years earlier had turned against the
king, was now turned against him. An additional motive
to bring peaceable Englishmen into line was found in the
capture of Berwick by Bruce in April, 1318. After this
negotiations for peace began. The king and Lancaster treated
as two independent princes. Lancaster was no longer supported by any prominent earl, and even his clerical friends
were falling from him. Ordainers as jealous as Arundel,
royalists as fierce as Mortimer, served along with trimmers
like Pembroke and Badlesmere, in acting as mediators. Lan-

caster could no more resist than Edward could in 1312. On August 9 he accepted at Leek, in Staffordshire, the conditions drawn up for him.

The treaty of Leek marks the triumph of the middle party and the removal of Lancaster from the first place in the royal council. A pardon was granted to him and his followers, but Thomas gained little else by the compact. Pembroke and his friends showed themselves as jealous of Edward as ever the ordainers had been. The ordinances were once more confirmed, and a new council of seventeen was nominated, including eight bishops, four earls, four barons, and one banneret. The earls were Pembroke, Arundel, Richmond, and Hereford. Of these the Breton Earl of Richmond was the most friendly to the king, but it was significant to find so truculent a politician as Hereford making common cause with Pembroke. The most important of the four barons was Roger Mortimer of Wigmore. Lancaster though not paramount was still powerful, but his habit of absenting himself from parliaments made it useless to offer him a place in the council, and he was represented by a single banneret, nominated by him. Of these councillors two bishops, one earl, one baron, and Lancaster's nominee were to be in constant attendance. They were virtually to control Edward's policy, and to see that he consulted parliament in all matters that required its assent. A few days after the treaty Edward and Lancaster met at Hathern, near Loughborough, and exchanged the kiss of peace. Roger of Amory and other magnates of the middle party reconciled themselves to Lancaster, and he condescendingly restored them to his favour. But he would not deign to admit Hugh Despenser to his presence, and declared that he was still free to carry on his quarrel against Warenne. In October, a parliament at York confirmed the treaty of Leek, adding new members to the council and appointing another commission to reform the king's household. From that time until 1321, Pembroke and his friends controlled the English state, though often checked both by the king and even more by Lancaster, who still stood ostentatiously aloof from parliaments and campaigns. These years, though neither glorious nor prosperous, were the most peaceable and uneventful of the whole of Edward II.'s reign. They are noteworthy for the only serious attempt made to check the progress of the Scots after

Bannockburn. From 1318 to 1320 king and court were almost continually in the north. York became the regular meeting-place of parliaments for even a longer period.

Since 1314, the Scots had mercilessly devastated the whole north of England. The population made little attempt at resistance, and sought to buy them off by large payments of money. The Scots took the cash and soon came again for more. They wandered at will over the open country, and only the castles and walled towns afforded protection against them. Their forays extended as far south as Lancashire and Yorkshire, and, so early as 1315, Carlisle and Berwick were regularly besieged by them. It was to no purpose that in 1317 the pope issued a bull insisting upon a truce. The English welcomed an armistice on any terms, but the Scots' interest was in the continuance of the war, and they paid no attention to the papal proposal. The result was a renewal of Bruce's excommunication, and the placing of all Scotland under interdict. Yet no papal censures checked Robert's career or lessened his hold over Scotland. Next year he showed greater activity than ever. In April, 1318, he captured the town of Berwick by treachery. Peter of Spalding, one of the English burgesses who formed the town guard, was bribed to allow a band of Scots to seize that section of the town wall of which he was guardian. Then the intruders captured the gates and admitted their comrades. Thus the last Scottish town to be held by the English went back to its natural rulers. The English burgesses were expelled, though Bruce showed wonderful moderation, and few of his enemies were slain. Berwick castle held out for a time, until lack of victuals caused its surrender. In May the Scots marched through Northumberland and Durham into Yorkshire, burnt Northallerton and Boroughbridge, and exacted a thousand marks from Ripon, as the price of respecting the church of St. Wilfred. They then spent three days at Knaresborough, and made their way home through Craven.

Such successes show clearly enough that the treaty of Leek was not signed a moment too soon. It was, however, too late for any great effort against the Scots in 1318. A strenuous endeavour was made to levy a formidable expedition for 1319. In strict accordance with the ordinances, the parliament, which met at York in May of that year, agreed that there should be

18 *

a muster at Berwick for July 22, and granted a liberal subsidy. An insolent offer of peace, coupled with a promise of freedom of life and limb to Bruce, should he resign his crown, provoked from the Scots king the reply that Scotland was his kingdom both by hereditary right and the law of arms, and that he was indifferent whether he had peace with the English king or not. On July 22, the feast of St. Mary Magdalen and the anniversary of Falkirk fight, the barons assembled at Newcastle. Thomas of Lancaster was there with his brother Henry. Warenne, newly reconciled with Lancaster by a large surrender of lands, also attended, as did Pembroke, Arundel, Hereford, and the husbands of the three Gloucester co-heiresses. There was a braver show of earls than even in 1314. An offer of lands, when Scotland was conquered, attracted a large number of volunteer infantry, while the cupidity of the seamen was appealed to by a promise of ample plunder. In August the host and fleet moved northwards, and closely beset Berwick.

The Scots were too astute to offer battle. While the English were employed at Berwick, Sir James Douglas led their main force into the heart of Yorkshire. Douglas hoped to capture Queen Isabella, who was staying near York. A spy betrayed this design to the English, and Isabella was hurried off by water to Nottingham, while Douglas pressed on into the heart of Yorkshire. The Yorkshiremen had to defend their own shire while their best soldiers were with the king at Berwick. A hastily gathered assembly of improvised warriors flocked into York. Archbishop Melton put himself at their head, and the clergy, both secular and religious, formed a considerable element in the host. Then they marched out against the Scots, and found them at Myton in Swaledale. The Scots despised the disorderly mob of squires and farmers, priests and canons, monks and friars. "These are not warriors," they cried, "but huntsmen. They will do nought against us." Concealing their movements by kindling great fires of hay, they bore down upon the Yorkshiremen and put them to flight with much loss. The fight was called "the white battle of Myton" on account of the large number of white-robed monks who took part in it. The archbishop escaped with the utmost difficulty. Many fugitives were drowned in the Swale, and not one would have escaped had not night stopped the Scots' pursuit. The victors then pushed as far south as Pontefract. On the news of the battle, the besiegers of Berwick were dismayed. There was talk of dividing the army, and sending one part to drive Douglas out of Yorkshire while the other continued the siege. But the magnates, in no mood to run risks, insisted on an immediate return to England. Before Edward had reached Yorkshire, Douglas had made his way home over Stainmoor and Gilsland. Thereupon the king sent back his troops, each man to his own house. The magnificent army had accomplished nothing at all. So inglorious a termination of the campaign naturally gave rise to suspicions of treason. A story was spread abroad that Lancaster had received £4,000 from the King of Scots and had consequently done his best to help his ally. The rumour was so seriously believed that the earl offered to purge himself by ordeal of hot iron. In despair Edward made a two years' truce with the Scots. It was the best way of avoiding another Bannockburn.

Troublous times soon began again. Since Edward surrendered himself to the guidance of Pembroke and Badlesmere, he had enjoyed comparative repose and dignity. It was only when a great enterprise, like the Scots campaign, was attempted that the evil results of anarchy and the still abiding influence of Lancaster made themselves felt. But Edward bore no love to Pembroke and his associates, and was quietly feeling his way towards the re-establishment of the court party. His chief helpers in this work were the two Despensers, father and son, both named Hugh. The elder Despenser, then nearly sixty years of age, had grown grey in the service of Edward I. A baron of competent estate, he inherited from his father, the justiciar who fell at Evesham, an hereditary bias towards the constitutional tradition, but he looked to the monarch or to the popular estates, rather than to the baronage, as the best embodiment of his ideals. Ambitious and not over-scrupulous, he saw more advantage to himself in playing the game of the king than in joining a swarm of quarrelsome opposition lords. From the beginning of the reign he had identified himself with Gaveston and the courtiers, and had incurred the special wrath of Lancaster and the ordainers. Excluded from court, forced into hiding, excepted from several pacifications as he had been, Despenser never long absented himself from the court. His ambition was kindled by the circumstance that his eldest son had become the most intimate personal friend of the king. Brought up as a boy in the household of Edward when Prince of Wales, the ties of old comradeship gradually drew the younger Hugh into Gaveston's old position as the chief favourite. Neither a foreigner nor an adventurer, Despenser had the good sense to avoid the worst errors of his predecessor. As chamberlain, he was in constant attendance on the king ; and having married Edward's niece Eleanor, the eldest of the Gloucester co-heiresses, he sought to establish himself among the higher aristocracy. Royal grants and offices rained upon father and son. The household officers were changed at their caprice. The only safe way to the king's favour was by purchasing their good-will. Their good fortune stirred up fierce animosities, and the barons showed that they could hate a renegade as bitterly as a foreign adventurer.

The Despensers' ambition to attain high rank was the more natural from the havoc which death had played among the earls. "Time was," said the monk of Malmesbury, "when fifteen earls and more followed the king to war ; but now only five or six gave him their assistance." The five earldoms of Thomas of Lancaster meant the extinction of as many ancient houses. The earldoms of Chester, Cornwall, and Norfolk had long been in the king's hands. If the comital rank was not to be extinguished altogether, it had to be recruited with fresh blood. And who were so fit to fill up the vacant places as these well-born favourites ?

A little had been done under Edward II. to remedy the desolation of the earldoms. The revival of the earldom of Cornwall in favour of Gaveston had not been a happy experiment. But the king's elder half-brother, Thomas of Brotherton, invested with the estates and dignities of the Bigods, was made earl marshal and Earl of Norfolk. In 1321 the earldom of Kent, extinct since the fall of Hubert de Burgh, was revived in favour of Edmund of Woodstock, the younger half-brother of the king. The titular Scottish earldoms of some English barons, such as the Umfraville earls of Angus, kept up the name, if not the state of earls, and we have seen the reward of the victor of Dundalk in the creation of a new earldom of Louth in Ireland. But there were certain hereditary dignities whose suspension seemed unnatural. Conspicuous among these was the Gloucester earldom which, from the days of the valiant son of Henry I. to the death of the last male Clare at Bannockburn, had played a unique part in English history.

Both the Despensers desired to be earls, and the younger Hugh wished that the Gloucester earldom should be revived in his favour. Assured of the good-will of the king, both had to contend against the jealousy of the baronage and the exclusiveness of the existing earls. The younger Hugh had also to reckon with his two brothers-in-law, with whom he had divided the Clare estates. These were Hugh of Audley, who had married Margaret the widow of Gaveston, and Roger of Amory, the husband of Elizabeth, the youngest of the Clare sisters. There had been difficulty enough in effecting the partition of the Gloucester inheritance among the three co-heiresses. In 1317 the division was made, and Despenser had become lord of Glamorgan, which politically and strategically was most important of all the Gloucester lands.[1] Yet even then, Despenser was not satisfied with his position. His rival Audley had been allotted Newport and Netherwent, while Amory had been assigned the castle of Usk and estates higher up the Usk valley. Annoyed that he should be a lesser personage in south Wales than Earl Gilbert had been, Despenser began to intrigue against his wife's brothers-in-law. Each of the co-heirs had already become deadly rivals. Their hostility was the more keen since the three had already taken different sides in English politics. Despenser was the soul of the court faction; Amory was the ally of Pembroke and Badlesmere, the men of the middle party; and Audley was an uncompromising adherent of Thomas of Lancaster. There was every chance that each one of the three would have competent backing. To each the triumph of his friends meant the prospect of his becoming Earl of Gloucester.

Despenser, abler and more restless than the others, and confident in the royal favour, was the first to take the aggressive. He wished to base his future greatness upon a compact marcher principality in south Wales, and to that end not only laid his hands upon the outlying possessions of the Clares but coveted the lands of all his weaker neighbours. He took advantage of

---

[1] See for this, W. H. Stevenson, *A Letter of the Younger Despenser in* 1321 in *Engl. Hist. Rev.*, xii. (1897), 755-61.

a family arrangement for the succession to Gower, to strike the first blow. The English-speaking peninsula of Gower, with the castle of Swansea, was still held by a junior branch of the decaying house of Braose, whose main marcher lordships had been divided a century earlier between the Bohuns and the Mortimers. Its spendthrift ruler, William of Braose, was the last male of his race. He strove to make what profit he could for himself out of his succession, and had for some time been treating with Humphrey of Hereford. Gower was immediately to the southwest of Hereford's lordship of Brecon. Its acquisition would extend the Bohun lands to the sea, and make Earl Humphrey the greatest lord in south Wales. At the last moment, however, Braose broke off with him and sought to sell Gower to John of Mowbray, the husband of his daughter and heiress. When Braose died in 1320, Mowbray took possession of Gower in accordance with the "custom of the march". The royal assent had not been asked, either for licence to alienate, or for permission to enter upon the estate. Despenser coveted Gower for himself. He had already got Newport, had he Swansea also he would rule the south coast from the Lloughor to the Usk. Accordingly, he declared that the custom of the march trenched upon the royal prerogative, and managed that Gower should be seized by the king's officers, as a first step towards getting it for himself.

Despenser's action provoked extreme indignation among all the marcher lords. They denounced the apostate from the cause of his class for upsetting the balance of power in the march, and declared that in treating a lordship beyond the Wye like a landed estate in England, Hugh had, like Edward I., "despised the laws and customs of the march". It was easy to form a coalition of all the marcher lords against him. The leaders of it were Humphrey of Hereford, Roger Mortimer of Chirk, justice of Wales, and his nephew, Roger Mortimer of Wigmore, the head of the house, who had overthrown Edward Bruce's monarchy of Ireland. As Braose co-heirs their position was unassailable. But every other baron had his grievance. John of Mowbray resented the loss of Gower; Henry of Lancaster feared for Monmouth and Kidwelly; Audley wished to win back Newport, and Amory, Usk. Behind the confederates was Thomas of Lancaster himself, eager to regain his lost position of leadership.

The league at once began to wage war against Despenser in south Wales, and approached the court with a demand that he should be banished as a traitor.

Edward made his way to Gloucester in March, 1321, and strove to protect Despenser and to calm the wild spirits of the marchers. But private war had already broken out after the marcher fashion, and the king retired without effecting his purpose. Left to themselves the marcher allies easily overran the Despenser lands, inherited or usurped. Neither Cardiff nor Caerphilly held out long against them: the Welsh husbandmen, like the English knights and barons of Glamorgan, were hostile to the Despensers. The king could do nothing to help his friends. In May, Lancaster formed a league of northern barons in the chapter-house of the priory at Pontefract. In June, another northern gathering was held in the Norman nave of the parish church of Sherburn-in-Elmet, a few miles to the north of Pontefract. This was attended by the Archbishop of York and two of his suffragans, and a great number of clergy, secular and regular, as well as by many barons and knights. It was in fact an informal parliament of the Lancastrian party. A long list of complaints were drawn up which, under fair words, demanded the removal of bad ministers, and among them the chamberlain. The clerical members of the conference met separately at the rectory, where they showed more circumspection, but an equally partisan bias.[1]

The conferences at Pontefract and Sherburn showed that Lancaster and the northerners were in full sympathy with the men of the west. The middle party again made common cause with the followers of Lancaster. Amory's interests were sufficiently involved to make him an eager enemy of Despenser, and Badlesmere was almost as keen. Though Pembroke still professed to mediate, it was generally believed that he was delighted to get rid of the Despensers. Even Warenne took sides against them, though the discredited earl was fast becoming of no account. Such being the drift of opinion, the fate of the favourites was settled when the estates assembled in London in July. Edward had delayed a meeting of parliament as long as he could, and was helpless in its hands. Great pains were taken this time to prevent the repetition of the informalities

---

[1] Bp. Stubbs works all this out, *Chron. Ed. I. and II.*, ii., pref., lxxxvi.-xc.

which had attended the attack on Gaveston. There was an unprecedented gathering of magnates, who came to the parliament with a large armed following, encamped like an army in all the villages to the north of the city. The commons were fully represented, and the clerical estate was expressly summoned. Articles were at once drawn up against the Despensers. They had aspired to royal power ; had turned the heart of the king from his subjects ; had excited civil war, and had taught that obedience was due to the crown rather than to the king. This last charge came strangely from those who had urged that doctrine as a pretext for withdrawing support from Gaveston. It is a good illustration of the tendency of the Despensers to cloak their personal ambitions with loud-sounding constitutional phrases.

The peers pronounced sentence of banishment and forfeiture against both the elder and the younger Hugh. They were not to be recalled save by consent of the peers in parliament assembled. The easy revolution was completed by the issuing of pardons to nearly five hundred members of the triumphant coalition. The elder Despenser at once withdrew to the continent. The younger Hugh found friends among the mariners of the Cinque Ports. These at first protected him in England, and then put at his disposal a little fleet of vessels with which, when driven from the land, he took to piracy in the narrow seas.

The fall of the Despensers was brought about very much after the same fashion as the first exile of Gaveston. Like Gaveston, they speedily returned, and in circumstances which suggest an even closer parallel with the events that led to the recall of the Gascon. The triumphant coalition in each case fell to pieces as soon as it had done its immediate work. Once more the loss of his friend and comrade stirred up Edward to an energy and perseverance such as he never displayed on other occasions. But the second triumph of the king assumed a more complete character than his earlier snatched victory. Accident favoured Edward's design of bringing back his favourites, and throwing off once more the baronial thraldom. On October 13, 1321, Queen Isabella, on her way to Canterbury, claimed hospitality at Leeds castle, situated between Maidstone and the archiepiscopal city. The castle belonged to Badlesmere, whose wife was then residing there, with his kinsman, Bartholomew Burghersh, and a competent garrison. Lady Badlesmere refused to admit the queen, declaring that, without her lord's orders, she could not venture to entertain any one. Bitterly indignant at the insult, the queen took up her quarters in the neighbouring priory and attempted to force an entrance. The castle, however, was not to be taken by the hasty attack of a small company. Six of Isabella's followers were slain, and the attempt was abandoned. Isabella called upon her husband to avenge her; and the king at once resolved to capture Leeds castle at any cost, and prepared to undertake the enterprise in person. He offered high wages to all crossbowmen, archers, knights, and squires who would follow him to Leeds, and summoned the levies of horse and foot from the towns and shires of the south-east. His trust in the loyalty of his subjects met with an unexpectedly favourable response. In a few days a large army gathered round the king under the walls of Leeds. Among the many magnates who appeared among the royal following were six earls: Pembroke, Badlesmere's own associate; the king's two brothers, Norfolk and Kent; Warenne, Richmond, and Arundel, who as Despenser's kinsman felt himself bound to fight on his side. On October 23 the castle was closely besieged by this overwhelming force, and on October 31 was forced to surrender. Burghersh was shut up in the Tower and Lady Badlesmere in Dover castle. Thirteen of the garrison, "stout men and valiant," were hanged by the angry king.

During the siege of Leeds, the magnates of the march, headed by Hereford and Roger Mortimer, collected a force at Kingston-on-Thames, where they were joined by Badlesmere. But they dared not advance towards the relief of the Kentish castle, and after a fortnight they dispersed to their own homes. Lancaster hated Badlesmere so bitterly that he made no move against the king, and sullenly bided his time in the north. His inaction paralysed the barons as effectively as in earlier days it had hindered the plans of the king. Flushed with his victory, Edward gradually unfolded his designs. His tool, Archbishop Reynolds, summoned a convocation of the southern province for December 1 at St. Paul's, and obtained from the assembled clergy the opinion that the proceedings against the Despensers were invalid. On January 1, 1322, Reynolds solemnly declared this sentence in St. Paul's. Edward did not wait for the archbishop. Attended by many of the warriors who had fought at Leeds, he marched to the west, occupying on his journey the lands and castles of his enemies. He kept his Christmas court at Cirencester, and thence advanced towards the Severn. As the inaction of Lancaster kept the northern barons quiet, Edward's sole task was to wreak his revenge on the marcher lords. They were unprepared for resistance, and waited in vain for Lancaster to come to their help. Without a leader, they made feeble and ill-devised efforts to oppose the king's advance. Their command of the few bridges over the Severn prevented the king from crossing the river, and leading his troops directly into the march. Foiled at Gloucester, Worcester, and Bridgnorth, Edward made his way up the stream to Shrewsbury. The two Mortimers, who held the town and the passage of the river, could have stopped him if they had chosen. But they feared to undertake strong measures while Lancaster's action remained uncertain. They suffered Edward to cross the stream and surrendered to him. The collapse of the fiercest of the marcher lords frightened the rest into surrender. Edward wandered back through the middle and southern marches, occupying without resistance the main strongholds of his enemies. At Hereford, he sharply rebuked the bishop for upholding the barons against their natural lord. At Berkeley, he received from Maurice of Berkeley the keys of the stately fortress which was so soon to be the place of his last humiliation. Early in February, he was back at Gloucester, where, on February 11, he recalled the Despensers.

Humphrey of Hereford, Roger of Amory, and a few other marchers managed to escape the king's pursuit, and rode northwards to join Thomas of Lancaster. Thomas had long been ready at Pontefract with his followers in arms. But he let the time for effective action slip, and was only goaded into doing anything when the fugitives from the march impressed him with the critical state of affairs. The quarrel of king and barons was not the only trouble besetting England. The two years' truce with Scotland had expired, and Robert Bruce was once more devastating the northern counties. But neither Edward nor Lancaster cared anything for this. Andrew Harclay, the governor of Carlisle, strongly urged the king to defend his subjects from the Scots rather than make war against them. Edward answered that rebels must be put down before foreign enemies could be encountered, and pressed northwards with his victorious troops.

Lancaster was then besieging Tickhill, a royal castle in southern Yorkshire. After wasting three weeks before its walls, he led his force south to Burton-on-Trent, which he occupied on March 10. Edward soon approached the Trent on his northward march. The barons thereupon lost courage, and, abandoning the defence of the passage over the river, fled northwards to Pontefract, the centre of Lancaster's power in Yorkshire. Edward advanced against them, taking on his road Lancaster's castle of Tutbury, where Roger of Amory was captured, mortally wounded. The Lancastrians were panic-stricken. They fled from Pontefract as they had fled from Burton, retreating northwards, probably simply to avoid the king, possibly to join hands with Robert Bruce. On March 16 the fugitives reached Boroughbridge, on the south bank of the Ure, where a long narrow bridge, hardly wide enough for horsemen in martial array, crossed the stream. The north bank of the river, and the approaches to the bridge, were held in force by the levies of Cumberland and Westmoreland which Harclay had summoned at the king's request, in order to prevent a junction between the Lancastrians and the Scots. Harclay was a brave and capable commander and had well learnt the lessons of Scottish warfare.[1] He dismounted all his knights and men at arms, and arranged them on the northern side of the river, along with some of his pikemen. The rest of the pikemen he ordered to form a "schiltron" after the Scottish fashion, so that their close formation might resist the cavalry of which the Lancastrian force consisted. He bade his archers shoot swiftly and continually at the enemy.

Seeing this disposition of the hostile force, the Lancastrian army divided. One band, under Hereford and Roger Clifford, dismounted and made for the bridge, which was defended by the schiltron of pikemen. The rest of the men-at-arms remained on horseback and followed Lancaster to a ford near the bridge, whence, by crossing the water, they could take the schiltron in flank. Neither movement succeeded. Hereford and Clifford advanced, each with one attendant, to the bridge.

[1] For the tactics of Boroughbridge see *Engl. Hist. Review*, xix. (1904), 711-13.

No sooner had the earl entered upon the wooden structure than he was slain by a Welsh spearman, who had hidden himself under it, and aimed a blow at Humphrey through the planking. Clifford was severely wounded, and escaped with difficulty. Discouraged by the loss of their leaders, the rest of the troops made only a feeble effort to force the passage. The same evil fortune attended the division that followed Lancaster. The archers of Harclay obeyed his orders so well that the Lancastrian cavalry scarcely dared enter the water. Lancaster lost his nerve, and besought Harclay for a truce until the next morning. His request was granted, but during the night all the followers of Hereford dispersed, thinking that there was no need for them to remain after the death of their lord. Lancaster's own troops were likewise thinned by desertions. The sheriff of York came up early in the morning with an armed force from the south, joined Harclay, and cut off the last hope of retreat. Further resistance being useless, Lancaster, Audley, Clifford, Mowbray, and the other leaders surrendered in a body.

Edward was then at Pontefract in the chief castle of his deadliest enemy. Thither the prisoners of Boroughbridge were sent for their trial, and there they were hastily condemned by a body of seven earls and numerous barons, presided over by the king himself. Lancaster, not allowed to say a word in his defence, was at once sentenced to death as a rebel and a traitor. In consideration of his exalted rank, the grosser penalties of treason were commuted, as in the case of Gaveston, to simple decapitation. On the morning of March 22 Thomas was led out of his castle, clad in the garb of a penitent and mounted on a sorry steed. He was conducted to a little hill outside the walls. The crowd mocked at his sufferings and in scorn called him " King Arthur ". In two or three blows of the axe, his head was struck off from his body. Nor was he the only victim. Audley, spared his life by reason of his marriage to the king's niece, was, like the two Mortimers, consigned to prison. Clifford and Mowbray were hanged at York, and Badlesmere at Canterbury. In all, more than twenty knights and barons paid the penalty of death.

It is hard to waste much pity on Lancaster. He was the victim of his own fierce passions and, still more, of his own utter incompetence. His attitude all through the crisis had been inept in the extreme, and the poor fight that he made for

his life at Boroughbridge was a fitting conclusion to a feeble CHAP.
career. But with all his faults he remained popular to the end, XIII.
especially with the clergy and commons. He was hailed as a
martyr to freedom and sound government. Pilgrimages were
made to the scene of his death, and miracles were wrought
with his relics. A chapel arose on the little hill dedicated to
his worship, and a loud cry arose for his canonisation. The
abuse made by his enemies of their victory only strengthened
his reputation among the people. The tragedy of his fall appealed to the rude sympathies of the north-countrymen, and the
merit of the cause atoned in their minds for the weakness of the
man.

A parliament met at York on May 2, where the triumph
of the king received its consummation. The Despensers had
more advanced constitutional ideas than Lancaster, and pains
were taken that this parliament should completely represent
the three estates. It was a novel feature that twelve representatives of the commons of north Wales and twelve of the
commons of south Wales attended, on this occasion, to speak
on behalf of the region where the troubles had first begun.
With the full approval of the estates, the ordinances were
solemnly revoked, as infringing the rights of the crown. The
important principle was laid down that " matters which are to
be established for the estate of the king and for the estate of
the realm shall be treated, accorded, and established in parliament by the king and by the council of the prelates, earls, and
barons, and the commonalty of the realm ". Thus, while the
repeal of the ordinances seemed based upon their infringement
of the royal prerogative, it was at least implied that they were
also invalid because they were the work of a council of barons
only, and not of a full parliament of the estates. This declaration of the necessity of popular co-operation in valid legislation
is the most important constitutional advance of the reign of
Edward II. It is a significant comment on the limitations of
the baronial opposition that the ordinances should be the last
great English law in the passing of which the commons were not
consulted, and that a royalist triumph should be the occasion
of the declaration of a vital principle.

The king's friends then received their rewards. Harclay
was made Earl of Carlisle and the elder Despenser became Earl

of Winchester.   Fear of the marcher lords, even in their prison, withheld from the younger Hugh the title, though hardly the authority, of Earl of Gloucester.   In other ways also the Despensers were anxious to prevent their victory suggesting too much of a reaction.   Before parliament separated, it adopted a new series of ordinances confirming the Great Charter and re-enacting in more constitutional fashion some portions of the laws of 1312, which aimed at protecting the subject and strengthening the administration.   Grants of men and money were made to fight the Scots, and once more the new customs were allowed to swell the royal revenue.   Thus the revolution was completed.   Edward, Gaveston, Lancaster, and Pembroke had each in their turn been tried and found wanting.   Thanks to the jealousies of the barons, his own spasmodic energy, and the acuteness of the Despensers, Edward was still to have another chance, under the guidance of his new friends.   We shall see how the restored rule of the Despensers was blighted by the same incompetence and selfishness which had ruined their predecessors in power.   The triumph of the Despensers proved but the first act in the tragic fall of Edward II.

CHAPTER XIV.

THE FALL OF EDWARD II. AND THE RULE OF ISABELLA AND MORTIMER.

DURING the deliberations of the parliament of York, the truce with Bruce expired, and forthwith came the news that the Scots had once more crossed the border. On this occasion Bruce raided the country from Carlisle to Preston, burning every open town on his way, though sparing most of the religious houses. At Cartmel, Lancaster, and Preston, favoured monastic buildings alone stood entire amidst the desolation wrought by the Scots. No effective opposition was offered to them, and after a three weeks' foray, they recrossed the Solway.

As in 1314 and 1318, the restoration of order was followed by an attempt to put down Bruce. In August, 1322, Edward assembled his forces at Newcastle and invaded Scotland. Berwick was unsuccessfully besieged and the Lothians laid waste. The Scots still had the prudence to withdraw beyond the Forth, and avoid battle in the open field. By the beginning of September, pestilence and famine had done their work on the invaders. Unable to find support in the desolate fields of Lothian, the English returned to their own land, having accomplished nothing. The Scots followed on their tracks, but with such secrecy that they penetrated into the heart of Yorkshire before Edward was aware of their presence. In October they suddenly swooped down on the king, when he was staying at Byland abbey. Some troops which accompanied him were encamped on a hill between Byland and Rievaux. They were attacked by the Scots and defeated; their leader, John of Brittany, was taken prisoner, and Edward only avoided capture by a precipitate flight from Byland to Bridlington. All Yorkshire was reduced to abject terror, and Edward's hosts, the canons of Bridlington, removed with all their valuables to Lincolnshire, and sent one of their number to Bruce at Malton to purchase immunity for their estates. After a month the Scots went home, leaving famine, pestilence, and misery in their train. The Despensers thus proved themselves not less incompetent to defend England than Thomas of Lancaster.

As the state afforded no protection, each private person had to make the best terms he could for himself. Even the king's favourite, Louis of Beaumont, the illiterate Bishop of Durham, entered into negotiations with the Scots, while the Archbishop of York issued formal permission to religious houses of his diocese to treat with the excommunicated followers of Bruce. Not only timid ecclesiastics, but well-tried soldiers found in private dealings with the Scots the only remedy for their troubles. After the Byland surprise, Harclay, the new Earl of Carlisle, the victor of Boroughbridge, and the warden of the marches, dismissed his troops, sought out Bruce at Lochmaben, and made an arrangement with him, by which it was resolved that a committee of six English and six Scottish magnates should be empowered to conclude peace between the two countries on the basis of recognising him as King of Scots. There was great alarm at court when Harclay's treason was known. A Cumberland baron, Anthony Lucy, was instructed to apprehend the culprit, and forcing his way into Carlisle castle by a stratagem, captured the earl with little difficulty. In March, 1323, Harclay suffered the terrible doom of treason. He justified his action to the last, declaring that his only motive was a desire to procure peace, and convincing many of the north-countrymen of the innocence of his motives. To such a pass had England been reduced that those who honestly desired that the farmers of Cumberland should once more till their fields in peace, saw no other means of gaining their end than by communication with the enemies of their country.

The disgrace of Byland and the tragedy of Carlisle showed that it was idle to pretend to fight the Scots any longer. Negotiations for peace were entered upon; Pembroke and the younger Despenser being the chief English commissioners. Peace was found impossible, as English pride still refused to recognise the royal title of King Robert, but a thirteen years' truce was arranged without any difficulty. This treaty of 1323 practically concluded the Scottish war of independence. Bruce then easily obtained papal recognition of his title, though English ill-will long stood in the way of the remission of his sentence of excommunication. His martial career, however, was past, and he could devote his declining years to the consolidation of his kingdom and the restoration of its material prosperity. He reorganised the national army, built up a new nobility by distributing among his faithful followers the estates of the obstinate friends of England, and first called upon the royal burghs of Scotland to send representatives to the Scottish parliament. He had made Scotland a nation, and nobly redeemed the tergiversation and violence of his earlier career.

Among Harclay's motives for treating with the Scots had been his distrust of the Despensers. As generals against the Scots and as administrators of England, they manifested an equal incapacity. Their greed and insolence revived the old enmities, and they proved strangely lacking in resolution to grapple with emergencies. Nevertheless they ruled over England for nearly five years in comparative peace. This period, unmarked by striking events, is, however, evidence of the exhaustion of the country rather than of the capacity of the Earl of Winchester and the lord of Glamorgan. The details of the history bear witness to the relaxation of the reins of government, the prevalence of riot and petty rebellion, the sordid personal struggles for place and power, the weakness which could neither collect the taxes, enforce obedience to the law, nor even save from humiliation the most trusted agents of the government.

The Despensers' continuance in power rested more on the absence of rivals than on their own capacity. The strongest of the royalist earls, Aymer of Pembroke, died in 1324. As he left no issue, his earldom swelled the alarmingly long roll of lapsed dignities. None of the few remaining earls could step into his place, nor give Edward the wise counsel which the creator of the middle party had always provided. Warenne was brutal, profligate, unstable, and distrusted; Arundel had no great influence; Richmond was a foreigner, and of little personal weight, and the successors of Humphrey of Hereford and Guy of Warwick were minors, suspected by reason of their fathers' treasons. The only new earl was Henry of Lancaster, who in 1324 obtained a partial restitution of his brother's estates and the title of Earl of Leicester. Prudent, moderate, and high-minded, Henry stood in strong contrast to his more famous brother. But the tragedy of Pontefract and his unsatisfied claim on the Lancaster earldom stood between Henry and the government, and the imprudence of the Despensers soon utterly estranged him from the king, though he was the last man to indulge in indiscriminate opposition, and Edward dared not push his powerful cousin to extremities. In these circumstances, the king had no wise or strong advisers whose influence might counteract the Despensers. His loneliness and isolation made him increasingly dependent upon the favourites.

The older nobles were already alienated, when the Despensers provoked a quarrel with the queen. Isabella was a woman of strong character and violent passions, with the lack of morals and scruples which might have been expected from a girlhood passed amidst the domestic scandals of her father's household. She resented her want of influence over her husband, and hated the Despensers because of their superior power with him. The favourites met her hostility by an open declaration of warfare. In 1324 the king deprived her of her separate estate, drove her favourite servants from court, and put her on an allowance of a pound a day. The wife of the younger Hugh, her husband's niece, was deputed to watch her, and she could not even write a letter without the Lady Despenser's knowledge. Isabella bitterly chafed under her humiliation. She was, she declared, treated like a maidservant and made the hireling of the Despensers. Finding, however, that nothing was to be gained by complaints, she prudently dissembled her wrath and waited patiently for revenge.

The Despensers' chief helpers were among the clergy. Conspicuous among them were Walter Stapledon, Bishop of Exeter, the treasurer, and Robert Baldock, the chancellor. The records of Stapledon's magnificence survive in the nave of his cathedral church, and in Exeter College, Oxford; but the great builder and pious founder was a worldly, greedy, and corrupt public minister. So unpopular was he that, in 1325, it was thought wise to remove him from office. Thereupon another building prelate, William Melton, Archbishop of York, whose piety and charity long intercourse with courtiers had not extinguished, abandoned his northern flock for London and the treasury. But the best of officials could do little to help the unthrifty king.　Edward was so poorly respected that he could not even obtain a bishopric for his chancellor.　On two occasions the envoys sent to Avignon, to urge Baldock's claims on vacant sees, secured for themselves the mitre destined for the minister.　In this way John Stratford became Bishop of Winchester and William Ayermine, Bishop of Norwich.　Edward had not even the spirit to show manifest disfavour to these self-seeking prelates, but his inaction was so clearly the result of weakness that it involved no gratitude, and the two bishops secretly hated the ruling clique, as likely to do them an evil turn if it dared.　Nor were the older prelates better contented or more loyal.　The primate Reynolds was deeply irritated by Melton's appointment as treasurer.　Burghersh, the Bishop of Lincoln, was a nephew of Badlesmere, and anxious to avenge his uncle.　Adam Orleton, Bishop of Hereford, was a dependant of the Mortimers, who took his surname from one of their Herefordshire manors.　Forgiven for his share in the revolt of 1322, he cleverly contrived in 1324 the escape of his patron, Roger Mortimer of Wigmore, from the Tower.　The marcher made his way to France, but his ally felt the full force of the king's wrath.　He was deprived of his temporalities, and, when the Church spread her ægis over him, the court procured the verdict of a Herefordshire jury against him.　Thus the impolicy of the crown combined the selfish worldling with the zealot for the Church in a common opposition.　Like Isabella, Orleton bided his time, and Edward feared to complete his disgrace.

In such ways the king and the Despensers proclaimed their incapacity to the world.　The Scottish truce, the wrongs of Henry of Lancaster, the humiliation of the queen, the alienation of the old nobles, the fears of greedy prelates,—each of these was remembered against them.　Gradually every order of the community became disgusted.　The feeble efforts of Edward to conciliate the Londoners met with little response.　Weak rule and the insecurity of life and property turned away the heart of the commons from the king.　It was no wonder that men went on pilgrimage to the little hill outside Pontefract, where Earl Thomas had met his doom, or that rumours spread that the king was a changeling and no true son of the great Edward.　But though the power of the king and the

Despensers was thoroughly undermined, the absence of leaders and the general want of public spirit still delayed the day of reckoning. At last, the threatening outlook beyond the Channel indirectly precipitated the crisis.

The relations of France and England remained uneasy, despite the marriage of two English kings in succession to ladies of the Capetian house. The union of Edward I. and Margaret of France had not done much to help the settlement of the disputed points in the interpretation of the treaty of Paris of 1303, and the match between Edward II. and his stepmother's niece had been equally ineffective. The restoration of Gascony in 1303 had never been completed, and in the very year of the treaty a decree of the parliament of Paris had withdrawn the homage of the county of Bigorre from the English duke. Within the ceded districts, the conflict of the jurisdictions of king and duke became increasingly accentuated. Having failed to hold Gascony by force of arms, Philip the Fair aspired to conquer it by the old process of stealthily undermining the traditional authority of the duke. Appeals to Paris became more and more numerous. The agents of the king wandered at will through Edward's Gascon possessions, and punished all loyalty to the lawful duke by dragging the culprits before their master's courts. The ineptitude which characterised all Edward's subordinates was particularly conspicuous among his Gascon seneschals and their subordinates. While the English king's servants drifted on from day to day, timid, without policy, and without direction, the agents of France, well trained, energetic, and determined, knew their own minds and gradually brought about the end which they had clearly set before themselves. In vain did bitter complaints arise of the aggressions of the officers of Philip. It was to no purpose that conferences were held, protocols drawn up, and much time and ink wasted in discussing trivialities. Neither Edward nor Philip wished to push matters to extremities. To the former the policy of drift was always congenial. The latter was content to wait until the pear was ripe. It seemed that in a few more years Gascony would become as thoroughly subject to the French crown as Champagne or Normandy.

Philip the Fair died in 1314, and was followed in rapid succession by his three sons. The first of these, Louis X., had,

like Edward II., to contend against an aristocratic reaction, and CHAP.
died in 1316, before he could even receive the homage of his XIV.
brother-in-law. A king of more energy than Edward might
have profited by the difficult situation which followed Louis'
death. For a time there was neither pope, nor emperor, nor
King of France. But Philip V. mounted the French throne
when his brother's widow had given birth to a daughter, and
continued the policy of his predecessors with regard to Gascony. Again the disputes between Norman and Gascon sailors
threatened, as in 1293, to bring about a rupture. The ever-increasing aggressions of the suzerain culminated in summoning
Edward's own seneschal of Saintonge to appear before the French
king's court. Edward neglected to do homage, alleging his
preoccupation in the Scottish war and similar excuses. But the
threatened danger soon passed away, for again the interests and
fears of both parties postponed the conflict. In avoiding any
alliance with the Scots, the French king showed a self-restraint
for which Edward could not but be grateful. In 1320 Edward
performed in person his long-delayed homage at Amiens,
though his grievances against his brother-in-law still remained
unredressed. In 1322 the death of Philip V. renewed the
troublesome homage question in a more acute form.[1]

The obligation of performing homage to a rival prince
weighed with increasing severity on the English kings at each
rapid change of occupants of the throne of France. The same
pretexts were again brought forward, as sufficient reasons for
postponing or evading the unpleasant duty. But before the
question was settled a new source of trouble arose in the affair of
Saint-Sardos, which soon plunged the two countries into open war.
The lord of Montpezat, a vassal of the Duke of Gascony, built a
bastide at Saint-Sardos upon a site which he declared was held
by himself of the duke, but which the French officials claimed
as belonging to Charles IV. The dispute was taken before the
parliament of Paris, which decided that the new town belonged
to the King of France. Thereupon a royal force promptly
took possession of it. Irritated at this high-handed action, the
lord of Montpezat invoked the aid of Edward's seneschal of
Gascony, who attacked and destroyed the *bastide* and massacred

[1] For the relations of Edward II. and Philip V. see Lehugeur, *Hist. de
Philippe le Long*, pp. 240-66 (1897).

the French garrison.[1] The answer of Charles the Fair to this aggression was decisive. Gascony was pronounced sequestrated and Charles of Valois, the veteran uncle of the king, was ordered to enforce the sentence at the head of an imposing army.

Thus, in the summer of 1324 England and France were once more at war. But while England remonstrated and negotiated, France acted. Norman corsairs swept the Channel and pillaged the English coasts. Ponthieu yielded without resistance. Early in August, Charles of Valois entered the Agenais, and on the 15th Agen opened its gates. The victorious French soon appeared before La Réole, where alone they encountered real resistance. Edmund, Earl of Kent, who had made vain attempts to procure peace at Paris, had been sent in July to act as lieutenant of Aquitaine. He had not sufficient force at his command to venture to meet the Count of Valois in the open field, and threw himself into La Réole. The rocky height, crowned with a triple wall, and looking down on the vineyards and cornfields of the Garonne, defied for weeks the skill of the eminent Lorrainer engineers who directed Charles of Valois' siege train. But when Charles announced to Edmund that he would carry the town by assault, if not surrendered within four days, the timid earl signed a truce from September to Easter, and was allowed to withdraw to Bordeaux. A mere fringe of coast-land still remained faithful to the English duke, when Charles of Valois went back to Paris, having victoriously terminated his long and chequered career. Before the end of 1325 he died.[2]

The truce involved a renewal of the negotiations. Bishop Stratford and William Ayermine, the astute chancery clerk, were commissioned in November, 1324, to treat with the French, but made little progress in their delicate task. At this stage Isabella, inspired probably by Adam Orleton, came forward with a proposal. She besought her husband to allow her to visit her brother, the French king, and use her influence with him to procure peace and the restitution of Gascony. With

---

[1] See for this affair Bréquigny, *Mémoire sur les différends entre la France et l'Angleterre sous Charles le Bel*, in *Mém. de l'Acad. des Inscriptions et Belles Lettres*, xli. (1780), pp. 641-92. M. Déprez is about to publish a Chancery Roll of Edward II. which includes all the official acts relating to it.

[2] Petit, *Charles de Valois*, pp. 207-15 (1900), gives the fullest modern account of these transactions.

the strange infatuation which marked all the acts of Edward and his favourites, Isabella's proposal was adopted, and in March, 1325, the queen crossed the Channel and made her way to her brother's court. The summer was consumed in negotiating a treaty, by which Edward's French fiefs were to be restored to him in their integrity, as soon as he had performed homage to the new king. Meanwhile the English garrison of Gascony was to withdraw to Bayonne, leaving the rest of the duchy in the hands of a French seneschal. Edward agreed to these terms, and put Gascony into Charles's hands. He was still unwilling to compromise his dignity by performing homage, while the Despensers were mortally afraid of his going to France, lest it should remove him from their influence. Isabella then made a second suggestion. She persuaded her brother to excuse the personal homage of her husband, if Edward would invest his young son, Edward, with Gascony and Ponthieu, and send him in his stead to tender his feudal duty. This also was agreed to by the English king, and in September the young prince, then about thirteen years old, was appointed Duke of Aquitaine and Count of Ponthieu, and despatched to join his mother at Paris, where he performed homage to his uncle.

It was expected that Gascony and Ponthieu would then be restored, and that the queen and her son would return to England. But Charles IV. perpetrated a clever piece of trickery which showed how far off a real settlement still was. He "restored" to Edward those parts of Gascony which had been peacefully surrendered to him in the summer, and announced that he should keep the Agenais and La Réole, as belonging to France by right of Charles of Valois' recent conquest. Bitterly mortified at this treachery, Edward took upon himself the title of "governor and administrator of his first-born, Edward, Duke of Aquitaine, and of his estates". By this technical subtlety, he thought himself entitled to resume the control of the ceded districts and resist the attack which was bound to follow hard upon the new breach. Once more Charles IV. pronounced the sequestration of the duchy, and despite Edward's efforts, his power crumbled away before the peaceful advent of the French troops, charged with the execution of their master's edict.

Long before the last Gascon castles had opened their gates

to Charles's officers, new developments at Paris made the question of Aquitaine a subordinate matter. Despite the breach of the negotiations, Isabella and her son still tarried at the French court. In answer to Edward's requests for their return, she sent back excuse after excuse, till his patience was fairly exhausted. At last, on December 1, 1325, Edward peremptorily ordered his wife to return home, and warned her not to consort with certain English traitors in the French court. The Duke of Aquitaine was similarly exhorted to return, with his mother if he could, but if not, without her. The reference to English traitors shows that Edward was aware that Isabella had already formed that close relation with the exiled lord of Wigmore which soon ripened into an adulterous connexion. Inspired by Roger Mortimer, Isabella declared that she was in peril of her life from the malice of the Despensers, and would never go back to her husband as long as the favourites retained power. A band of the exiles of 1322 gathered round her and her paramour, and sought to bring about their restoration as champions of the loudly expressed grievances of the queen, and the rights of her young son. The king's ambassadors at Paris, Stratford and Ayermine, recently made Bishop of Norwich by a papal provision which ignored the election of Robert Baldock the chancellor, united themselves with the queen and the fugitive marcher. With them, too, was associated Edmund of Kent, who was allowed by the treaty to return from Gascony through France. Bishop Stapledon, who had accompanied the queen to France, was so alarmed at the turn events were taking, that he fled in disguise to reveal his suspicions to the king. Thus England, already exposed to a danger of a French war, was threatened with the forcible overthrow of the Despensers and the reinstatement of Isabella by armed invaders.

By the spring of 1326 the scandalous relations of Isabella and Mortimer were notorious all over England and France. Charles IV. grew disgusted at his sister's doings, and gave no countenance to her schemes. Isabella accordingly withdrew from Paris with her son and her paramour, and made her way to the Netherlands. There she found refuge in the county of Hainault, whose lord, William II., of Avesnes, was won over to support her by a contract to marry the Duke of Aquitaine to his daughter Philippa. A large advance from Philippa's marriage portion was employed in hiring a troop of knights and squires of Hainault and Holland. John of Hainault, brother of the count, took joint command of this band with Roger Mortimer. The ports of Holland and Zealand, both of which counties were united with Hainault under William II.'s rule, offered ample facilities for their embarkation.

On September 23, 1326, the queen and her followers took ship at Dordrecht in Holland. Next day the fleet cast anchor in the port of Orwell, and that same day the expedition was landed and marched to Walton, where it spent the first night on English soil. The gentry of Suffolk and Essex flocked to the standard of the queen, who declared that she had come to avenge the wrongs of Earl Thomas of Lancaster and to drive the Despensers from power. Thomas of Brotherton, the earl marshal, made common cause with the invaders, and Henry, Earl of Leicester, hastened to associate himself with the champions of his martyred brother. A great force of native Englishmen swelled the queen's host, and reduced to insignificance the little band of Hainaulters and Hollanders. There was no resistance. Isabella marched to Bury St. Edmunds, "as if on a pilgrimage," and thence to Cambridge, where she tarried several days with the canons of Barnwell. From Cambridge she moved on to Baldock, where she despoiled the chancellor's manors and took his brother captive. At Dunstable, her next halt, she was on a great highway, within thirty-three miles of London.

On hearing of his wife's landing, Edward threw himself on the compassion of the Londoners, but met with so cold a reception that early in October he withdrew to Gloucester. Besides the chancellor and the two Despensers, the only magnates of mark who remained faithful to him were the brothers-in-law, Edmund, Earl of Arundel, and Earl Warenne. On Edward's retreat from London, Bishop Stratford made his way to the capital, where he joined with Archbishop Reynolds in a hollow pretence of mediation. The Londoners gladly welcomed the queen's messengers and soon rose in revolt in her favour. They plundered and burnt the house of the Bishop of Exeter, who fled in alarm to St. Paul's. Seized at the very door of the church, Stapledon was brutally murdered by the mob in Cheapside, where his naked body lay exposed all day. Immediately after this, Reynolds fled in terror to his Kentish estates, where he waited to see which was the stronger side. The king's younger son, John of Eltham, a boy of nine, who had been left behind by his father in the Tower, was proclaimed warden of the capital.

On hearing of Edward's flight to the west, Isabella went after him in pursuit. On the day of Stapledon's murder, she had advanced as far as Wallingford, where, posing as the continuer of the policy of the lords ordainers, she issued a proclamation denouncing the Despensers. Thence she made her way to Oxford, where Bishop Orleton, who had already joined her, preached a seditious sermon before the university and the leaders of the revolt. Taking as his text, " My head, my head," he demonstrated that the sick head of the state could not be restored by all the remedies of Hippocrates, and would therefore have to be cut off. This was the first intimation that the insurgents would not be content with the fall of the Despensers. From Oxford, Isabella and Mortimer hurried to Gloucester, whence Edward had already fled to the younger Despenser's palatinate of Glamorgan. From Gloucester, they passed on through Berkeley to Bristol, where the elder Despenser, the Earl of Winchester, was in command. The feeling of the burgesses of the second town in England was so strongly adverse that the earl was unable to defend either the borough or the castle. In despair he opened the gates on October 26 to the queen, and was immediately consigned, without trial or inquiry, to the death of a traitor. After proclaiming the Duke of Aquitaine as warden of the realm during his father's absence, the queen's army marched on Hereford, where Isabella remained, while the Earl of Leicester, accompanied by a Welsh clerk, named Rhys ap Howel, was sent with part of the army to hunt out the king.

After his flight from Gloucester, Edward had wandered through the Welsh march to Chepstow, whence he took ship, hoping to make sail to Lundy, which Despenser had latterly acquired, and perhaps ultimately to Ireland. But contrary winds kept him in the narrows of the Bristol Channel, and on October 27 he landed again at Cardiff. A few days later he was at Caerphilly, but afraid to entrust himself to the protection of the mightiest of marcher castles, he moved restlessly from place to place in Glamorgan and Gower, imploring the help of the tenants of the Despensers, and issuing vain summonses and commissions that no one obeyed. Discovered by the local

knowledge of Rhys ap Howel, or betrayed by those whom the
Welshman's gold had corrupted, Edward was captured on
November 16 in Neath abbey. With him Baldock and the
younger Despenser were also taken. On November 20 the
favourite was put to death at Hereford, while Baldock, saved
from immediate execution by his clerkly privilege, was consigned to the cruel custody of Orleton, only to perish a few
months later of ill-treatment. To Hereford also was brought
Edmund of Arundel, captured in Shropshire, and condemned
to suffer the fate of the Despensers. The king was entrusted
to the custody of Henry of Leicester, who conveyed him to his
castle of Kenilworth, where the unfortunate monarch passed
the winter, "treated not otherwise than a captive king ought
to be treated".

It only remained to complete the revolution by making
provision for the future government of England. With this
object a parliament was summoned, at first by the Duke of
Aquitaine in his father's name, and afterwards more regularly
by writs issued under the great seal. It met on January 7,
1327, at Westminster, and, after the York precedent of 1322,
contained representatives of Wales as well as of the three estates
of England. Orleton, the spokesman of Mortimer, asked the
estates whether they would have Edward II. or his son as
their ruler. The London mob loudly declared for the Duke of
Aquitaine, and none of the members of parliament ventured to
raise a voice in favour of the unhappy king, save four prelates
of whom the most important was the steadfast Archbishop
Melton. The southern primate, deserting his old master, declared that the voice of the people was the voice of God.
Stratford drew up six articles, in which he set forth that Edward of Carnarvon was incompetent to govern, led by evil
counsellors, a despiser of the wholesome advice of the "great
and wise men of the realm," neglectful of business, and addicted
to unprofitable pleasures ; that by his lack of good government
he had lost Scotland, Ireland, and Gascony ; that he had injured
Holy Church, and had done to death or driven into exile many
great men ; that he had broken his coronation oath, and that it
was hopeless to expect amendment from him.

Even the agents of Mortimer shrunk from the odium of
decreeing Edward's deposition, and the more prudent course

was preferred of inducing the king to resign his power into his son's hands. An effort to persuade the captive monarch to abdicate before his estates, was defeated by his resolute refusal. Thereupon a committee of bishops, barons, and judges was sent to Kenilworth to receive his renunciation in the name of parliament. On January 20, Edward, clothed in black, admitted the delegates to his presence. Utterly unmanned by misfortune, the king fell in a deep swoon at the feet of his enemies. Leicester and Stratford raised him from the ground, and, on his recovery, Orleton exhorted him to resign his throne to his son, lest the estates, irritated by his contumacy, should choose as their king some one who was not of the royal line. Edward replied that he was sorry that his people were tired of his rule, but that being so, he was prepared to yield to their wishes, and make way for the Duke of Aquitaine. On this, Sir William Trussell, as proctor of the three estates, formally renounced their homage and fealty, and Sir Thomas Blount, steward of the household, broke his staff of office, and announced that the royal establishment was disbanded. Thus the calamitous reign of Edward of Carnarvon came to a wretched end. His utter inefficiency as a king makes it impossible to lament his fate. Yet few revolutions have ever been conducted with more manifest self-seeking than that which hurled Edward from power. The angry spite of the adulterous queen, the fierce vengeance and greed of Roger Mortimer, the craft and cruelty of Orleton, the time-serving cowardice of Reynolds, the stupidity of Kent and Norfolk, the party spirit of Stratford and Ayermine, can inspire nothing but disgust. Among the foes of Edward, Henry of Leicester alone behaved as an honourable gentleman, anxious to vindicate a policy, but careful to subordinate his private wrongs to public objects. Though his name and wrongs were ostentatiously put forward by the dominant faction, it is clear from the beginning that he was only a tool in its hands, and that the reversal of the sentence of Earl Thomas was but the pretext by which the schemers and traitors sought to capture the government for their own selfish ends.

The resignation of the king was promptly reported to parliament. On January 24 the Duke of Aquitaine was proclaimed Edward III., and from the next day his regnal years were reckoned as beginning. Henry of Leicester dubbed him knight, and on January 29 he was crowned in Westminster Abbey. A few days later the young king met his parliament. A standing council was appointed to carry on the administration during his nonage. Of this body the Earl of Leicester acted as chief, though most of his colleagues were partisans of Mortimer and the queen. Orleton, who was made treasurer, continued to pull the wires as the confidential agent of Isabella and Mortimer. A show of devotion to the good old cause was thought politic, and therefore the sentences of 1322 were revoked, so that Earl Henry, restored to all his brother's estates, was henceforth styled Earl of Lancaster. The commons went beyond this in petitioning for the canonisation of Earl Thomas and Archbishop Winchelsea. The revolution was consummated by a new confirmation of the charters.

Even in the first flush of victory, Isabella and Mortimer were too insecure and too bitter to allow Edward of Carnarvon to remain quietly in prison under the custody of the Earl of Lancaster. As long as he was alive, he might always become the possible instrument of their degradation. At Orleton's instigation the deposed king was transferred in April from his cousin's care to that of two knights, Thomas Gurney and John Maltravers. He was promptly removed from Kenilworth and hurried by night from castle to castle until, after some sojourn at Corfe, he was at last immured at Berkeley. Every indignity was put upon him, and the systematic course of ill-treatment, to which he was subjected, was clearly intended to bring about his speedy death. But the robust constitution of the athlete rose superior to the persecutions of his torturers, and to save further trouble he was barbarously murdered in his bed on the night of September 21. Piercing shrieks from the interior of the castle told the peasantry that some dire deed was being perpetrated within its gloomy walls. Next day it was announced that the lord Edward had died a natural death, and his corpse was exposed to the public view that suspicion might be averted. He was buried with the state that became a crowned king in the Benedictine Abbey Church of St. Peter, Gloucester. A few years later the piety or remorse of Edward III. erected over his father's remains the magnificent tomb which still challenges our admiration by the delicacy of its tabernacle work and the artistic beauty of the sculptured effigy of the murdered monarch.

The tragedy of Edward's end soon caused his misdeeds to be forgotten, and ere long the countryside flocked on pilgrimage to his tomb, as to the shrine of a saint. By a curious irony the burial place of Edward of Carnarvon rivalled in popularity the chapel on the hill at Pontefract where Thomas of Lancaster had perished by Edward's orders. Like his cousin, Edward became a popular, though not a canonised, saint. From the offerings made at his tomb the monks of Gloucester were in time supplied with the funds that enabled them to recast their romanesque choir in the newer "perpendicular" fashion of architecture, and embellish their church with all the rich additions which contrast so strangely with the grim impressiveness of the stately Norman nave. There was only one impediment to the people's worship of the dead king. The secrecy which enveloped his end led to rumours that he was still alive, and the prevalence of these reports soon proved almost as great a source of embarrassment to his supplanters, as his living presence had been in the first months of their unhallowed power.

It was not easy for Isabella and Mortimer to restore the waning fortunes of England at home and abroad. We shall see that it was only by an almost complete surrender that they procured peace with France and a partial restoration of Gascony. In Scotland they were even less fortunate. Robert Bruce, though broken in health and spirits, took up an aggressive attitude, and it was found necessary to summon the feudal levies to meet on the border in the summer of 1327 in order to repel his attack. While the troops were mustering at York, a fierce fight broke out in the streets, between the Hainault mercenaries, under John of Hainault, and the citizens. So threatening was the outlook that it was thought wise to send the Hainaulters back home. From this accident it happened that the young king went forth to his first campaign, attended only by his native-born subjects. The Scots began operations by breaking the truce and overrunning the borders. The campaign directed against them was as futile as any of the last reign, and the English, though three times more numerous than the enemy, dared not provoke battle. This inglorious failure may well have convinced Mortimer that the best chance of maintaining his power was to make peace at any price. Early in 1328, the negotiations for a treaty were concluded at York. During

their progress, Edward, who was at York to meet his parliament, was married to Philippa of Hainault.

The Scots treaty was confirmed in April by a parliament
that met at Northampton. All claim to feudal superiority over
Scotland was withdrawn; Robert Bruce was recognised as King
of Scots, and his young son David was married to Joan of the
Tower, Edward III.'s infant sister. This surrender provoked
the liveliest indignation, and men called the treaty of Northampton the "shameful peace," and ascribed it to the treachery
or timorousness of the queen and her paramour. But it is hard
to see what other solution of the Scottish problem was practicable. For many years Bruce had been *de facto* King of Scots,
and any longer hesitation to withhold the recognition which he
coveted would have been sure to involve the north of England
in the same desolation as that which he had inflicted before
the truce of 1322. But the founder of Scottish independence
was drawing near to the end of his career. His health had long
been undermined by a terrible disease which the chroniclers
thought to be leprosy. He died in 1329, and on his death-bed
he bethought him of how he, who had shed so much Christian
blood, had never been able to fulfil his vow of crusade. Accordingly he entreated James Douglas, his faithful companion-
in-arms, to go on crusade against the Moors of Granada, taking
with him the heart of his dead master. Douglas fulfilled the
request, and perished in Spain, whither he had carried the heart
of the Scottish liberator. With the accession of the little
David Bruce, new troubles began for Scotland, though danger
from England was for the moment averted by the English
marriage and the treaty of Northampton.

The ill-will produced by the "shameful peace" spread far
and wide the profound dislike for Mortimer which pity for
the fate of Edward had first aroused in the breasts of Englishmen. The greedy marcher was at no pains to make himself
popular. Holding no great office of state, he strove to rule
through his creatures Orleton, the treasurer, and the hardly less
subservient chancellor, Bishop Hotham of Ely, or through lay
partisans such as Sir Oliver Ingham and Sir Simon Bereford.
But his best chance of remaining in power was through the be-
sotted infatuation of the queen-mother, whose relations with
him were not concealed from the public eye by any elaborate

parade of secrecy.   He still posed as the inheritor of the tradition of the lords ordainers, and never failed to put as much of the responsibility of his rule as he could on Henry of Lancaster and the old baronial leaders.   But with all his force and energy, he was too narrowly selfish and grasping to take much trouble to frame an elaborate policy.   As an administrator he was as incompetent as either Thomas of Lancaster or the Despensers.

Mortimer's chief care was to add office to office, and estate to estate, in order that he might establish his house as supreme over all Wales and its march.   Besides his own enormous inheritance, he ruled over Ludlow and Meath in the right of his wife, Joan of Joinville, the heiress of the Lacys.   He had inherited Chirk and the other lands of his uncle, the sometime justice of Wales, who had died in Edward II.'s prison ; and he procured for himself a grant of his uncle's old office for life, so that, while as justice of Wales he lorded it over the principality, as head of the Mortimers he could dominate the whole march. To complete his ascendency in the march became his great ambition.   He obtained the custody of Glamorgan, the stronghold of his sometime rival, Hugh Despenser the younger.   To this were added Oswestry and Clun, the Fitzalan march in western Shropshire, forfeited to the crown by the faithfulness with which Edmund Fitzalan, the late Earl of Arundel, had laid down his life for Edward II.   Minor grants of lands, offices, wardships, and pensions were constantly lavished upon him by the complacency of his mistress.   In Ireland he received complete palatine franchises over Trim, Meath, and Louth, along with the custody of the estates of the infant Earl of Kildare, the chief of the Leinster Geraldines.   He extended his connexions by marrying his seven daughters to the heads of great families, and where possible to men of marcher houses.   He soon numbered among his sons-in-law the representatives of the Charltons of Powys, the Hastingses of Abergavenny, now the chief heirs of Aymer of Pembroke, the Audleys of the Shropshire march, the Beauchamps of Warwick, the Berkeleys, the Grandisons, and the Braoses.   Anxious to extend his dignity as well as his power, he procured his nomination as Earl of the March of Wales, "a title," says a chronicler, "hitherto unheard of in England".   As earl of the march and justice of the principality, he ruled the lands west of the Severn with little less than

regal sway. His banquets, his tournaments, his pious founda-   CHAP.
tions even, dazzled all men by their splendour.   XIV.

Mortimer was created Earl of March in the parliament held
in October, 1328, at Salisbury, where John of Eltham was made
Earl of Cornwall and James, Butler of Ireland, Earl of Ormonde.
His assumption of this new title at last roused the sluggish
indignation of Earl Henry of Lancaster, who felt that his own
marcher interests were compromised, and bitterly resented the
vain use made of his name, while he was carefully kept without any control of policy. He refused to attend the Salisbury
parliament, though he and his partisans mustered in arms in
the neighbourhood of that city. Civil war seemed imminent,
and Mortimer's Welshmen devastated Lancaster's earldom of
Leicester, but Archbishop Meopham (who had lately succeeded
Reynolds in the primacy) managed to patch up peace. Not
long afterwards Lancaster was smitten with blindness, and
was thenceforth unable to take an active part in public
affairs. Mortimer again triumphed for the moment, and, with
cruel malice, excepted Lancaster's confidential agents from the
pardon which he was forced to extend to the earl. His success
over Lancaster was materially facilitated by the weakness of
Edmund, Earl of Kent, who, after joining with Earl Henry in
his refusal to attend the Salisbury parliament, deserted him
at the moment of the capture of Leicester by the Earl of
March. But his treachery did not save him from Mortimer's
revenge. In conjunction with the queen, Mortimer plotted to
lure on Earl Edmund to ruin. Their agents persuaded him
that Edward II. was still alive and imprisoned in Corfe castle,
and urged him to restore his brother to liberty. The earl rose
to the bait, and agreed to be party to an insurrection which was
to restore Edward of Carnarvon to freedom, if not to his throne.
When Kent was involved in the meshes, he was suddenly
arrested in the Winchester parliament of March, 1330, and
accused of treason. Convicted by his own speeches and letters,
he was adjudged to death by the lords, and on March 19 beheaded outside the walls of the city.

The fall of Kent convinced Lancaster that his fate would
not be long delayed, and that his best chance of saving himself
and his cause lay in stirring up the king to energetic action
against the Earl of March. The death of his uncle irritated

Edward, who at seventeen was old enough to feel the degrading nature of his thraldom, and was eager to govern the kingdom of which he was the nominal head. In June, 1330, the birth of a son, the future Black Prince, to Edward and Philippa seems to have impressed on the young monarch that he had come to man's estate. Lancaster accordingly found him eager to shake off the yoke of his mother's paramour. The opportunity came in October, 1330, when the magnates assembled at Nottingham to hold a parliament there. Isabella and Mortimer took up their abode in the castle, where Edward also resided. Suspicions were abroad, and the castle was closely guarded by Mortimer's Welsh followers. Sir William Montague, a close friend of Edward's, was chosen to strike the blow, and lay outside with a band of troops. Some rumour of the plot seems to have leaked out, and on October 19 Mortimer angrily denounced Montague as a traitor, and accused the king of complicity with his designs. But Montague was safe outside the castle, and, when evening fell, all that Mortimer could do was to lock the gates and watch the walls. William Eland, constable of the castle, had been induced to join the conspiracy, and had revealed to Montague a secret entrance into the stronghold. On that very night, Montague and his men-at-arms effected an entrance through an underground passage into the castle-yard, where Edward joined them. They then made their way up to Mortimer's chamber, which as usual was next to that of the queen. Two knights, who guarded the door, were struck down, and the armed band burst into the room. After a desperate scuffle, the Earl of March was secured. Hearing the noise, the queen rushed into the room, and though Edward still waited without, cried, with seeming consciousness of his share in the matter, " Fair son, have pity on the gentle Mortimer ". Her entreaties were unavailing, and the fallen favourite was hurried, under strict custody, to London.

Edward then issued a proclamation announcing that he had taken the government of England into his own hands. Parliament, prorogued to Westminster, met on November 26, and its chief business was the trial of Mortimer before the lords. He was charged with accroaching to himself the royal power, stirring up dissension between Edward II. and the queen, teaching Edward III. to regard the Earl of Lancaster as his enemy, deluding

Edmund of Kent into believing that his brother was alive and with procuring his execution, accepting bribes from the Scots for concluding the disgraceful peace, and with perpetrating grievous cruelties in Ireland. The lords, imitating the evil precedents set during Mortimer's time of power, condemned him without trial or chance of answer to the accusations made against him. On November 29 the fallen earl was paraded through London from his prison in the Tower to Tyburn Elms, and was there hanged on the common gallows. His vast estates were forfeited to the crown. His accomplice, Sir Simon Bereford, suffered the same fate; but Sir Oliver Ingham, another of his associates, was pardoned. Edward discreetly drew a veil over his mother's shame. Mortimer's notorious relations with her were not enumerated in the accusations brought against him, and Isabella, though removed from power and stripped of some of her recent acquisitions, was allowed to live in honourable retirement on her dower manors. Scrupulously visited by her dutiful son, she wandered freely from house to house, as she felt disposed. She died in 1358 at her castle of Hertford, in the habit of the Poor Clares—a sister order of the Franciscans. The later tradition that she was kept in confinement at Castle Rising has only this slender foundation in fact that Castle Rising was one of her favourite places of abode. With her withdrawal from public life Edward III.'s real reign begins.

CHAPTER XV.

THE PRELIMINARIES OF THE HUNDRED YEARS' WAR.

CHAP. XV.
EDWARD III. had just entered upon his nineteenth year when he became king in fact as well as in name. In person he was not unworthy of his father and grandfather. Less strikingly tall than they, he was nobly built and finely proportioned. In full manhood, long hair, a thick moustache and a flowing beard adorned his regular and handsome countenance. His graciousness and affability were universally praised. His face shone, we are told, like the face of a god, so that to see him or to dream of him was certain to conjure up joyous images.[1] He delighted in the pomp of his office, wore magnificent garments, and played his kingly part with the same majesty and dignity as his grandfather. Despite the troubles of his youth, he was well educated. Richard of Bury is said to have been his tutor, and the early lessons of the author or instigator of the *Philobiblon* were never entirely lost by the prince who took Chaucer and Froissart into his service. More conspicuous was his love of art, his taste for sumptuous buildings and their magnificent embellishment, which left memorials in the stately castle of Windsor and its rich chapel of St. George, in St. Stephen's chapel at Westminster, and the Eastminster for Cistercian nuns hard by Tower hill. A fluent and eloquent speaker in French and English, Edward was also conversant with Latin, and perhaps Low-Dutch. Yet no king was less given to study or seclusion. Possessed, perhaps, of no exceptional measure of intellectual capacity, and not even endowed to any large extent with firmness of character, he won a great place in history by the extraordinary activity of his temperament and the vigour and energy with which he threw himself

---

[1] *Continuation of Murimuth* (Engl. Hist. Soc.), pp. 225-27, which gives the best contemporary description of Edward's character.

into whatever work he set his hand to do. He was a consummate master of knightly exercises, delighting in tournaments,
and especially in those which were marked by some touch of
quaintness or fancy. He had the hereditary passion of his house
for the chase. In his youthful campaigns in Scotland and in
his maturer expeditions in France, he was accompanied by a
little army of falconers and huntsmen, by packs of hounds, and
many hawks trained with the utmost care. He honoured with
his special friendship an Abbot of Leicester, famed throughout
England as the most dexterous of hare-coursers.[1]

Edward's abounding energy was even more gladly devoted
to war than to the chase. He was an admirable exponent of
those chivalric ideals which are glorified in the courtly pages
of Froissart. Not content with the easy victories which fall in
the tiltyard to the crowned king, Edward was anxious to show
that his triumphs belonged to the knight and not to the
monarch, and more than once jousted victoriously in disguise.
The same spirit led him to challenge Philip of France to decide
their quarrel by single combat, and to win a personal triumph
when masking as a knight attached to the service of Sir
Walter Manny. He was liberal to the verge of prodigality,
good-tempered, easy of access, and, save when moved by deep
gusts of fierce anger, kindly and compassionate. His easy good
nature endeared him both to foreigners and to every class of
his own subjects. Not only did he enter fully into the free-
masonry which regarded the knights of all Christian nations as
equal members of a sworn brotherhood of arms, but he extended
his favours to the London vintner's son who earned his bread in
his service, and entertained the wives of the leading London
citizens, side by side with the noble ladies in whose honour he
gave the most quaint and magnificent of his banquets. Pious after
a somewhat formal fashion, he was unwearied in going on pilgrimage and lavish in his religious foundations. Though no prince
was more careful to protect the state from the encroachments
of churchmen, his orthodoxy and devoutness kept him in good
repute with the austerest champions of the Church. He could
choose fit agents to carry out his policy, and his campaigns were
a marvellous training ground for gallant and capable warriors.

[1] Knighton, ii., 127.

Edward seldom lost sight of the material and economic interests of his subjects. He was the friend of merchants, the
father of English commerce, the patron of the infant woollen
manufactures, and a zealous champion of the maritime greatness of his island realm, which boasted that he was " king of
the sea ". Though his financial exigencies often led him to
sell excessive privileges to alien traders, this policy did little
harm to his subjects, for few of them were ready as yet to
embark in foreign commerce. A true patriot, who declared
that his land of England was " nearer to his heart, more delight-
ful, noble, and profitable than all other lands," he succeeded
in making Englishmen conscious of their national life as they
had never been before ; and he won for his fatherland a foremost
place among the kingdoms of the world. His network of diplomatic alliances was dexterously fashioned, and enabled him
to supplement the resources of his own subjects.

The breadth of Edward's ambitions hindered their complete
accomplishment. Like Edward I., he undertook more than he
could carry through, and, though his panegyrists praise his
patience in adversity no less than his moderation in prosperity,
his merely animal courage and vigour broke down under the
weight of misfortune. Thus the glorious king, who in his youth
vied with his grandfather, seemed in his old age to have nearly
approached the fate of his wretched father. In early life he won
the love of his subjects. It was only in the first years of his reign
that the violence and greed of his disorderly household, which
inherited the evil traditions of the previous generation, bore so
heavily upon the people that Englishmen fled at his approach
in dread of the purveyors, who confiscated every man's goods
for the royal use.[1] The somewhat shallow opportunism which
abandoned, with little attempt at resistance, every royal right
that stood in the way of his receiving the full support of his
parliament, at least had the merit of keeping Edward in general
touch with his estates. The wanton breaches of good faith, by
which he sometimes strove to win back what he had lightly conceded, were regarded as efforts to save the sovereign's dignity,

---

[1] The *Speculum regis Edwardi* (ed. Moisant) was written before 1333, and
the attribution of its composition to Archbishop Islip and the inferences drawn in
Stubbs' *Const. Hist.*, ii., 394, are therefore unwarranted ; see Professor Tait's
note in *Engl. Hist. Review*, xvi. (1901), 110-15.

rather than as insidious attempts to restore the prerogative. Un-
just as was the very basis of his French pretensions, they were
backed up by a show of legal claim that satisfied the conscience of
king and subject, and to contemporaries Edward seemed a king
regardful of his honour and mindful of his plighted word. If his
generosity verged on extravagance, and his affectation of popular manners and graciousness on unreality, Englishmen of the
fourteenth century were no severe critics of a crowned king. It
was only when in his later years Edward laid aside the soldier's
life, and abandoned himself to the frivolous distractions and
degrading amours[1] which provoked the censure even of his
admirers, that the self-indulgent traits inherited from his unhappy father stood revealed.

Edward was before all things a soldier. He was not only
the consummate knight, the mirror of chivalry, but a capable
tactician with a general's eye that took in the essential points
of the situation at a glance. His restless energy ensured the
rapidity of movement and alertness of action which won him
many a triumph over less mobile and less highly trained antagonists ; while they inspired his followers with faith in their cause
and with the courage which succeeds against desperate odds.
Yet the victor of Crecy cannot be numbered among the consummate generals of history. His campaigns were ill-planned ;
and he lacked the self-restraint and sense of proportion which
would have prevented him from aiming at objects beyond his
reach. The same want of relation between ends and means, the
same want of definite policy and clear ideals, marred his statecraft.
Yet contemporaries, conscious of his faults, magnified Edward
as the brilliant and successful king who had won for himself an
assured place among the greatest monarchs of history. "Never,"
says Froissart, "had there been such a king since the days of
Arthur King of Great Britain." [2] Even to his own age his
senile degradation pointed the moral of the triumphs of his
manhood. The modern historian, who sees, beneath the superficial splendour of the days of Edward III., the misery and
degradation that underlay the wreck of the dying Middle Ages,
is in no danger of appraising too highly the merits of this

---

[1] *Chron. Angliæ*, 1328-1388, p. 401.
[2] Froissart (ed. Luce), viii., 231 ; *cf.* Canon of Bridlington, p. 95.

showy and ambitious monarch. Perhaps in our own days the reaction has gone too far, and we have been taught to undervalue the splendid energy and robustness of temperament which commanded the admiration of all Europe, and personified the strenuous ideals of the young English nation.

The internal history of the first few years of Edward's reign was uneventful. John Stratford became chancellor after Mortimer's fall, and remained for ten years the guiding spirit of the administration. Translated on Meopham's death in 1333 to Canterbury, he continued, as primate, to take a leading part in politics. His chief helper was his brother Robert, rewarded in 1337 by the see of Chichester. The brothers were capable but not brilliant politicians. The worst disorders of the times of anarchy were put down, and parliaments readily granted sufficient money to meet the king's necessities. After a few years, the strife of parties was so far hushed that Burghersh was suffered to return to office, and it looks as if the balance between the Lancastrian party, upheld by the Stratfords, and the old middle party of Pembroke and Badlesmere, with which Burghersh had hereditary connexions, was maintained, as it had been during the least unhappy period of the preceding reign. The country was growing rich and prosperous. The annalists tell us of little save tournaments and mummings, and the setting up of seven new earldoms to remedy the gaps which death and forfeiture had made in the higher circle of the baronage. The earldom of Devon was revived for the house of Courtenay; that of Salisbury in favour of the trusty William Montague, and an Audley, son of Despenser's rival, was raised to the earldom of Gloucester. William Bohun, a younger son of the Humphrey slain at Boroughbridge, became Earl of Northampton, an Ufford, Earl of Suffolk, a Clinton Earl of Huntingdon, a Hastings Earl of Pembroke, and Henry of Grosmont, the Earl of Lancaster's first born, Earl of Derby. A new rank was added to the English peerage when the king's little son, Earl of Chester in 1333, was made Duke of Cornwall in 1337. The old feuds seemed dead and with them the old disorder. But Edward was ambitious of military glory, and it was natural that he should seek to reverse the degrading part which he had been forced to play in relation to Scotland and France. His hands being tied by treaties, it was not easy for him to make the first move.

Before long, however, circumstances arose which gave him a CHAP. chance of taking up a line of his own with regard to Scotland. XV. From that time Scottish affairs mainly absorbed his attention until the outbreak of troubles with France.

The establishment of Robert Bruce on the Scottish throne had been attended by a considerable disturbance of the territorial balance in the northern kingdom. Many Scottish magnates, deprived of their lands and driven into exile, had abodes in England, and all might well look for the favour of the king in whose service they had been ruined. The treaty of Northampton made no provision for their restoration, and Edward showed himself disposed to uphold it. Their estates were in the hands of their supplanters, the nobles who had gathered round the throne of the Bruces. Thus it was that the exiles were cut off from all hope of return, and saw their only possibility of restitution in the break-up of the friendship of Edward and David. In like case were the English magnates who still entertained hopes of making effective the grants of Scottish estates which they had received from Edward I. and Edward II. For both classes alike every fresh year of peace between the realms decreased their chances of obtaining their desires. They failed to persuade Edward to go to war with his brother-in-law and repudiate formally the obligations imposed upon him by his mother and her paramour. But the minority of King David had unloosed the spirits of disorder in Scotland. Though the vigorous and capable regent, Sir Thomas Randolph, Earl of Moray, showed himself competent to stem the tide of aristocratic reaction which swelled round the throne of his infant cousin, he was one of the old generation of heroes that had aided King Robert to gain his throne. Were he to die, or become incapable of acting, there was no one who could supply his place. The Disinherited—thus they styled themselves— were encouraged both by the apathy of Edward III. and the weakness of Scotland to make a bold stroke on their own behalf.

At the head of the disinherited was Edward Balliol, the son of the deposed King John. Brought up in England, first under the care of his cousin, Earl Warenne, and afterwards in the household of the half-brothers of Edward II., Edward Balliol, who succeeded in 1315 to the French estates on which his father spent his latter years, divided his time between England

and France. The forfeiture of his father still kept him out of
Barnard Castle and the other Balliol lands in England. Young
and warlike, poor and ambitious, with few lands and great pretensions, he never formally abandoned either the lordship of
Galloway or the throne of Scotland. In 1330 he received permission to take up his quarters in England during pleasure. He
soon associated himself with his fellow-exiles in a bold attempt to
win back their patrimony. Chief among his followers were three
titular Scottish earls, closely related by intermarriage, each of
whom was also a baron of high rank in England. Of these the
French-born Henry of Beaumont, kinsman of Eleanor of Castile,
and brother of Bishop Louis of Durham, was the oldest and
most experienced. As the husband of a sister of the last of the
Comyn Earls of Buchan, he posed as the heir of the greatest
of the Scottish houses which had paid the penalty of its opposition to King Robert, and was summoned to the English
parliament as Earl of Buchan. Beaumont's great-nephew, the
young Gilbert of Umfraville, lord of Redesdale, was a grandson
of another Comyn heiress, and his ancestors had inherited in the
middle of the thirteenth century the ancient Scottish earldom
of Angus, though they also had incurred forfeiture for their
adhesion to the English policy. David of Strathbolgie, Earl of
Athol, had a better right to be called a Scot than Umfraville or
Beaumont. But his father abandoned Bruce, and was driven
into England, where he held the Kentish barony of Chilham,
and sat in the English parliament under his Scottish title. The
younger Athol was son-in-law to the titular Earl of Moray, and
all three kinsmen were bound by common interests to embrace
the policy of Edward Balliol. Many lesser men associated
themselves with the three earls and the claimant to a throne.
Nearly every nobleman of the Scottish border made himself a
party to a scheme of adventure which had its best parallels
in the Norman invasions of Wales and Ireland.

The object of the disinherited was to raise an army and
prosecute their Scottish claims by force. Edward III. gave
them no open countenance, and took up an ostentatiously correct attitude. He solemnly forbade all breach of the peace,
and prevented the adventurers from adopting the easy course
of marching from England to an open attack on Scotland. No
obstacles, however, were imposed to hinder their raising a

small but efficient army of 500 men-at-arms and 1,000 archers.
Mercenaries, both English and foreign, were hired to supplement their scanty numbers, and among those who took service
with them was a young gentleman of Hainault, Walter Manny,
whose father had a few years before perished in the service of
Edward II. in Gascony, and who had first come to England
in the service of his countrywoman, Queen Philippa. Ships
were collected in the Humber, and on the last day of July,
1332, the disinherited and their followers sailed from Ravens-
spur on a destination which was officially supposed to be unknown. A week later, on August 6, they landed at Kinghorn
in Fife.

Scotland was singularly unready to meet invasion. The
regent Moray had died a few weeks earlier, and his successor,
Donald, Earl of Mar, incompetent to carry on his vigorous
policy, had perhaps already been intriguing with the adventurers. The only resistance to Balliol's landing, made by
the Earl of Fife, was altogether unsuccessful. The little army
established itself easily in the enemies' territory, and, after two
days' rest at Dunfermline, advanced over the Ochils towards
Perth. The regent had by that time gathered together an imposing army. As the invaders approached Strathearn on their
way northwards, they found Mar encamped on Dupplin Moor,
on the left bank of the Earn, and holding in force the only
bridge available for crossing the river. There was some parley-
ing between the two hosts. "We are sons of magnates of this
land," declared the disinherited to Mar. "We are come hither
with the lord Edward of Balliol, the right heir of the realm, to
demand the lands which belong to us by hereditary right."
Mar returned a warlike answer to their words, and both armies
made preparation for battle.

The disinherited, though few in number, were well trained
in warfare, and from the beginning showed capacity to out-
general the unwieldy host and feeble leader opposed to them.
At sunset, some of their forces crossed the Earn by a ford
which the Scots had neglected to guard, and falling upon
an outlying portion of the enemies' camp, where the infantry
were quartered, slaughtered the surprised Scots at their leisure.
Luckily for Mar, the whole of his knights and men-at-arms
were far away, uselessly watching the bridge, over which they

had expected the disinherited to force a passage.   Thus saved
from the night ambuscade, the kernel of the Scottish army
prepared next morning, August 12, to attack the disinherited.
Puffed up by the memory of Bannockburn and the consciousness of superior numbers, they marched to battle as if certain of
victory.   All fought on foot, and the men-at-arms were drawn
up in a dense central mass, supported at each side by wings.
The disinherited were sufficiently schooled in northern warfare
to adopt the same tactics.   Save for a few score of horsemen
in reserve, their heavily armed troops, leaving their horses in
the rear, formed a compact column after the Scottish fashion.
But archers were distributed in open order on the right and
left flanks, with both extremities pushed forward, so that they
formed the horns of a half-moon.   Then the Scots advanced
to the charge, and both sides joined in battle.   The irresistible
weight of the Scottish main phalanx forced back the little
column of the disinherited, and for a moment it looked as if
the battle were won.   Meanwhile the archers on the flanks
poured a galling shower on the collateral Scottish columns.
The unvisored helmets of the Scots made them an easy prey
to the storm of missiles, and they were driven back on to the
main body.   By this time the disinherited had rallied from the
first shock; and still the deadly hail of arrows descended from
right and left, until the whole of the Scottish army was thrown
into panic-stricken disorder.   Escape was impossible for the
foremost ranks by reason of the closeness of their formation.
At last, the rear files sought safety in flight, and were closely
pursued by the victors, mounted on their fresh horses.   A
huge mass of slain, piled up upon each other, marked the place
of combat.   As at Bannockburn, the small disciplined host prevailed, but discipline was now with the English and numbers
only with the Scots.[1]

The victory of Dupplin Moor was for the moment decisive.
Balliol occupied Perth, and received the submission of many of the
Scottish magnates, among them being that Earl of Fife who first
opposed his landing.   A few weeks later, on September 24, Balliol
was crowned King of Scots at Scone by the Bishop of Dunkeld.

---

[1] The significance of the battle of Dupplin was first pointed out by Mr. J.
E. Morris in *Engl. Hist. Review*, xii. (1897), 430-31.

It was a soldier's coronation, and the magnates sat at the coronation feast in full armour, save their helmets.   The disinherited
then received the lands for which they had striven; and thereupon quitted the new king, either to secure their estates or to
revisit their property in England.   But the Scots, of no mind
to receive a king from the foreigner, chose a new regent in Sir
Andrew Moray, son of the companion of Wallace; and prepared
to maintain King David.   On December 16, Balliol was surprised at Annan by a hostile force under the young Earl of
Moray, son of the late regent, and by Sir Archibald Douglas.
His followers were cut off, his brother was slain, and he himself
had the utmost difficulty in effecting his escape to England.
He had only reigned four months.

During Balliol's brief triumph, Edward III. had declared
himself in his favour.   Debarred by the treaty of Northampton
from questioning the independence of King David, he was able
to make what terms he liked with David's supplanter.   In
November a treaty was drawn up at Roxburgh, by which
Balliol recognised the overlordship of Edward, and promised
him the town, castle, and shire of Berwick.   In return for these
concessions, Edward III. acknowledged his namesake as lawful
King of Scots.   When, a few weeks later, his new vassal
appeared as a fugitive on English soil, Edward had no longer
any scruples in openly supporting him in an attempt to win
back his throne.   In the spring of 1333, Balliol and the disinherited once more crossed the frontier in sufficient force to
undertake the siege of Berwick.   The border stronghold held
out manfully, but the Scots failed in an attempt to divert the
attention of the English by an invasion of Cumberland.   After
Easter, Edward III. went in person to Berwick, and devoted
the whole resources of England to ensuring its reduction.   The
siege lasted on until July, when the garrison, at the last gasp,
offered to surrender, unless the town were relieved within fifteen
days.   The Scots made a great effort to save Berwick from
capture, and the English king was forced to fight a pitched
battle, before he could secure its possession.

On July 19 Edward, leaving a sufficient portion of his army
to maintain the blockade of Berwick, took up a position with
the remainder on Halidon Hill, a short distance to the west of
the town.   The lessons of Bannockburn, Boroughbridge, and

Dupplin were not forgotten, and the English host was arranged much after the fashion which had procured the first victory of the disinherited. Knights and men-at-arms sent their horses to the rear and, from the king downwards, all, save a small reserve of horse, prepared to fight on foot. Edward divided his forces into three lines or "battles," each of which consisted of a central column of dismounted heavily armed troops, flanked by a right and a left wing of archers in open order. John of Eltham and the titular Earl of Buchan commanded the right battle, the king the centre, and Edward Balliol the left. The Scots still employed the traditional tactics which had failed so signally at Dupplin. Sir Archibald Douglas led his followers up the slopes of the hill in three dense columns. But a pitiless rain of arrows spread havoc among their ranks, and there were no answering volleys to disturb their foes. The battle was won for the English almost before the two lines had joined in close combat. It was only on Edward's right that the Scots were strong enough to push home their attack. On the centre and left, the English easily drove the enemy in panic flight down the slopes which they had ascended so confidently. The pursuit was long and bloody; few were taken prisoners, but many were slain or driven into the sea. Seven Scottish earls were believed by the English to have fallen, while the victors lost one knight, one squire, and a few infantry soldiers. Thus, for a second time the tactics, which had served the Scots so well in the defensive fight of Bannockburn, failed in offence to secure victory for them. The experience of this day completed the evolution of the new English battle array of men-at-arms fighting on foot and supported by wings of archers, which was soon to excite the wonder of Europe, when its possibilities were demonstrated on continental fields.

Next day Berwick opened its gates, and was handed over to the English, according to the treaty of Roxburgh, to be for the rest of its history an English frontier town. Edward Balliol again conquered Scotland as easily as he had done on the former occasion, and far more effectually. It was no longer possible for the few remaining champions of the house of Bruce to safeguard the person of the little king and queen. David and Joan were accordingly sent off to France, where they were to grow up as good friends of King Philip. But Balliol had

so clearly regained his throne through English help that he was CHAP.
no longer an independent agent. No sooner was his conquest   XV.
assured than he was forced not only to confirm the surrender
of Berwick, but to yield up the whole of south-eastern Scotland as the price of the English assistance. The depth of his
humiliation was sounded when, in the treaty of Newcastle,
June 12, 1334, Edward, King of Scots, granted Edward, King
of England, lands worth two thousand pounds a year in the
marches of Scotland, and in part payment thereof yielded up to
him, besides Berwick and its shire, the castle, town, and county
of Roxburgh, the forests of Jedburgh Selkirk, and Ettrick,
the town and county of Selkirk, and the towns, castles, and
counties of Peebles, Dumfries, and Edinburgh. Of these Dumfries then included the Stewartry of Kirkcudbright, while the
shire of Edinburgh took in the constabularies, the modern
shires, of Haddington and Linlithgow. Thus the whole of
Lothian, the whole of the central upland region, and Balliol's
own inheritance of Galloway east of the Cree were directly
transferred to the English crown, and were divided into sheriffdoms, and officered after the English fashion. On June 18
Balliol personally performed homage for so much of Scotland
as Edward chose to leave him. The wrongs of the disinherited
had been the means of re-opening the whole Scottish question,
and Edward III. seemed assured of a position as supreme as
that which had once been held by Edward I.

It was always easier in the Middle Ages to conquer a
country than to keep it. And the experience of forty years
might well have convinced Englishmen that no land was more
difficult to hold than the stubborn and impenetrable northern
kingdom, with its strenuous population, ever willing to cry a
truce between local feuds when there was an opportunity of
uniting against the southerners. Edward overshot his mark in
grasping too eagerly the fairest portions of Balliol's realm.
He needed for his policy a Scottish king, strong enough to
maintain himself against his subjects, and loyal enough to remain true to the English connexion. Any faint chance of
Balliol occupying such a position was completely destroyed
by his studied humiliation. Henceforward the King of Scots,
who had fought so well at Dupplin and Halidon, was but a pawn
in Edward's game. Hated by the Scots as the betrayer of his

country, distrusted by the English who henceforth spied his actions and commanded his armies in his name, the gallant victor of Dupplin lost faith in himself and in his cause. After all, he was his father's son, and in no wise capable of bearing adversity and indignity with equanimity. His helplessness soon proved the worst obstacle in the way of the success of Edward's plans. Even with the aid of a large Scottish party, Edward I. had failed to bring about the subjection of Scotland. It was clearly impossible for his grandson to succeed in the same task when all Scotland was united against him, and braced to action by a series of glorious memories.

Difficulties arose almost from the first. Not only had Balliol to contend against the implacable hostility of the Scottish patriots; the disinherited split up into rival factions after their triumph, and their divisions played the game of the partisans of the Bruces. The Earls of Athol and Buchan quarrelled with Balliol. Buchan, besieged by the partisans of David Bruce in a remote castle, was forced to surrender and quit Scotland for good. Athol was distinguished by the violence and suddenness of his tergiversations. After deserting Balliol for the patriots, he once more declared for the two Edwards, and persuaded many of the Scottish magnates to submit themselves to them. So long as the English king remained in Scotland, Athol was safe. On Edward's retirement to his kingdom in November, 1335, the nationalist leaders took the earl prisoner and put him to death. The war dragged on from year to year, with startling vicissitudes of fortune, but at no time was Balliol really established on the Scottish throne, and at no time did Edward III. really govern all the ceded districts.

Scottish business detained the English king and court mainly in the north. Edward was in Scotland for most of the winter of 1334-5, keeping his Christmas court at Roxburgh. In the summer of 1335 he led an army into Scotland and penetrated as far as Perth. Again in 1336, he marched from Perth along the east coast, as far as Elgin and Inverness. The Scots refused to give him battle, and their tactics of evasion and guerilla warfare soon exhausted his resources and demoralised his armies. This was Edward's last personal intervention in the business. He had long been irritated by the persistent interference of the French king in Scottish affairs, and his anger was not lessened by his hard plight forcing him, on more than one occasion, to grant short truces to the Scottish insurgents at Philip's intervention. His relations with France were becoming so strained that he preferred to spend 1337 in the south and entrust Thomas Beauchamp, Earl of Warwick, with the conduct of the fruitless campaign of that year. Early in 1338, Edward made his way once more to Berwick, but his intention of invading Scotland was suddenly abandoned on the news of a threatened French expedition to England recalling him to the south. This was the decisive moment of the long struggle. Henceforth the English king could only devote a small share of his resources to an undertaking which he had not been able to compass when his whole energies were absorbed in it. The patriots, who had always dominated the open country, now attacked the castles and fortified towns, which were the bulwarks of the Edwardian power. Within three years all the more important of these fell into their hands. In 1339 Edward Balliol's capital of Perth was beset by Robert, the Steward of Scotland, who had recently undertaken the regency for his uncle David. On the approach of danger, Balliol was ordered to England, and Sir Thomas Ughtred, an English knight and one of the disinherited of 1332, was entrusted with the command. By August he had been forced to surrender, and Stirling soon afterwards opened its gates to the gallant and energetic steward. In 1341 Edinburgh castle was captured by a clever stratagem, and a few weeks later David and Joan returned from France. The king, then seventeen years old, henceforth undertook the personal administration of his kingdom. Once more there was a King of Scots whom the Scottish people themselves desired. The first military enterprise of Edward's reign ended in complete failure.

During the years of Edward Balliol's attempt on Scotland, it was the obvious interest of the English king to maintain such relations with France as to prevent the tightening of the traditional bond between the French and the Scottish courts. There were plenty of outstanding points of difference between England and France, but neither country was anxious for war, and the result of this mutual forbearance enabled Edward III. to deal with the Scots at his leisure. A survey of the relations of the two realms during the first ten years of Edward III.'s reign will show how, despite the reluctance of either party to force matters to a crisis, the Kings of France and England gradually drifted into the hostility which, from 1337 onwards, paralysed the progress of the English cause in Scotland.

At the moment of the fall of Edward II., England and France were still nominally engaged in the war which had followed the second seizure of Guienne by Charles IV. The difficulties experienced by Isabella and Mortimer in establishing their power made them as willing to give way to the French as to the Scots. Accordingly, on March 31, 1327, a treaty of peace was signed at Paris. By this treaty Edward only gained the restoration of certain of his Gascon vassals to the estates of which they had been deprived through their loyalty to the English connexion. He pledged himself to pay a large war indemnity, and accepted a partial restitution of his Gascon lands. Like so many of the treaties since 1259, it was a truce rather than a peace. Many details still remained for settlement, and it was pretty clear that the French, having the whip hand, would drive Gascony towards the goal of gradual absorption which had been so clearly marked out by Philip the Fair.

Charles IV. restored to Edward such parts of Gascony as he chose to surrender. He retained in his hands Agen and the Agenais, and Bazas and the Bazadais, on the ground that Charles of Valois had won them by right of conquest in 1324. This policy reduced Edward's duchy to two portions of territory, very unequal in size and separated from each other by the lands conquered by the French king's uncle. The larger section of the English king's lands extended along the coast from the mouth of the Charente to the mouth of the Bidassoa. It included Saintes with Saintonge south of the Charente, Bordeaux and the Bordelais, Dax and the diocese of Dax, and Bayonne and its territory. But in no place did the boundaries go very far inland. Along the Dordogne, Libourne and Saint-Emilion were the easternmost English towns. Up the Garonne, the French were in possession of Langon, while, in the valley of the Adour, Saint-Sever, perched on its upland rock, was the landward outpost of the diminished Gascon duchy. In the east of the Agenais the two *châtellenies* of Penne and Puymirol formed a little *enclave* of ducal territory which extended from the Lot to the Garonne. But this second fragment of the ancient duchy was of no military and little commercial value, being commanded on all sides by the possessions of the French king. Moreover, the fiefs dependent on the Gascon duchy had fallen away with the attenuation of the duke's domain. In particular the viscounty of Béarn, now held by the Count of Foix, repudiated all allegiance to its English overlord. Even a thoroughly Gascon seigneur, such as the lord of Albret, was wavering in his fidelity to his duke. It was no longer safe for Gascons to risk the hostility of the king of the French.

Within a year of the treaty of Paris, the death of Charles IV. further complicated Anglo-French relations. Like his brothers, Louis X. and Philip V., Charles the Fair left no male issue ; but the pregnancy of his queen prevented the settlement of the succession being completed immediately after his decease. The barons of France, however, had no serious doubts as to their policy. The inadmissibility of a female ruler had already been determined at the accession of both Philip V. and Charles IV., and it was clear that the nearest male heir was Philip, Count of Valois, who had recently succeeded to the great appanage left vacant by the death in 1325 of his father, Charles of Valois, the inveterate enemy of the English. As the next representative of the male line, the French at once recognised Philip of Valois as regent. When his cousin's widow gave birth to a daughter, the regent was proclaimed as King Philip VI. without either delay or hesitation. Thus the house of Valois occupied the throne of France in the place of the direct Capetian line in which son had succeeded father since the days of Hugh Capet.

Even Isabella and Mortimer protested against the succession of Philip of Valois. Admitted that the exclusion of women from the monarchy was already established by two precedents, could it not be plausibly argued that a woman, incapable herself of reigning, might form " the bridge and plank "[1] (as a contemporary put it) by which her sons might step into the rights of their ancestors ? Strange as such a conception seems to our ideas, it was not unfamiliar to the jurists of that day. It was

---

[1] Viollet, *Hist. des Institutions politiques et administratives de la France*, ii., 74, from a MS. source. See also Viollet, *Comment les Femmes ont été exclues en France de la Succession à la Couronne*, in *Mém. de l'Acad. des Inscriptions*, xxxiv., pt. ii. (1893).

in this fashion that the Capetian house claimed its boasted descent and continuity from the race of Charlemagne. Such a principle was actually the law in some parts of France, and it was a matter of every-day occurrence in the Parisis to transmit male fiefs to the sons of heiresses, themselves incapable of succession. Edward, as the son of Charles IV.'s sister, was nearer of kin to his uncle than Philip, the son of Charles's uncle. Surely a man's nephew had a better right to his succession than his first cousin could ever claim? From the purely juridical point of view, the claim put forward by Isabella on her son's behalf was not only plausible but strong.

Happily for France, the magnates of the realm dealt with the succession question as statesmen and not as lawyers. A later age imagined that the French barons brought forward a text of the law of the Salian Franks, as a complete answer to Edward's claim from the juridical point of view. But the famous Salic law was a figment, forged by the next generation of lawyers who were eager to give a complete refutation of the elaborate legal pleadings of the partisans of the English claim. No authentic Salic law dealt with the question of the succession to the throne,[1] and the bold step of transferring a doctrine of private inheritance to the domain of public law was one of the characteristic feats of the medieval jurist, anxious to heap up at any risk a mass of arguments that might overwhelm his antagonists' case. The barons of 1328 rose superior to legal subtleties. To them the question at issue was the preservation of the national identity of their country. The vital thing for them was to secure the throne of France, both at the moment and at future times, for a Frenchman. Any admission, however guarded, of the right of women to transmit claims to their sons opened out a vista of the foreign offspring of French princesses, married abroad, ruling France as strangers, and it might be as enemies. They chose Philip of Valois because he was a Frenchman born and bred, and because he had no interests or possessions outside the French realm. They could not endure the idea of being ruled by the English king. He was not only a stranger, but the hereditary enemy. The Capetian monarchy must at all costs be kept French.

[1] Viollet, *op. cit.*, pp. 55-57 ; *cf.* Désprez, *Les Préliminaires de la Guerre de Cent Ans*, p. 32.

Isabella did what she could on her son's behalf. She ex- CHAP.
cited the *noblesse* of Aquitaine to support Edward's claim; XV.
but the lords of the south paid no heed to her exhortations.
She was more successful with the Flemings, then in revolt
against their Count, Louis of Nevers. Twelve notables of
Bruges, headed by the burgomaster, William de Deken, visited
England and offered to recognise Edward as King of France
if he would support the Flemish democracy against their feudal
lord.[1] But Philip VI.'s first act was to unite with the Count of
Flanders, and the fatal day of Cassel laid low the fortunes of
Bruges and restored the fugitive Louis to power. Isabella was
forced to resign herself to simple protests.

The inevitable demand from Philip VI. for Edward's
homage for Guienne and Ponthieu soon brought the English
government face to face with realities. The request for his
vassal's submission, conveyed to England by Peter Roger,
Abbot of Fécamp, the future Clement VI., was even more unwelcome than such demands commonly were. At first Isabella
used brave words : " My son, who is the son of a king, will
never do homage to the son of a count ".[2] But a threat of a
third seizure of Gascony soon brought the queen to her senses.
Further insistence on the part of Philip was met with polite
apologies for delay. At last, in May, 1329, the young king
crossed the Channel, and on June 6 performed homage to
Philip in the choir of the cathedral of Amiens. But even at
the last moment there were explanations and reservations on
both sides. Philip made it clear that he acknowledged no
claim of his vassal to any territories, beyond those which he
actually possessed. Edward's advisers protested that they
abandoned no pretension to the whole by performing homage
for a part. Moreover, the act of homage was couched in such
ambiguous phrases that it remained doubtful whether Edward
had performed " liege homage," as the King of France demanded, or only " simple homage," such as seemed to him less
offensive to the dignity of a crowned king. Thus, though the
cousins parted amicably and discussed proposals of a marriage

---

[1] See Pirenne, *La première Tentative pour reconnaître Édouard I. comme Roi
de France* in *Ann. de la Soc. d'Hist. de Gand,* 1902.
[2] *Grandes Chroniques de France,* v., 323 (ed. P. Paris).

treaty between the English and French houses, the homage at
Amiens settled nothing.

The diplomatists still had plenty of work before them. The
French statesmen insisted on the necessity of the ceremony at
Amiens being interpreted as liege homage, involving the obligation of defending the overlord "against all those who can live
or die". The English politicians complained of the "injustice
and unreason of the King of France, who seeks the disinherit-
ance of their master in Aquitaine". It was only by limiting the
demands of both parties to points of detail, that a compromise
was arrived at in the convention of the Wood of Vincennes on
May 8, 1330. Further negotiations were still necessary; and at
the moment when everything was trembling in the balance, the
sudden occupation of Saintes by the Count of Alençon, brother
of Philip VI., brought matters within a measurable distance of
war. But Edward, then at the beginning of his real reign, had
no mind for fighting. A more satisfactory convention, drawn
up on March 9, 1331, at Saint-Germain-en-Laye, was ratified
by Edward at Eltham on March 30, when he recognised that
he owed liege homage, and not merely simple homage, to the
King of France. Next month, he crossed over to France so
secretly that his subjects believed that he went disguised as
a merchant or a pilgrim. At Pont-Sainte-Maxence, a little
town on the Oise, a few miles below Compiègne, Edward
held an interview with Philip VI., who came thither with equal
privacy. The French king does not seem to have insisted
upon a renewal of homage, being content with the assurance
already given as to the character of the previous ceremony.
The informal interview, which the modern historian can
only ascertain by painful scrutiny of the royal itineraries,
proved more fertile in friendship than all the pomp of
Amiens. Before Edward went home, Philip gave him complete satisfaction for the outrage at Saintes, and arrived at a
financial settlement. Thus Edward and Philip at last became
friends "so far as outside appearances went," as a chronicler
of the time phrased it. The fundamental difference of interests and standpoint could be glossed over by no facile
compromise, and the calm of the next six years was only
the prelude to a storm destined to end the policy that had
regulated the relations of the two courts from the days

of the peace of 1259 to those of the meeting at Pont-Sainte- CHAP.
XV.
Maxence.

At first there was talk of further cementing the newly
established friendship. There were suggestions of a marriage
of Edward's infant son with Philip's daughter, a fresh interview between the monarchs, a treaty of perpetual alliance
and a common crusade against the Turks. The last, and
the most fantastic, of these projects was the one which was
most seriously discussed. The chivalrous spirit of Philip of
Valois rose eagerly to the idea of a great European expedition
against the infidel, of which he was to be the chief commander.
Inspired by John XXII., he took the cross, made preparations
for an early start, and invoked Edward's co-operation. Edward
cleverly utilised his kinsman's zeal as another lever for enforcing the settlement of outstanding differences. "Tell your
master," he said to the French ambassador, Peter Roger, now
Archbishop of Rouen, "that when he has fulfilled his promises,
I will be more eager to go on the holy voyage than he is himself." But the chronic troubles, arising from the unceasing
extension of the suzerain's claims in Aquitaine, and from the
shelter given by Philip to David Bruce, had continued all
through the years of professed friendship, and in 1334 an embassy to Paris, presided over by Archbishop Stratford, failed to
establish a *modus vivendi*. In the same year John XXII. died
without having either procured the crusade or crushed Louis
of Bavaria. His successor, James Fournier of Foix, who took
the name of Benedict XII., pursued his general policy, though
in a more diplomatic and self-seeking spirit. Benedict's great
wish was to unite France and England against his enemy,
the Emperor Louis of Bavaria, and he dexterously played
upon Philip's eagerness for the crusade to persuade him to
abandon to the papacy the position, which he had assumed,
of arbiter of the differences between Edward and the Scots.
It was a signal, though transitory, triumph of this policy that
a truce between England and Scotland was brought about
by the mediation of the pope and not of the French king.
But Benedict found that a crusade was impossible so long as
the chief powers of the west were hopelessly estranged from
each other. In 1336, he vetoed the crusading scheme until
happier times had dawned. Philip, bitterly disappointed, sought

out Benedict at Avignon, but utterly failed to change his purpose. He was in his own despite released from the crusader's
vow, though exhorted still to continue his preparations. The
galleys, purchased from the crusading tenths of the Church,
were transferred from the Mediterranean to the Channel. The
French king might well find consolation for the abandonment
of the holy war in a sudden descent on England.

From that moment the horizon darkened. Philip VI. once
more took up the cause of the Scots, and once more the
Aquitanian troubles became acute. His irritation at Benedict
led him to open up negotiations with Louis of Bavaria, whereat
Benedict was greatly offended. Edward III. then sought to
find friends who would help him against Philip. He was as
much disgusted with the pope as was his French rival. The
crusading fleet, equipped with the money of the Roman Church,
threatened the English coast, and the *curia* was even more
French in its sympathies than the temporising pontiff. It is no
wonder then that both kings looked coldly on Benedict's offer
of mediation between them. Yet, notwithstanding the indifference manifested by both courts, two cardinals, Peter Gomez, a
Spaniard, and Bertrand of Montfavence, a Frenchman, were
sent in the summer of 1337 as papal legates to France and
England to settle the points in dispute. For the next three
years these prelates pursued their mission with energy and
persistence, though with little result.

A fresh dispute further embittered the personal relations
of Philip and Edward. In 1336, Edward offered a refuge
in England to Robert of Artois, Philip's brother-in-law and
mortal enemy. The grandson of the Count Robert of Artois
who was slain in 1302 at Courtrai, Robert of Artois was indignant that the rich county of Artois should, according to local
custom, have devolved upon his aunt Maud, the wife of Otto,
Count of Burgundy, or Franche Comté, and the mother-in-law of
the last two kings of the direct Capetian line. Though he had
failed in several suits to obtain it, Robert renewed his claim after
his brother-in-law became King of France. It was soon proved
that the charters upon which he relied to prove his title had
been forged. The sudden death of the Countess of Artois,
followed quickly by that of her daughter and heiress, added
the suspicion of poisoning to the certainty of forgery. Robert

was deprived of all his possessions and was exiled from France.
Driven from his first refuge in Brabant by Philip's indignant
hostility, he found shelter in England, where he was received
with a favour which Philip bitterly resented. Condemned in
his absence as a traitor, and devoured by a ferocious hatred of
Philip and his Burgundian wife, Robert did all that he could
to inflame the mind of Edward against the French king. French
romance of the next generation, in the poem of the *Vow of
the Heron*,[1] tells how Robert, returning to Edward's court from
the chase, brought as his only victim a heron, which he offered
to the king as the most timid of birds to the most cowardly of
kings ; "for, sire," he declared, "you have not dared to claim
the realm of France which belongs to you by hereditary right".
Stirred up by this challenge, Edward swore to God and the
heron that within a year he would place the crown of France
on Queen Philippa's brow. This famous legend is, however, a
fiction. It was not until later that Edward seriously renewed
the claim which he had advanced in 1328. But when once war
became certain, the challenge of the French throne was bound
to be made, and the dissolution of the friendly personal relations
of the two kings, which had so long prevented either from proceeding to extremities, was certainly in large part the work of
Robert of Artois. For the moment, Edward probably thought
that his welcome of Robert was only a fair return for Philip's
reception of David Bruce.

War being imminent, Edward looked beyond sea for foreign
allies. Commercial and traditional ties closely bound England
to the county of Flanders, but our friendship had latterly
been with its people rather than with its princes. Louis of
Nevers, the Count of Flanders, had been expelled in 1328 by a
rising of the maritime districts of the county, and had been
restored by force of arms through the agency of Philip of
Valois. Gratitude and interest accordingly combined to make
Count Louis a strong partisan of Philip of Valois. Though far
from absolute, he was still possessed of sufficient authority
over his unruly townsmen to make it impossible for Edward to
negotiate successfully with them. In 1336 the count answered
Edward's advances by prohibiting all commercial relations be-

---

[1] *Les voeus du héron* in Wright, *Political Poems and Songs*, i., 1-25 (Rolls Ser.).

tween his subjects and England. Bitterly disgusted at the hostility of Flanders, Edward in 1337 passed a law through parliament which prohibited the export of wool to the Flemish weaving centres. This measure provoked an economic crisis at Ghent and Ypres; but for the moment such a catastrophe could only accentuate the differences between England and the count. It was otherwise, however, with the neighbouring princes of the imperial obedience. Count William I. of Hainault, Holland, and Zealand was Edward III.'s father-in-law, and, during the last months of his strenuous career, he welcomed Bishop Burghersh, Edward's chief diplomatist, to his favourite residence of Valenciennes, where from April, 1337, the English ambassadors kept great state, "sparing as little as if the king were present there in his own person," and striving with all their might to build up an alliance with the princes of the Low Countries. When the count died, his son and successor, William II., persisted, though with less energy, in his father's policy, and the Hainault connexion became the nucleus of a general Low German alliance. Burghersh was lavish in promises, and soon a large number of imperial vassals took Edward's pay and promised to fight his battles. Among these were Count Reginald of Gelderland, who since 1332 had been the husband of Edward III.'s sister Eleanor, and with him came the Counts of Berg, Jülich, Cleves, and Mark, the Count Palatine of the Rhine, and a swarm of minor potentates.

Hardest to win over of the Netherlandish princes was Duke John III. of Brabant, a crafty statesman and a successful warrior, who had recently conquered Limburg, and won a signal victory over a formidable coalition of his neighbours. Among his former foes had been the house of Avesnes, but he had reconciled himself with Hainault, by reason of his greater hatred for Louis of Flanders. The Flemish cities were the rivals in trade of his own land, and their count's friendship for his French suzerain ensured the establishment of Philip of Valois as temporary lord of Mechlin, the possession of which had long been indirectly disputed between Brabant and Flanders. The hesitating duke was at last won over by a favourable commercial treaty, which made Antwerp the staple of English wools, and ensured for the looms of Louvain and Brussels the advantages denied by Edward's hostility to the clothworkers of Ghent and Ypres.

Convinced that war with Philip was the surest way of adding
Mechlin to his dominions, he then joined the circle of Edward's
stipendiaries.   The excommunicated and schismatic emperor,
Louis of Bavaria, welcomed the advances of Burghersh.   More
than one tie already bound the Bavarian to England.   The
English Franciscan, William of Ockham, proved himself the
most active and daring of the literary champions of the
imperial claims against John XXII.   Moreover, the emperor
and Edward had married sisters, and their brother-in-
law, the new Count of Hainault, Holland, and Zealand, was
childless, so that they had common interests in keeping on
good terms with him.   Louis' bitter enemy, Benedict XII., forbade all hope of French support, and blocked the way to all
prospect of reconciliation with the Church.   It was natural
that Louis should take his revenge by an alliance with the
prince who ignored the advice of the pontiff, and hated the
Valois king.   As the result of all this, an offensive and defensive alliance between Edward on the one hand and Louis and
his Low German vassals on the other was signed at Valenciennes in the summer of 1337.

The die seemed cast.   Philip VI. pronounced the forfeiture
of Gascony and Ponthieu.   The French at once invaded Edward's duchy and county, while the French sailors in the
Channel plundered the Anglo-Norman islands and the towns
on the Sussex and Hampshire coasts.   Edward redoubled his
preparations for war, and issued a long manifesto to his subjects in which he set forth in violent language his grievances
against Philip.   It was at this unlucky moment that the two
cardinal legates came upon the scene, reaching Paris in August,
intent on arranging a pacification.   The irritation, which Benedict showed against Edward for concluding an alliance with the
schismatic emperor, did not make him more disposed to the
work of conciliation.   But the pope saw in the outbreak of a
great war the destruction of his last hopes of humiliating the
Bavarian, and once more played upon the weakness and impolicy of Philip.   Though France was more ready than England,
and Philip had everything to lose by delay, the French king
allowed himself to be persuaded by the two legates to enter
once more upon the paths of conciliation.   As a preliminary
measure, he revoked the order for the confiscation of Gascony,

and accepted a temporary armistice. As before in the Scottish business, Philip again played the game of the papacy. Unlike his adversary, Edward continued steadily in the line which he had determined upon, while welcoming any delay that gave him opportunity to get ready. He employed the interval in making peace more impossible than ever. On October 7, he renewed his claim to the French crown, repudiated the homage into which he had been tricked during his infancy, and sent Bishop Burghersh straight from Valenciennes to Paris as bearer of his defiance. Thus the autumn of 1337 saw a virtual declaration of war. In November the first serious hostilities took place. Sir Walter Manny devastated the Flemish island of Cadzand, taking away with him as prisoner the bastard brother of the Count of Flanders.

Papal diplomacy had not yet exhausted its resources. Benedict XII. was deeply concerned at the conclusion of the Anglo-imperial alliance. He was convinced that the only possible way of avoiding its perils was to persuade Edward and Philip to bury their differences and unite with him against the emperor. He succeeded in obtaining short prolongations of the existing armistice and, in December, 1337, the two cardinal legates landed in England, and were gladly received by Edward, who was delighted to gain time by negotiations. For the next six months they tarried in England, hoping against hope that something definite would result from their efforts. Meanwhile the English hurried on their preparations for war, and Edward made ready to cross over to the continent. As months slipped away, the tension became more severe, and in May Edward denounced the truces, though he still kept up the pretence of negotiations, and so late as June appointed ambassadors to treat with Philip of Valois. The real interest centred in the hard fighting which at once broke out at sea between the rival seamen of England and Normandy. At first the advantage was with the Normans. Not only were many English ships captured, but repeated destructive forays were made on the coasts of the south-eastern counties. Portsmouth was burnt ; the Channel Islands were ravaged ; and so alarming were the French corsairs that, in July, 1338, the dwellers on the south coast were ordered to take refuge in fortresses, or withdraw their goods to a distance of four leagues from the sea.

At last the army and fleet were ready. On July 12, 1338,
Edward appointed his son, the eight-year-old Duke of
Cornwall, warden of England, and a few days later sailed
from Orwell on a great ship named the *Christopher*. A
favourable wind quickly bore the royal fleet to the mouth
of the Scheldt. Thence the king and his army sailed
up the river to Antwerp, the chief port of Brabant, where
they landed on July 16. There, on July 22, Edward revoked all commissions addressed to the King of France, and
withheld from his agents all power to prejudice his own pretensions to the throne of the Valois. He passed more than a
month at Antwerp, holding frequent conferences with his imperial allies, and thence proceeded through Brabant and Jülich
to Cologne. From that city he went up the Rhine to Coblenz,
where on September 5 he held an interview with his queen's
imperial brother-in-law. Their meeting was celebrated with all
the pomp and stateliness of the heyday of chivalry. Edward was
accompanied by the highest nobles of his land, the emperor by
all the electors, save King John of Bohemia, who, as a Luxemburger, was a convinced partisan of the French. Louis received
his ally clothed in a purple dalmatic, with crown on head
and with sceptre and orb in hand, surrounded by the electors
and the higher dignitaries of the empire, and seated on a lofty
throne erected in the Castorplatz, hard by the Romanesque
basilica that watches over the junction of the Moselle with
the Rhine. Another throne, somewhat lower in height, was
occupied by the King of England, clothed in a robe of scarlet
embroidered with gold, and surrounded by three hundred
knights. Then, before the assembled crowd, Louis declared
that Philip of France had forfeited the fiefs which he held of
the empire. He put into Edward's hands a rod of gold and
a charter of investiture, by which symbols he appointed him
as " Vicar-general of the Empire in all the Germanies and in
all the Almaines ". Next day the allies heard a mass celebrated by the Archbishop of Cologne in the church of St.
Castor. After the service the emperor swore to aid Edward
against the King of France for seven years, while the barons of
the empire took oaths to obey the imperial vicar and to march
against his enemies. Thereupon the English king took farewell
of the emperor, and returned to Brabant.

All was ready for war. The interview at Coblenz was the deathblow to the papal diplomacy, and the sluggish Philip awaited in the Vermandois the expected attack of the Anglo-imperial armies. Yet the best part of a year was still to elapse before lances were crossed in earnest. The lords of the empire had no real care for the cause of Edward. They were delighted to take his presents, to pledge themselves to support him, and to insist upon the regular payment of the subsidies he had promised. But John of Brabant was more intent on winning Mechlin than on invading France, and even William of Avesnes was embarrassed by the ties which bound him to Philip, his uncle, even more than to Edward, his brother-in-law. They contented themselves with taking Edward's money and giving him little save promises in return. It became evident that an imperial vicar would be obeyed even less than an emperor. Every week of delay was dangerous to Edward, who had exhausted his resources in the pompous pageantry of his Rhenish journey, and in magnificent housekeeping in Brabant. It was then Edward's interest, as it had previously been Philip's, to bring matters to a crisis. That he failed to do this must be ascribed to the lukewarmness of his allies, the poverty of his exchequer, and, above all, to the still active diplomacy of Benedict XII.

The cardinal legates appeared in Brabant, but their tone was different from that which they had taken in the previous spring in England. Profoundly irritated by the alliance of Edward and Louis, Benedict lectured the English king on the iniquity of his courses. The empire was vacant; the Coblenz grant was therefore of no effect; if Edward persisted in acting as vicar of the schismatic, he would be excommunicated. Benedict stood revealed as the partisan of France. It was in vain that Edward offered peace if France gave up the Scots and made full restitution of Gascony. Benedict ordered his legates to refuse to discuss the latter proposal, and, as the Gascon question lay at the root of the whole matter, an amicable settlement became more impossible than ever. Edward hotly defended his right to make what alliances he chose with his wife's kinsmen, and bitterly denounced the employment of the wealth of the Church in equipping the armies of his enemies. Though the cardinals, Peter and Bertrand, remained in Edward's camp, they might, for all practical purposes, as well have been at Avignon.   The papal diplomacy had failed.

Edward employed the leisure forced upon him by these events in elaborating his claim to the French throne.   His lawyers ransacked both Roman jurisprudence and feudal custom that they might lay before the pope and Christendom plausible reasons for their master's pretensions.   They advanced pleas of an even bolder character.   Was not the right of Edward to the French throne the same as that of Jesus Christ to the succession of David?   The Virgin Mary, incapable of the succession on her own behalf, was yet able to transmit her rights to her Son.   These contentions, sacred and profane, did not touch the vital issue.   It was not the dynastic question that brought about the war, though, war being inevitable, Edward might well, as he himself said, use his claim as a buckler to protect himself from his enemies.   The fundamental difference between the two nations lay in the impossible position of Edward in Gascony.   He could not abandon his ancient patrimony, and Philip could not give up that policy of gradually absorbing the great fiefs which the French kings had carried on since the days of St. Louis.   The support given to the Scots, the Anglo-imperial alliance, the growing national animosity of the two peoples, the rivalry of English and French merchants and sailors, all these and many similar causes were but secondary.[1] At this stage the claim to the French throne, though immensely complicating the situation, and interposing formidable technical obstacles to the conduct of negotiations, loomed larger in talk than in acts.   It was only in 1340, when Edward saw in his pretensions the best way of commanding the allegiance of Philip's sworn vassals, that the question of the French title became a serious matter.

On which side did the responsibility for the war rest? National prejudices have complicated the question.   English historians have seen in the aggression of Philip in Gascony, his intervention in Scottish affairs, and the buccaneering exploits of the Norman mariners, reasons adequate to provoke the patience even of a peace-loving monarch.   French writers, unable to deny these facts, have insisted upon the slowness of

[1] Déprez, *Les Préliminaires de la Guerre de Cent Ans,* pp. 400-406, admirably elucidates the situation.

Philip to requite provocation, his servile deference to papal authority, his willingness to negotiate, and his dislike to take offence even at the denial of his right to the crown which he wore. Either king seems hesitating and reluctant when looked at from one point of view, and pertinaciously aggressive when regarded from the opposite standpoint. It is safer to conclude that the war was inevitable than to endeavour to apportion the blame which is so equally to be divided between the two monarchs. The modern eye singles out Edward's baseless claim and makes him the aggressor, but there was little, as the best French historians admit, in Edward's pretension that shocked the idea of justice in those days. Moreover this view, held too absolutely, is confuted by the secondary position taken by the claim during the negotiations which preceded hostilities. If in the conduct of the preliminaries we may assign to Edward the credit of superior insight, more resolute policy, and a more clearly perceived goal, the intellectual superiority, which he possessed over his rival, was hardly balanced by any special moral obliquity on his part; though to Philip, with all his weakness, must always be given the sympathy provoked by the defence of his land against the foreign invader. It is useless to refine the issue further. The situation had become impossible, and fighting was the only way out of the difficulty. When in the late summer of 1339 the curtain was rung down on the long-drawn-out diplomatic comedy, Edward had not yet finally assumed that title of King of France, which made an inevitable strife irreconcilable, and so prolonged hostilities that the struggle became the Hundred Years' War.

CHAPTER XVI.

THE EARLY CAMPAIGNS OF THE HUNDRED YEARS' WAR.

IN the late summer of 1339 Edward III. was at last able to take the offensive against France. During the negotiations England strained every effort to provide her absent sovereign with men and money, but neither the troops nor the supplies were adequate. The army which assembled in September in the neighbourhood of Brussels consisted largely of imperial vassals, hired by the English King, and clamorous for the regular payment of their wages. Already Edward told his ministers that, had not "a good friend in Flanders" advanced him a large sum, he would have been obliged to return with shame to England. As it was, enough was raised to set the unwieldy host in motion, and on September 20 he marched from Valenciennes, and thence advanced into the bishopric of Cambrai, whose lord, though an imperial vassal, had declared for France and the papacy.

The rolling uplands of the Cambrésis were devastated with fire and sword. One night an English baron took the Cardinal Bertrand, who with his comrade Peter still accompanied Edward's host, to the summit of a high tower, whence they could witness the flaming homesteads and villages of the fertile and populous district. In that woeful spectacle the churchman saw the futility of his last two years of constant labour, and fell in a swoon to the ground. But the confederates could do little more than devastate the open country. Cambrai itself was besieged to no purpose, and Edward pressed on to the invasion of France. On October 9 he spent his first night on French soil at the abbey of Mont Saint-Martin. He learnt how slender was the tie which bound his foreign allies to him, for his brother-in-law, William of Hainault, refused to serve, except on imperial soil, against his uncle Philip VI. Consoled for this

22 *

defection by the arrival of the sluggish Duke of Brabant and of the Elector of Brandenburg, the eldest son of the emperor, Edward marched through the Vermandois, the Soissonais, and the Laonnais, burning and devastating, without meeting any serious resistance. Philip of Valois timidly held aloof in the neighbourhood of Péronne.

By the middle of October, when Edward was near St. Quentin on the Oise, the Duke of Brabant suggested the expediency of seeking out winter quarters. The slow-moving host was almost in mutiny, when the master crossbowman of the King of France brought a challenge from his lord. " Let the King of England," ran the message, "seek out a field favourable for a pitched battle, where there is neither wood, nor marsh, nor river." Edward cheerfully accepted a day for the combat, and chose his ground higher up the Oise valley, among the green meadowlands and hedgerows of the Thiérache. The appointed day passed by, and the French came not. At last, when Edward almost despaired of a meeting, he was told that the French were arrayed at Buironfosse, on the plateau between the Oise and the upper Sambre, and that Philip was ready to fight the next day, Saturday, October 23. Edward once more chose a suitable field of action in a plain between La Flamangrie and Buironfosse, a league and a half from the French. " On the Saturday," wrote Edward to his son in England, "we were in the field, a full quarter of an hour before dawn, and took up our position in a fitting place to fight. In the early morning some of the enemy's scouts were taken, and they told us that his advanced guard was in battle array and coming out towards us. The news having come to our host, our allies, though they had hitherto borne themselves somewhat sluggishly, were in truth of such loyal intent that never were folk of such goodwill to fight. In the meantime one of our scouts, a knight of Germany, was taken, and he showed all our array to the enemy. Thereupon the foe withdrew his van, gave orders to encamp, made trenches around him, and cut down large trees in order to prevent us from approaching him. We tarried all day on foot in order of battle, until towards evening it seemed to our allies that we had waited long enough. And at vespers we mounted our horses and went near to Avesnes, and made him to know that we would await him there all the Sunday.

On the Monday morning we had news that the lord Philip
had withdrawn. And so would our allies no longer afterwards
abide."

Thus ended the inglorious campaign of the Thiérache.
Edward returned to Brussels "like a fox to his hole," and
each side denounced the other for failing to keep the appointed
tryst. The chivalry of the fourteenth century saw something
ignoble in the sluggishness of Philip ; but no modern soldier
would blame him for his inactivity. Without striking a blow, he
obtained the object of his campaign, for the enemy abandoned
French territory. Had Edward been fully confident of victory,
he could easily have forced a battle by advancing on Buironfosse ; but he preferred to run the risk of a fiasco rather than
abandon the defensive tactics on which he relied. Thus, even
from the chivalrous point of view, he was by no means blame-
less. From the material standpoint, his first French campaign
was a failure. It left its only mark on the devastated countryside, the beggared peasantry, the desolated churches and monasteries, the farmsteads and villages burnt to ashes.

Edward seemed ruined both in reputation and purse. He had
exhausted his resources in meeting the extravagant demands of
his allies, and their help had profited him nothing at all. Yet
his inexhaustible energy opened up a surer means of foreign
assistance than had been supplied by the unruly vassals of Louis
of Bavaria. At the moment when the imperial alliance was
tried and found wanting, the way was opened up for close
friendship between Edward and the Flemish cities. In earlier
years the chivalrous devotion of Louis of Nevers to his overlord had secured the political dependence of Flanders upon
the King of France. If the action of their count made the
Flemings the tools of French policy, their commercial necessities
bound them to England by chains forged by nature itself.
Alone of the lands of northern and western Europe, Flanders
was not a self-sufficing economic community.[1] Its great ports
and weaving towns depended for their customers on foreign
markets, and the raw material of their staple manufacture was
mainly derived from England. When in 1337 Edward prohibited the export of wool to Flanders, his action at once

---

[1] See for this Pirenne, *Histoire de Belgique*, vols. i. and ii., and Lamprecht,
Deutsche Geschichte, iii., 304-324, and iv., 134-142.

brought about the same result that the cessation of the supplies of American cotton would cause in the manufacturing districts of Lancashire. A wool famine, like the Lancashire cotton famine of 1862-65, plunged Ghent, Ypres, and Bruges into grievous distress. The starving weavers wandered through the farms begging their bread, and, when charity at home proved inadequate, they exposed their rags and their misery in the chief cities of northern France. Even wealthy merchants felt the pinch of the crisis which ruined the small craftsmen.

A common desire to avoid calamity bound together the warring classes and rival districts of Flanders, as they had never been united before. Bruges and Ypres had borne the brunt of earlier struggles, and had not even yet recovered from the exhaustion of the wars of the early years of the century. Their exhaustion left the way open to Ghent, where the old patricians and the rich merchants, the weavers and the fullers, forgot their ancient rivalries and worked together to remedy the crisis. A wealthy landholder and merchant-prince of Ghent, James van Artevelde, made himself the spokesman of all classes of that great manufacturing city. He was no demagogue nor artisan, though his eloquence and force had wonderful power over the impressionable craftsmen of the trading guilds. He was no Netherlandish patriot, as some moderns have imagined, though he was anxious to unite Flanders with her neighbour states, on the broad basis of their identity of economic and political interests. A man of Ghent, above all things, his policy was to save the imperilled industries of his native town, and to make it the centre of a new movement for the vindication of commercial liberty against feudal domination. By the winter of 1337 this rich capitalist allied himself with the turbulent democracy of the weavers' guilds, and put himself at the head of affairs. Early in 1338 he began to negotiate with Edward III., and his loans to the distressed monarch had the result of removing the embargo on English wool. The famished craftsmen hailed the enemy of their class as a god who had come down from heaven for their salvation.

Louis of Nevers and Philip of Valois took the alarm. Seeing in the ascendency of Artevelde the certainty that Flanders would join the English alliance, they left no stone unturned to avoid so dire a calamity. Artevelde, conscious of the narrow basis of his own authority, was prudent enough to be moderate. Instead of pressing the English alliance to a conclusion, he accepted the suggestion of Philip VI., that Flanders should remain neutral. Louis of Nevers hated the notion ; but in June, 1338, Edward and Philip agreed to recognise Flemish neutrality, and he was forced to acquiesce in it. Both monarchs promised to avoid Flemish territory, and offered free commercial relations between Flanders and their respective dominions.

Artevelde and the men of Ghent were the real masters of Flanders. They kept their count in scarcely veiled captivity, forcing him to wear the Flemish colours and to profess acceptance of the policy that he disliked. In such circumstances the neutrality of Flanders could not last long. Both Edward and Artevelde regarded it simply as a step towards a declared alliance. Before long Philip became uneasy, and lavished concession on concession to keep the dominant party true to its promises. He gave up the degrading conditions which since the treaty of Athis had secured the subjection of Flanders. But Edward could offer more than his rival. He proposed to the count and the "good towns" of Ghent, Bruges, and Ypres that, in return for their alliance, he would aid them to win back the towns of Lille, Douai, Béthune, and Tournai, which the French king had usurped from the Flemings, as well as the county of Artois, which had been separated from Flanders since the days of Philip Augustus. He also offered ample commercial privileges, the establishment of the staple of wool at Bruges as well as at Antwerp, free trade for Flemish cloth with the English markets, and a good and fixed money which was to be legal tender in Flanders, Brabant, France, and England. The Flemings demanded in return that Edward, by formally assuming the title of King of France, should stand to them as their liege lord, and thus free themselves and their count from the ecclesiastical penalties and dishonour involved in their waging war against a king of France. Late in 1339, these terms were mutually accepted, and Count Louis avoided further humiliations by flight into France.

In January, 1340, Edward entered Flemish territory and was magnificently entertained in the abbey of Saint Bavon at Ghent. "The three towns of Flanders," declared Artevelde to his guest, "are ready to recognise you as their sovereign lord, provided

that you engage yourself to defend them." The deputies of
the three towns took oaths to Edward as their suzerain, and
thereupon Edward was proclaimed King of France with much
ceremony in the Friday market of Ghent. A new great seal
was fashioned and new royal arms assumed, in which the lilies
of France were quartered with the leopards of England. The
new regnal year of Edward, which began on January 25, was
styled the fourteenth of his reign in England, and the first of
his reign in France. Urgent affairs called Edward back to his
kingdom, but his debts to the Flemings were already so heavy
that they only consented to his departure on his pledging
himself to return before Michaelmas day, and on his leaving as
hostages his queen, his two sons, and two earls. At last, on
February 20, he crossed over from Sluys to Orwell. He had
been absent from home for nearly a year and a half.

From February 21 to June 22, 1340, Edward remained in
England. During that period, formal treaties with the Flemings
confirmed the hasty negotiations of Ghent. Benedict XII. still
pursued Edward with remonstrances. He warned the English
king to have no trust in allies like the Flemings, who had
shamefully driven away their natural lords and whose faithless-
ness and inconstancy were by-words. He told him that his
strength was not enough to conquer France, and reproached
him with calling himself king of a land of which he possessed
nothing. Somewhat inconsistently, he offered his mediation between Edward and Philip. But Philip was only less weary than
Edward of the self-seeking pontiff. Benedict was forced to
drink the cup of humiliation, for after the rejection of his
mediation, he was confronted with a proposal that the schismatic
Bavarian should arbitrate between the two crowns. Meanwhile,
after many delays, Edward embarked a gallant army on a fleet
of 200 ships, and on June 22 a favourable west wind bore them
from the Orwell towards Flanders. On arriving next day off
Blankenberghe, he learned that a formidable French squadron
was anchored in the mouth of the Zwyn, and that he could
only land in Flanders as the reward of victory.

From the outbreak of hostilities in 1337, there had been
a good deal of fighting by sea, and in the first stages of warfare the advantage lay with the French. Since the days of
Edward I. and Philip the Fair, the maritime energies of the two

countries had developed at an almost equal rate, and the parallel growth had been marked by bitter rivalry between the seamen of the two nations. The Normans had taken the leading share in this expansion of the French navy.[1] They welcomed the outbreak of war with enthusiasm, as giving them a chance of measuring their forces with their hated foes. Alone among the provinces of France, Normandy seems already to have experienced that intense national bitterness against the English which was soon to spread to all the rest of the country. Not content with the vigorous war of corsairs which had inflicted so much mischief on our southern coast and on English shipping, the Normans formed bold designs of a new Norman Conquest of England, and in return for the permanent establishment of the local estates of Normandy, agreed with Philip and his son John, who bore the title of Duke of Normandy, to equip a large fleet and army, with which England was to be invaded in the summer of 1339. Normandy, which monopolised the glory, was to monopolise the spoil. If England were conquered, Duke John, like Duke William before him, was to be King of England as well as Duke of Normandy. Thus the aggressions of Edward in France were to be answered by Norman aggressions in England.[2]

Nothing came of this grandiose project, though the burning ruins of Southampton, the capture of the great *Christopher*, which had borne Edward in 1338 to Antwerp, and the occupation of the Channel Islands—the last remnants of the old duchy still under English rule—showed that the Normans were in earnest. The chief result of their energy was the equipment of the strongest French fleet that had ever been seen in the Channel. Though a few Genoese galleys under Barbavera and a few great Spanish ships swelled the number of the armada, 160 of the 200 ships that formed the fleet were Norman.[3] Of the two Frenchmen in command, one, Hugh Quièret, was a Picard knight, but the other, the more popular, was Nicholas Béhuchet, a Norman of humble birth, then a knight and the chief confidant of Philip VI. Quièret and Béhuchet had long challenged the command of the narrow seas. But for their

[1] C. de la Roncière, *Hist. de la Marine Française ;* cf. Nicolas, *Hist. of the Royal Navy.*

[2] See on this subject A. Coville, *Les États de Normandie,* pp. 41-52 (1894).

[3] S. Luce, *La Marine normande à l'Écluse,* in *La France pendant la Guerre de Cent Ans,* 3-21.

error of dividing their forces and preferring a piratical war of reprisals, they might have cut off communications between England and the Netherlands. They had learnt wisdom by experience, and their ships were massed in Zwyn harbour to prevent the passage of Edward to his new allies.

The coast-line between Blankenberghe and the mouth of the Scheldt was strangely different in the fourteenth century from what it is at present.[1] The sandy flats, through which the Zwyn now trickles to the sea, formed a large open harbour, accessible to the biggest ships then known. It was protected on the north by the island of Cadzand, the scene of Manny's exploit in 1337, while at its head stood the town of Sluys, so called from the locks, or sluices, that regulated the waters of the ship canal, which bore to the great mart of Bruges the merchantmen of every land. It was in this harbour that Edward, on arriving off Blankenberghe, first spied the fleet of Quièret and Béhuchet. He anchored at sea for the night, and on the afternoon of June 24, the anniversary of Bannockburn, he bore down on the French, having the sun, the tide, and the wind in his favour. On his approach Barbavera urged that the French should take to the open sea; but Quièret and Béhuchet preferred to fight in the harbour. As an unsatisfactory compromise, however, the French moved a mile or so towards the enemy. Then they lashed their ships together and awaited attack.

The English, unable to break the serried mass of their enemies, feigned a retreat, whereupon the Normans unlashed their ships and hurried in pursuit into the open water. At once the English turned and met them. The battle began when the English admiral, Robert Morley, lay alongside the *Christopher*, which, after its capture, had been taken into the enemy's service. Soon the ships of both fleets were closely grappled together in a fierce hand-to-hand fight which lasted until after nightfall. The desperate eagerness of the combatants strangely contrasted with the slackness of the campaign in the Thiérache. "This battle," says Froissart, "was right fierce and horrible, for battles by sea are more dangerous and fiercer than battles by land, for at sea there is no retreat nor fleeing; there is no remedy but to fight and abide fortune, and

[1] For this see Professor Tait's inset map of the district in *Oxford Historical Atlas*, plate lvi.

every man to show his prowess."   In the end the English won
an overwhelming victory, which was completed next morning
after more hard fighting.   During the night Barbavera and his
Genoese put to sea and escaped, but the magnificent Norman
fleet was in the hands of the victor.   The English loss was
small, though it included Thomas of Monthermer, a son of
Joan of Acre, and Edward himself was wounded in the thigh.
The Norman force was almost annihilated.   Quièret fell mortally
wounded into Edward's hands ; Béhuchet was captured unhurt.
A later Norman legend tells how Béhuchet, when brought before the English king, answered some taunt by boxing the
king's ears, whereupon the angry monarch hanged him forthwith
from the mast of his ship.[1]   But the tradition is unsupported by
English authorities, and, with all his faults, Edward was not the
man to deal thus with a captive knight who had fought his best.
Master at last of the sea, Edward landed at Sluys amidst the
rejoicings of the Flemings, and made his way to Ghent, where
he greeted his wife, and first saw his infant son John, born
during his absence, to whom Artevelde stood as godfather.

Edward's military fame was established over all Europe,
and, says the Flemish writer, John van Klerk, "all who spoke
the German tongue rejoiced at the defeat of the French".
Yet the victory at Sluys was the prelude to a land campaign as ineffective as the raid into the Thiérache.   Eager to
restore their lost lands to the Flemings, Edward made the
mistake of dividing his army.   He sent Robert of Artois to
effect the reconquest of Artois, while he himself besieged
Tournai, which was then in French hands.   Robert's attempt
to win back the lands of his ancestors was a sorry failure.
Defeated outside Saint Omer, he was unable even to invest
that town.   Almost equally unsuccessful was Edward's siege
of Tournai, which resisted with such energy that he was soon
at the end of his resources.   At last, in despair, Edward challenged Philip VI. to decide their claim to France by single
combat.   The Valois answered that he would gladly do so if,
in the event of his winning, he might obtain Edward's kingdom.
In the same spirit of caution, Philip tarried half-way between
Saint Omer and Tournai, watching both armies and afraid to

---

[1] Luce, *Le Soufflet de l'Écluse*, in *La France pendant la Guerre de Cent Ans,*
2nd série, pp. 3-15.

strike at either. The armies wore themselves out in this game of waiting until the widowed Countess of Hainault, then abbess of the Cistercian nuns of Fontenelles, was moved by the desolation of the country to intervene between the two kings. The mother of the Queen of England and the sister of the King of France, she succeeded not only by reason of her prayers, but through the refusal of the Duke of Brabant, the Count of Hainault, and the other imperial vassals to remain longer at the war. On September 25, 1340, a truce was signed at the solitary chapel of Esplechin, situated in the open country a little south of Tournai. By it hostilities between both kings and their respective allies were suspended, until midsummer day, 1341. Each king was to enjoy the lands actually in his possession, and commerce was to be carried on as if peace had been made. The most significant clause of the truce was that by which both kings pledged themselves that they " procure not that any innovation be done by the Church of Rome, or by others of Holy Church on either of the said kings. And if our most holy father the pope will do that, the two kings shall prevent it, so far as in them lies."

The truce of Esplechin, renewed until 1345, put an end to the first, or Netherlandish, period of the Hundred Years' War. The imperial alliance, which had failed Edward, was soon to be solemnly dissolved. Early in 1341, Louis of Bavaria revoked Edward's vicariate, and announced his intention of becoming henceforth the friend of his uncle, the King of France. This alliance between Philip and Louis completed the discomfiture of Benedict XII. In 1342 he died, and his successor was Peter Roger, the sometime Archbishop of Rouen, who assumed the title of Clement VI. By persuading Brabant and Hainault to be neutral between France and England, the new pontiff broke up the last remnant of the Anglo-imperial alliance. Even Flanders and England became estranged. Artevelde, who found it a hard matter to govern Flanders after the truce, would willingly have supported Edward. But Edward had henceforth less need of Artevelde than Artevelde had of him. In 1345 Edward again appeared at Sluys and had an interview with him, and then returned to his own country without setting foot on Flemish soil. Artevelde soon afterwards met his death in a popular tumult. His family fled to England,

where they lived on a pension from Edward. This was the CHAP.
XVI.
end of the Anglo-Flemish alliance.

After the treaty of Esplechin, Edward returned to Ghent.
The conclusion of military operations was a signal to all his
creditors to clamour for immediate settlement of their debts.
Neither subsidies nor wool came from England, though the
king wrote in piteous terms to his council. Edward was convinced that the real cause of his failure was the remissness of
the home government, and resolved to wreak his vengeance on
his ministers. He was encouraged to this effect by Bishop
Burghersh, who still remembered his old feuds with Archbishop
Stratford, and may well have believed that the archbishop, who
had a financier's dread of war, had wilfully ruined his rival's
diplomacy. But Edward dared not openly return to England,
for his Flemish creditors regarded his personal presence as the
best security for his debts. He was therefore reduced to the
pitiful expedient of running away from them. One day he rode
out of Ghent on the pretext of taking exercise, and hurried
secretly and without escort to Sluys. Thence he took ship
for England, and, after a tempestuous voyage of three days
and nights, sailed up the Thames, and landed at the Tower on
November 30, 1340, after nightfall. At cockcrow next morning,
he summoned his ministers before him, denounced them as false
traitors and drove them all from office. The judges were thrown
into prison, and with them some of the leading merchants, including William de la Pole of Hull. A special commission,
like that of 1289, scrutinised the acts of the royal officials
throughout the kingdom, and exacted heavy fines from the
many who were found wanting. Nothing but fear of provoking
the wrath of the Church prevented Edward from consigning
to prison the dismissed chancellor, Robert Stratford, Bishop of
Chichester, and the late treasurer, Roger Northburgh, Bishop
of Coventry. Their successors were lay knights, the new chancellor, Sir Robert Bourchier, being the first keeper of the great
seal who was not a clerk.

Earlier in the year the king had quarrelled with Archbishop
Stratford, who resigned the chancellorship. But before Edward
sailed from Orwell in June there had been a partial reconciliation, and the king left Stratford president of the council during
his absence. When his brother and colleagues were dismissed,

the archbishop was at Charing. Conscious that he was the chief object of Edward's vengeance, he at once took sanctuary with the monks of his cathedral. Every effort was made to drag him from his refuge. Some Louvain merchants, to whom he had bound himself for the king's debts, demanded that he should be surrendered to their custody until the money was paid. He was summoned to court and afterwards to parliament. But he prudently remained safe within the walls of Christ Church, and preached a course of sermons to the monks, in which he compared himself to St. Thomas of Canterbury, and hinted at the danger of his incurring his prototype's fate. Edward replied to this challenge by a lengthy pamphlet, called the *libellus famosus*. The violence and unmeasured terms of the tractate suggest the hand of Bishop Orleton, Stratford's lifelong foe, who had by Burghersh's recent death become the most prominent of the courtly prelates. The archbishop was declared to be the sole cause of the king's failures. He had left Edward without funds, and in trusting to him the king had leant on a broken reed. Stratford justified himself in another sermon in which he invited inquiry and demanded trial by his peers.

Edward so far relented as to issue letters of safe-conduct enabling the archbishop to attend the parliament summoned for April 23, 1341. But when Stratford took his place, the king refused to meet him, and ordered him to answer in the exchequer the complaints brought against him. The lords upheld the primate's cause, and declared that in no circumstances could a peer of parliament be brought to trial elsewhere than in full parliament. Edward's fury abated when he saw that he would get no grant unless he gave way. He restored Stratford to his favour, and acceded to his request that he should answer in parliament and not in the exchequer. The childish controversy ended with the personal victory of the primate and the formal re-assertion of the important principle of trial by peers. But not even then was Edward able to get a subsidy. He was further forced to embody in the statute of the year the doctrines that auditors of the accounts of the royal officers should be elected in parliament, and that all ministers should be chosen by the king, after consultation with his estates, and should resign their offices at each meeting of parliament and be prepared to answer all complaints before it.

Thus the fallen minister brought the estates the greatest triumph over the prerogative won during Edward's reign. Before long Edward was magnanimous enough to resume friendly relations with him, but he was never suffered to take a prominent part in politics. He died in 1348, after spending his later years in the business of his see. It was a strange irony of fate that this worldly and politic ecclesiastic should have perforce become the champion of the rights of the Church and the liberties of the nation. His victory established a remarkable solidarity between the high ecclesiastical party and the popular opposition, which was to last nearly as long as the century. Disgust at this alliance moved Edward to take up the anti-clerical attitude which henceforth marks the policy of the crown until the accession of the house of Lancaster.

The victory of the estates of 1341 was too complete to last. For a medieval king to hand over the business of government to a nominated ministry was in substance a return to the state of things in 1258 or 1312. Edward was not the sort of man to endure the thraldom that his father and great-grandfather had both found intolerable. Even at the moment of sealing the statute, he and his ministers protested that they were not bound to observe laws contrary to the constitution of the realm. Five months later, on October 1, 1341, the king issued letters, revoking the laws of the previous session. "We have never," he impudently declared, "really given our consent to the aforesaid pretended statute. But inasmuch as our rejecting it would have dissolved parliament in confusion, without any business having been transacted, and so all our affairs would have been ruined, we dissembled, as was our duty, and allowed the pretended statute to be sealed." For more than two years he did not venture to face a parliament, but the next gathering of the estates in April, 1343, repealed the offensive acts of 1341. Parliament was so reluctant to ratify the king's high-handed action, that he did not venture to ask it for any extraordinary grant of money. The only other important act of this parliament was a petition from lords and commons, urging the king to check the claims of a French pope, friendly to the "tyrant of France," to exercise ever-increasing rights of patronage over English benefices. The anti-clerical tide was still flowing.

Before parliament met in 1343, the French war had been renewed on another pretext. A new source of trouble arose in a disputed succession to the duchy of Brittany. The duke John III., the grandson of John II. and Edward I.'s sister Beatrice, died in April, 1341. He left no legitimate children, and his succession was claimed by his half-brother, John of Montfort, and his niece Joan of Penthièvre. Montfort, the son of Duke Arthur II. by his second wife, had inherited from his mother the Norman county of Montfort l'Amaury, which became her possession as the representative on the spindle side of the line of Simon de Montfort the Albigensian crusader. Joan was the daughter of Guy, John III.'s brother of the full blood, in whose favour the great county of Penthièvre-Tréguier, including the whole of the north coast of the duchy from the river of Morlaix to within a few miles of the Rance, had been dissociated from the demesne and reconstituted as an appanage.[1] The heiress of Penthièvre thus ruled directly over nearly a sixth of Brittany, and her power was further strengthened by her marriage with Charles of Blois, who, though a younger son, enjoyed great influence as the sister's son of Philip VI., and also by reason of his simple, saintly, honourable, and martial character. The house of Penthièvre not only stood to Brittany as the house of Lancaster stood to England, as the natural head of the higher nobility; it also enjoyed the favour and protection of the French king, who was ever anxious to find friends among the chief sub-tenants of his great vassals. Against so formidable an opponent John of Montfort could only secure his rights by promptitude. Accordingly he made his way to Nantes and, receiving a warm welcome from his burgesses, proclaimed himself duke. Very few of the great feudatories threw in their lot with him. His strength was in the petty *noblesse*, the townsmen, and the enthusiasm of the Celtic population of *La Brétagne bretonnante*, which made Léon, Cornouailles, and Vannes the strongholds of his cause. Yet the Penthièvre influence took with it the Breton-speaking inhabitants of the diocese of Tréguier, and the piety of Charles made the clergy, and especially the friars, devoted to him.

The fight was not waged in Brittany only. Montfort had to

---

[1] On the importance of Penthièvre, see A. de la Borderie, *La Géographie féodale de la Bretagne* (1889), pp. 60-65.

contend against the general sentiment of the French nobility and the strong interest and affection which bound Philip VI. to uphold the claims of Charles of Blois. After a few months the parliament of Paris decided in favour of the king's nephew against Montfort. Charles's wife was the nearest heir of the deceased duke, and had therefore a prior claim over her uncle. Montfort urged in vain that the superior rights of the male, which had made the Count of Valois King of France, equally gave the Count of Montfort the duchy of Brittany. He had to fight for his duchy. John, Duke of Normandy, the heir of France, marched to Brittany with a strong force, to secure the establishment of his cousin in accordance with the decree of parliament. The union of the royal troops, with the levies of Penthièvre and the great feudatories of Brittany, was too powerful a combination to withstand. Montfort was shut up in Nantes, was forced to capitulate, and sent prisoner to Paris. His place was taken by his wife, Joan of Flanders, a daughter of Louis of Nevers. This lady shewed "the heart of a man and of a lion," as Froissart says. Her efforts, however, did not prevail against her formidable enemies. Bit by bit she was driven from one stronghold to another, until at last she was closely besieged in Hennebont by Charles of Blois. Before that, she had recognised Edward as King of France, and offered him the homage of her husband and son.

Edward III. readily took up the cause of Montfort. He recked little of the inconsistency involved in the prince, who claimed France through his mother, supporting in Brittany a duke, whose pretensions were based upon grounds similar to the claim advanced by Philip of Valois on the French throne. As in Flanders, he found two rival nations contending in the bosom of a single French fief. He at once supported the Celtic party in Brittany as he had supported the Flemish party in Flanders. Both his allies had the same enemies in feudalism, the French monarchy, and the pretensions of high clericalism. Afraid to renew the attack in France without allies, Edward welcomed the support of the Montfort party, as giving him a chance of renewing his assaults on his adversary of Valois. He invested Montfort with the earldom of Richmond, of which John III. had died possessed. He sent Sir Walter Manny with a force sufficient to raise the siege of Hennebont.

The heroic Joan of Flanders was almost at the end of her

resources, when on an early June morning, in 1342, she espied
the white sails of Manny's fleet working its way from the
sea up the estuary of the Blavet, which bathes the walls of
Hennebont. After the arrival of the English, Charles of Blois
abandoned the siege in despair. For the rest of the year the
war was waged on a more equal footing. In August Edward
sent to Brest an additional force under William Bohun, Earl
of Northampton, who attempted, though with little success, to
invade the domains of the house of Penthièvre. A hard-won
victory against great odds near Morlaix was made memorable
by Northampton's first applying the tactics of Halidon Hill to a
pitched battle on the continent.[1] But the earl's troops were
so few that they were forced to withdraw after their success
into more friendly regions. Léon and Cornouailles then resumed
allegiance to the house of Montfort. In the midst of the struggle
Robert of Artois received a wound which soon ended his tempestuous career.

Edward was eager to enter the field in person. Since his
return to England in 1340, his only military experience had
been a luckless winter campaign in the Lothians against King
David. In October, 1342, he left the Duke of Cornwall as
warden of England during his absence, and took ship at Sandwich for Brittany. He remained in the country until the early
months of 1343, raiding the land from end to end, receiving
many of the greater barons into his obedience, and striving in
particular to conquer the regions included in the modern de-
partment of the Morbihan. There he besieged Vannes, the
strongest and largest city of Brittany, says Froissart, after
Nantes. The triumphs of his rival at last brought Philip VI.
into Brittany. While Edward laboriously pursued the siege of
Vannes, amidst the hardships of a wet and stormy winter, Philip
watched his enemy from Ploermel, a few miles to the north.
For a third time the situation of Buironfosse and Tournai was
renewed. The rivals were within striking distance, but once
more both Edward and Philip were afraid to strike. History
still further repeated itself; for the cardinal-bishops of Palestrina
and Frascati, sent by Clement VI. to end the struggle, travelled
from camp to camp with talk of peace. The sufferings of both

---

[1] Baker, p. 76, gives the place, Knighton, ii., 25, the details. See also
my note in *Engl. Hist. Review*, xix. (1904), 713-15.

armies gave the kings a powerful reason for listening to their advances. At last, on January 19, 1343, a truce for nearly four years was signed at Malestroit, midway between Ploermel and Vannes, " in reverence of mother church, for the honour of the cardinals, and that the parties shall be able to declare their reasons before the pope, not for the purpose of rendering a judicial decision, but in order to make a better peace and treaty". Scotland and the Netherlands were included in the truce, and it was agreed that each belligerent should continue in the enjoyment of the territories which he held at the moment. Vannes, the immediate apple of discord, was put into the hands of the pope.

The spring of 1343 saw Edward back in England. The scene of interest shifted to the papal court at Avignon, where ambassadors from Edward and Philip appeared to declare their masters' rights. The protracted negotiations were lacking in reality. The English, distrusting Clement as a French partisan, did their best to complicate the situation by complaints against papal provisions in favour of aliens " not having knowledge of the tongue nor condition of those whose governance and care should belong to them ". English indignation rose higher when, despite the terms of the truce and the promise of the cardinals, Montfort remained immured in his French prison, while Breton nobles of his faction were kidnapped and put to death by Philip. Clement declared himself against Edward's claims to the French throne, and, long before the negotiations had reached a formal conclusion, it was clear that nothing would come of them. At last in 1345 the English King denounced the truce and prepared to renew the war. His first concern was necessarily finance, and he had already exhausted all his resources as a borrower. The financial difficulties, which had stayed his career in the Netherlands five years before, had reached their culmination. Stratford was avenged for the outrages of 1340, for Edward was in worse embarrassments than on that winter night when the glare of torches illuminated the sovereign's sudden return to the Tower. The king's Netherlandish, Rhenish, and Italian creditors would trust him no longer and vainly clamoured for the repayment of their advances. " We grieve," he was forced to reply to the Cologne magistrates, " nay, we blush, that we are unable to meet our obligations at the due time." Edward's anxiety to prepare for fresh campaigns made him careless as to his former obligations. His wholesale neglect to repay his debts drove the great banking houses of the Bardi and the Peruzzi into bankruptcy, and the failure of the English king's creditors plunged all Florence into deep distress.

One good result came from the king's dishonour. The foreign sources of supply having dried up, Edward was forced to lean more exclusively upon his English subjects. A wealthy family of Hull merchants, recently transferred to London, became very flourishing. Its head, William de la Pole, who had financed every government scheme since the days of Mortimer, became a knight, a judge, a territorial magnate, and the first English merchant to found a baronial house. And as the credit of the English merchants was limited, Edward was forced more and more to rely upon parliamentary grants. The memory of the king's want of faith to the estates of 1341 had died away, and a parliament, which met in 1344, once more made Edward liberal contributions. Secure of his subjects' support, the frivolous king largely employed his resources in the chivalrous pageantry which stirred up the martial ardour of his barons and made the war popular. It was then that he resolved to set up a "round table" at Windsor after the fabled fashion of King Arthur. From this came the foundation of the Round Tower which Edward was to erect in his favourite abode, and the organised chivalry that was soon to culminate in the Order of the Garter.

In the summer of 1345 Edward made that journey to Sluys, which has already been noted, and he held on ship-board his last interview with James van Artevelde. His immediate return to England showed that he had no mind to renew his Flemish alliances. In the same year the death of the queen's brother, William of Avesnes, established the rule of Louis of Bavaria in the three counties of Holland, Zealand, and Hainault in the right of his wife, Philippa's elder sister. Edward put in a claim on behalf of his queen, which further embittered his already uneasy relations with Louis, and led him to seek his field of combat anywhere rather than in the Netherlands. In Brittany the murder of the nobles of Montfort's faction had given an excuse for the renewal of partisan warfare as early as 1343, but Montfort was still under surveillance in France, even after his release from Philip's prison, and Joan of Flanders, the heroic defender of Hennebont, was hopelessly insane in England. At last in

1345 Montfort ventured to flee from France to England, where CHAP.
he did homage to Edward as King of France for the duchy XVI.
which he claimed.   He then went to Brittany, and there shortly
afterwards died.   The new Duke of Brittany, also named
John, was a mere boy when he was thus robbed of both his
parents' care, and his cause languished for want of a head.
Edward took upon himself the whole direction of Brittany as
tutor of the little duke.   Northampton was once more sent
thither, but for a time the war degenerated into sieges of castles
and petty conflicts.

While action was thus impracticable in the Netherlands, and
ineffective in Brittany, Gascony became, for the first time during
the struggle, the scene of military operations of the first rank.
The storm of warfare had hitherto almost spared the patrimony of the English king in southern France.   No great effort
was made either by the French to capture the last bulwarks of
the Aquitanian inheritance, or by Edward to extend his duchy
to its ancient limits.   Cut off from other fields of expansion,
Edward threw his chief energies into the enlargement of his power
in southern France.   He won over many of those Gascon nobles,
including the powerful lord of Albret, who had been alienated
by his former indifference.   All was ready for action, and in
June, 1345, Henry of Grosmont, Earl of Derby, the eldest son
of Henry of Lancaster, landed at Bayonne with a sufficient
English force to encourage the lords of Gascony to rally round
the ducal banner.   Soon after his landing, the death of his blind
father made Derby Earl of Lancaster.   During the next eighteen
months, the earl successfully led three raids into the heart of
the enemies' territory.[1]   The first, begun very soon after his landing, occupied the summer of 1345.   Advancing from Libourne,
the limit of the Anglo-Gascon power, Henry made his way up
the Dordogne, a fleet of boats co-operating with his land forces.
He took the important town of Bergerac, and thence, mounting
the stream as far as Lalinde, he crossed the hills separating the
Dordogne from the Isle, and unsuccessfully assaulted Périgueux.
Thence he advanced still further, and captured the stronghold of
Auberoche, dominating the rocky valley of the Auvézère.   Leav-

---

[1] For these campaigns, see Ribadieu, *Les Campagnes du Comte de Derby en
Guyenne, Saintonge et Poitou* (1865).

CHAP.
XVI.

ing a garrison at Auberoche, Henry returned to his base, but upon his withdrawal the French closely besieged his conquest, and the earl made a sudden move to its relief. On October 21 he won a brisk battle outside the walls of Auberoche before the more sluggish part of his army had time to reach the scene of action. This famous exploit again established the Gascon duke in Périgord.

Early in 1346 the victor of Auberoche led his forces up the Garonne valley. La Réole, lost since 1325, was taken in January, and thence Earl Henry marched to the capture of many a town and fortress on the Garonne and the lower Lot. His most important acquisition was Aiguillon, commanding the junction of the Lot and the Garonne, for its possession opened up the way for the reconquest of the Agenais, the rich fruit of the last campaign of Charles of Valois. Duke John of Normandy then appeared upon the scene, and Henry of Lancaster withdrew before him to the line of the Dordogne. Aiguillon stood a siege from April to August, when the Duke of Normandy, then at the end of his resources, solicited a truce. News having come to Lancaster at Bergerac that Edward had begun his memorable invasion of Normandy, he contemptuously rejected the proposal. Before long, Duke John raised the siege and hurried to his father's assistance. Thereupon Lancaster returned to the Garonne and revictualled Aiguillon. Immediately after he started on his third raid. This time he bent his steps northwards, and late in September was at Châteauneuf on the Charente, whence he threatened Angoulême, and finally obtained its surrender. Crossing the Charente, he entered French Saintonge, where the important town of Saint-Jean-d'Angely opened its gates and took oaths to Edward as duke and king. Then he boldly dashed into the heart of Poitou, marching by Lusignan to Poitiers. "We rode before the city," wrote Lancaster, "and summoned it, but they would do nothing. Thereupon on the Wednesday after Michaelmas we stormed the city, and all those within were taken or slain. And the lords that were within fled away on the other side, and we tarried full eight days. Thus we have made a fair raid, God be thanked, and are come again to Saint-Jean, whence we propose to return to Bordeaux." This exploit ended Lancaster's Gascon career. In January, 1347, he was back in England, having restored the

reputation of his king in Gascony, and set an example of heroism
soon to be emulated by his cousin, the Black Prince.

Edward resolved to take the field in person in the summer of 1346. Special efforts were made to equip the army, and lovers of ancient precedent were dismayed when the king called upon all men of property to equip archers, hobblers, or men-at-arms, according to their substance, that they might serve abroad at the king's wages. But the nation responded to the king's call, and a host of some 2,400 cavalry and 10,000 archers and other infantry collected at Portsmouth between Easter and the early summer.[1] There were the usual delays of a medieval muster, and it was not until July was well begun that Edward, having constituted his second son Lionel of Antwerp, a boy of six, as regent, took ship at Portsmouth with his eldest son, then sixteen years of age, and, since 1343, Prince of Wales as well as Duke of Cornwall. The destination of the army was a secret, but Edward's original idea seems to have been to join Henry of Lancaster in Gascony, though we may well believe that the resources of medieval transport were hardly adequate to convey so large a force for so great a distance. Moreover, a persistent series of south-westerly winds prohibited all attempts to round the Breton peninsula, while Godfrey of Harcourt, a Norman lord who had incurred the wrath of Philip VI. and had been driven into exile, persistently urged on Edward the superior attractions of his native coast. When the fleet set sail from Portsmouth, it was directed to follow in the admiral's track; and as soon as the open sea was gained, the ships were instructed to make their way to the Côtentin. On July 12 the English army reached Saint-Vaast de la Hougue, and spent five days in disembarking and ravaging the neighbourhood.[2] Immediately on landing, Edward dubbed the Prince of Wales a knight, along with other young nobles, one of whom was Roger

[1] On the details of this force, see Wrottesley, *Crecy and Calais*, in *Collections for a History of Staffordshire*, vol. xviii. (1897); *cf.* J. E. Morris in *Engl. Hist. Review*, xiv., 766-69.

[2] Besides the sources for this campaign mentioned in Sir E. M. Thompson, *Chronicle of Geoffrey le Baker*, pp. 252-57, the disregarded *Acta bellicosa Edwardi*, etc., published in Moisant, *Le Prince Noir en Aquitaine*, pp. 157-74, from a Corpus Christi Coll. Cambridge MS., should be mentioned. It has first been utilised in H. Prentout's valuable paper, *La prise de Caen par Édouard III. en 1346*, in *Mémoires de l'Académie de Caen* (1904).

Mortimer, the grandson and heir of the traitor Earl of March. At last, on July 18, the English army began to move by slow stages to the south. It met with little resistance, and plundered and burnt the rich countryside at its discretion. The English marvelled at the fertility of the country and the size and wealth of its towns. Barfleur was as big as Sandwich, Carentan reminded them of Leicester, Saint-Lô was the size of Lincoln, and Caen was more populous than any English city save London.

It was only at Caen that any real resistance was encountered. On July 26 Edward's soldiers entered the northern quarter of the town without opposition, to find the fortified enclosures of the two great abbeys of William the Conqueror and his queen undefended and desolate, the *grand bourg*, the populous quarter round the church of St. Peter open to them, and only the castle in the extreme north garrisoned. Caen was not a walled town, and the defenders preferred to limit themselves to holding the southern quarter, the *Ile Saint-Jean*, which lay between the district of St. Peter's and the river Orne, but was cut off from the rest by a branch of the Orne that ran just south of St. Peter's church. There was sharp fighting at the bridge which commanded access to the island ; but the English archers prepared the way, and then the men-at-arms completed the work. After a determined conflict, the Island of St. John was captured, and its chief defenders, the Count of Eu, Constable of France, and the lord of Tancarville, the chamberlain, were taken prisoners. Meanwhile the English fleet, which had devastated the whole coast from Cherbourg to Ouistreham, arrived off the mouth of the Orne, laden with plunder and eager to get back home with its spoils. Edward thought it prudent to avoid a threatened mutiny by ordering the ships to recross the Channel, and take with them the captives and the loot which he had amassed at Caen. During a halt of five days at Caen, Edward discovered a copy of the agreement made between the Normans and King Philip for the invasion of England eight years before. This also he despatched to England, where it was read before the Londoners by the Archbishop of Canterbury in order to show that the aggression was not all on one side.

On July 31, Edward resumed his eastward march. At

Lisieux, the next important stage, came the inevitable two cardinals with their inevitable proposals of mediation, which Edward put aside with scant civility. The army was soon once more on the move, and on August 7 struck the Seine at Elbeuf, a few miles higher up the river than Rouen. Here Edward was at last in touch with his enemy. During the English march through lower Normandy, Philip VI. had assembled a considerable army, with which he occupied the Norman capital. Nothing but the Seine and a few miles of country separated the two forces. But as at Buironfosse, at Tournai, and at Vannes, the French declined to attack, and Edward would not depart from his tradition of acting on the defensive. The English slowly made their way up the left bank of the Seine, avoiding the stronger castles and walled towns, and devastating the open country. The French followed them on the right bank, carefully watching their movements, and breaking all the bridges. So things went until, on August 13, Edward reached Poissy, a town within fifteen miles of the capital.

The English advanced troops plundered up to the walls of Paris, whose citizens, watching in terror the flames that made lurid the western sky, implored their king to come to their help. From Saint-Denis Philip issued a challenge to Edward to meet him in the open field on a fixed day. Edward, however, was not to be tempted by such appeals to his chivalry. The day after Philip's message was sent, he repaired the bridge at Poissy, crossed the Seine, sent a stinging reply to Philip's letter, and moved rapidly northwards. Avoiding Pontoise, Beauvais, and other towns, he was soon within a few miles of the Somme. Long marching had fatigued his army, and he resolved to retreat to the Flemish frontier. The French soon followed him by a route some miles further towards the east. They reached the Somme earlier than the English, and were pouring into Amiens and Abbeville, while Edward's scouts were vainly seeking for an unguarded passage over the river. If the Somme could not be crossed, there was every chance of Edward's war-worn army being driven into a corner at Saint-Valéry, between the broad and sandy estuary of the Somme and the open sea. When affairs had become thus critical, local guides revealed to the English a way across the estuary, where a white band of chalk, called the *Blanche taque*, cropping out of the sandy river bed, forms a hard, practicable ford from one bank of the river to the other. "Then," writes an official reporter, "the King of England and his host took that water of the Somme, where never man passed before without loss, and fought their enemies, and chased them right up to the gate of Abbeville." That night Edward and his troops slept on the outskirts of the forest of Crecy. After traversing this, they took up a strong position on the northern side of the wood on Saturday, August 26. There, in the heart of his grand-mother's inheritance of Ponthieu, Edward elected to make a stand, and, for the first time in all their campaigning, Philip felt sufficient confidence to engage in an offensive battle against his rival.

Ponthieu is a land of low chalk downs, open fields, and dense woods, broken by valleys, through which the small streams that water it trickle down to the sea, and by the waterless depressions characteristic of a chalk country. The village of Crecy-en-Ponthieu is situated on the north bank of the little river Maye. Immediately to the east of the village, a lateral depression, running north and south, called the *Vallée aux Clercs*, falls down into the Maye valley, and is flanked with rolling downs, perhaps 150 to 200 feet in height. On the summit of the western slopes of this valley, Edward stationed his army. Its right was held by the first of the three traditional "battles," under the personal command of the young Prince of Wales. Its front and right flank were protected by the hill, while still further to the right lay Crecy village embowered in its trees, beyond which the dense forest formed an excellent protection from attack. The second of the English battles, under the Earls of Northampton and Arundel, held the less formidable slopes of the upper portion of the *Vallée aux Clercs*, their left resting on the enclosures and woods of the village of Wadicourt. The third battle, commanded by the king himself, and stationed in the rear as a reserve, held the rolling upland plain, on the highest point of which was a windmill, commanding the whole field, in which Edward took up his quarters. The English men-at-arms left their horses in the rear. The archers of each of the two forward battles were thrown out at an angle on the flanks, so that the enemy, on approaching the serried mass of men-at-arms, had to encounter a severe discharge of arrows both from the right and the left. It was the tactics of Halidon hill, perfected by experience and for the first time applied on a large scale against a continental enemy. The credit of it may well be assigned to Northampton, fresh from the fight at Morlaix, where similar tactics had already won the day.

The English were in position early in the morning of Saturday, August 26, and employed their leisure in further strengthening their lines by digging shallow holes, like the pits at Bannockburn, in the hope of ensnaring the French cavalry, if they came to close quarters with the dismounted men-at-arms. The summer day had almost ended its course before the French army appeared. Philip and his men had passed the previous night at Abbeville, and had not only performed the long march from the capital of Ponthieu, but many of them, misled by bad information as to Edward's position, had made a weary detour to the north-west. It was not until the hour of vespers that the mass of the French host was marshalled in front of the village of Estrées on the eastward plateau beyond the *Vallée aux Clercs.* John of Hainault, who had become a thorough-going French partisan, advised Philip to delay battle until the following day. The French were tired ; all the army had not yet come up ; night would soon put an end to the combat ; the evening sun, shining brightly after a violent summer storm, was blazing directly in the faces of the assailants. But the French nobles demanded an immediate advance. Confident in their numbers and prowess, they had already assured themselves of victory, and were quarrelling about the division of the captives they would make. Philip, too sympathetic with the feudal point of view to oppose his friends, ordered the advance.

The battle began by the French sending forward a strong force of Genoese crossbowmen, to prepare the way for the cavalry charge. But the long bows of the English outshot the obsolete and cumbrous weapons of the Genoese, whose strings had been wetted by the recent storm. The Italians descended into the valley, but were soon demoralised by seeing their comrades fall all round them, while their own bolts failed to reach the enemy. They were already in full retreat back up the slope, when the impatience of the French horsemen burst all bounds. The reckless cavalry charge swept right through the disordered ranks of the crossbowmen, whose groans and cries as they were trampled underfoot by the mail-clad steeds, inspired the rear ranks of the French with the vain belief that the English were hard pressed, and made them eager to join the fray. The charge, as disorderly and as badly directed as the fatal attack of Bannockburn, never reached the English ranks. Shot down right and left by archers, terrified by the fearful booming of three small cannon that the English had dragged about during their wanderings, the French line soon became a confused mob of furious horsemen on panic-stricken horses. With gallantry even more conspicuous than their want of discipline, the French made no less than fifteen attempts to penetrate the enemies' lines. At one point only did they get near their goal, and that was on the right battle where the Prince of Wales himself was in command. A timely reinforcement sent by King Edward relieved the pressure, and the French were soon in full retreat, protected, as the English boasted, from further attack by the rampart of dead that they left behind them. The darkness, which ended the struggle, forbade all pursuit. Next day the fight was renewed by fresh French forces, but a fog hampered their movements, and they fell easy victims to the English. Then the defeated force retreated to Abbeville. The English loss was insignificant, but the field was covered with the bravest and noblest of the French. Among those who perished on the side of Philip were Louis of Nevers, the chivalrous Count of Flanders, who had sacrificed everything save his honour on the altar of feudal duty, and the blind King John of Bohemia, whose end was as romantic and futile as his life. Both these princes left as their successors sons of very different stamp in Louis de Male and Charles of Moravia. Charles, who had recently been set up as King of the Romans by the clerical party against Louis of Bavaria, was present at Crecy, but a prudent retreat saved him from his father's fate.

In the midst of the Norman campaign, Philip urgently besought David, King of Scots, to make a diversion in his favour. Since 1341 David, then a youth of seventeen, had been back in Scotland. Prolonged truces gave him little opportunity of trying his skill as a soldier, and his domestic rule was not particularly successful. The full effects of the Franco-Scottish alliance were revealed when, early in October, the Scottish king invaded the north of England, confident that, as all the fighting-

men were in France, he would meet no more formidable opponents than monks, peasants, and shepherds.   The five days'
resistance of Lord Wake's border peel of Castleton in Liddes-
dale showed the baselessness of this imagination.   At its capture
on October 10, David put to death its gallant captain, a knight
named Walter Selby.   Then the Scots streamed over the hills
into Upper Tynedale, and soon devastated Durham.   Such
of the border lords as were not with the king in France had
now prepared for resistance.   Beside the Nevilles, Percys, and
other great houses of the north, the Archbishop of York,
William de la Zouch, took a vigorous part in organising the
local levies, and in a very short space of time a sufficient
army assembled to make head against the invaders.   From
their muster at Richmond, the northern barons marched into
the land of St. Cuthbert, many priests following their archbishop as of old their predecessors had followed Melton or
Thurstan.   On October 17 the forces joined battle at Neville's
Cross, a wayside landmark on the Red hills, a rough and
broken region sloping down to the Wear, immediately to the
west of the city of Durham.   Neither host was large in size,
and each stood facing the other, with the archers at either
wing, after the fashion that had become Scottish as well as
English.   For a time neither army was willing to begin.   At last
the English archers, irritated at the delay, advanced upon the
Scots with showers of missiles.   Then the struggle grew general
and after a fierce hand-to-hand fight the English prevailed.
David was taken prisoner and was lodged in the Tower, and
many of the noblest of the Scots lay dead on the field.   The
diversion was a failure ; the local levies had proved amply
sufficient to cope with the enemy.   In thus playing the game
of the French king, David began a policy which, from Neville's
Cross to Flodden, brought embarrassment to England and desolation to Scotland.   It was the inevitable penalty of two independent
and hostile states existing in one little island.

So war-worn were the victors of Crecy that all the profit
they could win from the battle was the power to continue their
march undisturbed to the sea coast.   On September 4, Edward
reached the walls of Calais, the last French town on the frontiers of Flanders, and the port whose corsairs had inflicted exceptional damage on English shipping during the whole of the war,

With a keen eye to the military importance of the place, the King abandoned the easy course of returning with his troops to England, and at once sat down before Calais. It was an arduous and prolonged siege. Calais was girt by double walls and ditches of exceptional strength and was bravely defended by John de Vienne and a numerous garrison. Moreover the yielding soil of the sands and marshes around the town made it impossible for Edward to erect against the fortifications the cumbrous machines by which engineers then sought to batter down the walls of towns. The only method of taking the place was by starvation. At first Edward was not able to block every avenue of access to the beleaguered fortress. Winter came on; the troops demanded permission to go home; the sailors threatened mutiny, and the French were actively on the watch.

Amidst these troubles, Edward III. showed a persistence worthy of his grandfather. He remained at the seat of war, transacting much of the business of government in the town of wooden huts which, growing up round the besiegers' lines, made the winter siege endurable. In the worst period of the year sufficient forces to man the trenches could only be secured by wholesale charters of pardon to felonious and offending soldiers, on condition that they did not withdraw from service without the king's licence, so long as Edward himself remained beyond the seas.[1] A parliament of magnates met in March, 1347, and granted an aid. Instead of summoning the commons, Edward preferred to raise his chief supplies by another loan of 20,000 sacks of wool from the merchants, by additional customs dues voted by a merchant assembly, and by considerable loans from ecclesiastics and religious houses. In April and May all England was alive with martial preparation, and gradually a force far transcending the Crecy army was gathered round the walls of Calais, while a great fleet held the sea and prohibited the access of French ships to the doomed garrison. Northampton, ever fertile in expedients, discovered that, even after the high seas were blocked, boats still crept into Calais port by hugging the shallow shore. He ran long jetties of piles from the coast line into deep water, and thus cut off the last means of communication and of supplies. By June the town was suffering severely from famine.

[1] See for this, *Rotulus Normanniæ* in *Cal. Patent Rolls*, 1345-48, especially pp. 473-526. For the vast force gathered later, see Wrottesley and Morris, *u.s.*

The French made a great effort, both by sea and land, to relieve Calais. On June 25 Northampton went out with his ships as far as the mouth of the Somme, where off Le Crotoy he won a naval victory which made the English command of the sea absolutely secure. A month later Philip, at the head of the land army, looked down upon the lines of Calais from the heights of Guînes. The two cardinals made their usual efforts for a truce, but the English would not allow their prey to be snatched from them at the eleventh hour. Then Philip challenged the enemy to a pitched battle, and four knights on each side were appointed to select the place of combat. The French, however, were of no mind to risk another Crecy, and on the morning of July 31 the smoke of their burning camp told the English that once more Philip had shrunk from a meeting. Then at last the garrison opened its gates on August 3, 1347. The defenders were treated chivalrously by the victor, who admired their courage and endurance. But the mass of the population were removed from their homes, and numerous grants of houses and property made to Englishmen. Edward resolved to make his conquest an English town, and, from that time onwards, it became the fortress through which an English army might at any time be poured into France, and the warehouse from which the spinners and weavers of Flanders were to draw their supplies of raw wool. For more than two hundred years, English Calais retained all its military and most of its commercial importance. Later conquests enabled a ring of forts to be erected round it which strengthened its natural advantages.

Crecy, Neville's Cross, Aiguillon, and Calais did not exhaust the glories of this strenuous time. The war of the Breton succession, which Northampton had waged since 1345, was continued in 1346 by Thomas Dagworth, a knight appointed as his lieutenant on his withdrawal to join the army of Crecy and Calais. The Montfort star was still in the ascendant, and even the hereditary dominions of Joan of Penthièvre were assailed. An English garrison was established at La Roche Derien, situated some four miles higher up the river Jaudy than the little open episcopal city of Tréguier, and communicating by the river with the sea and with England. So troublesome did Montfort's garrison at La Roche become to the vassals of Penthièvre, that in the summer of 1347 Charles of Blois col-

CHAP.
XVI.

lected an army, wherein nearly all the greatest feudal houses of Brittany were strongly represented, and sat down before La Roche. Dagworth, one of the ablest of English soldiers, was at Carhaix, in the heart of the central uplands, when he heard of the danger of the single English post within the lands of Penthièvre. He at once hurried northwards, and on the night of June 19 rested at the abbey of Bégard, about ten miles to the south of La Roche. From Bégard two roads led to La Roche, one on each bank of the Jaudy. Thinking that Dagworth would pursue the shorter road on the left bank, Charles of Blois stationed a portion of his army at some distance from La Roche on that side of the Jaudy, while the rest remained with himself on the right bank before the walls of the town. Dagworth, however, chose the longer route, and before daybreak, on the morning of June 20, fell suddenly upon Charles. A fierce fight in the dark was ended after dawn in favour of Montfort by a timely sally of the beleaguered garrison. In the confusion Charles forgot to recall the division uselessly stationed beyond the Jaudy, and this error completed his ruin. Charles fought like a hero, and, after receiving seventeen wounds, yielded up his sword to a Breton lord rather than to the English commander. When his wounds were healed, Charles was sent to London, where he joined David of Scotland, the Count of Eu, and the Lord of Tancarville. It looked as if Montfort's triumph was secured.

In the midst of his successes Edward made a truce, yielding to the earnest request of the cardinals, " through his reverence to the apostolic see ". The truce of Calais was signed on September 28, and included Scotland and Brittany as well as France within its scope. On October 12 Edward returned to his kingdom. Financial exhaustion, the need of repose, the unwillingness of his subjects to continue the combat, and the failure of the Flemish and Netherlandish alliances sufficiently explain this halt in the midst of victory. Yet from the military standpoint Edward's action, harmful everywhere to his partisans, was particularly fatal in Brittany, where most of Penthièvre and nearly all upper Brittany were still obedient to Charles of Blois.[1] But Edward had embarked upon a course infinitely beyond his material resources. When a special effort could only give him the one town of Calais, how could he ever conquer all France?

[1] See on this A. de la Borderie, *Hist. de Bretagne*, iii., 507, *et seq.*

CHAPTER XVII.

FROM THE BLACK DEATH TO THE TREATY OF CALAIS.

AT the conclusion of the truce of Calais in 1347, Edward III. and England were at the height of their military reputation. Perhaps the nation was in even a stronger position than the monarch. Edward had dissipated his resources in winning his successes, but the danger which faced the ruler had but slightly impaired the fortunes of his subjects. The country was in a sufficiently prosperous condition to bear its burdens without much real suffering. The widespread dislike of extraordinary taxation, which so often assumed the form of the familiar cry that the king must live of his own, had taken the shape of unwillingness to accept responsibility for the king's policy and a growing indisposition to meet his demands. But since the rule of Edward began, England enjoyed a prosperity so unbroken that far heavier burdens would hardly have brought about a diminution of the well-being which stood in glaring contrast to the desolation long inflicted by Edward's wars on France. A war waged exclusively on foreign soil did little harm to England, and offered careers whereby many an English adventurer was gaining a place among the landed classes. The simple archers and men-at-arms, who received high wages and good hopes of plunder in the king's foreign service, found in it a congenial and lucrative, if demoralising profession. In England, though wages were low, provisions were cheap and employment constant. The growth of the wool trade, then further stimulated by refugees from the "three towns of Flanders," against which Louis de Male was waging relentless war, was bringing comfort to many, and riches to a few. The maritime greatness of England that found its first results in the battle of Sluys was the fruit of a commercial activity on the sea which enabled English shipmen to deprive the Italians, Netherlanders, and Germans of the overwhelming share they had hitherto enjoyed of our foreign trade. The dark shadows of medieval life were indeed never absent from the picture ; but medieval England seldom enjoyed greater well-being and tranquillity than during the first eighteen years of the personal rule of Edward III. One sign of the increasing attention paid to suppressing disorder was an act of 1344, which empowered the local conservators of the peace, already an element in the administrative machinery, to hear and determine felonies. A later act made this a part of their regular functions, and gave them the title of justices of the peace, thus setting up a means of maintaining local order so effective that the old machinery of the local courts gradually gave way to it.

A rude ending to this period of prosperity was brought about by the devastations of the pestilence known to modern readers as the Black Death, which since 1347 had decimated the Levant. This was the bubonic plague, almost as familiar in the east of to-day as in the mid-fourteenth century. It was brought along the chief commercial highways which bound the western world to the markets of the east. First introduced into the west at the great ports of the Mediterranean, Venice, Genoa, Marseilles, it spread over France and Italy by the early months of 1348. Avignon was a chief centre of the infection, and, amidst the desolation around him, Clement VI. strove with rare energy to give peace to a distracted world. The regions of western and northern France, which had felt the full force of the war, were among the worst sufferers. Aquitaine, too, was cruelly desolated, and among the victims was Edward III.'s daughter, Joan, who perished at Bordeaux on her way to Castile, as the bride of the prince afterwards infamous as Peter the Cruel. Early in August, 1348, the scourge crossed the channel, making its first appearance in England at Weymouth. Thence it spread northwards and westwards. Bristol was the first great English town to feel its ravages. Though the Gloucestershire men prohibited all intercourse between the infected port and their own villages, the plague was in no wise stayed by their precautions. The disease extended, by way of Gloucester and Oxford, to London, reaching the capital early in November, and continuing its ravages until the following Whitsuntide. When it had almost died out in London, it began, in the spring of 1349, to rage

severely in East Anglia,[1] while in Lancashire the worst time
seems to have been from the autumn of 1349 to the beginning
of 1350.[2] Scotland was so long exempt that the Scots, proud
of their immunity, were wont to swear " by the foul death of
England ". In 1350 they gathered together an army in Ettrick
forest with the object of invading the plague-stricken border
shires. But the pestilence fell upon the host assembled for the
foray, and all war was stopped while Scotland was devastated
from end to end. Ireland began to suffer in August, 1349, the
disease being at first confined to the Englishry of the towns,
though, after a time, it made its way also to the pure Irish.[3]

The wild exaggerations of the chroniclers reflect the horror
and desolation wrought by the epidemic. There died so many, we
are told, that the survivors scarcely sufficed to bury the victims,
and not one man in ten remained alive. The more moderate
estimate of Froissart sets down the proportion dead of the
plague as one in three throughout all Christendom, and some
modern inquirers have rashly reckoned the mortality in England
as amounting to a half or a third of the population. In truth,
complete statistics are necessarily wanting, and if the records of
the admissions of the clergy attest that, in certain dioceses, half
the livings changed hands during the years of pestilence, it is not
permissible to infer from that circumstance that there was a
similar rate of mortality from the plague over the whole of the
population. The sudden and overwhelming character of the
disorder increased the universal terror. One day a man was
healthy : within a few hours of the appearance of the fatal
swelling, or of the dark livid marks which gave the plague its
popular name, he was a corpse. The pestilence seemed to single
out the young and robust as its prey, and to spare the aged
and sick. The churchyards were soon overflowing, and special
plague pits had to be dug where the dead were heaped up by

---

[1] A. Jessopp, *The Black Death in East Anglia*, in *The Coming of the Friars
and Other Essays* (1889). For general details see F. Seebohm, *The Black Death*,
in *Fortnightly Review* (1865 and 1866) ; J. E. T. Rogers, *England before and after
the Black Death*, in *Fortnightly Review* (1866) ; F. A. Gasquet's *Great Pestilence*
(1893) ; and C. Creighton, *History of Epidemics in Britain*, i., 114-207 (1891).

[2] A. G. Little, *The Black Death in Lancashire*, in *Engl. Hist. Review*, v.
(1890), 524-30.

[3] See for Ireland, however, the vivid details in J. Clyn of Kilkenny, *Annales
Hiberniæ ad annum 1349*, ed. R. Butler, *Irish Archæological Soc.* (1849).

the hundred.   Comparatively few magnates died, but the poor, the religious, and the clergy were chief sufferers.   The law courts ceased to hold regular sessions.   When the people had partially recovered from the first visitations of the plague, others befel them which were scarcely less severe.   The years 1362 and 1369 almost rivalled the horrors of 1348 and 1349.

The immediate effects of the calamity were overwhelming. At first the horror of the foul death effaced all other considerations from men's minds.   There were not enough priests to absolve the dying, and special indulgences, with full liberty to choose confessors at discretion, were promulgated from Avignon and from many diocesan chanceries.   The price of commodities fell for the moment, since there were few, we are told, who cared for riches amidst the general fear of death.   The pestilence played such havoc with the labouring population that the beasts wandered untended in the pastures, and rich crops of corn stood rotting in the fields from lack of harvesters to gather them.   There was the same lack of clergy as of labourers, and the priest, like the peasant, demanded a higher wage for his services by reason of the scarcity of labour.   A mower was not to be had for less than a shilling a day with his food, and a chaplain, formerly glad to receive two marks and his board, demanded ten pounds, or ten marks at the least.   Non-residence, neglect of cures, and other evils followed.   As Langland wrote :—

> Persones and parisch prestes · playneth to heore bisschops,
> That heore parisch hath ben pore · seththe the pestilence tyme,
> And asketh leue and lycence · at Londun to dwelle,
> To singe ther for simonye · for seluer is swete.[1]

The lack of clergy was in some measure compensated by the rush of candidates for orders.   Some of these new clerks were men who had lost their wives by the plague ; many of them were illiterate, or if they knew how to read their mass-book, could not understand it.   The close social life of the monasteries proved particularly favourable to the spread of the disease ; the number of monks and nuns declined considerably, and, since there was no great desire to embrace the religious profession, many houses remained half empty for generations.

No one in the Middle Ages believed in letting economic laws work out their natural results.   If anything were amiss, it

---

[1] *Vision of Piers Plowman*, i., p. 9, ed. Skeat.

was the duty of kings and princes to set things right. Accordingly Edward and his council at once strove to remedy
the lack of labourers by ordinances that harvesters and other
workmen should not demand more wages than they had been
in the habit of receiving, while the bishops, following the royal
example, ordered chaplains and vicars to be content with their
accustomed salaries. As soon as parliament ventured to assemble,
the royal orders were embodied in the famous statute of
labourers of 1351. This measure has been condemned as an
attempt of a capitalist parliament to force poor men to work
for their masters at wages far below the market rates. But it
was no new thing to fix wages by authority, and the medieval
conception was that a just and living wage should be settled
by law, rather than left to accident. The statute provided that
prices, like wages, should remain as they had been before the
pestilence, so that, far from only regarding the interests of the
employer, it attempted to maintain the old ratio between the
rate of wages and the price of commodities. Moreover it sought
to provide for the cultivation of the soil by enacting that the
sturdy beggar, who, though able, refused to work, should be
forced to put his hand to the plough. Futile as the statute of
labourers was, it was not much more ineffective than most laws
of the time. Though real efforts were made to carry it out, the
chronic weakness of a medieval executive soon recoiled before
the hopeless task of enforcing impossible laws on an unwilling
population. Class prejudices only showed themselves in the
stipulation that, while the employer was forbidden to pay the
new rate of wages under pain of heavy fines, the labourers
who refused to work on the old terms were imprisoned and
only released upon taking oath to accept their ancient wages.
In effect, however, the king's arm was not long enough to reach
either class. The labourers, says a chronicler, were so puffed
up and quarrelsome that they would not observe the new
enactment, and the master's alternative was either to see his
crops perish unharvested, or to gratify the greedy desires of the
workmen by violating the statute. While labourers could
escape punishment through their numbers, the employer was
more accessible to the royal officers.

Thus the labourers enjoyed the benefits of the scarcity of
labour, while the employers suffered the full inconveniences of

the change.   Producers were to some extent recompensed by
a great rise in prices, more especially in the case of those commodities into whose cost of production labour largely entered.
For example the rise in the price of corn and meat was in-
considerable, while clothing, manufactured goods, and luxuries
became extraordinarily dear.   Of eatables fish rose most in
value, because the fishermen had been swept away by the
plague.   Rents fell heavily.   Landlords found that they could
only retain their tenants by wholesale remissions.   When farmers
perished of the plague, it was often impossible to find others
to take up their farms.   It was even harder for lords, who
farmed their own demesne, to provide themselves with the
necessary labour.   Hired labour could not be obtained except
at ruinous rates.   It was injudicious to press for the strict perfor-
mance of villein services, lest the villein should turn recalcitrant
and leave his holding.   The lord preferred to commute his villein's
service into a small payment.   On the whole the best solution
of the difficulty was for him to abandon the ancient custom of
farming his demesne through his bailiffs, and to let out his
lands on such rents as he could get to tenant farmers.   Thus
the feudal method of land tenure, which, since the previous
century, had ceased to have much political significance, became
economically ineffective, and began to give way to a system more
like that which still obtains among us.

Struck by these undoubted results of the pestilence, some
modern writers have persuaded themselves that the Black Death
is the one great turning-point in the social and economic history
of England, and that nearly all which makes modern England
what it is, is due to the effects of this pestilence.   A wider
survey suggests the extreme improbability of a single visitation
having such far-reaching consequences.   Moreover the Black
Death was not an English but a European calamity, and it is
strange to imagine that the effects of the plague in England
should have been so much deeper than in France or Germany,
and so different.   In the fourteenth century there was little
that was distinctly insular in the conditions of England, as compared with those of the continent.   A trouble common to both
regions alike could hardly have been the starting-point of such
differentiation between them as later ages undoubtedly witnessed.
There was a French counterpart to the statute of labourers,

In truth the Black Death was no isolated phenomenon. There were already in the air the seeds of the decay of the ancient order, and those seeds fructified more rapidly in England by reason of the plague.[1]   It is only because of the impetus which it gave to changes already in progress that the pestilence had in a fashion more lasting results in England than elsewhere. The last thirty years of the reign of Edward were an epoch of social upheaval and unrest contrasting strongly with the uneventful times that had preceded the Black Death. It is not right to regard the period as one of misery or severe distress. The war of classes, which was beginning, sprang not so much from material discomfort of the poor, as from what unsympathetic annalists called their greediness, their pride, and their wantonness. The wage-earner was master of the situation and did not hesitate to make his power felt. While the spread of manufactures, the rise of prices, and the opening out of wider markets still secured the prosperity of the shopkeeper, the merchant, or the artisan of the towns, the whole brunt of the social change fell upon the landed classes, and most heavily upon the ecclesiastics and especially upon the monks. Broken down by the heavy demands of the state, unable to share with the layman in the new avenues to wealth opened up by the expanding resources of the country, the monks saw the chief sources of their prosperity drying up. Their rents were shrinking and it became increasingly difficult to cultivate their lands. They never recovered their ancient welfare, and were already getting out of touch with the national life.

One immediate result of the plague was a renewed activity in founding religious houses. Upon the two plague pits west and east of the city of London, Sir Walter Manny set up his Charterhouse in Smithfield, and Edward III. his foundation for Cistercian nuns between Tower Hill and Aldgate. More characteristic of the times was the foundation of secular colleges, which were established either with mainly ecclesiastical objects or to encourage study at the universities. Both at Oxford and Cambridge there were more colleges set up in the first than in

---

[1] See for this W. Cunningham, *Growth of English Industry and Commerce*, vol. i., p. 330 ff. (ed. 4) ; T. W. Page, *The End of Villainage in England* (American Economic Association, 1900) ; and, above all, P. Vinogradoff in *Engl. Hist. Review*, xv. (1900), 774-781.

the second half of the fourteenth century ; and it is noteworthy that several Cambridge colleges incorporated after the plague were founded with the avowed motive of filling up the gaps in the secular clergy occasioned by it.   The riots between the Oxford townsmen and the clerks of the university on St. Scholastica's day, 1354, resulted in the victory of the former because of the recent diminution in the number of the scholars.   Yet even as regards the monasteries, it is easy to exaggerate the effects of the plague.   Five years after the Black Death, the Cistercians of the Lancashire abbey of Whalley boasted that they had added twenty monks to their convent, and were busy in enlarging their church.[1]

Change was in the air in religion as well as in society.   Along with democratic ideas filtering in with the exiles from the great Flemish cities, came a breath of that restless and unquiet spirit which soon awakened the concern of the inquisition in the Netherlands.   There brotherhoods, some mystical and quietistic, others enthusiastic and fanatical, were growing in numbers and importance.   Some of these bodies, Beguines, Beghards, and what not, were harmless enough, but the whole history of the Middle Ages bears testimony to the readiness with which religious excitement, unchastened by discipline or direction, grew into dangerous heresy.   The strangest of the new communities, the Flagellants, made its appearance in England immediately after the pestilence.   In the autumn of 1349, some six score men crossed over from Holland and marched in procession through the open spaces of London, chanting doleful litanies in their own tongue.   They wore nothing save a linen cloth that covered the lower part of their body, and on their heads hats marked with a red cross behind and before.   Each of them bore in his right hand a scourge, with which he belaboured the naked back and shoulders of his comrade in the fore rank.   Twice a day they repeated this mournful exercise, and even at other times were never seen in public but with cap on head and discipline in hand.   Few Englishmen joined the Flagellants, but their appearance is not unworthy of notice as the first concrete evidence of the religious unrest which soon became more widespread.   Before long the Yorkshireman, John Wy-

---

[1] *Cal. Papal Registers, Petitions,* i., 264.   Professor Tait, however, informs me that the monks took a sanguine view of their numbers.   After the plague of 1362, we know that they were not much more numerous than in the previous century.

cliffe, was studying arts at the little north-country foundation of the Balliols at Oxford, and John Ball, the Essex priest, was preaching his revolutionary socialism to the villeins. "We are all come," said he, "from one father and one mother, Adam and Eve. How can the gentry show that they are greater lords than we?"[1] In 1355 there were heretics in the diocese of York who maintained that it is impossible to merit eternal life by good works, and that original sin does not deserve damnation.[2]

The Flagellants were denounced as heretics by Clement VI.; the Archbishop of York proceeded against the northern heretics, and in 1366 the Archbishop of Canterbury forbade John Ball's preaching. But there were more insidious, because more measured, enemies of the Church than a handful of fanatics. The English were long convinced that the Avignon popes were playing the game of the French adversary, and Clement VI.'s efforts for peace never had a fair hearing. Since the beginning of the war, the king laid his hand on the alien priories, and, though in his scrupulous regard for clerical rights he had allowed the monks to remain in possession, he diverted the stream of tribute from the French mother houses to his own treasury. Bolder measures against papal provisions were taken in the years which immediately followed the pestilence. Finding remonstrances futile, the parliament of 1351, which passed the statute of labourers, enacted also the first statute of provisors. It recited that the anti-papal statute of Carlisle of 1307 was still law, and that the king had sworn to observe it. It claimed for all electing bodies and patrons the right to elect or to present freely to the benefices in their gift. It declared invalid all appointments brought about by way of papal provision. Provisors who had accepted appointments from Avignon were to be arrested. If convicted, they were to be detained in prison, until they had made their peace with the king, and found surety not to accept provisions in the future, and also not to seek their reinstatement by any process in the Roman *curia*. Two years

---

[1] The sentiment, or its equivalent in Ball's famous distich, was not new; it was employed for mystical purposes in Richard Rolle's
   " When Adam delf and Eue span, spir, if þou wil spede,
   Whare was þen the pride of man, þat now merres his mede ? "
Library of Early English Writers. Richard Rolle of Hampole and his followers, ed. Horstman, i., 73 (1895).

[2] *Cal. Papal Registers, Letters*, iii., 565.

later this measure was supplemented by the first statute of *præmunire*, which enacted that those who brought matters cognisable in the king's courts before foreign courts should be liable to forfeiture and outlawry.   Though the papal court is not specially mentioned, it is clear that this measure was aimed against it.

General measures proving insufficient, more specific legislation soon followed.   In 1365 a fresh statute of *præmunire* was drawn up on the initiative of the crown, enacting that all who obtained citations, offices, or benefices from the Roman court should incur the penalties prescribed by the act of 1353. The prelates dissociated themselves from so stringent a law, but did not actively oppose it.   When in 1366, Edward requested the guidance of the estates as to how he was to deal with the demand of Urban V. for the arrears of King John's tribute, withheld altogether for more than thirty years, the prelates joined the lay estates in answering that neither John nor any one else could put the realm into subjection without their consent.   Even the ancient offering of Peter's pence ceased to be paid for the rest of Edward's reign.   If these laws had been strictly carried out, the papal authority in England would have been gravely circumscribed.   But medieval laws were too often the mere enunciations of an ideal.   The statutes of provisors and *præmunire* were as little executed as were the statutes of labourers, or as some elaborate sumptuary legislation passed by the parliament of 1363.   The catalogue of acts of papal interference in English ecclesiastical and temporal affairs is as long after the passing of these laws as before.   Litigants still carried their suits to Avignon : provisions were still issued nominating to English benefices, and Edward himself set the example of disregarding his own laws by asking for the appointment of his ministers to bishoprics by way of papal provision.   Papal ascendency was too firmly rooted in the fourteenth century to be eradicated by any enactment.   To the average clergyman or theologian of the day the pope was still the " universal ordinary," the one divinely appointed source of ecclesiastical authority, the shepherd to whom the Lord had given the commission to feed His sheep.   This theory could only be overcome by revolution ; and the parliaments and ministers of Edward III. were in no wise of a revolutionary temper.

The antipapal laws of the fourteenth century were the acts of the secular not of the ecclesiastical power. They were not simply antipapal, they were also anticlerical in their tendency, since to the men of the age an attack on the pope was an attack on the Church. No doubt the English bishop at Edward's court sympathised with his master's dislike of foreign ecclesiastical interference, and the English priest was glad to be relieved from payments to the *curia*. But the clergyman, whose soul grew indignant against the curialists, still believed that the pope was the divinely appointed autocrat of the Church universal. Being a man, a pope might be a bad pope; but the faithful Christian, though he might lament and protest, could not but obey in the last resort. The papacy was so essentially interwoven with the whole Church of the Middle Ages, that few figments have less historical basis than the notion that there was an antipapal Anglican Church in the days of the Edwards. However, before another generation had passed away, ecclesiastical protests began.

Monasticism no less than the papacy was of the very essence of the Church of the Middle Ages. Yet the monastic ideal had no longer the force that it had in previous generations, and even the latest embodiments of the religious life had declined from their original popularity. Pope John XXII. himself, in his warfare against William of Ockham and the Spiritual Franciscans who had supported Louis of Bavaria, denied in good round terms the Franciscan doctrine of "evangelical poverty". Ockham was now dead, and with him perished the last of the great cosmopolitan schoolmen, of whose birth indeed England might boast, but who early forsook Oxford for Paris. Conspicuous among the younger academical generation was Richard Fitzralph, Archbishop of Armagh, whose bitter attacks on the fundamental principles underlying the mendicant theory of the regular life are indicative of the changing temper of the age. A distinguished Oxford scholar, a learned and pungent writer, a popular preacher, a reputed saint, and a good friend of the pope, Fitzralph made himself, about 1357, the champion of the secular clergy against the friars by writing a treatise to prove that absolute poverty was neither practised nor commended by the apostles.[1] The indignant mendicants procured

[1] See his *De Pauperie Salvatoris*, lib. i.-iv., printed by R. L. Poole, as appendix to Wycliffe, *De Dominio Divino*.

the archbishop's citation to Avignon, and it was a striking proof of the ineffectiveness of recent legislation that Edward III. allowed him to plead his cause before the *curia*. By 1358 the friars gained the day, but their efforts to get Fitzralph's opinions condemned were frustrated by his death in 1360. Fitzralph had the sympathy not only of the seculars, but of the "possessioners," or property-holding monks.

The period of experiments in economic and anti-clerical legislation was also marked by other important new laws, such as the ordinance of the staple of 1354, providing that wool, leather, and other commodities were only to be sold at certain *staple* towns, a measure soon to be modified by the law of 1362, which settled the staple at Calais ; the ordinance of 1357 for the government of Ireland, to which later reference will be made ; the statute making English thè language of the law courts in 1362, and a drastic act against purveyance in 1365. The statute of treasons of 1352, which laid down seven several offences as alone henceforth to be regarded as treason, also demands attention. Its classification is rude and unsystematic. While the slaying of the king's ministers or judges, and the counterfeiting of the great seal or the king's coin, are joined with the compassing the death of the king or his wife or heir, adherence to the king's enemies, the violation of the queen or the king's eldest daughter, as definite acts of treason, its omission to brand other notable indications of disloyalty as traitorous, inspired the judges of later generations to elaborate the doctrine of constructive treason in order to extend in practice the scope of the act. It was, however, an advance for nobles and commons to have set any limitations whatever to the wide power claimed by the courts of defining treason.

Partial respite from war did not diminish the martial ardour of the king and his nobles. The period of the Black Death was precisely the time when Edward completed a plan which he had begun by the erection of his Round Table at Windsor in 1344. By 1348 he instituted a chapel at Windsor, dedicated to St. George, served by a secular chapter, and closely connected with a foundation for the support of poor knights. Within a year this foundation also included the famous Order of the Garter, the type and model of all later orders of chivalry. On St. George's day the king celebrated the new institution by special solemnities. The most famous of his companions-at-arms were associated with him as founders and first knights. Clad in russet coats sprinkled with blue garters, a blue garter on the right leg, and a mantle of blue ornamented with little shields bearing the arms of St. George, the Knights of the Garter heard mass sung by the Archbishop of Canterbury in St. George's chapel, and then feasted solemnly in their common hall. Ten years later the glorification of the king's birthplace was completed by the erection of new quarters for the king, more sumptuous and splendid than were elsewhere to be seen. The fame of the Knights of the Garter excited the emulation of King John of France, who set up a Round Table which grew in 1351 into the knightly Order of the Star.

The rival brethren of the Garter and the Star found plenty of opportunities of demonstrating their prowess. Though between 1347 and 1355 there was, so far as forms went, an almost continuous armistice for the space of eight years, its effect was not so much to stop fighting as to limit its scale. In reality the years of nominal truce were a period of harassing warfare in Brittany, the Calais march, Gascony, and the narrow seas, which even the ravages of the Black Death did not stop.

In Brittany affairs were in a wretched condition. The nominal duke, John, was a child brought up in England under the guardianship of Edward III. Edward was not in a position to spend either men or money upon Brittany. As an easy way of discharging his obligations to his ward, he handed over the duchy to Sir Thomas Dagworth, the governor, who maintained the war from local resources and had a free hand as regards his choice of agents and measures. In return for power to appropriate to his own purposes the revenues of the duchy, Dagworth undertook the custody of the fortresses, the payment of the troops, the expenses of the administration, and the conduct of the war. In short, Brittany was leased out to him as a speculation, like a farm left derelict of husbandmen after the Black Death. Dagworth sublet to the highest bidders the lordships, fortresses, and towns of Brittany. He established at various centres of his influence a military adventurer, whose chief business was to make war support war and, moreover, bring in a good profit. The consequences were disastrous. Dagworth's captains were for the most part Englishmen, men of character, energy, and resources, but utterly without scruples and with no other ambition than to raise a good revenue and maintain themselves in authority. The most famous of them were members of gentle but obscure houses, whose poverty debarred them from the ordinary avenues to fame and fortune, and whose vigour and ability made good use of their exceptional positions. Two Cheshire kinsmen, Hugh Calveley and Robert Knowles, thus won, each for himself, a place in history. Some of the adventurers were of obscurer origin, some were foreigners, German, French, or Netherlandish, and some few Breton gentlemen of Montfort's faction. Of these Crockart, the German, and Raoul de Caours, the Breton, were the most famous.

The results of the system bore heavily on the Breton peasantry. Each lord of a castle levied systematic blackmail on the neighbouring parishes. These payments, called ransoms, were exacted as a condition of protection. The governor, though severely maltreating those who neglected to pay their ransom, did little to save his dependants from the ravages of the partisans of Charles of Blois. Despite such misdeeds, the war of partisans was brightened by many feats of heroism. The friends of Charles of Blois disregarded the truce and waged war as well as they could. Among them was already conspicuous the son of a nobleman of the neighbourhood of Dinan, the ugly, able, restless Bertrand du Guesclin, whose enterprise and valour won for him a great local reputation. In 1350 Dagworth was slain. The history of the following years is not to be found in the acts of his successor, Sir Walter Bentley, but in the private deeds of daring of the heroes of both sides. Conspicuous among these is the famous Battle of the Thirty, well known from the detailed narrative of Froissart, and the stirring verses of a contemporary French poem. This fight was fought on March 27, 1351, between thirty Breton gentlemen of the Blois faction, drawn from the garrison of Josselin, and a less noble but even more strenuous band of thirty English and other adventurers of the Montfort party, from the garrison of Ploermel, seven miles to the east. Beaumanoir, the commandant at Josselin, had been moved to indignation at the cruel treatment of peasants who had refused to pay ransom by Robert Bembro, the commander of Ploermel. He challenged the tyrant to combat, and thirty heroes of each party fought out their quarrel at a spot marked by the half-way oak, equidistant from the two garrisons. After a long struggle, in which Bembro was slain, victory fell to the men from Josselin. Among the vanquished were Knowles, Calveley, and Crockart. This fight had absolutely no influence on the fortune of the war.

In 1352 the French strove to carry on the Breton war on a grander scale, and a large army, commanded by Guy of Nesle, marshal of France, was sent to reinforce the partisans of Charles of Blois. They met Bentley at Mauron, a few miles north of Ploermel, where one of the most interesting battles of the war was fought. Taught by the lesson of Crecy, Nesle had already, in obscure fights in Poitou, ordered the French knights and men-at-arms to fight on foot.[1] He here adopted the same plan for the first time in a battle of importance, but, after a severe struggle, Bentley won the day. In 1353 Edward III. made a treaty with his captive, Charles of Blois. In return for a huge ransom Charles was to obtain his liberty, be recognised as Duke of Brittany, marry one of Edward's daughters, and promise to remain neutral in the Anglo-French struggle. The treaty involved too great a dislocation of policy to be carried out. Charles, after visiting Brittany, renounced the compact and returned to his London prison. Thus the weary war of partisans still went on, and thenceforth the fortunes of Charles depended less upon negotiations than on the growing successes of Bertrand du Guesclin.

During these years Calais was the centre of much fighting. Eager to win back the town, the French bribed an Italian mercenary, then in Edward's service, to admit them into the castle. The plot was discovered, and Edward and the Prince of Wales crossed over in disguise to help in frustrating the French assault. The French were enticed into Calais and taken as in a trap. Edward then sallied out of the town, and rashly engaged in personal encounter with a more numerous enemy. He was unexpectedly successful, and made wonderful display of his prowess as a knight. In revenge, the English devastated the neighbouring country by raids like that led by the Duke of Lancaster in 1351, which spread desolation from Thérouanne to Etaples. Of more enduring importance were the gradual

---

[1] See my paper on *Some Neglected Fights between Crecy and Poitiers* in *Engl. Hist. Review*, vol. xxi., Oct., 1905.

extensions of the English pale by the piecemeal conquest of the fortresses of the neighbourhood. The chief step in this direction was the capture of Guînes in 1352. An archer named John Dancaster, who escaped from French custody in Guînes, led his comrades to the assault of the town by a way which he learnt during his imprisonment. The attack succeeded, and Dancaster, to avoid involving his master in a formal breach of the truce, professed to hold the town on his own account and to be willing to sell it to the highest bidder. Of course the highest bidder was Edward III. himself, and thus Guînes became the southern outpost of the Calais march.

In Aquitaine and Languedoc there was no thought of repose. In 1349 Lancaster led a foray to the gates of Toulouse, which wrought immense damage but led to no permanent results. There was incessant border warfare. The Anglo-Gascon forces spread beyond the limits of Edward's duchy and captured outposts in Poitou, Périgord, Quercy, and the Agenais. In retaliation, the Count of Armagnac, a strong upholder of the French cause, did what mischief he could in those parts of Gascony adjacent to his own territories. On the whole the result of these struggles was a considerable extension of the English power.

The most famous episode of these years was a naval battle fought off Winchelsea on August 29, 1350, against a strong fleet of Spanish privateers commanded by Charles of La Cerda. The Spaniards having plundered English wine ships, Edward summoned a fleet to meet them, and himself went on board, along with the Prince of Wales, Lancaster, and many of his chief nobles. The fight that ensued was remarkable not more for the reckless valour of the king and his nobles than for the dexterity of the English tactics. The great busses of Spain towered above the little English vessels, like castles over cottages. Yet the English did not hesitate to grapple their adversaries' craft and swarm up their sides on to the decks. Edward captured one of the chief of the Spanish ships, though his own vessel, the *Cog Thomas*, was so severely damaged that it had to be hastily abandoned for its prize. The glory of the victory of the " Spaniards on the sea " kept up the fame first won at Sluys.

In these years of truce first appeared the worst scourge of the war, bands of mercenary soldiers, fighting on their own account and recklessly devastating the regions which they chose to visit. The cry for peace rose higher than ever. Innocent VI., who succeeded Clement VI. in 1352, took up with great energy the papal policy of mediation. Thanks to his legates' good offices, preliminary articles of peace were actually agreed upon on April 6, 1354, at Guînes. By them Edward agreed to renounce his claim to the French throne if he were granted full sovereignty over Guienne, Ponthieu, Artois, and Guînes. When the chamberlain, Burghersh, laid before parliament, which was then sitting, the prospect of peace, "the commons with one accord replied that, whatever course the king and the magnates should take as regards the said treaty, was agreeable to them. On this reply the chamberlain said to the commons: 'Then you wish to agree to a perpetual treaty of peace, if one can be had?' And the said commons answered unanimously, 'Yea, yea'."[1] Vexatious delays, however, supervened, and at last the negotiations broke down hopelessly. The French refused to surrender their over-lordship over the ceded provinces, and the Easter parliament of 1355 agreed with the king that war must be renewed. Two years of war were to follow more fierce than even the struggles which had culminated in Crecy, La Roche, and Calais.

Two expeditions were organised to invade France in the summer of 1355, one for Aquitaine under the Prince of Wales,[2] and the other for Normandy under Lancaster. Westerly winds long prevented their despatch. It was not until September that the Prince of Wales reached Bordeaux. The change of wind, which bore the prince to Gascony, enabled the host, collected by the King and Lancaster on the Thames, to make its way to Normandy. But the special reason which brought the English thither was already gone. The expedition was planned to co-operate with the King of Navarre. Charles, surnamed the Bad, traced on his father's side his descent to that son of Philip the Bold who obtained the county of Evreux in upper Normandy for his appanage. From his mother, the daughter of Louis X., he derived his kingdom of Navarre and a claim on the French monarchy of the same type as that of Edward III. Cunning, plausible, unscrupulous, and violent,

---

[1] *Rot. Parl.*, ii., 262.

[2] For the Black Prince's career in Aquitaine, see Moisant, *Le Prince Noir en Aquitaine* (1894).

Charles had quarrelled fiercely with King John, whose daughter he had married. His vast estates in Normandy made him a valuable ally to Edward, and he had suggested joint action in that duchy against the French. Unluckily, while the west winds kept the English fleet beyond the Straits of Dover, John made terms with his son-in-law. Lancaster was compensated for his disappointment by the governorship of Brittany. The army equipped for the Norman expedition was diverted to Calais, whence in November, Edward and Lancaster led a purposeless foray in the direction of Hesdin, which hastily ended on the arrival of the news that the Scots had surprised the town of Berwick, and were threatening its castle. Thereupon Edward hastened back home. He had to keep the Scots quiet, before he could attack the French.

When the Black Prince reached Bordeaux, he received a warm welcome from the Gascons, and at once set out at the head of an army, partly English and partly Gascon, on a foray into the enemy's territory. He made his way from Bazas to the upper Adour through the county of Armagnac, whose lord had incurred his wrath by his devotion to the house of Valois and his invasions of the Gascon duchy. Thence he worked eastwards, avoiding the greater towns, and plundering and devastating wherever he could. The Count of Armagnac, the French commander in the south, watched his progress from Toulouse, and prudently avoided any open encounter. The prince approached within a few miles of the capital of Languedoc, but found an easier prey in the rich towns and fertile plains in the valley of the Aude. He captured the "town" of Carcassonne, though he failed to reduce the fortress-crowned height of the "city". At Narbonne also he took the "town" and left the "city". His progress spread terror throughout the south, and the clerks of the university of Montpellier and the papal *curia* at Avignon trembled lest he should continue his raid in their direction. But November came, and Edward found it prudent to retire, choosing on his westward journey a route parallel to that which he had previously adopted. He had achieved his real purpose in desolating the region from which the French had derived the chief resources for their attacks on Gascony. The raiders boasted that Carcassonne was larger than York, Limoux not less great than Carcassonne, and Narbonne nearly as populous as London. Over this fair region, where wine and oil were more abundant than water, the black band of desolation, which had already marked so many of the fairest provinces of France, was cruelly extended.

The prince kept his Christmas at Bordeaux. Even during the winter his troops remained active. Most of the Agenais was conquered by January, 1356, while in February the capture of Périgueux opened up the way of invasion northwards. Meanwhile the prince mustered his forces for a vigorous summer campaign. While the towns on the Isle and the Lot were yielding to his son, Edward III. was avenging the capture of Berwick by a winter campaign in the Lothians. Before the end of January, 1356, Berwick was once more in his hands. Thence he passed to Roxburgh, where Edward Balliol surrendered to him all his rights over the Scottish throne. Thenceforth styling himself no longer overlord but King of Scotland, Edward mercilessly harried his new subjects. But storms dispersed the English victualling ships, and Edward's men could not live in winter on the country that they had made a wilderness. In a few weeks they were back over the border, though their raid was long remembered in Scottish tradition as the Burnt Candlemas.

Another breach between Charles of Navarre and his father-in-law again opened to the English the way to Normandy. John lost patience at Charles's renewed intrigues, and in April arrested him and his friends at Rouen. Thereupon his brother, Philip of Navarre, rose in revolt. With him were many of the Norman lords, including Geoffrey of Harcourt, lord of Saint-Sauveur. The English were once more invited to Normandy, and on June 18 Lancaster landed at La Hougue with the double mission of aiding the Norman rebels and establishing John of Montfort, then arrived at man's estate, in his Breton duchy. It was the first English invasion of northern France during the war, in which they had, as in Brittany, the co-operation of a strong party in the land. The Navarre and Harcourt influence at once secured them the Côtentin. Meanwhile, however, the French were besieging the fortresses of the county of Evreux. With the object of relieving this pressure, Lancaster, immediately after his landing, marched into the heart of Normandy, and soon reached Verneuil. It looked for the moment as if he were destined to emulate the exploits of Edward III. in 1346.   But he abruptly turned back, leaving the county of Evreux to fall into French hands.   The permanent result of his intervention was to reduce Normandy to a state of anarchy nearly as complete as that of Brittany.   In the autumn Lancaster at last made his way to the land of which he had had nominal charge since the previous year.   He left Philip of Navarre as commander in Normandy, and the war was supported from local resources.   The Côtentin being in friendly hands, Lancaster attacked the strongholds of the Blois party, which had hitherto been exempt from the war.   In October he laid siege to Rennes and was detained before its walls until July, 1357, when he agreed to desist from the attack in return for a huge ransom.   Lancaster then established young Montfort as duke.   At the same time Charles of Blois, released from his long imprisonment, once more reappeared in his wife's inheritance, though, as his ransom was still but partly paid, his scrupulous honour compelled him to abstain from personal intervention in the war.   Thus Brittany got back both her dukes.

The northern operations in 1356 sink into insignificance when compared with the exploits of the Black Prince in the south. After the capture of Périgueux, there had been some idea of the prince making a northward movement and joining hands with Lancaster on the Loire.   When Lancaster retired from Verneuil, however, the Black Prince was still in the valley of the Dordogne.   Even when all was ready, attacks on the Gascon duchy compelled him to divert a large portion of his army for the defence of his own frontiers.   Not until August 9 was he able to advance from Périgueux to Brantôme into hostile territory. It was a month too late to co-operate with Lancaster, and the 7,000 men, who followed his banners, were in equipment rather prepared for a raid than for a systematic conquest.

Edward's outward march was in a generally northerly direction.   Leaving Limoges on his right, he crossed the Vienne lower down the stream, and thence he led his troops over the Creuse at Argenton and over the Indre at Châteauroux.   When he traversed the Cher at Vierzon, his followers rejoiced that they had at last got out of the limits of the ancient duchy of Guienne and were invading the actual kingdom of France.   On penetrating beyond the Cher into the melancholy flats of the Sologne, the prince encountered the first serious resistance.   He then turned

abruptly to the west, and chased the enemy into the strong castle
of Romorantin, which he captured on September 3. There he
heard that John of France, who had gathered together a huge
force, was holding the passages over the Loire. Edward marched
to meet the enemy, and on September 7 reached the neighbourhood of Tours, where he tarried in his camp for three days. But
the few bridges were destroyed or strongly guarded, and the
men-at-arms found it quite impossible to make their way over
the broad and swift Loire. Moreover the news came that John
had crossed the river near Blois, and was hurrying southwards.
Thereupon the Black Prince turned in the same direction, seeing
in this southward march his best chance of getting to close
quarters. The French host was enormously the superior in
numbers, but after Morlaix, Mauron, and Crecy, mere numerical
disparity weighed but lightly on an English commander.

For some days the armies marched in the same direction in
parallel lines, neither knowing very clearly the exact position of
the other. On September 14 Edward reached Châtelherault on
the Vienne. His troops were weary and war-worn, and his
transport inordinately swollen by spoils. He rested two days
at Châtelherault, but was again on the move on hearing that the
enemy was at Chauvigny, situated some twenty miles higher
up the Vienne. Edward at once started in pursuit, only to find
that the French had retired before him to Poitiers, eighteen
miles due west of Chauvigny. Careless of his convoy, he hurried
across country in the hope of catching the elusive enemy, but
was only in time to fight a rear-guard skirmish at a manor
named La Chaboterie, on the road from Chauvigny to Poitiers,
on September 17. That night the English lay in a wood hard by
the scene of action, suffering terribly from want of water. Next
day, Sunday, September 18, Edward pursued the French as
near as he could to Poitiers, halting in battle array within a league
of the town. A further check on his impatience now ensued.
Innocent VI.'s legate, the Cardinal Talleyrand, brother of the
Count of Périgord, who was with the French army, crossed to
the rival host with an offer of mediation. Edward received
the cardinal courteously and spent most of the day in negotiations. But the French showed no eagerness to bring matters to
a conclusion, and as every hour reinforcements poured into the
enemy's camp the scanty patience of the English was exhausted.

They declared that the legate's talk about saving the effusion of Christian blood was only a blind to gain time, so that the French might overwhelm them. Edward broke off the negotiations, and, retiring to a position more remote from the enemy, passed the night quietly. Early next morning the cardinal again sought to treat, but this time his offers were rejected. On his withdrawal, the French attack began.

The topographical details of the battle of Poitiers of September 19, 1356, cannot be determined with certainty. We only know that the place of the encounter was called Maupertuis, which is generally identified with a farm now called La Cardinerie, some six miles south-east of Poitiers, and a little distance to the north of the Benedictine abbey of Nouaillé. The abbey formed the southern limit of the field. On the west the place of combat was skirted by the little river Miausson, which winds its way through marshes in a deep-cut valley, girt by wooded hills. The French left their horses at Poitiers, having resolved, perhaps on the advice of a Scottish knight, Sir William Douglas, to fight on foot, after the English and Scottish fashion, and as they had already fought at Mauron and elsewhere. As at Mauron, a small band of cavalry was retained, both for the preliminary skirmishing which then usually heralded a battle, and in the hope of riding down some of the archers. But the French did not fully understand the English tactics, and took no care to combine men-at-arms with archers or crossbowmen, though these were less important against an army weak in archers and largely consisting of Gascons. Of the four " battles " the first, under the Marshals Audrehem and Clermont, included the little cavalry contingent ; the second was under Charles, Duke of Normandy, a youth of nineteen ; the third under the Duke of Orleans, the king's brother ; and the rear was commanded by the king.

The English army spent the night before the battle beyond the Miausson, but in the morning the prince, fearing an ambuscade behind the hill of Nouaillé on the east bank, abandoned his original position and crossed the stream in order to occupy it. He divided his forces into three "battles," led respectively by himself, Warwick, and William Montague, since 1343 by his father's death Earl of Salisbury. Though he found no enemy there, he remained with his "battle" on the hill, because it commanded the slopes to the north over on which the French were

now advancing. His remote position threw the brunt of the
fighting upon the divisions of Warwick and Salisbury. They
were stationed side by side in advance of him on ground lower
than that held by him, but higher than that of the enemy, and
beset with bushes and vineyards which sloped down on the left
towards the marshes of the Miausson. Some distance in front
of their position, a long hedge and ditch divided the upland, on
which the " battles " of Warwick and Salisbury were stationed,
from the fields in which the French were arrayed. At its upper
end, remote from the Miausson, where Salisbury's command lay,
the hedge was broken by a gap through which a farmer's track
connected the fields on each side of it. The first fighting began
when the English sent a small force of horsemen through the
gap to engage with the French cavalry beyond. While Audrehem, on the French right, suspended his attack to watch the
result, Clermont made his way straight for the gap, hoping to
take Salisbury's division, on the upper or right-hand station, in
flank. Before he reached the gap, however, he found the hedge
and the approaches to the cart-road held in force by the English
archers. Meanwhile the mail-clad men and horses of Audrehem's cavalry had approached dangerously near the left of
the English line, where Warwick was stationed. Their complete armour made riders and steeds alike impervious to the
English arrows, until the prince, seeing from his hill how things
were proceeding, ordered some archers to station themselves on
the marshy ground near the Miausson, in advance of the left
flank of the English army. From this position they shot at
the unprotected parts of the French horses, and drove the little
band of cavalry from the field. By that time Clermont's attack
on the gap had been defeated, and so both sections of the first
French division retired.

     Then came the stronger " battle " of the eldest son of the
French king. The fight grew more fierce, and for a long time
the issue remained doubtful. The English archers exhausted
their arrows to little purpose, and the dismounted French men-
at-arms, offering a less sure mark than the horsemen, forced
their way to the English ranks and fought a desperate hand-to-
hand conflict with them. At last the Duke of Normandy's
followers were driven back. Thereupon a panic seized the
division commanded by the Duke of Orleans, which fled from

the field without measuring swords with the enemy.   The victors themselves were in a desperate plight.   Many were wounded, and all were weary, especially the men-at-arms encased in heavy plate mail.   The flight of Orleans gave them a short respite: but they soon had to face the assault of the rear battle of the enemy, gallantly led by the king.   " No battle," we are told, "ever lasted so long.   In former fights men knew, by the time that the fourth or the sixth arrow had been discharged, on which side victory was to be.   But here a single archer shot with coolness a hundred arrows, and still neither side gave way." [1]   At last the bowmen had only the arrows they snatched from the bodies of the dead and dying, and when these were exhausted, they were reduced to throwing stones at their foes, or to struggle in the *mêlée*, with sword and buckler, side by side with the men-at-arms.   But the Black Prince from his hill had watched the course of the encounter, and at the right moment, when his friends were almost worn out, marched down, and made the fight more even.   Before joining himself in the engagement, Edward had ordered the Captal de Buch, the best of his Gascons, to lead a little band, under cover of the hill, round the French position and attack the enemy in the rear. At first the Anglo-Gascon army was discouraged, thinking that the captal had fled, but they still fought on.   Suddenly the captal and his men assaulted the French rear.   This settled the hard fought day.   Surrounded on every side, the French perished in their ranks or surrendered in despair.   King John was taken prisoner, fighting desperately to the last, and with him was captured his youngest son Philip, the future Duke of Burgundy, a boy of twelve, whose epithet of " the Bold " was earned by his precocious valour in the struggle.   Before nightfall the English host had sole possession of the field, and the best fought, best directed, and most important of the battles of the war ended in the complete triumph of the invaders.

As after Crecy, the victors were too weak to continue the campaign.   Next day they began their slow march back to their base.   On October 2 Edward reached Libourne, and a few days later conducted the captive king into the Gascon capital. They were soon followed by the Cardinal Talleyrand on whose insistence the prince agreed to resume negotiations.   On March

[1] *Eulogium Hist.*, iii., 225.

23, 1357, a truce to last until 1359 was arranged at Bordeaux. On May 24 the prince led the vanquished king through the streets of London.

The English, weary of the burden of war, strove to use their advantages to procure a stable peace. Though Charles of Blois was released, he was muzzled for the future, and when John joined his ally David Bruce in the Tower, it was the obvious game of Edward to exact terms from his prisoners. David's spirit was broken, and he was glad to accept a treaty sealed in October, 1357, at Berwick, by which he was released for a ransom of 100,000 marks, to be paid by ten yearly instalments. The task was harder for a poor country like Scotland than the redemption of Richard I. had been for England. On hostages being given, David was released, and Edward, without relinquishing his own pretensions to be King of Scots, took no steps to enforce his claim. The event showed that Edward knew his man. The instalments of ransom could not be regularly paid, and David never became free from his obligations. Nothing save the tenacity of the Scottish nobles prevented him from accepting Edward's proposals to write off the arrears of his ransom in return for his accepting either the English king himself or his son, Lionel of Antwerp, as heir of Scotland. This attitude brought David into conflict with his natural heir, Robert, the Steward of Scotland, the son of his sister Margaret. The tension between uncle and nephew forced the Scots king to remain on friendly terms with Edward. For the rest of the reign, Scottish history was occupied by aristocratic feuds, by financial expedients for raising the king's ransom, by the gradual development of the practice of entrusting the powers of parliament to those committees of the estates subsequently famous as the lords of the articles, by David's matrimonial troubles after Joan's death, and by his unpopular visits to the court of his neighbour. Warfare between the realms there was none, save for the chronic border feuds. When David died in 1371, the Steward of Scotland mounted the throne as Robert II. This first of the Stewart kings went back to the policy of the French alliance, but was too weak to inflict serious mischief on England.

In January, 1358, preliminaries of peace were also arranged with the captive King of France, and sent to Paris and Avignon for ratification. Innocent VI. was overjoyed at his success, and

Frenchmen were willing to make any sacrifices to bring back their monarch, for immediately after Poitiers a storm of disorder burst over France. The states general met a few weeks after the battle, and the regent, Charles of Normandy, was helpless in their hands. This was the time of the power of Stephen Marcel, provost of the merchants of Paris, and of Robert Lecoq, Bishop of Laon. But the movement in Paris was neither in the direction of parliamentary government nor of democracy, and few men have less right to be regarded as popular heroes than Marcel and Lecoq. The estates were manipulated in the interests of aristocratic intrigue, and, behind the ostensible leaders, was the sinister influence of Charles of Navarre, who availed himself of the desolation of France to play his own game. For a time he was the darling of the Paris mob. Innocent VI. was deceived by his protestations of zeal for peace. As grandson of Louis X. he aspired to the French throne, and was anxious to prevent John's return. Edward had no good-will for a possible rival, but it was his interest to keep up the anarchy, and he had no scruple in backing up Charles. There was talk of Edward becoming King of France and holding the maritime provinces, while Charles as his vassal should be lord of Paris and the interior districts. English mercenaries, who had lost their occupation with the truce, enlisted themselves in the service of Navarre. Robert Knowles, James Pipe, and other ancient captains of Edward fought for their own hand in Normandy, and built up colossal fortunes out of the spoils of the country. Some of these hirelings appeared in Paris, where the citizens welcomed allies of the Navarrese, even when they were foreign adventurers. However, Charles went so far that a strong reaction deprived him of all power. He was able to prevent the ratification of the preliminaries of 1358. But in that year the death of Marcel was followed by the return of the regent to Paris, the expulsion of the foreign mercenaries, the collapse of the estates, and the restoration of the capital to the national cause. The short-lived horrors wreaked by the revolted peasantry were followed by the more enduring atrocities of the nobles who suppressed them. Military adventurers pillaged France from end to end, but the worst troubles ended when Charles of Navarre lost his pre-eminence.[1]

---

[1] An admirable account of the state of France between 1356 and 1358 is in Denifle, *La Désolation des Églises en France pendant la Guerre de Cent Ans*, ii., 134-316 (1899).

When the truce of Bordeaux was on the verge of expiration, CHAP.
XVII. the French king negotiated a second treaty by which he bought off the threatened renewal of war. This was the treaty of London, March 24, 1359, by which John yielded up to Edward in full sovereignty the ancient empire of Henry II. Normandy, the suzerainty of Brittany, Anjou, and Maine, Aquitaine within its ancient limits, Calais and Ponthieu with the surrounding districts, were the territorial concessions in return for which Edward renounced his claim to the French throne. The vast ransom of 4,000,000 golden crowns was to be paid for John's redemption ; the chief princes of the blood were to be hostages for him, and in case of failure to observe the terms of the treaty he was to return to his captivity. The only provision in any sense favourable to France was that by which Edward promised to aid John against the King of Navarre.

The treaty of London excited the liveliest anger in France. "We had rather," declared the assembled estates, "endure the great mischief that has afflicted us so long, than suffer the noble realm of France thus to be diminished and defrauded." [1] Spurred up by these patriotic manifestations, the regent rejected the treaty, and prepared as best he could for the storm of Edward's wrath which soon burst upon his country. Anxious to unite forces against the national enemy, he made peace with Charles of Navarre, who, abandoned by Edward, was delighted to be restored to his estates.

Edward concentrated all his efforts on a new invasion of France. In November, 1359, he marched out of Calais with all his forces. His four sons attended him, and there was a great muster of earls and experienced warriors. Among the less known members of the host was the young Londoner, Geoffrey Chaucer, a page in Lionel of Antwerp's household. In three columns, each following a separate route, the English made their way from Calais towards the south-east. The French avoided a pitched battle, but hung on the skirts of the army and slew, or captured, stragglers and foragers. Chaucer was among those thus taken prisoner. Edward's ambition was to take Reims, and have himself crowned there as King of France. On December 4 he arrived at the gates of the city, and besieged it

---

[1] Froissart, v., 180, ed. Luce.

for six weeks. Then on January 11, 1360, the King despaired of
success, abandoned the siege, and marched southwards through
Champagne towards Burgundy. Despite the check at Reims,
he was still so formidable that in March Duke Philip of Burgundy concluded with him the shameful treaty of Guillon, by
which he purchased exemption from invasion by an enormous
ransom and a promise of neutrality.

Edward next turned towards Paris. The news that the
French had effected a successful descent on Winchelsea and
behaved with extreme brutality to the inhabitants, infuriated
the English troopers, who perpetrated a hundredfold worse
deeds in the suburbs of the French capital. It seemed as if
the war was about to end with the siege and capture of Paris.
The regent, unable to meet the English in the field, fell back
in despair on negotiation. Innocent VI. again offered his good
services. John sent from his English prison full powers to his
son to make what terms he would, and on April 3, which was
Good Friday, ambassadors from each power met under papal
intervention at Longjumeau; but Edward still insisted on the
terms of the treaty of London, for which the French were not
yet prepared. On April 7 Edward began the siege of Paris by
an attack on the southern suburbs, but was so little successful
that he withdrew five days later. A terrible tempest destroyed
his provision train and devastated his army. These disasters
made Edward anxious for peace, and the negotiations, after
two interruptions, were successfully renewed at Chartres, and
facilitated by the signature of a truce for a year. The work
of a definitive treaty was pushed forward, and on May 8, preliminaries of peace were signed between the prince of Wales
and Charles of France at the neighbouring hamlet of Brétigni,
whither the peacemakers had transferred their sittings.

There were still formalities to accomplish which took up
many months. King John was escorted in July by the Prince
of Wales to Calais, and in October he was joined by Edward
III., who had returned to England about the time that the negotiations at Brétigni were over. The peace took its final form
at Calais in October 24, 1360. Next day John was released,
and ratified the convention as a free man on French soil. This
permanent treaty is more properly styled the treaty of Calais
than the treaty of Brétigni; but the alterations between the

two were only significant in one particular respect. At Calais
the English agreed to omit a clause inserted at Brétigni by
which Edward renounced his claims to the French throne, and
John his claims over the allegiance of the inhabitants of the
ceded districts. As the Calais treaty of October alone had the
force of law, it was a real triumph of French diplomacy to have
suppressed so vital a feature in the definitive document.[1] Even
with this alleviation the terms were sufficiently humiliating to
France. Edward and his heirs were to receive in perpetuity,
"and in the manner in which the kings of France had held
them," an ample territory both in southern and northern France.
All Aquitaine was henceforth to be English, including Poitou,
Saintonge, Périgord, Angoumois, Limousin, Quercy, Rouergue,
Agenais, and Bigorre. The greatest feudatories of these districts,
the friendly Count of Foix as well as the hostile Count of Armagnac, and the Breton pretender to the viscounty of Limoges,
were to do homage to Edward for all their lands within these
bounds. Nor was this all. The county of Ponthieu, including
Montreuil-sur-mer, was restored to its English lords, and added
to the pale of Calais, which was to include the whole county of
Guînes, made up two considerable northern dominions for Edward. With these cessions were included all adjacent islands,
and all islands held by the English king at that time, so that
the Channel islands were by implication recognised as English.

The ransom of John was fixed at 3,000,000 gold crowns,
that is £500,000 sterling. The vastness of this sum can be
realised by remembering that the ordinary revenue of the
English crown in time of peace did not much exceed £60,000,
while the addition to that of a sum of £150,000 involved an
effort which only a popular war could dispose Englishmen to
make. Of this ransom 600,000 crowns were to be paid at once,
and the rest in annual instalments of 400,000 crowns until the
whole payment was effected. During this period the prisoners
from Poitiers, several of the king's near relatives, a long list
of the noblest names in France, and citizens of some of its
wealthiest cities, were to remain as hostages in Edward's hands.
As to the Breton succession, Edward and John engaged to do

[1] On the importance of this, see the paper of MM. Petit-Dutaillis and
P. Collier, *La Diplomatie française et le Traité de Brétigny* in *Le Moyen Age*,
2e serie, tome i. (1897), pp. 1-35.

their best to effect a peaceful settlement.   If they failed in attaining this, the rival claimants were to fight it out among themselves, England and France remaining neutral.   Whichever of the two became duke was to do homage to the King of France, and John of Montfort was, in any case, to be restored to his county of Montfort.   A similar care for Edward's friends was shown in the article which preserved for Philip of Navarre his hereditary domains in Normandy.   Forfeitures and outlawries were to be pardoned, and the rights of private persons to be respected.   Nevertheless Calais was to remain at Edward's entire disposal, and the burgesses, dispossessed by him, were not to be reinstated.   The French renounced their alliance with the Scots, and the English theirs with the Flemings.   Time was allowed to carry out these complicated stipulations, and, by way of compensating Edward for the significant omission which has been mentioned, elaborate provisions were made for the mutual execution at a later date of charters of renunciation, by which Edward abandoned his claim to the French throne and John the over-lordship of the districts yielded to Edward. These were to be exchanged at Bruges about a year later.

England rejoiced at the conclusion of so brilliant a peace, and laid no stress on the subtle change in the conditions which made the treaty far less definitive in reality than in appearance. In France the faithful flocked to the churches to give thanks for deliverance from the long anarchy.   The perfect courtesy and good feeling which the two kings had shown to each other gilded the concluding ceremonies with a ray of chivalry.   John was released almost at once, and allowed to retain with him in France some of the hostages, including his valiant son Philip, the companion of his captivity.   John made Edward's peace with Louis of Flanders, and Edward persuaded John to pardon Charles and Philip of Navarre.   At last the two weary nations looked forward to a long period of repose.

CHAPTER XVIII.

THE HUNDRED YEARS' WAR FROM THE TREATY OF CALAIS TO THE TRUCE OF BRUGES.

IT was an easier matter to conclude the treaty of Calais than to carry it out. Troubles followed the release of the French king and the expiration of the year during which the two parties were to yield up the ceded territory and effect the renunciations of their respective claims. John did his best to keep faith in both these matters. He ordered his vassals to submit themselves to their new lord, and appointed commissioners to hand over the lost provinces to the agents of the English king. In July, 1361, Sir John Chandos, Edward's lieutenant in France, received the special mission of taking possession of the new acquisitions in the name of his master. Chandos' reputation as a soldier made him acceptable to the French, and being recognised by the treaty as lord of Saint-Sauveur in the Côtentin, he was interested in maintaining good relations between the two realms. He began his work by taking possession of Poitiers and Poitou, but found that many of the descendants of the greedy lords, who, more than a hundred years before, had played off Henry III. against St. Louis, abandoned the rule of John with undisguised reluctance. It was worse with the towns, where national sentiment was stronger. La Rochelle held out for months, and, when its notables at last submitted, they declared: " We will accept the English with our lips but never with our hearts ". Much patriotic feeling was manifested in Quercy. The consuls of Cahors made their submission, weeping and groaning. " Alas ! " they declared, " how odious it is to lose our natural lord, and to pass over to a master we know not. But it is not we who abandon the King of France. It is he who, against our wishes, hands us over, like orphans, to the hands of the stranger." It was not until two years after the signing of the treaty that Edward entered into

399

CHAP.
XVIII.

possession of the bulk of the lands granted to him. Even then there were districts in Poitou, notably Belleville, which never became English at all. One of the last districts to yield was Rouergue, whose count, John of Armagnac, only made his submission under the compulsion of irresistible necessity.

It was even more difficult to get the English out of the lands which the treaty had assigned to the French. These districts were largely held by companies of mercenaries, little under Edward's control and indisposed to yield up the conquests won by their own hands because their nominal lord had thought fit to make a treaty with the French king. Despite the orders of Edward, the English garrisons in the north and centre of France flatly refused to surrender their strongholds. In Maine, Hugh Calveley took Bertrand du Guesclin prisoner when he sought to receive the submission of his castles, and only released him on payment of a heavy ransom. In Normandy, Du Guesclin had to buy off James Pipe, who dominated all the central district from the fortified abbey of Cormeilles, and to crush John Jowel in a pitched battle near Lisieux. Even when the castles were surrendered, the garrisons joined with each other to establish societies of warriors that now inflicted terrible woes on France. The exploits of these free companies hardly belong to English history, though many of their leaders and a large proportion of the rank and file were Englishmen. Cruel, fierce, and uncouth, they still preserved in all military dealings the strict discipline which had taught the English armies the way to victory. The combination of the order of a settled host with the rapacity of a gang of freebooters made them as irresistible as they were destructive. Though Edward formally repudiated them, it was more than suspected that they were secretly playing his game.

Before long, this guerilla warfare became consolidated into military operations on a large scale. Charles of Navarre once more profited by the disorder of France to bring himself to the front. In 1361 John had availed himself of the death of Philip of Rouvres to treat the duchy of Burgundy as a lapsed fief, and conferred it on his youngest son, Philip the Bold. Charles then claimed to be the heir of Burgundy, and while he personally directed the forces of disorder in the south, his agents united with the English *condottieri* in Normandy. John Jowel still

held tight to his Norman conquests, and was, by Edward's
direction, fighting openly for Charles of Navarre. The Captal
de Buch, the hero of Poitiers, hurried from Gascony to protect
the Navarrese lands from the invasion of Bertrand du Guesclin.
On May 16, 1364, the little armies of the captal and the Breton
partisan met at Cocherel on the Eure, where Du Guesclin
cleverly won the first important victory gained by the French
in the open field during the whole course of the war. The
captal was taken prisoner, and the establishment of Du Guesclin
in some of Charles of Navarre's Norman fiefs deprived the intriguer of his opportunities to do mischief in the north. Charles
of Navarre's career was not yet over ; but henceforth his chief
field was his southern kingdom.

The victorious Du Guesclin turned his attention to his native
Brittany, where the war of Blois and Montfort still went on,
for Joan of Penthièvre insisted so strongly upon her rights
that the efforts of Edward and John to end the contest had
been without result. In 1362 John de Montfort was at last
entrusted with the government of Brittany, and Du Guesclin
quitted the service of France for that of Charles of Blois, that
the treaty of 1360 might remain unbroken. But as in the early
wars, the army of Blois was mainly French, and the host of
Montfort was commanded by the Englishman, John Chandos,
and largely consisted of English men-at-arms and archers.
Calveley, Knowles, and the Breton Oliver de Clisson were
among the captains of Duke John's forces.

The decisive engagement took place on September 29, 1364,
on the plateau, north of Auray, which is still marked by the
church of St. Michael, erected as a thank-offering by the victor.
It was another Poitiers on a small scale. The Anglo-Breton
army held a good defensive position, facing northwards, with its
back on the town of Auray. The troops of Charles of Blois and
Du Guesclin advanced to attack them with more ardour than discipline or skill. Both sides fought on foot. The French knights
had at last learnt to meet the storm of English arrows by
strengthening their armour and by protecting themselves by
large shields. Thus, as at Poitiers, they had little difficulty in
making their way up to the enemy's ranks. But their order was
confused, and they thought of nothing but the fierce delights of
the *mêlée.* The Montfort party showed more intelligence, and

Chandos, like the captal at Poitiers, fell suddenly upon the flank of one of the enemy's divisions.   This settled the fight ; Charles of Blois was slain, Du Guesclin taken prisoner, and their army utterly scattered.   Auray ended the war of the Breton succession.   Even Joan of Penthièvre was at last willing to treat. In 1365 the treaty of Guérande was signed, by which· Montfort was recognised as John IV. of Brittany, and did homage to the French crown.   Joan was consoled by remaining in possession of the county of Penthièvre and the viscounty of Limoges.   Practically her defeat was an English victory, and Montfort remained in his duchy so long only as English influence prevailed.   A second step towards the pacification of the north was made when the troubles in Brittany were ended within a few months of the destruction of the power of Charles the Bad in Normandy.

The free companies lost their chief hunting-grounds; and a further relief came when some of them, like the White Company, found a better market for their swords in Italy.   With all their faults, the companies opened out a career to talent such as had seldom been found before.   John Hawkwood, the leader of the White Company, was an Essex man of the smaller landed class.   He had played but a subordinate figure beside Knowles, Calveley, Pipe, and Jowel ; but in Italy he won for himself the name of the greatest strategist of his age.   Thus, though at the cost of murder and pillage, the English made themselves talked about all over the western world.   " In my youth," wrote Petrarch, " the Britons, whom we call Angles or English, had the reputation of being the most timid of the barbarians.   Now they are the most warlike of peoples.   They have overturned the ancient military glory of the French by a series of victories so numerous and unexpected that those, who were not long since inferior to the wretched Scots, have so crushed by fire and sword the whole realm that, on a recent journey, I could hardly persuade myself that it was the France that I had seen in former years." [1]

It was to little purpose that King John laboured to redeem his plighted word and make France what it had been before the war.   Though in November, 1361, neither he nor Edward sent commissioners to Bruges, where, according to the treaty of

---

[1] *Epistolæ Familiares*, iii., Ep. 14, p. 162, ed. Fracassetti.

Calais, the charters of renunciation were to be exchanged, John CHAP.
offered in 1362 to carry out his promise.   Edward, however,   XVIII.
for reasons of his own, made no response to his advances.   The
result was that the renunciations were never made, and so the
essential condition of the original settlement remained unful-
filled.   The matter passed almost unnoticed at the time as a
mere formality, but in later years Edward's lack of faith brought
its own punishment in giving the French king a plausible excuse
for still claiming suzerainty over the ceded provinces.   Perhaps
Edward still cherished the ambition of resuscitating his pretensions to the French crown.   He found it as hard to give up
a claim as ever his grandfather had done.

John's good faith was conspicuously evinced by the efforts he
made to raise the instalments of his ransom.   His payments
were in arrears: some of the hostages left in free custody by
Edward's generosity broke their parole and escaped ; and among
them was his own son, Louis, Duke of Anjou.   The father felt
it his duty to step into the place thus left vacant.   In 1363
he returned to his English prison, where he died in 1364, surrounded with every courtesy and attention that Edward could
lavish upon him.   During the last months of his life, England
received visits from two other kings, David of Scotland and
the Lusignan lord of Cyprus, who still called himself King of
Jerusalem, and was wandering through the courts of Europe
to stir up interest in the projected crusade.

Charles of Normandy then became Charles V.   He was no
knight-errant like his father, and his diplomatic gifts, tact, and
patience made him much better fitted than John for outwitting
his English enemies and for restoring order to France.   Slowly
but surely he grappled with the companies, and at last an opening
was found for their skill in the civil war which broke out in
Castile.   Peter the Cruel, since 1350 King of Castile, had made
himself odious to many of his subjects.   At last his bastard
brother, Henry of Trastamara, rose in revolt against him.
Peter, however, was capable and energetic, and not without support from certain sections of the Castilians.   Moreover, he was
friendly with Charles of Navarre, and allied with Edward III.
On the other hand Henry found powerful backing from the
King of Aragon, and made an appeal to the King of France.
This gave Charles V. the chance he wanted.   He hated Peter,

26 *

CHAP.
XVIII.
who was reputed to have murdered his own wife, Blanche of Bourbon, sister of the Queen of France, and in 1365 he agreed to give Henry assistance. Du Guesclin welded the scattered companies into an army and led them against the Spanish king. The pope fell in with the scheme as an indirect way of realising his crusading ambition. When Henry had become King of Castile, the companies would go on to attack the Moors of Granada.

English and French mercenaries flocked gladly together under Du Guesclin's banner. Edward in vain ordered his subjects not to take part in an invasion of the lands of his friend and cousin, Peter of Castile. Though Chandos declined at the last moment to follow Du Guesclin into the peninsula, Sir Hugh Calveley would not desist from the quest of fresh adventure, even at the orders of his lord. Professional and knightly feeling bound Calveley to Du Guesclin more closely than their difference of nationality separated them, so that Calveley took his part in the Castilian campaign with perfect loyalty to his ancient enemy. In December, 1365, Du Guesclin and his followers made their way through Roussillon and Aragon into Castile. The spring of 1366 saw Peter a fugitive in Aquitaine, and Henry of Trastamara crowned Henry II. of Castile. Most of the companies then went home, though Du Guesclin and Calveley remained to support the new king's throne.

The deposed tyrant went to Bordeaux, where since 1363 the Black Prince had been resident as Prince of Aquitaine ; for in 1362 Edward had erected his new possessions into a principality and conferred it on his eldest son, in the hope of conciliating the Gascons by some pretence of restoring their independence. At Bordeaux Peter persuaded the prince to restore him to his throne by force. Edward also agreed to support Peter, and sent his third son, John of Gaunt, to march through Brittany and Poitou with a powerful English reinforcement to his brother's resources, while the lord of Aquitaine assembled the whole strength of his new principality for the expedition. At the bidding of his lord, Calveley cheerfully abandoned Du Guesclin, and thenceforth fought as courageously on the one side as he had previously done on the other. Charles of Navarre professed great desire to help forward the invaders, and his offers of friendship opened up to the prince the easiest way into Spain by way of the pass of Roncesvalles from Saint-

Jean-Pied-de-Port to Pamplona, the capital of Navarre. In
February, 1367, the prince's army made its way in frost and
snow through the valleys famous in romance. From Pamplona
two roads diverged to Burgos, the ancient Castilian capital. The
easier way ran south-westwards through Navarrese territory to
the Ebro at Logroño, where beyond the river lay the Castilian
frontier. The more difficult route went westwards through
rugged mountains and high valleys by way of Salvatierra and
Vitoria to a passage over the upper Ebro at Miranda. The
Black Prince chose the latter route, and reached Vitoria in
safety. Beyond the town King Henry's army held a position
so strong that Edward found it impossible to dislodge him.

The winter weather still held the upland valleys in its
grip when March was far advanced. Men and horses suffered
terribly from cold and hunger, and the prince, seeing that he
could not long maintain his position, boldly resolved to transfer
himself to the southern route. A flank march over snow-clad
sierras brought him to the vale of the Ebro, and, crossing the
stream at Logroño, he took up his position a few miles south-
west of that town, near the Castilian village of Navarrete. On
the prince's change of front King Henry also moved southward,
crossing the Ebro a few miles above Logroño, and then advanced to Nájera, a village about six miles west of Navarrete,
where he once more blocked the English path. The prince,
however, had the advantage of position and could afford to wait
until the Castilians attacked. On April 3 Henry advanced
over the little river Najarilla against the enemy. The Spanish
host fought after a different fashion from that practised by
both sides in the French wars. Only Du Guesclin and the
small remnant of the companies which still abode in Spain dismounted. The mass of the Castilians remained on their horses.
Their cavalry was of two sorts: besides a large number of
men-at-arms bestriding armoured steeds, there were swarms of
light horsemen, unencumbered by heavy armour and called *geni-
tours*, from being mounted on the fleet Spanish steeds called
jennets. The desperate valour of Du Guesclin and his followers
could not prevent utter disaster. Henry fled in panic from the
scene ; Du Guesclin was again a prisoner, and the Najarilla was
reddened by the blood of the thousands of fugitive Spaniards,
for, caught as in a trap at the narrow bridge which offered the

CHAP.
XVIII.

sole means of retreat, they were massacred without difficulty by the prince's troops. The victors marched on to Burgos, and, Don Henry having fled to France, Peter was restored with little further trouble to the Castilian throne.

The Black Prince remained in Castile all through the summer, waiting for the rewards which Don Peter had promised him. His army melted away through fever and dysentery, and the prince himself contracted the beginnings of a mortal disorder. Thus the crowning victory of his career was the last of his triumphs. Like many other leaders of chivalry, he had not understood the limitations of his resources, and had dissipated on this bootless Spanish campaign means scarcely sufficient to grapple with the spirit of disaffection already undermining his power in Aquitaine. With shattered health and the mere skeleton of his gallant army, he made his way back over the Pyrenees. Henceforth misfortune dogged every step of his career.

Since 1363 the constant residence of the Black Prince and his wife, Joan of Kent, in Gascony, had been broken only by his Castilian expedition. It was a wise policy to send the prince to hold a permanent court in Aquitaine, such as the land had never seen since Richard Cœur de Lion. All that affability, magnificence, and chivalry could do to make his domination attractive might be confidently anticipated from so brilliant and high-minded a knight as the prince of Aquitaine. The court of Bordeaux was as brilliant as the court of Windsor. "Never," boasted the Chandos Herald,[1] "was such good entertainment as his ; for every day at his table he had more than four-score knights and four times as many squires. There was found all nobleness, merriment, freedom, and honour. His subjects loved him, for he did them much good." The sulky magnates of the south-west, such as John of Armagnac and Gaston Phœbus of Foix, found their bitterness tempered by the prince's courtesy, while the boastful knights of Gascony looked forward to a career of honourable service under the descendant of their ancient dukes. Feastings and tournaments were not enough to win all his subjects' hearts ; and the Black Prince strove with some energy to show that he was a ruler of men as well as

---

[1] *Le Prince Noir, poème du héraut d'Armes Chandos*, pp. 107-108, ed. F. Michel.

the centre of a court.   It is to his credit that he cleared his inheritance from the free companies, so that Poitou and Limousin
enjoyed far more prosperity and tranquillity than in the days
of French ascendency.   Such new taxation as Gascon custom
allowed was only levied after grants from the three estates.
Great pains were taken to improve the administration, the
judicial system, and the coinage.   Edward saw that his best
policy was to rely upon the people of Gascony, and to look with
suspicion on the great lords.   But he did not understand how
limited was the authority which tradition gave to the dukes of
Aquitaine, and he was too stiff, too pedantic, too insular, to get
on really cordial terms with his subjects.   He never, like Gaston
Phœbus or Richard Cœur de Lion, threw himself into the local
life, language, and traditions of the country.

The Black Prince's greatest successes were with the towns,
and especially with those which had been continuously subject
to English rule.   The citizens of Bordeaux, who had feared lest
Edward's claim to the French crown should involve them in more
complete subjection, were appeased by promises that they should
in any case remain subject to the English monarchy.   Their liberties were increased and their wine trade was fostered, even to
the loss of English merchants.   The other towns were equally
contented.   Edward relied upon them as a counterpoise to the
feudal lords, and their liberties exempted them from the extraordinary taxes by which he strove to restore the equilibrium of
his finances.   The half-independent magnates were soon convinced that their chivalrous lord was no friend of aristocratic
privilege.   Edward, even when using their services in war,
carefully excluded them from the administration.   They saw
with disgust the chief offices monopolised by Englishmen.
An English bishop, John Harewell of Bath, was Edward's
chancellor and confidential adviser.   An English knight, Thomas
Felton, was seneschal of Aquitaine and head of the administration.   The constableship was assigned to Chandos.   The sene-
schalships of the several provinces were mainly in English
hands.   With English notions of the rights of the supreme
power, the prince paid little attention to the franchises of either
lord or prelate.   He mortally offended John of Armagnac by
requiring a direct oath of fealty from the Bishop of Rodez, who
held all his lands of Armagnac as Count of Rouergue.   Clerks

of lesser degree were outraged by the prince's attempts to hinder students from attending the university of Toulouse.

The Spanish expedition immensely increased the Black Prince's difficulties. He exhausted his finances to equip his army, and both on their coming and going his soldiers cruelly pillaged the country. Edward now dismissed most of his troops and urged them to betake themselves to France. In January, 1368, he obtained from the estates of Aquitaine a new hearth tax of ten *sous* a hearth for five years. The tax was freely voted and collected from the great majority of the payers without trouble. The towns were mainly exempt from it by reason of their liberties; and the lesser lords were as yet not averse from English rule. But the greater feudatories saw in the new hearth-tax a pretext for revolt. They had no special zeal for the French monarchy, but the house of Valois was weak and far removed from their territories. Their great concern was the preservation of their independence, which seemed more threatened by a resident prince than by a distant overlord at Paris. Even before the imposition of the hearth-tax, the Count of Armagnac entered into a secret treaty with Charles V., who promised to increase his territories and respect his franchises, if he would return to the French allegiance. The lord of Albret married a sister of the French queen and followed Armagnac's lead. A little later the Counts of Périgord and Comminges and other lords associated themselves with this policy. Thus the rule of the Black Prince in Aquitaine, acquiesced in by the mass of the people, was threatened by a feudal revolt. Armagnac appealed to the parliament of Paris against the hearth-tax. Charles V. accepted the appeal on the ground of the non-exchange of the renunciations which should have followed the treaty of Calais. Cited before the parliament in January, 1369, the Black Prince replied that he would go to Paris with helmet on head and with sixty thousand men at his back. His father once more assumed the title of King of France, and war broke out again.

The relative positions of France and England were different from what they had been nine years before. Edward III. was sinking into an unhonoured old age, and the Prince of Aquitaine suffered from dropsy, and was incapable of taking the field. Of their former comrades some, like Walter Manny, were dead, and others too old for much more fighting. On the other side was

Charles V., who had tamed Navarre and the feudal lords, had CHAP.
cleared the realm of the companies, had put down faction and ^{XVIII.}
disorder, and had made himself the head of a strong national
party, resolved to effect the expulsion of the foreigner. His
chief military counsellors were Du Guesclin, and Du Guesclin's
old adversary in the Breton wars, Oliver de Clisson, now the
zealous servant of the king. A wonderful outburst of French
patriotism facilitated the reconquest of the lands that had passed
to English rule nine years before. Even the tradition of military
superiority availed little against commanders who were learning
by their defeats how to meet their once invincible enemies.

There was a like modification in the foreign alliances of
the two kingdoms. Dynastic changes in the Netherlands had
robbed Edward of supporters who, though costly and ineffective, had been imposing in outward appearance. Even after
the dissolution of the alliances of the early years of the war,
the temporising policy of Louis de Male at least neutralised the
influence of Flanders. During the peace both Edward and
Charles did their best to win the goodwill of the Flemish count.
Louis' relation to the two rivals was the more important since
his only child was a daughter named Margaret. In 1356, this
lady, to Edward's great disgust, was promised in marriage to
Philip de Rouvre, Duke and Count of Burgundy, and Count
of Artois. The death of Philip in 1361 saved Edward from the
danger of a great state with one arm in the Burgundies and the
other in Flanders and Artois ; and the irritation of Louis de
Male at Charles V.'s grant of the Burgundian duchy to his
youngest son, Philip the Bold, gave the English king a new
chance of winning his favour. At last, in 1364, Edward concluded a treaty with Flanders according to his dearest wishes.
Edmund of Langley, Earl of Cambridge, his youngest son, was
betrothed to the widowed Margaret, with Ponthieu, Guines, and
Calais as their appanage. Great as were Edward's sacrifices,
they were worth making if a permanent union could be established between England and Flanders, equally threatening to
France and to the lords of the Netherlands. Charles persuaded Urban V. to refuse the necessary dispensations for the
marriage. Edward and Louis, irritated at the success of this
countermove, waited patiently and renewed their alliance.

No sooner was his understanding with Armagnac completed

CHAP.
XVIII.

than Charles strove to secure the support of northern as well as of southern feudalism against Edward. He offered his brother, Philip of Burgundy, to Margaret, along with the restoration of the districts of French Flanders, which he still held. In June, 1369, the marriage took place. Edmund of Cambridge lost his last chance of the great heiress, and Charles V. bought off the enmity of the Count of Flanders at the price of that union of Burgundy and Flanders which, in the next century, was to make the descendants of Philip and Margaret the most formidable opponents of the French monarchy. For the moment, however, Charles gained little. Flemish ships, indeed, fought against the English at sea, notably in Bourgneuf Bay in 1371, but next year Louis made peace with them. Despite his daughter's marriage, the Count of Flanders still showed that his sympathies were with England.

The other princes of the Netherlands were much more decidedly on the French side than the Count of Flanders. Margaret of Hainault, Queen Philippa's sister, had, after the death of her husband the Emperor Louis of Bavaria, in 1347, fought with her son William for the possession of her three counties of Hainault, Holland, and Zealand, to which Philippa also had pretensions, naturally upheld by her husband. William obtained such advantages over his mother that Margaret was obliged to invoke the assistance of her brother-in-law. Eager to regain his influence in the Netherlands, Edward willingly agreed to be arbiter between Margaret and her son, and at his suggestion the disputed lands were divided between them. William was married to Maud of Lancaster, Duke Henry's elder daughter, and thus secured to the English alliance. On Margaret's death William inherited all the three counties : but Maud died, and William became insane, whereupon his brother and heir invoked the support of the Emperor Charles IV., and was duly established in his fiefs. The claims of Philippa were ignored, and the Lancaster marriage with the lord of Holland, like the projected union of Edmund with the heiress of Flanders, failed to fulfil Edward's hopes.

Meanwhile Edward had to face the constant hostility of the emperor. Wenceslaus of Luxemburg, brother of Charles IV., had married the daughter and heiress of John III. of Brabant, with the result of solidly establishing the house of Luxemburg in the strongest of the duchies of the Low Countries. With the Luxemburger

as with the Bavarian, Edward's relations were unfriendly. Two
only of the Low German lords, the dukes of Gelderland and Jülich,
were willing to take his pay. Early in the war they were assailed
by the Luxemburgers, and the contest occupied all their energies.
Thus Edward re-entered the struggle against France with no help
save that of his own subjects. Urban V. died at Avignon in 1370,
and his successor, Gregory XI., was as little friendly to English
claims in France as his predecessors had been. Pope, emperor,
and the Netherlandish princes, were all either French or neutral.
And in 1369 Peter of Castile lost his throne, and soon afterwards perished at his brother's hands. Henry of Trastamara,
henceforth King of Castile, became the firm ally of the French,
who had already the support of Aragon. Even Charles the Bad
thought it prudent to declare for France.

At each stage of the war the French took the initiative.
The appeal of the southern nobles was the beginning of a
national movement which, before March, 1369, was supported
by more than 900 towns, castles, and fortified places in Edward's allegiance. In April the French invaded Ponthieu and
were welcomed as deliverers at Abbeville and the other towns
of the county. John of Gaunt led an army during the summer
from Calais southwards. He marched through Ponthieu, crossed
the Somme at Blanchetaque, and ravaged the country up to the
Seine. Then he retired exhausted, having gained no real advantage by this mere foray. Charles announced that, as Edward
had supported the free companies, he fell under the excommunication threatened by the pope against the abettors of these pests
of society, and that the vassals of the English crown were therefore relieved from allegiance to him. Soon afterwards he declared that Edward had forfeited all his possessions in France.

Quercy and Rouergue, which had submitted last, were
the first districts of Aquitaine to revolt. Cahors declared for
France as soon as the Black Prince was cited to Paris. By
the end of 1369 all Quercy had acknowledged Charles V.,
and John of Armagnac ruled Rouergue as his vassal. It was
the same in the Garonne valley, where towns which had no
quarrel with English rule, were swept away by the strong tide
of national feeling that surged round their walls. A systematic
attack was made upon the English power in Aquitaine. Charles
V. fitted out new armies in which the townsmen and the country-

folk fought side by side with the nobility. Two of his brothers, John, Duke of Berri, and Louis, Duke of Anjou, prepared to assail the intruders, Berri in the central uplands, Anjou in the Garonne valley. It was not enough to recover what was lost. Aggression must be met by aggression, and the Duke of Burgundy, Charles' third brother, equipped a fleet in Norman ports, either to invade England or at least to cut off the Black Prince from his base. Portsmouth was burnt, before England had made any effort to defend her shores.

The English were strangely inactive. The Black Prince lay sick at Cognac, and of his subordinates Chandos, now seneschal of Poitou, alone showed vigour. Chandos, finding the lords of Poitou much more loyal to the English connexion than those of the south, was able to take the aggressive by invading Anjou. He was, however, soon recalled to protect Poitou, and on January 1, 1370, was mortally wounded at the bridge of Lussac. James Audley had already died of disease in another Poitevin town. While England was losing her best soldiers, Du Guesclin began a fresh series of raids in the Garonne valley. Soon the banner of the lilies waved within a few leagues of Bordeaux, and ancient towns of the English obedience, like Bazas and Bergerac, fell into the enemy's hands. With the capture of Périgueux, the Limousin was isolated from Gascon succour. In August the Duke of Berri appeared before the walls of the *cité*, or episcopal quarter, of Limoges, and the bishop promptly handed it over to him.

Disasters at last stirred up the English to action. In 1370 John of Gaunt was sent with one army to Gascony and Sir Robert Knowles with another to Calais. The Black Prince, though unable to ride, was eager to command. It was arranged that while Lancaster led one force from Bordeaux to Limoges, Edward should accompany another that marched from Cognac towards the same destination. To resist this combination Du Guesclin strove to combine the separate armies of the Dukes of Anjou and Berri. However, he failed to prevent the junction of Lancaster and Edward, and their advance to Limoges. On September 19, the anniversary of Poitiers, the city of Limoges opened its gates after a five days' siege. The English took a terrible revenge. Not a house in the *cité* was spared, and the cathedral rose over a mass of ruins. The whole population

was put to the sword, the Black Prince in his litter watching CHAP.
grimly the execution of his orders. A few gentlemen alone were XVIII.
saved for the sake of their ransoms. Among them was the
brother of Pope Gregory XI., who not unnaturally became a
warm friend of the patriotic party. The sack of Limoges
was the last exploit of the Black Prince. Early in 1371, he
returned to England, partly because of his state of health,
and partly because he had no money to pay his soldiers. It is
not unlikely that he was already on bad terms with John of
Gaunt, who had necessarily taken the chief share in the campaign and was nominated his successor. Too late, efforts were
made to conciliate the Gascons; in 1370 a supreme court was
set up at Saintes to save the necessity of appeals to London
which had become as onerous as the ancient frequency of resort
to the parliament of Paris; and the hearth-tax, the ostensible
cause of the rising, was formally renounced.

Sir Robert Knowles's expedition of 1370 was as futile as
that of Lancaster. He advanced from Calais into the heart
of northern France. Taught by long experience the danger
of joining battle, the French allowed him to wander where
he would, plundering and ravaging the country. Roughly
following the line of march of Edward III. in 1360, the English
advanced through Artois and Vermandois to Laon and Reims,
and thence southwards through Champagne. Then striking
northwards from the Burgundian border, they appeared, at
the end of September, before the southern suburbs of Paris.
To dissipate the alarm felt at the presence of the English,
Du Guesclin was summoned from the south and made constable of France. Before his arrival Knowles had moved on
westwards towards the Beauce, intending to reach his own
estates in Brittany for winter quarters. But his young captains
got out of control. Led by a Gloucestershire knight, Sir John
Minsterworth, "ready in hand but deceitful and perverse in
mind," a considerable section of the troops refused to follow the
old "tomb-robber" to Brittany, and determined to spend the
winter where they were, under Minsterworth's leadership.
Knowles would not give place to his subordinate, and made
his way to Brittany with the part of his army which was
still faithful to him. No sooner was he well started than Du
Guesclin, after a march of ninety miles in three days, fell upon

his rearguard at Pontvallain in southern Maine and overwhelmed it, on December 4, 1370. Knowles managed to reach Brittany with the bulk of his forces, and Minsterworth, the real cause of the disaster, ventured to go to England and denounce his leader as a traitor. He was forced to flee to France, where he openly joined the enemy. Seven years later he was captured and executed.

Minsterworth was not the only traitor. In the earlier part of the war, there had fought on the English side a grand-nephew of the last independent Prince of Wales, Sir Owen ap Thomas ap Rhodri,[1] whose grandfather, Rhodri or Roderick, the youngest brother of the princes Llewelyn and David, had after the ruin of his house lived obscurely as a small Cheshire and Gloucestershire landlord. In 1365 Owen was in France, engaged, no doubt, in one of the free companies, and on his father's death he returned to defend his inheritance from the claims of the Charltons of Powys. Having succeeded in this, he returned to France, and nothing more is heard of him until after the renewal of the war. In 1370 he appeared as a strenuous partisan of the French. Mindful of his ancestry he posed as the lawful Prince of Wales, and established communications with his countrymen, both in France and in Wales. Anxious to stir up discord in Edward's realm, the French king gladly upheld his claims. A gallant knight and an impulsive, energetic partisan, Sir Owen of Wales soon won a place of his own in the history of his time. In Gwynedd he was celebrated as Owain *Lawgoch*, Owen of the Red Hand. Conspiracies in his favour were ruthlessly stamped out, and a halo of legend and poetry soon encircled his name. In France Charles entrusted him and another Welshman, named John Wynn, with the equipment of a fleet at Rouen with which the champion was to descend on the principality and excite a rising. Bad weather caused the complete destruction of the expedition of the Welsh pretender. Two years later, however, another fleet was fitted out on his behalf, and in June, 1372, Owen took possession of Guernsey.

At that time the fortune of war was strongly in favour of France, though the initial successes of Charles V. were damped by the doubtful results of the petty struggles which filled the year 1371. During that year Du Guesclin, the soul of the French

---

[1] The place of Owen of Wales in history was for the first time clearly shown by Mr. Edward Owen in *Y Cymmrodor*, 1899-1900, pp. 1-105.

attack, ejected the English from many places in Normandy and Poitou. On the other hand, the English won the hard fought battle over a Flemish fleet in Bourgneuf Bay, which has already been mentioned. They also showed some power of recovery in Aquitaine, where their recapture of Figeac in upper Quercy gave them a base for renewing their attacks on Rouergue. On the whole then, the year left matters much as they had been.

The occupation of Guernsey by Owen of Wales was the beginning of a new series of French victories. Up to that time the northern coastlands of Aquitaine, lower Poitou, Saintonge, and Angoumois had remained almost entirely under their English lords. In the hope of resisting attack, the English projected the invasion of France both from Calais and from Guienne. To carry out the latter plan John Hastings, Earl of Pembroke, was despatched with a fleet and army from England, with a commission to succeed John of Gaunt as the king's lieutenant in Aquitaine. The Franco-Spanish alliance then began to bear its fruits. Henry of Trastamara equipped a strong Spanish fleet to meet the invaders in the Bay of Biscay. On June 23, 1372, the two fleets fought an action off La Rochelle. The light Spanish galleys out-manœuvred the heavy English ships, laden deep in the water with stores and filled with troops and horses. The Spaniards set on fire some of the English transports, which became unmanageable owing to the fright of the horses embarked upon them. The English fought valiantly, and night fell before the battle was decided. Next day, the Spaniards attacked again, and won a complete victory. The English fleet was destroyed, and Pembroke was taken a prisoner to Santander.

The news of Pembroke's defeat encouraged the French to attempt the conquest of Poitou. Du Guesclin invaded the county from the north in co-operation with the Spaniards at sea. Owen of Wales abandoned the siege of Cornet castle, in Guernsey, which still held out against him, and hurried to join the Spaniards. At Santander he met the captive Pembroke, and bitterly reproached the marcher earl with the part his house had taken in driving the Welsh from their lands. In August Owen and the Spaniards were lying off La Rochelle. Sir Thomas Percy, seneschal of Poitou, and the Captal de Buch were with a considerable force at Soubise, near the mouth of the Charente.

Owen ascended the river and fell unexpectedly on the English at night. The English were utterly defeated and both leaders were taken prisoners, Thomas Percy, the future ally of Owen Glendower, being captured by one of Sir Owen's Welsh followers. Meanwhile, Du Guesclin, after receiving the surrender of Poitiers on August 7, pressed forward to the coast and was soon in touch with Owen and the Spaniards. On the same September day Angoulême and La Rochelle opened their gates to the French. In the course of the same month all the other towns of the district declared for the winning side. The nobles of Poitou were still to some extent English in sympathy, and a considerable band of them and their followers took refuge in Thouars. On December 1 this last stronghold of Poitevin feudalism surrendered. The tidings of disaster roused the old English king to his final martial effort. A fleet was raised and sailed from Sandwich, having on board the king, the Prince of Wales, the Duke of Lancaster, and many other magnates. Contrary winds kept the vessels near the English coast, and the vast sums lavished on the equipment of the expedition were wasted. In despair the Black Prince surrendered to his father his principality of Aquitaine. When the king begged the commons for a further war subsidy, he was told that the navy had been ruined by his harsh impressment of seamen, and his refusal to give them pay when detained in port waiting for orders. When the command of the sea passed to the French and their Spanish allies, all hope of retaining Aquitaine was lost.

The final stages in the ruin of the English power in France need not detain us long. Despite his successes, Du Guesclin persevered in his policy of wearing down the English by delays and by avoiding pitched battles. He turned his attention to Brittany, where Duke John, in difficulties with his subjects, had invoked the aid of an English army. Thereupon the Breton barons called the French king to take possession of the duchy, whose lord was betraying it to the foreigner. The old party struggle was at an end : Celtic Brittany joined hands with French Brittany. Before the end of 1373, Duke John was a fugitive, and only a few castles with English garrisons upheld his cause. Of these Brest was the most important, and despite the Spaniards and Owen of Wales, the English were still strong enough at sea to retain possession of the place.

In July, 1373, John of Gaunt marched out of Calais with one CHAP.
of the strongest armies with which an English invader had ever XVIII.
entered France.   Pursuing a general south-easterly direction,
the English pitilessly devastated Artois, Picardy, and Champagne.   Du Guesclin hastened back from Brittany to command
the army engaged in watching Lancaster.   He still continued his
defensive tactics, but gave the enemy little rest.   Lancaster was
no match for so able a general as the Breton constable.   At the
end of September he moved from Troyes to Sens, and thence
pushed into Burgundy.   Then he turned westwards through the
Nivernais and the Bourbonnais, and led his army through the
uplands of Auvergne.   By the end of the year he had traversed
the Limousin, and made his way to Bordeaux.   Half his army
had perished of hunger, cold, and in petty warfare.   The horses
had suffered worse than the men, and the baggage train was
almost destroyed.   Without fighting a battle Du Guesclin had
put the enemy out of action.   Experience now showed how useless were the prolonged plundering raids which ten years before
had filled all France with terror.

Even in Gascony Lancaster could not hold his own.   After
declining battle with the Duke of Anjou, he returned to England, leaving Sir Thomas Felton as seneschal.   The enemy had
penetrated to the very heart of the old English district.   La
Réole opened its gates to them ;   Saint-Sever, the seat of the
Gascon high court, followed its example.   By 1374 the English
duchy was reduced to the coast lands around Bayonne and Bordeaux.   That year the French laid siege to Chandos's castle
of Saint-Sauveur-le-Vicomte.   The siege was as long and as
elaborately organised as the great siege of Calais.   A ring of
bastilles was erected round the doomed town, and cannon discharged huge balls of stone against its ramparts.   After nearly
a year's siege the garrison agreed to surrender on condition of a
heavy payment.   With the fall of the old home of the Harcourts
the English power in Normandy perished.   There was still, it
is true, the influence of Charles of Navarre ;   but that desperate
intriguer had compromised himself so much with both parties
that no confidence could be placed in him.

The misfortunes of the English inclined them to listen to
proposals of peace.   Though the papacy was more frankly on
the French side than ever, it had not lost its ancient solicitude

to put an end to the war. With that object Gregory XI., though eager to return to Rome, tarried in the Rhone valley. Two of his legates appeared in Champagne at the time of John of Gaunt's abortive expedition. From that moment offers of peace were constantly pressed on both sides. Lancaster was at Calais, and Anjou was not far off at Saint-Omer, when definite proposals were exchanged. Before long it was found more convenient that the envoys should meet face to face, and for this reason the two dukes accepted the hospitality of Louis de Male, and held personal interviews at Bruges. More than once the negotiations broke down altogether. At no time was there much hope of a permanent peace. The English insisted on the terms of 1360, and the French demanded the cession of Calais and the release of the unpaid ransom of King John. However, on June 27, 1375, a truce for a year was signed at Bruges, which was further extended until June, 1377, just long enough to allow the old king to end his days in peace. France had once more to wrestle with the companies set free by the truce, so that England could still enjoy possession of Calais, Bordeaux, Bayonne, Brest, and the other scanty remnants of the cessions of the treaty of Calais. Satisfied at putting an end to the war, Gregory XI. betook himself to Rome. Thus the truce outlasted the Babylonish captivity of the papacy as well as the life of Edward III.

CHAPTER XIX.

ENGLAND DURING THE LATTER YEARS OF EDWARD III.

NEVER was Edward's glory so high as in the years immediately succeeding the treaty of Calais. The unspeakable misery of France heightened his magnificence by the strength of the contrast. At eight-and-forty he retained the vigour and energy of his younger days, though surrounded by a band of grown-up sons. In 1362 the king celebrated his jubilee, or his fiftieth birthday, amidst feasts of unexampled splendour. Not less magnificent were the festivities that attended the visits of the three kings, of France, Cyprus, and Scotland, in 1364.

Of the glories of these years we have detailed accounts from an eye-witness, a writer competent, above all other men of his time, to set down in courtly and happy phrase the wonders that delighted his eyes. In 1361, John Froissart, an adventurous young clerk from Valenciennes, sought out a career for himself in the household of his countrywoman, Queen Philippa, bearing with him as his credentials a draft of a verse chronicle which was his first attempt at historical composition. He came to England at the right moment. The older generation of historians had laid down their pens towards the conclusion of the great war, and had left no worthy successors. The new-comer was soon to surpass them, not in precision and sobriety, but in wealth of detail, in literary charm, and in genial appreciation of the externals of his age. He recorded with an eye-witness's precision of colour, though with utter indifference to exactness, the tournaments and fêtes, the banquets and the *largesses* of the noble lords and ladies of the most brilliant court in Christendom. He celebrated the courtesy of the knightly class, their devotion to their word of honour, the liberality with which captive foreigners was allowed to share in their sports and pleasures, and the implicit loyalty with which nearly all the many captive

27 *

CHAP.
XIX.
knights repaid the trust placed on their word. To him Edward was the most glorious of kings, and Philippa, his patroness, the most beautiful, liberal, pious, and charitable of queens. For nine years he enjoyed the queen's bounty, and described with loyal partiality the exploits of English knights. With the death of his patroness and the beginning of England's misfortunes, the light-minded adventurer sought another master in the French-loving Wenceslaus of Brabant. The first edition of his chronicle, compiled when under the spell of the English court, contrasts strongly with the second version written at Brussels at the instigation of the Luxemburg duke of Brabant.

Even Froissart saw that all was not well in England. The common people seemed to him proud, cruel, disloyal, and suspicious. Their delight was in battle and slaughter, and they hated the foreigner with a fierce hatred which had no counterpart in the cosmopolitan knightly class. They were the terror of their lords and delighted in keeping their kings under restraint. The Londoners were the most mighty of the English and could do more than all the rest of England. Other writers tell the same tale. The same fierce patriotism that Froissart notes glows through the rude battle songs in which Lawrence Minot sang the early victories of Edward from Halidon Hill to the taking of Guînes, and inspired Geoffrey le Baker to repeat with absolute confidence every malicious story which gossip told to the discredit of the French king and his people. It was under the influence of this spirit that the steps were taken, which we have already recorded, to extend the use of English, notably in the law courts. Yet the old bilingual habit clave long to the English. Despite the statute of 1362, the lawyers continued to employ the French tongue, until it crystallised into the jargon of the later *Year Books* or of Littleton's *Tenures.* Under Edward III., however, French remained the living speech of many Englishmen. John Gower wrote in French the earliest of his long poems. But he is a thorough Englishman for all that. He writes in French, but, as he says, he writes for England.[1]

It was characteristic of the patriotic movement of the reign of Edward III. that a new courtly literature in the English

---

[1] "O gentile Engleterre, a toi j'escrits," *Mirour de l'Omme*, in John Gower's *Works*, i., 378, ed. G. C. Macaulay, to whom belongs the credit of recovering this long lost work.

language rivalled the French vernacular literature which as yet had by no means ceased to produce fruit. The new type begins with the anonymous poems, " Sir Gawain and the Green Knight," and the " Pearl ". While Froissart was the chief literary figure at the English court during the ten years after the treaty of Calais, his place was occupied in the concluding decade of the reign by Geoffrey Chaucer, the first great poet of the English literary revival. The son of a substantial London vintner, Chaucer spent his youth as a page in the household of Lionel of Antwerp, from which he was transferred to the service of Edward himself. He took part in more than one of Edward's French campaigns, and served in diplomatic missions to Italy, Flanders, and elsewhere. His early poems reflect the modes and metres of the current French tradition in an English dress, and only reach sustained importance in his lament on the death of the Duchess Blanche of Lancaster, written about 1370. It is significant that the favourite poet of the king's declining years was no clerk but a layman, and that the Tuscan mission of 1373, which perhaps first introduced him to the treasures of Italian poetry, was undertaken in the king's service. Thorough Englishman as Chaucer was, he had his eyes open to every movement of European culture. His higher and later style begins with his study of Dante, Petrarch, and Boccaccio. Though he wrote for Englishmen in their own tongue, his fame was celebrated by the French poet, Eustace Deschamps, as the "great translator" who had sown the flowers of French poesy in the realm of Æneas and Brut the Trojan. His broad geniality stood in strong contrast to the savage patriotism of Minot. In becoming national, English vernacular art did not become insular.

Chaucer wrote in the tongue of the southern midlands, the region wherein were situated his native London, the two universities, the habitual residences of the court, the chief seats of parliaments and councils, and the most frequented marts of commerce. For the first time a standard English language came into being, largely displacing for literary purposes the local dialects which had hitherto been the natural vehicles of writing in their respective districts. The Yorkshireman, Wycliffe, the west-countryman, Langland, adopted before the end of the reign the tongue of the capital for their literary language in preference to the speech of their native shires. The language of the extreme south, the descendant of the tongue of the West Saxon court, became the dialect of peasants and artisans. That a continuous life was reserved for the idiom of the north country, was due to its becoming the speech of a free Scotland, the language in which Barbour, Archdeacon of Aberdeen, commemorated for the court of the first Stewart king the exploits of Robert Bruce and the Scottish war of independence. The unity of England thus found another notable expression in the oneness of the popular speech. And the evolution of the northern dialect into the "Scottish" of a separate kingdom showed that, if England were united, English-speaking Britain remained divided.

Other arts indicate the same tendency. Even in the thirteenth century English Gothic architecture differentiated itself pretty completely from its models in the Isle de France. The early fourteenth century, the age of the so-called "decorated style," suggests in some ways a falling back to the French types, though the prosperity of England and the desolation of France make the English examples of fourteenth century building the more numerous and splendid. The occasional tendency of the later "flowing" decorated towards "flamboyant" forms, to be seen in some of the churches of Northamptonshire, marks the culminating point of this fresh approximation of French and English architecture. But the division between the two countries brought about by war was illustrated before the end of the reign in the growth of the most local of our medieval architectural types, that "perpendicular" style which is so strikingly different from the "flamboyant" art of the neighbouring kingdom. This specially English style begins early in the reign of Edward III., when the cult of the murdered Edward of Carnarvon gave to the monks of St. Peter's, Gloucester, the means to recast the massive columns and gloomy arcades of the eastern portions of their romanesque abbey church after the lighter and brighter patterns in which Gloucester set the fashion to all southern Britain. In the buildings of the later years of Edward's reign the old "flowing decorated" and the newer and stiffer "perpendicular" grew up side by side. If the two seem almost combined in the church of Edington, in Wiltshire, the foundation dedicated in 1361 for his native village by Edward's chancellor, Bishop Edington of Winchester, the triumph of the perpendicular is assured in the new choir which Archbishop

Thoresby began for York Minster, and in the reconstruction of the Norman cathedral of Winchester begun by Bishop Edington, and completed when his greater successor, William of Wykeham, carried out in a more drastic way the device already adopted at Gloucester of recasing the ancient structure so as to suit modern tastes. The full triumph of the new style is apparent in Wykeham's twin foundations at Winchester and Oxford. The separation of feeling between England and Scotland is now seen in architecture as well as in language. When the perpendicular fashion was carrying all before it in the southern realm, the Scottish builders erected their churches after the flamboyant type of their French allies. Thus while the twelfth and thirteenth century structures of the northern and southern kingdoms are practically indistinguishable, the differences between the two nations, which had arisen from the Edwardian policy of conquest, expressed themselves ultimately in the striking contrast between the flamboyant of Melrose or St. Giles' and the perpendicular of Winchester or Windsor.

English patriotism, which had asserted itself in the literature and art of the people long before it dominated courtly circles, continued to express itself in more popular forms than even those of the poems of Chaucer. The older fashions of instructing the people were still in vogue in the early part of Edward's reign. Richard Rolle, the hermit of Hampole, whose *Prick of Conscience* and vernacular paraphrases of the Bible illustrate the older didactic literature, was carried off in his Yorkshire cell in the year of the Black Death. The cycles of miracle plays, which edified and amused the townsfolk of Chester and York, crystallised into a permanent shape early in this reign, and were set forth with ever-increasing elaborateness by an age bent on pageantry and amusement. The vernacular sermons and popular manuals of devotion increased in numbers and copiousness. In this the time of the Black Death is, as in other aspects of our story, a deep dividing line.

The note of increasing strain and stress is fully expressed in the earlier forms of *The Vision of Piers Plowman*, which were composed before the death of Edward III. Its author, William Langland, a clerk in minor orders, debarred by marriage from a clerical career, came from the Mortimer estates in the march of Wales: but his life was mainly spent in London, and he wrote

in the tongue of the city of his adoption. The first form of
the poem is dated 1362, the year of the second visitation of the
Black Death, while the troubles of the end of the reign perhaps
inspired the fuller edition which saw the light in 1377. It is a
commonplace to contrast the gloomy pictures drawn by Langland with the highly coloured pictures of contemporary society
for which Chaucer was gathering his materials. Yet this contrast may be pressed too far. Though Langland had a keen
eye to those miseries of the poor which are always with us, the
impression of the time gathered from his writings is not so much
one of material suffering, as of social unrest and discontent. The
poor ploughman, who cannot get meat, still has his cheese, curds,
and cream, his loaf of beans and bran, his leeks and cabbage, his
cow, calf, and cart mare.[1] The very beggar demanded "bread
of clean wheat" and "beer of the best and brownest," while the
landless labourer despised "night-old cabbage," "penny-ale," and
bacon, and asked for fresh meat and fish freshly fried.[2] There
is plenty of rough comfort and coarse enjoyment in the England
through which "Long Will" stalked moodily, idle, hopeless,
and in himself exemplifying many of the evils which he condemned. The England of Langland is bitter, discontented, and
sullen. It is the popular answer to the class prejudice and reckless greed of the lords and gentry. Langland's own attitude
towards the more comfortable classes is much that of the self-
assertive and mutinous Londoner whom Froissart looked upon
with such bitter prejudice. He boasts that he was loath to do reverence to lords and ladies, or to those clad in furs with pendants
of silver, and refuses to greet "sergeants" with a "God save you".
Every class of society is flagellated in his scathing criticisms.
He is no revolutionist with a new gospel of reform, but, though
content to accept the old traditions, he is the ruthless denouncer
of abuses, and is thoroughly filled with the spirit which, four
years after the second recension of his book, found expression
in the Peasants' Revolt of 1381. With all the archaism of his
diction and metre, Langland, even more than Chaucer, reflects
the modernity of his age.

Even the universities were growing more national, for the
war prevented Oxford students from seeking, after their English

---

[1] *Vision of Piers Plowman*, i., 220, ed. Skeat.
[2] *Ibid.*, i., 222.

graduation, a wider career at Paris. William of Ockham, the last of the great English schoolmen that won fame in the European rather than in the English world, died about 1349 in the service of the Bavarian emperor. In the same year the plague swept away Thomas Bradwardine, the "profound doctor," at the moment of his elevation to the throne of Canterbury. Bradwardine, though a scholar of universal reputation, won his fame at Oxford without the supplementary course at Paris, and lived all his career in his native land. As an English university career became more self-sufficient, Oxford became the school of the politician and the man of affairs as much as of the pure student. The new tendency is illustrated by the careers of the brothers Stratford, both Oxford scholars, yet famous not for their writings but for lives devoted to the service of the State, though rewarded by the highest offices of the Church. His conspicuous position as a teacher of scholastic philosophy first brought John Wycliffe into academic prominence. But he soon won a wider fame as a preacher in London, an adviser of the court, an opponent of the "possessioner" monks, and of the forsworn friars, who, deserting apostolic poverty, vied with the monks in covetousness. His attacks on practical abuses in the Church marked him out as a politician as well as a philosopher. His earlier career ended in 1374, the year in which he first became the king's ambassador, not long after proceeding to the degree of doctor of divinity,[1] His later struggles must be considered in the light of the political history of the concluding episodes of Edward's reign. In a few years we shall find the Oxford champion abandoning the Latin language of universal culture, and appealing to the people in homely English. With Wycliffe's entry upon his wider career, it is hardly too much to say that Oxford ceased to be merely a part of the cosmopolitan training ground of the schoolmen, and became in some fashion a national institution. Cambridge, too young and obscure in earlier ages to have rivalled Oxford, first began to enjoy an increasing reputation.

Hitherto culture had been not only cosmopolitan but clerical. Every university student and nearly every professional man was a clerk. But education was becoming possible for laymen, and

---

[1] This was before Dec. 26, 1373. See Twemlow in *Engl. Hist. Review*, xv. (1900), 529-530.

there were already lay professions outside the clerical caste. The wide cultivation and the vigorous literary output of laymen of letters like Chaucer and Gower are sufficient evidence of this. But the best proof is the complete differentiation of the common lawyers from the clergy. The inns of court of London became virtually a legal university, where highly trained men studied a juristic system, which was not the less purely English in spirit because its practitioners used the French tongue as their technical instrument. There were no longer lawyers in England who, like Bracton, strove to base the law of the land on the forms and methods of Roman jurisprudence. There were no longer kings, like Edward I., with Italian trained civilians at their court ready to translate the law of England into imperialist forms. The canonist still studied at Oxford or Cambridge, but his career was increasingly clerical, and the Church, unlike the State, was unable to nationalise itself, though the whole career of Wycliffe and the strenuous efforts of the kings and statesmen who passed the statutes of Provisors and Præmunire, showed that some of the English clergy, and many of the English laity, were willing to make the effort. English law, in divorcing itself from the universities and the clergy, became national as well as lay. There were no longer any Weylands who concealed their clerical beginnings, and hid away the subdeacon under the married knight and justice, the founder of a landowning family. The lawyers of Edward's reign were frankly laymen, marrying and giving in marriage, establishing new families that became as noble as any of the decaying baronial houses, and yet cherishing a corporate ideal and common spirit as lively and real as those of any monastery or clerical association.

In enumerating the many convergent tendencies which worked together in strengthening the national life, we must not forget the growing importance of commerce. Merchant princes like the Poles could rival the financial operations of Lombard or Tuscan, and climb into the baronial class. The proud and mutinous temper of the Londoners was largely due to their ever-increasing wealth. We are on the threshold of the careers of commercial magnates, like the Philpots and the Whittingtons. Even when Edward III. was still on the throne, a London mayor of no special note, John Pyel, could set up in his native Northamptonshire village of Irthlingborough a college and church of remarkable stateliness and dignity.　The growth of the wool trade, and its gradual transfer to English hands, the development of the staple system, the rise of an English seaman class that knew all the havens of Europe, the beginnings of the English cloth manufacture, all indicate that English commerce was not only becoming more extensive, but was gradually emancipating itself from dependence on the foreigner.　Thus before the end of Edward's reign England was an intensely national state, proudly conscious of itself, and haughtily contemptuous of the foreigner, with its own language, literature, style in art, law, universities, and even the beginnings of a movement towards the nationalisation of the Church.　The cosmopolitanism of the earlier Middle Ages was everywhere on the wane.　A modern nation had arisen out of the old world-state and world-spirit.　In the England of Edward III., Chaucer, and Wycliffe, we have reached the consummation of the movement whose first beginnings we have traced in the early storms of the reign of Henry III.　It is in the development of this tendency that the period from 1216 to 1377 possesses such unity as it has.

During the years of peace after the treaty of Calais, Edward III. completed the scheme for the establishment of his family begun with the grant of Aquitaine to the Black Prince.　The state of the king's finances made it impossible for him to provide for numerous sons and daughters from the royal exchequer, and the system of appanages had seldom been popular or successful in England.　Edward found an easier way of endowing his offspring by politic marriages that transferred to his sons the endowments and dignities of the great houses, which, in spite of lavish creations of new earldoms, were steadily dying out in the male line.　Some of his daughters in the same way were married into baronial families whose attachment to the throne would, it was believed, be strengthened by intermarriage with the king's kin ; while others, wedded to foreign princes, helped to widen the circle of continental alliances on which he never ceased to build large hopes.　Collateral branches of the royal family were pressed into the same system, which was so systematically ordered that it has passed for a new departure in English history.　This is, however, hardly the case.

Many previous kings, notably Edward I., carried out a policy based upon similar lines, and only less conspicuous by reason of the smaller number of children that they had to provide for. The descendants of Henry III. and Edward I. in no wise kept true to the monarchical tradition, but rather gave distinction to the baronial opposition by ennobling it with royal alliances. But the martial and vigorous policy of Edward III. had at least the effect of reducing to inactivity the tradition of constitutional opposition which had been the common characteristic of successive generations of the royal house of Lancaster, the chief collateral branch of the royal family. Subsequent history will show that the Edwardian family settlement was as unsuccessful as that of his grandfather. The alliances which Edward built up brought neither solidarity to the royal house, nor strength to the crown, nor union to the baronage. But the working out of this, as of so many of the new developments of the later part of Edward's reign, can only be seen after his death.

Edward's eldest son became, as we have seen, Duke of Cornwall, Prince of Wales, and Earl of Chester even before he received Aquitaine. He was the first of the continuous line of English princes of Wales, for Edward III. never bore that title. The Black Prince's marriage with his cousin, Joan of Kent, was a love-match, and the estates of his bride were scarcely an important consideration to the lord of Wales and Cheshire. Yet the only child of the unlucky Edmund of Woodstock was no mean heiress, bringing with her the estates of her father's earldom of Kent, besides the inheritance of her mother's family, the Wakes of Liddell and Lincolnshire. The estates and earldom afterwards passed to Joan's son by a former husband, and the Holland earls of Kent formed a minor family connexion which closely supported the throne of Richard of Bordeaux. Though their paternal inheritance was that of Lancashire squires, the Hollands won a leading place in the history of the next generation.

Edward III.'s second son, William of Hatfield, died in infancy. For his third son, Lionel of Antwerp, when still in his childhood, Edward found the greatest heiress of her time, Elizabeth, the only daughter of William de Burgh, the sixth lord of Connaught and third Earl of Ulster, the representative of one of the chief Anglo-Norman houses in Ireland. Even before his marriage, Lionel was made Earl of Ulster, a title sunk after

1362 in the novel dignity of the duchy of Clarence. This
title was chosen because Elizabeth de Burgh was a grand-
daughter of Elizabeth of Clare, the sister of the last Clare
Earl of Gloucester, and a share of the Gloucester inheritance
passed through her to the young duke. His marriage gave
Lionel a special relation to Ireland, where, however, his two
lordships of Ulster and Connaught were largely in the hands
of the native septs, and where the royal authority had never
won back the ground lost during the vigorous onslaught of
Edward Bruce on the English power. In 1342 the estates of
Ireland forwarded to Edward a long statement of the shortcomings of the English administration of the island.[1] No effective steps were taken to remedy those evils until, in 1361, Edward
III. sent Lionel as governor to Ireland, declaring " that our Irish
dominions have been reduced to such utter devastation and ruin
that they may be totally lost, if our subjects there are not immediately succoured ". Lionel's most famous achievement was
the statute of Kilkenny. This law prohibited the intermix-
ture of the Anglo-Normans in Ireland with the native Irish,
which was rapidly undermining the basis of English rule and
confounding Celts and Normans in a nation, ever divided
indeed against itself, but united against the English. Lionel
wearied of a task beyond his strength. His wife's early death
lessened the ties which bound him to her land, and he went
back to England declaring that he would never return to Ireland
if he could help it. His succession as governor by a Fitzgerald
showed that the plan of ruling Ireland through England was
abandoned by Edward III. in favour of the cheaper but fatal
policy of concealing the weakness of the English power by com-
bining it with the strength of the strongest of the Anglo-Norman
houses. Under this faulty system, the statute of Kilkenny
became inoperative almost from its enactment.

The widowed Duke of Clarence made a second great marriage. The Visconti, tyrants of Milan, were willing to pay
heavily for the privilege of intermarriage with the great reigning
families of Europe, and neither Edward III. nor the French
king could resist the temptation of alliance with a family that
was able to endow its daughters so richly. Accordingly, the
Duke of Clarence became in 1368 the husband of Violante

[1] *Cal. of Close Rolls,* 1341-43, pp. 508-16,

Visconti, the daughter of Galeazzo, lord of Pavia, and the niece of Bernabò, signor of Milan, the bitter foe of the Avignon papacy. Five months later, Lionel was carried away by a sudden sickness, and thus the Visconti marriage brought little fruit to England. Lionel's only child, Philippa, the offspring of his first marriage, was married, just before her father's death, to Edmund Mortimer, Earl of March, great-grandson of the traitor earl beheaded in 1330. Lionel's death added to the vast inheritance of the Mortimers and Joinvilles the lands and claims of Ulster and Clarence, and so Edward III.'s magnanimity in reviving the earldom of March after the disgrace of 1330 was rewarded by the devolution of its estates to his grand-daughter's child. The Earl of March was invested with a new political importance, for his wife was the nearest representative of Edward III., save for the dying Black Prince and his sickly son. The fierce blood and broad estates of the great marcher family continued to give importance to Philippa's descendants; and finally the house of Mortimer mounted the throne in the person of Edward IV.

The estates of Lancaster were annexed to the reigning branch of the royal house by the marriage in 1359 of John of Gaunt, Edward's third surviving son, with Blanche of Lancaster, the heiress of Duke Henry, who became, after her sister Maud's death, the sole inheritor of the duchy of Lancaster. In 1362 John, who had hitherto been Earl of Richmond, yielded up this dignity to the younger John of Montfort, its rightful heir, and was created Duke of Lancaster at the same time that Lionel was made Duke of Clarence. Ten years after her marriage Blanche died, leaving John a son, Henry of Derby, the future Henry IV., whose wedding, after his grandfather's death, to one of the Bohun co-heiresses brought part of the estates of another great house within the grasp of Edward III.'s descendants. Moreover, the other Bohun co-heiress became in 1376 the wife of Thomas of Woodstock, the youngest of Edward's sons, the Gloucester of the next reign. The three Bohun earldoms of Hereford, Essex, and Northampton were thus absorbed by the old king's children and grandchildren. John of Gaunt, like Lionel, lost his wife early and sought a second bride abroad. In 1372 he married Constance of Castile, a natural daughter of the deceased Peter the Cruel. Henceforth he was summoned to parliament as King of Castile and Leon as well as Duke of

Lancaster, though it was not until the next reign that he took any actual steps to assert his claim.

John's next younger brother, Edmund of Langley, Earl of Cambridge in 1362, married Isabella, Constance of Castile's younger sister. He was the future Duke of York, and as the only one of Edward III.'s sons who did not marry an English heiress, was the most scantily endowed of them all. The union of his descendants with those of Lionel of Clarence gave the house of York a territorial importance which was, as we have seen, mainly derived from the Mortimer inheritance. Thus the two lines of descendants of Edward III. which had most future significance were those which represented through heiresses the rival houses of Lancaster and March. The history of the next century shows that the rivalry was only made more formidable by the connexion of both these lines with the royal family. In this, the most striking triumph of the Edwardian policy, is also the most signal indication of its failure. From it arose the factions of York and Lancaster.

The legislation of the years of peace, from 1360 to 1369, is largely anti-papal and economic, and is so intimately connected with the laws of the preceding period that it has been dealt with in an earlier chapter. But however anti-papal, and therefore anti-clerical, some of Edward's laws were, his government was still mainly controlled by great ecclesiastical statesmen. Simon Langham, though a Benedictine monk, had as chancellor demanded in 1366 the opinion of the estates as to the unlawfulness of the Roman tribute, and the clerical estate, if it did not help forward the anti-Roman legislation, was content to stand aside, and let it take effect without protest. Shortly after taking part in the movement against papal tribute, Langham was removed from the see of Ely to that of Canterbury in succession to Islip. His conversion into a purely monastic college of his predecessor's mixed foundation for seculars and regulars in Canterbury Hall, Oxford, showed a bias which might have been expected in a former abbot of Westminster, while his willingness to follow in the footsteps of Kilwardby, and exchange his archbishopric for the dignity of a cardinal and residence at Avignon showed that he was a papalist as well as an English patriot. His successor as primate, appointed in 1369 by papal provision, was William Whittlesea, a nephew of Archbishop Islip, whose weak health and colourless character made of little account his five years' tenure of the metropolitical dignity. With Canterbury in such feeble hands, the leadership in the Church and primacy in the councils of the crown passed to stronger men: such as John Thoresby, Archbishop of York till 1373; Thomas Brantingham, treasurer from 1369 to 1371, and Bishop of Exeter from 1370 to 1394; and above all to Edward's old servant, William of Wykeham, chancellor from 1367 to 1371, and Bishop of Winchester, in succession to Edington, from 1367 until 1404. Wykeham was a strenuous and hard-working servant of the crown, a vigorous and careful ruler of his diocese, a mighty pluralist, a magnificent builder, and the most bountiful and original of all the pious founders of his age. " Everything," says Froissart, " was done through him and without him nothing was done." [1]

The year of the breach of the treaty of Calais was also marked by the third great visitation of the Black Death, and the death of Queen Philippa. Parliament cordially welcomed the resumption by Edward of the title of King of France, and made liberal subsidies for the prosecution of the campaign. Disappointment was all the more bitter when each campaign ended in disaster, and in the parliament of February, 1371, the storm burst. The circumstances of the ministerial crisis of 1341 were almost exactly renewed. As on the previous occasion, the state was in the hands of great ecclesiastics, whose conservative methods were thought inadequate for circumstances so perilous. John Hastings, second Earl of Pembroke of his house, a gallant young warrior and the intended son-in-law of the king, made himself the spokesman of the anti-clerical courtiers, probably with the good-will of the king. At Pembroke's instigation the earls, barons, and commons drew up a petition that, "inasmuch as the government of the realm has long been in the hands of the men of Holy Church, who in no case can be brought to account for their acts, whereby great mischief has happened in times past and may happen in times to come, may it therefore please the king that laymen of his own realm be elected to replace them, and that none but laymen henceforth be chancellor, treasurer, barons of the exchequer, clerk of privy

[1] Froissart, *Chroniques*, ed. Luce, viii., 101.

seal, or other great officers of the realm ".¹ Edward fell in with this request. Wykeham quitted the chancery, and Brantingham the treasury. Of their lay successors the new chancellor, Sir Robert Thorpe, chief-justice of the court of common pleas, was a close friend of the Earl of Pembroke, while the new treasurer, Sir Richard le Scrope of Bolton, a Yorkshire warrior, represented the interests of John of Gaunt, whose long absences abroad did not prevent his ultimately becoming a strong supporter of the lay policy. A subsidy of £50,000 and a statute that no new tax should be laid on wool without parliamentary assent concluded the work of this parliament.

The lay ministers did not prove as efficient as their clerical predecessors. Want of acquaintance with administrative routine led them to assess the parliamentary grant so badly that an irregular reassembling of part of the estates was necessary, when it was found that the ministers had ludicrously over-estimated the number of parishes in England among which the grant of £50,000 had been equally divided. Meanwhile the French war was proceeding worse than before. Thorpe died in 1372, and another lay chief-justice, Sir John Knyvett, succeeded him in the chancery. Pembroke, as we have seen, was taken prisoner to Santander within a few weeks of Thorpe's death. Fresh taxation was made necessary by every fresh defeat, and the clergy, who looked upon the misfortunes of the anti-clerical earl as God's punishment for his enmity to Holy Church, had their revenge against their lawyer supplanters, for the parliament of 1372 petitioned that lawyers, who used their position in parliament to advance their clients' affairs, should not be eligible for election as knights of the shire. Next year, the discontent of the estates came to a head after the failure of John of Gaunt's march from Calais to Bordeaux. The commons, by that time definitely organised as an independent house, answered the demand for fresh supplies by requesting the lords to appoint a committee of their number to confer with them on the state of the realm. The composition of the committee was not one that favoured the existing administration, and, guided by men like William of Wykeham, it made only a limited and conditional grant, which was strictly appropriated to the payment of the expenses of the war. The anti-clerical party was still

¹ *Rot. Parl.*, ii., 304.

strong enough to send up denunciations of papal assumptions, and the anxiety to adjust the relations between the papacy and the crown led to some abortive negotiations with the legates of Gregory XI. at Bruges in 1374, which were mainly memorable for the appearance of John Wycliffe as one of the royal commissioners. Disgust at the attitude of the commons may well have postponed the next parliament for nearly three years. But the truce of Bruges made frequent parliaments less necessary.

The truce brought John of Gaunt back to England, and the rivalry between him and his elder brother, which had begun during their last joint campaigns in France, crystallised into definite parties the discordant tendencies that had been well marked since the crisis of 1371. The old king was a mere pawn in the game. His health had been broken by the debauchery and frivolity to which he had abandoned himself after the death of Queen Philippa. He was now entirely under the influence of Alice Perrers, a Hertfordshire squire's daughter, whose venality, greed, and shamelessness made her the fit tool for the self-seeking ring of courtiers. John of Gaunt sought her support as the best means of withdrawing the old king from the influence of the Prince of Wales, and the lay ministers were glad to maintain themselves in their tottering power by means of such powerful allies. Prominent among their party were courtier nobles—such as the chamberlain, Lord Latimer, and the steward of the household, Lord Neville of Raby,—and rich London financiers, chief among whom was Richard Lyons, men who made exorbitant profits out of the necessities of the administration. Faction sought to appear more respectable by professions of zeal for reform. The cry against papal encroachments was extended to a denunciation of the wealth and power of the clergy. John Wycliffe was called from his Oxford classrooms to expound the close connexion between dominion and grace, and to teach from London pulpits that the ungodly bishop or priest has no right to the temporal possessions given him on trust for the discharge of his high mission.[1]

[1] Until recently all historians have dated the beginning of Wycliffe's political career from 1366, but J. Loserth has proved that 1374, the date of the last demand for the Roman tribute, to be the right year. See his *Studien zur Kirchenpolitik Englands im 14ten Jahrhundert*, in *Sitzungsberichte der Academie der Wissenschaften in Wien*, philos.-histor. classe, cxxxvi., 1897, and, more briefly, in *Engl. Hist. Review*, xi. (1896), 319-328.

A vigorous opposition to the dominant faction was formed. At its head was the Black Prince. Hardly less important and much more active than the dying hero of Poitiers was Edmund Mortimer, Earl of March, the husband of Philippa of Clarence, and the father of the little Roger Mortimer whom nothing but the uncertain lives of the Prince of Wales and the sickly Richard of Bordeaux separated from the English throne. Hereditary antagonism accentuated incompatibility of personal interests. The ancient feuds of the houses of Mortimer and Lancaster still lived on in the hostility of their representatives. The understanding between the Prince of Wales and the Earl of March seems to have been complete. They had as their most powerful supporters the outraged dignitaries of the Church, who saw themselves kept out of office and threatened in their temporalities by the dominant faction. William of Wykeham, who had been the guardian of the Earl of March during his long minority, was the most experienced and wary of the clerical opposition to the lawyers and courtiers of the Lancaster faction. He had an eager and enthusiastic backer in the young and high-born Bishop of London, William Courtenay, the son of the Earl of Devon, and through his mother, Margaret Bohun, a great-grandson of Edward I. Office and descent combined to make Bishop Courtenay the custodian of the constitutional tradition, which was equally strong among the great baronial houses of ancient descent and such highly placed ecclesiastics as were zealous for the nation as well as for their order. His support was the more necessary since Simon of Sudbury, who in 1375 succeeded Whittlesea on the throne of St. Augustine, was a weak and time-serving politician.

The storm, which had long been brewing, burst at last in the parliament of April, 1376. Of the acts of this memorable assembly, famous as the Good Parliament, and of the other concluding troubles of the reign we are fortunate in possessing not only copious official records, but a minute and highly dramatic account from the pen of a St. Alban's monk, who, alone of the monastic chroniclers of his age, represented the spirit which, in the days of Matthew Paris, made the great Hertfordshire abbey so famous a school of historiography.[1]

---

[1] *Chron. Angliæ*, 1328-88, ed. E. M. Thompson (Rolls Ser.). Compare Mr. S. Armitage-Smith's *John of Gaunt* for an unfavourable estimate of its value.

28 *

CHAP.
XIX.

The Good Parliament showed from the beginning a strong animosity against the courtiers. The time was not yet come when the commons could take the initiative, or supply leaders from its own ranks, and even among the commons capacity was unequally divided. Authority and influence were exclusively with the knights of the shire, and the citizens and burgesses were content to allow the country gentry to speak and act in their name. The knights of the shire demanded that, in accordance with the precedent of 1373, a committee of magnates should be associated with them in determining the policy to be adopted. The lords spiritual and temporal were as eager as the knights to attack the government, and a committee, of which the leading spirits included the Earl of March and the Bishop of London, supplied the element of direction and initiation in which the commons were lacking. The resolution which prevailed was shown by the estates agreeing to make no grant until grievances had been redressed, and by the choice of Sir Peter de la Mare as spokesman of the commons before the king. Sir Peter was elected, we are told, because he possessed abundant wisdom and eloquence, and enough boldness to say what was in his mind, regardless of the good-will of the great. Perhaps a further and more weighty reason was that he was steward of the Earl of March. He was the first person to hold an office indistinguishable in all essentials from that of the later Speaker. Under his guidance the commons worked out an elaborate policy of revenge and reform. The contempt with which John of Gaunt and the courtiers had at first regarded their action, gave place to fear. The duke found it prudent to stand aside, while a clean sweep of the administration was made.

Charges were brought against the leading ministers of state, after a fashion in which the constitutional historian sees the beginnings of the process of the removal of great offenders by impeachment. Lord Latimer was the first victim. He had appropriated the king's money to his own uses ; he had shown remissness and treachery during the last campaign in Brittany ; he had taken bribes ; he was, in a word, "useless to king and kingdom". His fate was promptly shared by Lyons, the London merchant, the accomplice of his frauds, who had availed himself of his court influence to make a "corner" in nearly all imported articles, to the impoverishment of the common people and the

disorganisation of trade.   Lord Neville, whose eager partisanship
of Latimer had led him to insult Sir Peter de la Mare, was
threatened with similar proceedings.   Even Alice Perrers was
attacked, though, says the chronicler, the natural affection of
Englishmen for their king was so great that they were slow to
molest the lady whom the king loved.   However, Alice's un-
blushing interference with the course of justice, her appearance in the courts at Westminster, sitting on the judges' bench,
clamouring for the condemnation of her enemies and the ac-
quittal of her friends, roused the knights of the shire to action.
An ordinance against women being allowed to practise in the
law courts was made the pretext for her removal from court,
and Alice, fearful that worse might happen, took oath that she
would have no further dealings with the king.   Meantime Latimer
and Lyons were condemned to forfeiture and imprisonment.

In the midst of these proceedings the knights lost their
strongest support by the death of the Black Prince on June 8.
John of Gaunt at once went down to the house of commons,
and boldly suggested that the English should follow the example of the French and allow no woman to become heiress
of the kingdom.   This was a direct assertion of his own claims
to stand next to the throne after Richard of Bordeaux, and
before Roger Mortimer.   Alarmed at the blow thus levelled
against their chief remaining champion, the knights courageously held to their position.   "The king," said they, "though
old is still healthy, and may outlive us all.   Moreover he has
an heir in the ten-year-old prince Richard.   While these are
alive there is no need to discuss the question of the succession."
They completed the drawing up of the long list of petitions,
whose grudging and partial acceptance by the crown made the
roll of the parliament of 1376 memorable as asserting principles,
if not as vindicating practical ends.   They forced Lancaster
to agree to a council of twelve peers nominated in parliament to
act as a standing committee of advisers, without which the king
might do nothing of any importance.   After this revival of the
methods of the Mad Parliament and the lords ordainers, the
Good Parliament separated on July 6.   It had sat longer than
any previous parliament of which there is record.   It had persevered to the end in the teeth of discouragements of all kinds,
and, even after his brother's death, Duke John dared not lift
up his hand against it so long as the session continued.

CHAP.
XIX.

When the estates separated Lancaster threw off the mask. The king, sunk in extreme dotage, was entirely in the hands of his unscrupulous son. The old man was kept quiet by the return of Alice Perrers to court. She had sworn on the rood never to see the king again, but the prelates were "like dumb dogs unable to bark" against her; and no effort was made to prosecute her for perjury. Latimer and Lyons returned from their luxurious imprisonment in the Tower to their places at court. The duke roundly declared that the late parliament was no parliament at all. No statute was based upon its petitions, the council of twelve was rudely dissolved, and Sir Peter de la Mare was imprisoned in Nottingham castle. William of Wykeham was deprived of his temporalities, and the rumour spread that his disgrace was due to his possession of a state secret, revealed to him by the dying queen Philippa, that John of Gaunt was no true son of the royal pair but a changeling. So timid was the disgraced bishop that he vied with the weak primate in his subserviency to Alice. The Earl of March, who was marshal of England, was ordered to inspect the fortresses beyond sea, whereupon, fearing a plot to assassinate him, he resigned his office, "preferring," says a friend, "to lose his marshal's staff rather than his life". The powerful north-country lord, Henry Percy, who had hitherto acted with the opposition, was bribed by the office of marshal to join the Lancastrian party.

Grave difficulties still beset the government, and in January, 1377, John of Gaunt had to face another parliament. Every precaution was taken to pack the commons with his partisans. Of the knights of the shire of the Good Parliament only eight were members of its successor,[1] while in the place of the imprisoned De la Mare, Sir Thomas Hungerford, steward of the Duke of Lancaster, was chosen Speaker, on this occasion by that very name. A packed committee of lords was assigned to advise the commons. In these circumstances it was not difficult to procure the reversal of the acts against Alice Perrers and Latimer, and the grant of a poll tax of a groat a head. The only measure of conciliation was a general pardon, a pretext for which was found in the jubilee of the king's accession. From this William of Wykeham was expressly excepted.

[1] *Return of Members of Parliament*, pt. i., 193-97; *Chron. Angliæ*, p. 112, understates the case.

The convocation of Canterbury proved less accommodating than the parliament. Under the able leadership of Bishop Courtenay, it took up the cause of the Bishop of Winchester, refused to join in a grant of money until he had taken his place in convocation, and, triumphing at last over the time-serving of Sudbury and the hesitation of Wykeham himself, persuaded the bishop to join their deliberations. Lancaster met the opposition of convocation by calling to his aid the Oxford doctor whom the clergy had already begun to look upon as the enemy of the privileges of their order. Wycliffe was not as yet under suspicion of direct dogmatic heresy. He had not yet clothed himself in the armour of his Balliol predecessor, Fitzralph, to wage war against the mendicant orders. But he had already formulated his theory that dominion was founded on grace, had declared that the pope had no right to excommunicate any one, or if he had that any simple priest could absolve the culprit from his sentence, and he had shown a hatred so bitter of clerical worldliness and clerical property that he was looked upon as the special enemy of the great land-holding prelates and of the "possessioner" monks, whose lands, he maintained, could be resumed by the representatives of the donors at their will. The strenuous advocate for reducing the clergy to apostolic poverty was not likely to find favour among the prelates. Wycliffe's only clerical supporters at this stage were the mendicant friars, from whose characteristic opinions as regards "evangelical poverty" he never at any time swerved.[1] He was, however, eloquent and zealous, and he had a following. Fear either of Wycliffe or of his mendicant allies forced the bishops to take decisive action. Even Sudbury awoke, "as from deep sleep".[2] The duke's dangerous supporter was summoned to answer before the bishops at St. Paul's.

On February 19 Wycliffe appeared in Courtenay's cathedral. Four mendicant doctors of divinity, chosen by Lancaster, came

---

[1] Shirley (preface to *Fasciculi Zizaniorum*, Rolls Ser., p. xxvi.) thought that Wycliffe was "the sworn foe of the mendicants" in 1377, and E. M. Thompson's emphatic words repudiating the contrary statement of the St. Alban's writer, *Chron. Angliæ*, p. liii., illustrate the view prevalent in England in 1874. Lechler's *Wiclif und die Vorgeschichte der Reformation*, published in 1873, proves that it was not until Wycliffe denied the doctrine of transubstantiation in 1379 or 1380 that the friars deserted him.

[2] *Chron. Angliæ*, p. 117.

with him to defend him against the "possessioners," while the Duke of Lancaster himself, and Henry Percy, the new marshal, also accompanied him to overawe the bishops by their authority. The court was to be held in the lady chapel at the east end of the cathedral, and Wycliffe and his friends found some difficulty in making their way through the dense crowd that filled the spacious nave and aisles. Percy, irritated at the pressure of the throng, began to force it back in virtue of his office. Courtenay ordered that the marshal should exercise no authority in his cathedral. Thereupon Percy in a rage declared that he would act as marshal in the church, whether the bishop liked it or not. When the lady chapel was reached, there was further disputing as to whether Wycliffe should sit or stand, and Lancaster taunted Courtenay for trusting overmuch to the greatness of his family. When the bishop replied with equal spirit, John muttered : " I would liefer drag him out of his church by the hair of his head than put up with such insolence ". The words were overheard, and the Londoners, who hated the duke, broke into open riot at this insult to their bishop. It was rumoured that the duke had come to St. Paul's, hot from an attack on the liberties of the city that very morning in parliament. The court broke up in wild confusion, and the riot spread from church to city. Next day Percy's house was pillaged, and John's palace of the Savoy attacked. The duke and the marshal were forced to seek the protection of their opponent, the Princess of Wales, at Kennington. The followers of Lancaster could only escape rough treatment by hiding away their lord's badges. The citizens cried that the Bishop of Winchester and Peter de la Mare should have a fair trial. At last the personal authority of Bishop Courtenay restored his unruly flock to order. The old king performed his last public act by soothing the spokesmen of the citizens with the pleasant words and easy grace of which he still was master. The Princess of Wales used her influence for peace, and matters were smoothed over.

At some risk of personal humiliation, Lancaster secured a substantial triumph. Convocation followed the lead of parliament and gave an ample subsidy. William of Wykeham purchased the restoration of his temporalities by an unworthy deference to Alice Perrers. Wycliffe remained powerful, flattered, and consulted, though his enemies had already drawn up secret articles against him, which they had forwarded to the papal *curia*. Perhaps in the rapidly declining health of the king all parties saw that their real interest lay in the postponement of a crisis.

In June Edward lay on his deathbed at Sheen. To the last his talk was all of hawking and hunting, and his mistress carefully kept from him all knowledge of his desperate condition. When he sank into his last lethargy, his courtiers deserted him, and Alice Perrers took to flight after robbing him of the very rings on his fingers. A simple priest, brought to the bedside by pity, performed for the half-conscious king the last offices of religion. Edward was just able to kiss the cross and murmur " Jesus have mercy ". On June 21, 1377, he breathed his last.

With Edward's death we break off a narrative whose course is but half run. John of Gaunt's rule was not over ; Wycliffe was advancing from discontent to revolt ; Chaucer was yet to rise for a higher flight ; Langland had not yet put his complaint into its permanent form ; the French war was renewed almost on the day of Edward's death ; popular irritation against bad government, and social and economic repression were still preparing for the revolt of 1381. With all its defects the age of Edward is pre-eminently a strong age. Greedy, self-seeking, rough, and violent it may be ; its passions and rivalries combined to make futile the exercise of its strength ; it sounded the revolutionary note of all abrupt ages of transition, and it ends in disaster and demoralisation at home and abroad. But government is not everything, and least of all in the Middle Ages when what was then thought vigorous government appears miserably weak to modern notions. The strong rule decayed with the failure of the king's personal vigour. The ministers of Edward's dotage could not hold France nor even keep England quiet. England had grown impatient of the rule of a despot, though she was not yet able to govern herself after a constitutional fashion. It is in the incompatibility of the political ideals of royal authority and constitutional control, not less than in the want of purpose of her ruler and in the factions of her nobles that the explanation of the period must be sought. The age of Edward III. has been alternatively decried and exalted. Both verdicts are true, but neither contains the whole truth. The explanation of both is to be found in the annals of a later age.

APPENDIX.

ON AUTHORITIES.

(1216-1377.)

OUR two main sources of knowledge for medieval history are records and chronicles. Chronicles are more accessible, easier to study, more continuous, readable, and coloured than records can generally be. Yet the record far excels the chronicle in scope, authority, and objectivity, and a prime characteristic of modern research is the increasing reliance on the record rather than the chronicle as the sounder basis of historical investigation. The medieval archives of England, now mainly collected in the Public Record Office, are unrivalled by those of any other country. From the accession of Henry III. several of the more important classes of records have become copious and continuous, while in the course of the reign nearly all the chief groups of documents have made a beginning. The whole of the period 1216 to 1377 can therefore be well studied in them.

A large proportion of our archives is taken up with common forms, technicalities, and petty detail. It will never be either possible or desirable to print the mass of them *in extenso*, and most of the efforts made to render them accessible have taken the form of calendars, catalogues, and inventories. Such attempts began with the costly and unsatisfactory labours of the Record Commission (dissolved in 1836) ; and in recent years the work has again been taken up and pursued on better lines. The folio volumes of the Record Commission only remain so far of value as they have not been superseded by the more scholarly octavo calendars which are now being issued under the direction of the deputy-keeper of the records. These latter are all accompanied by copious indices which, though not always to be trusted implicitly, immensely facilitate the use of them. The records were preserved by the various royal courts. Of special importance for the political historian are the records of the Chancery and Exchequer.

APP.   Prominent among the Chancery records are the PATENT ROLLS, strips of parchment sewn together continuously for each regnal year, whereon are inscribed copies of the letters patent of the sovereign, so called because they were sent out open, with the great seal pendent. Beginning in 1200, they present a continuous series throughout all our period, except for 23 and 24 Henry III. The publication of the complete Latin text of the *Patent Rolls of Henry III.* is now in progress, and two volumes have been issued, including respectively the years 1216-1225 and 1225-1232. From the accession of Edward I. onwards the bulk of the rolls renders the method of a calendar in English more desirable. The *Calendars of the Patent Rolls* are now complete from 1272 to 1324 and from 1327 to 1348 (Edward I., 4 vols.; Edward II., 4 vols.; Edward III., 7 vols.). For the years not thus yet dealt with the unsatisfactory *Calendarium Rotulorum Patentium* (1802, fol.) may still sometimes be of service.

The letters close, or sealed letters addressed to individuals, usually of inferior public interest to the letters patent, are preserved in the CLOSE ROLLS, compiled in the same fashion as the Patent Rolls. The whole extant rolls from 1204 to 1227 are printed in *Rotuli Literarum Clausarum* (2 vols. fol., 1833 and 1844, Rec. Com.), and it is proposed to continue the integral publication of the text for the rest of Henry III.'s reign on the same plan as that of the Patent Rolls. One volume of this continuation, 1227-1231 (8vo, 1902), has been issued. For the subsequent periods a calendar in English is being prepared similar in type to the *Calendar of Patent Rolls*. The periods at present covered by the *Calendar of Close Rolls* (1892-1905) are, Edward I., 1272-1296 (3 vols.); Edward II., the whole of the reign (4 vols.), and Edward III., 1327-1349 (8 vols.).

A third series of records preserved by the Chancery officials is the ROLLS OF PARLIAMENT, including the petitions, pleas, and other parliamentary proceedings. None of these are extant before 1278, and the series for the succeeding century is often interrupted. Many of them are printed in the first two folios (vol. i., Edward I. and II.; vol. ii., Edward III.) of *Rotuli Parliamentorum* (1767-1777). A copious index volume was issued in 1832. A specimen of what may still be looked for is to be found in Professor Maitland's edition of one of the earliest rolls of parliament in *Memoranda de Parliamento* (1305) (Rolls series, 1893) with an admirable introduction. For the reigns of Edward I. and II. the deficiencies of the published rolls are supplemented by SIR F. PALGRAVE'S *Parliamentary Writs and Writs of Military Service* (vol. i., 1827, Edward I.; vol. ii., 1834, Edward II., fol., Rec. Com.) with alphabetical digests and indices.

Formal grants under the great seal called *Charters*, characterised by a "salutation" clause, the names of attesting witnesses, and, under Henry III. after 1227, by the final formula *data per manum nostram apud*, etc., and implying normally the presence of the king, are contained in the CHARTER ROLLS, extant from the reign of John onwards. They are roughly analysed in the *Calendarium Rotulorum Chartarum* (1803, Rec. Com.); and the *Rotuli Chartarum* (fol., 1837, Rec. Com.) contains the rolls *in extenso* up to 1216. Vol. i., 1226-1257, of an English *Calendar of Charter Rolls*, printing some of the documents in full, was published in 1903.

The documents formerly known as ESCHEAT ROLLS, or INQUISITIONES POST MORTEM, are concerned with the inquiries made by the Crown on the death of every landholder as to the extent and character of his holding. Some of the information contained in these inquests was made accessible in the *Calendarium Inquisitionum sive Eschæt-arum* (vol. i., Henry III., Edward I. and II., 1806; vol. ii., Edward III., 1808, fol., Rec. Com.). The errors and omissions of these volumes were partially remedied for the reigns of Henry III. and Edward I. by C. ROBERTS's *Calendarium Genealogicum* (2 vols. 8vo, 1865). A scholarly guide to all this class of documents has been begun in the new *Calendar of Inquisitions Post Mortem and other Analogous Documents*, of which vol. i. (Henry III.) was issued in 1904. The first volume of a separate list of the analogous inquisitions *Ad quod damnum* is also announced.

Of the FINE ROLLS containing the records of fines[1] made with the Crown for licence to alienate, exemption from service, wardships, pardons, etc., those of Henry III. have been made accessible in C. ROBERTS's *Excerpta e Rotulis Finium*, 1216-1272 (1835-36, 8vo). Other rolls such as the LIBERATE ROLLS have not yet been published for the reigns here treated.

Of special or local rolls, preserved in the Chancery, the most important for our period are the GASCON ROLLS. The earlier documents called by this name are not exclusively concerned with the affairs of Gascony; they are miscellaneous documents enrolled for convenience in common parchments by reason of the presence of the king in his Aquitanian dominions. Of these are F. MICHEL's *Rôles Gascons*, vol. i., published in the French government series of *Documents Inédits sur l'Histoire de France* (1885), including a "fragmentum rotuli Vasconiæ," 1242-1243, and "patentes littere facte in Wasconia," 1253-1254, years in which Henry III. was actually in Gascony. This publication was resumed in 1896 by M. CHARLES

---

[1] A *fine* in this technical sense is an agreement arrived at by a money transaction.

APP.   BÉMONT'S *Supplément* to Michel's imperfect volume, containing innumerable corrections, an index, introduction, and some additional
rolls of 1254 and 1259-1260.   The later of these, the roll of Edward's delegated administration, is the first exclusively devoted to
the concerns of Gascony.   " Gascon Rolls " in this later sense begin
with Edward I.'s accession, and M. Bémont has undertaken their
publication for the whole of Edward's reign from photographs of the
records supplied by the English to the French government.   In 1900
vol. ii. of the *Rôles Gascons*, containing the years 1273-1290, was
issued.   Other classes of Chancery Rolls accessible in print are *Rotuli
Scotiæ*, 1291-1516 (2 vols., 1814-1819, Rec. Com.), and *Rotuli
Walliæ*, 5-9 Edward I., privately printed by Sir Thomas Phillipps
(1865).   Among isolated Chancery records the *Rotuli Hundredorum*
(Rec. Com., 2 vols. fol., 1812-1818), containing the very important
inquests made by Edward I.'s commissioners into the franchises of
the barons, may specially be noticed here.

Of not less importance than the Chancery records are those handed
down from the Court of Exchequer.   The most famous of these, the
PIPE ROLLS, which, unlike the Chancery Enrolments, were "filed"
or sewn skin by skin, are decreasingly important from the thirteenth
century onwards as compared with their value for the twelfth.   For this
reason the Pipe Roll Society, founded in 1883, only undertook their
publication up to 1200.   Fragments of Pipe Rolls for our period can
be seen in print in various local histories and transactions, as *e.g.*,
"Pipe Rolls of Northumberland" up to 1272 in HODGSON-HINDE'S
History of Northumberland, pt. iii., vol. iii., and 1273-1284, ed.
Dickson (Newcastle, 1854-60), and of Notts and Derby (translated
extracts) in YEATMAN'S *History of Derby* (1886).   The only gap in
our series is for 1 Henry III.   Of other Exchequer records we may
mention : (1) the ORIGINALIA ROLLS, containing the estreats or documents from the Chancery informing the Exchequer of moneys due
to it, beginning in 20 Henry III., a summary of which is published in *Rotulorum Originalium in Curia Scaccarii Abbreviatio*,
20 Henry III.—51 Edward III. (2 vols. fol., Rec. Com., 1805-1810);
(2) the MEMORANDA ROLLS, containing records of charges upon the
Exchequer, etc., are complete for this period.   They were kept by the
king's and the treasurer's remembrancer, and are illustrated in print by
extracts from the Memoranda Rolls, 1297, in *Transactions of the Royal
Hist. Soc.*, new series, iii., 281-291 (1886), and by the roll of 3 Henry
III. in COOPER'S *Proceedings of the Record Commissioners* (1833); (3)
MINISTERS ACCOUNTS, *i.e.*, accounts of royal bailiffs, etc., for royal
manors, etc., not included in the sheriffs' accounts, beginning with

Edward I., of which a list is given in the *P. R. O. Lists and Indexes*,
Nos. v. and viii.; (4) of the PELL RECORDS, recording issues and
payments, samples given in DEVON'S *Issues of the Exchequer* (Rec.
Com., 8vo, 1837), DEVON'S *Issue Roll of Thomas of Brantingham
in* 1370 (Rec. Com., 8vo, 1835). The pells of receipt were entered
on the (5) RECEIPT ROLLS, specimens of which, along with the
corresponding issues, are to be found in SIR JAMES RAMSAY'S ab-
stracts of issue and receipt rolls for certain years of Edward III. in
the *Antiquary* (1880-1888); (6) SUBSIDY ROLLS of various types,
illustrated by *Nonarum Inquisitiones tempore Edwardi III.* (Rec.
Com., 1807), the record of a subsidy of a ninth collected by Edward
III. in 1340-1341; (7) WARDROBE and HOUSEHOLD ACCOUNTS containing for the thirteenth and fourteenth centuries information on
national as well as private royal finance; specimens in print include
the important *Liber Quotidianus Contra-rotulatoris Garderobæ*, 28 *Ed.
I.* (1299-1300), (1787, Soc. Antiq.).

From the Exchequer records come also the following: (1) *Testa
de Neville sive Liber Feodorum temp. Hen. III. et Edw. I.* (Rec. Com.,
fol., 1807), a miscellaneous and ill-digested but valuable collection
of thirteenth century inquisitions; (2) *Nomina Villarum*, 9 Ed. II.,
published in PALGRAVE'S *Parl. Writs*, ii., iii., 301-416; (3)
Kirkby's Quest, a survey made by Bishop Kirkby, the treasurer, in
1284-85, of which the Yorkshire portion has been printed by the
Surtees Soc., ed. Skaife (1867), and other portions elsewhere; (4)
Taxatio Ecclesiastica Angliæ et Walliæ, 1291 (Rec. Com., 1802), the
taxation of benefices by Nicholas IV. by which assessments of papal
and ecclesiastical taxes were long made. A very useful compilation,
recently undertaken under the direction of the deputy-keeper, is *Inquisitions and Assessments relating to Feudal Aids*, 1284-1431, of which
three volumes, dealing in alphabetical order with the shires from
Bedford to Norfolk, are published. Cheshire and Durham are entirely omitted and Lancashire very scantily dealt with as exceptional
jurisdictions. The work is based upon the various lay records enumerated above and other analogous inquests. Ancient compilations
of miscellaneous documents by officials of the Exchequer are exem-
plified in *Liber Niger Scaccarii* (ed. Hearne, 2 vols., 1774), and in the
Red Book of the Exchequer (ed. H. Hall, 3 vols., Rolls ser., 1896).

The records of the common law courts, the King's Bench and the
Court of Common Pleas, are of less direct historical value than those
of the Chancery and the Exchequer. Extraordinarily bulky, they
require a good deal of sifting to sort the wheat from the chaff. As
yet a very small proportion of them has been printed, and few have

APP. even been calendared. A brief index of them has been compiled in the useful *List of Plea Rolls* (1894, *P. R. O. Lists and Indexes,* No. iv.). Of the various types of these records the FEET OF FINES have been largely used by the topographer and genealogist, and the feet of fines for many counties during this period have been calendared, summarised, excerpted, and printed, wholly or in part, by local archæological societies, as for example, W. FARRER's *Lancashire Final Concords till* 1307 (Rec. Soc. for Lancashire and Cheshire, 1899), and many others. The PLEA ROLLS are of wider importance. For the days of Henry III. *Placita Coram Rege* (*i.e.*, of the King's Bench) and the *Placita de Banco* (*i.e.*, of the Common Pleas in later phrase) are classified as *Rotuli Curiæ Regis*, while the rolls of the local eyres for the same period are called *Assize Rolls*. Separate series for each court begin with Edward I. Specimens of most of these types have been printed. *Placitorum Abbreviatio Ric. I.—Edw. II.* (Rec. Com., fol., 1811) is a careless seventeenth century abstract. *Placita de Quo Warranto,* Edward I. to Edward III. (Rec. Com., fol., 1818), is a record of local eyres of particular importance for the reign of Edward I. as the corollary of the Hundred Rolls and the attack on the local franchises. HUNTER's *Rotuli Selecti* (Rec. Com., 1834) contains pleas of the reign of Henry III. A typical year's pleadings of the King's Bench for 1297 is given in full in PHILLIMORE's *Placita coram rege,* 25 Edward I. (1898, British Rec. Soc.). Selections from the proceedings of the commission appointed by Edward I. in 1289 to hear complaints against judges and officials will shortly be published by Miss Hilda Johnstone and myself for the Royal Historical Society. Of special importance are the plea rolls issued by the Selden Society, which include for our period F. W. MAITLAND's *Select Pleas of the Crown,* 1200-1225 ; BAILDON's *Select Chancery Pleas,* 1364-1471 ; J. M. RIGG's *Select Pleas of the Jewish Exchequer ;* and G. J.TURNER's *Select Pleas of the Forest ;* all have translations and introductions, of which those of Professor Maitland are of exceptional value.

To these types must be added the records of the local courts, now largely also in the Public Record Office, though vast numbers of court rolls and manorial documents are still in private hands, and among the archives of ecclesiastical and secular corporations. The Selden Society has done excellent work in publishing such muniments ; as in particular, MAITLAND's *Select Pleas in Manorial Courts,* vol. i., Henry III. and Edward I., illustrating the social and legal life of a medieval village ; MAITLAND and BAILDON's *Court Baron ;* HUNTER's *Leet Jurisdiction of Norwich ;* C. GROSS's *Select Cases from the Coroners' Rolls,* 1265-1413. The records of the

Bishopric of Durham, the County Palatine of Chester, the Principality APP.
of Wales, and the Duchy of Lancaster are deposited in the Public
Record Office, and calendars and lists scattered over the *Deputy-
Keeper of the Records' Reports* throw some light on their contents.
Unluckily these records of franchise are incompletely preserved and
often in bad condition.   The best preserved for our period are the
Durham records, described in LAPSLEY's *County Palatine of Durham*,
pp. 327-337 (Harvard Historical Studies) ; some of the most important
are printed in *Registrum Palatinum Dunelmense*, ed. Hardy (Rolls
Series, 4 vols.), which is also an Episcopal register.   Welsh records
may be illustrated by the *Record of Carnarvon* (Rec. Com., fol.,
1838).   Academic records are illustrated by the Oxford *Munimenta
Academica* (ed. Anstey), Rolls Series.   Municipal records are very
numerous and important ; full particulars as to them can be found in
C. Gross's *Bibliography of British Municipal History* (Harvard Hist.
Studies).   Admirably edited examples of our wealth of municipal
records for this period are to be found in *Records of the Borough of
Nottingham* (ed. W. H. Stevenson), vol. i. (1882) ; *Records of the
Borough of Leicester* (ed. Mary Bateson), vols. i. and ii. (1899 and
1901) ; and *Munimenta Gildhallæ Londoniensis* (ed. H. T. Riley),
Rolls Series.   The *Reports of the Historical Manuscripts Commission*
afford much information as to every type of document in private or
local custody.   Ireland and Scotland have archives of their own ;
but there are no systematic records in the Register House at Edinburgh before the War of Independence.   Among the enterprises now
abandoned of the Public Record Office were *Calendars of Documents
relating to Scotland and Ireland*.   The Scottish series covers all this
period (vols. i.-iv.), the Irish was stopped at 1307.   They are derived, by a rather arbitrary selection, from various classes of English
records, but contain much valuable material.   JOSEPH STEVENSON'S
Documents illustrating the History of Scotland (1286-1306) (Scot. Rec.
Publications, 1870), and PALGRAVE's *Documents and Records illustrating the History of Scotland* (Rec. Com., 1837), are useful for the
reign of Edward I. as are for limited periods of it the *Wallace Papers*
(Maitland Club, 1841) and *Scotland in 1298* (ed. Gough, 1888).

    A new class of records begins in the thirteenth century with
BISHOPS' REGISTERS.   These, so far as they survive, are preserved in
the diocesan registries.   Of printed registers for this period the most
important is MARTIN's *Registrum Epistolarum J. Peckham* (3 vols.,
Rolls Series, 1882-1886), the earliest surviving Canterbury register.
Other registers printed or calendared are HINGESTON-RANDOLPH's
Exeter Registers, 1257-1291, 1307-1326, and 1327-1369 (5 vols., 1889,

etc.) ; excerpts, particularly from the York registers, in RAINE'S *Letters from the Northern Registers,* Rolls Series; the two oldest York *Registers* of ARCHBISHOPS WALTER GREY (1215-1255) and WALTER GIFFARD (1266-1279), both in Surtees Society ; the Wells *Registers* of BPS. DROKENSFORD, 1309-1329, and RALPH OF SHREWSBURY, 1329-1363 (Somerset Record Society) ; the Worcester *Register* of BP. GIFFARD, 1268-1302 (Worcester Historical Society) ; the Winchester *Registers* of BISHOPS SANDALE and RIGAUD, 1316-1323, and WYKEHAM, 1366-1404 (Hampshire Record Society). A society called the Canterbury and York Society has recently been started to set forth episcopal registers systematically in print. It has begun to publish the earliest Lincoln *Register* extant, that of Hugh of Wells, bishop of Lincoln, 1209-1235, whose *Liber Antiquus de Ordinatione Vicariorum* was printed in 1888. Analogous documents are LUARD'S *Rob. Grosseteste Epistolæ* (Roll Series, 1861), and the like.

Monastic CARTULARIES are less important for general history in this than in previous periods ; large masses of monastic records of this age have survived, not a tithe of which is to be found in DUGDALE'S *Monasticon.* Some monastic records illustrate the domestic economy or religious life of the house as KIRK'S *Accounts of the Obedientiaries of Abingdon,* 1322-1479 (Camden Soc.) ; J. W. CLARK'S *Observances in use at Barnwell Priory,* 1295-1296 (1897), and the like.

For this period by far the most important series of foreign records is the magnificent collections of the papacy. A summary of many of these is to be found in BLISS, JOHNSON, and TWEMLOW'S *Calendars of Papal Registers illustrating the History of Great Britain and Ireland; Papal Letters* (vols. i.-iv., 1198-1404), and *Petitions to the Pope* (vol. i., 1342-1419), of special importance for the fourteenth century. These useful calendars, however, do not always dispense us from consulting the grand series of papal records published or analysed under the care of the French School of Rome, which has not yet sufficiently been studied in this country. This enterprise is divided into two sections. In the first the *Registers from Gregory IX. to Benedict XI.* are in course of publication; in the second the letters of the Avignon popes relating to France are printed or analysed. Portions of the letters of John XXII., Benedict XII. and Clement VI. are already issued. PRESSUTI has published one volume of the *Registers of Honorius III.* (1888). From the Vatican archives also comes THEINER'S *Vetera Monumenta Hib. et Scot. Historiam illustrantia* (1864), beginning in 1216.

Extracts from various archives are found in such collections as RYMER'S *Fœdera,* of which the Record Commission's edition in folio

reaches just beyond the end of this period ; WILKINS's *Concilia* (1737),   APP.
containing many extracts from episcopal registers and canons of
councils ; HADDAN and STUBBS's *Councils*, vol. i. (for the thirteenth
century Welsh Church) ; CHAMPOLLION-FIGEAC's *Lettres des Rois et
des Reines d'Angleterre* (2 vols., 1847, *Doc. Inédits*) ; STUBBS's *Select
Charters* (Henry III. and Edward I.), and BÉMONT's excellent *Chartes
des Libertés anglaises* in the *Collection de Textes pour l'Étude et
l'Enseignement de l'Histoire*. Equally useful is COSNEAU's *Grands
Traités de la Guerre de Cent Ans* also in the same *Collection de
Textes*. The *Statutes of the Realm* (vol. i., fol., 1810) contains the
text of the laws and of the great charters of this period.

Chronicles, with all their deficiencies, must ever be largely used as
sources of continuous historical narrative. For the thirteenth century
our chief reliance must still be placed upon the annals drawn up in
various monasteries, some based upon little more than gossip or hear-
say, others showing real efforts to acquire authentic information. The
greatest centre of historical composition in thirteenth-century England
was the Abbey of St. Alban's, whose chronicles form so important
a series that they may appropriately be considered as a whole, before
the other chroniclers are dealt with in approximately chronological
order. The fame of St. Alban's as a school of history had its origin
in the order of Abbot Simon (d. 1183) that the house should always
appoint a special historiographer. The first of these whose work is
now extant is ROGER OF WENDOVER (d. 1236), whose *Flores Historiarum* (ed. H. O. Coxe, Engl. Hist. Soc., 1842, or ed. Hewlett,
Rolls Series, 1886-89—this latter edition is unscholarly) becomes original in 1216 and remains a chief source, copious and
interesting, if not always precise, until 1235. On Wendover's
death, MATTHEW PARIS, who took the monastic habit in 1217, became
the official St. Alban's chronicler. His great work, the *Chronica
Majora*, is, up to 1235, little more than an expansion and embellishment of Wendover. He re-edited Wendover's work with a patriotic
and anti-curialist bias quite alien to the spirit of the earlier writer,
whose version should preferably be followed. Paris's book is a first-
hand source from 1235 to 1259. The narrative of the years 1254-1259
is considerably later in composition to the history of the period 1235-
1253, since on reaching 1253 Paris devoted himself to an abridgment of what he had already written, called the *Historia Minor*. On
completing this he resumed his earlier book, and carried it on to the
eve of his death in 1259, though he did not live to complete its final
revision ; that was the work of another monk who added a picture of
his death-bed. The *Chronica Majora* has been excellently edited by

29 *

APP. Dr. H. R. Luard in seven volumes for the Rolls Series, with elaborate introductions tracing the literary history of the work and a magnificent index. The *Historia Minor* has been published in three volumes by Sir F. Madden in the Rolls Series. Paris also wrote the lives of the abbots of his house up to 1255, a work not now extant, and the basis of the later *Gesta Abbatum S. Albani*, compiled by Thomas Walsingham (d. 1422 ?) and likewise issued in the Rolls Series. The thirteenth century biographies have some original value. Paris's *Life of Stephen Langton* is printed in LIEBERMANN's *Ungedruckte Anglo-Normannische Geschichtsquellen* (1870).

Paris, perhaps the greatest historian of the Middle Ages, has literary skill, a vivid though prolix style, a keen eye for the picturesque, bold and independent judgment, wonderful breadth and range, and an insatiable curiosity. He was a man of the world, a courtier and a scholar ; he took immense pains to collect his facts from documents and eye-witnesses, and had great advantages in this respect through the intimate relations between his house and the court. Henry III. himself contributed many items of information to him. His details are extraordinarily full, and he tells us almost as much about continental affairs as about those of his own country. He wrote with too flowing a pen to be careful about precision, and had too much love of the picturesque to resist the temptation of embellishing a good story. His narrative of continental transactions is in particular extremely inexact. But the chief cause of his offending also gives special value to his work ; he was a man of strong views and his sympathies and prejudices colour every line he wrote. His standpoint is that of a patriotic Englishman, indignant at the alien invasions, at the misgovernment of the king, the greed of the curialists and the Poitevins, and with a professional bias against the mendicants. His writings make his age live.

The falling off in the St. Alban's work of the next generation is characteristic of the decay of colour and detail which makes the chroniclers of the age of Edward I. inferior to those of his father's reign. The years after 1259 were briefly chronicled by uninspired continuators of Matthew Paris, and the reputation of St. Alban's as a school of history led to the frequent transference of their annals to other religious houses, where they were written up by local pens. This led to the dissemination of the series of jejune compilations which in the ages of Edward I. and II. were widely spread under the name of *Flores Historiarum.* Dr. Luard has published a critical edition of these *Flores* in three volumes of the Rolls Series, which range from the creation to 1326, with an introduction determining their complicated relations to each other. They are of no real value before 1259, and for the next sixty-seven years are only important by reason of the defects of our other sources. No unity or colour can be expected in books handed from house to house and kept up to date by jottings by different hands. The ascription of these *Flores* to a conjectural Matthew of Westminster by earlier editors is groundless. Dr. C. Horstmann, *Nova Legenda Anglie*, i., pp. xlix. *seq.* (1901), maintains that John of Tynemouth's *Historia Aurea*, still in manuscript, is the official St. Alban's history from 1327 to 1377.

In the reign of Edward I. the credit of the school of St. Alban's was revived to some extent by WILLIAM RISHANGER, who made his profession in 1271 and died early in the reign of Edward II. To him is assigned a chronicle ranging from 1259 to 1306 published by H. T. Riley in the volume *Willelmi Rishanger et Anonymorum Chronica et Annales* (Rolls Series). Rishanger's authorship of the portion 1259-1272 is more probable than that of the section 1272-1306, which, not compiled before 1327, is almost certainly by another hand, and the attribution of even the earlier section to Rishanger is doubted by so competent an authority as M. Bémont. The compilation is frigid and unequal. Of the miscellaneous contents of Mr. Riley's volume, the short *Gesta Edwardi I.* (pp. 411-423), of no great value, is clearly Rishanger's work. We may also ascribe to Rishanger the *Narratio de Bellis apud Lewes et Evesham* (ed. Halliwell, Camden Soc., 1840), which tells the story of the Barons' Wars with vigour, detail, and insight. Written by a true inheritor of the prejudices of Matthew Paris, this chronicle is a eulogy of Montfort. It was put together not before 1312.

Another volume of *Chroniclers of St. Alban's* was edited by Mr. Riley for the Rolls Series in 1860. Three of its chronicles concern our period. These are: (1) *Opus Chronicorum*, 1259-1296, a source of "Rishanger's" chronicle; (2) J. DE TROKELOWE'S *Annales*, 1307-1322; (3) H. DE BLANEFORDE'S *Chronica* (1323). These last two are important for Edward II.'s reign. After these works, historical writing further declined at St. Alban's. At the end of our period, however, another true disciple of Matthew Paris was found in the St. Alban's monk who added to a jejune compilation for the years 1328 to 1370 a vivid and personal narrative of the years 1376-1388, our chief source for the history of the last year of Edward III.'s reign. In his bitter prejudice against John of Gaunt and his clerical allies, such as Wycliffe and the mendicants, the monk is so outspoken that his book was suppressed, and most manuscripts leave out the more offensive passages. It has been edited by Sir E. Maunde

Thompson as *Chronicon Angliæ*, 1328-1388 (Rolls Series). Before that its contents, like that of other St. Alban's annals, were partially known through the fifteenth century compilation under the name of a St. Alban's monk, THOMAS OF WALSINGHAM, whose *Historia Anglicana* (2 vols., Rolls Series, ed. Riley) is not an authority for our period.

For the early years of Henry III. we have besides Wendover's *Flores* : (1) The CANON OF BARNWELL's continuation of Howden published in STUBBS's *Memoriale Fratris Walteri de Coventria* (Rolls Series), written in 1227 and copious for the years 1216-1225. (2) RALPH OF COGGESHALL'S *Chronicon Anglicanum* (ed. Stevenson, Rolls Series), ending at 1227 and important for its last twelve years. (3) The *Histoire des Ducs de Normandie et des Rois d'Angleterre*, which, published by F. Michel in 1840 (Soc. de l'histoire de France), was first appreciated at its full value by M. Petit-Dutaillis in the *Revue Historique*, tome 2 (1892). (4) The *Chronique de l'Anonyme de Béthune* printed in 1904 in vol. xxiv. of the *Recueil des Historiens de la France*. (5) A French rhyming chronicle, the *Histoire de Guillaume le Maréchal*, discovered and edited by P. Meyer for the Soc. de l'histoire de France. Written by a minstrel of the younger Marshal from materials supplied by the regent's favourite squire, it is, though poetry and panegyric, an important source for Marshal's regency.

St. Alban's was not the only religious house that concerned itself with the production of chronicles. Other *Annales Monastici* have been edited in five volumes (Rolls Series, vol. v. is the index) by Dr. Luard. They are of special importance for the reign of Henry III. In vol. i. the meagre annals of the Glamorganshire abbey of Margam only extend to 1232. The *Annals of Tewkesbury* are useful from 1200 to 1263, and specially for the history of the Clares, the patrons of that house. The *Annals of Burton-upon-Trent* illustrate the years 1211 to 1261 with somewhat intermittent light, and are of unique value for the period of the Provisions of Oxford, containing many official documents. Vol. ii. includes the *Annals of Winchester* and *Waverley*. The former, extending to 1277, though mainly concerned with local affairs are useful for certain parts of the reign of Henry III., and particularly for the years 1267-1277. The annals of the Cistercian house of Waverley, near Farnham, go down to 1291. From 1219 to 1266 the narrative is contemporary and valuable ; from 1266 to 1275, and partly from 1275 to 1277 it is borrowed from the Winchester Annals ; from 1277 to its abrupt end it is again of importance. The *Annals of Bermondsey* in vol. iii. are a fifteenth century compilation. The *Annals* of the Austin canons of *Dunstable* are of great value, especially from the year 1201, when they become original, down to 1242. This section is written by RICHARD DE MORINS, prior of Dunstable from 1202 to 1242. After his death the annals become more local, though they give a clear narrative of the puzzling period 1258-1267. They stop in 1297. The chief contents of vol. iv. are the parallel *Annals of Oseney* and the *Chronicle* of THOMAS WYKES, a canon of that house, who took the religious habit in 1282. To 1258 the two histories are very similar, that of Wykes being slightly fuller. They then remain distinct until 1278, and again from 1280 to 1284 and 1285-1289. In the latter year Wykes stops, while Oseney goes on with independent value until 1293, and as a useless compilation till 1346. Wykes is of unique interest for the Barons' Wars, as he is the only competent chronicler who takes the royalist side. The Oseney writer, much less full and interesting, represents the ordinary baronial standpoint. Wykes is occasionally useful for the first years of Edward I.; after 1288 his importance becomes small. The *Annals of Worcester* are largely a compilation from the Winchester Annals and the *Flores;* the local insertions have some value for the period 1216-1258, and more for the latter part of the reign of Edward I., at whose death they end.

Other monastic chronicles of the thirteenth century, of small importance, enumerated by Dr. Luard (*Ann. Mon.*, iv., liii.) are not yet printed in full. Extracts from many are given in PERTZ'S *Monumenta Germaniæ Hist. Scriptores*, vols. xxvii. and xxviii. The *Annales Cestrienses* (to 1297) have been edited by R. C. Christie (Record Soc. of Lancashire and Cheshire) ; EDMUND OF HADENHAM'S *Chronicle* (down to 1307) is given in part in WHARTON'S *Anglia Sacra*, and M. Bémont publishes in an appendix to his *Simon de Montfort* (pp. 373-380) a valuable fragment of a *Chronicle of Battle Abbey* on the Barons' Wars, 1258-1265. For the latter part of that period we have some useful notices in HENRY OF SILEGRAVE'S brief *Chronicle* (ed. Hook, Caxton Soc., 1849), whose close relationship to the *Battle Chronicle* M. Bémont has first indicated. To these may be added the *Annals of Stanley Abbey* (1202-1271) in vol. ii. of *Chronicles of Stephen, Henry II. and Richard I.* (ed. Hewlett, Rolls Series, 1885), and the *Chronicle* of the Bury monk, JOHN OF TAXSTER or TAYSTER, which becomes copious from the middle of the thirteenth century and ends in 1265 ; it was partly printed in 1849 by Benjamin Thorpe as a continuation of Florence of Worcester (English Historical Society), and the years 1258-1262 are best read in Luard's edition of Bartholomew Cotton (Rolls Series). Taxster's work became the basis of several later compilations of the eastern counties, includ-

APP.   ing: (1) JOHN OF EVERSDEN, another Bury monk, independent from
1265 to 1301, also printed without his name by Thorpe, up to 1295, as
a further continuation of Florence.   (2) JOHN OF OXNEAD, a monk of
St. Benet's, Hulme, a reputed continuator of Taxster and Eversden
up to 1280, who adds a good deal of his own for the years 1280-
1293, edited somewhat carelessly by Sir Henry Ellis as *Chronica J.
de Oxenedes* (Rolls Series).   (3) BARTHOLOMEW COTTON, a monk of
Norwich, whose *Historia Anglicana*, original from 1291 to 1298, and
specially important from 1285 to 1291, is edited by Luard (Rolls Series).
Some thirteenth and early fourteenth century Bury chronicles are also
in *Memorials of St. Edmund's Abbey*, ed. T. Arnold (vols. ii. and iii.,
Rolls Series).   The *Chronicon de Mailros* (Bannatyne Club), from the
Cistercian abbey of Melrose, goes to 1270; though utterly untrust-
worthy, it may be noticed as almost the only Scottish chronicle before
the war of independence, and as containing a curious record of the
miracles of Simon de Montfort.

Among the historians of Edward I.'s reign is WALTER OF HEM-
INGBURGH, Canon of Guisborough in Cleveland (ed. H. C. Hamilton,
2 vols., Engl. Hist. Soc.).   His account of Henry III.'s reign is worthless, but from 1272 to 1312 his work is of great value, though never
precise and full of gaps.   It contains many documents and is remarkable for its stirring battle pictures.   Hemingburgh probably laid
down his pen when the narrative ceases early in the reign of Edward
II.   Another writer, identified by Horstmann with John of Tynemouth, carries the story from 1326 to 1346.

In striking contrast to the flowing periods of Hemingburgh is the
well-written and chronologically digested *Annals* of the Dominican
friar NICHOLAS TREVET or TRIVET, the son of a judge of Henry
III.'s reign (ed. Hog, Engl. Hist. Soc.).   Beginning in 1138, his
work assumes independent value for the latter years of Henry III.
and is of first-rate importance for the reign of Edward I., at whose
death it concludes, though Trevet was certainly alive in 1324.   It
was largely used by the later St. Alban's chroniclers.

Franciscan historiography begins earlier than Dominican with the
remarkable tract of THOMAS OF ECCLESTON, written about 1260, *De
Adventu Fratrum Minorum in Anglia*, published with other Minorite
documents (including Adam Marsh's letters) in BREWER'S *Monumenta
Franciscana* (Rolls Series, continued in a second volume by R. How-
lett).   The first important Franciscan chronicle, called the *Chronicon
de Lanercost* (ed. J. Stevenson, Bannatyne Club, 2 vols.), really comes
from the Minorite convent of Carlisle.   It covers the years 1201 to
1346.   The early part is derived from the valueless chronicle of

Melrose, and its incoherent cult of the memory of Montfort does not save it from the grossest errors in dealing with his history. It becomes important for northern affairs from Edward I. onwards, giving full details with a strong anti-Scottish bias. Another north-country chronicle is Sir T. GREY's *Scalacronica* (ed. Stevenson, Maitland Club, 1836), useful for the Scottish wars and for Edward III.'s reign up to 1362.

A sign of the times is the beginning of civic chronicles. The London series alone is important for English history. It begins with the *Liber de Antiquis Legibus*, or *Chronica Majorum et Vicecomitum Londoniarum* (1188-1274, ed. T. Stapleton, Camden Soc.). The work of ARNOLD FITZTHEDMAR, alderman of the German merchants in London, it is copious for the years 1236 to 1274, and is, with Wykes, the only chronicle of the Barons' Wars written with a royalist bias. Fourteenth century civic chronicles, based upon *Flores His-toriarum*, and continued independently, form the main contents of the two volumes of *Chronicles of the Reigns of Edward I. and II.* (ed. by Dr. Stubbs for the Rolls Series). These are : (1) *Annales Lon-donienses*, perhaps written by ANDREW HORN, chamberlain of London, and compiler of the *Liber Horn ;* they have much general value for the period 1301 to 1316, and deal more narrowly with London his-tory from 1316 to 1330, when they conclude. (2) *Annales Paulini*, 1307-1341, compiled by one of the clergy of St. Paul's, but not by Adam Murimuth. These take up Dr. Stubbs's first volume. The second contains : (1) JOHN OF LONDON's *Commendatio Lamentabilis in Transitu magni Regis Edwardi quarti*, a funeral eulogy containing the most elaborate contemporary analysis of Edward's character. (2) The CANON OF BRIDLINGTON's *Gesta Edwardi de Carnarvon*, with a continuation down to the death of Edward III., of little value after 1339. It has frequent reference to the vaticinations of the local prophet, John of Bridlington, and was not put in its present shape before 1377. Its first part is based on earlier sources, and it is, for lack of better, a prime authority for north-country history and Anglo-Scottish relations ; the continuation contains the best account of Edward Balliol's attempts on the Scottish throne. (3) *Vita Edwardi II.*, from 1307 to 1325, attributed by Hearne on slight grounds to a MONK OF MALMESBURY, with many notices of the history of Glouces-tershire and Bristol, of which the famous rising is described at length. The writer is the most human of the annalists of the reign, prolix, self-conscious, moralising, and somewhat incoherent. He is the most outspoken of all the fourteenth century critics of the Roman curia, and has more insight than most of his contemporaries.

APP.   The following are of primary importance for the early years of
Edward III.; it is significant that they are nearly all secular, not
monastic, in origin.   (1) *Continuatio Chronicorum*, 1303-1347, by
ADAM MURIMUTH, a canon of St. Paul's much employed by Edward
III. (ed. E. M. Thompson in Rolls Series), a mere continuation of the
Flores until 1325, thence enlarged from personal sources, but still
meagre until 1337, when it becomes a first-rate authority to 1346.
Murimuth's adoption of Michaelmas day as the beginning of the year
has often confused those who have imitated him.   Chief among these
is (2) GEOFFREY LE BAKER of Swinbrooke, an Oxfordshire man, and
like Murimuth, a secular clerk, whose *Chronicon* (ed. E. M. Thompson), beginning in 1303 on the basis of Murimuth, has independent
value after 1324, and is noteworthy for its touching details of Edward
II.'s fall and death.   It ends in 1356 with an excellent account of
the battle of Poitiers.   The early part of Baker's chronicle, widely
circulated as *Vita et Mors Edwardi II.*, was previously assigned
to Sir Thomas de la Moor, and was so edited by Stubbs, but
Sir E. M. Thompson showed clearly that this Oxfordshire
knight was Baker's patron and not the writer of a chronicle.
With many defects, Baker can tell a story picturesquely.   (3)
ROBERT OF AVESBURY, a canon lawyer, wrote *De mirabilibus Gestis
Edwardi III.*, of special importance for the war from 1339 to 1356,
and containing many state documents.   It is edited by E. M. Thompson in the same volume as Murimuth.   (4) HENRY KNIGHTON,
Canon of Leicester, wrote a *Chronicle* about 1366 which is valuable
for the period 1336-1366 and includes the best contemporary account of the Black Death.   The latest edition by Lumby in the
Rolls Series is not a scholarly work.   (5) *Eulogium Historiarum*
(ed. Haydon, Rolls Series) is contemporary and valuable for 1356-
1366 only.   There is a great dearth of English chronicles for the
latter years of Edward III.   The signal exception is the important
St. Alban's *Chronicon Angliæ* already mentioned.

In the age of Edward III. the *Flores Historiarum* were superseded
by the *Polychronicon* (often called the " Brute " after WACE'S *Brut
d'Angleterre*), the voluminous compilation (to 1352) of RANDOLPH
HIGDEN, a monk of Chester (edited by Babington and Lumby,
Rolls Series).   ROBERT OF GLOUCESTER, PETER LANGTOFT, and
ROBERT MANNYNG have been referred to elsewhere.   The first is
of some original value for the Barons' Wars and Edward I., while
Langtoft, a Yorkshire canon specially interested in the Scottish wars,
is a contemporary for all Edward I.'s reign.   Among rhyming chronicles, French in tongue but English in origin, may be mentioned *Le*

Siège de Carlaverock, 1300 (ed. Nicolas, 1828), of value for heraldry,
and CHANDOS HERALD's *Prince Noir* (ed. H. O. Coxe, whose edition
was pillaged by F. Michel for his more accessible version of 1883).
L'Histoire de Foulques Fitz Warin (d. 1260?), a picturesque marcher
hero, a prose romance of the end of the thirteenth century, can be
read in Stevenson's edition of COGGESHALL (Rolls Series), or Eng-
lished by A. Kemp-Welch (1904).

No contemporary Scottish chronicles of importance deal with the
War of Independence, though fairly full Scottish versions of it exist in
later books. The earliest of these is the *Bruce* of JOHN BARBOUR,
Archdeacon of Aberdeen. Written in 1375 at the instigation of
Robert II., Barbour's spirited verses are inspired by patriotic rather
than historic motives. His details are minute, but impossible to control by other sources, and he is more valuable as the epic poet of
Scottish liberty than as an historical authority. He is edited by
Skeat (Early English Text Soc.), Jamieson, and Innes. The earliest
prose Scottish chronicle, that of JOHN FORDUN, who died about 1384
(ed. Skene, in *Historians of Scotland*), is of value for the fourteenth
century. ANDREW WYNTONN's *Originale*, a metrical history written
in the fifteenth century, has next to no authority until the end of
this period (ed. Laing, in *Historians of Scotland*). BLIND HARRY's
Wallace, written in 1488, is romance not history.

Wales is more fortunate than Scotland in preserving contemporary
thirteenth century annals, of which a Latin chronicle, *Annales Cam-
briæ*, extending to 1288, and a Welsh one, *Brut y Tywysogion* (*i.e.*,
Chronicle of the Princes), down to 1278, are edited by J. Williams in
the Rolls Series, the latter with an English translation. A more
critical version of the Welsh text of the *Brut* is that of J. RHYS
and J. G. EVANS' *Red Book of Hergest*, vol. ii. (1890).

The close relations between England and France for the whole of
this period render the French chronicles by far the most important
of foreign sources for English history. They are enumerated in detail by Auguste Molinier in vols. iii. (up to 1328) and iv. (after 1328)
of the first part of *Les Sources de l'Histoire de France* (*Manuels de
Bibliographie historique*). The chief French chronicles of the period
1226-1328 are collected in vols. xx.-xxiv. of the *Recueil des Historiens
de la France* begun by Dom Bouquet. Some of them are of special
importance for English history. For Anglo-Netherlandish relations
under Edward I. see *Annales Gandenses* (1296-1310), "la chronique
la plus remarquable de la fin du xiiie siècle," the French *Chronique
Artésienne* (1295-1304), and the *Chronique Tournaisienne* (1296-1314),
all edited by F. Funck-Brentano in the already mentioned *Collection*

APP.   *de Textes.* For the Hundred Years' War the French chroniclers are indispensable, especially for military history. The most famous of these writers, JEAN FROISSART, has been characterised in my text (p. 419). He can best be studied in Luce and Raynouart's excellent edition for the Soc. de l'Histoire de France (tomes i.-viii., 1869-1888) which completes the story up to Edward III.'s death. Luce's careful "sommaire et commentaire critique" often affords means of checking Froissart by other sources. The magnificent volumes of indexes of Kervyn de Lettenhove's complete edition (vols. xx.-xxv.) are still of immense use, though his text and comments are inferior to those of Luce. Froissart's spirit may well be caught in Lord Berners's racy English translation (Tudor Translations), or in G. C. Macaulay's useful abridgment. The three redactions of Froissart's first book (from 1327 to 1373-1377), which is all that concerns our period, have been clearly distinguished by Luce. (1) The first edition, written about 1373, at the request of Count Robert of Namur, is inspired by an English bias. Up to 1360 it is largely derived from the chronicle of JEAN LE BEL, Canon of St. Lambert of Liège ; after that date it is original. (2) The second edition, only represented by two MSS., of which one is incomplete, is a modification of the first with a French bias. The earlier part is more independent of Jean le Bel. (3) The third edition, preserved in a single MS., ends with the death of Philip VI. in 1350, and, written after 1400, is even more hostile to England than the second. The best edition of Jean le Bel is by Polain for the Académie royale de Belgique.

A few of the more important French chronicles after 1328 may be mentioned shortly. (1) *Grands Chroniques de France* (ed. Paulin Paris), original from 1350 to 1377, a work of first-rate importance, where, if truth is altered, it is altered deliberately from political motives. (2) JEAN DE VENETTE, 1340-1368, written with a popular bias, and partly favourable to Charles of Navarre (edited as a supplement to Géraud's edition of Guillaume de Nangis, ii., 178-378, Soc. de l'Hist. de France). (3) *Chronique Normande du xive siècle*, 1337-1372 (ed. Molinier, Soc. de l'Hist. de France, 1882), exact and very important for the wars 1337 to 1372. (4) *Chronique des quatre premiers Valois* (Soc. de l'Hist. de France). (5) CUVELIER's poetical *Vie de Bertrand du Guesclin* (2 vols., *Doc. inédits*). Further details can be found in Molinier's bibliography. Netherlandish sources for the Hundred Years' War are summarised in PIRENNE's *Bibliographie de l'Histoire de Belgique* (1895). Of special importance is JAN VAN KLERK's *Van den Derden Edewaert Rym Kronyk.* (1840), useful for 1337-1341, and written with an English bias.

The unofficial legal literature of the thirteenth and fourteenth centuries is of exceptional variety and value. Many lawyers' treatises throw light on matters far beyond legal technicalities. HENRY OF BRACTON or BRATTON'S *De Legibus et Consuetudinibus Angliæ* illustrates the union of English and Roman juridical ideas characteristic of the age of Henry III. It has been edited badly by Sir T. Twiss in six volumes (Rolls Series), and some portions well by Professor Maitland in his *Select Passages from Bracton and Azo* (Selden Soc.). Maitland's *Bracton's Note Book* includes extracts from plea rolls seemingly made by Bracton. Bracton's book on the laws was translated, condensed, and rearranged by a writer of the next generation called Britton. It may be studied in a modern edition in NICHOLLS'S *Britton on the Laws of England*, while *Fleta*, an almost contemporary Latin law book, must be read in Selden's seventeenth century edition. Another thirteenth century law-book, *Le Mirroir des Justices*, has been edited by Maitland and W. J. Whittaker for the Selden Society. From Edward I.'s time onwards unofficial reports of trials called YEAR BOOKS, written in French, become valuable for their vividness and detail, and for the light which they throw on the more technical records of the plea rolls. Many of them are printed in unsatisfactory seventeenth century editions, but the Year Books of five of Edward I.'s regnal years, between 1292 to 1307, together with the Year Book of 11-12 Edward III., are accessible in A. J. Horwood's editions in the Rolls Series. L. O. Pike has also edited in the Rolls Series the *Year Books of Edward III.* from 1338 to 1345, and Maitland's *Year Books of 1 and 2, and 2 and 3, Edward II.* for the Selden Society are the first two instalments of a scheme for publishing the Year Books of the reign. Besides their legal value, the Year Books are an almost unworked mine for social and economic, and often even political and ecclesiastical, history.

Of literary aids to history T. WRIGHT'S *Political Songs* (Camden Soc.) illustrate this period to the reign of Edward II. One of Wright's pieces has been more elaborately edited in C. L. KINGSFORD'S *Song of Lewes* (1890), and C. Hardwick published a *Poem on the Times of Edward II.* for the Percy Soc. (1849). With Edward III. such literature becomes copious. Of special importance are T. Wright's *Political Poems and Songs from the accession of Edward III.*, vol. i. (Rolls Series, 1859), J. Hall's *Poems of* LAURENCE MINOT, Skeat's editions of CHAUCER and LANGLAND, and G. C. Macaulay's edition of GOWER. The Latin works of Wycliffe, published by the Wycliffe Society, mainly belong to the succeeding period, but *De Dominio Divino* and *De Civili Dominio*, as well as some tracts

APP.   printed in the appendix to Lewis's *Life of Wiclif* and in Shirley's edition of *Fasciculi Zizanioram* (Rolls Series), were written before 1377.

Of modern works treating of this period, many monographs, dealing with particular points, have been mentioned in notes in the course of the narrative. Of general guides to the period the best by far are Stubbs and Pauli. STUBBS's *Constitutional History* (vol. ii.) is as valuable for the chapters summarising the political history as for the more strictly constitutional matter. R. PAULI's *Geschichte von England*, iii., 489-896, and iv., 1-505, 716-741, remains, after half a century, the fullest and most satisfactory working up in detail of these reigns, though the great additions to our material make parts of it a somewhat unsafe guide. It can be supplemented for particular aspects of history by the following : For legal history, POLLOCK and MAITLAND's *History of English Law before the time of Edward I.*, especially vol. i., book i. (chapters iv.-vi.), and book ii. ; and most of vol. ii. ; to which should be added the prefaces by Prof. Maitland and others to the volumes of the Selden Society. MAITLAND's *Roman Canon Law in the Church of England* (1898) is also of great importance. For economic history, W. J. ASHLEY's *Economic History*, parts i. and ii.; W.CUNNINGHAM's *Growth of English Industry and Commerce, Early and Middle Ages ;* VINOGRADOFF's *Villainage in England*, S. DOWELL's *History of Taxation* (2nd edition), H. HALL's *Customs Revenue of England*, and, as a collection of materials, J. E. THOROLD ROGERS' *History of Agriculture and Prices*, vols. i. and ii. For ecclesiastical history, W. R. W. STEPHENS's *History of the English Church*, 1066-1272 ; W. W. CAPES's *History of the English Church in the Fourteenth and Fifteenth Centuries*, and F. MAKOWER's *The Constitutional History and Constitution of the Church of England* (translated from the German). For academic history, DENIFLE's *Entstehung der Universitäten des Mittelalters bis* 1400, especially pp. 1-40, 237-251 (Oxford) and pp. 367-376 (Cambridge), HAURÉAU's *Histoire de la Philosophie scholastique* and RASHDALL's *Universities of the Middle Ages*, i., 1-74, and ii., part ii. (Oxford and Cambridge). For military history, KÖHLER's *Entwickelung des Kriegswesens in der Ritterzeit*, OMAN's *History of the Art of War in the Middle Ages*, CLARK's *Mediæval Military Architecture*, and (above all) J. E. MORRIS's *Welsh Wars of Edward I.* For naval history, NICOLAS's *History of the Royal Navy*, and C. DE LA RONCIÈRE's *Histoire de la Marine Française.* For particular reigns the following may be found useful : For Henry III., PETIT-DUTAILLIS's *Étude sur Louis VIII.*, GASQUET's *Henry III. and the Church* (1905), BÉMONT's *Simon de*

Montfort, PROTHERO'S *Simon de Montfort,* and BLAAUW'S *Barons'
Wars* (2nd ed., 1871). For the reign of Edward I., SEELEY'S
Life and Reign of Edward I. (1872), my *Edward I.;* GOUGH'S
Itinerary of Edward I., MAXWELL'S *Robert the Bruce* (Heroes
of the Nations), and MORRIS'S above - mentioned *Welsh Wars
of Edward I.* For some aspects of Edward II.'s reign, STUBBS'S
prefaces to *Chronicles of Edward I. and Edward II.* are of special
value. For Edward III.'s reign, BARNES'S *History of Edward III.*
(1688) is not quite superseded by LONGMAN'S *Life and Times of
Edward III.* (2 vols., 1869), and MACKINNON'S *History of Edward
III.* (1900). For the Hundred Years' War, E. DÉPREZ'S *Préliminaires
de la Guerre de Cent Ans* (1328-1342) (Bibl. de l'Ecole française de
Rome, 1902) for diplomatic history, and DENIFLE'S *Désolation des
Églises et Monastères de la France pendant la Guerre de Cent Ans*
(ii., part i., 1899) for the best general survey of the war to 1380.
See also LUCE'S *La Jeunesse de Bertrand de Guesclin* and *La France
pendant la Guerre de Cent Ans,* and (for Brittany) A. DE LA BORDERIE'S
Histoire de Bretagne (1899). The end of Edward III.'s reign is
illustrated by S. ARMITAGE SMITH'S *John of Gaunt* (1904), J. LECH-
LER'S *Wiclif und die Vorgeschichte der Reformation* (2 vols., 1873),
also translated, not very adequately, *Wycliffe and His English Precursors* (1878 and 1881), F. D. MATTHEW'S introduction to *Wyclif's
English Works* (Early English Text Society), and R. L. POOLE'S
Illustrations of the History of Mediæval Thought (1884), and *Wycliffe*
(1889). G. M. TREVELYAN'S *England in the Age of Wycliffe* (1899)
is interesting but not always very scholarly.

Some account of the general foreign history of the period can be
found in LAVISSE and RAMBAUD'S *Histoire générale* (tomes ii. and iii.),
LOSERTH'S *Geschichte des späteren Mittelalters* (good bibliographies),
and, briefly, in my *Papacy and Empire* (up to 1273), and LODGE'S
Close of the Middle Ages (after 1273). For French history of the
period LAVISSE'S *Histoire de France* (iii., pt. i., 1137-1226, by A.
LUCHAIRE; iii., pt. ii., 1226-1328, by C. V. LANGLOIS, and iv., pt. i.,
1328-1422, by A. COVILLE) cover the whole of the period. More detailed works are, PETIT-DUTAILLIS'S *Louis VIII.,* E. BERGER'S *Blanche
de Castile,* WALLON'S *Louis IX.,* BOUTARIC'S *Saint Louis et Alfonse
de Poitiers,* C. V. LANGLOIS'S *Philippe le Hardi,* BOUTARIC'S *France
sous Philippe le Bel,* LEHUGEUR'S *Philippe le Long,* PETIT'S *Charles
de Valois,* FOURNIER'S *Royaume d'Arles et de Vienne,* L. DELISLE'S
Hist. de Saint-Sauveur-le-Vicomte, and (for the south) the new edition
of DE VIC and VAISSÈTE'S *Hist. générale de Languedoc.* Much recent
work has been done by French scholars towards the reconstruction

APP.   of the external history of England during the whole of our period. For the Low Countries, PIRENNE'S *Hist. de Belgique*, ii., ASHLEY'S *James and Philip van Artevelde*, and VANDER KINDERE'S *Le Siecle des Arteveldt*. PAULI is good for the relations of England and Germany. Maps illustrating the period are to be found in POOLE'S *Oxford Historical Atlas*, LONGNON'S *Atlas historique de la France*, and SPRUNER-MENKE'S *Historischer Hand-Atlas ;* special maps of Edward I.'s Scottish expeditions in GOUGH'S *Itinerary of Edward I.*, of Edward III.'s and the Black Prince's campaigns in THOMPSON'S *Chronicon Galfridi le Baker*, and KERVYN'S *Froissart*, of John of Gaunt's in ARMITAGE-SMITH'S *John of Gaunt*, and of Wales in the thirteenth century in *Owens College Historical Essays*. VIDAL DE LA BLACHE'S *Tableau de la Géographie de la France* (LAVISSE, *Hist. de France*, i., pt. i.) is instructive for the physical features of the campaigns of the Hundred Years' War.

Further details as to English authorities, ancient and modern, can be found in GROSS'S excellent *Sources and Literature of English History* (1900). The *Monumenta Germaniæ Historica, Scriptores*, vols. xxvii., xxviii., consist of excerpts from English writers of the twelfth and thirteenth centuries ; the introductions (in Latin) by Pauli and Liebermann contain noteworthy estimates of the works from which the extracts are taken.

NOTE TO PAGES 390-92.

My reasons for my account of the battle of Poitiers demand longer explanation than can be given in a footnote. Like most modern writers, I have based my narrative on the *Chronicle* of Geoffrey le Baker as expounded by Sir E. M. Thompson, though I agree with Professor Oman in holding that Baker's " ampla profundaque vallis et mariscus, torrente quodam irriguus," must be the valley of the Miausson. I also, however, agree with Father Denifle in not setting great store on Chandos Herald, though I would not reject him altogether, as all prudent writers must reject Froissart. My conjectural account of the movements of the armies is an attempt to combine Baker with what may be true in the Herald. I hope elsewhere to be able to justify my narrative at length.

INDEX.

30 *

Methven, battle of, 234.
Metingham, John of, 201.
Meyer, Paul, his edition of the *Histoire de Guillaume le Maréchal*, 16, 454.
Miausson, the river, 390, 391.
Michel, Francisque, 445, 446, 459.
Milan, 61, 430.
Ministers' Accounts, 446, 447.
Minorites, the, 84, 87, 91, 455, 456. See also Franciscans.
Minot, Lawrence, 420, 421, 461.
Minsterworth, Sir John, 413.
Miracle plays, 423.
Mirambeau, 36.
Miranda, 405.
Mirroir des Justices, Le, 460.
Mise of Amiens, the, 112, 113.
Mise of Lewes, the, 119.
Model Parliament, the. See Parliament.
Mohammedans, the, 19.
Molinier, Auguste, *Sources de l'histoire de France*, 459.
Monasteries, 86-88, 94, 375, 376, 425.
Monasticon, Dugdale's, 449.
Monmouth, castle and town of, 47, 48, 267, 280.
Monnow, the river, 47.
Mont Cenis, the, 140.
Montague, Sir William, 308. See also Salisbury, Earls of.
Montague, the house of, 267.
Montfavence, Bertrand of, Cardinal, 330, 330, 339.
Montfichet, Richard of, 66.
Montfort l'Amaury, 352.
Montfort, county of, 398.
Montfort, Amaury of, 56, 113.
Montfort, the house of (Dukes of Brittany), 352. See also John IV. and John V., Dukes of Brittany.
Montfort, the house of (Earls of Leicester), 124, 246.
Montfort, Henry of, 114.
Montfort, John of, the elder. See Brittany, John, Duke of.
Montfort, John of, the younger. See Brittany, John, Duke of.
Montfort, Peter of, 100, 103, 112, 128.
Montfort, Simon of, Count of Toulouse, 55. See also Leicester.
Montfort, Simon of, Earl of Leicester. See Leicester.
Montfort, Simon of, the younger, son of Simon, Earl of Leicester, 113, 126, 127, 129.
Montgomery, castle and town of, 24, 37, 40, 133, 167.
Monthermer, Ralph of, 223, 241, 264.
Monthermer, Thomas of, 347.
Montjoie, 22.

Montmorenci, Matthew of, 192.
Montpellier, University of, 386.
Montpezat, lord of, 295, 296.
Montreuil-sur-mer, 143, 216, 397; treaty of, 216.
Montrose, 198.
Mont-Saint-Martin, Monastery of, 339.
Monumenta Franciscana, Brewer's, 456.
Monumenta Hist. Germaniæ, Scriptores, Pertz', 455, 464.
Moors of Granada, 90, 305, 404.
Moor, Sir Thomas de la, 458.
Moray, 208.
Moray, Randolph, Earl of, 315-317.
Moray, Sir Andrew, 319.
Morbihan, 354.
Morgan of Caerleon, 15.
Morgan, leader of Glamorganshire rebels, 189, 190, 192, 193.
Morgarten, battle of, 262.
Morlaix, 352, 354, 363, 389; battle of, 389.
Morley, Robert, 346.
Mortimer, Edmund (d. 1303), 163.
Mortimer, Edmund (d. 1381). See March, Edmund Mortimer, Earl of.
Mortimer, Roger, of Chirk, 267, 284, 286, 293, 306.
Mortimer, Roger, of Wigmore (d. 1282), 76, 100, 103, 111, 125, 128-133, 139, 163.
Mortimer, Roger, of Wigmore (d. 1330), 267, 271-274, 280, 283, 284, 286, 293, 298-303, 305-309, 314. See also March, Roger Mortimer, first Earl of.
Mortimer, Roger, grandson of Roger Mortimer, first Earl of March, 359,360.
Mortimer, Roger, son of Edmund, Earl of March, 435, 437.
Mortimer, the house of, 1, 126, 148, 423, 431.
Mortmain, Statute of, 174.
Moselle, the river, 335.
Mountchensi, Joan of, 65.
Mount Sorrel, 9.
Mowbray, John of (of Scotland), 227.
Mowbray, John of, 280.
Murimuth, Adam, 458.
Myton, battle of, 276.

Najarilla, the river, 405.
Nájera, battle of, 405.
Nantes, 35, 36, 352-354.
Naples, 78, 79.
Narbonne, 386, 387.
Nassau, Adolf of, King of the Romans. See Adolf, King of the Romans.
Navarre, Blanche of Artois, Queen of. See Blanche.
Navarre, Henry III., King of. See Henry.

CORRIGENDA.

Page 111, line 11 from top, *for* Roger Bigod *read* Hugh Bigod.
Page 188, line 14 from bottom, *for* Earl of Cornwall *read* Earl of Lancaster.